KAPLAN

T0293536

LSAT® Premium Prep

Our 80 years' expertise = Your competitive advantage

REAL LSAT QUESTIONS + STRATEGIES FOR EVERY SECTION + ONLINE

Acknowledgements

A great number of people were involved in the creation of the book you are holding. Glen Stohr was the primary author, with contributions from Kaplan LSAT experts Chris Cosci, Jesse Evans, Craig Harman, Rebecca Houck, and Bob Verini. Jack Chase contributed invaluable research, and Bonnie Wang created the graphics.

Prakash Jagannathan managed the production work for this book, with the help of editor Ananth Rajasekaran. Joanna Graham oversaw layout and design. Once typesetting was done, Joan R. Summerfold proofread the entire volume. Jeffrey Batzli designed the cover.

Published by Kaplan North America, LLC dba Kaplan Publishing
1515 West Cypress Creek Road
Fort Lauderdale, FL 33309

10 9 8 7 6 5 4 3 2 1

ISBN: 978-1-5062-9608-1

Kaplan Publishing print books are available at special quantity discounts to use for sales promotions, employee premiums, or educational purposes. For more information or to purchase books, please call the Simon & Schuster special sales department at 866-506-1949.

TABLE OF CONTENTS

▶ **GO ONLINE**
www.kaptest.com/booksonline

PREFACE

Getting Started

Let's start with an assumption: You have this book because you want to raise your LSAT score. Now, as you use this book, you'll discover that assumptions are often complicated, sometimes flawed, yet often necessary to reach the conclusions of many arguments, especially on the LSAT. Still, the assumption that you're here to improve on the LSAT feels pretty safe, and if you've made the assumption that this book will help, you're right.

This book covers every question type that you'll encounter on the LSAT score, those from the test's two scored Logical Reasoning sections and the passages and questions from its Reading Comprehension section. Many of them will be genuinely challenging, others only deceptively so. On some, you'll need to learn how to speed up, while others will be a lesson in patience and accuracy. As you use Kaplan's proven strategies to master them, you'll learn a lot about how to dissect arguments, make valid deductions, and recognize subtle errors in logic. You'll become a more strategic reader and thinker, and in the end, a better law student and legal professional down the road.

Let's get started!

HOW TO USE THIS BOOK

First—Get Acquainted with the LSAT

Start by reading the introductory "About the LSAT" chapter. There, you'll find details about the LSAT's structure and scoring, how to register for the test, how it is administered, and how best to study.

Second—Start Becoming an LSAT Expert

The LSAT is a skills-based exam. Its purpose is to show law schools what you can *do* more than what you know. Thus, the foundation of this book's pedagogy is **learning by doing**. You can't cram for the LSAT; there is no subject matter to memorize. Because of that, mastering the LSAT may feel more like learning a musical instrument or improving at a sport. You need to practice, review your practice with an expert coach, make adjustments, and practice some more. This book provides the practice, and the expert review. Take a look at how you'll be doing this.

Work with real questions. As you complete the subsequent chapters of this book, you'll do more than 200 official LSAT questions, covering every question type found in the Logical Reasoning sections. The Law School Admission Council (LSAC), the organization that makes the test, has released dozens of official full-length LSATs from previous administrations. These are called PrepTests (more on these terrific practice resources in a few pages). Kaplan licenses these official items so that you have more realistic practice available.

This book contains questions from PrepTests 101, 104, 105, 106, 107, 108, 123, 131, 140, and B, and every full LSAT question you'll do in the book is an official LSAC item. Whenever you see a question ID like this, you'll know the official PrepTest, section, and question numbers for the item.

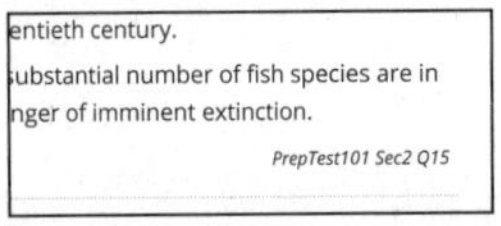

Have a Learning Objective. In each chapter of the book, Kaplan breaks down the skills you'll need for LSAT success. Some chapters have several Learning Objectives, others, just one or two. For every Learning Objective, you'll see pages marked [Prepare] and [Practice]. Prepare has the information you *need* to know about the skill or question type so that you can get to work. We'll keep Prepare sections as short and to-the-point as possible because Practice is where you want to spend your time. At the end of most chapters, you'll also have a section marked [Perform] where you can assess all of the skills you acquired and get recommendations for further practice. For Chapters 3, 4, 5, and 8, take the Perform quizzes under timed conditions to get an accurate assessment of your skills on each question type.

Review With Expert Examples. To learn new skills, you always need to try them out yourself. But then, reviewing your performance with an expert, and being able to *see*, not just hear about, how the expert performs can help you make big improvements. At Kaplan, our learning science team has put together *worked examples* that show you how an LSAT expert worked through any question you are asked to try. They look like this.

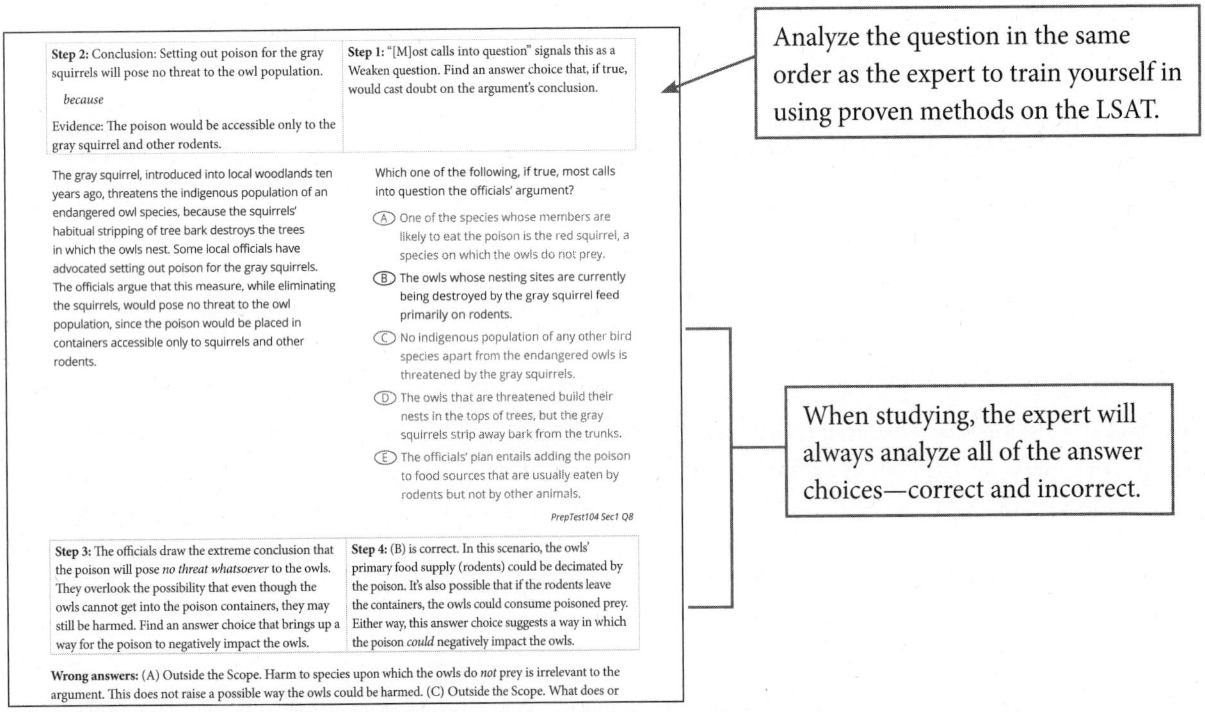

As you review, follow the expert's thinking step by step to see the patterns they spot and the strategies they deploy. When you practice full Logical Reasoning questions, Kaplan will help you reinforce the same method the expert uses by providing spaces for you to record your own thinking.

Step 2:	**Step 1:**
25. Laura: Harold is obviously lonely. He should sell his cabin in the woods and move into town. In town he will be near other people all the time, so he will not be lonely anymore. Ralph: Many very lonely people live in towns. What is needed to avoid loneliness is not only the proximity of other people but also genuine interaction with them.	Ralph responds to Laura by pointing out that (A) something needed for a certain result does not necessarily guarantee that result. (B) what is appropriate in one case is not necessarily appropriate in all cases. (C) what is logically certain is not always intuitively obvious. (D) various alternative solutions are possible for a single problem. (E) a proposed solution for a problem could actually worsen that problem. *PrepTest106 Sec3 Q10*
Step 3:	**Step 4:**

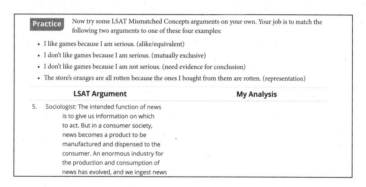

You won't be writing out these notes on test day, of course, because before then, you'll have absorbed and internalized these steps and strategies for yourself. In practice, however, consciously attending to each step will help you realize where you're going off-track or skipping an essential step.

Even in its skill-building exercises and drills, this book provides a space for you to record your own analysis, and then compare it to that of an expert.

Practice Now try some LSAT Mismatched Concepts arguments on your own. Your job is to match the following two arguments to one of these four examples:

- I like games because I am serious. (alike/equivalent)
- I don't like games because I am serious. (mutually exclusive)
- I don't like games because I am not serious. (need evidence for conclusion)
- The store's oranges are all rotten because the ones I bought from them are rotten. (representation)

LSAT Argument	My Analysis
5. Sociologist: The intended function of news is to give us information on which to act. But in a consumer society, news becomes a product to be manufactured and dispensed to the consumer. An enormous industry for the production and consumption of news has evolved, and we ingest news	

Expert Analysis

Take a look at how an LSAT expert would break down this argument.

LSAT Argument	Analysis
Press release: A comprehensive review evaluating the medical studies done up to the present time has found no reason to think that drinking coffee in normal amounts harms the coffee-drinker's heart. So coffee drinkers can relax and enjoy their beverage—it is safe to drink coffee. *PrepTest101 Sec2 Q1*	Keywords "studies" and "So" indicate evidence and conclusion, respectively. Conclusion: Drinking coffee is safe. *because* Evidence: Drinking coffee in normal amounts does not harm a coffee drinker's heart. The mismatched terms are *not harms the coffee-drinker's heart* and *safe to drink coffee.* So the author's assumption connects these terms: "What does not harm the heart is, overall, safe."

When it comes to Perform quizzes, however, you'll do things a little differently.

Assess Your Skills. Mastering new skills takes a little preparation and, sometimes, a lot of practice. To really know how you're doing, however, you need to [Perform]. You need to try your new skills under more test-like conditions, timed and without any hints. So, when you have Perform quizzes at the end of a chapter, you'll see the LSAT questions like this, more or less as they'll appear on-screen when you're taking the test.

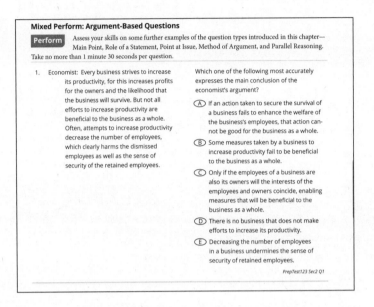

Mixed Perform: Argument-Based Questions

Perform Assess your skills on some further examples of the question types introduced in this chapter—Main Point, Role of a Statement, Point at Issue, Method of Argument, and Parallel Reasoning. Take no more than 1 minute 30 seconds per question.

1. Economist: Every business strives to increase its productivity, for this increases profits for the owners and the likelihood that the business will survive. But not all efforts to increase productivity are beneficial to the business as a whole. Often, attempts to increase productivity decrease the number of employees, which clearly harms the dismissed employees as well as the sense of security of the retained employees.

Which one of the following most accurately expresses the main conclusion of the economist's argument?

(A) If an action taken to secure the survival of a business fails to enhance the welfare of the business's employees, that action cannot be good for the business as a whole.

(B) Some measures taken by a business to increase productivity fail to be beneficial to the business as a whole.

(C) Only if the employees of a business are also its owners will the interests of the employees and owners coincide, enabling measures that will be beneficial to the business as a whole.

(D) There is no business that does not make efforts to increase its productivity.

(E) Decreasing the number of employees in a business undermines the sense of security of retained employees.

PrepTest123 Sec2 Q1

Take Perform quizzes under the timing recommended in the instructions; you need to know how you'd do on these questions in a real LSAT setting. When you're finished, assess yourself rigorously. Kaplan provides recommendations for additional practice after each Perform quiz. That practice will take place online where there are two vital resources: this book's online companion, and LSAC's LawHub.

HOW TO USE YOUR ONLINE BOOK COMPANION

First—Register Your Book to Access the Online Companion

The online book companion gives you access to even more prep, including the Spotlight video lessons from instructors on Kaplan's exclusive LSAT Channel, analysis and explanations for free, full-length PrepTests from LSAC, study planning guidance, video explanations, and more.

Register your book by following these simple steps:

1. Go to kaptest.com/booksonline and use this book's ISBN, or scan the QR code on the card inside the cover, to go to the appropriate book listing. Click the "Register" button next to it.
2. Enter the password as directed and click on "Next."
3. The online Study Plan will appear in your shopping cart free of charge. Click "Proceed to checkout" and complete your registration.
4. Once registered, click on the "personalized Student Homepage" link to access your online materials.

Please have your book with you because you will need information from the book to access your account. Access to the online Study Plan is limited to the original owner of this book and is not transferable. Kaplan is not responsible for providing access to the online Study Plan for customers who purchase or borrow used copies of this book. Access to the online Study Plan expires one year after you register.

Second—Getting Started Video

Kaplan's lead instructional designer explains how to make the most of your prep with the *LSAT Premium Prep, First Edition* book and its associated resources. You should watch the "Getting Started" video as soon as possible, in conjunction with this section of the book.

Third—Use Your Exclusive LSAT Prep Resources

With Kaplan's *LSAT Premium Prep, First Edition*, you've purchased much more than just a book. Here are the highlights of what's inside:

- **Study Planning Guidance and Sample Schedules**. Preparing for the LSAT is a lot of work, and LSAT test takers are busy people. For you, Kaplan's learning experience team has assembled best practices for planning your study and practice along with sample schedules for working through this book and incorporating other LSAT study resources.
- **LSAT Channel Spotlight Video Lessons**. This book features nine special Spotlight sections on special LSAT strategies and topics with accompanying video lessons from members of Kaplan's LSAT Channel faculty. In the online companion, you'll find the video lessons for the following Spotlight features:
  - *Secrets of LSAT Preparation*
  - *Great Moments in Formal Logic*
  - *The Denial Test*
  - *Flaw School*
  - *Logical Reasoning—Managing the Section*
  - *Same Road, Different Maps*

    - *Keywords are Road Signs*
    - *Reading Comprehension—Managing the Section*
    - *How Law Schools Use Your LSAT Argumentative Writing Essay*
- The LSAT Channel instructors are among Kaplan's highest-rated and most veteran teachers. The LSAT Channel has long been included in our comprehensive LSAT courses, where students benefit from live-instruction lessons five or six nights per week. Now, self-prep students can also subscribe to the LSAT Channel with full access to live lessons and a library of recorded sessions on nearly every LSAT topic imaginable. Learn more at **www.kaptest.com/lsat/courses/lsat-self-study**.
- **Additional Practice Recommendations** and the **LSAT Question Database**. In Kaplan's *LSAT Premium Prep, First Edition,* Chapters 3, 4, 5, and 8 cover all of the distinct question types found on the exam. Each of those chapters ends with a Perform quiz. Based on your performance, Kaplan provides recommendations for further practice using questions from official PrepTests. You'll find them in the book companion under *Additional Practice Recommendations*. In this part of the online companion, you'll also find a comprehensive index for every released LSAT question found in PrepTests 101 through 158 (more than 5,800 of them) with Question Type, Subtype, and Difficulty Rating to help you analyze your practice and find additional examples for any question type.
- **Full-Length PrepTest Analysis and Explanations**. The best full-length LSAT test practice experience is available through the testmaker, LSAC, on its LawHub platform. This is another vital online resource mentioned earlier. In LawHub, you can take released tests in the official digital interface, with the same tools and timing you'll see on test day. Register for LawHub at **www.lsac.org/lawhub**. There is a free version, LawHub Free, with (at the time of this writing) four released exams, PrepTests 140, 141, 157, and 158. Kaplan recommends that every self-prep student should use at least these free practice tests. To help you make the most of them, you'll find complete analysis and explanations for every question on these tests in your online companion to this book.

  For test takers who choose to upgrade to LSAC's paid option, called LawHub Advantage, Kaplan offers LSAT Link and Link+. These options are described in detail in the next section of this Preface called "Next-Level Self-Prep." The paid subscription to LawHub and Kaplan's LSAT Link are essentials for the serious self-prepping test taker. Once again, learn more at **www.kaptest.com/lsat/courses/lsat-self-study**.
- **Additional Free LSAT Resources.** This section contains links to additional free LSAT study and practice resources created by Kaplan. Click to see our latest free trials and assets.

There's an enormous amount of additional learning and practice in your online book companion for *LSAT Premium Prep, First Edition,* so don't miss out. Register your book as soon as possible!

NEXT-LEVEL SELF-PREP

Integrate Your Prep with LSAC's LawHub

LSAT Premium Prep, First Edition and its online companion contains expert strategies and tactics for every question type found on the test along with ample practice, but you'll almost certainly want to take additional tests and do additional practice.

As we mentioned in the discussion of your online companion resources, the best way to get additional practice with officially released LSAT questions is by subscribing to LSAC's LawHub Advantage. At the time of this writing, LawHub Advantage provides access to 58 released tests—that's more than 5,800 questions!—at a cost of $115 for a one-year subscription. LawHub will show you your scaled score for each test and what you got right and wrong. What LawHub does *not* offer, however, is detailed analysis of all those tests or explanations for all of those questions.

That's where Kaplan's LSAT Link comes in. When you *link* your LawHub Advantage subscription to Kaplan's LSAT Link, your answers from tests taken in LawHub automatically export to Link, where you'll get the same in-depth analysis and explanations for all 58 PrepTests. With our premium version, LSAT Link+, you'll also get access to more than 150 uniquely curated Mastery quizzes to target each LSAT question type at different levels of difficulty (including more than 1,500 officially released LSAT questions not available on LSAC's LawHub). Find out more about LSAT Link and LSAT Link+ in the next part of this Getting Started chapter under the heading Next-Level Self-Prep or by visiting **www.kaptest.com/lsat/courses/lsat-self-study**.

LawHub Lessons and Drill Sets

While the full-length PrepTests are the essential feature of LawHub for the self-prep LSAT test taker, LawHub also features a small library of lessons and drill sets originally designed in conjunction with Khan Academy, but no longer hosted on that company's website. These are available even on the free version of LawHub, so they're something literally anyone who registers with LSAC has access to.

The lessons include short, written "articles" about the different question types and skills on the test. Video assets include short introductory "video lessons" and "worked examples," each of which goes over a single question. To use these resources in conjunction with your Kaplan book and other resources, you'll need to know how the names and terminology on LawHub line up with those in the Kaplan LSAT universe. Here's a chart that should come in handy.

LOGICAL REASONING TERMS		READING COMPREHENSION TERMS	
LAWHUB	KAPLAN	LAWHUB	KAPLAN
Identify the conclusion	Main Point	Reading Comprehension Passage Types (subject matter)	
Identify an entailment	Inference	Humanities	Humanities
Infer what is most strongly supported		Law	Law
Identify or infer an issue in dispute	Point at Issue	Science	Natural Science
Identify the technique	Method of Argument	Social Science	Social Science
Identify the role	Role of a Statement	Reading Comprehension Passage Structures	
Identify the principle	Principle	N/A	Theory/Perspective
Match the structure	Parallel Reasoning	N/A	Event/Phenomenon
Match principles	Parallel Principle	N/A	Biography
Identify a flaw	Flaw	N/A	Debate
Match flaws	Parallel Flaw	Comparative Reading	Comparative Reading
Necessary Assumption	Assumption (Necessary Assumption)	Reading Comprehension Question Types	
Sufficient Assumption	Assumption (Sufficient Assumption)	Main point	Global
Strengthen	Strengthen	Recognition	Detail
Weaken	Weaken	Clarifying meaning	[Kaplan treats these as a subtype of Inference Qs.]
Identify what is most/least helpful to know	[Kaplan treats these as a subtype of Strengthen/ Weaken questions.]	Purpose of reference	Logic Function
Explain	Paradox	Organizing information	[Khan's category includes Q-types Kaplan would put under Global, Logic Function, and Inference.]
Resolve a Conflict		Inferences about views	Inference
		Inferences about information	
		Inferences about attitudes	
		Applying to new contexts	Logic Reasoning: Principle
		Discovering principles and analogies	Logic Reasoning: Parallel Logic Reasoning: Principle
		Additional evidence	Logic Reasoning: Strengthen/Weaken
		Primary purpose	Global

GO DEEPER IN YOUR AREAS OF GREATEST OPPORTUNITY FOR SCORE IMPROVEMENT

The LSAT Channel

Effective LSAT prep cannot be one-size-fits-all. Even two test takers with an identical score will have distinct strengths and weaknesses. As you learn yours from taking and reviewing practice tests and learning strategies and tactics from this book, you'll discover areas in which you need more work on the fundamentals and others where you're ready to challenge yourself with harder and harder questions. Enter the LSAT Channel, Kaplan's nightly live instruction platform for lessons on almost every conceivable concept and skill rewarded by the exam.

For years, students in Kaplan's comprehensive courses have enjoyed the LSAT Channel with dozens of distinct, hour-long episodes taught by some of the highest-rated instructors in the Kaplan faculty. Now, the LSAT Channel is available to self-prep students as well. You can attend live lessons where you can ask questions and interact with the instructor and online TAs. If you can't attend a live lesson, every episode is available in an archive of recordings available to stream on demand. You can search the upcoming schedule and the archive by subject matter, by difficulty level (Foundations, For Everyone, and Advanced lessons are available), and even by instructor (so that you can find more teaching from your newly discovered favorites).

With the LSAT Channel, you can personalize your instruction with the same specificity and nuance that LSAT Link+ provides for your test analyses and practice. Find out more about the LSAT Channel here: **www.kaptest.com/lsat/courses/lsat-self-study**.

The Hardest Real LSAT Questions

Diligent work with Kaplan's *LSAT Premium Prep, First Edition* and the supplemental tools and programs just outlined will raise your LSAT score, but what do you work on when you've already established a strong score and you're ready to push into the stratosphere? That's exactly the practice, analysis, and strategy Kaplan's LSAT Hardest Questions program provides.

Informed by the empirical results of tens of thousands of LSAT test takers, Kaplan experts have selected the 100 most challenging Logical Reasoning questions along with the 20 hardest Reading Comprehension passages of all time. With Kaplan's LSAT Hardest Questions, you'll try these head-scratchers on your own and then watch video analysis by elite instructors from Kaplan's LSAT faculty. They'll break down what makes each question or passage so challenging; reveal patterns found in the hardest LSAT items; and provide strategies you can use to crack the toughest questions with increased confidence and speed.

These are the kinds of questions that distinguish scores among the top percentile test takers. This means that LSAT Hardest Questions won't be for everyone, but if you're ready for the challenge, you can find more information at **www.kaptest.com/lsat/courses/lsat-self-study**.

Looking for Even More?

At Kaplan, we're thrilled you've chosen us to help you on your journey to law school. Beyond this book, there's a wealth of additional resources that we invite you to check out to aid you with your LSAT preparation and your law school application.

- ***LSAT Logical Reasoning Prep***—Kaplan's book *LSAT Logical Reasoning Prep* is a comprehensive guide to the LSAT exam's all-important Logical Reasoning sections with expert methods and strategies for every question type. It contains hundreds of officially released LSAC questions, along with the drills, exercises, and practice sets on all of the skills you'll need for Logical Reasoning mastery.
- **Comprehensive LSAT Courses**—Of course, we'd be remiss if we did not mention the world's most popular LSAT preparation courses. Visit our website to learn about our comprehensive prep options. Choose from Live Online, and Self-Paced options, depending on your needs and learning style. View course options and upcoming class schedules at **www.kaptest.com/lsat/lsat-courses**.
- **Private Tutoring**—After beginning their LSAT prep, students often realize the benefits of having some undivided, individual attention from an expert private tutor. At Kaplan, it is always easy to add a few hours of tutoring to your LSAT prep course enrollment. You may also realize that one of our comprehensive 10-, 20-, 30-, or 40-hour private tutoring packages is right for you. To find out more, ask your instructor, visit **www.kaptest.com/lsat/courses/lsat-tutoring,** or call us at 1-800-KAPTEST to discuss the best option for you.
- **Admissions Consulting**—A strong LSAT score is the foundation of a great law school application, but don't miss the opportunity to make the rest of your application stand out. An expert Kaplan admissions consultant can utilize your unique experiences, goals, and passions to help you make a convincing case for admission to the law school of your choice. Kaplan Admission Consulting packages include Personal Statement review, expert guidance, and unlimited email support, but consider adding premium features such as additional consulting hours, total application review (including the diversity statement, essay, and resume), and mock interview practice. Explore your options at **www.kaptest.com/lsat/practice/law-school-admissions-consulting** or call us at 1-800-KAPTEST.

You have a lot to do, so let's get to it. Up next: Take a closer look at the format, content, and scoring of the LSAT test.

INTRODUCTION

About the LSAT

Why the LSAT?

Each year, Kaplan surveys law school admissions officials, and consistently, over 60 percent say that the LSAT is their number-one consideration as they evaluate applications. Why do they put so much emphasis on this test? A breakdown of the components in the application offers the best explanation.

- 5 components of the standard law school application: LSAT score, undergraduate GPA, personal statement, letters of recommendation, and "resume factors," such as work experience, extracurricular activities, and so on
- 2 quantitative measures: LSAT score and undergraduate GPA
- 1 quantitative measure comparable for all applicants: LSAT score

The LSAT doesn't care what you majored in or where you went to school. It's the one element of the law school application that measures all applicants on a level playing field.

What the LSAT Tests

While the LSAT offers a standard, quantitative measure of all applicants, law school admissions officers would not value it so highly if the LSAT did not test skills relevant to—indeed, central to—an applicant's law school potential. Studies have consistently shown that LSAT score is more strongly correlated with law school performance, especially in a student's first year, than any other factor in the application.

THE FOUR CORE LSAT SKILLS

Reading Strategically—understanding the structure of a piece of text and the author's purpose for writing it

Analyzing Arguments—distinguishing an argument's conclusion from its evidence and identifying the implicit assumptions the author has made

Making Deductions—determining what follows logically from a set of statements or rules

Understanding Formal Logic—determining what must, can, or cannot be true on the basis of conditional "If/Then" statements

Law schools know that these skills are crucial to a student's success as a law student and in the practice of law later on. Because they are so fundamental to the test, these four core skills underlie all of the Learning Objectives found in this workbook.

Structure of the LSAT

The LSAT consists of four multiple-choice sections: two Logical Reasoning sections, one Reading Comprehension section, and one unscored "experimental" section that will look exactly like one of the other multiple-choice sections. These four multiple-choice sections can appear in any order on test day. A short break is offered between the second and third sections of the test. The unscored, 35-minute LSAT Argumentative Writing essay section is proctored separately. It is also done from the test taker's own computer and taken on-demand.

Here's how the four core skills align with the sections of the LSAT.

FOUR CORE LSAT SKILLS BY SECTION

Core Skill	Primary Section Tested	Secondary Section Tested
Reading Strategically	Reading Comprehension	Logical Reasoning
Analyzing Arguments	Logical Reasoning	Reading Comprehension
Making Deductions	Logical Reasoning	Reading Comprehension
Understanding Formal Logic	Logical Reasoning	

Note that Logical Reasoning is the primary section for three of the core skills and the secondary section for the other one. Indeed, Logical Reasoning is more-or-less the exclusive home of Formal Logic on the LSAT.

SECTION		NUMBER OF QUESTIONS		MINUTES
Logical Reasoning (2x)		24–26		35
Reading Comprehension		27		35
"Experimental"		24–27		35
LSAT Argumentative Writing		One essay		35

LSAC administers the LSAT in two modalities: remotely proctored/take-at-home or live-proctored/testing center administrations. The test content and format is identical regardless of the testing venue.

LSAT Scored Sections

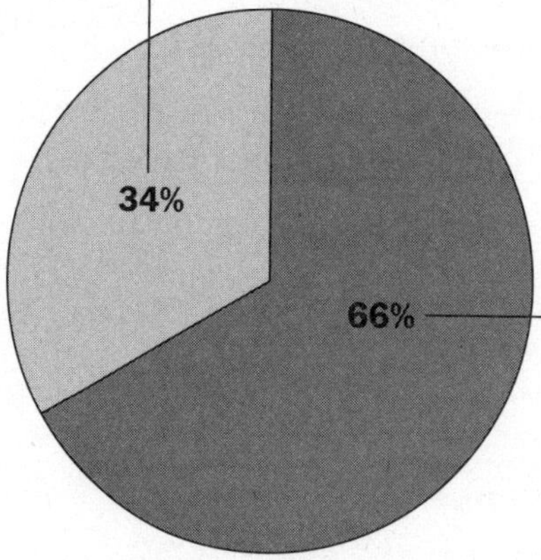

Reading Comprehension

One section with four passages and 27 questions

Reading Comp questions reward you for identifying the author's purpose and main idea, drawing valid inferences from the passage, and determining how and why the author uses certain details.

Logical Reasoning

Two sections with 24–26 questions each

Logical Reasoning rewards you for analyzing arguments to strengthen or weaken them or to identify their assumptions and flaws. Other LR questions require you to draw valid inferences from a set of facts.

LSAT Unscored Sections

Experimental

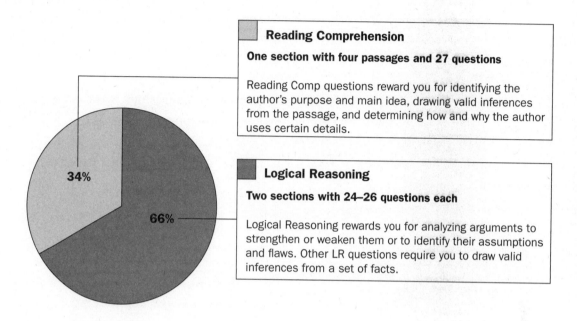

The Experimental section is an additional, unscored section of Logical Reasoning or Reading Comprehension. You will not know what type of section you will get, and it can show up anywhere, including after the break. You'll have to bring your A-game for the entire test, as there is no reliable way to determine which section is experimental while you're taking the test. The LSAT testmaker uses the unscored section to test questions for use as scored items on upcoming exams.

LSAT Argumentative Writing

Within one year after your official LSAT, you will write a short essay choosing between two possible courses of action. While unscored, your LSAT Argumentative Writing essay is submitted to all law schools to which you apply, and law schools use it as part of the evaluation process. Note: You need only one LSAT Argumentative Writing sample on record.

The Digital LSAT Interface

The official LSAT is administered digitally (taken on your personal device or at a testing center on the center's hardware), and getting practice with the interface and tools of the digital test is essential to your preparation. The most direct way to get familiar with the digital interface is to use the LSAC's officially released tests on LawHub: **lsac.org/lawhub**.

Make the most of those LSAC resources throughout your preparation. In the meantime, what follows is a quick introduction to the digital interface with some helpful strategy notes from Kaplan's expert instructors who have used it and have some best practices to pass on to test takers.

Here's a screenshot of a generic question, taken from the digital LSAT interface. The buttons are labeled to show you what each of them does.

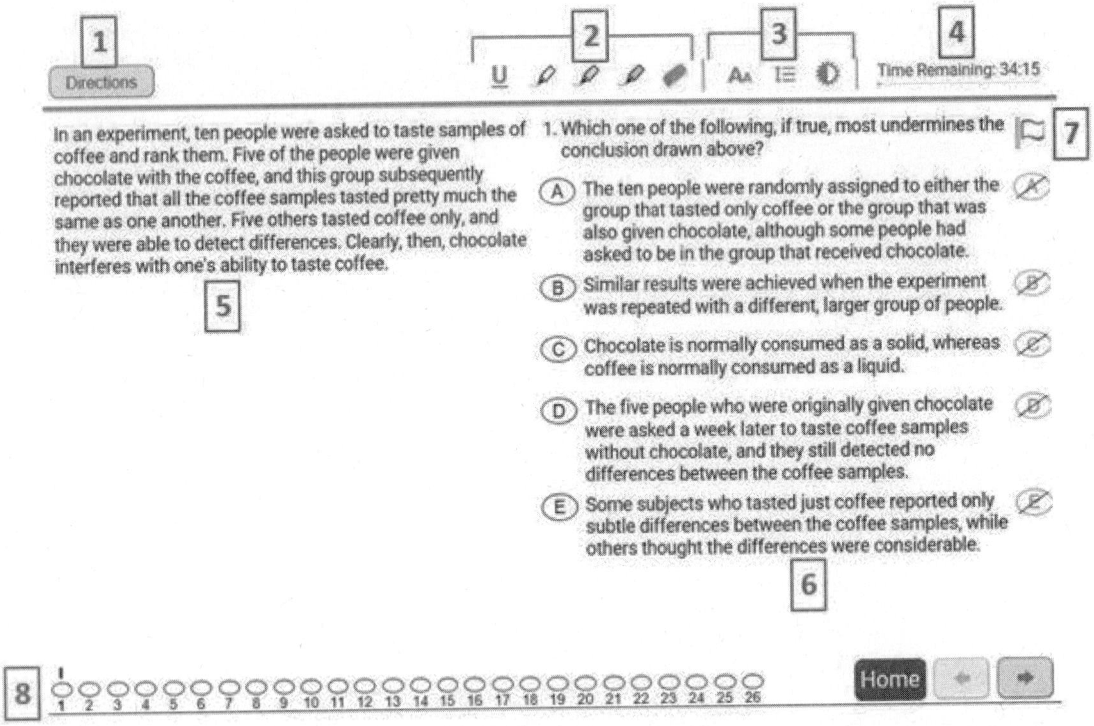

Digital LSAT screen layout LSAC.org

1. The "Directions" button will take you back to the Directions slide at the start of the test section. When you're on the Directions page, this button changes to say "Questions." If you click the button while you're on the Directions page, it will take you back to the last question at which you were looking.
2. These icons activate the underlining and highlighting tools (there are three highlighter colors), and an eraser tool to remove underlines or highlights you've made.

PRACTICE TIP

As you use the LSAC practice tests in the official interface, practice using your device. Do you prefer a mouse or touchpad? Or do you prefer to use your touchscreen or stylus? Make those decisions before test day.

3. These three tools allow you to adjust font size (four options), line spacing (three options), and brightness (a slider).

PRACTICE TIP

Practice using these tools until you're familiar and comfortable with them. That way, you'll know from the get-go how you want to adjust the view for each section of the test.

4. This is the section timer. It will start at 35:00 and count down to 00:00. For the first 30 minutes of the section, you can hide the timer by clicking on the numbers.

PRACTICE TIP

Some test takers like to see the timer. Others get anxious having the clock in their peripheral vision. There is no right or wrong way to use the timer. Try it out in practice to see what works best for you.

5. This is where the question's stimulus or prompt will be. For Logical Reasoning, that means the argument or paragraph on which the question is based, and for Reading Comprehension, it means the passage. For passages and paragraphs too long to fit on the screen, there will be a scroll bar that controls just the text in the left-hand column.
6. This column will always have the question stem and answer choices. Clicking a circle to the left of an answer choice selects that choice as the correct answer. Clicking a circle to the right of an answer choice will grey down that choice. Note: You must click a choice from the left-hand circles; greying down four answer choices does not automatically select the correct answer. This may look or sound confusing at first, but it's quite intuitive after just a few minutes of practice.

DIGITAL LSAT STRATEGY

Among the high-scoring LSAT experts we surveyed about their use of the digital interface, no feature gained as universally high praise as the "grey down" bubbles. Top scorers on the LSAT develop tremendous acumen and confidence that allows them to eliminate incorrect choices after one read-through. They all appreciated the added clarity of being able to visually eliminate the choice with one click.

6a. On questions in which the right-hand column text will not fit onscreen, you'll see upward arrows to the right of the answer choices. These allow you to collapse answer choices until the text no longer requires a scroll bar. Collapsing answers you've confidently eliminated will help you avoid rereading and confusion.

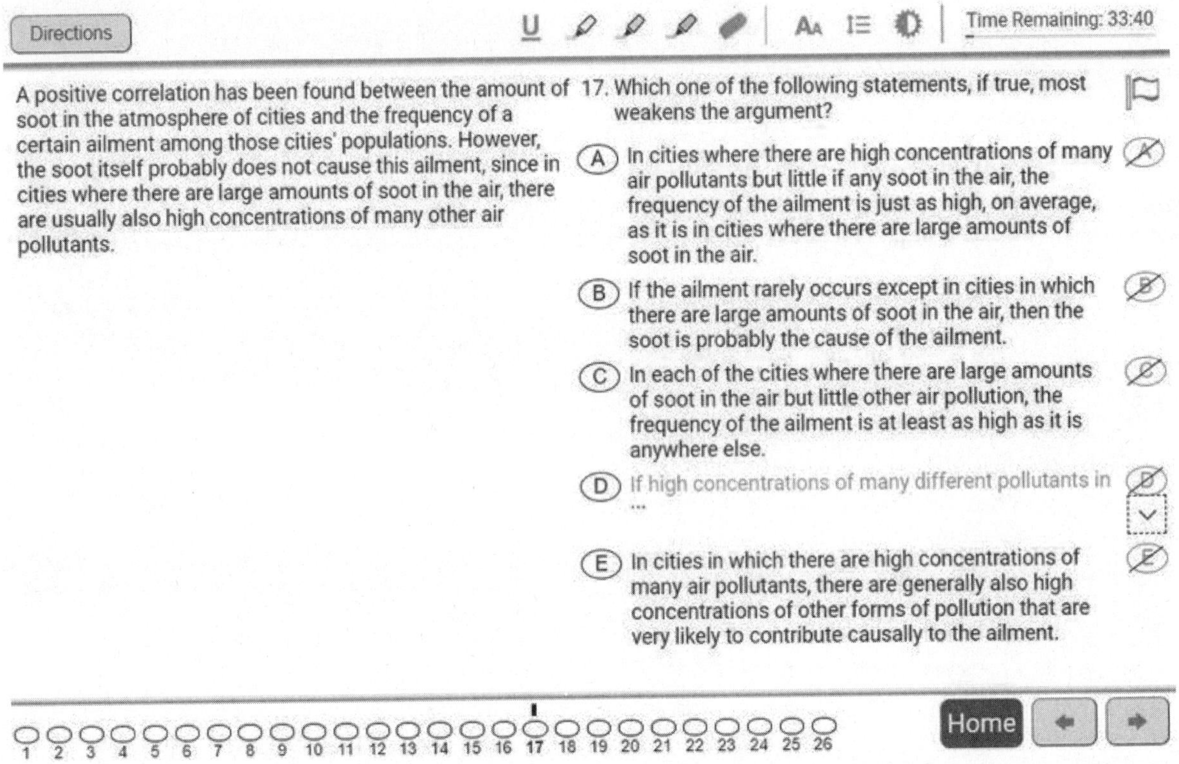

Collapsible answer choices LSAC.org

7. This flag allows you to mark questions. Our LSAT experts use it in two situations. Some flagged questions that they skipped or left unanswered. All of the experts, however, used the flag for questions to which they wanted to return, time permitting. In some cases, these were questions for which they had picked an answer, but had low confidence in their choice and wanted to give it one more look. In other cases, these were questions on which the expert had eliminated (greyed down) two or three of the answers and wanted to come back for a final decision on the remaining choices.

DIGITAL LSAT STRATEGY

Strategic skipping and guessing are important tactics for effective time management on the LSAT. Test experts know that all questions carry equal weight in calculating their final score, so they avoid wasting too much time on any single question. The flag tool provides an excellent way to keep track of skipped or incomplete questions.

8. The horizontal bar at the bottom of the screen is for navigation. This "bubble bar" indicates questions for which you've selected a correct answer, questions you've left blank, and any question you've flagged, answered or not. The current on-screen question is indicated by a small vertical bar above the bubble. Clicking on a bubble in the navigation bar will automatically advance you to that question. The forward and back buttons in the far bottom right will move you one question forward or back.

How the LSAT is Scored

To understand how the LSAT is scored, and the implications of your score for your law school application, it is helpful to think about three different scales.

Raw Score

Your raw score on the LSAT refers to the number of questions you got correct. Each question on the LSAT has one correct answer and four demonstrably incorrect ones. The raw score is simply the sum of your correct answers. Moreover, there is no wrong answer penalty on the LSAT and no partial credit for any question, so you should answer every question, even if your answer is a pure guess.

Scaled Score

Scaled scores make the scores of test takers who took different administrations of the LSAT comparable. The score-conversion table for a given exam distributes raw scores on a standard bell curve. Raw-to-scaled conversions vary *very* slightly from test to test to account for slight differences in the difficulty of different administrations.

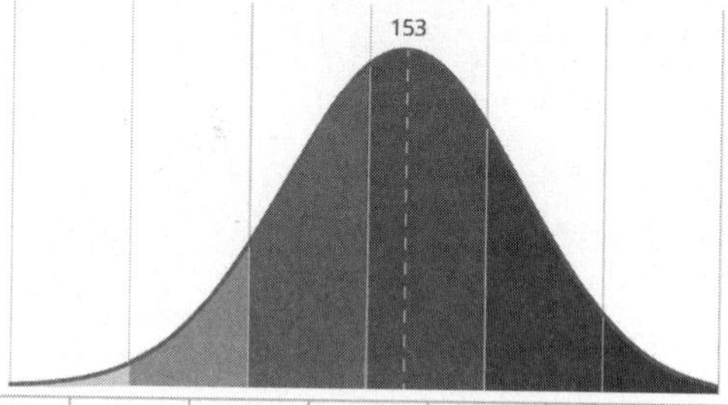

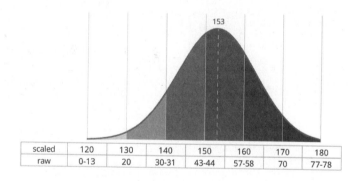

scaled	120	130	140	150	160	170	180
raw	0-13	20	30-31	43-44	57-58	70	77-78

Percentile Score

Percentile rankings allow schools to compare an applicant to their cohort. Your percentile score (or more accurately, your percentile *rank*) shows the percentage of test takers who had scaled scores below yours over the previous three testing years (July to June).

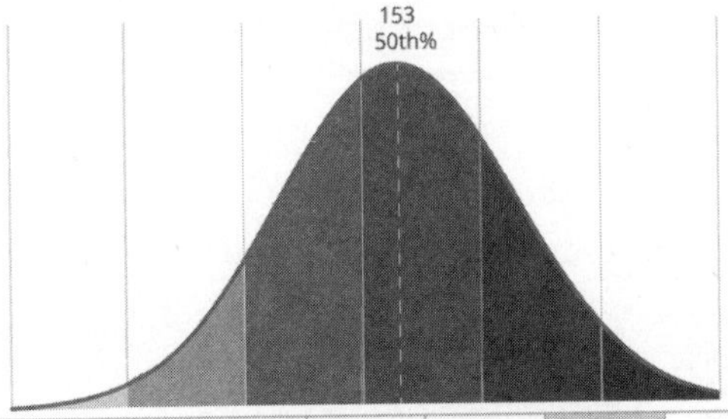

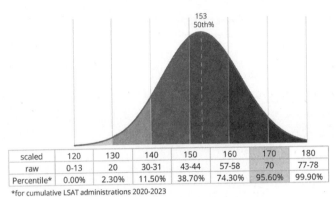

scaled	120	130	140	150	160	170	180
raw	0-13	20	30-31	43-44	57-58	70	77-78
Percentile*	0.00%	2.30%	11.50%	38.70%	74.30%	95.60%	99.90%

*for cumulative LSAT administrations 2020-2023

Note: 50th percentile is approximately 153 (~47 correct answers).
90th percentile is approximately 166 (~65 correct answers).

Adding percentile ranking to the chart illustrates the enormous power of even small improvements to your raw score, especially when you are scoring in the middle range of the bell curve.

Here's a table aligning percentile rankings with scaled scores and raw scores. In the raw score column, you see also the number of additional correct answers needed on average to move up by 10 percentile points.

Percentile	Scaled	Raw
99.90%	180	77-78 (+12)
95%	**170**	**70**
90%	166-167	65 (+5)
80%	162	60 (+4)
70%	159	56 (+5)
60%	156	51 (+4)
50%	153	47 (+3)
40%	150-151	44 (+5)
30%	147	39 (+4)
20%	144	35 (+6)
10%	139	29 (+16)
0%	120	0-13

Let it sink in that, depending on where you're scoring, adding just seven correct responses can move you past approximately 15,000 other test takers. That makes a huge difference to any law school considering your application. Use this as motivation to keep studying and practicing even when your initial score gains feel modest.

What's a Good LSAT Score?

What you consider a good LSAT score depends on your own expectations and goals, but here are a few interesting statistics: Getting about half of all of the scored questions right (a raw score of roughly 39) will earn a scaled score of roughly 146 or 147, around the 30th percentile—not a great performance. However, getting only three additional questions right per section (that's less than one additional right answer every 10 minutes during the test) would produce a raw score of 48, or a scaled score of approximately 153, around the 50th percentile—a huge improvement.

So, you don't have to be perfect to do well. On a typical LSAT, you can still get 20 questions wrong and end up in the 160s, or about 13 wrong and get a 167, typically a 90th percentile score. Even a perfect score of 180 often allows for a question to be missed.

Here is a chart detailing some law schools and the scores of their admitted students:

RANK*	SCHOOL	25TH–75TH %ILE LSAT* (SCALED)	25TH–75TH %ILE UGPA*	25TH–75TH %ILE LSAT** (RAW)
1	Yale University	171–178	3.87–3.99	71–76
5 (tied)	New York University	169–174	3.72–3.94	69–73
5 (tied)	Duke University	168–171	3.73–3.94	68–71
10	University of California–Berkeley	167–172	3.74–3.9	67–71
16 (tied)	University of Texas–Austin	166–171	3.71–3.92	65–71
16 (tied)	University of Southern California	165–169	3.76–3.94	64–69
22	University of Florida	162–170	3.52–3.97	60–70
29	Boston College	162–167	3.55–3.81	60–67
32	Arizona State University	158–168	3.42–3.94	55–68
45	Pepperdine University	159–166	3.54–3.93	56–65
54	Temple University	160–165	3.38–3.74	57–64
56	University of Colorado—Boulder	159–166	3.45–3.83	56–65
71	Tulane University	157–163	3.42–3.76	53–62

** U.S. News & World Report, 2023–2024 Best Law Schools*
*** Estimated score conversion*

Registration for and Administration of the LSAT

The LSAT is administered nine times per testing cycle (July–June).

LSAT FACTS

The typical testing cycle features LSAT administrations in the following months:

- July or August
- September
- October
- November
- January
- February
- March or April
- June

Check **lsac.org/LSATdates** for complete, accurate, and up-to-date test administration information.

Test takers choose either to take the test on their own device or to appear at a testing center and use the center's hardware. For each administration, there are multiple days and time slots from which to schedule their individual test. Dates and times may be different for tests administered outside the United States, Canada, and the Caribbean.

How do I register for the LSAT? Register for the LSAT online at **lsac.org**. Check the LSAC website for details on the procedures, deadlines, and fee schedules.

When should I register? Register as soon as you have chosen your test date. Registration is typically due about five weeks before test day. As of 2018, there is no longer a "Late Registration" period.

Can I change my test date? You can change your test date (subject to an additional fee) via the LSAC website. Timely changes of test date are not reported to schools; "no-shows," however, are reported.

What is the CAS? Upon signing up for the LSAT, you also need to register with the Credential Assembly Service (CAS) as part of the application process required by every ABA-approved law school. CAS receives your undergraduate transcripts and distributes a summary of your undergraduate performance, along with your letters of recommendation, evaluations, and LSAT score report to each of the law schools to which you apply. **lsac.org/applying-law-school/jd-application-process/credential-assembly-service-cas** lists the fees and sign-up details for CAS.

When are law schools' application deadlines? All law schools provide their application deadlines on their websites. A small number of schools require the LSAT be taken by December for admission the following fall; most will accept a later LSAT score. Because most schools use a "rolling admissions" process, taking the test earlier is preferable; also, taking the test earlier gives the test taker a chance to repeat the LSAT prior to most application deadlines.

Can I repeat the LSAT? Yes. Test takers are limited to five administrations within any period of five testing years, and seven administrations in their lifetime. If you cancel your score (including cancellations under the Score Preview option) after taking the test, that test administration still counts toward your total allowed administrations, but absences and withdrawals prior to testing do not. Any test taker who achieves a score of 180 may not take another LSAT in her lifetime (but why would anyone want to?).

How do law schools view multiple LSAT scores? What is Score Preview? It is now standard practice for schools to evaluate candidates based on their highest LSAT score from the five-year period preceding the date of their application. Schools do, however, see all of your scores and cancellations, so you may wish to explain the circumstances of low scores or cancellations in an addendum. LSAC's Score Preview option allows you (for a fee) to cancel your score within five days of receiving your score report. No schools see that score, but they do see that you canceled (and the administration will count against your testing limit).

Can I receive accommodations? The LSAC grants accommodated testing for physical, learning, and cognitive impairments, and there are a wide variety of accommodations available. A test taker must be registered for a test date before requesting accommodations. Full information about accommodated testing is available at **lsac.org/lsat/register-lsat/accommodations/accommodations-may-be-available-lsat**.

LSAT Study Skills

The LSAT is a skills-based test. For this reason, improving your score is, in some ways, more like mastering a musical instrument or an athletic skill than it is like learning a subject in school. The LSAT is very practical, testing what you can do above what you know. As such, it is also *practice-able* and coachable. Expect Kaplan to show you the best ways to practice. Expect us to show you the patterns of the test and how to tackle every question type. Expect us to show you how to manage every section. Expect us to show you how, when, and why to use your resources. In return, you're going to need to work—hard. Reaching your full potential on the LSAT takes lots of practice. We will show you precisely what you need to do, but ultimately it's up to you to do it.

LSAT Strategy and the Three Levels of Practice

On test day, you'll be asked to deal with stringent testing policies and procedures and answer approximately 104–105 multiple-choice questions (of which typically 77–78 will count toward your score). It's a grueling and intense two-and-one-half hours.

A strategic approach to the LSAT means increasing your speed only to the extent you can do so without sacrificing accuracy. Your goal is not to attempt as many questions as possible; your goal is to get as many questions right as possible. If you had unlimited time to take this test, you'd likely perform quite well. But you don't. You have a strict 35 minutes to complete each section, and many students are not able to tackle every question in the time allotted. For you, this means three things:

- It's important that you learn not only how to answer the questions effectively, but also how to answer them efficiently.
- It's important to approach each section strategically, knowing which questions to attack first and which questions to save for last.
- It's important that you prepare for the rigors of 2½ hours of testing. You'll want to maintain your focus in the final section as well as you did in the first.

To achieve your goals, you'll want to incorporate three levels of practice: Mastery, Timing, and Endurance.

Mastery is about learning the patterns of the exam and how to identify them in new questions. Kaplan provides a proven method for the questions in each section of the test. You will gain command of the method and master efficient, effective strategies and tactics through repeated practice on skill-based drills and individual questions. You'll study the answers and explanations to learn how the testmaker builds questions and answer choices. You'll identify why right answers are right, why wrong answers are wrong, what traps you consistently fall into, and how to avoid them. That's what Mastery practice is for.

Once you've learned the skills, you'll try section practice, or **Timing** practice. At about two-and-one-half hours of active testing, the LSAT can seem like a marathon, but it's really a series of sprints—four 35-minute tests. Learning section management—how to recognize and apply the patterns you've learned efficiently, maximizing the number of questions you get correct—is what Timing practice teaches you to do.

Finally, there's **Endurance** practice. Can you maintain your ability to identify and apply these patterns through the whole exam? Some test takers lose focus during the second hour of testing and struggle through the last two sections of the test. Others need warm-up time and underperform on the first section. Taking full-length practice tests will help you build your stamina and focus. As you'll learn in your course, practice tests are very important to your score improvement. Look for places in your schedule where you have an uninterrupted 2.5 hours and block them out for full-length practice. Then, the hours or days immediately following, look for at least two more hours (they do not need to be uninterrupted) and schedule them for test review. The process of reviewing the tests—especially with Kaplan's thorough and strategy-focused explanations—greatly enhances the benefits of testing.

By approaching your practice in this way—using Mastery practice to internalize the strategies for each new question type you learn, layering in Timing practice to build efficiency, and using consistent full-length Endurance practice throughout your preparation—you'll be fully and properly prepared by test day.

LSAT Attitude

In the main chapters, you'll learn, practice, and master the methods, strategies, and tactics that lead to test day success. Nevertheless, two students with equal LSAT proficiency still might not produce the same score. Of those two "equal" test takers, the one with greater confidence and less stress will likely outperform the other. You can develop these positive psychological characteristics just as you can your LSAT skill set.

Stay Positive

Those who approach the LSAT as an obstacle and rail against the necessity of taking it generally don't fare as well as those who see the LSAT as an opportunity, a chance to show law schools their proficiency with the four core skills. A great LSAT score will distinguish your application from those of your competition.

- Look at the LSAT as a challenge, but try not to obsess over it; you certainly don't want to psych yourself out of the game.
- Remember that the LSAT is important, but this one test will not single-handedly determine the outcome of your life.
- Try to have fun with the test. Learning how to unlock the patterns of the test and approach the content in the way the testmakers have crafted the exam can be very satisfying, and the skills you'll acquire will benefit you in law school and your career.

Confidence and Stress Management

Confidence in your ability leads to quick, sure answers and a sense of well-being that translates into more points. Confidence feeds on itself; unfortunately, so does self-doubt. If you lack confidence, you end up reading sentences and answer choices two, three, or four times, until you confuse yourself and get off-track. This leads to timing difficulties that perpetuate a downward spiral of anxiety, rushing, and poor performance. If you subscribe to the proper LSAT mind-set, however, you'll gear all of your practice toward taking control of the test. When you've achieved that goal—armed with the principles, techniques, strategies, and methods Kaplan has to offer—you'll be ready to face the LSAT with confidence. Your online resources have more good information, explanations, and other resources to help you minimize test anxiety, manage stress, and maximize your performance.

CHANNEL SPOTLIGHT

Secrets of LSAT Preparation

By The LSAT Channel Faculty

Watch the video lesson for this Spotlight in your online Study Plan.

Students who come to *The LSAT Channel* get to hear from some of Kaplan's most experienced and highly rated LSAT faculty. The message they hear most clearly is: Kaplan knows the LSAT—inside out, forward and backward—and we've got the method and strategies that will (with practice) help you master it. Each of these coaches and mentors has his or her own special insights, as well. In the video that accompanies this Spotlight, you'll meet the LSAT Channel faculty, and hear what each of them tells students at the beginning of their logic games prep. Here are a few of the themes they hit upon:

You Use LSAT Skills All the Time

It is often remarked that the LSAT is like no other test you've ever taken. It is entirely skills-based and requires little to no outside knowledge. The skills tested here, however, are more familiar than you may realize. If you've ever ranked the *Star Wars* movies from best to worst, chosen teams for a pick-up basketball game, or separated clothes into laundry and dry cleaning, you've done a logic game. If you've ever pointed out an unwarranted assumption in a friend's argument, you've engaged in logical reasoning. Likewise, if you've ever combined two statements to make a valid deduction. If you've ever questioned a pundit's point of view in an editorial, or analyzed an author's support for a position in an academic paper, you've tackled LSAT-style reading comprehension. So, while it may be true that you've never had to answer questions quite like these *on a test*, you engage in LSAT-related tasks every day. LSAT questions, games, and passages present you with small, real-world puzzles that may, at first, seem abstract or technical, but are really quite practical—and, you *can* do them.

There Is Always Enough Information to Answer Every Question

There are two criteria for a good game—not just for logic games, but even games we play with friends or against the computer: They need to be challenging, and they need to be fair. If we're honest, challenging games are more fun. We quickly lose interest in puzzles that are too easy to solve, or in games we always win. LSAT questions (not just those in the Logic Games section, but throughout the test) are challenging, but always fair. Before a question appears on an official LSAT, it has been tested on thousands of test takers to ensure it has all the information needed to produce exactly one correct answer and four demonstrably incorrect ones. The experts on the LSAT Channel are fond of stating "One right, four rotten" as a principle of every LSAT question. As you gain experience and expertise with the test, you, too, will gain confidence that you can identify the correct answer and reject the incorrect ones, efficiently and effectively.

Patience Can Make You Faster

The scored sections of the LSAT are 35 minutes long, and they contain between 23 and 27 questions. In Logical Reasoning, you have approximately 1 minute 20 seconds per question. In the Logic Games and Reading Comprehension sections, you have approximately 8½ minutes for each game or passage and its accompanying questions. The time pressure is real, but the best response to that pressure is counterintuitive. To increase your efficiency on the LSAT, you need patience. LSAT experts know that a methodical approach—untangling the stimulus of a Logical Reasoning question, accurately sketching a logic game's setup and rules, Roadmapping a Reading Comprehension passage—reduces confusion, eliminates wasteful rereading, and makes you faster and more accurate overall.

Small Improvements Produce Big Results

You saw this demonstrated earlier, in the section about LSAT scoring. There are only 101 questions on the typical LSAT test, and given that the LSAT is scored on a curve, adding just five more correct answers to your score can move you past 10 percent of test takers. Depending on your starting score, 10 additional correct answers could move your score past a quarter of all law school applicants (that's thousands of other test takers vying for admission). That means the improvements you make—even if it is "just" 2–3 more correct answers per section—can have an enormous impact on your law school application.

The LSAT Channel

Kaplan launched the LSAT Channel in 2015 to bring nightly live instruction from our most highly rated LSAT teachers to every student enrolled in a comprehensive LSAT prep course. Since then, students all over the country (and the world) have had access to over 100 unique hours of instruction for every testing cycle. The LSAT Channel faculty is constantly creating new lessons on special topics to provide their strategic insights to ambitious test takers.

Now, the LSAT Channel instructors have developed several Spotlight lessons exclusively for *LSAT Premium Plus*. Whenever you see one of these Spotlight features in the book, you'll not only get the expertise provided on the page, but also have a chance to practice the strategies explained there, and to learn directly from the instructors through the videos in your online Study Plan.

Take a few minutes to meet the faculty, both on the following page and in the accompanying video. They'll motivate you and set you on the path to LSAT success. Let's get started . . .

JEFF BOUDREAU

BEST ADVICE FOR STUDENTS: If this is truly your dream, don't put an expiration date on it.

DESCRIBES TEACHING STYLE AS: Excited, fun-loving, caring

BOBBY GAUTAM

BEST ADVICE FOR STUDENTS: Work hard to get ready for the test, but when the test begins don't work harder than you have to.

DESCRIBES TEACHING STYLE AS: Clear, compassionate, lively, humorous, passionate

HANNAH GIST

BEST ADVICE FOR STUDENTS: So many students come to class and do the homework, but they keep using the same flawed methods they used on the Diag. If you want better results, have the courage to CHANGE.

DESCRIBES TEACHING STYLE AS: Patient, energetic, encouraging, accessible, proficient

GED HELM

BEST ADVICE FOR STUDENTS: The LSAT is not an IQ test, a test of character, or a test of worth. The LSAT tests a specific set of skills that are learned.

DESCRIBES TEACHING STYLE AS: Energetic, positive, strategic, honest

MELANIE TRIEBEL

BEST ADVICE FOR STUDENTS: It feels good to get everything right, but you learn more when you get things wrong. When you make a mistake, celebrate! Then learn. If you can figure out why you made the mistake, that's one fewer mistake on test day.

DESCRIBES TEACHING STYLE AS: Enthusiastic, simplified, geeky, detailed

PART ONE

Formal Logic

CHAPTER 1

Formal Logic

Welcome to your LSAT studies! By the time you get to the end of this book, you'll have learned all of the skills and strategies necessary to master the LSAT. You'll begin in this chapter, however, by building the foundational skills associated with Formal Logic. On the LSAT, this means learning to identify, untangle, and combine conditional statements to make valid deductions. These skills are tested extensively in the test's Logical Reasoning sections.

You need very little "content" knowledge for the LSAT. There's no math, science, or history you're supposed to know. The LSAT is a test of the skills you'll use in law school and in legal practice. By working with dozens of expert LSAT test takers, psychometricians, and learning scientists, Kaplan has identified the most important of these skills and devised methods and strategies that you can use to master them on the test. There is little doubt that you'll think, read, and analyze information differently (and more skillfully) when you've mastered the LSAT.

CHANNEL SPOTLIGHT

Great Moments in Formal Logic

By The LSAT Channel Faculty

Watch the video lesson for this Spotlight in your online Study Plan.

Let's tell it like it is: Formal Logic is abstract. Indeed, that is its strength. The goal of Formal Logic is to provide a precise, systematic, almost mathematical way to analyze the inferences derived from formal rules and conditions. In its pure form, Formal Logic has no "real world" content at all; it's just "If A → B" and "If ~B → ~A." On the LSAT, however, you can apply Formal Logic to statements and rules written in natural language by reducing those statements to their formal content. A rule such as "If Aloysius is selected for the committee, then Benjamin is also selected for the committee," for example, can be reduced to the more manageable "If A → B."

That abstract expression of the rule is valuable on the LSAT because after you memorize a few rules about how inferences work, you know confidently that if Benjamin is *not selected* for the committee, then neither is Aloysius. Perhaps more importantly, based on that one statement alone, the fact that Benjamin is selected for the committee implies nothing about whether Aloysius is selected, and the fact that Aloysius is rejected implies nothing about whether Benjamin is selected. On many Logical Reasoning questions, the correct answer amounts to nothing more than the correct application of basic Formal Logic rules, and one or more of the wrong answers contain flawed applications of those same rules.

Depending on your experience and comfort level with Formal Logic, it can take some time to embrace the power of its abstract appearance. As you learn and practice the basics of Formal Logic in the course of your LSAT preparation, however, you will realize that conditional statements and rules are everywhere in your day-to-day life. "No admittance without proper ID" is simply "If ~I → ~A," and "Only club members may vote in the election for next year's officers" amounts to "If V → M."

In this Spotlight's video, an LSAT expert will take you on a journey through time that reveals some noteworthy (and humorous) examples of conditional statements made in history, politics, and culture. You may be surprised to realize that some of these familiar statements can be expressed in abstract terms, and that some of their contrapositives sound pretty bizarre. But, hey, that's going to be your life now. As an LSAT student, you'll start to realize that Formal Logic is with us all the time, and you'll be practicing whenever you spot an "If-then" statement. Embrace the abstract, my friend.

Formal Logic: Conditional Statements

On the LSAT, you are often rewarded for making valid deductions from conditional statements—that is, statements that can be expressed in "if...then" form (though conditional statements in Logical Reasoning questions rarely contain those exact words). Before going deeper into that parenthetical note in the preceding sentence, take a closer look at what an "if...then" statement is and what it means.

LEARNING OBJECTIVES

In this section, you'll learn to:

- Identify what is and is not a conditional statement (that is, understand what it means for a statement to be a conditional statement).
- Understand conditional statements that include *and* or *or*.
- Translate a sentence that expresses a conditional relationship into If/Then format.
- Make deductions on the basis of conditional statements.

Identifying Conditional Statements

Prepare

Consider this conditional statement:

If you are in New York, then you are in the United States.

What does that statement mean? It expresses a relationship of *logical necessity:* Being in New York logically necessitates—that is, requires—that you be in the United States. On the other hand, "if... then" language does not necessarily express a causal relationship: Being in New York doesn't *cause* you to be in the United States. (Consider the case of someone who flies from Atlanta to New York: They were in the United States the whole time.) And the word "then" doesn't express a chronological relationship: You aren't in New York *before* you're in the United States.

Every conditional statement has two parts: the "sufficient term" and the "necessary term":

- The *sufficient term* is the part that immediately follows "if." "Sufficient" means "enough," and this part of a conditional statement is sufficient—it's enough—to require the other part. You don't need any additional information to know that the other part is true. Being in New York is enough to know that you are in the United States. In this book, we may also sometimes call this sufficient term the *trigger* because it precipitates the occurrence or truth of something else, logically speaking.
- The *necessary term* is the part that immediately follows the "then." "Necessary" means "required," and this part of a conditional statement is required whenever the sufficient term is present. Being in the United States is required—it's necessary—whenever you're in New York. If you're not in the United States, you simply cannot be in New York. We may also call this term the *result* because it's the logical consequence of the "trigger" in the sufficient term. Whenever you have the trigger, you've got to have the result.

Let's focus a little more on what a conditional statement does and doesn't mean. In the previous example, you absolutely cannot be in New York without being in the United States (because being in the United States is necessary to being in New York). But can you be in the United States without being in New York? Sure—you could be in California, South Dakota, or Texas. So, the necessary term doesn't serve as a logical trigger.

Let's look at another real-world example to clarify this further. Consider this statement: If you're driving your car, then your car has an engine.

You driving your car logically necessitates that it have an engine. And you driving it is sufficient—that is, it's all we need to know—to determine that your car has an engine. But can it have an engine without you driving it? Obviously! At times when your car is sitting in the garage, cold and unused, it still most likely has an engine.

Do you find yourself nevertheless tempted to tease out the logical possibilities by beginning a sentence like this:

> "So if your car has an engine, then . . ."

If so, resist that temptation! There's no way, given only the original statement, to complete that sentence. There's no logical result of your car having an engine other than, well, your car having an engine.

The fact that the necessary term by itself doesn't logically trigger anything is a tremendously important concept to remember on the LSAT. Unless the LSAT argument or stimulus explicitly tells you otherwise, always assume that it's possible to have the necessary term without having the sufficient term. Moreover, the LSAT uses many examples that involve fictional people or ambiguous terms, which means that you can't rely on real-world knowledge to sort out what triggers something else or what is necessary for the trigger as you could with the previous examples. Let's demonstrate how to think about this using a conditional rule. Here's how an expert test taker would understand such a conditional statement:

Conditional Statement	Analysis
If James volunteers, then so does Rebekkah.	If James volunteers, that's sufficient to know that Rebekkah must volunteer. Or, to put that another way, if James volunteers, it is necessary that Rebekkah volunteers also. So James cannot be the only person who volunteers. But Rebekkah could volunteer without James volunteering. Given only this rule, Rebekkah could volunteer alone.

We identify and understand conditional statements all the time in the real world. Each of the following expresses a relationship of sufficiency and necessity:

> No shirt, no shoes, no service.
>
> You can't legally drink unless you're 21 or older.
>
> You must be over 48 inches tall to ride the roller coaster.

Most likely, you intuitively understand statements like this in real life. They're simply relationships in which one thing is needed for another to happen, and that's the essence of a conditional relationship. However, you'll notice that none of them contain the words *if* or *then*. And just as in real life, many conditional statements on the LSAT are phrased in ways that don't involve the specific words *if* and *then*. On the test, it's important for you to spot conditional relationships when they appear, regardless of how they're phrased.

Consider whether each of the following statements contains a trigger-and-result ("if" . . . "then") relationship. Keep in mind there are a couple of ways to think about spotting these: if one thing is sufficient—is enough—to make the other happen, then they have a trigger-and-result relationship. Similarly, if one thing is necessary—is required—whenever something else happens, that also signals a trigger-and-result relationship. In the Analysis here, the LSAT expert categorizes the statements "Yes, it contains a sufficient-necessary relationship" or "No, it does not."

Statement	Analysis
Drivers must pay a toll to cross the bridge.	Yes. Paying a toll is *necessary* for anyone wishing to cross the bridge.
The company ought to adopt the consultant's proposal.	No. This is a recommendation. It doesn't contain a condition necessary for another condition to occur.
How many tomatoes did you buy?	No. Like recommendations, questions do not express a Formal Logic relationship.
The state of California requires that all passengers wear a seatbelt when riding in a moving vehicle.	Yes. The word *requires* indicates wearing a seatbelt is *necessary* for passengers riding in a moving vehicle in California.
Any student in the halls after the bell rings will get a detention slip.	Yes. Regardless of the student's status or reason for being in the hallway, the fact that he is there after the bell rings is *sufficient* to tell us that he will receive a detention slip.
The LSAT is a prerequisite for getting into law school.	Yes. The word *prerequisite* indicates that the LSAT is *required* for getting into law school.
You can't make an omelet without breaking a few eggs.	Yes. *Without* is the word to pay attention to here. In order to make an omelet, it is *necessary* to break a few eggs.
Let them have cake.	No. This is simply a declarative statement with neither a necessary nor a sufficient condition.
Cheaters never prosper.	Yes. The knowledge that someone is a cheater is *sufficient* to know that she will never prosper.
Sara cannot go to the movies unless she cleans her room.	Yes. The word *unless* makes a clean room a *necessary* condition that must be met for Sara to go to the movies.

Each of the statements that received a "yes" answer—that is, every conditional statement—can be expressed in If/Then format. A bit later in this chapter, we'll devote a section to learning how to make those translations. For now, though, it's critical to hone your ability to spot trigger-and-result relationships in prose.

Practice Here's your chance to practice this. Take a look at each of the following statements and note to yourself whether it expresses a relationship of sufficiency and necessity and how you know whether it does or not. After each one, you can look ahead to see the expert thinking.

Statement	My Analysis
22. There's a strong possibility the election will oust the incumbent senator.	
23. The car cannot run without gasoline.	
24. Each of the apples in the basket has been rinsed off.	
25. Make it so.	
26. It may be the case that germs cause your headaches.	
27. Everything on the menu is vegan-friendly.	
28. Mammals don't have gills.	
29. Only members of the book club receive that discount.	

Statement	My Analysis
30. Did you pick up milk on your way home?	
31. Unless they beat the Eagles, the Lions won't make it to the playoffs.	
32. The car needs an oil change before your trip.	
33. Some wildcats are striped.	

Expert Analysis

Here's how an LSAT expert would evaluate the statements on the basis of whether each is an example of a conditional Formal Logic statement.

Statement	Analysis
22. There's a strong possibility the election will oust the incumbent senator.	No. This is a possibility and contains no condition sufficient or necessary for another to occur. No Formal Logic here.
23. The car cannot run without gasoline.	Yes. Gasoline is *necessary* for the car to run. The car running is *sufficient* to tell you it has gas.
24. Each of the apples in the basket has been rinsed off.	Yes. Telling me an apple is in that basket is enough, or *sufficient*, for me to know that it has been rinsed off. If it's in the basket, it's required for it to have been rinsed off.
25. Make it so.	No. This is just a command.
26. It may be the case that germs cause your headaches.	No. Because it only "may" be the case, you can't say that either term is sufficient for or requires the other.
27. Everything on the menu is vegan-friendly.	Yes. Knowing that an item appears on this menu is *sufficient* to tell you that it's vegan-friendly. "Vegan-friendly" is a status *required* of any item that is on the menu.
28. Mammals don't have gills.	Yes. Knowledge that an animal is a mammal is *sufficient* to know that it does not have gills. Likewise, it is *necessary* for mammals to lack gills. (Having gills would be a sure sign that an animal is not a mammal.)
29. Only members of the book club receive that discount.	Yes. Being a member of the book club is *necessary* to receive this discount, and if a person is getting the discount, that's enough (*sufficient*) to guarantee that the person is in the book club.

Statement	Analysis
30. Did you pick up milk on your way home?	No. Questions do not express conditional statements.
31. Unless they beat the Eagles, the Lions won't make it to the playoffs.	Yes. Beating the Eagles is a *necessary* condition for the Lions to make it to the playoffs. The Lions making the playoffs is *sufficient* to know that the Lions beat the Eagles.
32. The car needs an oil change before your trip.	Yes. An oil change is *necessary* if this car goes on a trip. If you're driving this car on your trip, that's enough to guarantee that this car had an oil change.*
33. Some wildcats are striped.	No. It is not necessary for a wildcat to be striped because only some of them are.

*Note that in day-to-day experience we often use *need* very loosely in place of *ought* or *should*. On the LSAT, you must treat a word such as *need* very strictly.

Again, each one of the exercises that is a conditional statement can be expressed in If/Then format, and later in this chapter, you'll get lots of practice with making those translations.

Reflect Look back over your practice.

- Did you accurately identify which statements were conditional statements and which weren't?
- What words were helpful to you in identifying that relationship of logical necessity?
- Did you notice all of the different ways in which sufficient-and-necessary relationships can be phrased?

Practice identifying conditional, Formal Logic statements in everyday life. Even simple interactions often reveal our understanding of necessary-sufficient relationships. Have you ever responded to someone who told you some electrical device wasn't working by asking, "Are you sure it's plugged in?" Your response is based on the fact that you know that a power source is necessary for the electrical device to operate. In no time, you'll treat all sorts of statements—"I can't serve you unless I see an ID," "Registration required," and so on—as indicative of Formal Logic.

A Note About Cause-and-Effect Relationships

We're going to steadily build on our understanding of conditional statements because you're going to see multiple instances of them on every section of the LSAT. Before we proceed, however, take a moment for an important caveat about conditional statements and cause-and-effect relationships. In a causal relationship, one thing is the reason *why* another happens. Examples of statements indicating cause-and-effect relationships include these:

Mike gets good grades because he studies every night.

Low pressure systems can cause headaches.

Many house fires are the result of faulty wiring.

The cause is the reason why the effect occurred, and the effect is what the cause brought about.

It's tempting to assume that causal relationships can be expressed in If/Then terms. Indeed, *sometimes* they can. For example, imagine a scientific experiment in which every time, without exception, pressing a button causes a bell to ring. In that case, you could say:

If you press the button, then the bell will ring.

The cause here (pressing the button) becomes the sufficient term, and the effect (the bell ringing) becomes the necessary term.

At other times, however, it is inappropriate to express causal relationships using conditional If/Then terms. Consider another example:

Colds are caused by exposure to germs.

Germs are the cause, and colds are the effect. Can we validly say the following?

If someone is exposed to germs, then he gets a cold.

The If/Then terminology doesn't fit here because the statement isn't true in all cases. We're exposed to cold germs all the time without necessarily getting colds; we only get colds a small percentage of the time. However, it is the case that every single person who has a cold has been exposed to cold germs, so we can say:

If you have a cold, then you have been exposed to germs.

Notice that in this case, the cause becomes the necessary term, and the effect becomes the sufficient term—very different from the example about the button and bell.

Take another example:

Throwing a brick at the window may cause the window to break.

Can we put that into If/Then format, like this?

If you throw a brick at the window, then the window will break.

No, because of that word *may*. It's possible that in some circumstances the window doesn't break when someone throws a brick at it. So it isn't always a true statement. (Now, it would be legitimate to say, "If you throw a brick at the window, then the window *may* break." But If/Then statements with *maybe* in them usually aren't terribly useful and, thus, are not very common on the LSAT.)

If you're confused at this point, don't worry about it. The takeaway here is that *you must not automatically conflate cause-and-effect relationships with sufficient-necessary relationships.* Remember that throughout your LSAT studies.

Understanding Conditional Statements with "And" or "Or"

Prepare Let's look at a variation some conditional statements can display. So far, we've seen conditional statements of the form "If *x*, then *y*," but sometimes a conditional statement can involve more than two items, linked with *and* or *or*. It's important to understand what those simple conjunctions mean in logical statements:

LSAT STRATEGY

In Formal Logic

- *And* means you need both terms for the conditional to be relevant or fulfilled.
- *Or* means you need at least one of the terms (the first or the second or both) for the conditional to be relevant or fulfilled. *Or* does not express a mutually exclusive relationship unless you're explicitly told otherwise.

Let's explain a little further about *and. And* might appear in the trigger:

If X and Y, then Z.

In that case, both X and Y must be true to apply the conditional statement. X by itself doesn't ensure that Z will happen; neither does Y by itself. So the conditional statement simply isn't relevant unless we have *both* X and Y.

And could also appear in the result:

If A, then B and C.

Here, whenever we have A, we have to have *both* B and C. Once we have A, it's just not possible that we could have B without C, or C without B. Given A, the statement can't be fulfilled without both B and C.

What about *or*? *Or* could appear in the trigger:

If G or H, then J.

Either G or H by itself is sufficient to ensure that you've got to have J. And if you have both G and H, this conditional still applies: You still have to have J.

Or could also appear in the result:

If M, then N or P.

Given M, then we have to have at least one of either N or P. If we have M, we don't *have* to have both N and P, but we do have to have one of them. And we *might* even have all three: M, N, and P all happening doesn't violate this rule.

Notice that in the last two examples, the word *or* doesn't preclude the possibility of having both of the terms linked by *or*. In other words, *or* doesn't express a relationship of mutual exclusivity. If the LSAT wants you to know that two items joined by *or* do have a relationship of mutual exclusivity, it will make this explicit as follows:

If S, then T or V, *but not both*.

Here, if we have S, we have to have either T or V. But, given S, we *can't* have both T and V. Whenever you *do not* see language that explicitly expresses *but not both*, however, you should assume that the two things joined by *or* could go together.

Let's see how an expert test taker would think through some conditional statements containing *and* or *or*.

Conditional Statement	Analysis
If Miranda goes to the store, then she will buy apples or bananas.	Miranda going to the store logically necessitates that she buy either apples, or bananas, or *both* apples and bananas. This statement allows her to buy both, but she doesn't have to. Say that Miranda went to the store and that she didn't buy apples. In that case, she definitely did buy bananas. No logical deductions stem from a statement beginning "If Miranda buys apples or bananas or both," because those are necessary but not sufficient conditions for Miranda's going to the store. Miranda might buy her fruit elsewhere.
If the league doesn't approve the new contract, then the players will go on strike and the city will lose valuable revenue.	The league's failure to approve the contract would necessitate both a strike by the players and the loss of revenue by the city. Suppose the players were on strike and the city had lost valuable revenue. No deduction about whether the league had approved or denied the new contract would follow from that. (And if the league actually did approve a new contract, the players could still strike or the city could still lose revenue for other reasons.)

Conditional Statement	Analysis
If Fatima does the grocery shopping and Pablo cleans the house, then the chores will be done before noon.	Fatima's grocery shopping and Pablo's house cleaning logically guarantee that the chores will be done before noon. If Fatima does the grocery shopping but Pablo doesn't clean the house, this statement simply doesn't apply. It's impossible to deduce whether the chores will get done before noon or not. (For example, someone else might clean the house.) Likewise, if the chores are finished before noon, it's not certain that Pablo cleaned the house or that Fatima went grocery shopping. Those two activities are sufficient to know that the chores are done before noon but not necessary to the completion of the chores by that time. (So, if the chores are done by noon, perhaps a third person pitched in to help or Pablo did everything himself. Who knows?)
If the chicken is soaked in buttermilk or brine, then it will stay moist while cooking.	A soak in either buttermilk or brine will ensure that the chicken stays moist while cooking. Do either one and the chicken will be moist. What would happen if the chicken was soaked in BOTH buttermilk and brine? Again, the chicken would be moist, guaranteed! (Although it might not taste that good.) The "or" here is not exclusive; it doesn't have to be just one or the other.

You'll notice, both on the LSAT and in life, that *and* and *or* relationships can be expressed in a variety of ways. In particular, when those terms are negated, you might see them joined by *neither... nor*. Just make a mental note now that *neither x nor y* means *not x and not y*. Like this:

Conditional Statement	Analysis
If it neither rains nor snows, then we'll go on our trip tomorrow.	If it does not rain and it does not snow, then we'll go on our trip tomorrow.
Neither Jane nor Thomas will go to the dinner if it starts later than 8 p.m.	If the dinner starts later than 8 p.m., then Jane will not go and Thomas will not go.

What if a conditional statement includes a phrase like *but not both*? We have to work that into our understanding of the statement, and the easiest way to do that is to think of it as being two statements.

Conditional Statement	Analysis
If the sous chef makes the soup, she will also make either the salad or the dessert but not both.	(1) The sous chef making the soup is sufficient to tell us that she must also make the salad or the dessert. (2) The sous chef making the soup also requires that she NOT make both salad and dessert.

Practice Check your understanding of each of the following conditional statements.

Conditional Statement	My Analysis
34. If Meagan buys a juicer, then she buys kale or mangos. What do we know if Meagan buys a juicer? What do we know if Meagan buys kale? What do we know if Meagan buys mangos? What do we know if Meagan buys neither mangos nor kale?	
35. If Ian draws a spaceship, he gives it lasers or a tractor beam, but not both. What do we know if we are told Ian is drawing a spaceship? What do we know if Ian is drawing lasers? What do we know if Ian is drawing a tractor beam? What do we know if Ian is drawing both lasers and a tractor beam?	
36. If Patricia makes nachos, then she'll also make salsa and bean dip. What do we know if we are told that Patricia makes nachos? What do we know if we are told that Patricia doesn't make salsa? What do we know if we are told that Patricia makes salsa and bean dip?	

Expert Analysis

Here's how an LSAT expert would analyze the conditional statements you just analyzed.

Conditional Statement	Analysis
34. If Meagan buys a juicer, then she buys kale or mangos.	
What do we know if Meagan buys a juicer?	She buys kale or mangos or both.
What do we know if Meagan buys kale?	Nothing additional.
What do we know if Meagan buys mangos?	Nothing additional.
What do we know if Meagan buys neither mangos nor kale?	Then she can't have bought a juicer.
35. If Ian draws a spaceship, he gives it lasers or a tractor beam, but not both.	
What do we know if we are told Ian is drawing a spaceship?	He gives his spaceship either lasers or a tractor beam, but he absolutely won't give it both lasers and a tractor beam.
What do we know if Ian is drawing lasers?	Nothing additional. Indeed, he may not even be drawing them on a spaceship in this case.
What do we know if Ian is drawing a tractor beam?	Nothing additional. Indeed, he may not even be drawing them on a spaceship in this case.
What do we know if Ian is drawing both lasers and a tractor beam?	Then he can't have drawn a spaceship.
36. If Patricia makes nachos, then she'll also make salsa and bean dip.	
What do we know if we are told that Patricia makes nachos?	Then she'll make both salsa and bean dip. She can't make just one of those—she has to make both.
What do we know if we are told that Patricia doesn't make salsa?	Then she can't have made nachos.
What do we know if we are told that Patricia makes salsa and bean dip?	Nothing additional.

Translating Conditional Statements into If/Then Format

Prepare It's helpful at this point to develop a simple system of notation for conditional statements. (The value of a uniform notation will become very clear when you start working with real LSAT problems.) Whenever you see a conditional statement on the LSAT, translate it into something that looks like this:

If Trigger (sufficient) → Result (necessary)

Write the sufficient term on the left, the necessary term on the right, and an arrow in the middle pointing from left to right (to indicate which direction the logical trigger-and-result relationship flows). If the statement includes a negative (*not* or *no*), there are a couple of ways to handle this. Some people write out the word *not*, others use a tilde symbol to mean *not*, and still others strike through a negated term. So you might write the statement "if A then not B," in shorthand in any of these ways:

If A → not B

If A → ~B

If A → ~~B~~

Symbolize negated terms however you like, but be consistent about it and make sure the entire term is legible. We'll alternate between using the word *not* and using the tilde in this book and in our online materials.

Armed with that simple notation, you're ready to learn how to distill conditional relationships from sometimes complicated prose into clear, brief shorthand notes. You've already learned that conditional statements can be phrased in lots of different ways; you'll see that some of those are more common than others on the LSAT, but they all appear from time to time. This section will give a library of ways that the testmaker phrases conditional statements so that you can quickly and easily translate them into If/Then form.

Think of If/Then statements as generalizations (or rules) that do not admit any exceptions. In the example we started with, every single time anybody is in New York, she has to be in the United States. The test could express this "rule" in a number of ways:

All people in New York are in the United States.

Everyone who is in New York is in the United States.

When (or whenever) someone is in New York, he is in the United States.

A person is in the United States every time he is in New York.

In these sentences, the word that tells you you're looking at a generalization (*all*, *any*, *every*, etc.) also serves to denote the sufficient term. Let's make a short catalog:

LSAT STRATEGY

Words that denote that one thing is sufficient for another to happen:

- *all*
- *any* (*any time*, *any place*, *anybody*, etc.)
- *every* (*every time*, *everybody*, etc.)
- *whenever*
- *each*

Negatives

The same is true for the opposites of those words: Words such as *none* or *no one* or *never* also signal a generalization without exceptions—that is, they also signal a sufficient-and-necessary relationship. These deserve special discussion, however, because sentences containing these negative words frequently employ a word order that can be confusing if you aren't familiar with how to parse it. Consider an example:

No one who is in New York is in Europe.

It may be tempting, if you just glance at the word order, to start your If/Then translation with "If not in New York . . ." But think about the statement's subject: The sentence isn't about people who are not in New York. Rather, it's about people who *are* in New York, and it's saying that those people are *not* in Europe.

If in New York → NOT in Europe

Be very careful about the way sentences are worded. A good practice is to always ask yourself: Who or what is this sentence *about*? That will point you to the sufficient term.

LSAT STRATEGY

Negative words that indicate a sufficient-necessary relationship include:

- None
- Never
- Not
- No one

Only

Just as there are words and phrases that signal that one thing is sufficient for another to happen, there are words and phrases that signal conditional relationships by denoting the necessary term, and a common one on the LSAT is the word *only*. Return to the original example:

> Only people in the United States can be in New York.

Whom is this sentence about? It's about people in New York. Thus, "[o]nly" signals the necessary term. You can translate *only* to *then*:

> If in New York → in United States

Consider a similar example:

> A person can be in New York only if she is in the United States.

Who is the subject of this sentence? The sentence is about people in New York. Don't let the word "if" throw you off there; when "if" follows "only" to make "only if," it always signals a necessary term:

> If in New York → in United States.

Treat this as another rule to memorize: "Only if" equals *only* equals *then*.

There is one use of the word *only*, however, that produces a different interpretation. *When only is preceded* by the definite article, the ensuing phrase—the only—signals the sufficient term in a conditional relationship:

> The only people who are in New York are people who are in the United States.

Again, whom is this sentence about? People in New York, so that's the sufficient term. The translation now looks familiar:

> If in New York → in United States.

Note: The meaning of the statement remains the same throughout all three examples. (Of course it does, as it is a statement we know to be true from real life in this case.) The part of the conditional logic signaled by the word *only*, however, was different: "Only" (by itself) and "only if" indicated necessity, whereas "the only" indicates sufficiency.

LSAT STRATEGY

The word *only* in Formal Logic

- *Only* signals the necessary term.
- *Only if* signals the necessary term.
- *The only* signals the sufficient term.

(By the way, notice that, in the prose previous examples, the sufficient and necessary terms appear in either order; the sufficient term doesn't always appear first in the plain-language English sentence. Nevertheless, in every Formal Logic "translation," the order was identical: If sufficient → necessary.)

Unless/Without

Take a look at another way of expressing the same sufficient-necessary relationship we've been illustrating throughout this section:

No one can be in New York unless he's in the United States.

Once again, this translates to our familiar If/Then statement:

If in New York → in United States.

This one needs some unpacking, but close examination will show you that it conforms to the way you use *unless* all the time in day-to-day conversation. *Unless* signals a requirement—that is, it signals the necessary term—so you can think, "*unless* equals *then*." But notice what "unless" does to the phraseology in the sufficient clause—we've had to add the negation "no one." The original statement ("If a person is in New York, then he is in the United States") didn't have a *no* in it. Do you see why? The word "unless" indicates that were the necessary condition to be absent, the sufficient condition would have to be absent as well. That means that to fit the sufficient condition into a sentence containing *unless*, you must negate the sufficient term.

If this seems tricky, just put it into an easily understandable real-life situation. Most people don't want to eat dry cereal without milk. For them, "I will not eat cereal unless I have milk" is an easy rule to articulate. Now, just think through what that means in Formal Logic terms. Because the person won't eat cereal unless she has milk, "milk" is *necessary* for her to eat cereal. Thus, the rule could just as easily be expressed in If/Then terms: If eat cereal → have milk.

What does a sentence containing *unless* mean if the sufficient term is not negated? Again, apply a real-world example and work it out. Imagine you hear a friend say, "I will go to the mall unless it rains." (Notice that this time, the term at the beginning of the sentence is positive—"I *will* go to the mall"—as opposed to the "I will *not* eat cereal" in the example above.) Treat your friend's statement as a rule; he means precisely what he says. His statement means "I will go to the mall in every case except one: rain." So, you can translate your friend's rule into "If I do *not* go to the mall, then it is raining."

As the following Strategy Box illustrates, you can translate any Formal Logic statement with *unless* by negating the sufficient statement and substituting *then* for the word *unless*.

LSAT STRATEGY

The word *unless* in Formal Logic

- "No X unless Y" translates to "If X then Y."
- "A unless B" translates to "If not A then B."

Note: The word *without* functions exactly the same way as *unless* in conditional Formal Logic statements. For example, "I will not eat cereal without having milk" has the same meaning as "I will not eat cereal unless I have milk."

If, But Only If

One other Formal Logic structure you'll occasionally see on the LSAT is *if, but only if.* Here's an example:

Piper goes to the beach if, but only if, Kinsley goes to the beach.

This means that Piper's going to the beach is sufficient *and* necessary for Kinsley's going. (Notice that the term "Kinsley goes to the beach" is preceded in the sentence by "if" [sufficient] and by "only if" [necessary].) It can be broken down into two statements:

If Piper goes to the beach → Kinsley goes to the beach

If Kinsley goes to the beach → Piper goes to the beach

Ultimately, the impact is this: Either they both go or neither of them does.

LSAT STRATEGY

The phrases "if, but only if" and "if, and only if" indicate a biconditional relationship. Each term in the relationship is both sufficient AND necessary for the other term.

"X if, and only if Y" can be written:

If X → Y

If Y → X

or, alternatively

X ↔ Y

The expert LSAT test taker automatically (either mentally or in simple shorthand) translates all conditional statements into If/Then format. Follow the expert's lead by practicing these skills until they are second nature. Here are a number of conditional statements along with the expert's translations:

Conditional Statement	Analysis
All visitors must check in at the front desk.	"All" is modifying "visitors," which makes that term sufficient: If visitor → check in at the front desk
Each of the contestants has been given one hour to prepare a dish.	"Each" indicates that being a contestant is sufficient: If contestant → one hour to prepare a dish
Every building on this street was built before the turn of the century.	"Every" is a modifier for the entire phrase "building on this street" and indicates sufficiency: If building on this street → built before the turn of the century
Anyone not on the list will be asked to leave.	"Anyone" is categorical language pertaining to all people not on the list; it indicates sufficiency: If NOT on the list → asked to leave
In order to start the car, the key must be in the ignition.	The phrase "in order to" and the word "must" combine to indicate that the key is required (necessary) for the car to start: If start the car → key in the ignition
The children in Ms. Hatcher's class all speak French.	The word order of this sentence is a little tricky. Whom is this sentence about? It's about students who are in Ms. Hatcher's class. Accordingly, "all" (which indicates sufficiency) is modifying the children in Ms. Hatcher's class: If in Ms. Hatcher's class → speaks French

Conditional Statement	Analysis
No one in Ms. Hatcher's class speaks German.	Whom is this sentence about? The kids in Ms. Hatcher's class. "No one" indicates that being in that class is sufficient to know a student does not speak German: If in Ms. Hatcher's class → NOT speak German
The only people allowed on the field at this time are members of the press.	"The only," because it has the definite article, indicates sufficiency: If allowed on the field → member of the press at this time
Everyone in the audience will get a copy of my new book.	"Everyone" indicates that being a person in the audience is sufficient to receive a copy of the new book: If in the audience → book
In order for us to make a diagnosis, we need an accurate patient history.	The phrase "in order to" and the word "need" combine to indicate that an accurate patient history is necessary for a diagnosis: If diagnosis → accurate patient history
They will name the baby Maya if, but only if, it's a girl.	"If but only if" indicates that a statement is both sufficient and necessary for the other and vice versa. If baby named Maya → girl If girl → baby named Maya

Practice Using the previous pages as a glossary, translate each of the following statements, each of which expresses a sufficient-and-necessary relationship, into If/Then format. Note them down in simple shorthand relationships using arrows.

Conditional Statement	My Analysis
37. All employees are required to attend the meeting.	
38. I'll skip the party only if I'm sick.	
39. Malinda will not win the race unless she trains hard and avoids injuries.	
40. All of those in the path of the tornado are being evacuated.	
41. Everyone in the cinema must turn their cell phones off now.	
42. Only if you have proper identification and a ticket will you be allowed to board the plane.	
43. All of those in attendance this evening are asked to give generously to the scholarship fund.	

Conditional Statement	My Analysis
44. Anyone over the age of fifty can remember disco music.	
45. Every city in the tristate region is currently suffering through the worst flu epidemic in twenty years.	
46. Candace will sign up for softball this year only if Jarvis or Tempest signs up as well.	
47. School is not canceled for bad weather unless there is snow accumulation in excess of three feet.	
48. A lake has experienced an infestation of Frankenfish if, but only if, it's in Travis County.	
49. Any fruit we received in the last shipment is bound to be spoiled by now.	
50. The only rooms big enough to accommodate the wedding party are booked for that weekend.	
51. Only when spring arrives and warmer weather returns do the swallows return to Capistrano.	

Expert Analysis

Here's how an LSAT expert would notate each of the examples you just worked on. In every case, the shorthand employs the format "If [sufficient] → [necessary]."

Conditional Statement	Analysis
37. All employees are required to attend the meeting.	If employee → attend
38. I'll skip the party only if I'm sick.	If skip party → sick
39. Malinda will not win the race unless she trains hard and avoids injuries.	If Malinda wins → trained hard AND avoided injuries
40. All of those in the path of the tornado are being evacuated.	If path of tornado → evacuated
41. Everyone in the cinema must turn their cell phones off now.	If in cinema → turn cell phone off
42. Only if you have proper identification and a ticket will you be allowed to board the plane.	If allowed to board the plane → proper ID AND a ticket
43. All of those in attendance this evening are asked to give generously to the scholarship fund.	If in attendance → asked to give to scholarship
44. Anyone over the age of fifty can remember disco music.	If over 50 → remember disco
45. Every city in the tristate region is currently suffering through the worst flu epidemic in twenty years.	If city in tristate region → suffering flu epidemic
46. Candace will sign up for softball this year only if Jarvis or Tempest signs up as well.	If candace signs up → Jarvis signs up OR Tempest signs up

Conditional Statement	Analysis
47. School is not canceled for bad weather unless there is snow accumulation in excess of three feet.	If school canceled for bad weather → more than 3 feet of snow
48. A lake has experienced an infestation of Frankenfish if, but only if, it's in Travis County.	If lake in Travis County → infested with Frankenfish If infested with Frankenfish → lake in Travis County
49. Any fruit we received in the last shipment is bound to be spoiled by now.	If fruit from last shipment → spoiled
50. The only rooms big enough to accommodate the wedding party are booked for that weekend.	If big enough to hold the party → booked
51. Only when spring arrives and warmer weather returns do the swallows return to Capistrano.	If swallows return → spring arrives AND warmer weather returns

Reflect Review your practice. Consider these questions:

- How well did you spot the sufficient and necessary terms? What words or phrases tended to mislead you?
- When noting the statements down in shorthand, did you always keep the sufficient term on the left and the necessary term on the right, with an arrow pointing to the necessary term?
- If you were able to spot which thing is needed for another in some of the examples, did you remember what that means about which one is necessary and which one is sufficient?

Translating conditional, Formal Logic statements is something you can practice every day. When you hear friends, coworkers, or others use words like *all, every, none, never, if, only if, unless,* and so on, treat their statements as rules and determine how the statements they've made would translate into If/Then statements.

Making Valid Deductions from Conditional Statements

Prepare Now that you understand conditional relationships and know how to spot them when you come across them in prose, you're ready to think about how to combine them to make deductions. You will see this skill tested routinely in Logical Reasoning questions on the LSAT.

The idea is simple: You can combine conditional statements when the same term appears in more than one statement. Where the sufficient terms are the same, they can be combined like this:

If A, then B.

If A, then C.

Deduction: If A, then both B and C.

If the same term appears in the necessary parts of two conditional statements, you can combine them like this:

If T, then V.

If W, then V.

Deduction: If either T or W (or both), then V.

Finally, by far the most useful opportunity to combine conditional statements occurs when the same term appears in the necessary part of one conditional statement and in the sufficient part of another. In that case, those two statements allow you to deduce an altogether new idea:

If X, then Y.

If Y, then Z.

Deduction: If X, then Z.

(That pattern of three statements is called a syllogism, by the way. You certainly won't have to know that word on the LSAT, but the test will definitely reward your ability to accurately combine statements in this way.)

More than two premises with shared terms can produce multiple deductions:

If D, then E.

If E, then F.

If F, then G.

If G, then H.

Deductions:

If D, then E and F and G and H.

If E, then F and G and H.

If F, then G and H.

By the way, what can you deduce if you know that you have H? Answer: not a thing. Remember, the necessary term of an If/Then doesn't trigger any results.

Take a look at how an LSAT expert might draw deductions from a set of conditional statements:

Conditional Statements	Analysis
If Jane goes to the movies, she'll also go to the beach.	If movies → beach
If Jane goes to the beach, she won't go to the museum.	If beach → ~museum
If Jane goes to the beach, she'll go to the amusement park.	If beach → amusement park
If Jane goes to the amusement park, she will buy a funnel cake.	If amusement park → buy funnel cake

If we know that Jane . . .	then we also know that she . . .
goes to the movies	—goes to the beach —does not go to the museum —goes to the amusement park —buys a funnel cake
goes to the beach	—does not go to the museum —goes to the amusement park —buys a funnel cake We don't know whether she goes to the movies or not.
doesn't go to the museum	We can't deduce anything.
buys a funnel cake	We can't deduce anything.

Practice In the following exercise, first translate the given conditional statements so that you can use them to create a chain of logic. Then, answer questions about what we must know, given our new chain. The expert analysis is found on the next page.

Conditional Statements	My Analysis
52. If John doesn't bake a pie, he doesn't buy apples. If John bakes chocolate chip cookies, he does not bake a pie. If John doesn't buy apples, he doesn't have applesauce or doesn't have jelly. If John buys bananas, then he bakes chocolate chip cookies. If John goes to the store, then he buys bananas.	

If we know that John . . .	then we also know that John . . .
bought bananas	
bakes chocolate chip cookies	
does not bake a pie	
doesn't have applesauce or jelly	

Expert Analysis

Here's how the LSAT expert translated the logic along with the valid deductions she drew from it.

Conditional Statements	Analysis
52. If John doesn't bake a pie, he doesn't buy apples. If John bakes chocolate chip cookies, he does not bake a pie. If John doesn't buy apples, he doesn't have applesauce or doesn't have jelly. If John buys bananas, then he bakes chocolate chip cookies. If John goes to the store, then he buys bananas.	If NOT bake pie → NOT buy apples If bake c/c cookies → NOT bake pie If NOT buy apples → NOT have applesauce OR NOT have jelly If buy bananas → bakes c/c cookies If goes to store → buy bananas

If we know that John . . .	then we also know that John . . .
bought bananas	baked chocolate chip cookies, did not bake a pie, didn't buy apples, and doesn't have applesauce or doesn't have jelly
bakes chocolate chip cookies	does not bake a pie, didn't buy apples, and doesn't have applesauce or doesn't have jelly
does not bake a pie	didn't buy apples and doesn't have applesauce or doesn't have jelly
doesn't have applesauce or doesn't have jelly	We can't deduce anything.

Formal Logic: Contrapositives

You've seen that, despite the many ways to express a conditional statement in prose, the logic underlying such statements is remarkably consistent. You're about to learn one more feature of these statements: the contrapositive. The contrapositive is simply another way to express any If/Then statement, but your ability to quickly and accurately form a statement's contrapositive is an incredibly important tool for you to have in your LSAT toolkit.

LEARNING OBJECTIVES

In this section, you'll learn to:

- Translate a conditional statement into its contrapositive.
- Make valid deductions from the contrapositive of a conditional statement.
- Analyze correctly the implications of conditional statements containing *and* and *or*.
- Analyze correctly the implications of conditional statements containing an "exclusive or."

While a conditional statement and its contrapositive express exactly the same logical premise, forming contrapositives explicitly is valuable to the LSAT test taker because the contrapositive provides another logical trigger to work with.

Translating If/Then Statements into Contrapositives

Prepare Let's return to our very first example to start thinking about contrapositives.

If you're in New York, then you are in the United States.

Every single time you are in New York, then you absolutely have to be in the United States. Being in the United States is necessary for a person to be in New York. So, if someone is not in the United States, there's no way he can be in New York. Put another way, negating the necessary term means negating the sufficient term. Contrapositives are built on this insight, and forming the contrapositive is pretty straightforward:

- Reverse the terms—put the term on the left of the arrow on the right and vice versa.
- Negate the terms—where a negation word (like *not*, *no*, or *never*) appears, take it out; where such a word does not appear, put it in.

Like this:

Original statement: If in New York → in the United States

- Reverse: If in the United States → in New York, *and*
- Negate: If not in the United States → not in New York

That's the contrapositive: If not in the United States → not in New York. If you're not in the United States, then you're not in New York.

Note: You must always reverse *and* negate simultaneously. Doing just one of those two actions distorts the meaning of the original statement:

- Reversing without negating produces "If you're in the United States, then you're in New York." Well, we know that to be wrong in real life, and it's a logical fallacy to do this to any conditional statement. The resulting sentence doesn't mean the same thing as the original. In fact, it confuses the necessary term for the sufficient one.
- Negating without reversing gives "If you're not in New York, then you're not in the United States." Again, we know that sentence is incorrect in real life as well as being a distortion of the original.

The test will include numerous wrong answers—in Logical Reasoning especially—that reflect both of those mistakes. Learning to avoid those wrong answers can be just as important as learning to spot correct answers that translate Formal Logic statements correctly.

It's very important to fully absorb that you can never negate without reversing or reverse without negating. This is easy to remember when you're dealing with a real-life example but easy to forget when you're plowing through a Logical Reasoning argument with unfamiliar scientific terms. Make sure you wrap your head around this principle now so it doesn't trip you up later.

We said earlier that a conditional statement and its contrapositive express exactly the same idea. As proof, notice that the contrapositive can be contraposed into the original statement:

If not in United States → not in New York
Reverse and negate: If in New York → in United States

Before you practice this, there's one more consideration for forming valid contrapositives: Along with reversing and negating, you must, whenever relevant, also change *and* to *or* and *or* to *and*. To see why, and to discern when this is the case, consider an example. Treat the following statement as a rule:

If it doesn't rain, then we will go to the park or we will go to the beach.

In other words, a lack of rain is sufficient to know that we will go to either the park or the beach (or maybe both, if we have time). Now, translate into simple shorthand:

If not rain → park or beach

Do the first two operations needed to form the contrapositive:

- Reverse: If park or beach → not rain, *and*
- Negate: If not park or not beach → rain

But that's mistaken. What would the statement mean if we left it like that? Not going to the park would be enough to absolutely require that it rain. But that's not consistent with the original statement. According to the original statement, if it doesn't rain, we might choose to go to the beach and not to the park. Preserving the *or* in the contrapositive has warped the meaning of the original statement. But watch how the meaning of the original is preserved if we change *or* to *and* in the contrapositive:

If not park and not beach → rain

If we're neither at the park nor at the beach, it's raining. Now we have a statement that is logically equivalent to the original.

Our example involved an *or* in the necessary term, but you must change *and* to *or* and vice versa regardless of whether those terms appear in the sufficient or necessary term.

Another important note here: When you're dealing with multiple terms in a conditional statement, negate *each one* to avoid confusion. If we formed our contrapositive by saying, "if not beach and park → rain," that could have gotten very confusing.

LSAT STRATEGY

To form the contrapositive of an If/Then statement:

- Reverse the terms.
- Negate *each* term.
- Change *and* to *or* and change *or* to *and* (whenever applicable).

Study the LSAT expert's work as she translates the following If/Then statements and forms the correct contrapositive for each. Note that, in every case, it would not matter whether the expert translated the original statement in negative or positive terms because, having formed the contrapositive, both the negative and positive equivalent statements would be clear.

Conditional Statement	Analysis
If the skies stay clear and the wind remains calm, we set sail tomorrow.	If skies clear AND winds calm → we sail tomorrow If NOT sail tomorrow → skies NOT clear OR winds NOT calm
There are no vacancies at the hotel unless we have a cancellation.	If vacancies → cancellation If NO cancellation → NO vacancies
If Joan is late for dinner, then either traffic is bad or she's lost her way.	If Joan is late → bad traffic OR lost If NOT bad traffic AND NOT lost → Joan is NOT late
Only the best players were invited to the tournament.	If invited → one of the best players If NOT one of the best players → NOT invited
If this substance is properly classified as a mineral, then it is neither animal nor vegetable.	If mineral → NOT animal AND NOT vegetable* If animal OR vegetable → NOT mineral

*NOTE: Remember that *neither x nor y* translates to *not x AND not y*.

Now, you're ready to pull together all of the thinking that an LSAT expert does whenever she encounters a statement indicating a sufficient-necessary relationship. She recognizes the presence of Formal Logic, translates it into If/Then format, and forms the contrapositive explicitly. When you're able to do these things accurately and quickly—in other words, when these processes become second nature—you'll be well on your way to getting a number of LSAT points that may have eluded you before (and will continue to elude your less well-trained competition).

Practice Translate each of the following statements into simple shorthand and form the contrapositives. After each one, you can turn the page to see the work of an LSAT expert with these same statements.

Conditional Statement	My Analysis
53. Each of the boys is wearing blue and yellow.	
54. When it rains, it pours.	
55. If we have turkey for dinner, we won't have ham.	
56. Any bowl that doesn't contain goldfish contains bettas.	
57. Arianna drives to Rochester only if she visits Syracuse.	
58. If the exhibition comes to the city zoo, then it will feature elephants but not pandas.	
59. If the talent show does not have a magician, then it will have either a dance number or a comedian.	

Conditional Statement	My Analysis
60. All triathlon participants must undergo a physical and sign a waiver.	
61. All the horses in the stable are either roan or palomino.	
62. If the train is late, then Bret won't make it to Chicago today.	
63. None of the coffee in this room is decaf.	
64. All sodas in the cupboard are either diet or cherry.	
65. We visit the Colosseum today only if we also visit the Pantheon but not the Roman Forum.	

Conditional Statement	My Analysis
66. Pre-med students must take organic chemistry and biology.	
67. Unless it rains, we will go to either the beach or the park.	
68. If she injured her anterior cruciate ligament or her medial collateral ligament, then she won't be able to play for the remainder of the season.	
69. Greg can join neither the swim team nor the debate team unless he brings up his grades.	
70. If Matt wins the lottery, then he will buy a boat and sail around the world.	
71. Only faculty or staff are allowed in the lounge.	

Expert Analysis

Here's how the LSAT expert translated and contraposed each of the statements you just worked with.

Conditional Statement	Analysis
53. Each of the boys is wearing blue and yellow.	If boy → wearing blue AND wearing yellow If NOT wearing blue OR NOT wearing yellow → NOT boy
54. When it rains, it pours.	If rains → pours If NOT pour → NOT rain
55. If we have turkey for dinner, we won't have ham.	If turkey → NOT ham If ham → NOT turkey
56. Any bowl that doesn't contain goldfish contains bettas.	If NOT goldfish → bettas If NOT bettas → goldfish
57. Arianna drives to Rochester only if she visits Syracuse.	If Arianna drives to Rochester → visits Syracuse If NOT visit Syracuse → Arianna NOT drive to Rochester
58. If the exhibition comes to the city zoo, then it will feature elephants but not pandas.*	If city zoo → elephants AND NOT pandas If NOT elephants OR if pandas → NOT city zoo**
59. If the talent show does not have a magician, then it will have either a dance number or a comedian.	If NOT magician → dance number OR comedian If NOT dance number AND NOT comedian → magician

Conditional Statement	Analysis
60. All triathlon participants must undergo a physical and sign a waiver.	If triathlon participant → undergo physical AND sign waiver If NOT sign waiver OR NOT undergo physical → NOT triathlon participant
61. All the horses in the stable are either roan or palomino.	If horse in stable → roan OR palomino If NOT roan AND NOT palomino → NOT horse in stable
62. If the train is late, then Bret won't make it to Chicago today.	If train late → Bret NOT make it to Chicago If Bret makes it to Chicago → train NOT late
63. None of the coffee in this room is decaf.	If coffee in this room → NOT decaf If decaf → NOT coffee in this room
64. All sodas in the cupboard are either diet or cherry.	If soda in the cupboard → diet OR cherry If NOT diet AND NOT cherry → NOT soda in the cupboard
65. We visit the Colosseum today only if we also visit the Pantheon but not the Roman Forum.*	If Colosseum → Pantheon AND NOT Roman Forum If NOT Pantheon OR if Roman Forum → NOT Colosseum

Conditional Statement	Analysis
66. Pre-med students must take organic chemistry and biology.	If pre-med student → take organic chemistry AND take biology If NOT take organic chemistry OR NOT take biology → NOT pre-med student
67. Unless it rains, we will go to either the beach or the park.	If NOT beach AND NOT park → rain If NOT rain → beach OR park
68. If she injured her anterior cruciate ligament or her medial collateral ligament, then she won't be able to play for the remainder of the season.	If ACL OR MCL → NOT play rest of season If plays (at all during the) rest of season → NOT ACL AND NOT MCL***
69. Greg can join neither the swim team nor the debate team unless he brings up his grades.	If swim team OR debate team → brings up grades If NOT bring up grades → NOT swim team AND NOT debate team
70. If Matt wins the lottery, then he will buy a boat and sail around the world.	If Matt wins lottery → buy boat AND sail around the world If NOT buy boat OR NOT sail around the world → Matt NOT win lottery
71. Only faculty or staff are allowed in the lounge.	If allowed in the lounge → faculty OR staff If NOT faculty AND NOT staff → NOT allowed in the lounge

*The word *but*, though rhetorically different from *and*, actually functions the same as *and* in Formal Logic translations.

**Be careful with statements like this one. In the contrapositive here, the expert has jotted down "If NOT elephants or if pandas. . . ." The "if" before pandas there helps to avoid the mistaken interpretation that would result from the prose clause "If not elephants or pandas," which makes it sound as if both terms are negated. In this contrapositive, elephants are not present, but pandas *are*.

***Note that the expert has included the idea of playing at any point during the rest of the season. This makes clear, in the contrapositive, that if the athlete plays at all during the rest of the season, you can be certain she didn't injure her ACL or MCL.

Reflect Review your practice.

- Were you careful to translate each sentence into shorthand before forming the contrapositive?
- What did you find challenging about forming the contrapositives?
- In cases involving *and* or *or*, did you convert them correctly? And did you negate each term?

In the coming days, use every opportunity you encounter to spot conditional reasoning in day-to-day life. The next time you see a sign such as "No Shirt, No Shoes, No Service," for example, translate it into If/Then terms. "If a person is not wearing shoes or is not wearing a shirt, then the person will not be served." Treat that as a rule without exceptions and practice forming the contrapositive: "If a person is being served, then he is wearing shoes and is wearing a shirt." You'll find it remarkable how often you engage in Formal Logic reasoning without even noticing it. You'll be noticing it a lot between now and test day.

Making Valid Deductions from the Contrapositive of a Conditional Statement

Prepare As you've seen (and practiced), a conditional statement and its contrapositive express exactly the same idea, but the contrapositive has a different trigger. Therefore, it's useful to write out the contrapositive for reference as you're thinking through how you can combine conditional statements to reveal further deductions. To start with, notice how a conditional statement and its contrapositive nicely define the field of what you do and don't know. Take a simple (and likely fictional) example:

If a creature is a cat, then that creature has nine lives.

Start by translating that into simple shorthand and then making the contrapositive:

If cat → nine lives
If NOT nine lives → NOT cat

You've already learned that you can have the result without the trigger (that is to say, the necessary term without the sufficient term), so a creature could have nine lives without being a cat. In fact, you don't know about any creature other than a cat. If someone asked you whether a unicorn has nine lives, you'd have to respond—based solely on the statement above—"I don't know." It can be useful mental shorthand on the LSAT to remember that the necessary terms of an If/Then statement and its contrapositive are not mutually exclusive. In the previous example, a creature that's not a cat may or may not have nine lives.

The contrapositive (and its implications) broadens your ability to make deductions from a set of conditional statements. Look again at the exercise about Jane and her entertainment choices and see how an expert LSAT test taker looks at the statements and their contrapositives:

Conditional Statements	Analysis
If Jane goes to the movies, she'll also go to the beach.	If movies → beach If NOT beach → NOT movies
If Jane goes to the beach, she won't go to the museum.	If beach → NOT museum If museum → NOT beach
If Jane goes to the beach, she'll go to the amusement park.	If beach → amusement park If NOT amusement park → NOT beach
If Jane goes to the amusement park, she will buy a funnel cake.	If amusement park → funnel cake If NOT funnel cake → NOT amusement park*
	All the deductions made earlier are still valid, but by including the contrapositives, the following deductions are also now clear: If Jane doesn't buy a funnel cake, then she doesn't go to the amusement park, she doesn't go to the beach, *and* she doesn't go to the movies. It's possible for Jane to choose none of these activities: movies, beach, museum, amusement park. The negated version of each (for example, "not movies") appears in the "results" column, but none of those negated versions is a trigger that forces her to do another of the activities. Suppose that Jane chooses none of the activities: that is, she doesn't go to the movies, beach, museum, or amusement park. In that case, does she buy a funnel cake? She may or may not.

*Notice that our expert LSAT test taker has kept all of the arrows aligned. That really makes it easier for her to run her eye down the list of triggers to search for additional deductions. You'll want to get into that habit whenever you are working with a set of related conditional statements.

Practice It's time to get some practice using contrapositives to make all the possible deductions from a set of conditional statements. For each statement below, turn it into shorthand, form the contrapositive, and then make notes about how each one can be combined with other conditional statements in the same set to make deductions. At any time, you can turn the page to see the expert test taker's approach.

Conditional Statements	My Analysis
72. If it is Tuesday, Mary is playing tennis.	
If Mary plays tennis, she is playing with John.	
If Mary does not play tennis, then she buys golf shoes.	
If Mary does not buy golf shoes, then she is in Hawaii.	

Expert Analysis for the Practice exercise may be found on the following page. ▶ ▶ ▶

CHAPTER 1

Expert Analysis

Here's the LSAT expert's thorough analysis of the example you just practiced. Compare your work to his by making sure you translated all of the rules and formed all of the contrapositives correctly. Then, compare your list of deductions to those made by the expert.

Conditional Statements	Analysis
72. If it is Tuesday, Mary is playing tennis.	If Tuesday → tennis If NOT tennis → NOT Tuesday
If Mary plays tennis, she is playing with John.	If tennis → plays with John If NOT play with John → NOT tennis
If Mary does not play tennis, then she buys golf shoes.	If NOT tennis → golf shoes If NOT golf shoes → tennis
If Mary does not buy golf shoes, then she is in Hawaii.	If NOT golf shoes → in Hawaii If NOT in Hawaii → golf shoes

If we know that . . .	then we also know that . . .
if it is Tuesday	Mary plays tennis and John plays tennis with her.
Mary plays tennis	John plays tennis with her.
John plays tennis	We can't deduce anything.
John is not playing tennis	It is not Tuesday, Mary is not playing tennis, and Mary buys golf shoes.
Mary does not play tennis	It is not Tuesday and Mary buys golf shoes.
Mary does not buy golf shoes	Mary plays tennis, John plays tennis with her, and Mary is in Hawaii.
Mary buys golf shoes	We can't deduce anything.
Mary is in Hawaii	We can't deduce anything.

Reflect Look back over your practice.

- Did you carefully note each If/Then statement in shorthand?
- Did you carefully and correctly make all the contrapositives before trying to combine statements?
- Did you remember that a result doesn't trigger anything?
- Did you miss logical deductions that were available?

Start to pay attention to "chains" of logic that you encounter in the real world. You'll hear them in business meetings at work: "If we are able to cut shipping costs, we'll have additional capital. With additional capital, we can hire another developer. With another developer, the new product line can reach the market before our competitor's product." You might encounter something like this watching a news channel: "Without reductions in spending, programs for education will fail. Without adequate education, our nation's students won't obtain crucial skills for the global marketplace. If we lack talent for companies trying to compete globally, we will need to reform immigration laws." The more you pay attention to this kind of reasoning wherever you might see or hear it, the better you'll be at spotting mistakes and gaps in the logic. These are exactly the skills the LSAT rewards on test day.

Making Valid Deductions from Conditional Statements Containing "And" and "Or"

Prepare We saw previously in this chapter that the inclusion of *and* or *or* in a conditional statement adds a layer of complexity. We also saw that you have to be careful when forming the contrapositive of a statement containing *and* or *or*, to exchange those conjunctions consistently and in the right way. This warrants additional practice. In this section, we'll look at how a test taker can make deductions by combining conditional statements that contain conjunctions and get some more practice translating these statements in the bargain.

As a reminder, to form the contrapositive of a conditional statement, do the following:

- Reverse the terms.
- Negate the terms.
- Change *and* to *or* and change *or* to *and* (whenever applicable).

Now, when we first discussed conditional statements with the word *or*, we noted that the word *or* does not express a relationship of mutual exclusivity unless the LSAT explicitly tells you otherwise. As another reminder, here's how to think about these statements in terms of Formal Logic:

Given the statement:

If *x*, then *y* or *z*

we understand it to mean:

If we have *x*, then we have to have at least *y* or *z*, and we might also have both.

Given the statement:

If *a* or *b*, then *c*

we understand it to mean:

Whenever we have *a*, then we have *c*.
Whenever we have *b*, then we have *c*.
Whenever we have both *a* and *b*, then we have *c*.

That's an important point to remember when you're employing conditional statements with *or* to draw further deductions. That's your next task: making logical deductions from sets of conditional statements in which some of the statements contain *and* or *or*.

Review the LSAT expert's thorough analysis of the following set of statements:

Conditional Statements	Analysis
Thomas can take a road trip only if he fills up his car with gas and gets the oil changed.	If road trip → gas AND oil change If NOT gas OR NOT oil change → NOT road trip
If Thomas's friend comes to town, the two will take a road trip to Big Sur.	If friend in town → road trip If NOT road trip → NOT friend in town
If Thomas fills up his car with gas, he will also get a car wash or buy snacks.	If gas → car wash OR snacks If NOT car wash AND NOT snacks → NOT gas
Thomas cannot get an oil change unless he schedules an appointment to do so.	If oil change → appointment If NOT appointment → NOT oil change

If we know that...	then we also know that...
Thomas's friend comes to town	Thomas goes on road trip, changes oil in car, gets gas for car, makes appointment to change oil, and gets a car wash or snacks or both
Thomas does not make an appointment for an oil change	Thomas doesn't get oil change and does not go on road trip. His friend does not come to town We don't know whether he gets gas or not.
Thomas does not get an oil change OR does not fill his car up with gas or both	does not go on a road trip, and friend not in town
Thomas does not get his car washed	We can't deduce anything.
Thomas does not buy any snacks	We can't deduce anything.
Thomas does not get a car wash and also does not get snacks	doesn't get gas, doesn't go on a road trip, and his friend doesn't come to town

Practice Now, get some practice translating and contraposing conditional statements containing *and* or *or*.

For each of the following statements, translate it into simple shorthand in the format: If sufficient → necessary. Then, form the contrapositives and take a moment to absorb what each one means. You can turn the page at any time to compare your work to the expert thinking.

Conditional Statement	My Analysis
73. If a white knight slays the green dragon or the purple ogre, he will save the princess.	
74. If Barry drinks his juice, he will become strong and mean.	
75. Jack will not have a lot of friends unless Jill or Jenny dates him.	
76. The flight will depart later than scheduled if the pilot and copilot fall asleep.	

Expert Analysis for the Practice exercise may be found on the following page. ▶ ▶ ▶

Expert Analysis

Here's how the LSAT expert interpreted the If/Then statements, formed her contrapositive, and drew valid deductions about what was certain, possible, and/or impossible given each one.

Conditional Statement	Analysis
73. If a white knight slays the green dragon or the purple ogre, he will save the princess.	If slays green dragon OR slays purple ogre → saves the princess If NOT save the princess → NOT slays green dragon AND NOT slays the purple ogre So if he slays just one of the two, he will save the princess. If he slays both, the princess will also be saved. If he doesn't save the princess, neither the dragon nor the ogre will be slain.
74. If Barry drinks his juice, he will become strong and mean.	If juice → strong AND mean If NOT strong OR NOT mean → NOT juice So if Barry drinks his juice, he becomes both strong and mean. We also know that if Barry becomes neither strong nor mean, he did not drink his juice.
75. Jack will not have a lot of friends unless Jill or Jenny dates him.	If has a lot of friends → dates Jill OR dates Jenny If NOT date Jill AND NOT date Jenny → NOT a lot of friends So if Jack has a lot of friends, either Jill or Jenny dates him, and possibly both. If neither Jill nor Jenny dates Jack, Jack does not have a lot of friends.
76. The flight will depart later than scheduled if the pilot and copilot fall asleep.	If pilot sleeps AND copilot sleeps → flight late If flight NOT late → pilot does NOT sleep OR copilot does NOT sleep So if both the pilot and copilot fall asleep, the flight will depart late. If the flight departs on time or even early, at least one of the pilot and copilot did not fall asleep.

Reflect Look back over your practice.

- Did you carefully make shorthand translations of each statement and contrapositives for each?
- Did you remain clear in your mind about the meaning of *or* in each one?
- Were there logical deductions you missed?

Spot conditional statements in day-to-day life and work through their implications. If you hear someone say something along the lines of "If I forget to call my mom on her birthday, I'll have to send flowers or take her out to dinner next weekend," what does he mean? Treat the statement as a rule. If he's forgetful, could he do both? Sure. If you know this fellow didn't send flowers and didn't take his mother out for dinner, what could you validly deduce? In that case, you'd know that he didn't forget to call.

Making Valid Deductions from Conditional Statements Containing an "Exclusive Or" Provision

Prepare So far we've emphasized the fact that *or*, by itself, does not denote a relationship of mutual exclusivity. Put simply, you can have both of the things connected by an *or* unless the LSAT explicitly tells you otherwise, as in the following example from earlier in the chapter:

Conditional Statement	Analysis
If the sous chef makes the soup, she will also make either the salad or the dessert, but not both.	(1) The sous chef making the soup is sufficient to tell us that she must also make the salad *or* the dessert. (2) The sous chef making the soup also requires that she NOT make both the salad *and* the dessert.

When we first showed this example, we discussed the fact that it's most easily understood when broken into two statements, as the LSAT expert did in the previous example. But now that you've expanded your Formal Logic skills to the point that you're habitually making contrapositives for all conditional statements, it's time to get some practice with contraposing this type of "exclusive or" statement. The simplest way: Break it out into two statements, translate them both into simple shorthand, and contrapose both, like this:

Conditional Statement	Analysis	
If the sous chef makes the soup, she will also make either the salad or the dessert, but not both.	If soup	→ salad OR dessert
	If NOT salad AND NOT dessert	→ NOT soup
	If soup	→ NOT [salad/dessert combo]
	If [salad/dessert combo]	→ NOT soup

Notice how the expert test taker, when turning the second part of this statement into shorthand, found a way to express that the *combination* of salad and dessert (rather than salad or dessert separately) was the necessary term. If he'd noted it down like this...

If soup → not salad and dessert

then his automatic contrapositive-making habits might have kicked in, and he might have been tempted to make the contrapositive like this:

If salad or not dessert → not soup

...which is not at all correct. Thus, decide for yourself on a shorthand you'll use whenever a term in a conditional statement is a combination of two things so that you won't get confused and start treating them separately. That shorthand will usually only be necessary in statements like this that have an "exclusive or" clause—that is, with the phrase "but not both" appended to a clause containing *or*. You won't see many of these on the LSAT, but when you do, you'll want to know that you have the logical implications of the statement worked out perfectly.

Clear notation will be your best friend when it comes to combining conditional statements, some of which contain "exclusive or" clauses.

Consider the following demonstration of an LSAT expert's work with a set of If/Thens:

Conditional Statements	Analysis
If today is a holiday, then Marisol does not work.	If holiday → NOT work If work → NOT holiday
If the post office is closed, then today is a holiday.	If post office closed → holiday If NOT holiday → post office open
If the post office is open, then Marisol collects her mail.	If post office open → collects mail If NOT collect mail → post office closed
If it is not the weekend, Marisol goes to bed early.	If NOT weekend → bed early If NOT bed early → weekend
If today is not a holiday, then it is the weekend or the post office is open, but not both.	If NOT holiday → weekend OR post office open If NOT weekend AND post office closed → holiday If NOT holiday → NOT [both weekend AND post office open] If [both weekend AND post office open] → holiday

The final statement contains an "exclusive or." When it is not a holiday, two mutually exclusive possibilities are offered: Either it is the weekend or the post office is open, but both together cannot be true. ["But not both" statements can be broken down into two separate statements, with contrapositives for each.]

Translating these statements and forming the contrapositives allows for further deductions.

For instance, if Marisol does not collect her mail, then the post office is closed. And when the post office is closed, it must be a holiday, and when it's a holiday, Marisol does not work.

What would happen if Marisol were at work? First, it is not a holiday. And when it's not a holiday, the post office is open. But "not a holiday" appears in more than one of our conditional statements. It also triggers the "exclusive or." When it's not a holiday, either it is the weekend or the post office is open, but not both. Because the post office is open, it can't be the weekend. And when it's not the weekend, Marisol collects her mail and she goes to bed early.

Practice Here's an opportunity to practice forming contrapositives and making deductions with conditional statements, some of which contain "exclusive or" clauses. Record each of the following statements in If/Then shorthand and form their contrapositives. You can turn the page at any time to check your work.

Conditional Statement	My Analysis
77. When we go to the amusement park, we always ride either the teacups or the Himalayan, but we never ride both.	
78. I've noticed something about life: If you ask, you get what you asked for—but it'll be either at the right time or in the right place but never both at once!	
79. In Professor Smith's class, you'll get an A if you write an extra paper or if you do a presentation in class. Oddly enough, though, if you both write an extra paper and do a presentation, then Smith will think you're just trying to curry favor, and in that case you definitely won't get an A!	

Conditional Statements	My Analysis
80. If Maria is selected for the team, then Kevin or Charles will be selected but not both.	
Unless Vivian is selected, Kevin will not be selected.	
David is not selected for the team if Charles is selected.	
If Kevin and Charles are both selected for the team, Angela will also be selected.	

If we know that . . .	then we also know that . . .
Kevin is selected	
Charles is not selected	
Maria is selected	
David is selected	
Angela is selected	
Kevin and Charles are selected	

Expert Analysis

Here's how the LSAT expert looked at those two exercises. Compare your work recording the If/Then statements and forming the contrapositives. Check to see if you made all of the available deductions.

Conditional Statement	Analysis
77. When we go to the amusement park, we always ride either the teacups or the Himalayan, but we never ride both.	If amusement park → teacups OR Himalayan If NOT teacups AND NOT Himalayan → NOT amusement park If amusement park → NOT [teacups AND Himalayan combo] If [teacups AND Himalayan combo] → NOT amusement park [So, if we are somewhere and we have just ridden both a teacups ride and a Himalayan ride, then we're somewhere other than the amusement park—the county fair, perhaps?]
78. I've noticed something about life: If you ask, you get what you asked for—but it'll be either at the right time or in the right place but never both at once!	If ask → right time OR right place If NOT right time AND NOT right place → NOT ask If ask → NOT [right time AND right place combo] If [right time AND right place combo] → NOT ask [So, if you get what you want in the right place and at the right time, you must not have asked for it (paradoxically enough).]

Conditional Statement	Analysis
79. In Professor Smith's class, you'll get an A if you write an extra paper or if you do a presentation in class. Oddly enough, though, if you both write an extra paper and do a presentation, then Smith will think you're just trying to curry favor, and in that case you definitely won't get an A!	If extra paper OR presentation → A If NOT A → NOT extra paper AND NOT presentation If [extra paper AND presentation combo] → NOT A If A → NOT [extra paper AND presentation combo]
80. If Maria is selected for the team, then Kevin or Charles will be selected but not both.	If Maria → Kevin OR Charles If NOT Kevin AND NOT Charles → NOT Maria If Maria → NOT [Kevin AND Charles combo] If [Kevin AND Charles combo] → NOT Maria
Unless Vivian is selected, Kevin will not be selected.	If Kevin → Vivian If NOT Vivian → NOT Kevin
David is not selected for the team if Charles is selected.	If Charles → NOT David If David → NOT Charles
If Kevin and Charles are both selected for the team, Angela will also be selected.	If Kevin AND Charles → Angela If NOT Angela → NOT Kevin OR NOT Charles

If we know that...	then we also know that...
Kevin is selected	Vivian is selected There are no further deductions.
Charles is not selected	We can't deduce anything.
Maria is selected	Kevin or Charles is selected, and the other one is not Because we don't know which one is selected, there are no further deductions.
David is selected	Charles is not selected There are no further deductions.
Angela is selected	We can't deduce anything. Angela's being selected is never a trigger.
Kevin and Charles are selected	Maria and David are not selected, and Angela and Vivian are selected

Formal Logic: Numerical Deductions from Conditional Statements

Prepare

LEARNING OBJECTIVES

In this section, you'll learn to:

- Determine the valid deductions from a Conditional Statement with the "If X → ~Y" Structure.
- Determine the valid deductions from a Conditional Statement with the "If ~X → Y" Structure.

You've already gotten some practice in making deductions from conditional statements. Now, we're going to devote a section of this chapter to two particular types of deductions because both are very common on the LSAT. You'll find it immensely helpful to be able to think through them quickly and accurately.

Determining the Valid Deduction from a Conditional Statement with the "If X → ~Y" Structure

This type of conditional is very common on the LSAT:

> If Charlene acts in the play, then Daisy will not act in the play.

The trigger involves something that *does* happen, and the result is that something else *cannot* happen.

In dealing with this, let's put the statement into our standard shorthand and make the contrapositive, just as we always will when we encounter conditional statements:

> If C → ~D
>
> If D → ~C

Now, if you don't push your understanding of the rule beyond that point, you'll still be able to get through the logical reasoning stimulus... slowly. But you can distill the logic further, and doing so will save you from having to write it all out. Take another look at the statement and its contrapositive together. Every time you have either one of these entities acting in the play, you can't have the other one. In other words, you can't ever include both of them in the play. Be very clear, however, that it's possible for neither one to act in the play. They can't be together in the play, but they could both sit in the audience. So, there are three possible outcomes from this statement:

- C in, D out
- D in, C out
- Both C and D out

Thus, if you prefer, instead of writing out the statement and its contrapositive, you could simply note the one result that cannot happen:

> Never C and D in together

Already you've saved yourself some time. But there's another deduction to be drawn here. Before you were given this rule, it may have been possible that all actors available to be in the play are, in fact, *in* the play. This rule, however, has made that impossible. The maximum number of actors who can be in the play is now at least one less than the total pool of actors. This type of rule reduces the acceptable maximum number, which may be an invaluable deduction in a Logical Reasoning question.

You'll get to practice making this type of deduction after we cover the other type of rule that commonly affects numbers on the LSAT.

Determining the Valid Deduction from a Conditional Statement with "If ~X → Y" Structure

We just got to know a common format for a rule in which two things can't go together or can't both happen. That rule always reduces the maximum number of things that can happen. There's a sort of corollary rule that also affects numbers, and it has this structure:

If Edith doesn't act in the play, then Frank will.

The trigger is something *not* happening, and the result is that something *does* happen.

In dealing with this, let's once again put the statement into standard shorthand and make the contrapositive, just as we always will with conditional statements:

If ~E → F

If ~F → E

As before, if you don't push your understanding of this rule beyond that point, you'll still be able to get through the logical reasoning stimulus. But you can become more efficient in your treatment of this type of rule by noticing something about it right now: The absence of one of the entities requires the presence of the other one—every single time. Thus, one or the other of them must always be included. If either one is left out, then the other one must be in as a consequence. And can they both be in the play? Of course, because you can have the logical results without the triggers.

So we could have...

- E out, F in
- F out, E in
- Both E and F in

Thus, if you find it easier, you could skip the Formal Logic translation and note the rule in shorthand with something like this:

At least one of E or F in the play (maybe both)

Think for a moment about what this rule does to the numbers. Prior to this rule, it may have been possible that we were dealing with an avant-garde play in which no one appears on stage and the audience is treated to five minutes of darkness and the sound of rain. Can that happen now? No. This rule establishes a minimum: This play has at least one actor, if not more, who appears. And knowledge of the minimum acceptable number, just like knowledge of the maximum, is priceless when reasoning through LSAT questions.

Practice Here's an opportunity to practice working with conditional statements that affect maxima and minima, as well as everything else you've learned in this chapter.

For each of the following, translate any conditional statements into simple shorthand. You can do this by forming the If/Then and its contrapositive, or you can cut straight to one of the simpler shorthand notes described above, if appropriate. Not all of the statements will fit the two patterns discussed in this section, but part of the object here is to recognize a minimum-increaser or a maximum-reducer when you see it. If there's more than one statement, note down any logical deductions that can be made by combining them. It is possible that some of these statements might not be conditional Formal Logic statements at all. If that's the case, note that no If/Then translation is possible. Expert thinking follows on the page immediately after your practice.

Conditional Statement	My Analysis
81. If Bob gets gouda at the store, he won't also get emmenthaler.	
82. Wherever mosquitoes are not prevalent, rates of malaria drop significantly.	
83. If your sophomore students aren't assigned the time-consuming *War and Peace*, they will be assigned both *Anna Karenina* and *Resurrection*.	
84. If I don't get my taxes done by a professional, I will use tax-preparation software.	
85. Sheila can't go to the event if her husband doesn't stay home with the kids.	
86. If you can't say something nice, then just nod and smile.	
87. Paul won't eat anything that has mushrooms or mayonnaise.	
88. No one who really cares would ever just give to a charity without understanding how the charity operates.	

Conditional Statement	My Analysis
89. If Bob can't find gouda at the store, then he'll get edam instead. If he can't get gouda and can't get edam, then he will yell at the guy at the cheese counter.	
90. Soup that doesn't taste spicy needs a lot of salt.	
91. We can reopen the unused factory unless it's either sitting on a fault line or is contaminated with mercury.	
92. We ought to go to the memorial service.	
93. Whenever I am in Paris, I see lights reflected in the Seine and I can't get a decent taco!	
94. Mary does a great improvised barbeque, but she can cook indoors only if you give her a very specific recipe.	
95. No one who wants to be a doctor should set a bad example by smoking.	
96. Don't bother getting eggs at the store unless you also get butter in which to cook them. Don't get margarine unless they're out of butter or the butter is more than $4.	
97. The X organization won't support a bill if the Y organization is backing it. The Y organization refuses to support anything backed by the Z organization.	
98. I never believe what I read in the *Menda City Daily News.*	
99. I will make the phone call if, but only if, I can find my cell phone.	

Expert Analysis

Here's how an LSAT expert would diagram each of the statements you just worked with. In some cases, the expert has added an additional comment to remind you of easily overlooked exceptions to or implications of these statements.

Conditional Statement	Analysis
81. If Bob gets gouda at the store, he won't also get emmenthaler.	If G → NOT E If E → NOT G OR Never both G AND E
82. Wherever mosquitoes are not prevalent, rates of malaria drop significantly.	If mosquitoes NOT prevalent → malaria rates sig. drop If malaria rates NOT sig. drop → mosquitoes prevalent OR Either malaria rates sig. drop OR mosquitoes are prevalent, OR both

Conditional Statement	Analysis
83. If your sophomore students aren't assigned the time-consuming *War and Peace*, they will be assigned both *Anna Karenina* and *Resurrection*.	If NOT WP → AK AND R If NOT AK OR NOT R → WP OR Either WP OR [AK AND R combo] Note: Students could be assigned *War and Peace* and one of the other two books, or they could be assigned all three. The triggers in the original statement and its contrapositive are all negative statements, so there's no way to determine what happens if they *are* assigned one or more of these books. Another helpful way to translate this statement would be to break it down into smaller pieces: If ~WP → AK If ~AK → WP If ~WP → R If ~R → WP Notice how that translation covers all of the triggers and results in the statement.
84. If I don't get my taxes done by a professional, I will use tax-preparation software.	If NOT pro → software If NOT software → pro OR Either a professional OR software OR both
85. Sheila can't go to the event if her husband doesn't stay home with the kids.	If husband NOT home → Sheila NOT at event If Sheila at event → husband home [Remember: It is possible for Sheila's husband to stay home and for her not to go to the event.]

Conditional Statement	Analysis
86. If you can't say something nice, then just nod and smile.	If NOT say something nice → nod AND smile If NOT nod OR NOT smile → say something nice Either say something nice OR [nod AND smile combo] Note: A person could say something nice and do one of the other two gestures, or they could do all three. The triggers in the original statement and its contrapositive are all negative statements, so there's no way to determine what happens if they *do* say something nice or if they *do* nod or smile. Another helpful way to translate this statement would be to break it down into smaller pieces: If ~say something nice → nod If ~nod → say something nice If ~say something nice → smile If ~smile → say something nice Notice how that translation covers all of the triggers and results in the statement.
87. Paul won't eat anything that has mushrooms or mayonnaise.	If mushrooms OR mayo → Paul NOT eat If Paul eat → NOT mushrooms AND NOT mayo
88. No one who really cares would ever just give to a charity without understanding how the charity operates.	If really cares → does NOT give without understanding If gives without understanding → does NOT really care [Remember: You can't have "really cares" and "gives without understanding" at the same time (that is, in the same individual).]

Conditional Statement	Analysis
89. If Bob can't find gouda at the store, then he'll get edam instead. If he can't get gouda and can't get edam, then he will yell at the guy at the cheese counter.	If NOT G → E If NOT E → G Either E OR G OR both at all times If NOT G AND NOT E → yell If NOT yell → G OR E [If the first rule is obeyed, the second one will never be triggered. Note that it's possible for Bob to buy gouda or edam or both and still yell at the guy at the cheese counter without violating these rules.]
90. Soup that doesn't taste spicy needs a lot of salt.	If NOT spicy → salt If NOT salt → spicy [Soup must always be either salty or spicy *or both* by the conditions of this rule.]
91. We can reopen the unused factory unless it's either sitting on a fault line or is contaminated with mercury.	If can NOT reopen → fault line OR mercury If NOT fault line AND NOT mercury → can reopen [Either we can reopen the factory, or it is sitting on a fault line, or it has mercury. Remember, though, that it is possible for the factory to sit on a fault line and be contaminated with mercury and still be reopened. "Can reopen" is not a trigger in this rule. Sitting on a fault line or mercury contamination are necessary to the factory's remaining closed. Their absence is not required for its reopening.]
92. We ought to go to the memorial service.	Not a conditional; no translation. This is a statement of opinion.

Conditional Statement	Analysis
93. Whenever I am in Paris, I see lights reflected in the Seine and I can't get a decent taco!	If Paris → see lights AND can't-get-taco If NOT see lights OR NOT can't-get-taco (can-get-taco) → NOT Paris
94. Mary does a great improvised barbeque, but she can cook indoors only if you give her a very specific recipe.	[First clause is not a conditional. Second clause translates:] If can cook indoors → give specific recipe If NOT give specific recipe → can NOT cook indoors
95. No one who wants to be a doctor should set a bad example by smoking.	If want to be doctor → should NOT smoke If smoke → NOT want to be doctor
96. Don't bother getting eggs at the store unless you also get butter in which to cook them. Don't get margarine unless they're out of butter or the butter is more than $4.	If eggs → butter If NOT butter → NOT eggs If margarine → NOT butter OR butter = $4+ If butter AND NOT butter = $4+ → NOT margarine That is, if the store has butter *and* it's not $4 or more, then don't get margarine. [Consider the following: —If I get eggs at the store, then I bought butter. Did I also buy margarine? If I paid $4 or less for the butter, then I did not buy margarine. If I paid more than $4 for the butter, then maybe I did buy margarine, but I don't know for sure. —If they have butter for $3, I could buy it, but I don't know that I do. I also don't know whether I buy eggs, though I do know I don't buy margarine.]

Conditional Statement	Analysis
97. The X organization won't support a bill if the Y organization is backing it. The Y organization refuses to support anything backed by the Z organization.	If Y supports → X NOT support If X supports → Y NOT support That is, X and Y never support the same bill. If Z supports → Y NOT support If Y supports → Z NOT support That is, Y and Z never support the same bill. [Deductions: • If Y supports a bill, both X and Z will refuse to support it. • If Z supports a bill, Y will not support it, but we don't know about X. • If X supports a bill, Y will not also support it, but we don't know about Z. • At any time, all three could oppose the same bill.]
98. I never believe what I read in the *Menda City Daily News.*	If read in MCDN → NOT believe If believe → NOT read in MCDN OR An item can never be both printed in MCDN AND believed by me
99. I will make the phone call if, but only if, I can find my cell phone.	If make the phone call → can find my cell phone If can NOT find my cell phone → will NOT make the phone call If can find my cell phone → make the phone call If NOT make the phone call → can NOT find my cell phone [Deduction: Either both events will happen or neither will.]

Reflect Look back over your practice.

- Did you take the time to understand each conditional statement before noting it down in shorthand?
- If you couldn't immediately see how to write it down in one sentence, did you make the If/Then and its contrapositive? (If so, that's great!)
- Did you tend to get confused about the side of the arrow on which *not* should appear?
- Did you remember that you can have the result without the trigger in each case?

Now, take a moment to look back over all of Chapter 1. You may not have even been thinking about it, but you've successfully employed a great many essential LSAT skills, skills you'll continue to use in law school and in the practice of law. Now that you've built this foundation, you're ready to tackle a range of LSAT material. Chapters 2–6 cover the Method and strategies for the Logical Reasoning sections. Finally, Chapters 7–9 outline what you need to know to master Reading Comprehension. You may be tackling any of those sections in the next part of your practice. Regardless, we strongly encourage you to return to Chapter 1 whenever you feel you need a refresher about these Formal Logic fundamentals that form the heart of LSAT reasoning.

PART TWO

Logical Reasoning

CHAPTER 2

The Kaplan Logical Reasoning Method

The most important skills you'll learn and master for the LSAT are those pertaining to the Logical Reasoning sections. The reason is pretty clear: With two scored sections on every test, Logical Reasoning accounts for half of your LSAT score. Recent Logical Reasoning sections have had 25 or 26 questions, but unlike the Reading Comprehension questions, each question in the Logical Reasoning sections is self-contained. What's more, the Logical Reasoning sections test more distinct question types than the Reading Comprehension section does. The questions may ask you to identify what is missing in a short argument or ask you to identify a fact that would strengthen or weaken the argument. Other Logical Reasoning questions reward you for describing an argument's logical flaw or its author's argumentative strategy. Still others contain no argument but instead ask you to draw valid deductions from a set of statements. In Chapters 3, 4, and 5, you'll learn to identify each of the Logical Reasoning question types, and you'll practice all of the skills you need to answer them quickly and accurately. In this chapter, however, we'll focus on two features that all Logical Reasoning questions have in common: (1) their overall structure and (2) the way their incorrect answer choices are devised.

Logical Reasoning Question Format and the Kaplan Logical Reasoning Method

The first and most important commonality among LSAT Logical Reasoning questions is their structure. Every Logical Reasoning question will begin with a *stimulus*, usually a paragraph-length argument or set of assertions. The stimulus is the text you need to untangle or analyze to understand the author's argument or his set of premises. Next to the stimulus, the *question stem* describes the task that the LSAT asks you to perform in relation to the stimulus. Finally, there are always five *answer choices*, exactly one of which is correct, while the other four are demonstrably incorrect.

The Kaplan Logical Reasoning Method leverages the consistent structure of Logical Reasoning questions to allow you to approach each one in the most efficient and effective manner possible.

THE KAPLAN LOGICAL REASONING METHOD

STEP 1 Identify the Question Type

STEP 2 Untangle the Stimulus

STEP 3 Predict the Correct Answer

STEP 4 Evaluate the Answer Choices

There is nothing abstract about this approach. In fact, take a look at the Method mapped onto a Logical Reasoning question and you'll see just how, well, *logical* this way of attacking the questions is.

Step 2: Untangle the Stimulus	**Step 1: Identify the Question Type**
Zero in on what is relevant. Here, the expert has highlighted the conclusion and underlined the evidence.	Start here, so you know what to look for in the stimulus.

Health officials claim that because <u>the foods and beverages mentioned or consumed on many television programs are extremely low in nutritional value</u>, watching television has a bad influence on the dietary habits of television viewers.

The claim by health officials depends on the presupposition that

(A) the eating and drinking habits of people on television programs are designed to mirror the eating and drinking habits of television viewers

(B) seeing some foods and beverages being consumed on, or hearing them mentioned on, television programs increases the likelihood that viewers will consume similar kinds of foods and beverages

(C) the food and beverage industry finances television programs so that the foods and beverages that have recently appeared on the market can be advertised on those programs

(D) television viewers are only interested in the people on television programs who have the same eating and drinking habits as they do

(E) the eating and drinking habits of people on television programs provide health officials with accurate predictions about the food and beverages that will become popular among television viewers

PrepTest101 Sec Q13

Step 3: Predict the Correct Answer	**Step 4: Evaluate the Answer Choices**
In your own words, state what the correct answer must say.	Identify the answer that matches your prediction. Eliminate those that do not.

Notice that the LSAT expert always starts with the question stem. After all, there's no reason to read through the stimulus unless you know what you're looking for. As you learn to identify the various Logical Reasoning questions used by the testmaker, you'll start to recognize words and phrases that signal your task and, in turn, you'll be able to anticipate the relevant portions of the stimulus before you even start reading and untangling it.

Note, too, that the LSAT expert takes a moment to reflect on the information from the stimulus and to predict the correct answer before wading into the answer choices. If you've taken the LSAT before picking up this book, you know that tackling the answer choices unprepared can lead you to reread the stimulus over and over, double-checking what it said and comparing it to each choice. The Method you'll learn here avoids all of that unnecessary repetition. By predicting the meaning or content of the correct answer first, you can evaluate each choice by asking, "Does this match my prediction?" If not, eliminate that answer choice. If it matches your prediction, you've got the right answer.

Let's walk through a Logical Reasoning question step by step and see the LSAT expert's analysis as it develops using this approach.

Step 1: The "presupposition" an argument "depends on" indicates a Necessary Assumption question. Determine an unstated assumption that the author believes must be true for the evidence to lead logically to the conclusion.

Health officials claim that because the foods and beverages mentioned or consumed on many television programs are extremely low in nutritional value, watching television has a bad influence on the dietary habits of television viewers.

The claim by health officials depends on the presupposition that

(A) the eating and drinking habits of people on television programs are designed to mirror the eating and drinking habits of television viewers

(B) seeing some foods and beverages being consumed on, or hearing them mentioned on, television programs increases the likelihood that viewers will consume similar kinds of foods and beverages

(C) the food and beverage industry finances television programs so that the foods and beverages that have recently appeared on the market can be advertised on those programs

(D) television viewers are only interested in the people on television programs who have the same eating and drinking habits as they do

(E) the eating and drinking habits of people on television programs provide health officials with accurate predictions about the food and beverages that will become popular among television viewers

PrepTest101 Sec3 Q13

You'll learn all about Assumption questions in Chapter 4. For now, follow the LSAT expert as he untangles the argument in the stimulus.

Step 2: Conclusion: Watching television negatively influences viewers' diets. *because* Evidence: Food and beverages consumed on television are low in nutrition.	**Step 1:** The "presupposition" an argument "depends on" indicates a Necessary Assumption question. Determine an unstated assumption that the author believes must be true for the evidence to lead logically to the conclusion.

Health officials claim that because the foods and beverages mentioned or consumed on many television programs are extremely low in nutritional value, watching television has a bad influence on the dietary habits of television viewers.

The claim by health officials depends on the presupposition that

(A) the eating and drinking habits of people on television programs are designed to mirror the eating and drinking habits of television viewers

(B) seeing some foods and beverages being consumed on, or hearing them mentioned on, television programs increases the likelihood that viewers will consume similar kinds of foods and beverages

(C) the food and beverage industry finances television programs so that the foods and beverages that have recently appeared on the market can be advertised on those programs

(D) television viewers are only interested in the people on television programs who have the same eating and drinking habits as they do

(E) the eating and drinking habits of people on television programs provide health officials with accurate predictions about the food and beverages that will become popular among television viewers

PrepTest101 Sec3 Q13

As you'll see in the upcoming chapters, your reading and untangling of the stimulus will vary, depending on the type of information relevant to the answer. Here, because the LSAT expert recognized this as a Necessary Assumption question, he focused on analyzing the health officials' argument. In particular, he zeroed in on first identifying the officials' conclusion, and then finding the evidence used to support that claim. Now he's ready to predict the correct answer for this question.

Step 2: Conclusion: Watching television negatively influences viewers' diets. *because* Evidence: Food and beverages consumed on television are low in nutrition.	**Step 1:** The "presupposition" an argument "depends on" indicates a Necessary Assumption question. Determine an unstated assumption that the author believes must be true for the evidence to lead logically to the conclusion.

Health officials claim that because the foods and beverages mentioned or consumed on many television programs are extremely low in nutritional value, watching television has a bad influence on the dietary habits of television viewers.

The claim by health officials depends on the presupposition that

(A) the eating and drinking habits of people on television programs are designed to mirror the eating and drinking habits of television viewers

(B) seeing some foods and beverages being consumed on, or hearing them mentioned on, television programs increases the likelihood that viewers will consume similar kinds of foods and beverages

(C) the food and beverage industry finances television programs so that the foods and beverages that have recently appeared on the market can be advertised on those programs

(D) television viewers are only interested in the people on television programs who have the same eating and drinking habits as they do

(E) the eating and drinking habits of people on television programs provide health officials with accurate predictions about the food and beverages that will become popular among television viewers

PrepTest101 Sec3 Q13

Step 3: The health officials must assume that simply *seeing* or *hearing about* foods consumed on TV will somehow *influence* the dietary choices of those watching TV.

After you read the expert's prediction in Step 3, look back at the question stem for a moment. The words "depends on the presupposition" tell you that the correct answer must be a fact that the author believes *must be true* in order for the argument's conclusion to be drawn. In a question like this, the expert knows to look for a gap between the concepts discussed in the evidence and those in the conclusion. The correct answer will tie together the idea of watching television to the idea of being influenced by television. Wrong answer choices will connect these ideas in an illogical way, discuss factors that are irrelevant to the argument, or state facts that are stronger or more extreme than what the author is assuming.

Step 2: Conclusion: Watching television negatively influences viewers' diets. *because* Evidence: Food and beverages consumed on television are low in nutrition.	**Step 1:** The "presupposition" an argument "depends on" indicates a Necessary Assumption question. Determine an unstated assumption that the author believes must be true for the evidence to lead logically to the conclusion.

Health officials claim that because the foods and beverages mentioned or consumed on many television programs are extremely low in nutritional value, watching television has a bad influence on the dietary habits of television viewers.

The claim by health officials depends on the presupposition that

(A) the eating and drinking habits of people on television programs are designed to mirror the eating and drinking habits of television viewers

(B) seeing some foods and beverages being consumed on, or hearing them mentioned on, television programs increases the likelihood that viewers will consume similar kinds of foods and beverages

(C) the food and beverage industry finances television programs so that the foods and beverages that have recently appeared on the market can be advertised on those programs

(D) television viewers are only interested in the people on television programs who have the same eating and drinking habits as they do

(E) the eating and drinking habits of people on television programs provide health officials with accurate predictions about the food and beverages that will become popular among television viewers

PrepTest101 Sec3 Q13

Step 3: The health officials must assume that simply *seeing* or *hearing about* foods consumed on TV will somehow *influence* the dietary choices of those watching TV.	**Step 4:** (B) is correct. This matches the prediction that viewers' diets are influenced by what viewers see on TV.

Wrong answers: (A) 180. Rather than viewers copying what they see on TV, this answer suggests that TV mimics viewers' eating habits. (C) Outside the Scope. The argument is only concerned with TV's influence on viewers, not why certain foods got on TV in the first place. (D) Extreme and 180. The argument states that viewers are influenced by what they see on TV. How viewers decide what to view reverses the logic of the argument. (E) Extreme. It is necessary to the argument that foods shown on TV influence viewers' diets, not that these foods accurately predict future trends.

There you see the Method in action. As you practice it on the various question types, you'll find that you'll get faster and more accurate throughout the Logical Reasoning sections. For the sake of completeness, we included the analysis of all five answer choices, but, on the test, our LSAT expert would have been able to stop evaluating the answer choices as soon as he reached (B). That's the power of making a prediction in Step 3. It's a bit like making a list of features you must have in a new car before you go to the dealership. You're able to rule out any number of choices that won't fit your needs and zero in on the model that's going to make you happy. It won't happen on every Logical Reasoning question, but you'll find that a great majority of questions can be tackled effectively and efficiently by utilizing this exact approach.

Take note of the paragraph following the example. There, the expert has mentally labeled the wrong answer choices, describing why each one does not fit the task set out by the question stem. Choice (A) reverses the direction of causation in the argument; choice (C) drifts out of the scope of the argument by describing why certain foods might appear on TV; choice (D) again gets the direction of causation wrong by explaining why people might watch certain shows; and choice (E) is extreme—there is nothing in the original argument suggesting that health officials will begin to predict the popularity of certain foods among TV viewers. This ability to recognize wrong answers and define why they are incorrect is an invaluable skill to LSAT experts. In addition to consistently creating the same types of questions, the LSAT also repeatedly uses the same types of wrong answer choices. Quickly spotting these wrong answer types and eliminating them will help you become an even more confident test taker.

Wrong Answers in Logical Reasoning Questions

The LSAT is nothing if not consistent. Each test administration offers the same question types and even draws on much the same subject matter for passages and stimuli. It's no surprise, then, that the testmaker employs the same types of wrong answers as well. Because you get points only for selecting the correct answer on the LSAT, you may wonder why it's valuable to label the wrong answers by type. It is valuable because recognizing the common wrong answer patterns will make you more confident (and thus faster) when you eliminate choices.

Many students, when they practice, will simply check to see if they got a question right. If so, they'll move on, ignoring any analysis of the wrong answers. On test day, that's fine—get the right answer and go. But in practice, take the time to review the wrong answers as well. By doing so, you'll internalize the patterns—even the words and phrases—that repeatedly identify incorrect choices.

Take a look at two more Logical Reasoning questions worked out with the expert analysis. Read them through in order, from Step 1 through Step 4, so that you start to get the rhythm of the method. This time, though, pay special attention to the analysis of each wrong answer. At the end of these examples, we'll distill a list of the most common wrong answer types in Logical Reasoning. As you work through subsequent chapters, you'll see these same types of distractors appear over and over again, and in no time you'll be eliminating wrong answers without having to reread and double-check the stimulus to assuage your doubts.

Step 2: Conclusion: Setting out poison for the gray squirrels will pose no threat to the owl population.	Step 1: "[M]ost calls into question" signals this as a Weaken question. Find an answer choice that, if true, would cast doubt on the argument's conclusion.
because	
Evidence: The poison would be accessible only to the gray squirrel and other rodents.	

The gray squirrel, introduced into local woodlands ten years ago, threatens the indigenous population of an endangered owl species, because the squirrels' habitual stripping of tree bark destroys the trees in which the owls nest. Some local officials have advocated setting out poison for the gray squirrels. The officials argue that this measure, while eliminating the squirrels, would pose no threat to the owl population, since the poison would be placed in containers accessible only to squirrels and other rodents.

Which one of the following, if true, most calls into question the officials' argument?

(A) One of the species whose members are likely to eat the poison is the red squirrel, a species on which the owls do not prey.

(B) The owls whose nesting sites are currently being destroyed by the gray squirrel feed primarily on rodents.

(C) No indigenous population of any other bird species apart from the endangered owls is threatened by the gray squirrels.

(D) The owls that are threatened build their nests in the tops of trees, but the gray squirrels strip away bark from the trunks.

(E) The officials' plan entails adding the poison to food sources that are usually eaten by rodents but not by other animals.

PrepTest104 Sec1 Q8

Step 3: The officials draw the extreme conclusion that the poison will pose *no threat whatsoever* to the owls. They overlook the possibility that even though the owls cannot get into the poison containers, they may still be harmed. Find an answer choice that brings up a way for the poison to negatively impact the owls.	Step 4: (B) is correct. In this scenario, the owls' primary food supply (rodents) could be decimated by the poison. It's also possible that if the rodents leave the containers, the owls could consume poisoned prey. Either way, this answer choice suggests a way in which the poison *could* negatively impact the owls.

Wrong answers: (A) Outside the Scope. Harm to species upon which the owls do *not* prey is irrelevant to the argument. This does not raise a possible way the owls could be harmed. (C) Outside the Scope. What does or does not happen to any other species of birds is irrelevant to the connection between the poison and the owls. (D) Outside the Scope. The evidence established that bark-stripping is harmful to the trees in which the owls live; where on the tree the squirrels strip the bark is irrelevant. (E) 180. The fact that owls are unlikely to eat any poisoned food removed from the containers by rodents would strengthen, not weaken, this argument.

The LSAT expert quickly homes in on answer choice (B) as the only one that establishes a strong connection between the negative impact the poison will have on the rodents and the resulting impact on the owls. The expert quickly moves through and eliminates the other answer choices—each one just as irrelevant to the original argument as the next. As you become better at identifying why wrong answer choices are incorrect, you too will be able to move more quickly through answer choices, gaining speed and confidence along the way.

Step 2: Conclusion: Jones is the best qualified candidate for the position of president. *because* Evidence: Jones has a "unique set of qualifications."	**Step 1:** The phrase "vulnerable to criticism" indicates a Flaw question. Find an answer choice that describes the reasoning error the author makes as she moves from her evidence to her conclusion.

Several excellent candidates have been proposed for the presidency of United Wire, and each candidate would bring to the job different talents and experience. If the others are compared with Jones, however, it will be apparent that none of them has her unique set of qualifications. Jones, therefore, is best qualified to be the new president of United Wire.

The argument is vulnerable to criticism on the ground that it

(A) uses flattery to win over those who hold an opposing position

(B) refutes a distorted version of an opposing position

(C) seeks to distinguish one member of a group on the basis of something that applies to all

(D) supports a universal claim on the basis of a single example

(E) describes an individual in terms that appropriately refer only to the group as a whole

PrepTest101 Sec2 Q6

Step 3: The argument jumps from a discussion of *unique* qualifications in the evidence to a claim of the *best* qualifications in the conclusion. The author assumes that having a unique set of qualifications makes a candidate the best qualified. However, the author states that each candidate brings unique talents and experiences to the race. The correct answer will describe this inconsistency.	**Step 4:** (C) is correct. The author distinguishes Jones on the basis of having unique qualifications, even though she earlier indicates that all the candidates have unique qualifications.

Wrong answers: (A) Distortion. The author does not use flattery to win anybody over. (B) Distortion. The author does not characterize any opposing positions in her argument. (D) Distortion. The author does not jump to a universal claim. Both the evidence and the conclusion are about one person: Jones. (E) Distortion. The author describes Jones' qualifications as "unique," which just as appropriately applies to the other individuals in the group.

Notice that the LSAT expert takes her time in Step 3 of the method and articulates the reasoning flaw in the author's argument. While her prediction isn't an exact, word-for-word match with the right answer, a clear understanding of the overlooked possibility in the argument—that the other candidates' unique talents are superior to Jones's unique talents—allows the expert to quickly move through the answer choices and find the one that most closely fits. While an untrained test taker might be tempted by wrong answer choices that evocatively describe various reasoning errors, an LSAT expert knows that her task is not simply to find a description of any old flaw in reasoning. Instead, she is focused intensely on her task: to find the answer choice that describes the *specific* flaw present in the stimulus.

The Logical Reasoning Wrong Answer Types

Not every wrong answer you see will fit neatly into one of the types you see described here. After all, sometimes when a question asks for what the author assumes, the wrong answer will just be something she doesn't assume, without clearly being a 180 or Extreme. Other wrong answers might fit more than one category. Still, it's worth your time to learn the wrong answer types in the list that follows. You'll see them referred to many times in the questions illustrated in the coming chapters.

LOGICAL REASONING: WRONG ANSWER TYPES

- **Outside the Scope**—a choice containing a statement that is too broad, too narrow, or beyond the purview of the stimulus
- **Irrelevant Comparison**—a choice that compares two items or attributes in a way not germane to the author's argument or statements
- **Extreme**—a choice containing language too emphatic to be supported by the stimulus; extreme choices are often (though, not always) characterized by words such as *all*, *never*, *every*, or *none*
- **Distortion**—a choice that mentions details from the stimulus but mangles or misstates the relationship between them given or implied by the author
- **180**—a choice that directly contradicts what the correct answer must say (for example, a choice that strengthens the argument in a Weaken question)
- **Faulty Use of Detail**—a choice that accurately states something from the stimulus but in a manner that answers the question incorrectly; this type is rarely used in Logical Reasoning

Along the way, you'll see a handful of wrong answer types that apply to specific question types. In Assumption or Main Point questions, for example, it's common to see wrong answers that simply repeat the author's evidence instead of his unstated assumption or conclusion. We'll cover these wrong answers when they appear and explain why they aren't credited on the test.

It's also important to bring up Formal Logic statements here. Imagine a case in which the correct answer must say: "To vote in County Y, it is necessary to register 60 days prior to the election." A common wrong answer might say, "Anyone registered 60 days prior to the election can vote in County Y." For the purposes of our wrong answer types, that would be a Distortion. But if you think back to Chapter 1: Formal Logic, you'll recognize that the first statement, the one that matches the correct answer, holds that meeting the registration requirement is *necessary* for voting, while the wrong answer holds that the registration requirement is *sufficient* to be able to vote. Being clear with Formal Logic is important for success in Logical Reasoning. Anytime you need a brush up on necessity and sufficiency, return to Chapter 1 and review the examples and drills there.

Now that you have the big picture of Logical Reasoning in view, it's time to focus on specific questions and their associated skills. The argument-based questions in Chapter 3 provide a foundation for the more numerous (and often more difficult) assumption-based questions in Chapter 4. The non-argument-based questions in Chapter 5 reward you for different skills but still conform precisely to the question format, method, and wrong answer types you've learned in this chapter.

CHAPTER 3

Argument-Based Questions

In the Logical Reasoning sections of the LSAT, the majority of questions—indeed over 70 percent of Logical Reasoning questions on tests released from 2008 to 2014—reward your ability to analyze arguments. That's well over half of all the questions on the exam. So, the skills you'll acquire in this chapter and the next have the potential to make your LSAT score skyrocket.

As we'll discuss it here, the word *argument* does not refer to a dispute between two people, though occasionally, the LSAT will present a brief dialogue in which each party presents an argument. An LSAT argument is one person's attempt to convince the reader that some assertion is true or that some action is advisable. LSAT arguments are defined by two explicit components: (1) a *conclusion*, the author's main point, and (2) one or more pieces of *evidence*, the facts or analyses he offers in support of the conclusion.

LSAT STRATEGY

Every LSAT argument contains

- a conclusion—the assertion, evaluation, or recommendation of which the author is trying to convince his readers; and
- evidence—the facts, studies, or contentions the author believes support or establish the conclusion.

The testmaker has designed several Logical Reasoning question types—Main Point, Role of a Statement, Method of Argument, Point at Issue, and Parallel Reasoning questions—to test your ability to recognize, identify, and characterize the explicit parts of arguments or to describe how the author is putting the pieces of the argument together. In this chapter, you'll learn how to strategically attack and answer each of the five question types listed above. Together, they will account for roughly 9–11 of the Logical Reasoning questions you'll see on test day.

But notice that we keep referring to the conclusion and evidence as the *explicit* parts of each LSAT argument. That's because almost every argument used in the stimulus of a Logical Reasoning question also contains an implicit *assumption*. Three more question types—the extremely important Assumption, Strengthen/Weaken, and Flaw questions, which are all covered in Chapter 4—reward you for identifying the unstated premise in the argument. Together, those questions account for around 24 questions per test. While it might be tempting to leap ahead to these popular question types, you should take the time to first study and practice the learning objectives outlined in the present chapter. Without the skills to analyze the explicit parts of LSAT arguments, the all-important "Assumption Family" questions are nearly impossible.

Conclusions and Main Point Questions

LEARNING OBJECTIVES

In this section, you'll learn to:

- Identify the conclusion in an LSAT argument.
- Characterize and paraphrase the conclusion.
- Identify Main Point questions and characterize their correct and incorrect answer choices.

Here's a Main Point question. Feel free to try it now. You'll see a complete analysis later in this section. By the end of this section, you will have learned how to answer questions of this type.

The authors of a recent article examined warnings of an impending wave of extinctions of animal species within the next 100 years. These authors say that no evidence exists to support the idea that the rate of extinction of animal species is now accelerating. They are wrong, however. Consider only the data on fishes: 40 species and subspecies of North American fishes have vanished in the twentieth century, 13 between 1900 and 1950, and 27 since 1950.

Which one of the following is the main point of the argument?

(A) There is evidence that the rate of extinction of animal species is accelerating.

(B) The future rate of extinction of animal species cannot be determined from available evidence.

(C) The rate of extinction of North American fishes is parallel to the rate of extinction of all animal species taken together.

(D) Forty species and subspecies of North American fishes have vanished in the twentieth century.

(E) A substantial number of fish species are in danger of imminent extinction.

PrepTest101 Sec2 Q15

Main Point questions reward you for directly locating (and sometimes for accurately paraphrasing) the author's conclusion. Because spotting the conclusion forms the basis of all argument analyses on the test, jump right in and practice this important skill.

Identify the Conclusion

Prepare Think of the conclusion as the author's point, the statement she's trying to convince you is true. In our day-to-day lives, we identify conclusions all the time, though we're seldom aware that we're doing so. When your spouse or roommate says, "I don't feel like cooking; we should order something for delivery," the second part of that sentence is his conclusion. This is because the second part of the sentence is what he's trying to convince you to do, and he offers the first part of the sentence (the evidence) as a reason why you should accept his point. Indeed, conclusions are always statements that call out for a reason; they always elicit the question "Why?"

LSAT arguments are usually (though not always) a good deal more complex than that example, but they feature multiple ways in which to identify the conclusion.

Many LSAT arguments use Keywords to introduce the conclusion.

LSAT Question	Analysis
If you know a lot about history, it will be easy for you to impress people who are intellectuals. But unfortunately, you will not know much about history if you have not, for example, read a large number of history books. Therefore, if you are not well versed in history due to a lack of reading, it will not be easy for you to impress people who are intellectuals. *PrepTest104 Sec4 Q7*	"Therefore" signals the author's conclusion here: *If you are not well versed in history, then you won't easily impress intellectuals.* Everything else is either background or evidence.

Other conclusion Keywords or phrases include *hence, thus, consequently, as a result, so*, and *it follows that.* When conclusion Keywords are present, they can be the quickest way to spot the author's point. Don't become overly reliant on conclusion Keywords, however; sometimes the author may use one or more subsidiary conclusions as part of the evidence. Look at this example.

LSAT Question	Analysis
People in the tourist industry know that excessive development of seaside areas by the industry damages the environment. Such development also hurts the tourist industry by making these areas unattractive to tourists, a fact of which people in the tourist industry are well aware. People in the tourist industry would never knowingly do anything to damage the industry. Therefore, they would never knowingly damage the seaside environment, and the people who are concerned about damage to the seaside environment thus have nothing to fear from the tourist industry. *PrepTest101 Sec3 Q12*	In the last sentence, "[t]herefore" signals a conclusion in the argument: *people in the tourist industry would never knowingly damage the seaside environment.* But the sentence continues, and another conclusion Keyword, "thus," signals the ultimate conclusion: *People concerned about damage to the seaside environment should not worry about the tourist industry.* The first part of the last sentence, then, is the argument's subsidiary conclusion, used to support the second half of the last sentence, which is the argument's ultimate conclusion.

In other LSAT arguments, Keywords may signal the evidence. The most common examples are *because, after all, for*, and *since.*

LSAT Question	Analysis
All actions are motivated by self-interest, since any action that is apparently altruistic can be described in terms of self-interest. For example, helping someone can be described in terms of self-interest: the motivation is hope for a reward or other personal benefit to be bestowed as a result of the helping action. *PrepTest107 Sec4 Q18*	"[S]ince" indicates that the second half of the first sentence is evidence supporting the claim made in the first half of the sentence. "For example" simply points to an example that will be used to demonstrate the point that the author wishes to make. *All actions are motivated by self-interest* is the author's conclusion.

The toughest arguments in which to locate the conclusion are those with neither conclusion nor evidence Keywords. In these cases, you need to follow the logical flow of the argument by asking, "What is the author's point, and what is she offering to support that point?" We call this the One-Sentence Test because you're trying to strip away anything other than the one sentence or clause that constitutes the author's ultimate point.

LSAT Question	Analysis
Art Historian: Robbins cannot pass judgment on Stuart's art. While Robbins understands the art of Stuart too well to dismiss it, she does not understand it well enough to praise it. *PrepTest104 Sec4 Q20*	The art historian begins with a very strong opinion: Robbins cannot pass judgment on Stuart's art. She then gives two reasons, or pieces of evidence, to support this subjective claim: Robbins understands Stuart's art well enough to dismiss it, but not well enough to praise it. The conclusion then is the author's subjective, opinionated claim: *Robbins cannot pass judgment on Stuart's art.*

One special case—often associated with Main Point questions, by the way—occurs when the author's conclusion is an assertion that another person's position is incorrect. Arguments with this structure will often begin with language such as "some believe" or "biologists contend" or "it has been proposed." The author's rejection of whatever these other parties are arguing for is then signaled by a Contrast Keyword, such as *but* or *however*, or a flat-out refutation, such as "This is incorrect."

LSAT Question	Analysis
The authors of a recent article examined warnings of an impending wave of extinctions of animal species within the next 100 years. These authors say that no evidence exists to support the idea that the rate of extinction of animal species is now accelerating. They are wrong, however. Consider only the data on fishes: 40 species and subspecies of North American fishes have vanished in the twentieth century, 13 between 1900 and 1950, and 27 since 1950. *PrepTest101 Sec2 Q15*	In this argument, we learn that "[t]he authors of a recent article … say that no evidence exists to support the idea that the rate of extinction … is now accelerating." What does the person making this argument think of the scientists' claim? "They are wrong, however." The conclusion here can thus be summed: *There is evidence to suggest that the rate of animal extinctions is increasing.*

While the author's conclusion in the argument is the sentence containing the Contrast Keyword, your understanding of the author's overall main point requires an understanding of the position held by the "authors of a recent article." Imagine an argument that begins: "Members of the other party argue that we should adopt the proposed city budget. But, they are mistaken." Here, the author's conclusion is the second sentence, but the meaning of the conclusion is "we should not adopt the proposed budget." Notice, too, that the argument would continue with the author's evidence: Here's why we should not adopt the budget. You'll practice paraphrasing conclusions shortly, and you'll look more closely at authors' evidence in the next section. First, however, get in a little practice locating the conclusion in LSAT arguments.

TEST DAY TIP

Some test takers find it helpful to highlight or underline the conclusion in the question text on-screen. Try this in practice and see if it is a tactic you want to add to your Logical Reasoning routine.

Practice Now practice locating the conclusion in a handful of LSAT arguments.

In each of the following arguments, locate and mark the conclusion and, in your own words, explain how you knew that the sentence or clause you selected is the author's main point. After each, review the expert analysis on the pages following the exercise to check your work.

LSAT Question	My Analysis
1. Historian: We can learn about the medical history of individuals through chemical analysis of their hair. It is likely, for example, that Isaac Newton's psychological problems were due to mercury poisoning; traces of mercury were found in his hair. Analysis is now being done on a lock of Beethoven's hair. Although no convincing argument has shown that Beethoven ever had a venereal disease, some people hypothesize that venereal disease caused his deafness. Since mercury was commonly ingested in Beethoven's time to treat venereal disease, if researchers find a trace of mercury in his hair, we can conclude that this hypothesis is correct. *PrepTest106 Sec3 Q16*	
2. Press release: A comprehensive review evaluating the medical studies done up to the present time has found no reason to think that drinking coffee in normal amounts harms the coffee-drinker's heart. So coffee drinkers can relax and enjoy their beverage—it is safe to drink coffee. *PrepTest101 Sec2 Q1*	

LSAT Question	My Analysis
3. During the 1980s Japanese collectors were very active in the market for European art, especially as purchasers of nineteenth-century Impressionist paintings. This striking pattern surely reflects a specific preference on the part of many Japanese collectors for certain aesthetic attributes they found in nineteenth-century Impressionist paintings. *PrepTest104 Sec1 Q5*	
4. All potatoes naturally contain solanine, which is poisonous in large quantities. Domesticated potatoes contain only very small amounts of solanine, but many wild potatoes contain poisonous levels of solanine. Since most of the solanine in potatoes is concentrated in the skin, however, peeling wild potatoes makes them at least as safe to eat as unpeeled domesticated potatoes of the same size. *PrepTest105 Sec1 Q9*	

Expert Analysis

Here's how an LSAT expert looks at each of the arguments you've just examined.

LSAT Question	Analysis
1. Historian: We can learn about the medical history of individuals through chemical analysis of their hair. It is likely, for example, that Isaac Newton's psychological problems were due to mercury poisoning; traces of mercury were found in his hair. Analysis is now being done on a lock of Beethoven's hair. Although no convincing argument has shown that Beethoven ever had a venereal disease, some people hypothesize that venereal disease caused his deafness. Since mercury was commonly ingested in Beethoven's time to treat venereal disease, if researchers find a trace of mercury in his hair, we can conclude that this hypothesis is correct. *PrepTest106 Sec3 Q16*	"[W]e can conclude" signals the author's conclusion: *If researchers find mercury in Beethoven's hair, then this hypothesis is correct.* But what hypothesis? The hypothesis that "some people" have put forward. The author's conclusion can therefore be paraphrased: *If it's determined that traces of mercury were in Beethoven's hair, then his deafness was caused by a venereal disease.*
2. Press release: A comprehensive review evaluating the medical studies done up to the present time has found no reason to think that drinking coffee in normal amounts harms the coffee-drinker's heart. So coffee drinkers can relax and enjoy their beverage—it is safe to drink coffee. *PrepTest101 Sec2 Q1*	"So" signals the author's conclusion here: *Coffee drinkers can relax and enjoy their beverage—it is safe to drink coffee.*
3. During the 1980s Japanese collectors were very active in the market for European art, especially as purchasers of nineteenth-century Impressionist paintings. This striking pattern surely reflects a specific preference on the part of many Japanese collectors for certain aesthetic attributes they found in nineteenth-century Impressionist paintings. *PrepTest104 Sec1 Q5*	There are no conclusion or evidence Keywords here, so use the One-Sentence Test. The first sentence is a description of a pattern of behavior that occurred in the 1980s. The second sentence then introduces the author's voice through the phrase "[T]his ... surely reflects." This subjective, opinionated claim is therefore the conclusion: *Japanese art collectors preferred buying 19th century Impressionistic paintings because of their aesthetic attributes.*

LSAT Question	Analysis
4. All potatoes naturally contain solanine, which is poisonous in large quantities. Domesticated potatoes contain only very small amounts of solanine, but many wild potatoes contain poisonous levels of solanine. Since most of the solanine in potatoes is concentrated in the skin, however, peeling wild potatoes makes them at least as safe to eat as unpeeled domesticated potatoes of the same size. *PrepTest105 Sec1 Q9*	The Keyword "[s]ince" directs to the argument's evidence, and "however" pivots to the author's conclusion: *Peeling wild potatoes makes them at least as safe to eat as unpeeled domesticated potatoes of the same size.*

Paraphrase and Characterize the Conclusion

Prepare Now that you can spot conclusions, you're ready to tackle the task of understanding what they actually mean. LSAT arguments don't always use the simplest or most succinct wording, and as you've seen, sometimes you'll need to combine two sentences to accurately articulate the author's main point.

Being able to put the author's conclusion into your own words is important because, in some questions, the LSAT will paraphrase the author's conclusion in the correct answer. Indeed, it will directly quote another part of the argument in a wrong answer. Being able to zero in on and accurately capture the author's meaning is a skill you'll use in the Reading Comprehension section as well.

Here's how an LSAT expert sees a complex conclusion.

LSAT Question	Analysis
On a certain day, nine scheduled flights on Swift Airlines were canceled. Ordinarily, a cancellation is due to mechanical problems with the airplane scheduled for a certain flight. However, since it is unlikely that Swift would have mechanical problems with more than one or two airplanes on a single day, some of the nine cancellations were probably due to something else. *PrepTest106 Sec3 Q19*	The first sentence establishes a fact: Nine scheduled flights were canceled on one day. "Ordinarily" indicates the normal course of events, but the Keyword "[h]owever" in the next sentence suggests an anomaly. "[S]ince" points to more evidence: It is unlikely that Swift would have mechanical problems with more than a couple of planes, and that sets up the author's conclusion: *Some of the nine canceled flights were due to something other than mechanical problems.*

As you practice paraphrasing conclusions, it's valuable to know that the conclusions to every LSAT argument fall into one of six categories.

LSAT STRATEGY

Conclusions of LSAT arguments almost always match one of these six types:

- Value Judgment (an evaluative statement; e.g., Action X is unethical or Y's recital was poorly sung)
- If/Then (a conditional prediction, recommendation, or assertion; e.g., If X is true, then so is Y or If you are an M, you should do Y)
- Prediction (X *will* or *will not* happen in the future)
- Comparison (X is taller/shorter/more common/less common/etc. than Y)
- Assertion of Fact (X is true or X is false)
- Recommendation (we *should* or *should not* do X)

Learning to spot the category into which a conclusion falls is valuable for many Logical Reasoning question types. When the testmaker asks you to identify the conclusion in a Main Point question, the correct answer must, naturally, match the conclusion in the stimulus. In Parallel Reasoning questions, even though the arguments in the answer choices deal with different subject matter than does the stimulus argument, the conclusion type in the correct answer must match that in the stimulus. Even in the all-important Assumption Family questions, noting a particular conclusion type can help reveal the pattern in the argument, making your analysis more efficient. By the way, some conclusions fall into more than one of these categories. If an author concludes, for example, "If the city's budget is not balanced next year, the council should vote to cut funding to animal shelters," his conclusion is both an If/Then and a Recommendation.

Take a look at how an LSAT expert would recognize the conclusion types in these examples.

LSAT Question	Analysis
Alice will volunteer to work on the hospital fund-raising drive only if her brother Bruce also volunteers and a majority of the others working on the drive promise to select Bruce to manage the drive. However, although Bruce is willing to volunteer, none of the others working on the drive will promise to select Bruce to manage the drive. Thus it is certain that Alice will not volunteer. *PrepTest105 Sec1 Q12*	The conclusion here—*Alice will not volunteer*—is a prediction. The author is stating that a person will not do something in the future.
Press release: A comprehensive review evaluating the medical studies done up to the present time has found no reason to think that drinking coffee in normal amounts harms the coffee-drinker's heart. So coffee drinkers can relax and enjoy their beverage—it is safe to drink coffee. *PrepTest101 Sec2 Q1*	The conclusion here—*coffee is safe to drink*—is an assertion of fact. The author is simply stating a fact that she believes to be true, based on the evidence she has provided.
Formal performance evaluations in the professional world are conducted using realistic situations. Physicians are allowed to consult medical texts freely, attorneys may refer to law books and case records, and physicists and engineers have their manuals at hand for ready reference. Students, then, should likewise have access to their textbooks whenever they take examinations. *PrepTest107 Sec4 Q25*	The conclusion here—*students should have access to textbooks whenever they take exams*—is a recommendation. The author advocates for a change in policy.

LSAT Question	Analysis
If you know a lot about history, it will be easy for you to impress people who are intellectuals. But unfortunately, you will not know much about history if you have not, for example, read a large number of history books. Therefore, if you are not well versed in history due to a lack of reading, it will not be easy for you to impress people who are intellectuals. *PrepTest104 Sec4 Q7*	The conclusion here—*if you're not well versed in history then you won't be able to impress intellectuals*—is a classic if/then conditional statement.
All potatoes naturally contain solanine, which is poisonous in large quantities. Domesticated potatoes contain only very small amounts of solanine, but many wild potatoes contain poisonous levels of solanine. Since most of the solanine in potatoes is concentrated in the skin, however, peeling wild potatoes makes them at least as safe to eat as unpeeled domesticated potatoes of the same size. *PrepTest105 Sec1 Q9*	The conclusion here—*peeling wild potatoes makes them at least as safe to eat as unpeeled domesticated potatoes of the same size*—is a comparison that states that two things are equally safe.
Most people feel that they are being confused by the information from broadcast news. This could be the effect of the information's being delivered too quickly or of its being poorly organized. Analysis of the information content of a typical broadcast news story shows that news stories are far lower in information density than the maximum information density with which most people can cope at any one time. So the information in typical broadcast news stories is poorly organized. *PrepTest104 Sec4 Q19*	The conclusion here—*the information in typical broadcast news stories is poorly organized*—is a value judgment. The author is stating a personal opinion about the quality of a certain thing.

Practice Now that you're familiar with the types of conclusions, practice locating and paraphrasing the conclusions in the following arguments. Make sure to note into which of the six conclusion categories each one falls.

In each of the following arguments, locate the conclusion, identify the conclusion type, and give a simple, accurate paraphrase of the author's meaning in your own words. After each, you can turn to the pages following the exercise to see the expert thinking and check your work.

LSAT Question	My Analysis
5. Jim will go to the party only if both Sam and Elaine also go. Sam is going to the party, but Elaine is not going. So it is certain that Jim will not go to the party. *PrepTest105 Sec1 Q12*	
6. Sociologist: The intended function of news is to give us information on which to act. But in a consumer society, news becomes a product to be manufactured and dispensed to the consumer. An enormous industry for the production and consumption of news has evolved, and we ingest news with an insatiable appetite. Under such circumstances, news is primarily entertaining and cannot, therefore, serve its intended function. *PrepTest105 Sec1 Q18*	
7. Barnes: The two newest employees at this company have salaries that are too high for the simple tasks normally assigned to new employees and duties that are too complex for inexperienced workers. Hence, the salaries and the complexity of the duties of these two newest employees should be reduced. *PrepTest107 Sec1 Q5*	

LSAT Question	My Analysis
8. Maude is incessantly engaging in diatribes against people who are materialistic. But her hypocrisy is evinced by the sentimental treatment of the watch her grandmother gave her. She certainly is very fond of the watch—she worries about damaging it; in fact she always sets it carefully in a special box before going to bed. *PrepTest105 Sec4 Q4*	
9. Several excellent candidates have been proposed for the presidency of United Wire, and each candidate would bring to the job different talents and experience. If the others are compared with Jones, however, it will be apparent that none of them has her unique set of qualifications. Jones, therefore, is best qualified to be the new president of United Wire. *PrepTest101 Sec2 Q6*	
10. All actions are motivated by self-interest, since any action that is apparently altruistic can be described in terms of self-interest. For example, helping someone can be described in terms of self-interest: the motivation is hope for a reward or other personal benefit to be bestowed as a result of the helping action. *PrepTest107 Sec4 Q18*	

Expert Analysis

Here's how an LSAT expert looks at each of the arguments you've just examined.

LSAT Question	Analysis
5. Jim will go to the party only if both Sam and Elaine also go. Sam is going to the party, but Elaine is not going. So it is certain that Jim will not go to the party. *PrepTest105 Sec1 Q12*	The Keyword "[so]" marks the conclusion: *It is certain that Jim will not go to the party.* This is a strong prediction that someone will not do something in the future.
6. Sociologist: The intended function of news is to give us information on which to act. But in a consumer society, news becomes a product to be manufactured and dispensed to the consumer. An enormous industry for the production and consumption of news has evolved, and we ingest news with an insatiable appetite. Under such circumstances, news is primarily entertaining and cannot, therefore, serve its intended function. *PrepTest105 Sec1 Q18*	"[T]herefore" signals the conclusion, an assertion of fact: *News cannot serve its intended function.* But what is its intended function? Look back to the first sentence to fully understand the author's conclusion: *News cannot give us information on which to act.*
7. Barnes: The two newest employees at this company have salaries that are too high for the simple tasks normally assigned to new employees and duties that are too complex for inexperienced workers. Hence, the salaries and the complexity of the duties of these two newest employees should be reduced. *PrepTest107 Sec1 Q5*	"Hence" signals the conclusion here: *The salaries and the complexity of duties of the two newest employees should be reduced.* The Keyword "should" identifies this conclusion as a recommendation.

LSAT Question	Analysis
8. Maude is incessantly engaging in diatribes against people who are materialistic. But her hypocrisy is evinced by the sentimental treatment of the watch her grandmother gave her. She certainly is very fond of the watch—she worries about damaging it; in fact she always sets it carefully in a special box before going to bed. *PrepTest105 Sec4 Q4*	The first sentence tells us that Maude engages in diatribes against people who are materialistic. In the second sentence, the author calls out Maude for her hypocrisy, and provides evidence to prove it. So the conclusion here is a value judgment: *Maude is a hypocrite because she is also materialistic.*
9. Several excellent candidates have been proposed for the presidency of United Wire, and each candidate would bring to the job different talents and experience. If the others are compared with Jones, however, it will be apparent that none of them has her unique set of qualifications. Jones, therefore, is best qualified to be the new president of United Wire. *PrepTest101 Sec2 Q6*	"[T]herefore" points us to the conclusion here: *Jones is best qualified to be the new president of United Wire.* The author is making a comparison between Jones and the other candidates.
10. All actions are motivated by self-interest, since any action that is apparently altruistic can be described in terms of self-interest. For example, helping someone can be described in terms of self-interest: the motivation is hope for a reward or other personal benefit to be bestowed as a result of the helping action. *PrepTest107 Sec4 Q18*	The second half of the first sentence follows the evidence Keyword "since," so the first half of the first sentence is the author's conclusion: *All actions are motivated by self-interest.* This is a conditional, or "if-then," statement.

Identify and Answer Main Point Questions

Prepare Once you know how to locate and paraphrase conclusions, you're ready to answer Main Point questions. On tests released from 2008 through 2014, there were an average of 2–3 Main Point questions per test with a high count of four on two exams given in 2012. While Main Point questions do not constitute a great number of questions, keep in mind how fundamental the conclusion-based skills are. You'll be analyzing the author's conclusion on dozens of questions on test day.

Employing the Kaplan Method for Logical Reasoning, you begin with the question stem. Although the testmaker uses different wording from time to time, Main Point questions always call for the author's final conclusion. The correct answer either restates the conclusion or paraphrases it without changing the meaning. Incorrect answers often state a piece of the author's evidence or one of his subsidiary conclusions that serve as evidence in the argument. Other incorrect answers distort or contradict the author's conclusion. If another party's position is mentioned in the argument, the testmaker may include an incorrect answer that states the other party's point.

Here are a pair of Main Point question stems seen on officially released exams.

LSAT Question	Analysis
Which one of the following is the main point of the argument? *PrepTest101 Sec2 Q15*	"[T]he main point of the argument": a Main Point question. The correct answer will be a paraphrase of the author's conclusion.
Which one of the following most accurately expresses the main conclusion of the essayist's argument? *PrepTest106 Sec1 Q18*	"[E]xpresses the main conclusion of the ... argument": a Main Point question. The correct answer will be a paraphrase of the author's conclusion.

Once you've identified a Main Point question, untangle the stimulus to locate the author's conclusion. Remember that you can use conclusion Keywords, evidence Keywords, or the One-Sentence Test. Paraphrase the conclusion and use that paraphrase as your prediction of the correct answer. Evaluate the answer choices by finding the correct answer that mirrors your prediction or by eliminating choices that restate the evidence, distort or contradict the author's conclusion, or refer to another party's point of view.

Here's how an LSAT expert might analyze a full Main Point question.

Step 2: Conclusion: There *is* evidence that the rate of extinctions is accelerating. The author denies the claim ("They are wrong, however") of those who say there is no such evidence.	**Step 1:** The phrasing "main point of the argument" indicates that this is a Main Point question. The correct answer will paraphrase the author's conclusion.

The authors of a recent article examined warnings of an impending wave of extinctions of animal species within the next 100 years. These authors say that no evidence exists to support the idea that the rate of extinction of animal species is now accelerating. They are wrong, however. Consider only the data on fishes: 40 species and subspecies of North American fishes have vanished in the twentieth century, 13 between 1900 and 1950, and 27 since 1950.

Which one of the following is the main point of the argument?

(A) There is evidence that the rate of extinction of animal species is accelerating.

(B) The future rate of extinction of animal species cannot be determined from available evidence.

(C) The rate of extinction of North American fishes is parallel to the rate of extinction of all animal species taken together.

(D) Forty species and subspecies of North American fishes have vanished in the twentieth century.

(E) A substantial number of fish species are in danger of imminent extinction.

PrepTest101 Sec2 Q15

Step 3: The correct answer will match the author's conclusion: *There is evidence to support the idea that the rate of animal species extinction is accelerating.*	**Step 4:** (A) is correct. This matches the prediction perfectly.

Wrong answers: Wrong answers: (B) This is an extreme interpretation of what "the authors of a recent article" believe, but the person making the argument *disagrees* with those authors. Our author thinks that there *is* evidence to suggest that the rate is accelerating. (C) Extreme. The author does not claim that the rate of fish extinction is parallel with *all* other animal species, merely that fish provide a counterexample to her opponents' position. (D) This is evidence that the author uses to support her conclusion. (E) Extreme and Distortion. The argument makes no claim about whether a *substantial* number of species are in *imminent* danger. Instead, the argument simply states that the rate of extinction is increasing.

Notice that the correct answer mirrors the meaning, if not necessarily the exact wording, of the author's main point. And, just as we suspected, the wrong answers almost always do one of the following: restate the evidence instead of the conclusion, distort the conclusion or miss its scope, or state the view of someone other than the author.

Practice Now try some Main Point questions yourself. Use everything you've learned about locating, characterizing, and paraphrasing the conclusion. Take your time and record your thinking for each step in the Kaplan Method.

Apply the Kaplan Method to each Logical Reasoning question. To compare your work to the thinking of an LSAT expert, turn to the pages following this exercise.

Step 2:	**Step 1:**

11. It is well known that many species adapt to their environment, but it is usually assumed that only the most highly evolved species alter their environment in ways that aid their own survival. However, this characteristic is actually quite common. Certain species of plankton, for example, generate a gas that is converted in the atmosphere into particles of sulfate. These particles cause water vapor to condense, thus forming clouds. Indeed, the formation of clouds over the ocean largely depends on the presence of these particles. More cloud cover means more sunlight is reflected, and so the Earth absorbs less heat. Thus plankton cause the surface of the Earth to be cooler and this benefits the plankton.

Of the following, which one most accurately expresses the main point of the argument?

(A) The Earth would be far warmer than it is now if certain species of plankton became extinct.

(B) By altering their environment in ways that improve their chances of survival, certain species of plankton benefit the Earth as a whole.

(C) Improving their own chances of survival by altering the environment is not limited to the most highly evolved species.

(D) The extent of the cloud cover over the oceans is largely determined by the quantity of plankton in those oceans.

(E) Species such as plankton alter the environment in ways that are less detrimental to the well-being of other species than are the alterations to the environment made by more highly evolved species.

PrepTest107 Sec1 Q11

Step 3:	**Step 4:**

Step 2:	Step 1:

12. Essayist: The way science is conducted and regulated can be changed. But we need to determine whether the changes are warranted, taking into account their price. The use of animals in research could end immediately, but only at the cost of abandoning many kinds of research and making others very expensive. The use of recombinant DNA could be drastically curtailed. Many other restrictions could be imposed, complete with a system of fraud police. But such massive interventions would be costly and would change the character of science.

Which one of the following most accurately expresses the main conclusion of the essayist's argument?

(A) We should not make changes that will alter the character of science.

(B) If we regulate science more closely, we will change the character of science.

(C) The regulation of science and the conducting of science can be changed.

(D) The imposition of restrictions on the conduct of science would be very costly.

(E) We need to be aware of the impact of change in science before changes are made.

PrepTest106 Sec1 Q18

Step 3:	Step 4:

Expert Analysis

Here's how an LSAT expert would look at those two questions.

Step 2: Conclusion: [Keyword "However"] The characteristic of adapting to and altering their environment is not unique to highly evolved species; it is common to many species. The rest of the argument is an example that acts as evidence supporting the conclusion.	**Step 1:** The phrasing "accurately expresses the main point" indicates that this is a Main Point question. The correct answer will paraphrase the author's conclusion.

11. It is well known that many species adapt to their environment, but it is usually assumed that only the most highly evolved species alter their environment in ways that aid their own survival. However, this characteristic is actually quite common. Certain species of plankton, for example, generate a gas that is converted in the atmosphere into particles of sulfate. These particles cause water vapor to condense, thus forming clouds. Indeed, the formation of clouds over the ocean largely depends on the presence of these particles. More cloud cover means more sunlight is reflected, and so the Earth absorbs less heat. Thus plankton cause the surface of the Earth to be cooler and this benefits the plankton.

Of the following, which one most accurately expresses the main point of the argument?

(A) The Earth would be far warmer than it is now if certain species of plankton became extinct.

(B) By altering their environment in ways that improve their chances of survival, certain species of plankton benefit the Earth as a whole.

(C) Improving their own chances of survival by altering the environment is not limited to the most highly evolved species.

(D) The extent of the cloud cover over the oceans is largely determined by the quantity of plankton in those oceans.

(E) Species such as plankton alter the environment in ways that are less detrimental to the well-being of other species than are the alterations to the environment made by more highly evolved species.

PrepTest107 Sec1 Q11

Step 3: The correct answer will be a close paraphrase of the author's conclusion: *Adapting to their environment is not something that only highly evolved species do.*	**Step 4:** (C) is correct. This is a close match to the prediction.

Wrong answers: (A) How plankton affect the temperature of the Earth is used as evidence to support the conclusion. (B) Distortion. Plankton alter their environment in ways that benefit plankton. Also, in this argument, the example of plankton is evidence, not the conclusion. (D) How plankton affect cloud cover is used as evidence to support the conclusion. (E) Irrelevant Comparison. Whether alterations to a species' environment are positive or negative to other species is not discussed.

Step 2:	Step 1:
Step 2: Conclusion: [Keyword "But"] In order to determine whether changes to the way science is conducted and regulated are warranted, we need to take into account the cost of such changes.	**Step 1:** The phrasing "accurately expresses the main conclusion" indicates that this is a Main Point question. The correct answer will paraphrase the author's conclusion.

12. Essayist: The way science is conducted and regulated can be changed. But we need to determine whether the changes are warranted, taking into account their price. The use of animals in research could end immediately, but only at the cost of abandoning many kinds of research and making others very expensive. The use of recombinant DNA could be drastically curtailed. Many other restrictions could be imposed, complete with a system of fraud police. But such massive interventions would be costly and would change the character of science.

Which one of the following most accurately expresses the main conclusion of the essayist's argument?

(A) We should not make changes that will alter the character of science.

(B) If we regulate science more closely, we will change the character of science.

(C) The regulation of science and the conducting of science can be changed.

(D) The imposition of restrictions on the conduct of science would be very costly.

(E) We need to be aware of the impact of change in science before changes are made.

PrepTest106 Sec1 Q18

Step 3:	Step 4:
Step 3: The correct answer will be a close paraphrase of the author's conclusion: *While changes in science are possible, we must take into account the costs of such changes before we determine whether those changes are warranted.*	**Step 4:** (E) is correct. This matches the prediction.

Wrong answers: (A) Extreme. The author does not make a recommendation for or against the adoption of changes in science. (B) The author concedes that *massive* interventions would change the character of science, but this is evidence used to support the author's conclusion. (C) This is Sentence 1, and is background information that the author considers to be a fact. The conclusion does not come until the next sentence. (D) The fact that some restrictions may be costly is used as evidence.

FOR FURTHER PRACTICE

You'll find more Main Point questions in the Perform quiz at the end of this chapter.

Keep in mind that you'll practice locating, characterizing, and paraphrasing conclusions in all of the upcoming Assumption, Strengthen/Weaken, Flaw, Parallel Reasoning, and Method of Argument questions—and many Principle, Role of a Statement, and Point at Issue questions as well.

These are skills you'll reuse and reinforce throughout your Logical Reasoning practice.

Reflect Congratulations on developing a core set of Logical Reasoning skills and on mastering your first Logical Reasoning question type. Over the next few days, reflect on this session.

Take note of how often you or someone you're talking to makes an argument. What was his or her conclusion? What type was it? Even statements as simple and everyday as "We should go get some ice cream" or "The singing on this song is really weak" can help reinforce your mastery of LSAT conclusion types.

When you're watching TV or reading the news, keep an eye out for arguments. When you spot them, locate and characterize their conclusions. You'll be shocked by how many arguments you encounter on a daily basis.

Evidence and Arguments: Role of a Statement, Method of Argument, and Point at Issue Questions

Several question types besides Main Point questions reward your ability to understand argument structures and parts, and we're about to learn the skills necessary for grabbing those points. Taken together, the question types we'll cover in this chapter are worth 8–12 questions on an average LSAT. In addition, the more you know about working with arguments, the better prepared you'll be to start tackling Assumptions and other key question types in Chapter 4. Remember, argument-based questions make up over 70 percent of the Logical Reasoning sections and around half (or more) of the LSAT. Also, keep in mind that a strong understanding of arguments will serve you well in the Reading Comprehension section, too—not to mention in law school.

So far in this chapter, you've learned how to identify conclusions. Take a moment to look back at the questions you just practiced earlier in this chapter and notice how many different ways the authors tried to establish their main points. You're about to work in greater depth with these different ways of supporting a conclusion. In other words, you're ready to tackle *evidence*.

Evidence and Role of a Statement Questions

Prepare

LEARNING OBJECTIVES

In this section, you'll learn to:

- Distinguish evidence from background information.
- Identify Role of a Statement questions and characterize the correct and incorrect answers.

You learned in the previous section that evidence is the set of facts, analyses, or other considerations that an author uses to try to persuade her reader that her conclusion is correct. Evidence can be long or short, convincing or questionable, and accurate or wildly fictitious. Don't get hung up on comparing the claims you read on the LSAT with what you know about real life. You'll never be asked whether an author's evidence, by itself, is true or believable, but you will frequently be asked about how an author's evidence interacts with her conclusion: whether her evidence does a good job supporting her conclusion, how that support could be made stronger or weaker, or what additional evidence is needed to establish the conclusion. The first step in being able to answer those questions is to identify and paraphrase an author's evidence.

(By the way, evidence is sometimes referred to on the LSAT as the author's "premises." The premises of an argument are that argument's complete set of evidence, and "a premise" is a piece of evidence.)

Just as conclusions are sometimes marked with Keywords, evidence also is sometimes marked with a Keyword. Similarly, just as conclusions can come anywhere in an argument (first sentence, last sentence, in the middle), so too can evidence. Authors use evidence Keywords to say, "Here's why I think the conclusion is true."

Chicago is a great city. After all, there's so much fun stuff to do there.

Notice that there's no conclusion Keyword, but "after all" signals that the second sentence exists to support the first one. That second sentence is the author's evidence.

We could write that same argument a different way:

Because there's so much fun stuff to do there, Chicago is a great city.

Here the conclusion and evidence appear in the same sentence. The first clause of that sentence is evidence, and the second clause is the author's overall conclusion. Don't be thrown off when wording changes on the LSAT. Stay focused on the role played by each clause in the argument and take advantage of evidence Keywords like "because." Other common Keywords indicating evidence are *since* and *for*. Remember, too, that phrases like *this shows* and *from this one can conclude* indicate a conclusion and tell you that the main evidence comes just prior to this in the argument.

Restate the argument about Chicago using each of those Keywords. (Of course, you can substitute the city of your choice if you like.) How would you construct that same argument using the various evidence Keywords in this list? Which evidence Keywords work best *after* a conclusion, and which work best *before* a conclusion?

Practice using evidence Keywords to spot an author's evidence. Take a look at this example from a real LSAT question:

LSAT Question	Analysis
Historian: We can learn about the medical history of individuals through chemical analysis of their hair. It is likely, for example, that Isaac Newton's psychological problems were due to mercury poisoning; traces of mercury were found in his hair. Analysis is now being done on a lock of Beethoven's hair. Although no convincing argument has shown that Beethoven ever had a venereal disease, some people hypothesize that venereal disease caused his deafness. Since mercury was commonly ingested in Beethoven's time to treat venereal disease, if researchers find a trace of mercury in his hair, we can conclude that this hypothesis is correct. *PrepTest106 Sec3 Q16*	The conclusion here is indicated by the Keywords "we can conclude": *The hypothesis that Beethoven's deafness was caused by a venereal disease is correct.* This claim, however, is dependent on some lab results: *if researchers find a trace of mercury in his hair.* The evidence is signaled by the evidence Keyword "[s]ince": *mercury was commonly ingested in Beethoven's time to treat venereal disease.* Earlier in the argument we had more evidence, indicated by the common phrasing "for example": *it's likely Newton's psychological problems were due to mercury poisoning, since mercury was found in his hair.*

(By the way, did you have trouble buying the author's reasoning here? If so, good for you! Many LSAT arguments are flawed, and the LSAT frequently rewards you for spotting argumentative flaws. We'll discuss flaws thoroughly in Chapter 4.)

Sometimes evidence isn't marked with a Keyword. In those cases, you need to ask yourself which parts of the argument answer the question "What supports this?" That is, identify the author's conclusion using conclusion Keywords or the One-Sentence Test. Then imagine yourself saying to the author, "Here's your claim. Why so? What makes you believe that?" The parts of the argument that answer that question are the author's evidence. To see this, turn to the next page and revisit an argument you saw in the last section.

LSAT Question	Analysis
The authors of a recent article examined warnings of an impending wave of extinctions of animal species within the next 100 years. These authors say that no evidence exists to support the idea that the rate of extinction of animal species is now accelerating. They are wrong, however. Consider only the data on fishes: 40 species and subspecies of North American fishes have vanished in the twentieth century, 13 between 1900 and 1950, and 27 since 1950. *PrepTest101 Sec2 Q15*	The conclusion here is a rebuttal: *The authors of the article are wrong.* But what are they wrong about? Always articulate a full, clear understanding of an argument's conclusion: *There is evidence to support the idea that the rate of animal extinctions is increasing.* In the absence of clear evidence Keywords, look for the data and facts that the author presents in order to support her conclusion. "Consider only the data on fishes . . ." Aha! That's the evidence: *13 fish species vanished in the first half of the century, while 27 species vanished in the second half of the century.*

Did anything strike you about the nature of the evidence in that argument? The author used scientific data to back up her claim. (In fact, phrases such as "research has shown" and "consider the data" are subtle clues that you're looking at evidence.) It's frequently helpful on the LSAT to note what kind of evidence an author is using: Is it made up of examples? Research studies? General principles about how the universe works? Expert opinion? Something else? We'll practice characterizing an author's argumentative strategy later in this chapter. For now, get in the habit of making a mental note of the kind of evidence you're looking at.

LSAT Question	Analysis
The play *Mankind* must have been written between 1431 and 1471. It cannot have been written before 1431, for in that year the rose noble, a coin mentioned in the play, was first circulated. The play cannot have been written after 1471, since in that year King Henry VI died, and he is mentioned as a living monarch in the play's dedication. *PrepTest101 Sec3 Q9*	The first sentence, a strong assertion of fact, is the conclusion: Mankind *must have been written between 1431 and 1471.* The evidence here is the rest of the argument, but notice what the author does. In the second sentence she uses evidence pertaining to the year a coin was first circulated to support a subsidiary conclusion that the play could not have been written before 1431. In the third sentence, she uses evidence regarding the year King Henry VI died to support another subsidiary conclusion that the play could not have been written after 1471. So two distinct pieces of evidence support two subsidiary conclusions, both of which are then used to draw the main conclusion.

TEST DAY TIP

Some test takers mark the evidence on-screen as they're untangling a Logical Reasoning stimulus. In fact, some find it helpful to mark the evidence and conclusion differently, (e.g., highlighting the conclusion and underlining the evidence.) Try out these tactics, but don't let the digital test taking tools become time consuming. On test day, use only those that improve your overall efficiency.

Practice Now practice identifying the evidence in a handful of LSAT arguments.

In each of the following arguments, locate the evidence the author or speaker in question uses to support her conclusion. In your own words, explain how you knew that the sentence or clause you selected is evidence for the author's conclusion. After each, you can turn to the expert thinking and check your work.

LSAT Question	My Analysis
13. Recent research shows that sound change (pronunciation shift) in a language is not gradual. New sounds often emerge suddenly. This confounds the classical account of sound change, whose central tenet is gradualness. Since this classical account must be discarded, sound-change theory in general must also be. *PrepTest104 Sec1 Q16*	
14. The widespread staff reductions in a certain region's economy are said to be causing people who still have their jobs to cut back on new purchases as though they, too, had become economically distressed. Clearly, however, actual spending by such people is undiminished, because there has been no unusual increase in the amount of money held by those people in savings account. *PrepTest101 Sec3 Q17*	
15. Research indicates that 90 percent of extreme insomniacs consume large amounts of coffee. Since Tom drinks a lot of coffee, it is quite likely that he is an extreme insomniac. *PrepTest104 Sec1 Q23*	

Expert Analysis

Here's how an LSAT expert looks at each of the arguments you've just examined.

LSAT Question	Analysis
13. Recent research shows that sound change (pronunciation shift) in a language is not gradual. New sounds often emerge suddenly. This confounds the classical account of sound change, whose central tenet is gradualness. Since this classical account must be discarded, sound-change theory in general must also be. *PrepTest104 Sec1 Q16*	Conclusion: Sound-change theory in general must be discarded. *because* Evidence: The classical account of sound change must be discarded.

Notice that in the argument, the first sentence starts with the evidence Keywords "[r]ecent research shows." An untrained test taker might imagine that that is the only—or at least the most significant—piece of evidence in the argument. But keep reading. What role does the research play in the argument? It is used by the author to show that the classical account of sound change may be incorrect. The argument continues: because the classical account should be discarded, sound-change theory in general must be discarded. A well-trained LSAT expert separates the many different possible pieces of an argument—background information, evidence, subsidiary conclusions, main conclusions—by constantly asking: What role does this statement play? Why is it here? Is it supporting something else?

LSAT Question	Analysis
14. The widespread staff reductions in a certain region's economy are said to be causing people who still have their jobs to cut back on new purchases as though they, too, had become economically distressed. Clearly, however, actual spending by such people is undiminished, because there has been no unusual increase in the amount of money held by those people in savings account. *PrepTest101 Sec3 Q17*	Conclusion: People who still have jobs are still spending on new purchases. *because* Evidence: There has been no unusual increase in the savings accounts of people who still have jobs.

What purpose does the first sentence serve in this example? It's the opposing claim that we need in order to understand the author's argument, but does not, by itself, advance the author's conclusion.

LSAT Question	Analysis
15. Research indicates that 90 percent of extreme insomniacs consume large amounts of coffee. Since Tom drinks a lot of coffee, it is quite likely that he is an extreme insomniac. *PrepTest104 Sec1 Q23*	Conclusion: Tom is an extreme insomniac. *because* Evidence: [1] 90 percent of extreme insomniacs consume large amounts of coffee; and [2] Tom drinks a lot of coffee.

Did you notice what the author did in this argument? He provided evidence showing that overwhelmingly, insomniacs are people who drink a lot of coffee. He then drew a conclusion suggesting that a person who drinks a lot of coffee is likely an insomniac. Does that argument structure seem familiar to you? The author is confusing the sufficient and necessary terms of a conditional statement. Determining that a person is an insomniac is sufficient to know that that person likely drinks a lot of coffee, but being an insomniac is not necessarily an attribute of a person who drinks a lot of coffee. The stronger your grasp of the principles of Formal Logic (covered in Chapter 1), the more easily and quickly you'll be able to spot this common reasoning flaw.

Reflect Review the practice you just did: How efficiently were you able to identify the author's evidence? Did you paraphrase the evidence in your own words? Did you make a mental note of what kind of evidence the author was using? What, if anything, distracted you from homing in on the relevant evidence?

Did you make some mistakes? That's great! Mistakes are a tremendously valuable source of information for you: Every error tells you something about what you need to work on before test day. How did you misidentify the evidence in this practice? Do you see any patterns in your mistakes?

Identify and Answer Role of a Statement Questions

Prepare You've gotten some practice with identifying conclusions and evidence. Ready to put it to use? One LSAT question type, called Role of a Statement, rewards your ability to simply identify the various pieces of an argument—such as evidence, conclusion, opponent's argument, or background information. You know you're dealing with a Role of a Statement question if you see a question stem like this:

LSAT Question	Analysis
That consumers are buying more durable goods than before figures in the economist's argument in which one of the following ways? *PrepTest101 Sec2 Q10*	The question stem quotes a statement from the stimulus (here, "consumers are buying more durable goods than before") and then asks us to determine *how* the statement figures into the argument. This is a Role of a Statement question. Our task is to identify the statement as the argument's conclusion, evidence, background information, or something else.

As always when working with arguments on the LSAT, start with identifying and paraphrasing evidence and conclusion. Then formulate a prediction to use when looking at the answer choices. Your prediction on a Role of a Statement question will sound something like this: "the statement is evidence," "the statement is the author's conclusion," or "the statement is evidence cited by the author's opponents." Wrong answer choices on a Role of a Statement question will likely describe *other* parts of the author's argument or distort the argument in some way.

Let's look at an LSAT expert's analysis of a full LSAT Role of a Statement question.

Step 2: Conclusion: A society will not remain stable without the long-term stability of its citizens' goals. *because* Evidence: [Key phrase "This is clear from the fact"] [1] A legislature cannot make laws that satisfy citizens without most people having predictable aspirations; and [2] A society will remain stable only if its laws tend to make its citizens happier. [This is the statement in the question stem.]	**Step 1:** The phrasing "the claim ... plays which one of the following roles" indicates that this is a Role of a Statement question. The correct answer choice will describe how the statement functions in the overall argument.

The stable functioning of a society depends upon the relatively long-term stability of the goals of its citizens. This is clear from the fact that unless the majority of individuals have a predictable and enduring set of aspirations, it will be impossible for a legislature to craft laws that will augment the satisfaction of the citizenry, and it should be obvious that a society is stable only if its laws tend to increase the happiness of its citizens.

The claim that a society is stable only if its laws tend to increase the happiness of its citizens plays which one of the following roles in the argument?

(A) It is the conclusion of the argument.

(B) It helps to support the conclusion of the argument.

(C) It is a claim that must be refuted if the conclusion is to be established.

(D) It is a consequence of the argument.

(E) It is used to illustrate the general principle that the argument presupposes.

PrepTest104 Sec1 Q17

Step 3: The claim in the question stem is one of two pieces of evidence used to support the argument's conclusion.	**Step 4:** (B) is correct. This matches the prediction.

Wrong answers: (A) The conclusion is the first sentence in the argument. (C) 180. The conclusion is supported by the claim. (D) Distortion. The statement is simply evidence for the conclusion. A consequence is something that would *follow from* the argument. (E) The claim itself is a general rule, not a specific example.

On test day, you could stop with (B) once you've seen that it matches your prediction perfectly. As you're practicing for the LSAT, however, it's always valuable to review all four wrong answers and make sure you see why each is incorrect.

Practice Practice solving Role of a Statement questions using the approach just illustrated.

Apply the Kaplan Logical Reasoning Method to answer each of the following questions. Here, note clues in the question stem to determine that these are Role of a Statement questions. Then, untangle the stimulus by identifying the author's conclusion and evidence. Find the statement cited in the question stem and describe the role it plays in the argument. Use that as your prediction of the correct answer and evaluate the answer choices. After each question, you can turn to the expert thinking and check your work.

Step 2:	**Step 1:**

16. Economist: The economy seems to be heading out of recession. Recent figures show that consumers are buying more durable goods than before, indicating that they expect economic growth in the near future.

That consumers are buying more durable goods than before figures in the economist's argument in which one of the following ways?

(A) It is the phenomenon that the argument seeks to explain.

(B) Its truth is required in order for the argument's conclusion to be true.

(C) It is an inference drawn from the premise that the recession seems to be ending.

(D) It is an inference drawn from the premise that consumers expect economic growth in the near future.

(E) It is the primary evidence from which the argument's conclusion is drawn.

PrepTest101 Sec2 Q10

Step 3:	**Step 4:**

Step 2:	**Step 1:**

17. Ambiguity inspires interpretation. The saying, "We are the measure of all things," for instance, has been interpreted by some people to imply that humans are centrally important in the universe, while others have interpreted it to mean simply that, since all knowledge is human knowledge, humans must rely on themselves to find the truth.

That claim that ambiguity inspires interpretation figures in the argument in which one of the following ways?

(A) It is used to support the argument's conclusion.

(B) It is an illustration of the claim that we are the measure of all things.

(C) It is compatible with either accepting or rejecting the argument's conclusion.

(D) It is a view that other statements in the argument are intended to support.

(E) It sets out a difficulty the argument is intended to solve.

PrepTest107 Sec4 Q15

Step 3:	**Step 4:**

Expert Analysis

Here's how an LSAT expert looks at each of the arguments you've just examined.

Step 2: Conclusion: The economy seems to be heading out of recession. *because* Evidence: [Key phrase "Recent figures show"] [1] Consumers are buying more durable goods [this is the statement in the question stem], which indicates that [2] they expect economic growth in the near future.	**Step 1:** The phrasing "figures in the . . . argument in which one of the following ways" indicates that this is a Role of a Statement question. The correct answer choice will describe how the statement functions in the overall argument.

16. Economist: The economy seems to be heading out of recession. Recent figures show that consumers are buying more durable goods than before, indicating that they expect economic growth in the near future.

That consumers are buying more durable goods than before figures in the economist's argument in which one of the following ways?

(A) It is the phenomenon that the argument seeks to explain.

(B) Its truth is required in order for the argument's conclusion to be true.

(C) It is an inference drawn from the premise that the recession seems to be ending.

(D) It is an inference drawn from the premise that consumers expect economic growth in the near future.

(E) It is the primary evidence from which the argument's conclusion is drawn.

PrepTest101 Sec2 Q10

Step 3: The statement is used as evidence to support the economist's conclusion.	**Step 4:** (E) is correct. The first part of sentence 2 is a piece of evidence from which the author draws an inference; that inference is then used to reach the argument's conclusion.

Wrong answers: (A) Distortion. While the relevant statement is a phenomenon that has occurred, the author does not seek to explain what caused that phenomenon; instead, he uses it to make a prediction. (B) Extreme. While the statement is evidence for the conclusion, the argument does not claim that it must be true for the conclusion to be drawn. (C) 180. The fact that consumers are buying more durable goods is a premise used to support the claim that the recession seems to be ending. (D) 180. Again, the statement in the question stem is itself a premise and not an inference.

Step 2: Conclusion: Ambiguity inspires interpretation. [This is the statement in the question stem.] *because* Evidence: [Key phrase "for instance"] A certain saying has been interpreted in different ways.	**Step 1:** The phrasing "figures in the ... argument in which one of the following ways" indicates that this is a Role of a Statement question. The correct answer choice will describe how the statement functions in the overall argument.

17. Ambiguity inspires interpretation. The saying "We are the measure of all things," for instance, has been interpreted by some people to imply that humans are centrally important in the universe, while others have interpreted it to mean simply that, since all knowledge is human knowledge, humans must rely on themselves to find the truth.

That claim that ambiguity inspires interpretation figures in the argument in which one of the following ways?

(A) It is used to support the argument's conclusion.

(B) It is an illustration of the claim that we are the measure of all things.

(C) It is compatible with either accepting or rejecting the argument's conclusion.

(D) It is a view that other statements in the argument are intended to support.

(E) It sets out a difficulty the argument is intended to solve.

PrepTest107 Sec4 Q15

Step 3: The statement referenced in the question stem is the argument's conclusion.	**Step 4:** (D) is correct. The conclusion of an argument is the view or claim that the other statements in the argument are intended to support.

Wrong answers: (A) This describes evidence, not the conclusion. (B) The claim "We are the measure of all things" is used by the author as an example to show how statements can be interpreted differently. (C) Because the statement *is* the conclusion, this can't be right. (E) The argument does not intend to solve anything.

Look back over your practice. Did you identify and paraphrase the author's conclusion and evidence before making a prediction about the statement quoted in the question stem? Did you keep your prediction in mind as you evaluated answer choices?

If these questions didn't go well, treat that as a blessing in disguise by using your mistakes as powerful sources of information about what you need to work on. What led you to misidentify the role played by the statement you were asked about?

Outlining Complete Arguments and Point at Issue Questions

LEARNING OBJECTIVES

In this section, you'll learn to:

- Outline complete arguments.
- Identify Point at Issue questions and characterize the correct and incorrect answers.

Here you see a Point at Issue question. You'll review it piece by piece shortly. These questions reward you for zeroing in on the particular point about which two speakers disagree. Preparing to tackle this question type provides the perfect opportunity to learn another valuable LSAT Logical Reasoning skill: outlining complete arguments.

P: Complying with the new safety regulations is useless. Even if the new regulations had been in effect before last year's laboratory fire, they would not have prevented the fire or the injuries resulting from it because they do not address its underlying causes.

Q: But any regulations that can potentially prevent money from being wasted are useful. If obeyed, the new safety regulations will prevent some accidents, and whenever there is an accident here at the laboratory, money is wasted even if no one is injured.

A point at issue between P and Q is whether

(A) last year's fire resulted in costly damage to the laboratory

(B) accidents at the laboratory inevitably result in personal injuries

(C) the new safety regulations address the underlying cause of last year's fire

(D) it is useful to comply with the new safety regulations

(E) the new safety regulations are likely to be obeyed in the laboratory

PrepTest104 Sec4 Q11

Outline Complete Arguments

Prepare Expert LSAT test takers are able to sum up and paraphrase the arguments in Logical Reasoning questions logically and accurately. They sort out the complex prose and sometimes indirect sentence structure in a way that makes every argument as simple as saying, "The author believes *y* (his conclusion) because of *x* (his evidence)."

Recall some of the arguments you've seen already in this chapter. At times, the evidence appeared before the conclusion, and at other times, after it. You've even seen arguments that had two pieces of evidence, one before and one after the conclusion. Those can all be effective ways of expressing an argument, but when you're outlining the argument—summarizing and paraphrasing it for your own understanding—you'll want to arrange the premises and conclusion logically:

[Conclusion] because [Evidence]

or

[Evidence]. Thus, [Conclusion]

Take a look at how an LSAT expert would outline this LSAT Logical Reasoning argument.

LSAT Question	Analysis
Historian: We can learn about the medical history of individuals through chemical analysis of their hair. It is likely, for example, that Isaac Newton's psychological problems were due to mercury poisoning; traces of mercury were found in his hair. Analysis is now being done on a lock of Beethoven's hair. Although no convincing argument has shown that Beethoven ever had a venereal disease, some people hypothesize that venereal disease caused his deafness. Since mercury was commonly ingested in Beethoven's time to treat venereal disease, if researchers find a trace of mercury in his hair, we can conclude that this hypothesis is correct. *PrepTest106 Sec3 Q16*	Conclusion: If researchers find traces of mercury in Beethoven's hair, then a venereal disease caused his deafness. *because* Evidence: During his time, mercury was commonly ingested to treat venereal disease.

Like many of the arguments you'll see on the LSAT, the argument given here is, at its heart, quite simple. The author states that if it is determined that Beethoven had traces of mercury in his hair, then one can conclude that his deafness was caused by a certain type of disease. What's the evidence for this argument? Simply that during Beethoven's time, mercury was commonly used to treat that type of disease.

While the argument itself is relatively simple, the way it was presented on the LSAT is not. The author begins the argument by providing background information. The first sentence sets the stage by defining the scope of the argument to come. The next sentence, signaled by "for example," gives us historical information that provides support for the idea that chemical analysis of hair can be useful in determining the medical history of certain people. How necessary is all of that to the author's central argument? Not necessary at all. While untrained test takers might stumble over or get confused by such a lengthy preamble, a well-trained test taker cuts through the fluff and seeks out the conclusion and the direct evidence used to support that conclusion.

The argument is further complicated by the fact that the author does not explicitly state the argument's conclusion. Instead, the author describes the hypothesis of "some people," and then later confirms that hypothesis to be correct if a certain condition is met.

Don't be confused or frustrated by lengthy arguments. Instead, do what the LSAT expert above did: Seek out the conclusion and put it into your own words. Then find the evidence that most directly supports that conclusion.

Here are some more examples. Notice that the following arguments aren't constructed in exactly the same way as the preceding argument. No matter; focus on identifying the conclusion and the evidence and then reconstruct the argument with those pieces.

LSAT Question	Analysis
Plant Manager: We could greatly reduce the amount of sulfur dioxide our copper-smelting plant releases into the atmosphere by using a new process. The new process requires replacing our open furnaces with closed ones and moving the copper from one furnace to the next in solid, not molten, form. However, not only is the new equipment expensive to buy and install, but the new process also costs more to run than the current process, because the copper must be reheated after it has cooled. So overall, adopting the new process will cost much but bring the company no profit. *PrepTest107 Sec4 Q14*	Conclusion: Even though it would reduce sulfur dioxide, the new process (closed furnaces and moving copper in solid form) will cost a lot and not be profitable. *because* Evidence: The equipment for the new process is expensive to buy and install, and it costs more to run.
A recent study concludes that prehistoric birds, unlike modern birds, were cold-blooded. This challenges a widely held view that modern birds descended from warm-blooded birds. The conclusion is based on the existence of growth rings in prehistoric birds' bodily structures, which are thought to be found only in cold-blooded animals. Another study, however, disputes this view. It concludes that prehistoric birds had dense blood vessels in their bones, which suggests that they were active creatures and therefore had to be warm-blooded. *PrepTest106 Sec3 Q13*	Position #1: Conclusion: Prehistoric birds were cold-blooded. *because* Evidence: Presence of growth rings in prehistoric birds' bodily structures (thought to be only in cold-blooded animals). Position #2: Conclusion: Prehistoric birds were warm-blooded. *because* Evidence: Prehistoric birds had dense blood vessels in their bones, which suggests they were active.

Notice how, in the second stimulus, the test expert untangles and keeps separate two distinctly different arguments. The author of that stimulus never steps in and provides a judgment as to which of the two arguments is preferable, or more accurate. The test expert is unperturbed: She simply identifies both conclusions and the evidence for each, and will then approach the rest of the question accordingly.

In all three of the preceding examples, our LSAT expert maintains a singular focus: identifying, separating, and paraphrasing an argument's evidence and conclusion. You'll find that having the ability to summarize and outline LSAT arguments in this way is enormously helpful in many Logical Reasoning question types—Assumption, Strengthen/Weaken, and Flaw, as well as three question types still to come in this chapter, Point at Issue, Method of Argument, and Parallel Reasoning.

Practice Now, try untangling and outlining a handful of LSAT arguments on your own. Strive to make your summaries as clear and simple as the expert thinking you saw above.

For each of the following arguments, locate the conclusion and the relevant evidence. Then, outline the complete argument in the following format: [Conclusion] because [Evidence]. When the argument has more than one piece of evidence, make sure you can outline the logical progression of the author's reasoning. When you're done, you can check your work and review the expert thinking on the next page.

LSAT Question	My Analysis
18. Unplugging a peripheral component such as a "mouse" from a personal computer renders all of the software programs that require that component unusable on that computer. On Fred's personal computer, a software program that requires a mouse has become unusable. So it must be that the mouse for Fred's computer became unplugged. *PrepTest104 Sec4 Q10*	
19. Combustion of gasoline in automobile engines produces benzene, a known carcinogen. Environmentalists propose replacing gasoline with methanol, which does not produce significant quantities of benzene when burned. However, combustion of methanol produces formaldehyde, also a known carcinogen. Therefore the environmentalists' proposal has little merit. *PrepTest107 Sec4 Q1*	
20. The miscarriage of justice in the Barker case was due to the mistaken views held by some of the forensic scientists involved in the case, who believed that they owed allegiance only to the prosecuting lawyers. Justice was thwarted because these forensic scientists failed to provide evidence impartially to both the defense and the prosecution. Hence it is not forensic evidence in general that should be condemned for this injustice. *PrepTest105 Sec4 Q16*	

Expert Analysis for the Practice exercise may be found on the following page. ▶ ▶ ▶

Expert Analysis

Here's how an LSAT expert would untangle the arguments you just looked at.

LSAT Question	Analysis
18. Unplugging a peripheral component such as a "mouse" from a personal computer renders all of the software programs that require that component unusable on that computer. On Fred's personal computer, a software program that requires a mouse has become unusable. So it must be that the mouse for Fred's computer became unplugged. *PrepTest104 Sec4 Q10*	Conclusion: The mouse on Fred's computer is unplugged. *because* Evidence: A mouse must be plugged in for a certain software program to work. *and* Evidence: One of the programs on Fred's computer that requires a mouse doesn't work.
19. Combustion of gasoline in automobile engines produces benzene, a known carcinogen. Environmentalists propose replacing gasoline with methanol, which does not produce significant quantities of benzene when burned. However, combustion of methanol produces formaldehyde, also a known carcinogen. Therefore the environmentalists' proposal has little merit. *PrepTest107 Sec4 Q1*	Conclusion: We shouldn't replace gasoline with methanol. *because* Evidence: Combustion of methanol produces formaldehyde, a carcinogen. *even though* Evidence: Combustion of gasoline produces benzene, a carcinogen.
20. The miscarriage of justice in the Barker case was due to the mistaken views held by some of the forensic scientists involved in the case, who believed that they owed allegiance only to the prosecuting lawyers. Justice was thwarted because these forensic scientists failed to provide evidence impartially to both the defense and the prosecution. Hence it is not forensic evidence in general that should be condemned for this injustice. *PrepTest105 Sec4 Q16*	Conclusion: Forensic evidence in general should not be condemned for this miscarriage of justice. *because* Evidence: Justice was miscarried in this case because the forensic scientists, believing they owed allegiance only to the prosecution, were not impartial.

Identify and Answer Point at Issue Questions

Prepare As you master the skill of untangling and outlining complete arguments, you're ready to tackle another LSAT Logical Reasoning question type: Point at Issue questions. Point at Issue questions are relatively rare—a typical test will likely have 1–3 of them. Point at Issue questions always have a dialogue in the stimulus. Both speakers make arguments, and they always disagree about one particular aspect of their arguments. The correct answer states or paraphrases this point of disagreement. The wrong answers to these questions come in three flavors: (1) a point about which only one of the speakers has an opinion, (2) a point outside the scope of both speakers' arguments, or (3) a point over which the two speakers *agree*. That last wrong answer type can be tempting because it is something about which both speakers have expressed an opinion.

Take a look at a couple of typical Point at Issue question stems.

LSAT Question	Analysis
Steven and Miguel's statements provide the most support for holding that they would disagree about the truth of which one of the following statements? *PrepTest101 Sec2 Q14*	"[D]isagree about"—a Point at Issue question. The correct answer is a statement about which one speaker would say "yes, I agree," and the other "no, I disagree."
A point at issue between P and Q is whether *PrepTest104 Sec4 Q11*	"[P]oint at issue"—a Point at Issue question. The correct answer will be a statement about which the speakers have opposite opinions.

On very rare occasions, the testmaker will ask a Point of Agreement question, in which case the correct answer will be the one containing a statement on which the two speakers have the same point of view. Make sure that you always respond to the task the test has set out for you.

Once you've identified a Point at Issue question, untangle both speakers' arguments to make sure you understand their conclusions and how they're supporting them. The two parties in the dialogue won't always disagree with each other's conclusions. Here's a simple example:

Tom: Our football team will win this game because our quarterback is great.

Jenny: You're wrong. Our quarterback is pretty average. We're going to win because our defense is so strong.

Here, Tom and Jenny share the same conclusion: Their team is going to win. They disagree about why that will be the case. In particular, they are directly at odds in their assessment of the quarterback.

In other cases, the two speakers may share the same evidence but reach different conclusions.

Michelle: The expansion of Superior Corporation's factory will bring workers into the area. That means a lot of new houses will be built in our town.

Sundeep: But these aren't the kind of jobs that lead to housing starts. The workers coming for jobs at Superior will be seasonal, so they'll likely seek apartments or other rental options.

Michelle and Sundeep see eye to eye on the fact that the factory expansion will bring workers into the area, but from that information, they draw opposed inferences about what this means for the town's housing market.

When you're able to spot the issue over which the two speakers are at odds, you have predicted the correct answer and can evaluate the answer choices.

TEST DAY TIP

A great way to evaluate the answer choices in Point at Issue questions is to apply the questions in Kaplan's Point at Issue Decision Tree.

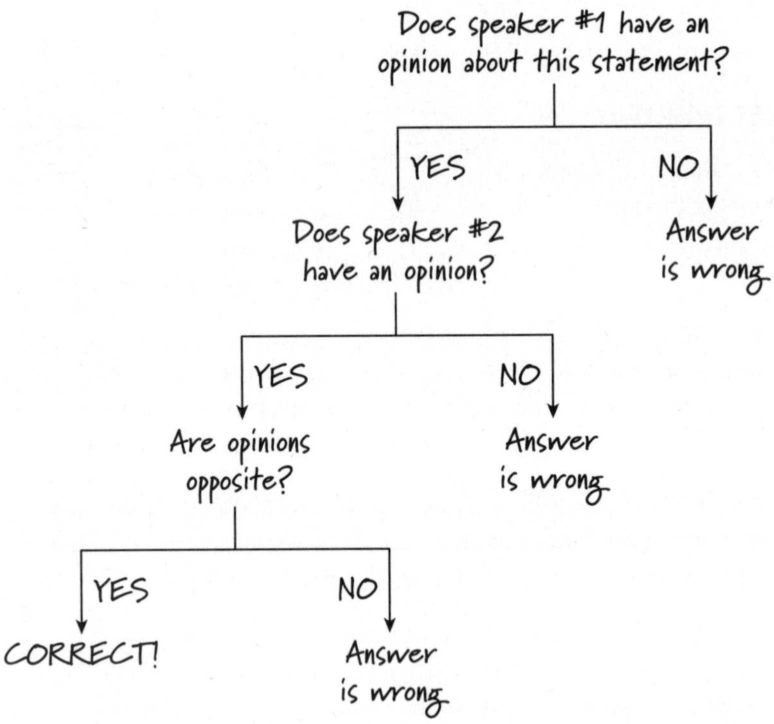

Because the correct answer must be the one statement over which the two speakers are committed to disagreeing, it will be the only choice that produces a "yes" to all three questions in the Decision Tree. In other words, if the speaker doesn't have an opinion about an answer choice, you can immediately eliminate it.

Take a look at how an LSAT expert approaches a Point at Issue question.

Step 2: P's argument: [conclusion] Complying with the new safety regulations is useless, because [evidence] the regulations do not address the underlying causes of accidents like last year's lab fire. Q's response: [conclusion] The regulations will be useful if they save the company money, because [evidence] anything that saves money is useful, and these new regulations will prevent costly accidents.	**Step 1:** The phrasing "point at issue between P and Q" indicates that this is a Point at Issue question. The correct answer choice will represent a point on which P and Q disagree. Wrong answer choices will represent statements that P and Q agree on, or statements upon which one of them has no opinion.

P: Complying with the new safety regulations is useless. Even if the new regulations had been in effect before last year's laboratory fire, they would not have prevented the fire or the injuries resulting from it because they do not address its underlying causes.

Q: But any regulations that can potentially prevent money from being wasted are useful. If obeyed, the new safety regulations will prevent some accidents, and whenever there is an accident here at the laboratory, money is wasted even if no one is injured.

A point at issue between P and Q is whether

(A) last year's fire resulted in costly damage to the laboratory

(B) accidents at the laboratory inevitably result in personal injuries

(C) the new safety regulations address the underlying cause of last year's fire

(D) it is useful to comply with the new safety regulations

(E) the new safety regulations are likely to be obeyed in the laboratory

PrepTest104 Sec4 Q11

Step 3: Q's response indicates that she disagrees with P's conclusion. While P believes that the new safety regulations are useless, Q believes they can be useful.	**Step 4:** (D) is correct. P believes compliance is useless, while Q believes compliance can be useful.

Wrong answers: (A) Q does not state her opinion of last year's fire. (B) Neither P nor Q hold this extreme position. (C) Q does not state whether she believes the regulations would have addressed the underlying cause of last year's fire. (E) Neither P nor Q offers an opinion on whether the regulations will be obeyed.

Notice how, once again, a strong prediction allows the test expert to quickly move through and eliminate wrong answer choices, and to quickly and confidently select the right answer choice once it is found.

Practice Now, try a couple of Point at Issue questions on your own. Remember to outline each side's argument before you evaluate the answer choices. Use the Decision Tree to help you eliminate wrong answers and zero in on the one credited response.

Apply the Kaplan Logical Reasoning Method to answer the following questions. When you're done, check your work and review the expert thinking on the pages that follow these questions.

Step 2:	Step 1:

21. Hospital auditor: The Rodriguez family stipulated that the funds they donated to the neurological clinic all be used to minimize patients' suffering. The clinic administration is clearly violating those terms, since it has allocated nearly one fifth of those funds for research into diagnostic technologies, instead of letting that money flow directly to its patients.

Clinic administrator: But the successful development of new technologies will allow early diagnosis of many neurological disorders. In most cases, patients who are treated in the early stages of neurological disorders suffer far less than do patients who are not treated until their neurological disorders reach advanced stages.

Which one of the following is the main point at issue between the hospital auditor and the clinic administrator?

(A) whether early treatment of many neurological disorders lessens the suffering associated with those disorders rather than completely eliminating such suffering

(B) whether the patients being treated at the neurological clinic are currently receiving adequate treatment for the neurological disorders from which they suffer

(C) whether the Rodriguez family clearly stipulated that the funds they donated to the neurological clinic be used to minimize patients' suffering

(D) whether the neurological clinic is adhering strictly to the conditions the Rodriguez family placed on the allocation of the funds they donated to the clinic

(E) whether the Rodriguez family anticipated that some of the funds they donated to the neurological clinic would be used to pay for research into new diagnostic technologies

PrepTest106 Sec1 Q6

Step 3:	Step 4:

Step 2:	**Step 1:**

22. Steven: The allowable blood alcohol level for drivers should be cut in half. With this reduced limit, social drinkers will be deterred from drinking and driving, resulting in significantly increased highway safety.

    Miguel: No, lowering the current allowable blood alcohol level would have little effect on highway safety, because it would not address the most important aspect of the drunken driving problem, which is the danger to the public posed by heavy drinkers, who often drive with a blood alcohol level of twice the current limit.

    Steven and Miguel's statements provide the most support for holding that they would disagree about the truth of which one of the following statements?

    (A) Social drinkers who drink and drive pose a substantial threat to the public.

    (B) There is a direct correlation between a driver's blood alcohol level and the driver's ability to drive safely.

    (C) A driver with a blood alcohol level above the current legal limit poses a substantial danger to the public.

    (D) Some drivers whose blood alcohol level is lower than the current legal limit pose a danger to the public.

    (E) A driver with a blood alcohol level slightly greater than half the current legal limit poses no danger to the public.

PrepTest101 Sec2 Q14

Step 3:	**Step 4:**

Expert Analysis

Here's how LSAT experts would answer the problems you just tried.

Step 2: Hospital auditor's argument: [Conclusion] The clinic is not using the Rodriguez family funds as the family intended ("to minimize patients' suffering"), because [evidence] it is allocating a lot of money to technology research instead of directly to patients. Clinic Administrator's response: [Conclusion] Using the money for technology research *will* reduce suffering, because [evidence] that technology will lead to early diagnoses, and patients treated in early stages of a neurological disorder will suffer far less than those treated later.	**Step 1:** The phrasing "the main point at issue" indicates that this is a Point at Issue question.

21. Hospital auditor: The Rodriguez family stipulated that the funds they donated to the neurological clinic all be used to minimize patients' suffering. The clinic administration is clearly violating those terms, since it has allocated nearly one fifth of those funds for research into diagnostic technologies, instead of letting that money flow directly to its patients.

Clinic administrator: But the successful development of new technologies will allow early diagnosis of many neurological disorders. In most cases, patients who are treated in the early stages of neurological disorders suffer far less than do patients who are not treated until their neurological disorders reach advanced stages.

Which one of the following is the main point at issue between the hospital auditor and the clinic administrator?

(A) whether early treatment of many neurological disorders lessens the suffering associated with those disorders rather than completely eliminating such suffering

(B) whether the patients being treated at the neurological clinic are currently receiving adequate treatment for the neurological disorders from which they suffer

(C) whether the Rodriguez family clearly stipulated that the funds they donated to the neurological clinic be used to minimize patients' suffering

(D) whether the neurological clinic is adhering strictly to the conditions the Rodriguez family placed on the allocation of the funds they donated to the clinic

(E) whether the Rodriguez family anticipated that some of the funds they donated to the neurological clinic would be used to pay for research into new diagnostic technologies

PrepTest106 Sec1 Q6

Step 3: The auditor and the administrator disagree over whether all of the donated money is being used to reduce suffering in patients at the neurological clinic. The auditor does not believe that the money set aside for research reduces suffering, while the administrator believes it does.	**Step 4:** (D) is correct. The auditor believes that *no*, the clinic is not adhering to the conditions set forth by the Rodriguez family (i.e., to reduce patients' suffering); the administrator believes that *yes*, the clinic is adhering to those conditions.

Wrong answers: (A) Irrelevant Comparison. The distinction between lessening suffering and eliminating suffering is not at issue in either argument. (B) Outside the Scope. The focus in each argument is the reduction of patients' suffering. Adequate treatment is not at issue in either argument. (C) While not explicitly mentioned by the administrator, it can be inferred that, if anything, she would agree with this statement. This is a point of agreement, not a point of disagreement. (E) Outside the Scope. What the Rodriguez family expected would happen with the money is not the point of disagreement here; instead, the issue is whether the clinic followed the family's instructions.

Step 2: Steven's argument: [Conclusion] Lowering the allowable blood alcohol level for drivers will increase highway safety, because [evidence] social drinkers won't drink and drive as much. Miguel's response: [Conclusion] Lowering the allowable blood alcohol level for drivers won't increase highway safety, because [evidence] it won't do anything to deter heavy drinkers from drinking past the legal limit.	**Step 1:** The phrasing "they would disagree about" indicates that this is a Point at Issue question.

22. Steven: The allowable blood alcohol level for drivers should be cut in half. With this reduced limit, social drinkers will be deterred from drinking and driving, resulting in significantly increased highway safety.

Miguel: No, lowering the current allowable blood alcohol level would have little effect on highway safety, because it would not address the most important aspect of the drunken driving problem, which is the danger to the public posed by heavy drinkers, who often drive with a blood alcohol level of twice the current limit.

Steven and Miguel's statements provide the most support for holding that they would disagree about the truth of which one of the following statements?

(A) Social drinkers who drink and drive pose a substantial threat to the public.

(B) There is a direct correlation between a driver's blood alcohol level and the driver's ability to drive safely.

(C) A driver with a blood alcohol level above the current legal limit poses a substantial danger to the public.

(D) Some drivers whose blood alcohol level is lower than the current legal limit pose a danger to the public.

(E) A driver with a blood alcohol level slightly greater than half the current legal limit poses no danger to the public.

PrepTest101 Sec2 Q14

Step 3: Steven and Miguel disagree over whether or not lowering the allowable blood alcohol level will result in safer highways. While Steven believes that deterring social drinkers will result in safer highways, Miguel doesn't consider the behavior of social drinkers to be a significant factor in the drunk driving problem.	**Step 4:** (A) is correct. Steven believes that they do pose a substantial threat; Miguel believes that they do not.

Wrong answers: (B) Both would presumably agree with this. (C) Both would presumably agree with this. (D) Outside the Scope. The danger posed by drivers who are below the legal limit is not at issue here. (E) Both Steven and Miguel believe drunk driving is a problem, so presumably both would disagree with this statement, and thus, agree with one another.

Reflect Pay attention to some of the arguments, disputes, and disagreements you see or hear. Are the parties actually talking about the same thing? Try to pinpoint the actual issue(s) over which they disagree.

When you're listening to disagreements, try to determine whether the two speakers accept the same facts but draw different conclusions from them or see the same result but attribute it to different causes. These are like LSAT dialogues, which almost always feature a disagreement involving the reasoning, that is, a dispute about what the facts mean. Distinguish these from day-to-day arguments in which the parties simply disagree about the facts. The LSAT almost never features a dispute of that kind.

Describing Argumentative Strategy and Method of Argument Questions

Prepare

LEARNING OBJECTIVES

In this section, you'll learn to:

- Describe an author's argumentative strategy.
- Identify Method of Argument questions and characterize the correct and incorrect answers.

Now that you've gotten some practice with describing arguments and their structures, you're ready to learn to characterize an author's argumentative strategy.

You saw as you were working with different kinds of evidence in the previous section that authors make choices about how to support their conclusions. One author might think that citing studies is really compelling, while another tries to persuade her readers by applying commonsense principles to the subject at hand. Another makes a generalization and backs it up with a handful of examples. Another author might claim that a statement must be true because Professor Thingummy, who's an expert, said so. Yet another might simply attack her opponent's position and figure that doing so will make her own position seem more compelling.

All those choices can be thought of as argumentative strategies, a phrase we'll use a great deal in this section. You've already gotten some good practice identifying *what* an author says and putting it into your own words. Now you'll learn how to describe in your own words *how* the author tries to convince the reader. Then, in a few pages, you'll meet a question type that rewards you for doing just that.

Always start by identifying and paraphrasing the author's conclusion, then the author's evidence. Then describe how the author has chosen to back up her conclusion.

LSAT Question	Analysis
It is well known that many species adapt to their environment, but it is usually assumed that only the most highly evolved species alter their environment in ways that aid their own survival. However, this characteristic is actually quite common. Certain species of plankton, for example, generate a gas that is converted in the atmosphere into particles of sulfate. These particles cause water vapor to condense, thus forming clouds. Indeed, the formation of clouds over the ocean largely depends on the presence of these particles. More cloud cover means more sunlight is reflected, and so the Earth absorbs less heat. Thus plankton cause the surface of the Earth to be cooler and this benefits the plankton. *PrepTest107 Sec1 Q11*	Conclusion: While it is "usually assumed" that only the most highly evolved species alter their environment, the author disputes this interpretation. The Keyword "[h]owever" points us to the author's claim: *It is quite common for species to alter their environment.* Evidence: "Certain species of plankton, for example . . ." The rest of the argument provides evidence by describing the behavior of types of plankton. Argumentative strategy: The author uses the specific example of plankton to counter a previously held belief.

LSAT Question	Analysis
The play *Mankind* must have been written between 1431 and 1471. It cannot have been written before 1431, for in that year the rose noble, a coin mentioned in the play, was first circulated. The play cannot have been written after 1471, since in that year King Henry VI died, and he is mentioned as a living monarch in the play's dedication. *PrepTest101 Sec3 Q9*	Conclusion: The first sentence gives a strong assertion of fact: *The play* Mankind *must have been written between 1431 and 1471.* Evidence: There are two pieces of evidence, each leading to two subsidiary conclusions. The first piece of evidence is that *1431 was the year the rose noble, a coin mentioned in the play, was first circulated.* From that the author concludes that the play could not have been written before 1431. The other piece of evidence, that *King Henry VI died in 1471 and yet the play mentions him as alive*, is used to draw the conclusion that the play could not have been written after 1471. Argumentative strategy: The author uses two separate pieces of evidence to draw two distinct subsidiary conclusions about the time range in which a play could have been written.

Again, stay focused on what the author *does*—not what the author says. This strategy could be applied in any number of arguments about any number of subjects.

LSAT STRATEGY

Common methods of argument on the LSAT include:

- Argument by analogy, in which an author draws parallels between two unrelated (but purportedly similar) situations
- Use of examples, in which an author cites specific cases to justify a generalization
- Use of counterexamples, in which an author seeks to discredit an opponent's argument by citing a specific case in which an opponent's conclusion appears to be invalid
- Appeal to authority, in which an author cites an expert or other authority figure as support for her conclusion
- Eliminating alternatives, in which an author lists possibilities and discredits all but one
- *Ad hominem* attack, in which an author attacks not her opponent's argument but rather her opponent's personal credibility
- Means/Requirement, in which the author argues that something is needed to achieve a desired result

Practice Practice describing argumentative strategies using the following LSAT questions.

In each of the following arguments, identify the author's conclusion and the relevant evidence. Once you've done so, describe in your own words *how* the author goes about supporting her conclusion. After each question, use the expert thinking on the next page to check your work.

LSAT Question	My Analysis
23. The miscarriage of justice in the Barker case was due to the mistaken views held by some of the forensic scientists involved in the case, who believed that they owed allegiance only to the prosecuting lawyers. Justice was thwarted because these forensic scientists failed to provide evidence impartially to both the defense and the prosecution. Hence it is not forensic evidence in general that should be condemned for this injustice. *PrepTest105 Sec4 Q16*	
24. Formal performance evaluations in the professional world are conducted using realistic situations. Physicians are allowed to consult medical texts freely, attorneys may refer to law books and case records, and physicists and engineers have their manuals at hand for ready reference. Students, then, should likewise have access to their textbooks whenever they take examinations. *PrepTest107 Sec4 Q25*	

Expert Analysis for the Practice exercise may be found on the following page. ▶ ▶ ▶

Expert Analysis

Here's how an LSAT expert looks at each of the arguments you've just examined.

LSAT Question	Analysis
23. The miscarriage of justice in the Barker case was due to the mistaken views held by some of the forensic scientists involved in the case, who believed that they owed allegiance only to the prosecuting lawyers. Justice was thwarted because these forensic scientists failed to provide evidence impartially to both the defense and the prosecution. Hence it is not forensic evidence in general that should be condemned for this injustice. *PrepTest105 Sec4 Q16*	Conclusion: Following the Keyword "Hence": *forensic evidence in general should not be condemned for this miscarriage of justice.* Evidence: The Keyword "because" helps us identify the evidence: *The forensic scientists in this case were partial to the prosecution over the defense.* Additionally, the miscarriage of justice was "due to" *the mistaken views of the forensic scientists.* Argumentative strategy: The author discredits a specific group of forensic scientists and attempts to demonstrate that they are not representative of their profession.
24. Formal performance evaluations in the professional world are conducted using realistic situations. Physicians are allowed to consult medical texts freely, attorneys may refer to law books and case records, and physicists and engineers have their manuals at hand for ready reference. Students, then, should likewise have access to their textbooks whenever they take examinations. *PrepTest107 Sec4 Q25*	Conclusion: A classic recommendation conclusion signified by the Keyword "should": *Students should be able to use textbooks during their exams, just like certain professionals.* Evidence: There aren't any strong evidence Keywords here, but the three examples provided in the second sentence provide the basis for the author's conclusion: *Physicians, lawyers, and scientists all get to consult texts during formal performance evaluations.* Argumentative strategy: The author uses an analogy to demonstrate why one group of people should be allowed to do the same thing as another group of people.

Reflect Look back over your practice. Did you identify and paraphrase the author's conclusion and evidence before describing the entire argument? Did you describe the argumentative strategy in your own words? Did you stay focused on what the author *does* instead of what the author *says*?

Did you make some mistakes? Good! Use those mistakes as sources of insight about what you need to work on. How did you mischaracterize the author's evidence? Do you see any patterns in your mistakes?

Identify and Answer Method of Argument Questions

Prepare Your ability to break down and analyze arguments will be rewarded with points throughout the Logical Reasoning and Reading Comprehension sections. One question type that rewards those skills in a very direct way is the Method of Argument question. There are typically 1–2 of these on an average LSAT. As you described argumentative strategies in the last section, you were (without knowing it perhaps) already applying the Kaplan method for Method of Argument questions.

Method of Argument questions on the LSAT reward you for describing an author's argumentative strategy. The following are examples of question stems that tell you you're looking at a Method of Argument question:

LSAT Question	Analysis
The argument in the passage proceeds by doing which one of the following? *PrepTest101 Sec3 Q17*	"The argument . . . proceeds by" tells you to focus on the argument's rhetorical moves rather than on the argument's content—to describe *how* the argument is constructed, not *what* the argument is about.
Which of the following accurately describes the argumentative strategy employed? *PrepTest107 Sec1 Q12*	"[D]escribes the argumentative strategy employed" directs you to identify and characterize the author's method of argumentation.

It's important to be able to predict what you're looking for in the correct answer choice. The right choice will match your description of the author's argumentative strategy. The wrong answers may describe argumentative strategies not used by the author, or they might distort the argument in some way.

Look at how an expert LSAT taker attacks a Method of Argument question:

Step 2: Conclusion: [Keyword "However"] The characteristic of adapting to and altering their environment is not unique to highly evolved species; it is common to many species. The rest of the argument is an example that acts as evidence supporting the conclusion.	**Step 1:** The phrasing "describes the argumentative strategy" indicates that this is a Method of Argument question.

It is well known that many species adapt to their environment, but it is usually assumed that only the most highly evolved species alter their environment in ways that aid their own survival. However, this characteristic is actually quite common. Certain species of plankton, for example, generate a gas that is converted in the atmosphere into particles of sulfate. These particles cause water vapor to condense, thus forming clouds. Indeed, the formation of clouds over the ocean largely depends on the presence of these particles. More cloud cover means more sunlight is reflected, and so the Earth absorbs less heat. Thus plankton cause the surface of the Earth to be cooler and this benefits the plankton.

Which of the following accurately describes the argumentative strategy employed?

(A) A general principle is used to justify a claim made about a particular case to which that principle has been shown to apply.

(B) An explanation of how a controversial phenomenon could have come about is given in order to support the claim that this phenomenon did in fact come about.

(C) A generalization about the conditions under which a certain process can occur is advanced on the basis of an examination of certain cases in which that process did occur.

(D) A counterexample to a position being challenged is presented in order to show that this position is incorrect.

(E) A detailed example is used to illustrate the advantage of one strategy over another.

PrepTest107 Sec1 Q12

Step 3: The author uses a detailed example of the characteristics of plankton to refute a commonly held belief.	**Step 4:** (D) is correct. This closely matches our prediction.

Wrong answers: (A) This gets the author's strategy a bit backward; the author is using an example of a particular situation to refute a general understanding. (B) The author is challenging a conventional belief, not supporting a claim about a phenomenon. (C) The author is not presenting an example to advance a generalization about species; instead, she is challenging that generalization. (E) Out of Scope. The author is concerned about determining how common a certain strategy is; whether it's more or less optimal to other strategies is not at issue here.

Sometimes the LSAT will give us two speakers in dialogue, and ask how one speaker responds to the other. Here's an example:

Step 2: P's argument: [Conclusion] Complying with the new safety regulations is useless, because [evidence] the regulations do not address the underlying causes of accidents like last year's lab fire. Q's response: [Conclusion] The regulations will be useful if they save the company money, because [evidence] anything that saves money is useful, and these new regulations will prevent costly accidents.	**Step 1:** The phrasing "responds ... by" indicates that this is a Method of Argument question. The correct answer will describe how Q constructs her response to P.

P: Complying with the new safety regulations is useless. Even if the new regulations had been in effect before last year's laboratory fire, they would not have prevented the fire or the injuries resulting from it because they do not address its underlying causes.

Q: But any regulations that can potentially prevent money from being wasted are useful. If obeyed, the new safety regulations will prevent some accidents, and whenever there is an accident here at the laboratory, money is wasted even if no one is injured.

Q responds to P's position by

(A) extending the basis for assessing the utility of complying with the new regulations

(B) citing additional evidence that undermines P's assessment of the extent to which the new regulations would have prevented injuries in last year's laboratory fire

(C) giving examples to show that the uselessness of all regulations cannot validly be inferred from the uselessness of one particular set of regulations

(D) showing that P's argument depends on the false assumption that compliance with any regulations that would have prevented last year's fire would be useful

(E) pointing out a crucial distinction, overlooked by P, between potential benefits and actual benefits

PrepTest104 Sec4 Q12

Step 3: Q responds by changing the definition of "useful" to include things that will save the company money. This more inclusive definition allows Q to conclude that the regulations will be useful.	**Step 4:** (A) is correct. "Extending the basis for assessing" is another way of saying that Q is broadening the scope of what is considered "useful."

Wrong answers: (B) Out of Scope. Q neither cites additional evidence nor discusses whether the regulations would have prevented injuries. (C) Q uses broad rules to demonstrate her point; she does not give examples. (D) Extreme. While Q might believe this, this is not her approach to responding to P. Instead, Q simply broadens the definition of a term to include more situations. (E) Distortion. While Q believes saving money is a real benefit, she does not infer that P overlooks the difference between potential benefits and actual benefits.

Practice Let's get some practice applying this method to Method of Argument questions.

In each of the following arguments, identify the author's conclusion and the relevant evidence. Once you've done so, describe in your own words *how* the author goes about supporting her conclusion. That description is the prediction you'll use to evaluate each answer choice. Find the answer choice that matches your prediction. Keep in mind the wrong answers will describe *other* argumentative strategies or somehow distort the argument. When you're done, check your work by reviewing the expert analysis that follows.

Step 2:	Step 1:

25. Laura: Harold is obviously lonely. He should sell his cabin in the woods and move into town. In town he will be near other people all the time, so he will not be lonely anymore.

Ralph: Many very lonely people live in towns. What is needed to avoid loneliness is not only the proximity of other people but also genuine interaction with them.

Ralph responds to Laura by pointing out that

(A) something needed for a certain result does not necessarily guarantee that result.

(B) what is appropriate in one case is not necessarily appropriate in all cases.

(C) what is logically certain is not always intuitively obvious.

(D) various alternative solutions are possible for a single problem.

(E) a proposed solution for a problem could actually worsen that problem.

PrepTest106 Sec3 Q10

Step 3:	Step 4:

Step 2:	Step 1:

26. The widespread staff reductions in a certain region's economy are said to be causing people who still have their jobs to cut back on new purchases as though they, too, had become economically distressed. Clearly, however, actual spending by such people is undiminished, because there has been no unusual increase in the amount of money held by those people in savings accounts.

The argument in the passage proceeds by doing which one of the following?

(A) concluding that since an expected consequence of a supposed development did not occur, that development itself did not take place

(B) concluding that since only one of the two predictable consequences of a certain kind of behavior is observed to occur, this observed occurrence cannot, in the current situation, be a consequence of such behavior

(C) arguing that since people's economic behavior is guided by economic self-interest, only misinformation or error will cause people to engage in economic behavior that harms them economically

(D) arguing that since two alternative developments exhaust all the plausible possibilities, one of those developments occurred and the other did not

(E) concluding that since the evidence concerning a supposed change is ambiguous, it is most likely that no change is actually taking place

PrepTest101 Sec3 Q17

Step 3:	Step 4:

Expert Analysis

Here's how an expert test taker works through the problems you just saw:

Step 2: Laura: [Conclusion] Harold won't be lonely if he sells his cabin and moves into town, because [evidence] in town he'll be around people. Ralph: [Conclusion] Just being near people isn't enough to avoid loneliness, because [evidence] to avoid loneliness, genuine interaction is also required.	**Step 1:** "*X* responds to *Y* by" indicates that this is a Method of Argument question. The rest of the question, "by pointing out that," indicates that the correct answer will be something that Ralph feels Laura has overlooked or failed to consider.

25. Laura: Harold is obviously lonely. He should sell his cabin in the woods and move into town. In town he will be near other people all the time, so he will not be lonely anymore.

Ralph: Many very lonely people live in towns. What is needed to avoid loneliness is not only the proximity of other people but also genuine interaction with them.

Ralph responds to Laura by pointing out that

(A) something needed for a certain result does not necessarily guarantee that result.

(B) what is appropriate in one case is not necessarily appropriate in all cases.

(C) what is logically certain is not always intuitively obvious.

(D) various alternative solutions are possible for a single problem.

(E) a proposed solution for a problem could actually worsen that problem.

PrepTest106 Sec3 Q10

Step 3: Ralph points out that Laura is incorrect in thinking that proximity to others is sufficient to avoid loneliness; instead, Ralph believes it is necessary. Look for an answer choice that describes a confusion of necessary and sufficient terms.	**Step 4:** (A) is correct. Ralph points out that something needed for a certain result [proximity to others] does not necessarily guarantee that result [avoiding loneliness].

Wrong answers: (B) Distortion. Ralph does not point to Harold as an exception to a rule. (C) Outside the Scope. What is logically certain and intuitively obvious is not at issue here. (D) Distortion. Ralph states that more than one requirement is necessary to prevent loneliness, but that is far from offering alternative solutions. (E) Distortion. Ralph never suggests that proximity to others will make Harold *more* lonely.

Step 2: Conclusion: [Keyword "Clearly"] People who still have jobs are not cutting back on spending due to concern over widespread staff reductions. Evidence: [Keyword "because"] There has been no "unusual" increase in the amount of money added to the savings accounts of the still-employed.	**Step 1:** The phrase "argument in the passage proceeds by" identifies this as a Method of Argument question. The correct answer will describe *how* the author makes her point.

26. The widespread staff reductions in a certain region's economy are said to be causing people who still have their jobs to cut back on new purchases as though they, too, had become economically distressed. Clearly, however, actual spending by such people is undiminished, because there has been no unusual increase in the amount of money held by those people in savings account.

The argument in the passage proceeds by doing which one of the following?

(A) concluding that since an expected consequence of a supposed development did not occur, that development itself did not take place

(B) concluding that since only one of the two predictable consequences of a certain kind of behavior is observed to occur, this observed occurrence cannot, in the current situation, be a consequence of such behavior

(C) arguing that since people's economic behavior is guided by economic self-interest, only misinformation or error will cause people to engage in economic behavior that harms them economically

(D) arguing that since two alternative developments exhaust all the plausible possibilities, one of those developments occurred and the other did not

(E) concluding that since the evidence concerning a supposed change is ambiguous, it is most likely that no change is actually taking place

PrepTest101 Sec3 Q17

Step 3: The author claims that the employed are spending just as much as before because they are not putting more money into their savings accounts. The author must assume that those worried about losing their jobs will increase their savings. The correct answer will say: "If we are not seeing x (the behavior of distressed people), then y (distress) isn't happening."	**Step 4:** (A) is correct. This answer choice describes the author's argumentative strategy in generic terms: The "expected consequence" being an increase in savings, and the "development" being a reduction in spending.

Wrong answers: (B) Distortion. The author does not make any claims about the result of an action; instead, the author claims that an action is not occurring. (C) Economic self-interest, misinformation, and error are all Outside the Scope of the argument. (D) Distortion. The author doesn't claim that something else happened *as a result of* people not adding money to their savings accounts. (E) The author never claims that the evidence is ambiguous.

By the way, did you notice in that last question a gap between the author's evidence and conclusion? You may have paused and said to yourself, "Wait a minute, spending money on new purchases and putting that money into a savings account aren't the only two things people can do with their income." If so, you're starting to think like an LSAT expert. Most LSAT arguments have gaps of this kind. In Chapter 4, we're going to start working in depth with those gaps, otherwise known as assumptions, and we're going to pick up a lot of points in doing so. But your work so far in this chapter—analyzing evidence and conclusions—has been necessary groundwork for getting those points. You should congratulate yourself for building a good foundation to tackle assumptions!

Reflect Look back over your practice in this section. Did you describe the argumentative strategy in your own words? Did you formulate a prediction regarding the author's argumentative strategy before looking at answer choices? Did you efficiently eliminate answer choices that didn't match your prediction?

If you made some mistakes in this practice section, good! You now have some valuable information about where you need to work on your skills before test day. How did you mischaracterize the arguments? Do you see any commonalities among the wrong answer choices you were drawn to?

Parallel Reasoning Questions

Prepare Another way in which you will be tested on your ability to recognize argument structures on the LSAT is to identify two different arguments that use the same pattern to reach a similar conclusion. Questions that ask you to spot two identically structured arguments are called Parallel Reasoning questions.

LEARNING OBJECTIVES

In this section, you'll learn to:

- Rule out incorrect answer choices in Parallel Reasoning questions based on conclusion type.
- Identify similar argument structures in Parallel Reasoning questions.

You won't see many Parallel Reasoning questions on test day. There has been an average of 3–4 per test over the past five years. For many students, however, their length and complexity can make these questions some of the most time-consuming questions they encounter. Parallel Reasoning questions are, on average, the longest questions in the Logical Reasoning sections. While the length of these questions is off-putting to many students, LSAT experts know that there is a way to tackle these questions quickly and efficiently. Because the correct answer choice in these questions will be an argument that is parallel to the argument in the stimulus, both arguments must have similar conclusions. More on that in a second. First, let's figure out how to identify Parallel Reasoning question stems.

The question stem for Parallel Reasoning questions will ask you to find the answer choice whose reasoning is "most parallel to," "most similar to," or "most like" the reasoning in the stimulus.

First, take a look at some typical Parallel Reasoning question stems as they appear on the LSAT.

LSAT Question Stem	Analysis
In which one of the following arguments is the pattern of reasoning most similar to the pattern of reasoning in the argument above? *PrepTest105 Sec1 Q12*	The phrase "reasoning most similar to" indicates this is a Parallel Reasoning question.
The reasoning in the passage is most similar to that in which one of the following? *PrepTest106 Sec1 Q13*	The phrase "reasoning in the passage is most similar to" indicates this is a Parallel Reasoning question.

Parallel Reasoning questions require you to find an answer choice that uses the same *kind* of evidence to reach the same kind of conclusion as in the stimulus. The *content* of the stimulus will likely be different from that in the correct answer; in fact, each answer choice will probably discuss material unrelated to the information in the stimulus. Additionally, the order in which the evidence and the conclusion are presented in the stimulus may be different from the order in which the evidence and conclusion appear in the correct answer. In other words, if the conclusion in the stimulus is the first sentence, the conclusion in the correct answer does not necessarily need to be the first sentence. In short, the correct answer will be similar in *structure* (though perhaps not in sequence of evidence and conclusion) to the stimulus—the only difference is that the answer will discuss different ideas and concepts.

The ability to correctly identify and characterize conclusions will help you tackle Parallel Reasoning questions. Remember the six different conclusion types discussed earlier in this chapter: value judgment, if/then, prediction, comparison, assertion of fact, and recommendation. Because the correct answer must have the same type of evidence leading to the same type of conclusion, any answer choice that has a different type of conclusion than does the stimulus is automatically incorrect and can be eliminated. And because checking the conclusion in each answer choice is faster than reading (and characterizing the structure of) the entire stimulus and of each answer choice, your first line of attack when faced with a Parallel Reasoning question should be to identify and characterize the conclusion in the stimulus, then eliminate any answer choices that do not contain the same conclusion type. This process will occasionally allow you to arrive at the correct answer, even without breaking down the evidence. While other test takers spend minutes wading through six separate arguments (the stimulus and five answer choices), experts are able to quickly evaluate just the conclusions. Even if this strategy doesn't always lead directly to the right answer, it will often, at the very least, eliminate a few wrong answer choices.

In addition to characterizing a conclusion's *type*, pay attention to two other things: whether the conclusion is positive or negative (does the author state that something is or will be true, or that something is not or won't become true) and the level of certainty that exists (whether the conclusion is forceful or uses qualified language). For example, a conclusion stating that something will definitely occur is very different from a conclusion stating that something might not occur. The former is a strong prediction that something will happen, while the latter is a qualified prediction that something might not happen.

Practice To sharpen your ability to characterize conclusions, try the following drill. You've seen some of these conclusions earlier in this chapter, so they may look familiar. Characterize each by type, level of certainty, positive or negative language, and any other unique qualities it may have. The more specific you can be in your description of the conclusion in a Parallel Reasoning stimulus, the more useful the conclusion-typing method will be when you attack the answer choices. Examine the conclusions in this drill closely, then turn the page and compare your thinking to the expert analysis that follows.

LSAT Conclusion	My Analysis
27. [W]atching television has a bad influence on the dietary habits of television viewers. *PrepTest101 Sec3 Q13*	
28. [H]owever, peeling wild potatoes makes them at least as safe to eat as unpeeled domesticated potatoes of the same size. *PrepTest105 Sec1 Q9*	
29. Hence, the salaries and the complexity of the duties of these two newest employees should be reduced. *PrepTest107 Sec1 Q5*	
30. Therefore, if you are not well versed in history due to a lack of reading, it will not be easy for you to impress people who are intellectuals. *PrepTest104 Sec4 Q7*	
31. [I]t is quite likely that he is an extreme insomniac. *PrepTest104 Sec1 Q23*	
32. Thus it is certain that Alice will not volunteer. *PrepTest105 Sec1 Q12*	
33. Thus, supertasters experience sharp cheddar as tasting more bitter than mild cheddar, but nontasters experience sharp cheddar as tasting no more bitter than mild cheddar. *PrepTest105 Sec4 Q22*	

LSAT Conclusion	My Analysis
34. Thus, the size of the interstitial nucleus determines whether or not male cats can contract disease X. *PrepTest106 Sec3 Q25*	
35. Hence, depictions of violence among teenagers should be prohibited from movies and television programs, if only in those programs and movies promoted to young audiences. *PrepTest106 Sec3 Q5*	
36. [I]t is likely that Steve will work alone at the sale. *PrepTest105 Sec1 Q12*	
37. So if Paula does not work, Arthur will work with both Jane and Elise. *PrepTest105 Sec1 Q12*	
38. [F]loors made out of narrow floorboards were probably once a status symbol, designed to proclaim the owner's wealth. *PrepTest101 Sec3 Q23*	
39. So the information in typical broadcast news stories is poorly organized. *PrepTest104 Sec4 Q19*	

Expert Analysis

Here's how an LSAT expert analyzed the conclusions you just characterized.

LSAT Conclusion	Analysis
27. [W]atching television has a bad influence on the dietary habits of television viewers. *PrepTest101 Sec3 Q13*	This is a Value Judgment ("bad").
28. [H]owever, peeling wild potatoes makes them at least as safe to eat as unpeeled domesticated potatoes of the same size. *PrepTest105 Sec1 Q9*	The phrasing "as safe . . . as" indicates a Comparison, with the qualifier "at least."
29. Hence, the salaries and the complexity of the duties of these two newest employees should be reduced. *PrepTest107 Sec1 Q5*	The word "should" makes this a Recommendation. This counts as a definite recommendation since there is no qualifier, such as "probably."
30. Therefore, if you are not well versed in history due to a lack of reading, it will not be easy for you to impress people who are intellectuals. *PrepTest104 Sec4 Q7*	This conclusion has clear If/Then phrasing.
31. [I]t is quite likely that he is an extreme insomniac. *PrepTest104 Sec1 Q23*	This is an Assertion of Fact, qualified by the phrase "quite likely." An "extreme insomniac" is merely a medical condition, not a value judgment.
32. Thus it is certain that Alice will not volunteer. *PrepTest105 Sec1 Q12*	The word "will" indicates a negative Prediction. More specifically, it is a definite prediction that something will *not* happen.
33. Thus, supertasters experience sharp cheddar as tasting more bitter than mild cheddar, but nontasters experience sharp cheddar as tasting no more bitter than mild cheddar. *PrepTest105 Sec4 Q22*	The word "than" indicates a Comparison. Note that this conclusion makes two separate comparisons.

LSAT Conclusion	Analysis
34. Thus, the size of the interstitial nucleus determines whether or not male cats can contract disease X. *PrepTest106 Sec3 Q25*	This is an Assertion of Fact claiming a causal relationship between two things.
35. Hence, depictions of violence among teenagers should be prohibited from movies and television programs, if only in those programs and movies promoted to young audiences. *PrepTest106 Sec3 Q5*	This conclusion contains If/Then phrasing, while the word "should" indicates a Recommendation. This is a conditional recommendation.
36. [I]t is likely that Steve will work alone at the sale. *PrepTest105 Sec1 Q12*	The word "will" indicates a Prediction, which is qualified by "likely."
37. So if Paula does not work, Arthur will work with both Jane and Elise. *PrepTest105 Sec1 Q12*	This conclusion contains If/Then phrasing, while the word "will" indicates a Prediction. This is a conditional prediction.
38. [F]loors made out of narrow floorboards were probably once a status symbol, designed to proclaim the owner's wealth. *PrepTest101 Sec3 Q23*	This is an Assertion of Fact qualified by the word "probably."
39. So the information in typical broadcast news stories is poorly organized. *PrepTest104 Sec4 Q19*	The word "poorly" indicates a Value Judgment.

LSAT STRATEGY

When approaching Parallel Reasoning questions:

- First, characterize the conclusion in the stimulus.
- Characterize the conclusion in each answer choice, and eliminate any answer choice that has a conclusion of a type different than that of the conclusion in the stimulus.
- If more than one answer choice remains, analyze the evidence in the stimulus; find the answer choice that presents an argument structurally identical to the stimulus.

Take a look at an LSAT expert's analysis of a full Parallel Reasoning question.

Step 2: Conclusion: [A strong comparison of one quantity over two different time periods] Millville consumed more energy this August than last August. *because* Evidence: 1) [A proportionality rule] Energy consumption is proportional to humidity. *and* 2) [A comparison of the relevant condition] Humidity in Millville was higher this August than last August.	**Step 1:** "[M]ost similar to"—this is a Parallel Reasoning question.

The amount of electricity consumed in Millville on any day in August is directly proportional to peak humidity on that day. Since the average peak humidity this August was three points higher than the average peak humidity last August, it follows that more energy was consumed in Millville this August than last August.

Which one of the following arguments has a pattern of reasoning most similar to the one in the argument above?

(A) The amount of art supplies used in any of the Aesthetic Institute's 25 classes is directly proportional to the number of students in that class. Since in these classes the institute enrolled 20 percent more students overall last year than in the previous year, more art supplies were used in the institute's classes last year than in the previous year.

(B) The number of courses in painting offered by the Aesthetic Institute in any term is directly proportional to the number of students enrolled in the institute in that term. But the institute offers the same number of courses in sculpture each term. Hence, the institute usually offers more courses in painting than in sculpture.

(C) The number of new students enrolled at the Aesthetic Institute in any given year is directly proportional to the amount of advertising the institute has done in the previous year. Hence, if the institute seeks to increase its student body it must increase the amount it spends on advertising.

(D) The fees paid by a student at the Aesthetic Institute are directly proportional to the number of classes in which that student enrolls. Since the number of students at the Aesthetic Institute is increasing, it follows that the institute is collecting a greater amount in fees paid by students that it used to.

(E) The number of instructors employed by the Aesthetic Institute in any term is directly proportional to the number of classes offered in that term and also directly proportional to the number of students enrolled at the institute. Thus, the number of classes offered by the institute in any term is directly proportional to the number of students enrolled in that term.

PrepTest101 Sec3 Q21

Step 3: The correct answer must contain a conclusion that makes a strong comparison of the same quantity over two different time periods. The evidence must also be of the same type as that in the stimulus.	**Step 4:** (A) is correct. The conclusion is a strong comparison of the same quantity over two different time periods. The evidence is a proportionality rule and a comparison of the relevant condition.

Wrong answers: (B) Here, the conclusion is weak ("usually") and compares two different quantities ("courses in painting" versus "courses in sculpture"), rather than the same quantity at two different times. (C) Here, the conclusion is conditional ("if"), and offers a recommendation for how to increase a number, rather than comparing a quantity at two different times. (D) Here, the conclusion is the comparison of a quantity at present to that same quantity "in the past." This is not as clear-cut as the comparison between "this August" and "last August." Moreover, the evidence does not align to that in the stimulus. Here, the proportionality rule is triggered by the "number of classes in which [a] student enrolls," but the next piece of evidence tells us that the overall number of students is increasing. (E) Here, the conclusion is a proportionality rule, not a comparison. The proportionality rule is part of the *evidence* in the stimulus.

Practice Now that we have covered the basics of Parallel Reasoning questions, try your hand at a couple of examples of this question type. Characterize the conclusion in the stimulus; then eliminate any choices that do not share the same conclusion type. Be sure to check each answer choice, as there may be more than one choice that has the same type of conclusion as the stimulus. If you are unable to rule out all incorrect choices based upon your characterization of the conclusion, then move back to the stimulus and examine the evidence. The correct answer will use the same type of evidence to support the same type of conclusion as the stimulus. If you need to, simplify the original argument by replacing the various terms and concepts with letters (such as "All X are Y, and no Y is Z . . ."). Then match that same structure to one of the answer choices.

When you're finished, compare your analyses to those of an LSAT expert.

Step 2:	**Step 1:**

40. People who say that Dooney County is flat are clearly wrong. On flat land, soil erosion by water is not a problem. Consequently, farmers whose land is flat do not build terraces to prevent erosion. Yet I hear that the farms in Dooney County are dotted with terraces.

The reasoning in the passage is most similar to that in which one of the following?

(A) If we paint the room white, it will get smudged, and we will have to paint it again soon. Therefore, we should paint it dark blue.

(B) People with children need more space than those without children. Yet people with no children can usually afford bigger houses.

(C) People who get a lot of exercise have no trouble falling asleep; hence, people who get a lot of exercise do not use medication to help them fall asleep. Jack is taking many kinds of medication, so he must not be getting a lot of exercise.

(D) If I go grocery shopping when I am hungry, I buy snack foods and cannot resist eating them. Therefore, I cannot lose weight.

(E) People who have many friends tend to go out often, so they need cars. Therefore, if Joe wants to have many friends, he must buy a car.

PrepTest106 Sec1 Q13

Step 3:	**Step 4:**

Step 2:	**Step 1:**

41. Carl's Coffee Emporium stocks only two decaffeinated coffees: French Roast and Mocha Java. Yusef only serves decaffeinated coffee, and the coffee he served after dinner last night was far too smooth and mellow to have been French Roast. So, if Yusef still gets all his coffee from Carl's, what he served last night was Mocha Java.

The argument above is most similar in its logical structure to which one of the following?

(A) Samuel wants to take three friends to the beach. His mother owns both a sedan and a convertible. The convertible holds four people so, although the sedan has a more powerful engine, if Samuel borrows a vehicle from his mother, he will borrow the convertible.

(B) If Anna wants to walk from her house to the office where she works, she must either go through the park or take the overpass across the railroad tracks. The park paths are muddy, and Anna does not like using the overpass, so she never walks to work.

(C) Rose can either take a two-week vacation in July or wait until October and take a three-week vacation. The trail she had planned to hike requires three weeks to complete but is closed by October, so if Rose takes a vacation, it will not be the one she had planned.

(D) Werdix, Inc., has offered Arno a choice between a job in sales and a job in research. Arno would like to work at Werdix but he would never take a job in sales when another job is available, so if he accepts one of these jobs, it will be the one in research.

(E) If Teresa does not fire her assistant, her staff will rebel and her department's efficiency will decline. Losing her assistant would also reduce its efficiency, so, if no alternative solution can be found, Teresa's department will become less efficient.

PrepTest101 Sec2 Q13

Step 3:	**Step 4:**

Expert Analysis

Here's how an LSAT expert worked through the questions you just completed.

Step 2: Conclusion: The *assertion of fact* that should be paraphrased as: Dooney County is definitely not flat. *Because* Evidence: 1) Dooney County is dotted with terraces; 2) farmers only use erosion control terraces on land that is not flat.	**Step 1:** The phrase "reasoning . . . most similar" indicates a Parallel Reasoning question.

40. People who say that Dooney County is flat are clearly wrong. On flat land, soil erosion by water is not a problem. Consequently, farmers whose land is flat do not build terraces to prevent erosion. Yet I hear that the farms in Dooney County are dotted with terraces.

The reasoning in the passage is most similar to that in which one of the following?

(A) If we paint the room white, it will get smudged, and we will have to paint it again soon. Therefore, we should paint it dark blue.

(B) People with children need more space than those without children. Yet people with no children can usually afford bigger houses.

(C) People who get a lot of exercise have no trouble falling asleep; hence, people who get a lot of exercise do not use medication to help them fall asleep. Jack is taking many kinds of medication, so he must not be getting a lot of exercise.

(D) If I go grocery shopping when I am hungry, I buy snack foods and cannot resist eating them. Therefore, I cannot lose weight.

(E) People who have many friends tend to go out often, so they need cars. Therefore, if Joe wants to have many friends, he must buy a car.

PrepTest106 Sec1 Q13

Step 3: Eliminate any answers with a conclusion that is not a definite assertion of fact.	**Step 4:** (C) is correct. This is the only answer that has the right type of conclusion. As in the stimulus, the evidence indicates the presence of something (the medication) and uses its presence to make an assertion about a present-tense condition.

Wrong answers: (A) The conclusion here is a *recommendation.* (B) This answer does not even contain an argument, so much as it states a paradox. Also, the qualifier "usually" has no correlate in the argument in the stimulus. (D) This conclusion is actually a statement of impossibility that extends into the future, rather than a mere assertion of a current state. The conclusion in the stimulus does not assert that Dooney County cannot be made flat, merely that it currently is not flat. Additionally, the evidence provides a chain of causation not present in the stimulus. (E) The conclusion here is a *conditional recommendation.*

Step 2: Conclusion: A *conditional* identification of a single specific result: "*If* Yusef still gets *all* his coffee from Carl's," it was Mocha Java. *because* Evidence: 1) Carl's only supplies two decaf varieties; 2) Yusef only serves decaf; and 3) reasons to eliminate one of the two varieties.	**Step 1:** The phrase "similar in its logical structure" indicates a Parallel Reasoning question.

41. Carl's Coffee Emporium stocks only two decaffeinated coffees: French Roast and Mocha Java. Yusef only serves decaffeinated coffee, and the coffee he served after dinner last night was far too smooth and mellow to have been French Roast. So, if Yusef still gets all his coffee from Carl's, what he served last night was Mocha Java.

The argument above is most similar in its logical structure to which one of the following?

(A) Samuel wants to take three friends to the beach. His mother owns both a sedan and a convertible. The convertible holds four people so, although the sedan has a more powerful engine, if Samuel borrows a vehicle from his mother, he will borrow the convertible.

(B) If Anna wants to walk from her house to the office where she works, she must either go through the park or take the overpass across the railroad tracks. The park paths are muddy, and Anna does not like using the overpass, so she never walks to work.

(C) Rose can either take a two-week vacation in July or wait until October and take a three-week vacation. The trail she had planned to hike requires three weeks to complete but is closed by October, so if Rose takes a vacation, it will not be the one she had planned.

(D) Werdix, Inc., has offered Arno a choice between a job in sales and a job in research. Arno would like to work at Werdix but he would never take a job in sales when another job is available, so if he accepts one of these jobs, it will be the one in research.

(E) If Teresa does not fire her assistant, her staff will rebel and her department's efficiency will decline. Losing her assistant would also reduce its efficiency, so, if no alternative solution can be found, Teresa's department will become less efficient.

PrepTest101 Sec2 Q13

Step 3: Eliminate choices that do not have a conclusion that conditionally results in the specific choice of a single option. If choices remain, the evidence should match the identification of only two possible options, and a reason that one of the options is impossible.	**Step 4:** (D) is correct. The evidence identifies two options and provides a reason that one will definitely not occur, with a conditional conclusion that specifically identifies the remaining option.

Wrong answers: (A) While the conclusion appropriately is the conditional selection of a specific one of two options, the evidence is not a match. There is no evidence that one of the options has to be eliminated from consideration. (B) The conclusion in this choice is not overtly conditional. One could reasonably argue that the conclusion is conditional—*if work, then not walk*—but choice (B) would still be wrong because, as with (C), the conclusion in choice (B) merely eliminates a possibility (rather than resulting in the selection of a specific option). (C) The conclusion, while conditional, does not result in the identification of a specific chosen option. Instead, this conclusion merely indicates that the choice, whatever it may be, will *not* be the one planned. (E) While this conclusion is conditional, the result, rather than indicating a specific choice of an option, has the relative relationship "become *less* efficient."

Mixed Perform: Argument-Based Questions

Perform Assess your skills on some further examples of the question types introduced in this chapter—Main Point, Role of a Statement, Point at Issue, Method of Argument, and Parallel Reasoning. Take no more than 1 minute 30 seconds per question.

1. Economist: Every business strives to increase its productivity, for this increases profits for the owners and the likelihood that the business will survive. But not all efforts to increase productivity are beneficial to the business as a whole. Often, attempts to increase productivity decrease the number of employees, which clearly harms the dismissed employees as well as the sense of security of the retained employees.

Which one of the following most accurately expresses the main conclusion of the economist's argument?

(A) If an action taken to secure the survival of a business fails to enhance the welfare of the business's employees, that action cannot be good for the business as a whole.

(B) Some measures taken by a business to increase productivity fail to be beneficial to the business as a whole.

(C) Only if the employees of a business are also its owners will the interests of the employees and owners coincide, enabling measures that will be beneficial to the business as a whole.

(D) There is no business that does not make efforts to increase its productivity.

(E) Decreasing the number of employees in a business undermines the sense of security of retained employees.

PrepTest123 Sec2 Q1

2. Antonio: One can live a life of moderation by never deviating from the middle course. But then one loses the joy of spontaneity and misses the opportunities that come to those who are occasionally willing to take great chances, or to go too far.

Marla: But one who, in the interests of moderation, never risks going too far is actually failing to live a life of moderation: one must be moderate even in one's moderation.

Antonio and Marla disagree over

(A) whether it is desirable for people occasionally to take great chances in life

(B) what a life of moderation requires of a person

(C) whether it is possible for a person to embrace other virtues along with moderation

(D) how often a person ought to deviate from the middle course in life

(E) whether it is desirable for people to be moderately spontaneous

PrepTest123 Sec3 Q7

---

3. A group of unusual meteorites was found in Shergotty, India. Their structure indicates that they originated on one of the geologically active planets, Mercury, Venus, or Mars. Because of Mercury's proximity to the Sun, any material dislodged from that planet's surface would have been captured by the Sun, rather than falling to Earth as meteorites. Nor could Venus be the source of the meteorites, because its gravity would have prevented dislodged material from escaping into space. The meteorites, therefore, probably fell to Earth after being dislodged from Mars, perhaps as the result of a collision with a large object.

The argument derives its conclusion by

(A) offering a counterexample to a theory

(B) eliminating competing alternative explanations

(C) contrasting present circumstances with past circumstances

(D) questioning an assumption

(E) abstracting a general principle from specific data

PrepTest101 Sec2 Q3

4. Suppose I have promised to keep a confidence and someone asks me a question that I cannot answer truthfully without thereby breaking the promise. Obviously, I cannot both keep and break the same promise. Therefore, one cannot be obliged both to answer all questions truthfully and to keep all promises.

Which one of the following arguments is most similar in its reasoning to the argument above?

(A) It is claimed that we have the unencumbered right to say whatever we want. It is also claimed that we have the obligation to be civil to others. But civility requires that we not always say what we want. So, it cannot be true both that we have the unencumbered right to say whatever we want and that we have the duty to be civil.

(B) Some politicians could attain popularity with voters only by making extravagant promises; this, however, would deceive the people. So, since the only way for some politicians to be popular is to deceive, and any politician needs to be popular, it follows that some politicians must deceive.

(C) If we put a lot of effort into making this report look good, the client might think we did so because we believed our proposal would not stand on its own merits. On the other hand, if we do not try to make the report look good, the client might think we are not serious about her business. So, whatever we do, we risk her criticism.

(D) If creditors have legitimate claims against a business and the business has the resources to pay those debts, then the business is obliged to pay them. Also, if a business has obligations to pay debts, then a court will force it to pay them. But the courts did not force this business to pay its debts, so either the creditors did not have legitimate claims or the business did not have sufficient resources.

(E) If we extend our business hours, we will either have to hire new employees or have existing employees work overtime. But both new employees and additional overtime would dramatically increase our labor costs. We cannot afford to increase labor costs, so we will have to keep our business hours as they stand.

PrepTest123 Sec2 Q12

5. Although the concept of free will is essential to that of moral responsibility, its role in determining responsibility is not the same in all situations. We hold criminals morally responsible for the damage they cause, assuming that they freely chose their activities. But we do not hold someone who has a heart attack while driving morally responsible for the damage caused, if any, even when we have good reason to believe that the heart attack could have been prevented by eating different foods and that one's choice of diet is made freely.

The claim that a choice of diet can affect whether or not one has a heart attack plays which one of the following roles in the argument?

(A) It is a subsidiary conclusion of the argument.

(B) It is used to show that we should hold someone morally responsible for damages caused by having a heart attack while driving.

(C) It is cited as evidence that our concept of moral responsibility should be the same in all situations.

(D) It is used to disprove the claim that we should not hold criminals morally responsible for damages.

(E) It is used in support of the conclusion of the argument.

PrepTest105 Sec1 Q11

6. Novel X and Novel Y are both semiautobiographical novels and contain many very similar themes and situations, which might lead one to suspect plagiarism on the part of one of the authors. However, it is more likely that the similarity of themes and situations in the two novels is merely coincidental, since both authors are from very similar backgrounds and have led similar lives.

Which one of the following most accurately expresses the conclusion drawn in the argument?

(A) Novel X and Novel Y are both semiautobiographical novels, and the two novels contain many very similar themes and situations.

(B) The fact that Novel X and Novel Y are both semiautobiographical novels and contain many very similar themes and situations might lead one to suspect plagiarism on the part of one of the authors.

(C) The author of Novel X and the author of Novel Y are from very similar backgrounds and have led very similar lives.

(D) It is less likely that one of the authors of Novel X or Novel Y is guilty of plagiarism than that the similarity of themes and situations in the two novels is merely coincidental.

(E) If the authors of Novel X and Novel Y are from very similar backgrounds and have led similar lives, suspicions that either of the authors plagiarized are very likely to be unwarranted.

PrepTest123 Sec3 Q12

7. Carolyn: The artist Marc Quinn has displayed, behind a glass plate, biologically replicated fragments of Sir John Sulston's DNA, calling it a "conceptual portrait" of Sulston. But to be a portrait, something must bear a recognizable resemblance to its subject.

Arnold: I disagree. Quinn's conceptual portrait is a maximally realistic portrait, for it holds actual instructions according to which Sulston was created.

The dialogue provides most support for the claim that Carolyn and Arnold disagree over whether the object described by Quinn as a conceptual portrait of Sir John Sulston

(A) should be considered to be art
(B) should be considered to be Quinn's work
(C) bears a recognizable resemblance to Sulston
(D) contains instructions according to which Sulston was created
(E) is actually a portrait of Sulston

PrepTest123 Sec3 Q3

8. Sam: In a recent survey, over 95 percent of people who purchased a Starlight automobile last year said they were highly satisfied with their purchase. Since people who have purchased a new car in the last year are not highly satisfied if that car has a manufacturing defect, Starlight automobiles are remarkably free from such defects.

Tiya: But some manufacturing defects in automobiles become apparent only after several years of use.

Which one of the following most accurately describes how Tiya's response is related to Sam's argument?

(A) It argues that Sam's conclusion is correct, though not for the reasons Sam gives.
(B) It provides evidence indicating that the survey results Sam relies on in his argument do not accurately characterize the attitudes of those surveyed.
(C) It offers a consideration that undermines the support Sam offers for his conclusion.
(D) It points out that Sam's argument presupposes the truth of the conclusion Sam is defending.
(E) It presents new information that implies that Sam's conclusion is false.

PrepTest106 Sec3 Q7

9. It is now a common complaint that the electronic media have corroded the intellectual skills required and fostered by the literary media. But several centuries ago the complaint was that certain intellectual skills, such as the powerful memory and extemporaneous eloquence that were intrinsic to oral culture, were being destroyed by the spread of literacy. So, what awaits us is probably a mere alteration of the human mind rather than its devolution.

The reference to the complaint of several centuries ago that powerful memory and extemporaneous eloquence were being destroyed plays which one of the following roles in the argument?

(A) evidence supporting the claim that the intellectual skills fostered by the literary media are being destroyed by the electronic media

(B) an illustration of the general hypothesis being advanced that intellectual abilities are inseparable from the means by which people communicate

(C) an example of a cultural change that did not necessarily have a detrimental effect on the human mind overall

(D) evidence that the claim that the intellectual skills required and fostered by the literary media are being lost is unwarranted

(E) possible evidence, mentioned and then dismissed, that might be cited by supporters of the hypothesis being criticized

PrepTest123 Sec2 Q11

10. Gamba: Muñoz claims that the Southwest Hopeville Neighbors Association overwhelmingly opposes the new water system, citing this as evidence of citywide opposition. The association did pass a resolution opposing the new water system, but only 25 of 350 members voted, with 10 in favor of the system. Furthermore, the 15 opposing votes represent far less than 1 percent of Hopeville's population. One should not assume that so few votes represent the view of the majority of Hopeville's residents.

Of the following, which one most accurately describes Gamba's strategy of argumentation?

(A) questioning a conclusion based on the results of a vote, on the grounds that people with certain views are more likely to vote

(B) questioning a claim supported by statistical data by arguing that statistical data can be manipulated to support whatever view the interpreter wants to support

(C) attempting to refute an argument by showing that, contrary to what has been claimed, the truth of the premises does not guarantee the truth of the conclusion

(D) criticizing a view on the grounds that the view is based on evidence that is in principle impossible to disconfirm

(E) attempting to cast doubt on a conclusion by claiming that the statistical sample on which the conclusion is based is too small to be dependable

PrepTest123 Sec2 Q20

11. Double-blind techniques should be used whenever possible in scientific experiments. They help prevent the misinterpretations that often arise due to expectations and opinions that scientists already hold, and clearly scientists should be extremely diligent in trying to avoid such misinterpretations.

Which one of the following most accurately expresses the main conclusion of the argument?

(A) Scientists' objectivity may be impeded by interpreting experimental evidence on the basis of expectations and opinions that they already hold.

(B) It is advisable for scientists to use double-blind techniques in as high a proportion of their experiments as they can.

(C) Scientists sometimes neglect to adequately consider the risk of misinterpreting evidence on the basis of prior expectations and opinions.

(D) Whenever possible, scientists should refrain from interpreting evidence on the basis of previously formed expectations and convictions.

(E) Double-blind experimental techniques are often an effective way of ensuring scientific objectivity.

PrepTest123 Sec2 Q10

12. Taylor: Researchers at a local university claim that 61 percent of the information transferred during a conversation is communicated through nonverbal signals. But this claim, like all such mathematically precise claims, is suspect, because claims of such exactitude could never be established by science.

Sandra: While precision is unobtainable in many areas of life, it is commonplace in others. Many scientific disciplines obtain extremely precise results, which should not be doubted merely because of their precision.

The statements above provide the most support for holding that Sandra would disagree with Taylor about which one of the following statements?

(A) Research might reveal that 61 percent of the information taken in during a conversation is communicated through nonverbal signals.

(B) It is possible to determine whether 61 percent of the information taken in during a conversation is communicated through nonverbal signals.

(C) The study of verbal and nonverbal communication is an area where one cannot expect great precision in one's research results.

(D) Some sciences can yield mathematically precise results that are not inherently suspect.

(E) If inherently suspect claims are usually false, then the majority of claims made by scientists are false as well.

PrepTest123 Sec2 Q16

Assess Use the following criteria to evaluate your results on the Argument-Based Questions Perform quiz.

If, under timed conditions, you correctly answered:

10–12 of the questions: Outstanding! You have demonstrated a strong skill level in Argument-Based questions. For further practice, use any of the Recommended Additional Practice sets, including the Advanced set. Then, move on to Chapter 4 on Assumption Family questions. After completing Chapter 4, timed practice with full Logical Reasoning sections should also become part of your study schedule.

7–9 of the questions: Good work! You have a solid foundation in Argument-Based questions. For further practice, begin with the Foundations or Mid-Level Recommended Additional Practice set (and, time permitting, work up through the Advanced set, as well). Then, move on to Chapter 4 on Assumption Family questions. After completing Chapter 4, timed practice with full Logical Reasoning sections should also become part of your study schedule.

0–6 of the questions: Keep working. The skills you use on Argument-Based questions form the foundation for success on Assumption Family questions, too. Begin by reviewing this chapter. Then, try the questions in the Foundations Recommended Additional Practice set. As you continue to progress, move on to the Mid-Level Recommended Additional Practice set, and then to Chapter 4 on Assumption Family questions.

Recommended Additional Practice: Argument-Based Questions

All of the following questions will provide good practice on recent Argument-Based questions. They are grouped by difficulty as determined from empirical student practice results. Foundations practice has 1- and 2-star questions; Mid-Level practice has 1-, 2-, and 3-star questions; Advanced practice has 2-, 3-, and 4-star questions. All the questions are from PrepTests that are available for digital practice on LawHub with an LSAC LawHub Advantage subscription. Complete explanations and analysis for these questions are available on Kaplan's LSAT Link and LSAT Link+. See **www.kaptest.com/LSAT** to learn more about LSAT Link and LSAT Link+.

Foundations

PrepTest 144, Section 3, Question 4
PrepTest 140, Section 2, Questions 5, 8, & 16
PrepTest 139, Section 1, Question 9; Section 4, Questions 1 & 4
PrepTest 138, Section 2, Question 9
PrepTest 137, Section 2, Questions 10 & 19; Section 4, Question 19
PrepTest 136, Section 4, Question 13
PrepTest 135, Section 1, Questions 2 & 10; Section 4, Questions 4, 12, & 25
PrepTest 134, Section 1, Questions 1 & 3; Section 3, Questions 5, 7, 10, & 25
PrepTest 133, Section 3, Questions 1, 4, 19, & 20
PrepTest 132, Section 4, Questions 1, 12, & 21

Mid-Level

PrepTest 144, Section 3, Question 18
PrepTest 140, Section 2, Question 24
PrepTest 139, Section 1, Questions 2 & 11; Section 4, Questions 10 & 25
PrepTest 138, Section 2, Questions 19 & 26; Section 3, Question 11
PrepTest 137, Section 2, Question 12; Section 4, Questions 1, 12, & 22

PrepTest 136, Section 4, Questions 5 & 19
PrepTest 135, Section 1, Questions 9 & 23; Section 4, Question 17
PrepTest 134, Section 1, Question 25; Section 3, Question 16
PrepTest 133, Section 1, Questions 8, 13, 17, & 21; Section 3, Question 10
PrepTest 132, Section 2, Questions 10 & 14; Section 4, Questions 4 & 25

Advanced

PrepTest 144, Section 3, Questions 17 & 19
PrepTest 140, Section 2, Questions 17 & 26
PrepTest 139, Section 1, Question 23; Section 4, Questions 12 & 24
PrepTest 138, Section 2, Questions 11, 17, 21, & 22; Section 3, Questions 8, 20, 22, & 25
PrepTest 137, Section 2, Questions 16, 20, & 22
PrepTest 136, Section 2, Questions 16, 18, 20, & 25; Section 4, Questions 9, 23, & 26
PrepTest 135, Section 1, Question 22; Section 4, Questions 14, 16, & 21
PrepTest 134, Section 1, Questions 14 & 21
PrepTest 133, Section 1, Question 14

Answers and Explanations

1. (B) Main Point ★★★★

Step 1: Identify the Question Type

The question stem directly asks for the main conclusion of the economist's argument.

Step 2: Untangle the Stimulus

A Contrast Keyword, in this case *but*, will often highlight the author's transition to her conclusion. In this argument, [*b*]*ut* precedes the conclusion that "not all efforts to increase productivity are beneficial to the business as a whole." The subsequent sentence provides a supporting example for this assertion.

Step 3: Make a Prediction

There is no need to analyze the evidence or formulate the assumption; the correct answer to a Main Point question should match what you identify as the conclusion of the argument.

Step 4: Evaluate the Answer Choices

(B) is correct. With minor rephrasing ("not all are beneficial" is equivalent in meaning to "some fail to be beneficial"), this choice is a match for the conclusion.

(A) works as the argument's sufficient assumption, linking the evidence of harm to employees with the conclusion's concern for the good of the business as a whole. This answer goes beyond simply identifying the argument's conclusion.

(C) discusses employees who are also owners, which goes well beyond the scope of the argument.

(D) rephrases the first phrase in the stimulus. Admittedly, this first idea that "every business strives to increase its productivity" is supported by the premise that "this increases profits for the owners and the likelihood that the business will survive." However, it is very common on the LSAT for the author to begin an argument with an alternative viewpoint or common belief before using a Contrast Keyword to segue to her main point.

(E) is a deduction implicit in the evidence at the end of the passage, which is support for the preceding conclusion.

2. (B) Point at Issue ★★★★

Step 1: Identify the Question Type

Because the correct answer will describe what Antonio and Marla "disagree over," this is a Point at Issue question.

Step 2: Untangle the Stimulus

Paraphrase each speaker's statements. Antonio suggests that you can achieve a moderate life by sticking to the middle course. The downside of this is that you would lose the benefits that come from taking great chances and going too far. Marla suggests that people who are always moderate are actually not moderate because they are extreme in their moderation.

Step 3: Make a Prediction

While you can always use the Point at Issue Decision Tree to work through the answer choices to a Point at Issue question, you may be able to predict the point of disagreement based on the content of the stimulus. Here, the disagreement seems to be about how one could actually achieve a life of moderation. Antonio thinks that always sticking to the middle course would lead to a life of moderation. Marla thinks that always sticking to the middle course would not lead to a life of moderation. The correct answer will reflect this point of disagreement.

Step 4: Evaluate the Answer Choices

(B) matches the prediction. Antonio and Marla disagree about how one could actually achieve a life of moderation.

(A) is Out of Scope because Marla voices no opinion on the desirability of taking chances.

(C) is Out of Scope because neither Antonio nor Marla discuss virtues other than moderation.

(D) is 180 because both speakers seem to agree that people should sometimes stray from the middle course, although neither states precisely how often they should do so.

(E) is a Distortion because neither really discusses "moderate spontaneity," which is essentially just a mixture of terms from the stimulus. Regardless, Marla states no opinion on the desirability of any sort of spontaneity.

3. (B) Method of Argument ★★★★

Step 1: Identify the Question Type

The phrase "derives its conclusion by" is a clear sign that this is a Method of Argument question. Keep your focus on *how* the author structures the evidence and conclusion rather than on *what* the argument specifically claims.

Step 2: Untangle the Stimulus

The Keyword *therefore* indicates the conclusion: The meteorites discovered in Shergotty, India, probably fell to Earth after being dislodged from Mars. The author reaches this conclusion in a linear fashion. First, the author says that the meteorites must have come from Mercury, Venus, or Mars. Then, she says the meteorites could not have come from Mercury (it is too close to the Sun) or Venus (its gravity would not have allowed the meteorites to reach space). So, Mars is their likely source.

Step 3: Make a Prediction

The argument concludes that Mars is the source of the meteorites by eliminating the other two possible sources.

Step 4: Evaluate the Answer Choices

(B) is correct. The argument claims that Mars is the source of the meteorites by eliminating Mercury and Venus as possible sources.

(A) is incorrect because no particular examples are cited and the author never offers a counterexample to anything.

(C) is Outside the Scope. The argument describes what must have been the case based on what is known about the planets. No contrast between past and present circumstances is ever made.

(D) is incorrect because the author never critiques an argument by questioning an assumption; the only view presented is her own.

(E) is Outside the Scope. There is no general principle in the argument; the author's conclusion is limited to the source of these specific meteorites in Shergotty, India.

4. (A) Parallel Reasoning ★★★★

Step 1: Identify the Question Type

The phrase "similar in its reasoning" indicates a Parallel Reasoning question. Characterize the conclusion and knock out any answer in which the conclusion doesn't match.

Step 2: Untangle the Stimulus

The author concludes that "one cannot be obliged both to answer all questions truthfully and to keep all promises" because there could be situations in which those obligations would conflict.

Step 3: Make a Prediction

Always start Parallel Reasoning questions by eliminating any answers that do not have the proper type of conclusion. The correct answer should have an Assertion of Fact conclusion that similarly indicates that two broad obligations or claims cannot always both be met on the grounds that circumstances can exist in which they would conflict.

Step 4: Evaluate the Answer Choices

(A) is correct. It concludes that two obligations or rights—free speech and the duty to be civil—contradict each other. That is the same type of conclusion as in the stimulus, while all the other choices contain deviations as described below.

(B) cannot be correct because the conclusion is different. This conclusion asserts that some politicians must deceive. To be the same type of conclusion, it would have to state something along the lines of "it cannot be true that a politician is always popular and never deceives." Additionally, the conclusion wouldn't be true universally, since the evidence is only about *some* politicians.

(C) also cannot be correct because the conclusion doesn't match. This answer choice presents a lose-lose situation; it does not state the general impossibility of always complying with two different claims or dictates. Additionally, the evidence—about what "might" occur—is too uncertain.

(D) also does not match the stimulus. The answer presents two Formal Logic statements and then uses the contrapositives to draw a conclusion. This conclusion states that one of two things must have occurred, whereas the conclusion in the stimulus says two things cannot always occur together. The difference is subtle, but important.

(E) also presents Formal Logic: If hours are extended, then employees must be hired or current employees must work overtime. The conclusion says the necessary condition is unacceptable, so the sufficient condition cannot happen. It doesn't argue that two broad rules can't always occur at the same time.

5. (E) Role of a Statement ★★★★

Step 1: Identify the Question Type

This question stem presents a claim from this stimulus and asks for its "role in the argument," making this a Role of a Statement question.

Step 2: Untangle the Stimulus

Start by browsing the stimulus for the claim in question (about how diet choices affect heart attacks). Mark that claim, then break the argument into evidence and conclusion, determining how the marked claim functions within that argument. This argument investigates the concept of free will by looking at two examples. In the first, a criminal is morally responsible for his actions because of free will. In the second, someone who has an accident while having a heart attack is not, even if that person's choice of diet (free will) directly contributed to the heart attack. These examples support the author's point that free will's role in assigning responsibility changes from situation to situation.

Step 3: Make a Prediction

The claim in question is part of the second example at the bottom. That example is merely used to back up the author's conclusion. The correct answer will identify the claim in question as part of this supporting evidence.

Step 4: Evaluate the Answer Choices

(E) accurately identifies the claim as part of the supporting evidence.

(A) is incorrect because the claim is not a conclusion of any kind; it's part of a hypothetical example. There is no supporting evidence for the claim in question.

(B) is a 180. The author claims that we do *not* hold such people morally responsible. No recommendation is made by the author otherwise.

(C) is also a 180. The author claims that responsibility is *not* determined the same way in all situations and never suggests it should be otherwise.

(D) is a Distortion. Criminal activity is part of the first example. The claim in question is part of the second example and does not address, let alone *disprove*, the first example in any way.

6. (D) Main Point ★★☆☆

Step 1: Identify the Question Type

Because the correct answer "accurately expresses the conclusion" of the argument, this is a Main Point question.

Step 2: Untangle the Stimulus

Paraphrase the stimulus. First, the author says that because two novels are similar, some people might suspect one of them is plagiarized. Next, the author suggests it is more likely that the similarities are coincidental, rather than a result of plagiarism. The reason for this is that there are many similarities between the lives of the two authors.

Step 3: Make a Prediction

The first sentence of the stimulus introduces the topic and puts forward a view that some people might have. The second sentence starts with the Contrast Keyword *however*, which introduces the author's point of view. This view, not surprisingly, goes against the view that some people might have. Finally, the author finishes by providing a reason why this new view is correct. Thus, the first clause of the second sentence is the author's conclusion. The main point is that the similarities between the two novels are more likely due to mere coincidence than to plagiarism.

Step 4: Evaluate the Answer Choices

(D) matches the prediction.

(A) is the evidence for why some people might think that the one of the authors plagiarized the other.

(B) is the view that some people might hold regarding the two authors as well as the reason why they might hold that view.

(C) is the author's evidence.

(E) distorts the argument by making the evidence a condition ("If the authors . . ."), and the conclusion a result. Moreover, it adds the Extreme word *very*. The author says it is "more likely" that the similarities are coincidental, which is not as strong as saying plagiarism is "very likely" not to be the case. Regardless, the correct answer to a Main Point question needs to be a paraphrase of just the author's conclusion, not of the evidence as well.

7. (E) Point at Issue ★☆☆☆

Step 1: Identify the Question Type

This is a Point at Issue question because the correct answer is the claim about which the two speakers *disagree*. Additionally, this stem directs you to the disagreement; it will have something to do with Sir John Sulston's *portrait*.

Step 2: Untangle the Stimulus

Paraphrase the argument made by each speaker. Carolyn's basic point is that the conceptual portrait is no portrait at all, because it does not look like Sir John Sulston. Arnold thinks that the conceptual portrait is a "maximally realistic" portrait, because it contains the genetic instructions for making Sulston.

Step 3: Make a Prediction

The two speakers disagree about their conclusions. Carolyn thinks the artwork is not a portrait. Arnold thinks it is. Additionally, they have differing ideas on what a portrait must entail. Carolyn thinks it has to resemble the subject, whereas Arnold does not.

Step 4: Evaluate the Answer Choices

(E) matches the prediction.

(A) is Out of Scope. Neither Carolyn nor Arnold mentions art.

(B) is Out of Scope. Neither speaker contests Quinn's authorship of the "conceptual portrait."

(C) is Out of Scope because even though Carolyn implies that the portrait fails to resemble Sulston, Arnold never contradicts her. Instead, Arnold disputes that the proper criteria for a portrait is that it resembles its subject.

(D) is Out of Scope because only Arnold addresses whether or not the portrait contains instructions for Sulston's creation.

8. (C) Method of Argument ★★★★

Step 1: Identify the Question Type

This question stem asks you to determine *how* Tiya's response is related to Sam's argument, which makes this a Method of Argument question.

Step 2: Untangle the Stimulus

Before you assess anything about Tiya's response, read and dissect Sam's argument. *Since* at the beginning of Sam's last sentence indicates evidence, so the second clause of that sentence is Sam's conclusion: The Starlight is quite free of manufacturing defects. Sam's evidence is that nearly all of last year's Starlight purchasers said they were satisfied, and no one would claim to be satisfied with a car if that car had a manufacturing defect. In response, Tiya points out that some defects can only be detected after several years.

Step 3: Make a Prediction

Tiya is implicitly disagreeing with Sam's assumption that if the cars had defects, the owners would know about them. What she's implying is that the cars may in fact have defects, contrary to Sam's optimistic conclusion, but those defects didn't affect the survey because they hadn't yet been discovered. Tiya is accusing Sam of committing the classic flaw of failing to consider alternative possibilities.

Step 4: Evaluate the Answer Choices

(C) matches the prediction. By undermining Sam's evidence, Tiya has cast doubt on his certainty that these cars are trouble-free. Knowledge of classic flaws will help with Method of Argument questions.

(A) is incorrect because nothing in Tiya's response indicates that she agrees with Sam's conclusion.

(B) is Out of Scope. Tiya never mentions either the survey results or the attitudes of others, so there's no way that **(B)** could describe her response to Sam. She doesn't contest the 95-percent-satisfaction figure from the survey; her opposition lies in the fact that the satisfaction could be misguided.

(D) has Tiya accusing Sam of circular logic, of assuming his conclusion to be true to prove it. However, his evidence and conclusion are different from each other, and all she does is attack an assumption he's making.

(E) may be tempting in that it picks up on the Tiya/Sam disagreement. It begins in a promising way, considering that Tiya does indeed bring up a new point. Contrary to **(E)**, however, Tiya stops short of saying, "No, Sam, you're wrong, those cars *do* have problems." She simply casts doubt on his *certainty* about the cars. Tiya would concede that Sam *could* be right and the cars *could* be defect-free, but she would argue that the survey results don't prove it.

9. (C) Role of a Statement ★★★★

Step 1: Identify the Question Type

A question stem that takes a portion of the stimulus and asks you what role it plays in the argument is a Role of a Statement question. Start by finding the referenced statement in the stimulus and underlining it. Then read the argument in full, breaking it down into the evidence and conclusion. Focus on the structure of the argument and how the underlined statement fits into that structure.

Step 2: Untangle the Stimulus

The question stem focuses on the "complaint of several centuries ago that powerful memory and extemporaneous eloquence were being destroyed," which is found in the second sentence. Underline it and then go back to the top and parse the argument's structure.

In the first sentence, the author identifies a common present-day complaint that electronic media has corroded intellectual skills fostered by literature. Then the author presents a similar complaint from centuries ago: The spread of the written word was destroying intellectual skills fostered by oral culture. The author then concludes that the human mind will merely change, not degrade.

Step 3: Make a Prediction

The referenced statement is an old complaint that the author uses to put into perspective the current complaint. The author uses both to support the conclusion that the human mind is evolving and adapting, not deteriorating. Therefore, the statement in question is evidence and being used as an analogy to dismiss the alleged coming harm to the human mind. As you move to the answer choices, make sure you understand the conclusion of the stimulus as well. Many Role of a Statement answer choices will indicate that the statement is "evidence in support of the claim that . . ." To be correct, the answer must *accurately* describe the conclusion that the evidence supports.

Step 4: Evaluate the Answer Choices

(C) correctly matches the role of the statement. The complaint from centuries ago did revolve around a cultural change, and the author uses it to downplay concerns that such changes are harmful to the human mind.

(A) incorrectly describes the conclusion of the argument. This answer choice actually describes the current complaint, which the author then proceeds to downplay.

(B) is Out of Scope. This choice makes up a conclusion that is found nowhere in the argument.

(D) is a tempting answer yet subtly distorts the conclusion. The author may actually accept that intellectual skills fostered by literary media *are* being lost in the shift to electronic media. But the author's point is that this loss of some skills (and likely replacement by others) should not be considered a degradation of the human mind, just a change.

(E) is incorrect because the author uses this example in support of her argument. The author does not dismiss it, nor is there any suggestion that the statement would be used by those the author counters.

10. (E) Method of Argument ★★★★

Step 1: Identify the Question Type

A question that asks you to identify the method, strategy, or technique employed by the author is a Method of Argument question. Focus on the structure, or *how* the author constructs the argument.

Step 2: Untangle the Stimulus

Gamba first points out someone else's claim: Muñoz believes that there is citywide opposition to a new water system, based on an *overwhelming* vote by a neighborhood association. Gamba then attacks Muñoz's evidence. Gamba points out that only 25 of 350 members voted, and only 15 of those opposed the new water system. Finally, Gamba asserts that "the 15 opposing votes represent far less than 1 percent of Hopeville's population." Gamba then concludes that "so few votes" should not be taken as representative of the majority of residents.

Step 3: Make a Prediction

With enough Flaw question practice, you should recognize the classic LSAT flaw of representativeness that Gamba highlights. Gamba attacks the assumption that a subset or survey group represents the broader population. Notice, however, that Gamba's conclusion is that Muñoz's claim is not *necessarily* correct; Gamba does *not* go so far as to say the claim is incorrect or, further, that the city *supports* the water system.

Step 4: Evaluate the Answer Choices

(E) is correct. This describes exactly what the author does. Gamba tries to cast doubt on Muñoz's conclusion by claiming that 15 opposing votes is too small a percentage of all voters to be representative.

(A) is a Distortion. The first part is accurate, but Gamba questions the vote by saying the number of voters is too *small* to be representative. Gamba does not suggest that the representativeness flaw is because people with certain views are more likely to vote.

(B) is a Distortion. Gamba argues that the statistical data is insufficient, not that it can be manipulated to support any view.

(C) is not an accurate description of what the author does. At a very general level, in LSAT arguments, the truth of the premises usually does not guarantee the truth of the conclusion. Gamba points out something more specific. Indeed, in this case, the author does not necessarily accept the truth of Muñoz's premise, which is that the neighborhood association *overwhelmingly* opposes the new water system. Muñoz uses the association's opposition to claim that there is citywide opposition. Gamba, however, points out that the vote was not *overwhelming*. Also, Gamba is not trying to *refute* Muñoz's conclusion; Gamba merely points out that it does not necessarily follow.

(D) is incorrect because Gamba accepts the accuracy of the numbers in the vote. Gamba merely says those numbers don't necessarily mean what Muñoz says they do. The possibility of confirming or disconfirming the evidence is Out of Scope.

11. (B) Main Point ★★★★

Step 1: Identify the Question Type

The question stem explicitly asks you for the main conclusion of the argument.

Step 2: Untangle the Stimulus

The first sentence is the author's conclusion: a recommendation. Identifying the conclusion may be somewhat difficult here because the last phrase in the argument is both a recommendation and emphasized by the word *clearly*. However, the entire last sentence provides reasons for using the double-blind techniques recommended in the first sentence. If unsure, ask yourself which piece supports the other. Which makes sense: (1) Scientists should use double-blind techniques because scientists should try to avoid misinterpretations, or (2) scientists should try to avoid misinterpretations because scientists should use double-blind techniques? The former does and the latter does not.

Step 3: Make a Prediction

Find the answer that matches the recommendation to use double-blind techniques whenever possible. Avoid answers that stray into the evidence, formulate the assumption, or speculate beyond the stated conclusion.

Step 4: Evaluate the Answer Choices

(B) is correct. It matches the recommendation to use double-blind techniques as much as possible.

(A) incorrectly focuses on the evidence describing what double-blind techniques help to prevent.

(C) incorrectly focuses on the evidence, and speculates beyond that evidence as well. The author doesn't mention what scientists *do*, just what they *should* do.

(D) fails to mention double-blind techniques, which are integral to the author's conclusion. **(D)** rephrases the final sentence, which is merely a piece of evidence.

(E) is Extreme and a Distortion. The author says double-blind techniques help *mitigate* subjectivity, but does not say that those techniques *ensure* objectivity.

12. (D) Point at Issue ★★★★

Step 1: Identify the Question Type

A question asking what two people "disagree" about is a Point at Issue question. Identify what both speakers address and where their opinions differ.

Step 2: Untangle the Stimulus

Taylor concludes that a specific claim, like all mathematically precise claims, is suspect because science cannot establish such exact claims.

Sandra, on the other hand, doesn't address the specific claim Taylor discusses. Instead, she asserts that precise claims need not always be doubted because some scientific disciplines can yield extremely precise results.

Step 3: Make a Prediction

The point of disagreement is about whether to doubt all precise scientific claims. If you do not recognize a point of disagreement, dive right into the answers, asking in turn whether each speaker has an opinion on the answer choice and whether those opinions conflict. Watch out for answers that mention topics that only one person addresses or on which they might actually agree.

Step 4: Evaluate the Answer Choices

(D) is correct. Taylor believes that *all* mathematically precise results are inherently suspect while Sandra believes that *some* sciences can yield precise results.

(A) is incorrect. While you know Taylor would be suspect of such results, Sandra doesn't mention this specific finding. You can't know whether Sandra would think this is one of those scientific disciplines for which she thinks precise results *can* be obtained.

(B) says the same thing as **(A)**, only slightly stronger. Again, you do not know Sandra's beliefs regarding the possibility of precision in this particular scientific discipline.

(C) is wrong for the same reason the first two answer choices are. It is unknown whether the study of verbal and nonverbal communication is one of the fields of scientific study within which Sandra believes precise results are possible.

(E) is Out of Scope. While Taylor mentions inherently suspect claims, Sandra doesn't. Moreover, neither speaker addresses the falsity of scientific claims in general.

CHAPTER 4

Assumption Family Questions

As you learned in Chapter 3, the ability to analyze arguments is a valuable skill for LSAT mastery. A student who is able to separate evidence from conclusion in an LSAT argument will dominate Main Point, Role of a Statement, and Method of Argument questions. But this skill is useful for other, even more important question types. In this chapter, you'll face Assumption, Flaw, Strengthen, Weaken, and select Principle questions—together known as the Assumption Family questions—that also require you to quickly and effectively analyze arguments into their constituent parts. There is one big difference, though, between the types of questions you saw in Chapter 3 and the types of questions you'll see in this chapter: here, the untangling of arguments into their explicit parts (evidence and conclusion) is an important but insufficient task. That's because Assumption Family questions also depend on your ability to determine the implicit assumption, or unstated premise, of an argument. They reward test takers who are constantly skeptical of the arguments presented and, more precisely, skeptical of the shift from the author's evidence to the author's conclusion.

One thing that is consistently true about arguments on the LSAT is that too little evidence is provided in support of a conclusion that the author reaches too hastily. This jump to the conclusion means that there is an informational gap between the evidence and the conclusion. Because of this gap in the argument's reasoning, the testmaker is able to generate questions that test your ability to do a number of things: to find the assumption in an argument, to point out the error in an author's reasoning, or to strengthen or weaken an argument.

LSAT STRATEGY

Every Assumption Family argument contains:

- A conclusion—the author's main point: an assertion, evaluation, or recommendation
- Evidence—the facts and information the author presents in support of the conclusion
- An assumption—the *unstated* premise that logically connects the evidence to the conclusion

Knowing the structure of these arguments is crucial to test takers. By learning and understanding the common ways in which an LSAT argument can move from evidence to conclusion and by developing strategies to identify an author's assumption (the unstated evidence in an argument), you are able to anticipate, or predict, the correct answer choice before you even begin evaluating the answer choices. For the vast majority of the questions discussed in this section, predicting the correct answer will help you earn more points, and earn them more quickly, than will a process of elimination or guesswork.

This chapter will focus on two big ideas: In the first half of the chapter, you'll learn to identify the common ways in which arguments on the LSAT move from evidence to conclusion. In the second half of the chapter, you'll learn to approach strategically the question types that reward the ability to analyze arguments. Understanding the structure of arguments and identifying authors' assumptions are the most valuable skills you can develop for the LSAT. In fact, more than a quarter of all questions on the LSAT test your ability to do just these things.

LEARNING OBJECTIVES

In this chapter, you'll learn to:

- Identify Mismatched Concepts in an argument.
- Identify Overlooked Possibilities in an argument.
- Identify the assumption in both types of arguments.
- Use an argument's assumption to predict a correct answer for each Assumption Family question type.

The first thing we'll do is discuss the ways in which arguments on the LSAT tend to be constructed. The jump from the evidence to the conclusion takes two basic forms: either (1) the author moves from a discussion of particular terms and concepts in the evidence to a conclusion that introduces a new, seemingly unrelated term or concept (what we will refer to as a "Mismatched Concepts" argument), or (2) the author uses relevant evidence to jump to a conclusion that is too extreme, without considering potential objections or alternatives to that conclusion (an "Overlooked Possibilities" argument).

Mismatched Concepts

Consider this argument:

> Chemical X is harmful because poison is harmful.

Does this argument seem completely sound to you? It probably doesn't. That's because, just like the arguments you will see on test day, this argument is incomplete. There is a gap between what the evidence states and what the author concludes. Assumption Family arguments always follow this pattern—the evidence presented is never enough to completely support the argument's conclusion. Your job, then, will be to determine *why* a particular argument's evidence isn't enough to establish its conclusion. Take a moment now and describe to yourself what's wrong with the Chemical X argument. Here's the catch, though: You have to do it without using any of the following words (or synonyms): chemical X, poison, harmful, or assumes.

Having a hard time? There's a good chance you already know what's missing in this argument: The piece of evidence that should be there but isn't. But how can you know what it is? And more importantly, how will you know what the missing piece is in more complicated LSAT arguments? To learn how to spot the problem in an argument, you first need to learn what those problems are.

Take a look at this argument from a different angle. Imagine a game in which a person is given a piece of evidence, and his task is to predict a conclusion based on that evidence. If he guesses correctly, he is awarded a million-dollar prize. Now, imagine that the person is given this piece of evidence: "poison is harmful." How long would it take him to guess that the conclusion is "Chemical X is harmful"? Frankly, that contestant is probably never going to see that million-dollar prize. The reason is simple: The concept *Chemical X* is, for all we know, completely unrelated to the concept *poison*. That's the problem with this argument: The author is using evidence that, without an additional, unstated assumption, may be unrelated to the conclusion.

Mismatched Concepts: The Basics

Prepare

LSAT STRATEGY

How can you tell an argument contains mismatched concepts?

- The terms or concepts in the evidence appear unrelated to the conclusion.
- A new term or concept—not related to the evidence—appears in the conclusion.

In Assumption Family questions, the LSAT consistently tests your ability to determine when an author is using evidence that is not inherently relevant (i.e., that may be unrelated) to the conclusion. Think of these as Apples and Oranges arguments: the author is concluding something about apples, while the evidence deals with oranges. Just because the author *assumes* that a relationship between the terms or concepts is apparent does not mean that the relationship is true. Our job then is to learn how to spot when the author is making this leap, then build a bridge that logically connects the mismatched concepts. If properly constructed, this bridge—the author's assumption—completes the argument by "filling in" the gap between the evidence and the conclusion. The good news is that there is a straightforward, repeatable process you can go through to derive the assumption when you're dealing with Mismatched Concepts arguments.

Let's go back to Chemical X to illustrate the process. First, one of the most common signs of a Mismatched Concepts argument is a conclusion that brings up a new concept that did not appear in the evidence. Taking a look at our argument, it's clear that the new, out-of-nowhere term in the conclusion is *Chemical X*.

Conclusion	Evidence
Chemical X is harmful	because poison is harmful

Next, take a look at the evidence and check for any mismatched concepts there—a concept that is in the evidence but never showed up in the conclusion. In this case, that would be *poison*.

Conclusion	Evidence
Chemical X is harmful	because **poison** is harmful

Now that you have your mismatched concepts, ask whether these two things are inherently related to each other. Usually the concepts *could* be related, but they don't *have to be* related—this is what creates the gap between the evidence and the conclusion. In this instance, given that we have no idea what Chemical X is, it's safe to say that it isn't by definition related to poison. It's possible, but without more evidence, there's no way to know for sure.

If you have mismatched concepts, then relate them to each other in a way that fixes the argument. Ask what the author must believe to be true about *Chemical X* and *poison* to fix this argument. The answer is that the author needs Chemical X *to be* a poison. If that's true, then the argument is complete! If Chemical X is a poison, and poisons are harmful, then it must be true that Chemical X is harmful:

Chemical X is harmful because

Chemical X is a poison and **poison is harmful.**

Mismatched Concepts arguments won't always use such straightforward terminology. In fact, many arguments on the LSAT contain academic, legal, or philosophical jargon that might make it difficult to understand the argument in full. Don't get flustered. Sometimes, the abstract nature of the concepts presented in arguments makes it easier for you to spot the mismatched concepts in the evidence and conclusion. Take this argument as an example:

Dweezil is a zulzey alien. Therefore, Dweezil can perform the amazing *yeerchta* move.

These are all made-up terms, of course—we have no real-world understanding of these things. Start by looking for any mismatched concepts in the conclusion. In both the evidence and conclusion, we have Dweezil; because there is no gap between Dweezil in the evidence and Dweezil in the conclusion, we don't have to "build a bridge" between them. The conclusion mentions the amazing *yeerchta* move, which never showed up in the evidence. From there, search the evidence for signs of a mismatch—zulzey aliens are discussed there, though such things are never mentioned in the conclusion. Because these concepts are made up, there is no inherent (i.e., "by definition") relationship between them. However, based on the structure of the argument, we can relate the two concepts in a way that makes sense of the argument. In this case, the author's assumption must be that all zulzey aliens are able to do the amazing *yeerchta* move. If the author had simply bothered to mention that in the evidence, then there would be no problem with this argument. With the assumption filled in, the argument becomes whole, and the conclusion makes sense; it follows logically from the evidence.

Mismatched Concepts arguments don't always use abstract or unfamiliar terms, though. In fact, the more realistic or understandable an argument is, the more cognizant you need to be of your *own* assumptions. There are times on the LSAT when it can be all too easy for you to mentally fill in an argument's assumption without even realizing it—you read the argument and think, "Oh, right, that makes sense." Take this argument as an example:

Kim is a nice person. Therefore, it's easy for Kim to make friends.

A quick look at the conclusion shows us that it's about making friends, but the evidence is about being a nice person. The next step is to ask ourselves if these things are necessarily related to each other. It's easy to think, "Okay, sure. Kim is a nice person. People tend to like other people who are nice, so Kim should be able to make friends easily. Makes sense to me!" The problem is that the relevance of being nice to the ease of making friends is not explicitly stated; it has not, *within this argument*, been established. Maybe being nice does affect your ability to make friends, but then again, maybe not. The argument's assumption, then, is that people who are nice make friends easily. Indeed, if this assumption were *not* true, then the evidence would not support the conclusion.

Even when an argument seems to make all the sense in the world, evaluate the evidence and conclusion with an eye toward spotting mismatched concepts. Are the terms and concepts presented in the evidence *inherently* relevant to those in the conclusion? When you are a lawyer, part of your job will be to expose the weaknesses in the other side's arguments. Looking at every argument and saying, "Sure, that argument makes all the sense in the world to me!" is, to put it mildly, an ineffective legal skill. Finding the gap in an argument, on the other hand, will expose its weakness. Starting today, train yourself to become a skeptical thinker.

LSAT STRATEGY

When tackling an argument containing Mismatched Concepts:

- Separate concepts in evidence from concepts in conclusion.
- Identify the mismatched concepts that the author assumes are somehow related.
- Find the assumption by making a sentence that logically relates the mismatched concepts—this sentence serves as a bridge to make the evidence relevant to the conclusion.

Mismatched Concepts: Sample Arguments

Here are some brief Mismatched Concepts arguments and the assumption of each. After reviewing these examples, you'll have a chance to try some others on your own.

Argument	Analysis
Cady attended North High School. Therefore, Cady is good at sculpture.	The author assumes North High School students are good at sculpture.
Spending time with pets relieves stress. Therefore, spending time with pets makes people happy.	The author assumes relieving stress makes people happy.
Ivan is an astronaut. Therefore, Ivan doesn't like jazz.	The author assumes astronauts don't like jazz.
You haven't done your homework. Therefore, you can't go to the concert.	The author assumes you need to do your homework before going to the concert.
People who play table tennis are also good at skiing. Therefore, the wealthy are good at skiing.	The author assumes that the wealthy play table tennis.
The city council members are all vegan. Therefore, Grace is vegan.	The author assumes Grace is a member of the city council.

Practice Practice your ability to spot the gap between concepts in the evidence and the conclusion by analyzing the following simple arguments. In each one of these arguments, follow this simple approach:

- Separate the evidence from the conclusion.
- Identify a term or concept in the conclusion that is not present in the evidence.
- Look in the evidence for an important term or concept not in the conclusion.
- Determine the relationship the author assumes exists between those terms.
- Put the mismatched terms or concepts into a sentence to form the author's assumption.

After each argument, feel free to look at the expert analysis on the next two pages. If you're feeling confident, try all four and then read the expert's thinking.

Argument	My Analysis
1. Brand D teddy bears are fluffy; therefore, children like Brand D teddy bears.	
2. Because Ariel likes to have fun, he enjoys amusement parks.	
3. Gopher tortoises burrow in the desert. Therefore, gopher tortoises don't eat grubs.	
4. People who text while driving are not safe drivers because one needs to be attentive in order to be a safe driver.	

Expert Analysis for the Practice exercise may be found on the following page. ▶ ▶ ▶

Expert Analysis

Now take a look at how an LSAT expert would analyze these arguments you've just evaluated.

Argument	Analysis
1. Brand D teddy bears are fluffy; therefore, children like Brand D teddy bears.	Conclusion: Children like Brand D teddy bears. Evidence: Brand D teddy bears are fluffy. Analyze: "[C]hildren like" is in the conclusion but not evidence. "[F]luffy" is in the evidence but not conclusion. The author assumes some sort of relationship exists between these distinct concepts. Connect the terms in a sentence to form the piece of evidence that the author assumes is true: "Children like things that are fluffy."
2. Because Ariel likes to have fun, he enjoys amusement parks.	Conclusion: Ariel enjoys amusement parks. Evidence: Ariel likes to have fun. Analyze: The conclusion is about "amusement parks," but there's nothing about them in the evidence. The evidence is about "having fun," but there's nothing in the conclusion about fun. The author assumes a relationship exists between these distinct concepts. Connect the terms in a sentence to form the piece of evidence that the author assumes is true: "Anyone who likes to have fun enjoys amusement parks."
3. Gopher tortoises burrow in the desert. Therefore, gopher tortoises don't eat grubs.	Conclusion: Gopher tortoises don't eat grubs. Evidence: Gopher tortoises burrow in the desert. Analyze: The conclusion is about "not eating grubs," but the evidence isn't about that at all. The evidence is about "burrowing in the desert," but that isn't in the conclusion. The author assumes some sort of relationship exists between these otherwise unrelated concepts. Connect the terms in a sentence to form the piece of evidence that the author assumes is true: "Creatures that burrow in the desert don't eat grubs."

Argument	Analysis
4. People who text while driving are not safe drivers because one needs to be attentive in order to be a safe driver.	Conclusion: Drivers who are texting aren't safe. Evidence: Safe drivers must be attentive. Analyze: The conclusion is about "drivers who text," but the evidence never mentions that. The evidence is about "being attentive," but that isn't in the conclusion. The author assumes some sort of relationship exists between these two concepts. Connect the terms in a sentence to form the piece of evidence that the author assumes is true: "Drivers who text aren't attentive."

The LSAT, of course, will present more difficult arguments than the ones you just saw, but the fundamental *structure* of arguments with mismatched concepts will remain the same. Regardless of the topic being discussed in the argument—whether it be on matters philosophical, legal, or scientific—your method and objective will always remain the same. First, separate evidence from conclusion. Then, analyze the concepts discussed in both. If the author introduces a distinct or unrelated term or idea in the conclusion, find the assumption by connecting a mismatched concept in the evidence to the mismatched concept in the conclusion.

Practice Try that now with an actual LSAT argument.

LSAT Argument	My Analysis
Press release: A comprehensive review evaluating the medical studies done up to the present time has found no reason to think that drinking coffee in normal amounts harms the coffee-drinker's heart. So coffee drinkers can relax and enjoy their beverage—it is safe to drink coffee. *PrepTest101 Sec2 Q1*	

Did you see a new term or concept in the conclusion that seemed to come out of the blue? Did the evidence contain terms that are not inherently relevant (i.e., might be unrelated) to those in the conclusion drawn by the author?

Expert Analysis

Take a look at how an LSAT expert would break down this argument.

LSAT Argument	Analysis
Press release: A comprehensive review evaluating the medical studies done up to the present time has found no reason to think that drinking coffee in normal amounts harms the coffee-drinker's heart. So coffee drinkers can relax and enjoy their beverage—it is safe to drink coffee. *PrepTest101 Sec2 Q1*	Keywords "studies" and "So" indicate evidence and conclusion, respectively. Conclusion: Drinking coffee is safe. *because* Evidence: Drinking coffee in normal amounts does not harm a coffee drinker's heart. The mismatched terms are *not harms the coffee-drinker's heart* and *safe to drink coffee.* So the author's assumption connects these terms: "What does not harm the heart is, overall, safe."

Even though this argument comes from an actual LSAT question, it is really no more complicated than the examples you saw earlier in this chapter. Once the expert has identified the evidence and conclusion, she simplifies the argument to herself: "Okay, so the press release says that because drinking normal amounts of coffee doesn't harm the heart, coffee is safe to drink." Phrased that way—that *simply*—the gap in the argument becomes much easier to spot. By equating "doesn't harm the heart" with "overall safe," the press release overlooks any number of possible objections: What about consuming more than normal amounts of coffee? What about the possibility that coffee harms some other part of the body? Note again the steps the expert works through to arrive at this point: logically separating and paraphrasing the evidence and conclusion, looking for a gap between terms discussed in each, then connecting those mismatched terms to formulate the argument's assumption.

Hopefully you're starting to get the hang of evaluating arguments that introduce a new, unrelated concept in the conclusion. Let's dive in even deeper and discuss some of the most common relationships you'll see between mismatched concepts in LSAT arguments.

Going Deeper: Common Relationships between Mismatched Concepts

Prepare By now, you've seen the benefit of skeptically looking at the relationship between the concepts in an argument's evidence and its conclusion. If the author introduces, seemingly out of nowhere, a new term or concept in an argument's conclusion, suspect a Mismatched Concepts argument. Connect those mismatched concepts in a sentence to identify the argument's assumption. Fortunately, a few relationships between the mismatched concepts will make up the bulk of the arguments you will see. Knowing what they are can make you faster and more efficient at tackling Assumption Family questions.

LSAT STRATEGY

The most commonly assumed relationships between mismatched concepts:

- The terms or concepts are alike/equivalent.
- The terms or concepts are mutually exclusive.
- One term or concept is needed for the other.
- One term or concept represents another.

For many questions, merely finding the mismatched concepts is enough to get you to the correct answer, as the correct answer will be the only choice to mention both of them. But for more challenging questions, you may be asked to choose between two or more answer choices, each one of which contains the same mismatched concepts. The difference between the answer choices will be the specific relationships between the mismatched concepts. One answer choice may say that the two concepts are mutually exclusive, while another may say that they are alike. As you go deeper into Assumption Family questions, the ability to determine the difference between an argument that assumes two things are equivalent and an argument that assumes one thing is representative of another, for example, will become increasingly important. Fortunately, the fact that most arguments make use of one of just a few relationships makes this easier than it may sound.

Consider the following statement:

> I like games because I am serious.

The conclusion is about liking games, but the evidence is about being serious. These two concepts are not inherently (i.e., "by definition") related to each other, so the author is making an assumption. In this case, the author assumes that liking games and being serious are equivalent to each other—that one leads to the other. But what if we change the wording slightly:

> I don't like games because I am serious.

The statement uses all the same terms as the previous one; it's still about liking games and being serious. Now, however, there's a very different relationship between liking games and being serious. The author in this example assumes that liking games and being serious are incompatible or mutually exclusive—you can't like games and be serious at the same time.

Now let's change the wording one last time:

> I don't like games because I am not serious.

This last example again has the same mismatched concepts as do the previous examples, but here, the terms have a different relationship: The author assumes that being serious is a necessary condition to liking games. It's worth noting that a Mismatched Concepts argument in the form of *Not X because Not Y* will always mean that the evidence concept (Y) is necessary for the conclusion concept (X). Expect answer choices in these arguments to test you on which concept is necessary!

While the three relationships just discussed are the most common, there is a fourth relationship that you will probably also see on the LSAT. In these arguments, the author assumes that one thing represents another. Representation arguments on the LSAT usually involve a mismatch between one group in the evidence and a different group in the conclusion. Consider the following argument:

> The oranges at my local store are all rotten. I know this because the three I just bought from that store are rotten.

Notice that the author uses information about the three oranges he bought to draw a conclusion about *all* of the oranges in the local store. The author assumes that the three oranges purchased must represent all of the oranges at the store. Be on the lookout for arguments in which the author uses a particular sample in the evidence and tries to draw an overly general conclusion from it. Though this kind of argument is most common in Flaw questions, it can show up in any of the Assumption Family questions.

The reality is that most Mismatched Concepts arguments on the LSAT are just more elaborate versions of the four arguments above. Your job isn't to find a new and unique relationship between mismatched concepts every time you see an Assumption Family argument—that would be frustrating and far too difficult. Instead, your goal is to spot the mismatched concepts, then connect the concepts in a way that matches up with other arguments like these.

Take a look at the following LSAT argument and try to match it up with one of the four relationships you just learned about:

Barnes: The two newest employees at this company have salaries that are too high for the simple tasks normally assigned to new employees and duties that are too complex for inexperienced workers. Hence, the salaries and the complexity of the duties of these two newest employees should be reduced.

PrepTest107 Sec1 Q5

The keyword "[h]ence" indicates the argument's conclusion. Notice that before *hence*, in the evidence, the author refers to the subjects of the argument as "inexperienced workers." After *hence*, those same people are referred to as the two "newest employees." These are the argument's mismatched concepts. The next question is this: Which stock relationship does the author need these two concepts to have? If you said alike/equivalent, then you are correct. Much like the author of the very first example (liking games and being serious), this author is assuming that the mismatched concepts are equivalent in some way—that being new entails being inexperienced. Now, you might have rephrased this a bit and thought the author assumes that being new is incompatible with having experience. That also would be a correct way of dealing with the negative phrasing in the argument.

Practice Now try some LSAT Mismatched Concepts arguments on your own. Your job is to match the following two arguments to one of these four examples:

- I like games because I am serious. (alike/equivalent)
- I don't like games because I am serious. (mutually exclusive)
- I don't like games because I am not serious. (need evidence for conclusion)
- The store's oranges are all rotten because the ones I bought from them are rotten. (representation)

LSAT Argument	My Analysis
5. Sociologist: The intended function of news is to give us information on which to act. But in a consumer society, news becomes a product to be manufactured and dispensed to the consumer. An enormous industry for the production and consumption of news has evolved, and we ingest news with an insatiable appetite. Under such circumstances, news is primarily entertaining and cannot, therefore, serve its intended function. *PrepTest105 Sec1 Q18*	
6. Art Historian: Robbins cannot pass judgment on Stuart's art. While Robbins understands the art of Stuart too well to dismiss it, she does not understand it well enough to praise it. *PrepTest104 Sec4 Q20*	

Expert Analysis

Having an understanding of the specific relationship between mismatched terms will help you form the correct assumption. Do the terms have a positive relationship? Are they mutually exclusive? Check out how an LSAT expert evaluated the same arguments.

LSAT Argument	Analysis
5. Sociologist: The intended function of news is to give us information on which to act. But in a consumer society, news becomes a product to be manufactured and dispensed to the consumer. An enormous industry for the production and consumption of news has evolved, and we ingest news with an insatiable appetite. Under such circumstances, news is primarily entertaining and cannot, therefore, serve its intended function. *PrepTest105 Sec1 Q18*	Conclusion: Under the described circumstances, news cannot serve its intended function to give us information to act on. *because* Evidence: Under the described circumstances, news is primarily entertaining. The author in the evidence refers to news as "primarily entertaining." The conclusion indicates that the news "cannot, therefore, serve its intended function." If the conclusion contains a vague term (*intended function*) that is defined elsewhere, it is important to build that definition into your paraphrase of the conclusion. So the author shifts from indicating that news is *primarily entertaining* to concluding that it **cannot** give us *information to act upon*, which assumes those concepts are mutually exclusive. This is just a more elaborate version of "I don't like games because I am serious."
6. Art Historian: Robbins cannot pass judgment on Stuart's art. While Robbins understands the art of Stuart too well to dismiss it, she does not understand it well enough to praise it. *PrepTest104 Sec4 Q20*	Conclusion: Robbins can't judge Stuart's art. *because* Evidence: 1) Robbins understands Stuart's art too well to dismiss it; 2) Robbins doesn't understand it well enough to praise it. The author jumps from evidence that Robbins can neither dismiss nor praise the art to a conclusion that he can't judge the art. This assumes that judging art requires being able at least to either dismiss or praise it, and is a match for: "I don't like games because I am not serious."

Whenever you are trying to link mismatched concepts for your prediction, keep the four common relationships in mind. The LSAT has a limited menu of relationships, and your job is to simply learn to recognize them in slightly different clothing.

Yet another tool for analyzing Mismatched Concepts arguments is in the toolbox of every LSAT expert: understanding Formal Logic.

Formal Logic in Mismatched Concepts

Formal Logic can be a valuable skill for untangling the arguments in LSAT Assumption Family questions. In this section, we'll lay out for you some of the most basic patterns of Formal Logic found in Mismatched Concepts arguments.

A quick word of warning before we begin: Though a mastery of Formal Logic is a valuable tool that will help you in this section, most Assumption Family questions don't have conditional statements at all. The most important skill you can develop in evaluating Mismatched Concepts arguments is the ability to recognize the gap between evidence and conclusion and then connect the mismatched terms or concepts. Looking at every argument as a Formal Logic puzzle that needs to be decoded will lead to frustration. Instead, think of tackling Mismatched Concepts arguments as a two-step process: Start by identifying the relationships between the mismatched terms or concepts and then, if needed, use Formal Logic to determine the directionality of the concepts in the assumption.

LEARNING OBJECTIVES

In this section, you'll learn to:

- Recognize common Formal Logic patterns in arguments containing Mismatched Concepts.
- Use knowledge of Formal Logic and contrapositives to determine an argument's assumption.
- Understand when directionality of terms is important.

When Mismatched Concepts arguments on the LSAT contain Formal Logic, the most basic structural pattern is as follows: "If A then B. Therefore, if A then C," where the letters A, B, and C represent unique terms.

	Sample Argument	My Analysis
evidence	If A → B	
assumption		
conclusion	If A → C	

First of all, how would you know that this argument contains mismatched concepts? The evidence discusses A and B, while the conclusion jumps to a discussion of A and C. This is about as straightforward as a Mismatched Concepts argument gets. The author must assume that B and C are in some way connected. Give it a shot: How would you fill in the assumption in this argument?

	Sample Argument	My Analysis
evidence	If A → B	If A → **B**
assumption		
conclusion	If A → C	If A → **C**

If you said that the assumption must be "If B then C" (or drew If B → C), then good work.

	Sample Argument	Analysis
evidence	If A → B	If A → **B**
assumption		**If B → C**
conclusion	If A → C	If A → **C**

This assumption, combined with the evidence, produces a chain of logic: If A → B → C. It is then clear that the author can conclude: If A → C. To see how this plays out in an argument that uses less abstract terms, consider this argument:

> Dolphins are social animals that live in groups. Therefore, dolphins are intelligent.

Both the evidence and the conclusion discuss dolphins, but only the evidence mentions "social animals," while the conclusion moves to a discussion of "intelligence." Therefore, it's easy to see that this is a Mismatched Concepts argument. But how would you know that the evidence and conclusion also use Formal Logic? Words like *are*, *every*, and *any* allow the statements to be turned into conditional statements:

	Sample Argument	My Analysis
evidence	If dolphins → social animals	
assumption		
conclusion	If dolphins → intelligent	

To make this argument work, we need to make a connection between "social animals" and "intelligent." But which direction? Is it that animals that are intelligent live in groups? Or that social animals are intelligent? The missing piece, the assumption, will not just connect the mismatched terms but connect them in the right direction:

	Sample Argument	Analysis
evidence	If dolphins → social animals	If dolphins → **social animals**
assumption		**If social animals → intelligent**
conclusion	If dolphins → intelligent	If dolphins → **intelligent**

As you can see, the argument fits the original pattern of "If A → B; therefore, If A → C." That means the assumption must be If B → C for the conclusion to be logically inferred. Now, based on the previous example, which of these would be an assumption that would allow the conclusion to be logically drawn?

(1) Social animals that live in groups are intelligent.

(2) All intelligent animals are social and live in groups.

In this case, the correct choice is (1), not (2). The assumption is that social animals living in groups must be intelligent, not that all animals that are intelligent are social animals living in groups. Although the testmaker won't always include answer choices with the same terms relating to each other in different ways, it does happen occasionally. By offering two answer choices that, to the unprepared test taker, appear nearly identical—and particularly by offering two distinct choices in which the relationship between concepts is alike/equivalent—the testmaker is able to increase the difficulty of a question. This shows up most often in Sufficient Assumption questions, which we will discuss later in the chapter. For now, just remember this: When you analyze an argument that contains Formal Logic, pay attention to which terms are sufficient and which are necessary.

To see why distinguishing mismatched concepts in the necessary terms from those in the sufficient terms is so valuable, consider another Formal Logic pattern often found in LSAT arguments: "If A, then B. Therefore, if C, then B."

	Sample Argument	My Analysis
evidence	If A → B	
assumption		
conclusion	If C → B	

This time, the mismatched terms or concepts are in the sufficient terms of the evidence and of the conclusion. Identify them.

	Sample Argument	My Analysis
evidence	If A → B	If **A** → B
assumption		
conclusion	If C → B	If **C** → B

In this case, the author assumes that if something is a C (or has the characteristic C), then that thing is an A (or has the characteristic A).

	Sample Argument	Analysis
evidence	If A → B	If **A** → B
assumption		**If C → A**
conclusion	If C → B	If **C** → B

You may recognize this pattern as fitting an argument we used earlier in the chapter: "Chemical X is harmful because poison is harmful." To match the diagrams above, rewrite the argument as "If poison (A), then harmful (B). Therefore, if Chemical X (C), then harmful (B)." As we clearly saw, the author assumes that Chemical X (C) is a poison (A).

Here's another argument, fleshed out in "real world" terms, that illustrates this pattern:

> All first-year associates at the firm will be mentored by a partner. Thus, Mark will be mentored by a partner.

Lay out this argument to match the diagrams above and determine the author's unstated assumption.

	Sample Argument	**My Analysis**
evidence	If 1st year assoc → partner mentors	
assumption		
conclusion	If Mark → partner mentors	

Here, the mismatched terms/concepts are in the sufficient terms of both the evidence and the conclusion.

	Sample Argument	**Analysis**
evidence	If 1st year assoc → partner mentors	If **1st year assoc** → partner mentors
assumption		**If Mark** → **1st year assoc**
conclusion	If Mark → partner mentors	If **Mark** → partner mentors

The author must assume that Mark is a first-year associate at the firm.

A quick note about the direction of connection between the mismatched terms in these formal logic diagrams. If the mismatched concepts are on the right side of the arrows (the necessary side) then the direction of connection goes downward from evidence to conclusion. This is the most common configuration. If the mismatched concepts are on the left side of the arrow (the sufficient side) then the direction of connection goes upward from conclusion to evidence. This could also be visualized and remembered by using clockwise arrows going around the diagram connecting the four terms (note: the clockwise rule only works when evidence is placed above the conclusion). This always shows you the proper direction of connection. Here are the two arguments you just analyzed with arrows to illustrate this approach:

If **1st year** assoc → partner mentors	If dolphin → **social animal**
If **Mark** → partner mentors	If dolphin → **intelligent**

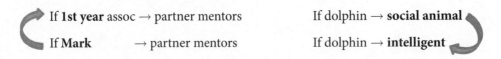

Making It More Difficult: Adding an Extra Concept in the Evidence

Though the most basic Formal Logic Mismatched Concepts argument structure includes three terms (two terms in the evidence and two terms in the conclusion, with one term in the evidence identical to one term in the conclusion), many arguments contain more than just three concepts. A common pattern is for the test-maker to construct arguments with one or more extra terms in the evidence. If the terms are necessary for each other, combine them and remove the redundant term. This makes the evidence simpler and, in turn, easier to compare to the conclusion. Here is the most common pattern for this type of argument on the LSAT:

	Sample Argument	My Analysis
evidence	If A → B If B → C	
assumption		
conclusion	If A → D	

Since the two statements in the evidence share term B—and note that B is the necessary term in one statement and the sufficient term in the other—they can be combined to simplify the evidence. Doing this reveals the terms that are unique to the evidence and to the conclusion.

	Sample Argument	My Analysis
evidence	If A → B If B → C	If A → **C**
assumption		
conclusion	If A → D	If A → **D**

That step reveals that we are back to the simple pattern illustrated by the argument about intelligent, social dolphins you saw above. The author assumes that all things C (or things with the attribute C) are things D (or things with the attribute D).

	Sample Argument	Analysis
evidence	If A → B If B → C	If A → **C**
assumption		**If C → D**
conclusion	If A →D	If A → **D**

Let's use another "real world" argument to illustrate this pattern as you will analyze it on the LSAT.

> All students in Dr. Peterson's class are juniors. Every junior has taken a public speaking class. Therefore, all students in Dr. Peterson's class have given a speech to a large crowd.

Start by laying out the argument in the diagram we've been using.

	Sample Argument	My Analysis
evidence	If Dr. P's student → junior If junior → speech class	
assumption		
conclusion	If Dr. P's student → speech to crowd	

Make sure that the two statements in the evidence can be combined. Once again, because the necessary term in the first statement is the same as the sufficient term in the second statement, they can. (Note that the order of the statements does not matter. The statements could still be combined if the original argument began "Every junior has taken a public speaking class. All students in Dr. Peterson's class are juniors.") Once the evidentiary statements are combined, identify the terms or concepts that are different between the evidence and the conclusion.

	Sample Argument	My Analysis
evidence	If Dr. P's student → junior If junior → speech class	If Dr. P's student → **speech class**
assumption		
conclusion	If Dr. P's student → speech to crowd	If Dr. P's student → **speech to crowd**

Finally, formulate the statement that logically links the author's evidence to his conclusion. That's the author's assumption.

	Sample Argument	Analysis
evidence	If Dr. P's student → junior If junior → speech class	If Dr. P's student → **speech class**
assumption		**If speech class → speech to crowd**
conclusion	If Dr. P's student → speech to crowd	If Dr. P's student → **speech to crowd**

Now, when you read through the argument, you can see that it is complete. If all of Dr. Peterson's students have had a speech class, and if everyone who has had a speech class has given a speech to a large crowd, then it is certain that anyone who is Dr. Peterson's student has given a speech to a large crowd. The additional term in the original argument ("junior") was just there to link up Dr. Peterson's students with the speech class attribute, but it plays no role in the author's unstated assumption. Recognizing this pattern will help you efficiently tackle Assumption Family questions in which the evidence contains two linked statements.

Mismatched Concepts in the Evidence

Mismatched Concepts arguments typically move from one concept in the evidence to a new concept in the conclusion, but it's also possible for an author to present two mismatched concepts in the evidence. Though this is rare, it does occasionally show up, so don't be surprised if you see such an argument on the exam. Here's the algebraic diagram for an argument of this type:

	Sample Argument	My Analysis
evidence	If A → B If C → D	
assumption		
conclusion	If A → D	

Notice two things. First, both of the terms in the conclusion are also present in the evidence; there is no mismatch there. Second, there is no way to link up the two evidentiary terms; they share no common terms. In such a case, the author's assumption (her missing, unstated "bridge") lies between the two pieces of evidence. Rewriting the diagram like this makes this clear.

	Sample Argument	My Analysis
evidence	If A → B	If A → **B**
assumption		
evidence	If C → D	If **C** → D
conclusion	If A → D	If A → D

Now you can see what the author has left out of the argument.

	Sample Argument	Analysis
evidence	If A → B	If A → **B**
assumption		**If B → C**
evidence	If C → D	If **C** → D
conclusion	If A → D	If A → D

Reading through this argument, you can see that it is complete and logical. If As are Bs, and Bs are Cs, and Cs are Ds, then it is valid to conclude that As are Ds.

For good measure, do the same analysis with a "real world" example.

> Whenever people watch a good movie, they get a happy feeling. And people always do the right thing when they feel the urge to help others. Therefore, watching a good movie makes people do the right thing.

Plug that argument into the diagram.

	Sample Argument	My Analysis
evidence	If good movie → happy feeling If urge to help → do the right thing	
assumption		
conclusion	If good movie → do the right thing	

Once again, both terms in the conclusion are found in the evidence, and there is no term shared between the two pieces of evidence. The author needs to bridge the two pieces of evidence; she is assuming they are linked.

	Sample Argument	My Analysis
evidence	If good movie → happy feeling	If good movie → **happy feeling**
assumption		
evidence	If urge to help → do the right thing	If **urge to help** → do the right thing
conclusion	If good movie → do the right thing	If good movie → do the right thing

Finally, determining the assumption, and reading it into the argument, reveals a complete, logical argument.

	Sample Argument	Analysis
evidence	If good movie → happy feeling	If good movie → **happy feeling**
assumption		**If happy feeling → urge to help**
evidence	If urge to help → do the right thing	If **urge to help** → do the right thing
conclusion	If good movie → do the right thing	If good movie → do the right thing

Again, an argument with mismatched concepts in the evidence is rare—in fact, you might not even see it on the LSAT you take. Just know that the testmaker *can* present an argument this way; to find the assumption, find the mismatched concepts in the evidence and connect them.

Strict Formal Logic statements tend to show up most often in Sufficient Assumption questions, which we will discuss in depth later in this chapter. In other Assumption Family questions, strict Formal Logic is less common. The thing to keep in mind is that the underlying Formal Logic structure of "If A → B (evidence); therefore, If A → C (conclusion)" *is* common. Knowing that this pattern underlies many of the Mismatched Concepts arguments you'll see on the LSAT will help you achieve mastery in Assumption Family questions. Remember to approach Mismatched Concepts arguments in two steps: Start by identifying the relationships between the mismatched terms or concepts and then, if needed, use Formal Logic to determine the directionality of the concepts in the assumption.

LSAT STRATEGY

Formal Logic in arguments containing Mismatched Concepts:

- The most common structure is: "If A → B; therefore, If A → C."
- When possible, connect multiple terms in the evidence and simplify.
- Difficult wrong answer choices may confuse necessary and sufficient terms.

You now have a more solid understanding of the common relationships and patterns you'll see in Mismatched Concepts arguments. Later in this chapter, you'll get much more practice identifying and analyzing these types of arguments in Assumption Family questions. Now, though, let's turn our attention to the other type of argument structure you'll see in Assumption Family arguments: Overlooked Possibilities.

Overlooked Possibilities

Consider this argument:

> Last night Maria parked her car in an area of town where many car thefts occur. This morning, Maria woke up and discovered that her car was no longer in its parking spot. Therefore, ________________.

Remember the million-dollar prize game we described earlier? Just like before, your job is to figure out what the conclusion is by filling in the blank. Take a moment and think about it.

Unlike in the argument you saw earlier about poison and Chemical X, you probably *would* be able to come up with the conclusion fairly quickly: "I bet the author's going to say that Maria's car was stolen." And if you guessed something along those lines, you're making a reasonable conjecture as to the author's conclusion. Remember, though, that the LSAT doesn't present complete, reasonable arguments—it presents incomplete arguments. Here's what an LSAT argument would likely say:

> Last night Maria parked her car in an area of town where many car thefts occur. This morning, Maria woke up and discovered that her car was no longer in its parking spot. Therefore, Maria's car *must* have been stolen.

Take a moment now and try to describe to yourself what is wrong with the LSAT version of this argument without using any of the words from the stimulus.

To understand what is wrong with the argument, begin by envisioning the author's argument as a road: The author is driving from the evidence to the conclusion. As far as she's concerned, it's a clear path, but an LSAT expert is trained to see all of the roadblocks along the way that the author can't. That's exactly what went wrong with the argument above: The author starts the trip with evidence that introduces the *possibility* of the car having been stolen, and from there she tries to reach a conclusion that it *must* be the explanation for the disappearance. Unfortunately for the author, there are many possible explanations for the car's disappearance, and if even one of them is possible, the author's entire conclusion falls apart. These are the roadblocks (in other words, the possible objections) to the argument. The only way the author's argument will work is if they're all removed.

Overlooked Possibilities: The Basics

Prepare Not all LSAT arguments have a problem of relevance. The reason why you could reasonably predict the conclusion in this argument is that it does use the right *kind* of evidence: The information given helps us figure out whether Maria's car was stolen. Contrast that with the Chemical X example from earlier in the chapter. In that argument, the evidence about poison didn't help us figure out whether Chemical X was harmful. In fact, on roughly half of the LSAT arguments you'll see on test day, the author is using pieces of evidence that *are* in some way related and relevant to the terms and concepts in the conclusion, but the author's conclusion will be too extreme for its evidence. Instead of a jump or shift in the *types* of concepts discussed, the author's shift will be one of *degree.*

LSAT STRATEGY

How can you identify an argument containing Overlooked Possibilities?

- The terms or concepts in the evidence *are* related to the conclusion.
- The conclusion reached is too strong or extreme based on the evidence.
- The author has failed to consider possible objections to the conclusion.

Finding the assumption in these arguments is fundamentally different from our approach to Mismatched Concepts problems. Instead of linking two concepts from within the stimulus, our job is to consider the potential objections to the author's conclusion: Any unconsidered information that would prove the conclusion false. Going back to Maria's vanishing car, for example, couldn't it also be true that Maria's car was towed? Or that she gave her keys to a friend, who took the car? Or that the car was impounded due to Maria's failure to make her loan payments in a timely manner? We could actually spend all day thinking of all of the various fates that could have befallen her poor car aside from being stolen, and there's often no way to know which one will be brought up in the correct answer. Overlooked Possibilities assumptions are thus best thought of as negative assumptions—they are about all of the things that the author *didn't* consider, or at least didn't mention considering or ruling out as possibilities. In this case, the author is assuming that there are *no* other reasons for the car's disappearance—if that's true, then all potential objections have been removed from the argument. Most of the time, the questions will specifically test you on these unconsidered objections.

LSAT STRATEGY

When tackling an argument containing Overlooked Possibilities:

- Focus on the conclusion.
- Determine the possible objections to that conclusion.
- Understand the assumption in negative terms: The author assumes that the possible objections are not present, or did not happen.

Overlooked Possibilities: Sample Arguments

Here are some brief Overlooked Possibilities arguments and the assumption of each. After reviewing these examples, you'll have a chance to try some others on your own.

Argument	Analysis
These berries taste delicious. Therefore, we should eat them!	The author assumes that there are no other considerations when determining whether or not to eat the berries.
When I wore a tracksuit to the party, I was ignored. Therefore, the tracksuit caused people to ignore me.	The author assumes that nothing else, besides the tracksuit, caused people to ignore him at the party.
Sad movies make my friend cry. She's crying now. Therefore, she must have watched a sad movie.	The author assumes that there is no other possible explanation for why her friend is crying.
There's no cash in William's wallet. Therefore, he won't be able to buy any gum.	The author assumes that there is no other possible way for William to pay for gum besides cash from William's wallet.
Our team has the best player in the game. Therefore, we will win the game.	The author assumes that there are no other considerations to take into account when determining the winner besides which team has the best player.

Practice Practice your ability to evaluate Overlooked Possibilities arguments by analyzing the following arguments. In each one of these arguments, follow this approach:

- Separate the evidence from the conclusion.
- Describe to yourself why the evidence is relevant.
- Ask yourself what the possible objections to the conclusion are.
- Phrase the assumption in negative terms (i.e., what didn't happen).

After each argument, feel free to turn to the next page to see the expert analysis.

Argument	My Analysis
7. Medication B has more side effects than Medication A. Therefore, we should use Medication A.	
8. The pet store down the street has only cats and dogs for sale. I'm definitely going to get a pet, but my parents won't let me get a cat. Clearly, then, I'm going to get a dog.	
9. Sally suggests driving to work on the highway, but the highway tends to have much more traffic than the side streets. So I am going to ignore Sally's advice and take the side streets instead.	

Expert Analysis for the Practice exercise may be found on the following page. ▶ ▶ ▶

Expert Analysis

Now take a look at how an LSAT expert would look at the arguments you've just evaluated.

Argument	Analysis
7. Medication B has more side effects than Medication A. Therefore, we should use Medication A.	Conclusion: We should use Med. A (instead of Med. B). Evidence: Med. B has more side effects than Med. A. The author considers only the side effects of the two medications in making a decision; therefore, the author is *not* considering any other reasons why Med. B might be preferable to Med. A. What if Med. A simply isn't effective? Or if Med. A is astronomically expensive? Phrase the assumption negatively: "There are no unconsidered benefits of Med. B and no unconsidered drawbacks of Med. A."
8. The pet store down the street has only cats and dogs for sale. I'm definitely going to get a pet, but my parents won't let me get a cat. Clearly, then, I'm going to get a dog.	Conclusion: I am going to get a dog. Evidence: The store down the street only has cats and dogs, and I can't get a cat. There's nothing new in the conclusion, but the conclusion goes too far. The unconsidered objections to this argument would be anything that says the author *doesn't* have to get a dog. Specifically, there may be other pet stores in the area that sell more than just cats and dogs. Phrase the assumption negatively: "There is no other place to get a pet aside from the pet store down the street."
9. Sally suggests driving to work on the highway, but the highway tends to have much more traffic than the side streets. So I am going to ignore Sally's advice and take the side streets instead.	Conclusion: I'm going to take the side streets to work. Evidence: The highway tends to have more traffic than side streets. There's nothing new in this conclusion either, but much as in the first argument, the author is not considering potential objections to the conclusion. Specifically, the author fails to rule out any additional reasons why the highway may be a good idea or additional information about potential cons of the side streets. Phrase the assumption negatively: "There are no unconsidered pros of the highway or cons of the side streets that would make the highway the better choice."

The LSAT, of course, will present more difficult arguments than the ones just shown, but the fundamental *structure* of Overlooked Possibilities arguments will remain the same. Regardless of the topic being discussed in the argument—whether it be on matters philosophical, legal, or scientific—your method and objective will always remain the same. First, separate evidence from conclusion. Then, evaluate the concepts discussed in both—if the author uses relevant information to draw a conclusion that is too strong or extreme, find the assumption by identifying the factors the author is not considering.

Practice Try that now with an actual LSAT argument.

LSAT Argument	My Analysis
10. Economist: In the interaction between producers and consumers, the only obligation that all parties have is to act in the best interests of their own side. And distribution of information about product defects is in the best interests of the consumer. So consumers are always obligated to report product defects they discover, while producers are never obligated to reveal them. *PrepTest105 Sec1 Q8*	

Did the terms and concepts in the evidence relate to the conclusion drawn? Did the author then overlook potential objections to the conclusion?

Expert Analysis

Take a look at how an LSAT expert would break down this argument.

LSAT Argument	Analysis
10. Economist: In the interaction between producers and consumers, the only obligation that all parties have is to act in the best interests of their own side. And distribution of information about product defects is in the best interests of the consumer. So consumers are always obligated to report product defects they discover, while producers are never obligated to reveal them. *PrepTest105 Sec1 Q8*	Conclusion: Consumers are always obligated to report product defects, but producers are never obligated to reveal them. *because* Evidence: 1) Producers must act in the best interest of producers and consumers must act in the best interest of consumers; 2) reporting defects is in the best interest of consumers. Though the evidence does relate to reporting defects, the author jumps to a very extreme conclusion that ignores the fact that the evidence, while indicating what is in the best interest of consumers, fails to indicate what is in the best interest of producers. The author assumes that it is in the best interest of producers to *not* have defects disclosed.

Hopefully you're starting to get the hang of evaluating these types of arguments. Let's dive in even deeper and discuss some of the most common types of Overlooked Possibilities arguments you'll see on the LSAT.

Going Deeper: Common Patterns and Relationships in Arguments with Overlooked Possibilities

By now, you've seen the benefit of skeptically looking at an argument in which the author uses relevant evidence to support a conclusion that goes too far. In doing so, the author chooses to overlook alternative possibilities that would hurt his conclusion. Indeed, the author's assumption is that no potential objections to the conclusion exist. Now we'll take a look at several of the most common patterns that show up in Overlooked Possibilities arguments.

No Other Explanation, Reason, or Outcome

Prepare One of the most common patterns within the Overlooked Possibilities argument class consists of a conclusion that posits only one explanation or reason for something or only one likely outcome. Invariably, the assumption will then be that there is no other possible explanation, reason, or outcome. For example, consider the following simple argument:

> Chlorophyll A is a type of green-pigmented chlorophyll abundant in plants. Clearly, the presence of chlorophyll A must be what gives plants their green coloration.

Notice that the conclusion provides only one explanation for the green color of plants: It must be due to the presence of chlorophyll A. Yet the evidence alludes to the fact that chlorophyll A might not be the only type of chlorophyll in existence. The author is overlooking the possibility that there are other kinds of chlorophyll—or other pigments unrelated to chlorophyll—that also contribute to the green color of plants. In other words, the possible objections to this argument are other explanations for the green color of plants.

Practice Now take a look at an LSAT stimulus built on this same pattern. You've seen this argument before, in Chapter 3. Here, see if you can spot the overlooked explanation or outcome; then compare your thinking to the expert analysis on the next page.

LSAT Argument	My Analysis
11. During the 1980s Japanese collectors were very active in the market for European art, especially as purchasers of nineteenth-century Impressionist paintings. This striking pattern surely reflects a specific preference on the part of many Japanese collectors for certain aesthetic attributes they found in nineteenth-century Impressionist paintings. *PrepTest104 Sec1 Q5*	

Does this conclusion strike you as particularly strong? "This striking pattern *surely* reflects a specific preference... for certain aesthetic attributes ..." Such a confident-sounding conclusion indicates that this is likely an Overlooked Possibilities argument.

Expert Analysis

Here's how an LSAT expert might analyze that argument.

LSAT Argument	Analysis
11. During the 1980s Japanese collectors were very active in the market for European art, especially as purchasers of nineteenth-century Impressionist paintings. This striking pattern surely reflects a specific preference on the part of many Japanese collectors for certain aesthetic attributes they found in nineteenth-century Impressionist paintings. *PrepTest104 Sec1 Q5*	Conclusion: Japanese art collectors were enticed by the aesthetic attributes of 19th-century Impressionist paintings during the 1980s. *because* Evidence: Japanese collectors purchased much 19th-century Impressionist art during the 1980s. The evidence is merely that a certain phenomenon occurred and the author's conclusion attributes a specific causal explanation, which is entirely reasonable but stated with far too much certainty. Overlooked possibilities include any other reasons that Japanese collectors might have purchased this specific type of art. The author assumes that no other explanations could apply.

Here, the author is overlooking the possibility that the Japanese collectors of the 1980s purchased significant amounts of this particular art for reasons other than aesthetic attributes. For example, perhaps the investors believed the artwork had strong investment potential. Or maybe a strong Japanese economy in the 1980s allowed the collectors to purchase significant amounts of many types of art. Indeed, there might be many alternative explanations for why the investors were purchasing such art.

Although the failure to consider alternative explanations is one of the most common overlooked possibilities, this argument class includes a number of other variants as well. The ability to recognize the following five patterns will give you an advantage over other test takers who have to reinvent the wheel each time they see an argument type they do not recognize. Try out the examples for each pattern and watch for them while you practice.

Necessity versus Sufficiency: Assuming that What is Sufficient is Actually Necessary

Prepare You've seen how Formal Logic statements can be tested in Mismatched Concepts arguments. Occasionally, though, an author will commit a Formal Logic error in an Overlooked Possibilities argument. This happens when an argument either confuses sufficient and necessary terms or incorrectly negates the terms. The result of both of these errors is that the author overlooks other potential causes for a given event. For instance, take a look at the following simple argument:

> Every time my cat jumps onto the coffee table, she knocks over the lamp. I just got home and found the lamp on the coffee table knocked over. Obviously my cat has been at it again.

This author concludes that there is only one possible cause for the lamp having been knocked over: the cat. But is that necessarily true? Just because the cat *can* cause the lamp to fall over doesn't mean that there are no other ways it could happen. Perhaps the dog is at fault, for example, or perhaps a human living in the house is responsible, or perhaps there was an earthquake. Think of it in terms of sufficiency and necessity: The fact that the cat is sufficient to cause the lamp to fall down does not mean that the cat is necessary for the lamp to fall down—there could be lots of other sufficient conditions as well.

Looking at this argument in clear Formal Logic terminology helps illuminate the error:

> Evidence: If cat on table → lamp down
>
> Conclusion: If lamp down → cat on table

As you remember from Chapter 1, you can't read the conditional statement "If the cat is on the table then the lamp gets knocked down" backward as "If lamp got knocked down then cat was on the table." Whenever an author switches the necessary and sufficient sides of a conditional statement without negating the terms, she automatically overlooks the fact that there could be other triggers for an event, just as the author of the cat-and-lamp argument assumes that no other factor besides the cat could have caused the lamp to be knocked over.

Practice Try out the following LSAT argument that confuses necessary and sufficient conditions:

LSAT Argument	My Analysis
12. If you know a lot about history, it will be easy for you to impress people who are intellectuals. But unfortunately, you will not know much about history if you have not, for example, read a large number of history books. Therefore, if you are not well versed in history due to a lack of reading, it will not be easy for you to impress people who are intellectuals. *PrepTest104 Sec4 Q7*	

The repeated use of the term *if* indicates that this argument uses Formal Logic. In such arguments, suspect either a Mismatched Concepts argument or an Overlooked Possibilities argument that confuses sufficient and necessary.

Expert Analysis

Here's how an LSAT expert might analyze that argument.

LSAT Argument	Analysis
12. If you know a lot about history, it will be easy for you to impress people who are intellectuals. But unfortunately, you will not know much about history if you have not, for example, read a large number of history books. Therefore, if you are not well versed in history due to a lack of reading, it will not be easy for you to impress people who are intellectuals. *PrepTest104 Sec4 Q7*	Conclusion: One who is not knowledgeable about history cannot easily impress intellectuals. *because* Evidence: Those who are knowledgeable about history can easily impress intellectuals. The evidence indicates that knowledge of history is sufficient to easily impress intellectuals. The author then concludes that a lack of knowledge about history will preclude easily impressing intellectuals. This is another way of stating that knowledge of history is necessary to impress intellectuals.

Assuming that There Are No Overlooked Advantages or Disadvantages that Impact a Recommendation

Prepare Consider the following:

The deli down the street is currently offering a lunch special, so we should eat lunch there today.

Okay, so the deli's running a special. But what if it's still more expensive than the pizza place across the street? Or what if the deli's been cited for food safety violations repeatedly during the past month and, in fact, your friend just got sick from eating there yesterday? Or what if the deli's food doesn't taste good? If the deli has any of these disadvantages, should you still eat there? Perhaps not.

Whenever the author of an LSAT argument cites an advantage (or disadvantage) and makes a recommendation based upon it, the possible objections to the argument are any disadvantages (or advantages) that could outweigh it. In the argument above, the author assumes that the deli offers no disadvantages that could tilt the scale in favor of eating elsewhere.

Practice Now try to spot the author's assumption in an LSAT argument that involves a recommendation based upon advantages or disadvantages:

LSAT Argument	My Analysis
13. Formal performance evaluations in the professional world are conducted using realistic situations. Physicians are allowed to consult medical texts freely, attorneys may refer to law books and case records, and physicists and engineers have their manuals at hand for ready reference. Students, then, should likewise have access to their textbooks whenever they take examinations. *PrepTest107 Sec4 Q25*	

Notice that the conclusion of this argument is a recommendation. If the author of the argument bases the recommendation on citing advantages or disadvantages to the proposal, suspect an Overlooked Possibilities argument.

Expert Analysis

Take a look at how an LSAT expert evaluates the argument.

LSAT Argument	Analysis
13. Formal performance evaluations in the professional world are conducted using realistic situations. Physicians are allowed to consult medical texts freely, attorneys may refer to law books and case records, and physicists and engineers have their manuals at hand for ready reference. Students, then, should likewise have access to their textbooks whenever they take examinations. *PrepTest107 Sec4 Q25*	Conclusion: Students should have access to their textbooks during their exams. *because* Evidence: Professionals are allowed to consult texts and manuals during performance evaluations. The author cites an analogy (to professional performance evaluations) that identifies a possible advantage of the recommendation to allow students to use textbooks during their examinations. The unconsidered objections here are any reasons why students should not be allowed to use textbooks, including any differences between the goals of professional evaluations and student examinations. As is typical with an argument with a recommendation conclusion, the author assumes that there are no disadvantages that outweigh the benefits.

Assuming that Something that Could Occur, Will Occur

Prepare The fact that something might happen doesn't necessarily mean that it actually will happen. Yet, authors of LSAT arguments sometimes wrongly assume the opposite—that is, they assume that something merely possible is definitely true. Here's a simplified example to illustrate:

> Skateboarding can cause all sorts of injuries. It follows that Aaron, who just went skateboarding, must be injured.

The fact that skateboarding *can* cause injuries does not mean that it *always* causes injuries. But that's exactly what this author assumes in concluding that Aaron must be injured just because he went skateboarding. Stated differently, the author overlooks the possibility that Aaron might have managed to go skateboarding without incurring an injury.

Practice See if you can recognize the shift from language of *possibility* in the evidence to language of *certainty* in the conclusion in this LSAT argument:

LSAT Argument	My Analysis
14. All actions are motivated by self-interest, since any action that is apparently altruistic can be described in terms of self-interest. For example, helping someone can be described in terms of self-interest: the motivation is hope for a reward or other personal benefit to be bestowed as a result of the helping action. *PrepTest107 Sec4 Q18*	

Expert Analysis

Now take a look at the same argument, through the lens of an LSAT expert:

LSAT Argument	Analysis
14. All actions are motivated by self-interest, since any action that is apparently altruistic can be described in terms of self-interest. For example, helping someone can be described in terms of self-interest: the motivation is hope for a reward or other personal benefit to be bestowed as a result of the helping action. *PrepTest107 Sec4 Q18*	Conclusion: All actions are motivated by self-interest. *because* Evidence: Any action can be described in terms of self-interest. The evidence is provisional: Actions "*can be* described in terms of self-interest." But the conclusion uses much stronger language: "*All* actions *are* motivated by self-interest." This over-looks the fact that just because something can be described a certain way doesn't mean that there isn't another (and maybe better or more accurate) way to describe it.

Causal Arguments: Assuming that Correlation Proves Causation

Prepare Thing A happens. At the same time (or soon after), Thing B happens. So A caused B. This is the classic argument of causation based on evidence of a correlation. Because they come with such a wealth of overlooked possibilities, causal arguments show up most frequently in Flaw, Strengthen, and Weaken questions. Here's a basic causal argument:

> Over the past half-century, worldwide sugar consumption has nearly tripled. During the same time period, there has been a marked increase in the rate of global technological advancement. It follows that the increase in global sugar consumption has caused the acceleration in technological advancement.

The author concludes that increased sugar consumption caused the acceleration in technological advancement. In doing so, the author assumes that there are *no other possible relationships* between sugar consumption and technological advancement. Specifically, the three possible objections to any causal argument are:

1. There is an **alternate cause**. Perhaps something else caused the accelerated technological advancement.
2. The causation is **reversed**. Perhaps it's the other way around: Technological advances allow for easier sugar refinement, which leads to higher sugar consumption.
3. The correlation is purely **coincidental**. Perhaps the fact that increased sugar consumption and technological innovation occurred at the same time is merely a coincidence.

The author of a causal argument assumes, then, that (1) there is no alternate cause, (2) the causation is not reversed, and (3) the correlation is not coincidental. In the future, remind yourself of these overlooked objections by using the acronym **ARC**. And, because the author isn't considering them, we can say that the flaw in these arguments is that the author improperly assumes that there is "**No ARC**."

Practice Try out an LSAT argument that includes a claim of causation based on evidence of a correlation and ask yourself which of these overlooked possibilities are most likely:

LSAT Argument	My Analysis
15. Unplugging a peripheral component such as a "mouse" from a personal computer renders all of the software programs that require that component unusable on that computer. On Fred's personal computer, a software program that requires a mouse has become unusable. So it must be that the mouse for Fred's computer became unplugged. *PrepTest104 Sec4 Q10*	

While this argument's conclusion does not explicitly assert a claim of causation, the author must believe that an unplugged mouse caused the program to stop working. If the author explicitly concludes or implicitly assumes that one thing is making another thing happen, you're dealing with a causal argument.

Expert Analysis

Take a look at one LSAT expert's analysis of the argument about Fred's computer and mouse.

LSAT Argument	Analysis
15. Unplugging a peripheral component such as a "mouse" from a personal computer renders all of the software programs that require that component unusable on that computer. On Fred's personal computer, a software program that requires a mouse has become unusable. So it must be that the mouse for Fred's computer became unplugged. *PrepTest104 Sec4 Q10*	Conclusion: The mouse on Fred's computer became unplugged. *because* Evidence: A program on Fred's computer that requires a mouse has stopped working. By concluding so definitively that the mouse on Fred's computer must have become unplugged, the author assumes that it is the only possible cause of the problem with the program.

Predictions: Assumptions about Circumstances

Prepare As you learned in Chapter 3, a conclusion stating that something is likely to happen in the future is called a "prediction." To illustrate the classic assumption underlying predictions, consider the following weather prediction:

> Due to the current prevailing northwesterly breeze, the weather in Flooville will remain clear and cold tomorrow.

The problem with this prediction is that if the northwesterly breeze unexpectedly shifts to, say, southeasterly, the weather in Flooville might not "remain clear and cold." The author assumes that the circumstances under which the prediction was made *will not change.*

Now consider this prediction:

> Despite the prevailing northwesterly breeze that is currently bringing clear and cold weather to Flooville, the weather in Flooville will shift tomorrow to overcast and warm.

This time, the author assumes that the northwesterly breeze will have changed direction by tomorrow—in other words, the assumption is that there *will be* a change in circumstances.

Anyone making a prediction is making an assumption about circumstances. Keep this in mind whenever you see that an argument's conclusion is a prediction.

Practice Analyze the following LSAT argument:

LSAT Argument	My Analysis
16. Plant Manager: We could greatly reduce the amount of sulfur dioxide our copper-smelting plant releases into the atmosphere by using a new process. The new process requires replacing our open furnaces with closed ones and moving the copper from one furnace to the next in solid, not molten, form. However, not only is the new equipment expensive to buy and install, but the new process also costs more to run than the current process, because the copper must be reheated after it has cooled. So overall, adopting the new process will cost much but bring the company no profit. *PrepTest107 Sec4 Q14*	

Notice how this conclusion is phrased: a confident prediction that something will definitely happen. Take a look at how an LSAT expert evaluates this argument:

Expert Analysis

Review an LSAT expert's analysis of that argument.

LSAT Argument	Analysis
16. Plant Manager: We could greatly reduce the amount of sulfur dioxide our copper-smelting plant releases into the atmosphere by using a new process. The new process requires replacing our open furnaces with closed ones and moving the copper from one furnace to the next in solid, not molten, form. However, not only is the new equipment expensive to buy and install, but the new process also costs more to run than the current process, because the copper must be reheated after it has cooled. So overall, adopting the new process will cost much but bring the company no profit. *PrepTest107 Sec4 Q14*	Conclusion: Even though adopting closed furnaces will greatly reduce the amount of sulfur dioxide it releases, doing so will cost much without earning a profit. *because* Evidence: 1) The new equipment is expensive to buy and install, and 2) the new process costs more to run because of an extra reheating step. The author assumes that no other circumstances or change of circumstances will affect the results of adopting the new process. This particular argument also reflects the assumption inherent in any recommendation conclusion that no other factors will figure into the equation.

As with Mismatched Concepts arguments, the better you can become at spotting these various Overlooked Possibilities argument patterns, the more efficient you will become at analyzing arguments. You'll be ahead of the game when you encounter Assumption, Strengthen, Weaken, and Flaw questions—which, taken together, constitute about one-fourth of the LSAT.

LSAT STRATEGY

Overlooked Possibilities tend to fit one of the following patterns:

- Fails to consider other explanations, reasons, or outcomes based on the evidence
- Confuses sufficient and necessary terms
- Does not consider potential advantages or disadvantages when making a recommendation
- Assumes that something *will* occur just because it *could* occur
- Author arrives at a claim of causation based on evidence that is only correlated
- Prediction is based on an assumption that circumstances will or will not change

On the next page, you get a chance to put all of this knowledge into practice and analyze some arguments.

Untangling and Analyzing LSAT Arguments

At this point, you should have more confidence in your ability to identify the assumption in LSAT arguments. If an argument contains a new concept in the conclusion that is not inherently relevant or related to the concept in the evidence, the author's assumption is that a logical relationship exists between mismatched concepts in the evidence and conclusion. On the other hand, if an argument uses clearly applicable or relevant evidence, but jumps to a conclusion that overlooks other potentially relevant factors, explanations, or criteria, then the author's assumption is that there are no possible objections to the conclusion. Understanding the common ways an LSAT argument moves from its evidence to its conclusion will help you tackle Assumption Family questions. Use this new knowledge to analyze a few LSAT arguments.

Practice In each of the following arguments, separate the evidence from the conclusion. Simplify each, and then compare them. Is the author assuming that two mismatched concepts are somehow related? Or is the author using relevant evidence to jump to an extreme conclusion without considering potential objections?

LSAT Argument	My Analysis
17. All potatoes naturally contain solanine, which is poisonous in large quantities. Domesticated potatoes contain only very small amounts of solanine, but many wild potatoes contain poisonous levels of solanine. Since most of the solanine in potatoes is concentrated in the skin, however, peeling wild potatoes makes them at least as safe to eat as unpeeled domesticated potatoes of the same size. *PrepTest105 Sec1 Q9*	
18. Recent research shows that sound change (pronunciation shift) in a language is not gradual. New sounds often emerge suddenly. This confounds the classical account of sound change, whose central tenet is gradualness. Since this classical account must be discarded, sound-change theory in general must also be. *PrepTest104 Sec1 Q16*	

LSAT Argument	My Analysis
19. On a certain day, nine scheduled flights on Swift Airlines were canceled. Ordinarily, a cancellation is due to mechanical problems with the airplane scheduled for a certain flight. However, since it is unlikely that Swift would have mechanical problems with more than one or two airplanes on a single day, some of the nine cancellations were probably due to something else. *PrepTest106 Sec3 Q19*	
20. The miscarriage of justice in the Barker case was due to the mistaken views held by some of the forensic scientists involved in the case, who believed that they owed allegiance only to the prosecuting lawyers. Justice was thwarted because these forensic scientists failed to provide evidence impartially to both the defense and the prosecution. Hence it is not forensic evidence in general that should be condemned for this injustice. *PrepTest105 Sec4 Q16*	

Expert Analysis

Now, take a look at how an LSAT expert would untangle and evaluate the arguments you've just examined.

LSAT Argument	Analysis
17. All potatoes naturally contain solanine, which is poisonous in large quantities. Domesticated potatoes contain only very small amounts of solanine, but many wild potatoes contain poisonous levels of solanine. Since most of the solanine in potatoes is concentrated in the skin, however, peeling wild potatoes makes them at least as safe to eat as unpeeled domesticated potatoes of the same size. *PrepTest105 Sec1 Q9*	Conclusion: Peeled wild potatoes are as safe to eat as unpeeled domesticated potatoes. *because* Evidence: 1) Solanine is poisonous in large quantities; 2) domesticated potatoes have small amounts; and 3) wild potatoes have poisonous levels, with most concentrated in the skin. The argument assumes that once "most" of the solanine in wild potatoes is removed by peeling, the solanine levels in wild potatoes will drop to the same or lower levels than in entire domesticated potatoes. This overlooks the possibility that the amount of solanine in the core of wild potatoes could still be higher than the overall amount in domesticated potatoes.
18. Recent research shows that sound change (pronunciation shift) in a language is not gradual. New sounds often emerge suddenly. This confounds the classical account of sound change, whose central tenet is gradualness. Since this classical account must be discarded, sound-change theory in general must also be. *PrepTest104 Sec1 Q16*	Conclusion: Sound theory generally must be discarded. *because* Evidence: The classical account of sound theory must be discarded. This is a classic Mismatched Concepts argument: While the evidence is about the classical account of sound theory, the conclusion is about sound theory generally. More specifically, the argument assumes that sound theory in general is dependent upon the classical account.

LSAT Argument	Analysis
19. On a certain day, nine scheduled flights on Swift Airlines were canceled. Ordinarily, a cancellation is due to mechanical problems with the airplane scheduled for a certain flight. However, since it is unlikely that Swift would have mechanical problems with more than one or two airplanes on a single day, some of the nine cancellations were probably due to something else. *PrepTest106 Sec3 Q19*	Conclusion: Some of the nine cancellations were due to something other than mechanical problems. *because* Evidence: It is unlikely that more than one or two airplanes on a single day would have mechanical problems. The Mismatched Concepts in this argument are the number of *planes* that have mechanical problems and the number of canceled *flights* that are due to mechanical problems. The argument assumes that there is no way that one or two planes being grounded could lead to nine canceled flights; this overlooks the possibility that all nine of the canceled flights could have been scheduled to use only one or two planes (such as in short commuter hops between nearby cities).
20. The miscarriage of justice in the Barker case was due to the mistaken views held by some of the forensic scientists involved in the case, who believed that they owed allegiance only to the prosecuting lawyers. Justice was thwarted because these forensic scientists failed to provide evidence impartially to both the defense and the prosecution. Hence it is not forensic evidence in general that should be condemned for this injustice. *PrepTest105 Sec4 Q16*	Conclusion: Forensic evidence in general is not to blame for the injustice in the Barker case. *because* Evidence: The forensic scientists on the case failed to be impartial. The Mismatched Concepts in the argument are individual forensic scientists and forensic science generally, with the author assuming that the failings of individual forensic scientists should not be attributed broadly as failings of forensic science generally.

You've now had a lot of practice breaking down LSAT arguments and identifying the author's central assumption. But just evaluating and analyzing arguments alone won't get you to your target score; to do that, you'll have to correctly answer the Assumption Family questions you'll face on test day. The good news is that the fundamental understanding you now have of the common ways LSAT arguments move from their evidence to their conclusion puts you light-years ahead of your competition. You'll soon see that Assumption, Strengthen, Weaken, and Flaw questions—which taken together constitute about 25 percent of the LSAT—will seem much easier to analyze, evaluate, and correctly answer.

Let's take a look now at the first of these question types.

Assumption Questions

Prepare

LEARNING OBJECTIVES

In this section, you'll learn to:

- Identify Assumption questions.
- Recognize Sufficient Assumption questions.
- Recognize Necessary Assumption questions.
- Phrase a prediction of the correct answer choice.

On test day, you will be asked to correctly answer roughly eight Assumption questions. Put plainly, these questions will ask you to determine an argument's assumption. This seems straightforward and easy enough; after all, you are now already in the habit of determining the unstated premise of each Assumption Family question argument you see. To identify an Assumption question, look for the words *assumption*, *assumes*, or *presupposes* in the question stem. The correct answer to these questions will always present a new piece of information that the author has not included in his argument. In fact, if an answer choice restates evidence that has already been explicitly stated in the argument, then it will never be correct in an Assumption question. The LSAT will phrase an Assumption question in one of two distinct ways. Take a look at these two LSAT question stems:

> Which one of the following, if assumed, allows the argument's conclusion to be properly drawn?
>
> *PrepTest101 Sec2 Q21*

> Which one of the following is an assumption on which the argument depends?
>
> *PrepTest104 Sec4 Q9*

Although both question stems include references to the assumption—the terms *assumed* and *assumption*—they actually ask for two distinctly different things. Notice that the first question stem asks you to determine an assumption that, if true, would allow for the conclusion to be properly drawn. This means that the correct answer will be an assumption that, when added to the evidence, will *guarantee* the conclusion. We will refer to these as Sufficient Assumption questions.

Now take a look at the second question stem. Here, the testmaker asks you to determine an assumption that the argument requires, or depends on. For this question stem, a correct answer doesn't need to guarantee the conclusion; instead, the correct answer choice to such a Necessary Assumption question will be an assumption that is *necessary* for the conclusion to make logical sense.

To understand the basic difference between Sufficient and Necessary Assumption questions, let's revisit the argument about Dweezil:

> Dweezil is a zulzey alien. Therefore, Dweezil can perform the amazing *yeerchta* move.

Previously, we said that the assumption of this argument is that zulzey aliens are able to perform the amazing *yeerchta* move. So what if an answer choice to an Assumption question said something like this: "Every type of alien is capable of performing the *yeerchta* move." Would that be correct? Actually, we don't know—it all depends on whether or not the question we're evaluating is a Sufficient Assumption or Necessary Assumption question. First, let's look at this assumption in the context of a Sufficient Assumption question:

> Which one of the following, if assumed, allows the argument's conclusion to be properly drawn?
>
> *PrepTest101 Sec2 Q21*

Here, "Every type of alien is capable of performing the *yeerchta* move" *would* be correct. Because we know that Dweezil is an alien (the type of alien doesn't really matter), we could add this assumption to the evidence and draw the conclusion that, yes, Dweezil can definitely perform the *yeerchta* move. But what about this next question? Will the assumption "Every type of alien is capable of performing the *yeerchta* move" be correct here, as well?

> Which one of the following is an assumption on which the argument depends?
>
> *PrepTest104 Sec4 Q9*

For this Necessary Assumption question, we don't need to find an assumption that guarantees the conclusion; instead, we need to find an assumption that is *necessary* or *required* for the conclusion to follow. The statement "Every type of alien is capable of performing the *yeerchta* move" doesn't satisfy this question because the author's argument doesn't *need* every alien to be able to do the *yeerchta* move, only zulzey aliens. So long as at least one zulzey alien is capable of doing it—and, particularly, so long as Dweezil herself is able to do it—the author's conclusion could still stand.

It is worth noting that a statement can be both necessary and sufficient to establish a conclusion. For example, in this fictional argument, the premise "Zulzey aliens named Dweezil can perform the amazing *yeerchta* move" is both necessary (the argument could not be completed if it were not true) and sufficient (it is enough to establish the conclusion beyond doubt on the basis of the evidence). Similarly, the premise "Nothing prevents a zulzey alien from performing the amazing *yeerchta* move" is necessary, but not sufficient, to establish the conclusion in that argument.

Though the two Assumption question subtypes are similar in some ways, you'll see that recognizing the distinction between the two will help you determine the right answer choice more efficiently and confidently.

Sufficient Assumption Questions

As you just saw, Sufficient Assumption questions will ask you to consider an assumption that, "if assumed," allows the conclusion to be drawn logically. In these questions, which make up about 40 percent of all Assumption questions, you are asked to find an assumption that would be *sufficient* to establish the conclusion from the evidence. In other words, when added to the evidence, the assumption will *guarantee* that the conclusion is true. The language of Sufficient Assumption question stems will include phrases like "if assumed," "conclusion follows logically," or "allows the conclusion to be drawn." You can also spot these questions by the words and terms they *don't* include; unlike Necessary Assumption questions, Sufficient Assumption questions won't use language like "needs," "requires," or "depends."

Take a look at some actual LSAT Sufficient Assumption question stems:

LSAT Question Stem	Analysis
Which one of the following, if assumed, enables the conclusion above to be properly inferred? *PrepTest105 Sec4 Q22*	Sufficient Assumption question. Find an answer choice that, when connected to the evidence, would guarantee the conclusion is true.
The conclusion of the argument follows logically if which one of the following is assumed? *PrepTest101 Sec3 Q19*	Sufficient Assumption question. Find an answer choice that, when combined with the evidence, will guarantee that the conclusion is true.

In Sufficient Assumption questions, the argument pattern is overwhelmingly Mismatched Concepts arguments that contain Formal Logic. Your goal for most of these questions, then, will be to find the mismatched terms between the evidence and the conclusion, connect those terms strongly, and eliminate any answer choices that bring in outside information. If you do come across the rare Sufficient Assumption question that uses an Overlooked Possibilities argument, be sure to find an answer choice that rules out *all* potential objections to the author's conclusion. Because the correct answer choice to a Sufficient Assumption question will, when added to the argument's evidence, definitely lead to the author's conclusion, it is acceptable for these assumptions to be broader than the argument itself.

LSAT STRATEGY

Some facts to remember about Sufficient Assumption questions:

- Recognize these questions by the phrasing "if assumed" or "conclusion follows logically."
- The correct answer, when combined with the evidence, will guarantee the conclusion.
- Mismatched Concepts arguments with Formal Logic dominate Sufficient Assumption questions.

To demonstrate how Sufficient Assumption questions operate, review an LSAT expert's work on the following LSAT question.

Step 2: Conclusion: "spirit is not a material body." *because* Evidence: 1) "All material bodies are divisible"; and 2) "everything divisible is imperfect" (which are combined by the author to: material → not perfect).	**Step 1:** The formulation "conclusion...follows logically if...assumed" indicates a Sufficient Assumption question.

All material bodies are divisible into parts, and everything divisible is imperfect. It follows that all material bodies are imperfect. It likewise follows that the spirit is not a material body.

The final conclusion above follows logically if which one of the following is assumed?

(A) Everything divisible is a material body.

(B) Nothing imperfect is indivisible.

(C) The spirit is divisible.

(D) The spirit is perfect.

(E) The spirit is either indivisible or imperfect.

PrepTest101 Sec3 Q10

Step 3: Contrapose the combined evidence deduction provided in the second sentence to yield: Evid: Perfect → Not Material Body Conc: Spirit → Not Material Body With the mismatched terms on the left of the arrows, the direction of connection is up, so the correct answer will indicate: Spirit → Perfect (or) Not Perfect → Not Spirit.	**Step 4:** (D) is correct. This is a precise match for the prediction.

Wrong answers: (A) The correct answer must at a minimum provide a connection to "spirit," which is the unique term in the conclusion. This is merely an incomplete contrapositive of one of the pieces of evidence. (B) As with (A), there is no connection to "spirit" and this is merely a Distortion of one of the pieces of evidence. (C) 180. In addition to the prediction above, which used the endpoints of the combined evidence, the conclusion could also be proved true by a rule that the "spirit is ***in***divisible." If the spirit were indivisible, the contrapositive of the first piece of evidence would dictate that it also would be not material. (E) 180. As discussed in (C), the spirit is indivisible proves the conclusion, or, as discussed in (D), the spirit is *perfect* proves the conclusion.

Later, in the Practice problems at the end of this section and in the Perform quiz at the end of the chapter, you'll have an opportunity to work on even more Sufficient Assumption questions. Now, though, let's discuss Necessary Assumption questions.

Necessary Assumption Questions

Necessary Assumption questions are different from Sufficient Assumption questions in that they ask for an assumption that is *necessary* for the argument's conclusion to make sense. Necessary Assumption questions are a bit more common than Sufficient Assumption questions and tend to make up about 60 percent of all Assumption questions. You can identify these questions because they will use the terms *depends*, *require*, or *is necessary* in the question stems.

Take a look at some actual LSAT Necessary Assumption question stems:

LSAT Question Stem	Analysis
Which one of the following is an assumption that the argument requires in order for its conclusion to be properly drawn? *PrepTest104 Sec4 Q19*	Necessary Assumption question. Find an assumption required for the conclusion to make logical sense.
The argument depends on which one of the following assumptions? *PrepTest106 Sec3 Q19*	Necessary Assumption question. Find an assumption required for the conclusion to make logical sense.
Which one of the following is an assumption required by the economist's argument? *PrepTest105 Sec1 Q8*	Necessary Assumption question. Find an assumption required for the conclusion to make logical sense.

In Necessary Assumption questions, the argument pattern is as likely to be Mismatched Concepts as Overlooked Possibilities. If it's a Mismatched Concepts argument, look for an assumption that establishes some sort of relationship between the mismatched concepts. If it's an Overlooked Possibilities argument, look for an assumption that removes at least one possible objection to the conclusion that the author has not considered. In both argument types, look for an assumption that is required or essential to the argument. Additionally, because you are looking for an assumption that is necessary for the argument, you can test the validity of answer choices by "denying" them. We'll talk about that strategy more later. Now, though, let's discuss Mismatched Concepts arguments in Necessary Assumption questions.

LSAT STRATEGY

Some facts to remember about Necessary Assumption questions:

- Recognize these questions by the phrasing "an assumption required by the argument" or "the argument depends on the assumption that."
- The correct answer doesn't have to be sufficient for the conclusion to be drawn, just necessary.
- Both Mismatched Concepts and Overlooked Possibilities arguments will be tested.
- Use the Denial Test to distinguish the correct answer.

Mismatched Concepts in Necessary Assumption Questions

To see the difference between necessary and sufficient assumptions in a Mismatched Concepts argument, evaluate the following test-like question and the two answer choices that follow:

> Bill: A recent book reviewer called Mary's novel "boring and prosaic." But the reviewer is clearly wrong because not only is the entire first half of Mary's novel all about pirates, but part of the second half is, as well.
>
> The argument depends on the assumption that
>
> (A) any novel that mentions pirates cannot be boring and prosaic
>
> (B) a novel that is mostly about pirates cannot be boring and prosaic

Start by untangling the argument. Bill's conclusion is that Mary's novel is not boring and prosaic. Why? Because more than half of Mary's novel is all about pirates. There is a disconnect here between the concepts "boring and prosaic" and "a novel mostly about pirates": Bill assumes that they are mutually exclusive. The correct answer will tie these two concepts together.

Both answer choices present assumptions formed from these mismatched concepts, and neither one brings in outside information. But are they both *necessary* assumptions? Answer choice (A) does give us a sufficient connection between the evidence and conclusion. After all, Mary's book mentions pirates, so if (A) is established, then it follows that her novel is not boring and prosaic. However, (A) is not a necessary assumption required for the conclusion to hold up. Bill's evidence is explicit: most of the novel is about pirates, and *that's* why it shouldn't be considered boring and prosaic. In fact, we have no idea what Bill thinks about novels that *only mention* pirates. It's possible that Bill would find a novel that discusses pirates once, in passing, to be boring and prosaic.

Now evaluate answer choice (B). Here, we see an assumption that *is* required by the argument. Bill's evidence directly states that a majority of Mary's novel is about pirates. It's not just because Mary's novel *mentions* pirates that Bill believes the reviewer to be wrong; it's because Mary's novel is *mostly* about pirates. To prove that this answer is correct, deny it and see what happens to the argument: "novels that are mostly about pirates *can* be boring and prosaic." If that's true, then Bill's entire argument falls apart, and his conclusion can no longer stand. We'll revisit this idea of "denying" the right answer choice to prove if it is correct later in the section.

Now, though, take a look an LSAT expert's analysis of a full Necessary Assumption question based on an argument that you've seen earlier in the chapter.

Step 2: Conclusion: Under the described circumstances, news cannot give us information to act on. *because* Evidence: Under the described circumstances, news is primarily entertaining.	**Step 1:** The phrase "assumption on which... argument depends" indicates a Necessary Assumption question.

Sociologist: The intended function of news is to give us information on which to act. But in a consumer society, news becomes a product to be manufactured and dispensed to the consumer. An enormous industry for the production and consumption of news has evolved, and we ingest news with an insatiable appetite. Under such circumstances, news is primarily entertaining and cannot, therefore, serve its intended function.

Which one of the following is an assumption on which the sociologist's argument depends?

(A) News that serves its intended function should not be entertaining.

(B) Most viewers prefer that news be entertaining.

(C) News has only one important function.

(D) News that primarily entertains does not give us information on which to act.

(E) A news industry that aims to make a profit inevitably presents news as entertainment.

PrepTest105 Sec1 Q18

Step 3: Both the evidence and conclusion relate to the news under the described circumstances, so the Mismatched Concepts unique to the evidence and conclusion respectively are: *primarily entertaining* and *cannot give information to act on.* The correct answer will indicate that news that is primarily entertaining will not provide information on which to act.	**Step 4:** (D) is correct. This choice matches the prediction in linking the Mismatched Concepts of *primarily entertain* and *not give information on which to act.*

Wrong answers: (A) Distortion. The argument assumes that news cannot be *primarily* entertaining—not that it shouldn't be entertaining at all—and still serve its intended function. (B) Outside the Scope. The argument is not concerned with viewer preferences, but with whether news serves its intended function of providing information on which to act. (C) This answer merely paraphrases—and arguably distorts—a stated premise, so it cannot be the unstated assumption. (E) Outside the Scope. The argument does not make the causal claim that the news industry's profit motive inevitably leads to the presentation of news as entertainment.

The assumption of this argument as articulated in choice (D) is necessary for the argument's conclusion to be drawn. If you were to deny that answer choice—if you were to state that news that primarily entertains *does* give us information on which to act—then the argument falls apart, and the conclusion can no longer stand.

You'll get more practice with Mismatched Concepts arguments in Necessary Assumption questions later in this section, as well as at the end of the chapter. Now, though, let's take a look at how Overlooked Possibilities arguments show up in Necessary Assumption questions.

Overlooked Possibilities in Necessary Assumption Questions

Not all Necessary Assumption questions contain mismatched concepts. In an Overlooked Possibilities argument that asks for a necessary assumption, your approach will change slightly. In these arguments, seek an answer choice that removes at least one possible objection to the author's conclusion. This is one of the reasons why learning to phrase the assumption of an Overlooked Possibilities argument in negative terms is so valuable.

To demonstrate, let's revisit this argument:

> Last night Maria parked her car in an area of town where lots of car thefts occur. This morning Maria woke up and discovered that her car was no longer in its parking spot. Therefore, Maria's car must have been stolen.

We said earlier that the possible objections to this argument include any other explanation for the vanishing car: Maria's friend Patty moving the car, her car being towed, that she moved the car to a different parking spot and forgot, and so on. The author's *sufficient* assumption is that none of the potential objections happened. In other words, the answer to a Sufficient Assumption question would say something like this:

- There are no other ways Maria's car could have vanished aside from theft.
- Theft is the only possible explanation for the disappearance of Maria's car.

Sufficient Assumption questions require you to rule out *all* other possible explanations to guarantee that the car was stolen. The correct answer to a Necessary Assumption question, on the other hand, only needs to rule out *one* possible objection. Consider the following answer choices:

- Maria's friend Patty didn't move the car.
- Maria's car was not towed.
- Maria didn't forget that she moved the car to a different parking spot in the middle of the night.

In a Necessary Assumption question, any one of the above answer choices would be correct because each one of them *needs* to be ruled out for this conclusion to be true. Unlike Mismatched Concepts arguments, the answers to Overlooked Possibilities arguments can and do routinely mention new, but relevant, information. But such answers should not be considered Outside the Scope of the argument because rather than bring in that new concept the answer identifies it as what the author is *not* considering. Because you can't always predict the exact objection that the answer choice will rule out, it's important to make a prediction that is broad enough that you can spot whichever one they choose.

The Denial Test

To test whether an answer choice in a Necessary Assumption question is actually necessary, you can use a strategy we call the "Denial Test." *Deny* in this context means to negate the assumption, or to say that it is not true. After all, if the assumption is *required* by the conclusion, then saying that the assumption is *not true* should directly undermine that conclusion. In the preceding example, let's deny the second answer choice and see what happens. As it is written, it reads, "Maria's car was not towed." Denied, that answer choice would say, "Maria's car *was* towed." If this newly denied assumption were true, then the author's conclusion could not stand. Therefore, it must be an assumption required by the argument and would be confirmed as the correct answer.

The Denial Test works only in Necessary Assumption questions and is not meant to be your initial approach to these questions. Tackling every Necessary Assumption question by denying each answer choice is ultimately a time-consuming and potentially confusing approach. Instead, use the Denial Test as a final strategy to "prove" the correct answer. If you are able to deny the assumption in an answer choice and still draw the conclusion, then that is not the right answer. Once you deny the assumption in the right answer, however, and add that newly denied assumption to the argument's evidence, you'll find that the argument crumbles and the conclusion no longer stands.Additionally, you can use the Denial Test on your prediction from Step 3 to determine whether you have predicted a valid Necessary Assumption.

To see how Overlooked Possibilities arguments are tested in Necessary Assumption questions, review an LSAT expert's work on the following question. Its stimulus contains an argument you saw earlier.

Step 2: Conclusion: Consumers are always obligated to report product defects, but producers are never obligated to reveal them. *because* Evidence: 1) Producers must act in the best interest of all producers and consumers must act in the best interest of all consumers; and 2) reporting defects is in the best interest of consumers.	**Step 1:** The phrase "assumption required by the... argument" indicates a Necessary Assumption question.

Economist: In the interaction between producers and consumers, the only obligation that all parties have is to act in the best interests of their own side. And distribution of information about product defects is in the best interests of the consumer. So consumers are always obligated to report product defects they discover, while producers are never obligated to reveal them.

Which one of the following is an assumption required by the economist's argument?

(A) It is never in the best interests of producers for a producer to reveal a product defect.

(B) No one expects producers to act in a manner counter to their own best interests.

(C) Any product defect is likely to be discovered by consumers.

(D) A product defect is more likely to be discovered by a consumer than by a producer.

(E) The best interests of consumers never coincide with the best interests of producers.

PrepTestB Sec1 Q8

Step 3: Combining the evidence about consumers (that exposure of defects is in their best interests and that consumers must do what is in the best interest of all consumers) logically leads to the portion of the conclusion that asserts consumers must report defects. In contrast, the evidence is silent as to what is in the best interest of producers. Thus, the author must assume that not exposing defects is in the best interest of the producers.	**Step 4:** (A) is correct. This matches the prediction. For the author to conclude that producers are not obligated to reveal defects requires that he assume that such exposure is *not* in the interest of producers.

Wrong answers: (B) Outside the Scope. The argument concerns what *should* be done, not what is *expected.* Also, the argument does not explicitly establish that hiding defects is in the producers' best interest. (C) Outside the Scope. The argument concerns what should be done regarding defects that *are* discovered, not the likelihood of discovery. (D) Irrelevant Comparison. As with (C), the relative likelihood of discovery is irrelevant. (E) Extreme. The argument only presumes that consumers and producers have divergent interests in regards to exposure of defects, not universally.

By identifying the structure of this argument as Overlooked Possibilities, the expert is able to predict the correct answer choice. Apply the Denial Test to answer choice (A): *It is at least sometimes in the best interests of producers for a producer to reveal a product defect.* If that were true, is it possible to conclude that producers are never obligated to reveal a defect, knowing that producers must act in the interest of all producers? No! Thus answer choice (A) is necessary to the argument.

Good work. You can go deeper into the valuable strategies associated with the Denial Test in the following LSAT Channel Spotlight. After that, it will be time to practice everything you've learned so far about Sufficient and Necessary Assumption questions.

CHANNEL SPOTLIGHT

The Denial Test

By The LSAT Channel Faculty

Watch the video lesson for this Spotlight in your online Study Plan.

When evaluating the answer choices in Necessary Assumption questions, LSAT experts often use a tactic we refer to as the Denial Test. It is easy to explain how the Denial Test works, but making efficient, effective use of it takes some practice. Let's start with the definition: When you deny, or negate, each of the answer choices in a Necessary Assumption question, only the negation of the correct answer will make the conclusion impossible based on the evidence. Now consider an example:

> My roommate promised that he was going to buy milk for the house today because we are entirely out of milk. However, when I left this morning, he was asleep on the couch, and when I got home, I found him asleep on the couch. Thus, I'm sure we are still entirely out of milk.

Consider whether any of the following statements constitutes an assumption *necessary* to the argument.

- My roommate was wearing the same clothes when I got home that he was wearing when I went out.
- It is not uncommon for the house to be out of milk for days at a time.
- My roommate always takes very long naps.
- No one else got any milk for the house today.

What happens when you deny (and, again, in this context, that means to negate) each of those assumptions? Here's what that would look like:

- My roommate was *not* wearing the same clothes when I got home that he was wearing when I went out.
- It is ~~not~~ uncommon for the house to be out of milk for days at a time.
- My roommate ~~always~~ *sometimes* takes ~~very long~~ *shorter* naps.
- ~~No one~~ *Someone* else got ~~any~~ *some* milk for the house today.

The negations of the first three statements weaken the author's conclusion, but they do not disprove it. If the roommate has different clothes on, you at least know that he got up at some point. You do not, however, know that he even left the house, let alone that he went and bought milk. If it is rare that the house is out of milk for days, it is less likely that the roommate would have ignored his promise, but not impossible that he would have done so. Similarly, if the roommate sometimes takes short naps, there is at least the chance that he got up and went to the store, but no guarantee that he did so.

When you negate the fourth statement, however, the argument falls apart. Notice that the conclusion was not that the roommate did not get milk, but that the house still had no milk. If someone else supplied the house with milk, then the author's conclusion just falls apart. What the alternate source was in this case doesn't matter; maybe there is a responsible third roommate, or maybe someone's mom stopped by with milk after going to the store. Who knows?!? The point of this example is a universal truth about Necessary Assumption questions: Denying the correct answer will simply obliterate the conclusion. The question stem tells you, after all, that the assumption is *required* by the conclusion.

In the video that accompanies this Spotlight, an LSAT Channel expert will explain why the Denial Test works only in Necessary Assumption questions, why it is not meant to be your initial approach to these questions, and how you can effectively use it as a final strategy to "prove" the correct answer. Here are two official LSAT questions that you'll go over in the video lesson.

8. Economist: In the interaction between producers and consumers, the only obligation that all parties have is to act in the best interests of their own side. And distribution of information about product defects is in the best interests of the consumer. So consumers are always obligated to report product defects they discover, while producers are never obligated to reveal them.

Which one of the following is an assumption required by the economist's argument?

(A) It is never in the best interests of producers for a producer to reveal a product defect.

(B) No one expects producers to act in a manner counter to their own best interests.

(C) Any product defect is likely to be discovered by consumers.

(D) A product defect is more likely to be discovered by a consumer than by a producer.

(E) The best interests of consumers never coincide with the best interests of producers.

PrepTest105 Sec1 Q8

17. When exercising the muscles in one's back, it is important, in order to maintain a healthy back, to exercise the muscles on opposite sides of the spine equally. After all, balanced muscle development is needed to maintain a healthy back, since the muscles on opposite sides of the spine must pull equally in opposing directions to keep the back in proper alignment and protect the spine.

Which one of the following is an assumption required by the argument?

(A) Muscles on opposite sides of the spine that are equally well developed will be enough to keep the back in proper alignment.

(B) Exercising the muscles on opposite sides of the spine unequally tends to lead to unbalanced muscle development.

(C) Provided that one exercises the muscles on opposite sides of the spine equally, one will have a generally healthy back.

(D) If the muscles on opposite sides of the spine are exercised unequally, one's back will be irreparably damaged.

(E) One should exercise daily to ensure that the muscles on opposite sides of the spine keep the back in proper alignment.

PrepTest123 Sec3 Q17

Complete answers and explanations are provided in the LSAT Channel Spotlight video "The Denial Test" in your online Study Plan.

Practice Try some Assumption questions on your own. Remember to follow the Logical Reasoning Method. In Step 1, identify the stem as a Sufficient or Necessary Assumption question. In Step 2, identify the evidence and the conclusion. In Step 3, ask: Does the author move from certain terms or concepts in the evidence to different terms or concepts in the conclusion? Or does the author use relevant evidence to draw a conclusion that is too strong? Determine the argument's assumption and then, in Step 4, match it to the correct answer. When you're finished, check the expert analyses on the pages that follow the exercise.

Step 2:	Step 1:

21. Health officials claim that because the foods and beverages mentioned or consumed on many television programs are extremely low in nutritional value, watching television has a bad influence on the dietary habits of television viewers.

The claim by health officials depends on the presupposition that

(A) the eating and drinking habits of people on television programs are designed to mirror the eating and drinking habits of television viewers

(B) seeing some foods and beverages being consumed on, or hearing them mentioned on, television programs increases the likelihood that viewers will consume similar kinds of foods and beverages

(C) the food and beverage industry finances television programs so that the foods and beverages that have recently appeared on the market can be advertised on those programs

(D) television viewers are only interested in the people on television programs who have the same eating and drinking habits as they do

(E) the eating and drinking habits of people on television programs provide health officials with accurate predictions about the food and beverages that will become popular among television viewers

PrepTest101 Sec3 Q13

Step 3:	Step 4:

Step 2:	Step 1:

22. The only physical factor preventing a human journey to Mars has been weight. Carrying enough fuel to propel a conventional spacecraft to Mars and back would make even the lightest craft too heavy to be launched from Earth. A device has recently been invented, however, that allows an otherwise conventional spacecraft to refill the craft's fuel tanks with fuel manufactured from the Martian atmosphere for the return trip. Therefore, it is possible for people to go to Mars in a spacecraft that carries this device and then return.

Which one of the following is an assumption on which the argument depends?

(A) The amount of fuel needed for a spacecraft to return from Mars is the same as the amount of fuel needed to travel from Earth to Mars.

(B) The fuel manufactured from the Martian atmosphere would not differ in composition from the fuel used to travel to Mars.

(C) The device for manufacturing fuel from the Martian atmosphere would not take up any of the spaceship crew's living space.

(D) A conventional spacecraft equipped with the device would not be appreciably more expensive to construct than current spacecraft typically are.

(E) The device for manufacturing fuel for the return to Earth weighs less than the tanks of fuel that a conventional spacecraft would otherwise need to carry from Earth for the return trip.

PrepTest104 Sec4 Q9

Step 3:	Step 4:

Step 2:	Step 1:

23. Most people feel that they are being confused by the information from broadcast news. This could be the effect of the information's being delivered too quickly or of its being poorly organized. Analysis of the information content of a typical broadcast news story shows that news stories are far lower in information density than the maximum information density with which most people can cope at any one time. So the information in typical broadcast news stories is poorly organized.

Which one of the following is an assumption that the argument requires in order for its conclusion to be properly drawn?

(A) It is not the number of broadcast news stories to which a person is exposed that is the source of the feeling of confusion.

(B) Poor organization of information in a news story makes it impossible to understand the information.

(C) Being exposed to more broadcast news stories within a given day would help a person to better understand the news.

(D) Most people can cope with a very high information density.

(E) Some people are being overwhelmed by too much information.

PrepTest104 Sec4 Q19

Step 3:	Step 4:

Step 2:	Step 1:

24. Children fall into three groups—nontasters, regular tasters, and supertasters—depending on how strongly they experience tastes. Supertasters strongly prefer mild cheddar cheese to sharp, regular tasters weakly prefer mild to sharp, and nontasters show no preference. Also, the more bitter a food tastes, the less children like it. Thus, supertasters experience sharp cheddar as tasting more bitter than mild cheddar, but nontasters experience sharp cheddar as tasting no more bitter than mild cheddar.

Which one of the following, if assumed, enables the conclusion above to be properly inferred?

(A) Supertasters like mild cheddar cheese more than do regular tasters.

(B) The age of the child is the most important factor in determining whether that child is a nontaster, a regular taster, or a supertaster.

(C) The sweeter a food tastes, the more children like it.

(D) Bitterness is the only factor relevant to how strongly children prefer sharp cheddar cheese to mild cheddar cheese.

(E) Nontasters tend to like a wider variety of foods than do regular tasters, who in turn like a wider variety of foods than do supertasters.

PrepTest105 Sec4 Q22

Step 3:	Step 4:

Step 2:	Step 1:

25. We ought to pay attention only to the intrinsic properties of a work of art. Its other, extrinsic properties are irrelevant to our aesthetic interactions with it. For example, when we look at a painting we should consider only what is directly presented in our experience of it. What is really aesthetically relevant, therefore, is not what a painting symbolizes, but what it directly presents to experience.

The conclusion follows logically if which one of the following is added to the premises?

(A) What an artwork symbolizes involves only extrinsic properties of that work.

(B) There are certain properties of our experiences of artworks that can be distinguished as symbolic properties.

(C) Only an artwork's intrinsic properties are relevant to our aesthetic interactions with it.

(D) It is possible in theory for an artwork to symbolize nothing.

(E) An intrinsic property of an artwork is one that relates the work to itself.

PrepTest106 Sec1 Q24

Step 3:	Step 4:

Step 2:	Step 1:

26. Maude is incessantly engaging in diatribes against people who are materialistic. But her hypocrisy is evinced by the sentimental treatment of the watch her grandmother gave her. She certainly is very fond of the watch—she worries about damaging it; in fact she always sets it carefully in a special box before going to bed.

Which one of the following is an assumption on which the argument depends?

(A) Possessions that come from relatives are treated with better care than those that do not.

(B) Sentimental attachment to a single possession indicates being materialistic.

(C) People who care about material things in general tend to take special care of all their possessions.

(D) Maude's watch is not the only material thing she especially cares for.

(E) People who are not materialistic tend to have merely sentimental attachments to things.

PrepTest105 Sec4 Q4

Step 3:	Step 4:

Step 2:	Step 1:

27. Historian: We can learn about the medical history of individuals through chemical analysis of their hair. It is likely, for example, that Isaac Newton's psychological problems were due to mercury poisoning; traces of mercury were found in his hair. Analysis is now being done on a lock of Beethoven's hair. Although no convincing argument has shown that Beethoven ever had a venereal disease, some people hypothesize that venereal disease caused his deafness. Since mercury was commonly ingested in Beethoven's time to treat venereal disease, if researchers find a trace of mercury in his hair, we can conclude that this hypothesis is correct.

Which one of the following is an assumption on which the historian's argument depends?

(A) None of the mercury introduced into the body can be eliminated.

(B) Some people in Beethoven's time did not ingest mercury.

(C) Mercury is an effective treatment for venereal disease.

(D) Mercury poisoning can cause deafness in people with venereal disease.

(E) Beethoven suffered from psychological problems of the same severity as Newton's.

PrepTest106 Sec1 Q16

Step 3:	Step 4:

Expert Analysis

Take a look at how an LSAT expert evaluates these arguments.

Step 2: Conclusion: Watching television negatively influences viewers' diets. *because* Evidence: Food and beverages seen on television are low in nutrition.	**Step 1:** The "presupposition" an argument "depends" on indicates a Necessary Assumption question.

21. Health officials claim that because the foods and beverages mentioned or consumed on many television programs are extremely low in nutritional value, watching television has a bad influence on the dietary habits of television viewers.

The claim by health officials depends on the presupposition that

(A) the eating and drinking habits of people on television programs are designed to mirror the eating and drinking habits of television viewers

(B) seeing some foods and beverages being consumed on, or hearing them mentioned on, television programs increases the likelihood that viewers will consume similar kinds of foods and beverages

(C) the food and beverage industry finances television programs so that the foods and beverages that have recently appeared on the market can be advertised on those programs

(D) television viewers are only interested in the people on television programs who have the same eating and drinking habits as they do

(E) the eating and drinking habits of people on television programs provide health officials with accurate predictions about the food and beverages that will become popular among television viewers

PrepTest101 Sec3 Q13

Step 3: The author jumps from *seeing* foods on TV to being *influenced* in dietary choices. The assumption here is that simply watching TV is enough to influence TV watchers' behavior.	**Step 4:** (B) is correct. This matches the prediction that viewers are influenced by TV in their food choices.

Wrong answers: (A) 180. Rather than viewers copying TV, this indicates TV mimics viewers' eating habits. (C) Outside the Scope. The argument is only concerned with TV's influence on viewers, not why certain foods got on TV in the first place. (D) Extreme ("only") and 180. This answer suggests that viewers are drawn to TV characters who dine as they do, while the argument assumes that seeing TV characters eat particular foods will lead viewers to dine on the same foods. (E) Extreme. It is merely necessary that foods shown on TV have some negative influence on viewers' diets, not that they are accurate predictors of future trends.

Step 2: Conclusion: The new device will allow for a return trip to and from Mars. *because* Evidence: 1) Weight is the only factor precluding such a trip; 2) fuel for round-trip travel is too heavy for the craft to launch; 3) a new device allows spacecraft to refuel with fuel manufactured on Mars.	**Step 1:** The "assumption on which the argument depends" indicates a Necessary Assumption question.

22. The only physical factor preventing a human journey to Mars has been weight. Carrying enough fuel to propel a conventional spacecraft to Mars and back would make even the lightest craft too heavy to be launched from Earth. A device has recently been invented, however, that allows an otherwise conventional spacecraft to refill the craft's fuel tanks with fuel manufactured from the Martian atmosphere for the return trip. Therefore, it is possible for people to go to Mars in a spacecraft that carries this device and then return.

Which one of the following is an assumption on which the argument depends?

(A) The amount of fuel needed for a spacecraft to return from Mars is the same as the amount of fuel needed to travel from Earth to Mars.

(B) The fuel manufactured from the Martian atmosphere would not differ in composition from the fuel used to travel to Mars.

(C) The device for manufacturing fuel from the Martian atmosphere would not take up any of the spaceship crew's living space.

(D) A conventional spacecraft equipped with the device would not be appreciably more expensive to construct than current spacecraft typically are.

(E) The device for manufacturing fuel for the return to Earth weighs less than the tanks of fuel that a conventional spacecraft would otherwise need to carry from Earth for the return trip.

PrepTest104 Sec4 Q9

Step 3: The argument assumes that eliminating fuel previously needed for a return trip will reduce weight enough to allow the spacecraft to launch. It further assumes that the positives of the device (fuel weight reduction) will not be outweighed by the negatives of the device (presumably it weighs something itself, but not as much as the fuel).	**Step 4:** (E) is correct. This matches the prediction. If the device weighs as much, or more, than the fuel it replaces, then a spacecraft would be too heavy to launch.

Wrong answers: (A) Irrelevant comparison. A balance between fuel use for outbound and inbound trips is not necessary to the argument. In fact, if the outbound trip uses less fuel, then an imbalance would make it easier to launch from Earth. (B) As with (A), such precision is not required. All that matters about the composition of the Martian fuel is that it suitably powers the craft. (C) Outside the Scope. The issue in the argument is weight, not living space. (D) Outside the Scope. Costs are irrelevant to the conclusion regarding the physical possibility of making the trip.

Step 2: Conclusion: Information in typical news broadcasts is poorly organized. *because* Evidence: 1) There are two potential sources of people's confusion from information in broadcast news: i) news is delivered too quickly or ii) news is poorly organized; and 2) there is a reason to believe the news is not delivered too quickly.	**Step 1:** The phrase "assumption that the argument requires" indicates a Necessary Assumption question.

23. Most people feel that they are being confused by the information from broadcast news. This could be the effect of the information's being delivered too quickly or of its being poorly organized. Analysis of the information content of a typical broadcast news story shows that news stories are far lower in information density than the maximum information density with which most people can cope at any one time. So the information in typical broadcast news stories is poorly organized.

Which one of the following is an assumption that the argument requires in order for its conclusion to be properly drawn?

(A) It is not the number of broadcast news stories to which a person is exposed that is the source of the feeling of confusion.

(B) Poor organization of information in a news story makes it impossible to understand the information.

(C) Being exposed to more broadcast news stories within a given day would help a person to better understand the news.

(D) Most people can cope with a very high information density.

(E) Some people are being overwhelmed by too much information.

PrepTest104 Sec4 Q19

Step 3: This argument identifies two explanations, discounts one, and concludes it must be the other. The assumption is that there can be no other explanation besides the two presented in the evidence. The correct answer may also eliminate a specific alternative explanation for the confusion.	**Step 4:** (A) is correct. This matches the prediction that a correct answer will eliminate an alternative explanation for the confusion. If it were the number of stories that causes the confusion, then it no longer makes sense to conclude that the poor organization is the cause.

Wrong answers: (B) Extreme. It is necessary to the argument that poor organization *can cause* confusion, not that it *makes it impossible* to understand the information. (C) This is consistent with poor organization being the cause of the confusion, but even if more exposure would not help understanding the news, poor organization could still be the cause of the confusion. Also, this potentially suggests (rather than excludes) an alternative cause of the confusion (too little exposure). (D) At most, this supports the premise that the news is not delivered too quickly. But since that premise should be accepted as true, this support is not necessary to the argument. (E) 180. While not contradictory, this runs counter to the argument's assertion that most people are *not* exposed to too much information too quickly.

Step 2: Conclusion: To a child supertaster, sharp cheddar tastes more bitter than mild cheddar; to nontasters, sharp cheddar tastes no more bitter than mild cheddar. *because* Evidence: 1) There are three types of child tasters (non, regular, and super); 2) the more bitter a food tastes, the less children like it; and 3) child supertasters strongly prefer mild cheddar, regular tasters weakly prefer mild, and nontasters have no preference.	**Step 1:** The formulation "if assumed... conclusion...properly inferred" indicates a Sufficient Assumption question.

24. Children fall into three groups—nontasters, regular tasters, and supertasters—depending on how strongly they experience tastes. Supertasters strongly prefer mild cheddar cheese to sharp, regular tasters weakly prefer mild to sharp, and nontasters show no preference. Also, the more bitter a food tastes, the less children like it. Thus, supertasters experience sharp cheddar as tasting more bitter than mild cheddar, but nontasters experience sharp cheddar as tasting no more bitter than mild cheddar.

Which one of the following, if assumed, enables the conclusion above to be properly inferred?

(A) Supertasters like mild cheddar cheese more than do regular tasters.

(B) The age of the child is the most important factor in determining whether that child is a nontaster, a regular taster, or a supertaster.

(C) The sweeter a food tastes, the more children like it.

(D) Bitterness is the only factor relevant to how strongly children prefer sharp cheddar cheese to mild cheddar cheese.

(E) Nontasters tend to like a wider variety of foods than do regular tasters, who in turn like a wider variety of foods than do supertasters.

PrepTest105 Sec4 Q22

Step 3: Based on the preferences of child supertasters and the rule that the more bitter a food tastes the less children like it, it is reasonable to conclude that child supertasters find sharp cheddar more bitter than mild, while nontasters do not. This assumes that there is no distinguishing factor in the taste of cheese other than its bitterness.	**Step 4:** (D) is correct. This matches the prediction and proves the conclusion by eliminating any other potential factor explaining the preferences among the groups.

Wrong answers: (A) While this is consistent with the information provided, it does not prove that bitterness is the factor explaining the relative preferences among the three types of tastes. (B) Outside the Scope. The argument is not concerned with what makes one a super, regular, or non-taster in the first place; it merely describes how those in the different groups experience tastes. (C) If one assumes that sweet is the opposite of bitter, then this is merely redundant with the rule stated in the evidence. If one considers sweetness a separate factor from bitterness that could alternatively explain the preferences, then this is a 180. Either way. (E) Irrelevant Comparison/Outside the Scope. The argument is concerned with what accounts for the cheddar cheese type preferences among the groups and not which group likes a wider variety of foods.

Step 2: Conclusion: One's direct experience of a painting is aesthetically relevant; a painting's symbolism is not aesthetically relevant. *because* Evidence: 1) Intrinsic properties are aesthetically relevant; 2) extrinsic properties are aesthetically irrelevant; 3) direct experience should be considered (i.e., is relevant).	**Step 1:** The formulation "conclusion follows logically... if which one of the following is added" indicates a Sufficient Assumption question.

25. We ought to pay attention only to the intrinsic properties of a work of art. Its other, extrinsic properties are irrelevant to our aesthetic interactions with it. For example, when we look at a painting we should consider only what is directly presented in our experience of it. What is really aesthetically relevant, therefore, is not what a painting symbolizes, but what it directly presents to experience.

The conclusion follows logically if which one of the following is added to the premises?

(A) What an artwork symbolizes involves only extrinsic properties of that work.

(B) There are certain properties of our experiences of artworks that can be distinguished as symbolic properties.

(C) Only an artwork's intrinsic properties are relevant to our aesthetic interactions with it.

(D) It is possible in theory for an artwork to symbolize nothing.

(E) An intrinsic property of an artwork is one that relates the work to itself.

PrepTest106 Sec1 Q24

Step 3: The new, unique concept appearing in the conclusion is *what a painting symbolizes*. Because the evidence states that *extrinsic properties* are irrelevant, and because the author concludes that *symbolism* is irrelevant, then the author must believe that extrinsic properties and symbolism are alike/equivalent.	**Step 4:** (A) is correct. This matches the prediction.

Wrong answers: (B) Distortion. This conflates one's experience of an artwork with its symbolic properties, contrary to the argument, which distinguishes them. This in no way shows that symbolic properties are irrelevant. (C) This merely reiterates one of the premises explicit in the argument. (D) Outside the Scope. The argument pertains to the symbolism in paintings, so an artwork that symbolizes nothing is irrelevant. (E) At most, this relates to the evidence, providing a definition of intrinsic, but it neither connects evidence to conclusion nor proves that symbolism is aesthetically irrelevant.

Step 2: Conclusion: Maude, herself, is materialistic. *because* Evidence: Maude gives sentimental treatment to a watch.	**Step 1:** The phrase "assumption on which the argument depends" indicates a Necessary Assumption question.

26. Maude is incessantly engaging in diatribes against people who are materialistic. But her hypocrisy is evinced by the sentimental treatment of the watch her grandmother gave her. She certainly is very fond of the watch—she worries about damaging it; in fact she always sets it carefully in a special box before going to bed.

Which one of the following is an assumption on which the argument depends?

(A) Possessions that come from relatives are treated with better care than those that do not.

(B) Sentimental attachment to a single possession indicates being materialistic.

(C) People who care about material things in general tend to take special care of all their possessions.

(D) Maude's watch is not the only material thing she especially cares for.

(E) People who are not materialistic tend to have merely sentimental attachments to things.

PrepTest105 Sec4 Q4

Step 3: The Mismatched Concepts in this argument are *sentimental treatment* of a possession and being *materialistic*. The assumption is that such sentimental treatment is equivalent to materialistic behavior.	**Step 4:** (B) is correct. This matches the prediction by linking sentimental attachment to materialism.

Wrong answers: (A) Irrelevant Comparison. This is consistent with the background details regarding the watch, but does nothing to connect such sentimentality to materialism. (C) Extreme. This argument involves a claim based on the treatment of a single possession and doesn't extend to people's treatment of all their possessions. (D) This supports the claim that Maude is materialistic, but it is not necessary to the argument. The author's claim that Maude is materialistic would not fall apart if Maude was only materialistic regarding the watch. (E) 180. This argument bases its claim of materialism on a sentimental attachment.

Step 2: Conclusion: If researchers find traces of mercury in Beethoven's hair, then he had venereal disease. *because* Evidence: In Beethoven's time, mercury was commonly ingested to treat venereal disease.	**Step 1:** The phrase "assumption on which the... argument depends" indicates a Necessary Assumption question.

27. Historian: We can learn about the medical history of individuals through chemical analysis of their hair. It is likely, for example, that Isaac Newton's psychological problems were due to mercury poisoning; traces of mercury were found in his hair. Analysis is now being done on a lock of Beethoven's hair. Although no convincing argument has shown that Beethoven ever had a venereal disease, some people hypothesize that venereal disease caused his deafness. Since mercury was commonly ingested in Beethoven's time to treat venereal disease, if researchers find a trace of mercury in his hair, we can conclude that this hypothesis is correct.

Which one of the following is an assumption on which the historian's argument depends?

(A) None of the mercury introduced into the body can be eliminated.

(B) Some people in Beethoven's time did not ingest mercury.

(C) Mercury is an effective treatment for venereal disease.

(D) Mercury poisoning can cause deafness in people with venereal disease.

(E) Beethoven suffered from psychological problems of the same severity as Newton's.

PrepTest106 Sec3 Q16

Step 3: The evidence identifies the treatment of venereal disease as a possible explanation for the presence of any mercury found in Beethoven's hair, while the conclusion treats it as the only reason for the presence of mercury. The correct answer will either indicate that the presence of mercury is not universal among people of that time, or it will eliminate an alternative explanation for the presence of any mercury.	**Step 4:** (B) is correct. The Denial Test proves that this assumption is necessary to the argument. If "everybody in Beethoven's time ingested mercury," then finding a trace of mercury in Beethoven's hair would not distinguish Beethoven from any of his contemporaries. It would not be more likely that he had venereal disease, or that venereal disease caused his deafness.

Wrong answers: (A) Extreme. The argument does not rely on the claim that no mercury, once ingested, can ever leave the body. Indeed, the conclusion is conditioned on finding even "a trace of mercury" in the hair. (C) Outside the Scope. Whether mercury was actually effective in treating venereal disease is irrelevant to explaining the presence of mercury in Beethoven's hair. (D) Outside the Scope. The argument concludes that a trace of mercury is evidence of venereal disease, not that Beethoven had mercury poisoning, or that mercury poisoning caused his deafness. (E) Outside the Scope. Newton's psychological problems merely provide context and are irrelevant to the argument regarding mercury and venereal disease in Beethoven.

Other Assumption Family Question Types

By now, you should have a good grasp of the two main argument structures you'll see on the LSAT: Mismatched Concepts and Overlooked Possibilities. You've also seen the ways in which the testmaker can evaluate your understanding of these argument types by asking you to identify an argument's sufficient or necessary assumption. But the LSAT can test you on more than just your ability to discern an argument's assumption. From the same argument, the testmaker can ask you a number of different questions: you may be asked to identify the flaw in an author's reasoning, to strengthen or weaken an argument, or even to determine an underlying principle of the argument. One thing to keep in mind is that even though different question types may change the format of the answers, the argument itself and the assumption of the argument will not change. Each of the arguments you see on the LSAT will be constructed in a similar way: an author fails to provide evidence sufficient to establish his conclusion. As such, the way in which you approach these questions will be the same as the way in which you approach Assumption questions. The only difference is in Step 3; here, you will use your knowledge of the different question types to create an appropriate and question-specific prediction.

As an example, let's take a look at an argument we've seen before.

> The miscarriage of justice in the Barker case was due to the mistaken views held by some of the forensic scientists involved in the case, who believed that they owed allegiance only to the prosecuting lawyers. Justice was thwarted because these forensic scientists failed to provide evidence impartially to both the defense and the prosecution. Hence it is not forensic evidence in general that should be condemned for this injustice.
>
> *PrepTest105 Sec4 Q16*

Previously, we used this argument to provide you practice in breaking down an argument and recognizing an author's assumption: that the Barker case is representative of forensic science generally. Indeed, this argument could have been used for an Assumption question on the LSAT. However, it actually appeared on the LSAT as a Strengthen question: "Which one of the following, if true, most strengthens the argument?" It also would have been right at home as the argument in a Weaken or Flaw question, as well.

Take a look at how an LSAT expert characterizes each question stem, and how she relates each to the stimulus about the Barker case.

LSAT Question Stem	Analysis
The reasoning in the argument is most vulnerable to criticism on the grounds that the argument	The correct answer to this **Flaw** question will describe the way in which the author's reasoning is flawed. For the argument about the Barker case, you might see an answer choice such as "Overlooks the possibility that the forensic scientists in the Barker case are representative of the practices of the vast majority of forensic scientists across the nation."
Which of the following, if true, most seriously weakens the argument?	The correct answer to this **Weaken** question will present a new piece of information that, if true, will make the author's conclusion less likely. For the argument about the Barker case, you might see an answer choice such as "In confidential surveys, a majority of forensic scientists acknowledge that they believe their primary obligations are to the prosecution in criminal cases."
Which of the following, if true, provides the most support for the argument?	The correct answer to this **Strengthen** question will present a new piece of information that, if true, will make the author's conclusion more likely. For the argument about the Barker case, you might see an answer choice such as "Most forensic scientists acknowledge a professional obligation to provide evidence impartially to both the defense and the prosecution."

In the next part of the chapter, we'll take a look at each one of these unique question types. By the end, you'll be able to (1) identify each question type based on the phrasing in the question stem and (2) turn any argument's assumption into a prediction that is appropriate for the specific question type.

Flaw Questions

Prepare

LEARNING OBJECTIVES

In this section, you'll learn to:

- Identify Flaw questions.
- Recognize and characterize the most common flawed argument patterns.
- Recognize an abstractly worded but correct answer choice in a Flaw question.

One of the ways the LSAT can test your ability to analyze arguments is by asking you to determine the error in the author's reasoning. These Flaw questions, as we call them, might be thought of as *describe the flaw* questions because that's what you are being asked to do. On test day, you'll face roughly eight of these questions. With a few notable exceptions discussed later in this section, the arguments you'll find in Flaw questions are identical to the ones you see in other Assumption Family questions.

As always in Logical Reasoning, your first step is to identify the question type from the stem. To recognize a Flaw question, look for language that uses words or phrases like "point out a flaw," "identify the error in reasoning," or "vulnerable to criticism." Take a look at the following to see some common Flaw question stems:

LSAT Question Stem	Analysis
The reasoning in the argument is questionable because the argument *PrepTest107 Sec4 Q25*	The correct answer to this Flaw question will describe the way in which the evidence fails to properly support the conclusion.
The argument's reasoning is flawed because the argument overlooks the possibility that *PrepTest104 Sec4 Q7*	The correct answer to this Flaw question will describe an overlooked possibility that the author did not take into account.
The plant manager's argument is most vulnerable to criticism on which one of the following grounds? *PrepTest107 Sec4 Q14*	The correct answer to this Flaw question will describe the way in which the evidence fails to properly support the conclusion.

Your approach to Flaw questions starts in the same way as your approach to other Assumption Family questions: Untangle the stimulus into evidence and conclusion, then identify the author's assumption. The types of arguments you'll see in Flaw questions are generally the same as those discussed earlier in the chapter—either the author uses evidence that is not necessarily related to the conclusion (Mismatched Concepts) or the author uses relevant evidence to draw an extreme conclusion (Overlooked Possibilities). Indeed, in Flaw questions, you're likely to run into the specific types of Mismatched Concepts and Overlooked Possibilities discussed earlier in the chapter. The good news is that the bulk of Flaw questions will ask you about just a handful of common argument types, which are listed on the next page. Being able to anticipate the likelihood of certain argument patterns based on the question type will help you untangle arguments and form predictions more quickly and efficiently.

Common Flaw Types

LSAT STRATEGY

Flaw questions are dominated by these common argument types:

- Overlooked Possibilities: Failure to consider alternative explanations
- Overlooked Possibilities: A conclusion of causation based on evidence of correlation
- Overlooked Possibilities: Confusing necessary and sufficient terms
- Mismatched Concepts (including alike/equivalent, mutually exclusive, and representation)

For many test takers, finding the assumption or determining the pattern of an argument in a Flaw question is not hugely challenging. Instead, the difficult part of correctly answering a Flaw question is matching a prediction to the correct answer choice. This is because the LSAT words the correct answers to Flaw questions differently than it does the correct answers to other Assumption Family questions. Consider, for example, the following argument:

> Joe started feeling sick a short while after eating at the restaurant around the corner. Clearly, he got food poisoning from the food he ate there!

This is a classic causal argument. The author takes two things that happened around the same time, eating at the restaurant and getting sick, and concludes that one of them must have caused the other. As you learned earlier in this chapter, the assumption of the argument is *No ARC*: There is no *alternative cause* for the illness; the illness isn't the reason why the author went out to eat (*reversal*); and, the fact that the author went out to eat right before getting ill isn't just a *coincidence*. The correct answer to a Necessary Assumption question would rule out *A*, *R*, or *C*. Consider:

> Joe did not catch a stomach virus from his neighbor.

This rules out an *alternative cause*. But a Flaw question's answer might say something like...

> Overlooks the possibility that Joe caught a stomach virus from his neighbor.

or even ...

> Mistakes a correlation between two events for one event causing the other.

The difference between the first two of these answer choices is not very great. The only distinction is that the Flaw answer choice is descriptive—it tells us that the author is overlooking something rather than ruling out a specific possibility. The difference between the Necessary Assumption answer and the second Flaw answer, however, is much bigger. The second Flaw answer is also describing the problem, but it is doing so in much more abstract terms. One key to success in Flaw questions is learning how to spot your prediction stated in different language.

Take a look at how an LSAT expert might analyze a Flaw question.

Step 2: Conclusion: The tourist industry will not damage the seaside environment. *because* Evidence: People in the tourist industry wouldn't knowingly damage the tourist industry, and so ... Subsidiary Conclusion: People in the tourist industry wouldn't knowingly damage the seaside environment.	**Step 1:** The phrase "vulnerable to criticism" indicates a Flaw question.

People in the tourist industry know that excessive development of seaside areas by the industry damages the environment. Such development also hurts the tourist industry by making these areas unattractive to tourists, a fact of which people in the tourist industry are well aware. People in the tourist industry would never knowingly do anything to damage the industry. Therefore, they would never knowingly damage the seaside environment, and the people who are concerned about damage to the seaside environment thus have nothing to fear from the tourist industry.

The reasoning in the argument is most vulnerable to criticism on which one of the following grounds?

(A) No support is provided for the claim that excessive development hurts the tourist industry.

(B) That something is not the cause of a problem is used as evidence that it never coexists with that problem.

(C) The argument shifts from applying a characteristic to a few members of a group to applying the characteristic to all members of that group.

(D) The possibility that the tourist industry would unintentionally harm the environment is ignored.

(E) The argument establishes that a certain state of affairs is likely and then treats that as evidence that the state of affairs is inevitable.

PrepTest101 Sec3 Q12

Step 3: The author concludes that the tourist industry will cause no harm to the seaside environment from evidence that people in the tourist industry would not knowingly do something that would harm their industry. This overlooks the possibility those in the industry might unintentionally harm the seaside environment.	**Step 4:** (D) is correct. This matches the prediction perfectly. The only difference is that this answer choice is written in the passive voice.

Wrong answers: (A) Outside the Scope. The author is not obligated to provide support for something he claims that people in the tourist industry already know. (B) Extreme. The argument does not conclude that excessive development *never coexists* with damage to the seaside environment, but simply that the tourist industry will not knowingly cause excessive development in this case. (C) Distortion. There is no shift from some members of the tourist industry to all. The evidence is about the tourist industry writ large. (E) 180. The argument does not shift from *likely* to definite; the author is quite definite throughout.

The correct answer choice (D) points out that the author ignores the possibility of *unintentional* harm to the seaside environment, which, if true, would undermine his argument. This is simply a twist on how the answer to an Assumption question would have been worded. The heart of prediction in Assumption Family questions is learning to say the same few things in a variety of different ways.

LSAT STRATEGY

Some facts to remember about Flaw questions:

- The correct answer will *describe* the error in the author's reasoning.
- You will be tested on your ability to identify flaws in both Mismatched Concepts arguments and Overlooked Possibilities arguments.
- Correct answer choices are often written in abstract language; form a prediction and match it to the closest answer choice.

Less Common Flaw Types

In addition to the common flaws previously listed (as well as the argument types you read about earlier in the chapter), the testmaker may ask you to identify a few rarer types of arguments. These are not included on the test often, but it's important to know them when you see them. The following are short descriptions of the most important ones:

Mismatched Concepts—Equivocation: On the LSAT, an error of equivocation means using the same word or phrase twice in an argument but with two different meanings. For example: "Jason says that when Alex is around, it drives him crazy; therefore, I have decided to have him evaluated by a psychologist who specializes in crazy people." Notice that the argument uses the word *crazy* in the evidence to mean "annoyed," but it uses the word *crazy* in the conclusion to mean "mentally disturbed." This pattern is quite rare in LSAT stimuli. However, wrong answer choices in Flaw questions frequently refer to equivocation, so it's important to understand the flaw this term describes.

Mismatched Concepts—Parts to Whole: A parts-to-whole argument is very similar to a representation argument. The author of an argument looks at one piece of something—say a chapter in a book—and uses that to make a conclusion about the entirety of that thing—say the book itself. Or the author of an argument will look at many pieces individually and then make a deduction regarding the pieces together: "Each of these seven energy drinks is safe to drink, and so I'll be fine if I drink them all at once." This argument is rare, but when it shows up on the LSAT, it is almost always in a Flaw question.

Circular Reasoning: Circular reasoning describes an argument in which the author uses equivalent statements for both the evidence and the conclusion, for example, "Chris must be in debt, for if Chris says he is not in debt, he is surely lying." Much like equivocation, circular reasoning almost never shows up on the LSAT as the correct answer describing the author's flaw in the stimulus argument, but it is a common wrong answer choice in Flaw questions.

Evidence Contradicts Conclusion: There have been very few instances of this particular argument on the LSAT. Here is a simple example: "This book didn't sell well at all; nearly all copies printed were returned to the publisher. It follows that the publisher should print more copies as soon as possible." If the book didn't sell, the logical inference is that more copies should *not* be printed. Again, this pattern is rare; though the evidence in any Assumption Family question will never fully prove the conclusion, it almost never happens that the evidence actually contradicts the conclusion. Despite the fact that this pattern has shown up only a handful of times, it is a common wrong answer choice in Flaw questions. Be wary of choosing such an answer if you didn't initially predict it.

That list is not exhaustive. Through the decades, LSAT Flaw questions have included rare instances of arguments flawed in the following ways.

LSAT STRATEGY

Some extremely rare flaw arguments you might see on the LSAT:

- Conflating numerical values with percentage values
- Using evidence of belief to draw a conclusion of fact
- Attacking the person making the argument instead of the argument (ad hominem)
- Stating that absence of evidence is evidence of absence
- Making an inappropriate appeal to authority
- Failing to address the other speaker's point

Of course, the odds of running into any of the flaws listed above are extremely low. At the end of the day, if you know the common argument patterns discussed earlier in the chapter, you should be able to tackle everything you will see on test day.

CHANNEL SPOTLIGHT

Flaw School

By The LSAT Channel Faculty

Watch the video lesson for this Spotlight in your online Study Plan.

This isn't talked about very much, but it's time for you to know. There's something a bit unpleasant that happens to a lot of students when they study for the LSAT. It may happen to you, too. In fact, it's something that gets even worse when you get to law school. It will annoy your friends, and maybe even your loved ones. Lively conversations may grind to a halt when you approach, and there will likely be a measurable uptick in eye rolling in your immediate vicinity. You, dear test taker, are going to start picking apart every argument you hear.

You see, as we mature, our argumentative skills develop. Childhood staples—like "No. You are!"—give way to more subtle approaches—such as the evergreen "She started it." Later, we learn to dispute the factual basis of an opponent's position, and with higher education comes the art of supporting contentions with citations and evidence.

What lies beyond that is reserved to a select group, and as someone bound for law school, you are definitely a member. These are the people able to attack an argument's reasoning. These are the people who actually know what they are talking about when they say things like, "You're mistaking necessity for sufficiency," "That conclusion is based on an unrepresentative sample," or "C'mon, man, you can infer the contrapositive, but not the converse." You'll use terms such as "ad hominem," "equivocation," and "circular reasoning" the way sportscasters use catchphrases. Yes, that's going to be you if it isn't already. Try not to be too hard on your friends' arguments . . . if you can help it.

In this Spotlight's video, an LSAT Channel expert (and some friends who make a lot of errors in their reasoning) will give you an introduction to the logical reasoning flaws most frequently tested on the LSAT. It's a fun way to start building some very important LSAT skills, skills that you will use throughout law school, and even in law practice. Welcome to Flaw School.

Drill: Identifying Argument Types in Flaw Question Answer Choices

Understanding the different ways in which the LSAT can describe familiar argument patterns requires a careful study of the answer choices in Flaw questions. When you study, be sure to spend time looking at answer choices and asking yourself which argument patterns they are referencing. Doing so will help you quickly eliminate tempting choices on test day. Let's start that process now with a short exercise. A list of sample answer choices follows. Your job is to match those answer choices to the flawed argument type they are describing.

Answer Choices	My Analysis
28. Overlooks the possibility that there are some red cars that do not take unleaded gas.	
29. Two events that merely occur together are taken as though one is the cause of the other.	
30. Bases a general claim on a few exceptional instances.	
31. Treats as similar two cases that may be different in a fundamental way.	
32. Allows a key term to shift in meaning during the course of the argument.	
33. Presupposes what it seeks to establish.	
34. Mistakes something that is necessary to bring about a situation for something that merely can bring about that situation.	

Expert Analysis

Now take a look at the expert analysis to see how you did:

Answer Choices	Analysis
28. Overlooks the possibility that there are some red cars that do not take unleaded gas.	"Overlooks the possibility that" is a classic phrase that is most often a reference to Overlooked Possibilities arguments. In this case, it would mean the author assumes that all red cars take unleaded gas, overlooking the possibility that some do not.
29. Two events that merely occur together are taken as though one is the cause of the other.	Describes the flaw of confusing correlation for causation.
30. Bases a general claim on a few exceptional instances.	Making a general claim about a group using evidence about a smaller group is the definition of Mismatched Concepts—Representation.
31. Treats as similar two cases that may be different in a fundamental way.	This is just another way of describing Mismatched Concepts–Alike/Equivalent. The author assumes that two different things are the same.
32. Allows a key term to shift in meaning during the course of the argument.	Any answer choice that says that a term is given more than one meaning in an argument is a reference to equivocation (and is probably wrong).
33. Presupposes what it seeks to establish.	This is the definition of circular reasoning.
34. Mistakes something that is necessary to bring about a situation for something that merely can bring about that situation.	The word "necessary" indicates that this is an Overlooked Possibilities—Necessary versus Sufficient problem.

Here's an LSAT expert's analysis of another full Flaw question. Review it to see how the expert uses the tactics and tools you've been learning.

Step 2: Conclusion: The mouse on Fred's computer became unplugged. *because* Evidence: A program on Fred's computer that requires a mouse has stopped working.	**Step 1:** The phrase "vulnerable to...criticism" indicates a Flaw question.

Unplugging a peripheral component such as a "mouse" from a personal computer renders all of the software programs that require that component unusable on that computer. On Fred's personal computer, a software program that requires a mouse has become unusable. So it must be that the mouse for Fred's computer became unplugged.

The argument is most vulnerable to which one of the following criticisms?

(A) It contains a shift in the meaning of "unusable" from "permanently unusable" to "temporarily unusable."

(B) It treats an event that can cause a certain result as though that event is necessary to bring about that result.

(C) It introduces information unrelated to its conclusion as evidence in support of that conclusion.

(D) It attempts to support its conclusion by citing a generalization that is too broad.

(E) It overlooks the possibility that some programs do not require a peripheral component such as a mouse.

PrepTest104 Sec4 Q10

Step 3: The evidence indicates that an unplugged mouse would cause the program to stop working, but that does not mean nothing else can be the cause. The correct answer could offer an overlooked possibility, but will more likely describe how the argument treats a condition *sufficient* to cause the program to crash as though it were *necessary* for the program to crash.	**Step 4:** (B) is correct. The evidence indicates that an unplugged mouse *can* cause the program to stop working (i.e., sufficient), but the conclusion treats an unplugged mouse as the *only* potential cause of the problem (i.e., necessary).

Wrong answers: (A) Distortion. The argument simply does not do this. (C) Distortion. The evidence *is* related to the conclusion; the conclusion merely goes too far with that evidence. (D) Distortion. The evidence is not overly broad. Rather, the conclusion interprets it more broadly than is warranted. (E) Outside the Scope. The argument is only concerned with a program that *does* require a mouse.

Common Wording of Flaw Types in Answer Choices

Take a moment now to look over some of the most common argument patterns and answer types in Flaw questions in the LSAT Strategy box. Feel free to return to this list from time to time to hone your ability to get through Flaw answer choices quickly and efficiently.

LSAT STRATEGY

Common Flaw Question Answer Choices by Argument Pattern

Overlooked Possibilities—General	"overlooks the possibility that"/"ignores the possibility that"/"fails to consider" "assumes only one possibility when more exist" "treats one explanation of many as though it were the only one"
Overlooked Possibilities—Causation	"mistakes a correlation for causation" "presumes that because one event was followed by another, the first event caused the second" "ignores the possibility that two things that occur together may be only coincidentally related"
Overlooked Possibilities—Necessary vs Sufficient	"confuses a result with a condition that is required to bring about that result" "mistakes something that is necessary for a particular outcome for something that is merely sufficient for that outcome" "ignores the possibility that a particular outcome may be sufficient but not necessary for another"
Mismatched Concepts—General	"facts that are not directly related to the case are used to support a conclusion about it" "draws an analogy between two things that are not alike enough in the ways they would need to be in order for the conclusion to be properly drawn"
Mismatched Concepts—Representation	"draws a general conclusion from a few isolated instances" "generalizes from an unrepresentative sample" "treats the children living in County X as though they were representative of all children that age living in State Y"
Mismatched Concepts—Equivocation	"relies on an ambiguity in the term *plant*" "allows a key phrase to shift in meaning from one use to the next" "fails to provide a sufficient definition of a key term"
Circular Reasoning	"the conclusion is no more than a restatement of the evidence used to support it" "restates its conclusion without providing sufficient justification for accepting it" "presupposes the truth of what it seeks to establish"
Evidence Contradicts the Conclusion	"the evidence given actually undermines the argument's conclusion" "some of the evidence given is inconsistent with other evidence presented" "draws a recommendation that is inconsistent with the evidence given to support it"

Practice Now that you've had a chance to learn the basics of Flaw questions, take some time to practice a few on your own. As always, follow the Kaplan Method and work to make a prediction in Step 3. After you've tried these on your own, check out the expert analyses on the following pages.

Step 2:	Step 1:

35. Television allows us to transmit images of ourselves that propagate into space. The earliest of these transmissions have by now reached all of our neighboring star systems. None of these transmissions, so far as we know, has been recognized; we have yet to receive any messages of extraterrestrial origin. We must conclude that there is no extraterrestrial intelligence in any of our neighboring star systems.

The reasoning in the argument is questionable because the argument

(A) fails to provide an adequate definition of the word "messages"

(B) infers that there is no extraterrestrial intelligence in neighboring star systems from the lack of proof that there is

(C) assigns too little importance to the possibility that there is extraterrestrial intelligence beyond our neighboring star systems

(D) neglects to mention that some governments have sent meticulously prepared messages and recordings on spacecraft

(E) overlooks the immense probability that most star systems are uninhabited

PrepTest105 Sec4 Q13

Step 3:	Step 4:

Step 2:	**Step 1:**

36. Several excellent candidates have been proposed for the presidency of United Wire, and each candidate would bring to the job different talents and experience. If the others are compared with Jones, however, it will be apparent that none of them has her unique set of qualifications. Jones, therefore, is best qualified to be the new president of United Wire.

The argument is vulnerable to criticism on the ground that it

(A) uses flattery to win over those who hold an opposing position

(B) refutes a distorted version of an opposing position

(C) seeks to distinguish one member of a group on the basis of something that applies to all

(D) supports a universal claim on the basis of a single example

(E) describes an individual in terms that appropriately refer only to the group as a whole

PrepTest101 Sec2 Q6

Step 3:	**Step 4:**

Step 2:	**Step 1:**

37. Research indicates that 90 percent of extreme insomniacs consume large amounts of coffee. Since Tom drinks a lot of coffee, it is quite likely that he is an extreme insomniac.

Which one of the following most accurately describes a flaw in the argument's reasoning?

(A) It fails to acknowledge the possibility that Tom is among the 10 percent of people who drink large amounts of coffee who are not extreme insomniacs.

(B) It fails to consider the possible contribution to extreme insomnia of other causes of insomnia besides coffee.

(C) It relies on evidence that does not indicate the frequency of extreme insomnia among people who drink large amounts of coffee.

(D) It draws an inference about one specific individual from evidence that describes only the characteristics of a class of individuals.

(E) It presumes without warrant that drinking coffee always causes insomnia.

PrepTest104 Sec1 Q23

Step 3:	**Step 4:**

Step 2:	**Step 1:**

38. A number of Grandville's wealthiest citizens have been criminals. So, since it is of utmost importance that the Grandville Planning Committee be composed solely of individuals whose personal standards of ethics are beyond reproach, no wealthy person should be appointed to that committee.

The argument is most vulnerable to the criticism that it

(A) confuses a result with something that is sufficient for bringing about that result

(B) mistakes a temporal relationship for a causal relationship

(C) assumes that because a certain action has a certain result the person taking that action intended that result

(D) judges only by subjective standards something that can be readily evaluated according to objective standards

(E) generalizes on the basis of what could be exceptional cases

PrepTest106 Sec3 Q2

Step 3:	**Step 4:**

Step 2:	Step 1:

39. Jane: Television programs and movies that depict violence among teenagers are extremely popular. Given how influential these media are, we have good reason to believe that these depictions cause young people to engage in violent behavior. Hence, depictions of violence among teenagers should be prohibited from movies and television programs, if only in those programs and movies promoted to young audiences.

Maurice: But you are recommending nothing short of censorship! Besides which, your claim that television and movie depictions of violence cause violence is mistaken: violence among young people predates movies and television by centuries.

Maurice's attempted refutation of Jane's argument is vulnerable to criticism on which one of the following grounds?

(A) It presupposes that an unpopular policy cannot possibly achieve its intended purpose.

(B) It confuses a subjective judgment of private moral permissibility with an objective description of social fact.

(C) It rules out something as a cause of a current phenomenon solely on the ground that the phenomenon used to occur without that thing.

(D) It cites purported historical facts that cannot possibly be verified.

(E) It relies on an ambiguity in the term "violence" to justify a claim.

PrepTest106 Sec3 Q5

Step 3:	Step 4:

Expert Analysis

Now that you've had a chance to do these on your own, check your reasoning against the expert analyses below.

Step 2: Conclusion: There is not intelligent extraterrestrial life in neighboring star systems. *because* Evidence: No extraterrestrials have responded to our televised messages.	**Step 1:** The phrase "argument is questionable" indicates a Flaw question.

35. Television allows us to transmit images of ourselves that propagate into space. The earliest of these transmissions have by now reached all of our neighboring star systems. None of these transmissions, so far as we know, has been recognized; we have yet to receive any messages of extraterrestrial origin. We must conclude that there is no extraterrestrial intelligence in any of our neighboring star systems.

The reasoning in the argument is questionable because the argument

(A) fails to provide an adequate definition of the word "messages"

(B) infers that there is no extraterrestrial intelligence in neighboring star systems from the lack of proof that there is

(C) assigns too little importance to the possibility that there is extraterrestrial intelligence beyond our neighboring star systems

(D) neglects to mention that some governments have sent meticulously prepared messages and recordings on spacecraft

(E) overlooks the immense probability that most star systems are uninhabited

PrepTest105 Sec4 Q13

Step 3: The author here uses the absence of any evidence demonstrating alien intelligence to prove that alien intelligence does not exist. The argument also assumes that any "intelligent" extraterrestrial life would have the capability or desire to respond to our calls.	**Step 4:** (B) is correct. Matches the prediction and describes how the argument commits the classic flaw of using "an absence of evidence as evidence of absence."

Wrong answers: (A) The LSAT does not generally consider it a logic flaw to fail to provide a definition for a word, and "messages" is not even an inherently ambiguous term. (C) Outside the Scope. The argument is limited to whether intelligent life exists in neighboring star systems. (D) 180. This fact would strengthen the conclusion that there is no life in neighboring systems. So it is not a logic flaw to fail to consider this information. (E) 180. This possibility supports the author's conclusion and it is not a logic flaw to fail to consider a possibility that supports one's argument.

Step 2: Conclusion: Jones is the best qualified candidate for president.	Step 1: The phrase "vulnerable to criticism" indicates a Flaw question.
because	
Evidence: Jones has a unique set of qualifications to be president.	

36. Several excellent candidates have been proposed for the presidency of United Wire, and each candidate would bring to the job different talents and experience. If the others are compared with Jones, however, it will be apparent that none of them has her unique set of qualifications. Jones, therefore, is best qualified to be the new president of United Wire.

The argument is vulnerable to criticism on the ground that it

(A) uses flattery to win over those who hold an opposing position

(B) refutes a distorted version of an opposing position

(C) seeks to distinguish one member of a group on the basis of something that applies to all

(D) supports a universal claim on the basis of a single example

(E) describes an individual in terms that appropriately refer only to the group as a whole

PrepTest101 Sec2 Q6

Step 3: The argument contains a mismatch between *unique qualifications* in the evidence and *best qualifications* in the conclusion. The assumption here is that a unique set of qualifications makes for the best qualified candidate. Additionally, the first sentence tells us that all of the candidates have their own unique qualifications, so it's not clear why Jones is being singled out.	Step 4: (C) is correct. The author distinguishes Jones on the basis of having *unique* qualifications, even though all of the candidates are themselves unique in their set of qualifications.

Wrong answers: (A) Distortion. The author simply does not use flattery to win anybody over. (B) Distortion. This classic rhetorical strategy, known as a "straw man" argument, is not something the author does. (D) Distortion. The author does not jump to a universal claim. The evidence is about Jones and the conclusion is about Jones. (E) Distortion. The author describes Jones's qualifications as "unique," a term appropriate to the individuals within the group. Indeed, the problem with the argument is that "unique" applies to all of the individuals within the group.

Step 2:	Step 1:
Step 2: Conclusion: Tom is likely an extreme insomniac. *because* Evidence: 1) Tom drinks lots of coffee; and 2) the vast majority of extreme insomniacs consume lots of coffee.	**Step 1:** The phrase "flaw in...reasoning" indicates a Flaw question.

37. Research indicates that 90 percent of extreme insomniacs consume large amounts of coffee. Since Tom drinks a lot of coffee, it is quite likely that he is an extreme insomniac.

Which one of the following most accurately describes a flaw in the argument's reasoning?

(A) It fails to acknowledge the possibility that Tom is among the 10 percent of people who drink large amounts of coffee who are not extreme insomniacs.

(B) It fails to consider the possible contribution to extreme insomnia of other causes of insomnia besides coffee.

(C) It relies on evidence that does not indicate the frequency of extreme insomnia among people who drink large amounts of coffee.

(D) It draws an inference about one specific individual from evidence that describes only the characteristics of a class of individuals

(E) It presumes without warrant that drinking coffee always causes insomnia.

PrepTest104 Sec1 Q23

Step 3:	Step 4:
Step 3: In the evidence, knowing that someone is an extreme insomniac is *sufficient* to know that that person is likely a heavy coffee drinker. In the conclusion, though, the author states that a heavy coffee drinker (Tom) is likely an insomniac. This argument confuses necessary and sufficient terms, and overlooks the possibility that there could be a vastly larger number of heavy coffee drinkers than extreme insomniacs.	**Step 4:** (C) is correct. This choice relates to the possibility that there could be many more heavy coffee drinkers than extreme insomniacs. If there were, say, only 10 extreme insomniacs but 100,000 heavy coffee drinkers, the fact that 9 of 10 extreme insomniacs were heavy coffee drinkers would only dictate that at least 9 of 100,000 heavy coffee drinkers were extreme insomniacs.

Wrong answers: (A) Distortion. The argument implies that 10 percent of extreme insomniacs don't drink coffee, not that 10 percent of people who drink a lot of coffee are not insomniacs. (B) Outside the Scope. This possibility, even if true, is irrelevant to the conclusion regarding the likelihood that Tom is an extreme insomniac. (D) This answer passes the baseline test of something the author does. However, this is not necessarily a logical flaw. The evidence that 90% of extreme insomniacs are heavy coffee drinkers could well be used to reach a conclusion that an individual extreme insomniac is "likely" a heavy coffee drinker. (E) Extreme and Outside the Scope. The argument does not assume any particular causal relationship, let alone that any level of coffee drinking always causes some level of insomnia.

Step 2: Conclusion: Not a single wealthy person should be appointed to the Grandville Planning Committee. *because* Evidence: 1) Everybody on the GPC must have ethics beyond reproach; and 2) some of Grandville's wealthy have been criminals.	**Step 1:** The phrase "vulnerable to . . . criticism" indicates a Flaw question.

38. A number of Grandville's wealthiest citizens have been criminals. So, since it is of utmost importance that the Grandville Planning Committee be composed solely of individuals whose personal standards of ethics are beyond reproach, no wealthy person should be appointed to that committee.

The argument is most vulnerable to the criticism that it

(A) confuses a result with something that is sufficient for bringing about that result

(B) mistakes a temporal relationship for a causal relationship

(C) assumes that because a certain action has a certain result the person taking that action intended that result

(D) judges only by subjective standards something that can be readily evaluated according to objective standards

(E) generalizes on the basis of what could be exceptional cases

PrepTest106 Sec3 Q2

Step 3: The argument makes a number of assumptions, including the assumption that members of the GPC must be from Grandville. However, the most dramatic scope shift is from evidence about an unspecified number of wealthy people from Grandville to a conclusion encompassing all wealthy people. In other words, the author generalizes from a sample that may be too small.	**Step 4:** (E) is correct. This choice matches the prediction by describing how the argument uses evidence that some wealthy people are criminals to reach a conclusion about all wealthy people.

Wrong answers: (A) Distortion. This answer is another way of saying the argument confuses cause and effect, but the argument is not about causation. (B) Distortion. The argument deals with neither temporal nor causal relationships. (C) Distortion. As with (A) and (B), cause and effect (actions and results) are not involved in this argument. (D) Outside the Scope. The author claims that some wealthy citizens have been criminals, but there is no indication that such a claim is subjective. The author's problem is that he wants all wealthy citizens banned when only some have been criminals.

Step 2: Jane's Conclusion: Movies and television programs promoted to young audiences shouldn't be allowed to depict violence among teenagers. *because* Evidence: There is "good reason to believe" that depictions of violence among teenagers "cause young people to engage in violent behavior." Maurice's Conclusion: Depictions of violence in movies does not cause violence. *because* Evidence: Violence among young people occurred for centuries before there were movies and television.	**Step 1:** The phrase "vulnerable to criticism" indicates a Flaw question. Note that you are directed to identify the flaw in *Maurice's* argument.

39. Jane: Television programs and movies that depict violence among teenagers are extremely popular. Given how influential these media are, we have good reason to believe that these depictions cause young people to engage in violent behavior. Hence, depictions of violence among teenagers should be prohibited from movies and television programs, if only in those programs and movies promoted to young audiences.

Maurice: But you are recommending nothing short of censorship! Besides which, your claim that television and movie depictions of violence cause violence is mistaken: violence among young people predates movies and television by centuries.

Maurice's attempted refutation of Jane's argument is vulnerable to criticism on which one of the following grounds?

(A) It presupposes that an unpopular policy cannot possibly achieve its intended purpose.

(B) It confuses a subjective judgment of private moral permissibility with an objective description of social fact.

(C) It rules out something as a cause of a current phenomenon solely on the ground that the phenomenon used to occur without that thing.

(D) It cites purported historical facts that cannot possibly be verified.

(E) It relies on an ambiguity in the term "violence" to justify a claim.

PrepTest106 Sec3 Q5

Step 3: Maurice's argument fails to consider that a new factor could contribute to or exacerbate the continuation of violence that has occurred for centuries.	**Step 4:** (C) is correct. This matches the prediction and is an accurate description of the argument.

Wrong answers: (A) Outside the Scope. Although he describes Jane's proposal as censorship, Maurice makes no comment about the proposal's popularity. (B) This profound sounding answer really does not directly relate to Maurice's argument. (D) Outside the Scope. Presumably, Maurice's claim could be verified. The problem is that, even if his claim is verified, Maurice's response doesn't damage Jane's argument. His response treats Jane's claim that video game violence is sufficient to cause violence among the young as though it were a claim that video game violence is necessary to cause such violence. (E) The argument is consistent in its use of the term "violence."

Weaken Questions

Prepare

LEARNING OBJECTIVES

In this section, you'll learn to:

- Identify Weaken questions.
- Turn an assumption into an accurate prediction for the correct answer.
- Recognize answer choices that weaken the author's assumption.

Another way in which the LSAT will test your ability to evaluate an argument is to ask you to identify a piece of information that, if true, would weaken the author's argument. Here, "weaken an argument" doesn't mean that you have to conclusively disprove the conclusion. All you need to do is find the answer choice containing a fact that makes the author's conclusion less likely to be true based on the evidence.

First, let's take a look at some typical Weaken question stems as they appear on the LSAT:

LSAT Question Stem	Analysis
Which one of the following, if true, most seriously weakens the argument? *PrepTest107 Sec1 Q16*	The correct answer will be a new piece of information that will weaken the author's argument.
The argument would be most seriously weakened if which one of the following were discovered? *PrepTest101 Sec3 Q9*	The correct answer will be a new piece of information that will weaken the author's argument.

Weaken questions tend to use the words *weakens, call into question,* or *undermines* in the question stem. Though most students are able to identify Weaken questions easily, some students occasionally confuse Weaken and Flaw questions. To keep the two question types straight, remember that in a Flaw question, you are being asked to *describe* that argument's error in reasoning. In a Weaken question, the testmaker wants you to identify a *new piece of information* that, if true, will undermine the author's assumption and thus weaken the conclusion. Accept the answer choices as true in a Weaken question and evaluate them by saying, "Okay, if this piece of information were true, would the author's conclusion be less likely to follow from her evidence?"

Your approach to Weaken questions begins in the same way as your approach to other Assumption Family questions: Start by untangling the stimulus into evidence and conclusion; then find the author's central assumption. Only occasionally will you see a Mismatched Concepts argument in a Weaken question. Instead, the nature of Weaken questions is such that you will largely be asked to evaluate Overlooked Possibilities arguments. By now, you are already in the habit of phrasing the assumption of these types of arguments in negative terms: "the author is assuming that *no other* explanation or potential objections to this conclusion exists." To weaken an Overlooked Possibilities argument, then, identify one of these possible objections in the answer choices. Review how the LSAT expert does that in the following Weaken question.

Here is an LSAT expert's analysis of a Weaken question. Take note of how the expert uses the argument type to predict the correct answer.

Step 2: Conclusion: Something is discouraging the potentially best-liked teachers from pursuing teaching. *because* Evidence: The personality type most correlated with being liked by students is found in 20 percent of the general public but only 5 percent of teachers.	**Step 1:** The phrase "most weakens the argument" indicates a Weaken question.

In a study in which secondary school students were asked to identify the teachers they liked the best, the teachers most often identified possessed a personality that constitutes 20 percent of the general public but only 5 percent of teachers. Thus something must discourage the people who would be the best-liked teachers from entering the profession.

Which of the following, if true, most weakens the argument?

(A) People with the personality type constitute 5 percent of the medical profession.

(B) People with the personality type constitute 5 percent of college students pursuing a degree in education.

(C) Students of teachers with the personality type are intensely recruited for noneducational professions.

(D) Students with the personality type are more likely to be liked by teachers than those with other personality types.

(E) Teachers with the personality type are more likely to quit teaching than those with other personality types.

PrepTest105 Sec4 Q18

Step 3: The conclusion seems to directly follow from the evidence, thus the correct answer will provide an overlooked possibility; it will cite a reason why those with the personality type are underrepresented in the teaching profession *other than* the argument's explanation that they are discouraged from *entering* the profession.	**Step 4:** (E) is correct. This choice provides an alternative explanation for the underrepresentation of this personality type among teachers. It is not that they are discouraged from entering the teaching profession; it's that they don't remain in the teaching profession.

Wrong answers: (A) Outside the Scope. Potential underrepresentation in the medical profession does nothing to explain their underrepresentation among teachers. (B) 180. Underrepresentation in education degree programs supports the claim that something is discouraging these people from going into teaching. (C) 180. This answer identifies what is discouraging them from going into teaching. (D) Irrelevant Comparison. How well liked by teachers those with the personality type are has no clear effect on the likelihood of the conclusion.

LSAT STRATEGY

Some facts to remember about Weaken questions:

- A correct answer doesn't have to disprove the conclusion, just weaken it.
- The most common argument type in Weaken questions is Overlooked Possibilities.
- Correct answer choices nearly always introduce a possible objection to the conclusion that the author has not considered.

If you find yourself getting lost or frustrated in a specific Weaken question, take a step back from the argument and focus solely on the argument's conclusion. While many Weaken questions require you to understand how the evidence relates to the conclusion, some Weaken questions do not. In these, simply understanding the conclusion will be enough to identify a correct answer choice.

Here's an LSAT expert's analysis of another Weaken question. Review it with an eye to the skills and strategies you've been learning.

Step 2: Conclusion: The size of the interstitial nucleus dictates the potential for male cats to contract disease X. *because* Evidence: In a sample of male cats that died from the extremely rare disease X, all had enlarged interstitial nuclei.	**Step 1:** The phrase "most . . . weakens the argument" indicates a Weaken question.

The interstitial nucleus, a subregion of the brain's hypothalamus, is typically smaller for male cats than for female cats. A neurobiologist performed autopsies on male cats who died from disease X, a disease affecting no more than .05 percent of male cats, and found that these male cats had interstitial nuclei that were as large as those generally found in female cats. Thus, the size of the interstitial nucleus determines whether or not male cats can contract disease X.

Which of the following statements, if true, most seriously weakens the argument?

(A) No female cats have been known to contract disease X, which is a subtype of disease Y.

(B) Many male cats who contract disease X also contract disease Z, the cause of which is unknown.

(C) The interstitial nuclei of female cats who contract disease X are larger than those of female cats who do not contract disease X.

(D) Of 1,000 autopsies on male cats who did not contract disease X, 5 revealed interstitial nuclei larger than those of the average male cat.

(E) The hypothalamus is known not to be causally linked to disease Y, and disease X is a subtype of disease Y.

PrepTest106 Sec3 Q25

Step 3: This argument jumps from evidence of correlation to a conclusion of some causal connection between the size of the interstitial nuclei and the occurrence of disease X in male cats. The Weaken answer will break the causal connection by suggesting one of three things: 1) an alternative cause; 2) reverse causation; or 3) coincidence (a lack of connection).	**Step 4:** (E) is correct. Breaking the causal connection between the hypothalamus and disease Y breaks (or at least undermines) any causal connection between their relative subparts and subtypes.

Wrong answers: (A) Outside the Scope. The argument is not concerned with occurrences of disease X in female cats. (B) Outside the Scope. This unspecified level of correlation of disease X and Z does not affect the likelihood of a causal connection between the size of the interstitial nucleus and disease X. (C) 180. The argument is not concerned with female cats, but this evidence would, if anything, strengthen the author's claim. (D) Finding a low correlation between enlarged interstitial nuclei and the absence of disease X does not damage the author's argument. If anything, it strengthens it.

Later, you'll get an opportunity to try some Weaken questions on your own and to compare your thinking to that of an LSAT expert. For now, though, take a look at a question type that is intimately related to Weaken questions: Strengthen questions.

Strengthen Questions

Prepare

LEARNING OBJECTIVES

In this section, you'll learn to:

- Identify and answer Strengthen questions.
- Turn assumptions into accurate predictions.
- Recognize answer choices that strengthen the author's assumption.

At this point, you've learned how to evaluate an LSAT argument, find its assumption, describe its flaw, and identify an answer choice that would weaken the argument. Here's yet another task: Identify a piece of information that, if true, would strengthen the argument. Strengthen, in this context, doesn't mean "prove" the argument or "confirm" the conclusion—that's too strong. Instead, Strengthen questions ask you to identify an answer choice that makes the conclusion more likely to be true. Combined, you will see about eight Strengthen and Weaken questions on test day.

First, let's take a look at some typical Strengthen question stems as they appear on the LSAT:

LSAT Question Stem	Analysis
Which one of the following, if true, most helps to strengthen the historians' argument? *PrepTest101 Sec3 Q23*	Since we're looking for something that, "if true," would most help to "strengthen" an argument, this is a Strengthen question.
Which one of the following, if true, most strongly supports the explanation above? *PrepTest104 Sec1 Q5*	The correct answer choice, "if true, most strongly supports" the stimulus above indicates that this is a Strengthen question.
Which one of the following, if true, provides the strongest additional support for the hypothesis above? *PrepTest104 Sec1 Q18*	"[I]f true, provides the strongest... support," marks this as a Strengthen question.

Your approach to Strengthen questions starts in the same way as your approach to other Assumption Family questions. Begin by untangling the author's argument into evidence and conclusion. Next, note the argument pattern and identify the assumption. Then predict an answer choice that would strengthen the argument's conclusion. For a Strengthen question that uses a Mismatched Concepts argument, that means looking for an answer choice that affirms the relationship the author assumes exists between mismatched terms. In a Strengthen question that uses an Overlooked Possibilities argument, seek an answer choice that removes a potential objection that the author is overlooking. And in both types of arguments, you may actually find that the correct answer choice simply provides information that directly strengthens the author's conclusion.

Take a look at an LSAT expert's analysis of a Strengthen question.

Step 2: Environmentalists' Conclusion: Replace gasoline with methanol. *because* Evidence: Methanol combustion does not produce significant quantities of benzene. Author's Conclusion: Don't listen to the environmentalists (stick with gasoline). *because* Author's Evidence: Methanol combustion does produce another known carcinogen, formaldehyde.	**Step 1:** The phrase "most supports the... proposal" indicates a Strengthen question. The question stem further specifies that the task is to strengthen the environmentalists' claim.

Combustion of gasoline in automobile engines produces benzene, a known carcinogen. Environmentalists propose replacing gasoline with methanol, which does not produce significant quantities of benzene when burned. However, combustion of methanol produces formaldehyde, also a known carcinogen. Therefore the environmentalists' proposal has little merit.

Which one of the following, if true, most supports the environmentalists' proposal?

(A) The engines of some automobiles now on the road burn diesel fuel rather than gasoline.

(B) Several large research efforts are underway to formulate cleaner-burning types of gasoline.

(C) In some regions, the local economy is largely dependent on industries devoted to the production and distribution of automobile fuel.

(D) Formaldehyde is a less potent carcinogen than benzene.

(E) Since methanol is water soluble, methanol spills are more damaging to the environment than gasoline spills.

PrepTest107 Sec4 Q1

Step 3: Based on the author's evidence and the environmentalists' evidence, the choice between methanol and gasoline comes down to a choice between the formaldehyde and benzene found in each, respectively. Thus, a reason to favor formaldehyde over benzene would strengthen the environmentalists' proposal to use methanol.	**Step 4:** (D) is correct. Matches the prediction by indicating a reason to prefer formaldehyde over benzene, and, thus, methanol over gasoline.

Wrong answers: (A) Outside the Scope. The argument is between gasoline and methanol, not diesel. (B) 180. This potentially minimizes the benefits of switching to methane, as the environmentalists propose. (C) Outside the Scope. The environmentalists' proposal is based on health concerns. (E) 180. Supports the author's rejection of the environmentalists' proposal to replace gasoline with methanol.

LSAT STRATEGY

Some facts to remember about Strengthen Questions:

- The correct answer, when added to the evidence, doesn't have to prove the conclusion—just make it more likely.
- Both Mismatched Concepts and Overlooked Possibilities arguments show up in Strengthen questions, although overlooked possibilities are more common.
- In a Mismatched Concepts argument, look for an answer choice that either affirms the author's assumption or directly supports the conclusion.
- In an Overlooked Possibilities argument, look for an answer choice that removes a potential objection that the author is not considering.

As in some Weaken questions, it's possible in some Strengthen questions to find the right answer by focusing solely on an argument's conclusion. If you get lost or frustrated by a Strengthen question, return to the conclusion and try to find an answer choice that most strengthens that conclusion.

Here's an LSAT expert's analysis of another Strengthen question. Review it to see the strategies and tactics in action.

Step 2: Conclusion: The explanation for motion sickness in astronauts is the conflicting information received by the brain about the body's motion. *because* Evidence: Astronauts see their motion, but, due to weightlessness, their inner ears indicate they are not moving.	**Step 1:** The phrase "support for the hypotheses" indicates a Strengthen question.

Astronauts who experience weightlessness frequently get motion sickness. The astronauts see their own motion relative to passing objects, but while the astronauts are weightless their inner ears indicate that their bodies are not moving. The astronauts' experience is best explained by the hypothesis that conflicting information received by the brain about the body's motion causes motion sickness.

Which one of the following, if true, provides the strongest additional support for the hypothesis above?

(A) During rough voyages ship passengers in cabins providing a view of the water are less likely to get motion sickness than are passengers in cabins providing no view.

(B) Many people who are experienced airplane passengers occasionally get motion sickness.

(C) Some automobile passengers whose inner ears indicate that they are moving and who have a clear view of the objects they are passing get motion sickness.

(D) People who have aisle seats in trains or airplanes are as likely to get motion sickness as are people who have window seats.

(E) Some astronauts do not get motion sickness even after being in orbit for several days.

PrepTest104 Sec1 Q18

Step 3: The conclusion provides a causal explanation for the phenomenon of motion sickness in astronauts. The correct answer will eliminate an alternative explanation or provide further support for the hypothesis that conflicting signals to the brain cause the motion sickness.	**Step 4:** (A) is correct. This answer provides an analogous situation in which motion sickness occurs in conjunction with conflicting signals to the brain.

Wrong answers: (B) Outside the Scope. This is an irrelevant situation that does not involve conflicting signals, so it cannot strengthen the conclusion. (C) 180. A small number of contrary examples would not technically weaken the argument, but generally this runs counter to the argument as it involves motion sickness in the absence of conflicting signals. (D) Irrelevant Comparison. Both people in window and aisle seats can see the motion of the background. (E) Outside the Scope. The mere existence of some astronauts who do not experience motion sickness provides no information relevant to the cause of motion sickness in those who do.

Rare Strengthen and Weaken Questions

Weaken and Strengthen EXCEPT Questions

In addition to asking straightforward Weaken and Strengthen questions, the LSAT may ask you to identify an answer choice that *does not* weaken or *does not* strengthen the author's conclusion. Though these Strengthen/Weaken EXCEPT questions are rare (constituting fewer than 5 percent of all Strengthen/Weaken questions), it's important to know how to tackle them when you see them. The first thing you need to be able to do is identify these question types. Take a look at the following typical Strengthen/Weaken EXCEPT question stems:

Question Stem	Analysis
Each of the following, if true, weakens the argument EXCEPT	The four wrong answer choices will weaken the conclusion. The right answer will strengthen the conclusion or have no impact.
Each of the following, if true, supports the claim above EXCEPT	The four wrong answer choices will strengthen the conclusion. The right answer will weaken the conclusion or have no impact.

In these Weaken and Strengthen EXCEPT questions, understand that the correct answer does not need to strengthen or weaken an argument. In fact, the correct answer to these EXCEPT questions may have no impact on the argument at all. The only thing you can be sure of in these questions is that the four incorrect answer choices will *definitely* weaken the argument in a Weaken EXCEPT question and *definitely* strengthen the argument in a Strengthen EXCEPT question.

For this reason, you need to be able to characterize what the correct answer choice requires in Strengthen/Weaken EXCEPT questions. In a Weaken EXCEPT question, the correct answer will either strengthen the argument or have no impact. Similarly, the correct answer to a Strengthen EXCEPT question will either weaken the argument or have no impact.

LSAT STRATEGY

Some facts to remember about Strengthen and Weaken EXCEPT questions:

- Always slow down and characterize what the right and wrong answer choices will look like.
- The correct answer in a Strengthen EXCEPT question will either weaken the argument or have no impact.
- The correct answer in a Weaken EXCEPT question will either strengthen the argument or have no impact.

Evaluate Questions

Evaluate Questions are an even rarer subspecies of Strengthen and Weaken questions. In fact, it's likely you won't see one on the LSAT. On the last 21 released LSATs (seven years' worth), only seven questions have fallen into this category. However, because they do show up on occasion, it's good to know about them and to have a plan, just in case. The first thing you need to be able to do is identify Evaluate questions. Take a look at the following typical Evaluate question stems:

Question Stem	Analysis
Which one of the following would be most useful to know in order to evaluate the legitimacy of the philosopher's argument?	The correct answer will provide a piece of information that, if true, would make the argument either stronger or weaker and, if false, would have the opposite effect. In other words, the correct answer is *relevant* to the argument's validity.
Information about which one of the following would be LEAST useful in evaluating the doctor's hypothesis?	Four of the answer choices will be useful in evaluating the hypothesis, while the correct answer choice won't be useful. That means it will be irrelevant or have no impact on the hypothesis.

As with other Assumption Family questions, start by breaking down the argument in an Evaluate question into evidence and conclusion. Determine the assumption and use that information to identify an answer choice that will help you evaluate the argument. Answer choices in Evaluate questions are not straightforward strengtheners or weakeners—instead, they are typically phrased as questions, whose answers may or may not help you evaluate the validity of the argument. Select the answer choice that allows you to say that the argument is strong or weak. In an Evaluate EXCEPT or Evaluate LEAST question, your goal is to find the answer choice that has *no impact* on the argument.

LSAT STRATEGY

Some facts to remember about Evaluate questions:

- These questions are similar to Strengthen and Weaken questions.
- Untangle the stimulus, and then determine the author's assumption.
- The correct answer will often present a question the answer to which has either a positive or negative impact on the argument.

Practice Now it's time to try some Strengthen and Weaken questions on your own. Use your knowledge of argument patterns to determine the author's assumption. In Weaken questions, the assumption is often that the author is overlooking potential objections to the conclusion, so be on the lookout for an answer choice that introduces one of these objections. In Strengthen questions, the correct answer affirms the assumption or removes a possible objection.

Step 2:	Step 1:

40. Historians of North American architecture who have studied early nineteenth-century houses with wooden floors have observed that the boards used on the floors of bigger houses were generally much narrower than those used on the floors of smaller houses. These historians have argued that, since the people for whom the bigger houses were built were generally richer than the people for whom the smaller houses were built, floors made out of narrow floorboards were probably once a status symbol, designed to proclaim the owner's wealth.

Which one of the following, if true, most helps to strengthen the historians' argument?

(A) More original floorboards have survived from big early nineteenth-century houses than from small early nineteenth-century houses.

(B) In the early nineteenth century, a piece of narrow floorboard was not significantly less expensive than a piece of wide floorboard of the same length.

(C) In the early nineteenth century, smaller houses generally had fewer rooms than did bigger houses.

(D) Some early nineteenth-century houses had wide floorboards near the walls of each room and narrower floorboards in the center, where the floors were usually carpeted.

(E) Many of the biggest early nineteenth-century houses but very few small houses from that period had some floors that were made of materials that were considerably more expensive.

PrepTest101 Sec3 Q23

Step 3:	Step 4:

CHAPTER 4

Step 2:	Step 1:

41. The play *Mankind* must have been written between 1431 and 1471. It cannot have been written before 1431, for in that year the rose noble, a coin mentioned in the play, was first circulated. The play cannot have been written after 1471, since in that year King Henry VI died, and he is mentioned as a living monarch in the play's dedication.

The argument would be most seriously weakened if which one of the following were discovered?

(A) The Royal Theatre Company includes the play on a list of those performed in 1480.

(B) Another coin mentioned in the play was first minted in 1422.

(C) The rose noble was neither minted nor circulated after 1468.

(D) Although Henry VI was deposed in 1461, he was briefly restored to the throne in 1470.

(E) In a letter written in early 1428, a merchant told of having seen the design for a much-discussed new coin called the "rose noble."

PrepTest101 Sec3 Q9

Step 3:	Step 4:

Step 2:	**Step 1:**

42. The most reliable way to detect the presence of life on a planet would be by determining whether or not its atmosphere contains methane. This is because methane completely disappears from a planet's atmosphere through various chemical reactions unless it is constantly replenished by the biological processes of living beings.

Which one of the following statements, if true, most seriously weakens the argument?

(A) There are other ways of detecting the presence of life on a planet.

(B) Not all living beings have the ability to biologically produce methane.

(C) We are incapable at present of analyzing a planet's atmosphere for the presence of methane.

(D) Some living beings biologically produce only very small amounts of methane.

(E) Earth is the only planet whose atmosphere is known to contain methane.

PrepTest105 Sec4 Q5

Step 3:	**Step 4:**

Step 2:	Step 1:

43. To allay public concern about chemicals that are leaking into a river from a chemical company's long-established dump, a company representative said, "Federal law requires that every new chemical be tested for safety before it is put onto the market. This is analogous to the federal law mandating testing of every pharmaceutical substance for safety."

Which one of the following, if true, most seriously weakens the representative's implied argument that the public need not be concerned about the leak?

(A) When pharmaceutical substances are tested for safety pursuant to federal requirements, a delay is imposed on the entry of potentially lifesaving substances onto the market.

(B) Leakage from the dump has occurred in noticeable amounts only in the last few months.

(C) Before the federal law requiring testing of nonpharmaceutical chemicals went into effect recently, there were 40,000 such chemicals being manufactured, many of them dangerous.

(D) The concentration of chemicals leaking into the river is diluted, first by rainwater and then by the water in the river.

(E) The water in the river is murky because of the runoff of silt from a number of nearby construction projects.

PrepTest105 Sec4 Q9

Step 3:	Step 4:

Step 2:	Step 1:

44. Surviving seventeenth-century Dutch landscapes attributed to major artists now equal in number those attributed to minor ones. But since in the seventeenth century many prolific minor artists made a living supplying the voracious market for Dutch landscapes, while only a handful of major artists painted in the genre, many attributions of seventeenth-century Dutch landscape paintings to major artists are undoubtedly erroneous.

Which one of the following, if true, most strengthens the argument?

(A) Technically gifted seventeenth-century Dutch landscape artists developed recognizable styles that were difficult to imitate.

(B) In the workshops of major seventeenth-century artists, assistants were employed to prepare the paints, brushes, and other materials that the major artists then used.

(C) In the eighteenth century, landscapes by minor seventeenth-century artists were often simply thrown away or else destroyed through improper storage.

(D) Seventeenth-century art dealers paid minor artists extra money to leave their landscapes unsigned so that the dealers could add phony signatures and pass such works off as valuable paintings.

(E) More seventeenth-century Dutch landscapes were painted than have actually survived, and that is true of those executed by minor artists as well as of those executed by major artists.

PrepTest106 Sec3 Q24

Step 3:	Step 4:

Step 2:	**Step 1:**

45. A recent study concludes that prehistoric birds, unlike modern birds, were cold-blooded. This challenges a widely held view that modern birds descended from warm-blooded birds. The conclusion is based on the existence of growth rings in prehistoric birds' bodily structures, which are thought to be found only in cold-blooded animals. Another study, however, disputes this view. It concludes that prehistoric birds had dense blood vessels in their bones, which suggests that they were active creatures and therefore had to be warm-blooded.

Which one of the following, if true, would most help to resolve the dispute described above in favor of one party to it?

(A) Some modern warm-blooded species other than birds have been shown to have descended from cold-blooded species.

(B) Having growth rings is not the only physical trait of cold-blooded species.

(C) Modern birds did not evolve from prehistoric species of birds.

(D) Dense blood vessels are not found in all warm-blooded species.

(E) In some cold-blooded species the gene that is responsible for growth rings is also responsible for dense blood vessels.

PrepTest106 Sec3 Q13

Step 3:	**Step 4:**

Expert Analysis

Now take a look at how an LSAT expert would approach and analyze these Strengthen and Weaken questions.

Step 2: Conclusion: The purpose of narrow floorboards was to show status and wealth. *because* Evidence: Bigger houses, which were generally built for wealthy people, contained more narrow floorboards than did smaller houses.	**Step 1:** The phrase "most helps to strengthen" indicates a Strengthen question.

40. Historians of North American architecture who have studied early nineteenth-century houses with wooden floors have observed that the boards used on the floors of bigger houses were generally much narrower than those used on the floors of smaller houses. These historians have argued that, since the people for whom the bigger houses were built were generally richer than the people for whom the smaller houses were built, floors made out of narrow floorboards were probably once a status symbol, designed to proclaim the owner's wealth.

Which one of the following, if true, most helps to strengthen the historians' argument?

(A) More original floorboards have survived from big early nineteenth-century houses than from small early nineteenth-century houses.

(B) In the early nineteenth century, a piece of narrow floorboard was not significantly less expensive than a piece of wide floorboard of the same length.

(C) In the early nineteenth century, smaller houses generally had fewer rooms than did bigger houses.

(D) Some early nineteenth-century houses had wide floorboards near the walls of each room and narrower floorboards in the center, where the floors were usually carpeted.

(E) Many of the biggest early nineteenth-century houses but very few small houses from that period had some floors that were made of materials that were considerably more expensive.

PrepTest101 Sec3 Q23

Step 3: Since the conclusion provides a causal explanation for the observation that bigger houses correlate with narrow floorboards, find an answer that either eliminates an alternative explanation (e.g., no structural reason for using narrow floorboards in big houses) or firms up the connection between narrow floorboards and wealth (e.g., narrow floorboards are costly).	**Step 4:** (B) is correct. This strengthens the argument by eliminating a possibility (narrow floorboards were cheaper) that would have weakened the argument.

Wrong answers: (A) Irrelevant Comparison. The age of the surviving houses has no relevance to why narrow floorboards were used in big houses. (C) Irrelevant Comparison. The number of rooms in a house, as with (A), has no relevance to why narrow floorboards were used in big houses. (D) 180. If narrow floorboards were hidden from view, then the assertion that narrow floorboards were a status symbol would be undermined. (E) Outside the Scope. At most, this would be marginally relevant as a weakener by indicating that the real status symbol flooring was made of other materials.

Step 2: Conclusion: The play *Mankind* was definitely written between 1431 and 1471.	Step 1: The phrase "most seriously weakened" indicates a Weaken question.
because	
Evidence: 1) A coin mentioned in the play was first circulated in 1431; and 2) the play's dedication indicates King Henry VI, who died in 1471, was living at that time.	

41. The play *Mankind* must have been written between 1431 and 1471. It cannot have been written before 1431, for in that year the rose noble, a coin mentioned in the play, was first circulated. The play cannot have been written after 1471, since in that year King Henry VI died, and he is mentioned as a living monarch in the play's dedication.

The argument would be most seriously weakened if which one of the following were discovered?

(A) The Royal Theatre Company includes the play on a list of those performed in 1480.

(B) Another coin mentioned in the play was first minted in 1422.

(C) The rose noble was neither minted nor circulated after 1468.

(D) Although Henry VI was deposed in 1461, he was briefly restored to the throne in 1470.

(E) In a letter written in early 1428, a merchant told of having seen the design for a much-discussed new coin called the "rose noble."

PrepTest101 Sec3 Q9

Step 3: The argument assumes that the two pieces of evidence preclude the possibility of the play being written before 1431 or after 1471. The correct answer to this Weaken question will provide new information that allows for the possibility that the play could have been written earlier or later. Perhaps the dedication to King Henry was written before the play itself, or the coin was known to exist before its circulation.	Step 4: (E) is correct. If people knew about the coin before it was first circulated, then the earliest circulation date is not a valid cut-off for dating the play.

Wrong answers: (A) Outside the Scope. A performance in 1480 does not call into question the author's claim that the play was written between 1431 and 1471. (B) Outside the Scope. Similar to (A), this merely indicates the play was written any time from 1422 on. (C) Similar to (A) and (B), this fact, if true, allows the play to have been written before, during or after the time frame purported by the author. (D) This information provides a distinction that would potentially eliminate nine of the years within the author's time frame for dating the play, but in no way undermines the conclusion that the play was written between 1431 and 1471.

Step 2: Conclusion: Checking the atmosphere for methane would be the most reliable way to detect life on a planet. *because* Evidence: The continuing presence of methane in the atmosphere requires living beings to constantly replenish it.	**Step 1:** The phrase "most seriously weakens" indicates a Weaken question.

42. The most reliable way to detect the presence of life on a planet would be by determining whether or not its atmosphere contains methane. This is because methane completely disappears from a planet's atmosphere through various chemical reactions unless it is constantly replenished by the biological processes of living beings.

Which one of the following statements, if true, most seriously weakens the argument?

(A) There are other ways of detecting the presence of life on a planet.

(B) Not all living beings have the ability to biologically produce methane.

(C) We are incapable at present of analyzing a planet's atmosphere for the presence of methane.

(D) Some living beings biologically produce only very small amounts of methane.

(E) Earth is the only planet whose atmosphere is known to contain methane.

PrepTest105 Sec4 Q5

Step 3: The author provides evidence that the production of methane by living creatures is *necessary* to sustain methane in a planet's atmosphere. He concludes, however, that the presence of methane in the atmosphere is *sufficient* to prove the existence of life on a planet. The correct answer will present a fact suggesting that there could be life on a planet that does not have methane in its atmosphere.	**Step 4:** (B) is correct. Checking for methane would not be a reliable method of detecting these forms of life, which would undercut the reliability of the method to at least some degree.

Wrong answers: (A) By asserting that checking for methane is the *most* reliable method, the argument does not dismiss the possibility of using other methods. (C) Outside the Scope. The conclusion is conditioned on an ability to detect methane (using the hypothetical *would be*, rather than asserting it *is* the most reliable method), thus an actual inability to detect methane is outside the scope of the argument. (D) Similar to (C), this possibility only increases the technical difficulty of detecting methane, and the author's argument is conditioned on being able to do so. (E) This is consistent with the argument, since currently Earth is also the only planet known to contain life.

Step 2: Conclusion: The public doesn't need to be concerned about chemicals leaking into a river from a dump. *because* Evidence: There is a program that requires the testing of new chemicals similar to the testing of pharmaceuticals.	**Step 1:** The phrase "most seriously weakens" indicates a Weaken question. The question stem further clarifies the conclusion to weaken: "the public need not be concerned about the leak."

43. To allay public concern about chemicals that are leaking into a river from a chemical company's long-established dump, a company representative said, "Federal law requires that every new chemical be tested for safety before it is put onto the market. This is analogous to the federal law mandating testing of every pharmaceutical substance for safety."

Which one of the following, if true, most seriously weakens the representative's implied argument that the public need not be concerned about the leak?

(A) When pharmaceutical substances are tested for safety pursuant to federal requirements, a delay is imposed on the entry of potentially lifesaving substances onto the market.

(B) Leakage from the dump has occurred in noticeable amounts only in the last few months.

(C) Before the federal law requiring testing of nonpharmaceutical chemicals went into effect recently, there were 40,000 such chemicals being manufactured, many of them dangerous.

(D) The concentration of chemicals leaking into the river is diluted, first by rainwater and then by the water in the river.

(E) The water in the river is murky because of the runoff of silt from a number of nearby construction projects.

PrepTest105 Sec4 Q9

Step 3: The argument assumes that the testing program for new chemicals, similar to the testing of pharmaceuticals, does not overlook any potential cause for concern. The correct answer will either distinguish these chemicals from pharmaceuticals or indicate an Overlooked Possibility of inadequacy in the testing program. Note that the testing only applies to *new* chemicals, so if older chemicals are at the *long established* dump, that would be a reason for concern.	**Step 4:** (C) is correct. Matches the prediction by pointing out an inadequacy in the testing program focused solely on *new* chemicals, especially for a *long established* dump.

Wrong answers: (A) Outside the Scope. This is a potential downside to the testing of pharmaceuticals, but in no way indicates a cause for concern regarding the leaking chemicals. (B) Outside the Scope. This may alleviate concerns of people who previously lived in the area, but the conclusion is focused on any present need for concern from the leak among the current public. (D) 180. This provides an additional reason, along with the testing, to *not* be concerned. (E) The effect of this information on the argument is unclear; while it could be a reason to not be concerned about further pollution, the combined effects of pollution on the river might be a cause for heightened concern.

Step 2: Conclusion: Many 17th century Dutch landscapes were not painted by the major artists attributed to them. *because* Evidence: 1) There are an equal number of such paintings attributed to major artists as to minor artists, while 2) there were many prolific minor artists in the genre but only a handful of major artists.	**Step 1:** The phrase "most strengthens the argument" indicates a Strengthen question.

44. Surviving seventeenth-century Dutch landscapes attributed to major artists now equal in number those attributed to minor ones. But since in the seventeenth century many prolific minor artists made a living supplying the voracious market for Dutch landscapes, while only a handful of major artists painted in the genre, many attributions of seventeenth-century Dutch landscape paintings to major artists are undoubtedly erroneous.

Which one of the following, if true, most strengthens the argument?

(A) Technically gifted seventeenth-century Dutch landscape artists developed recognizable styles that were difficult to imitate.

(B) In the workshops of major seventeenth-century artists, assistants were employed to prepare the paints, brushes, and other materials that the major artists then used.

(C) In the eighteenth century, landscapes by minor seventeenth-century artists were often simply thrown away or else destroyed through improper storage.

(D) Seventeenth-century art dealers paid minor artists extra money to leave their landscapes unsigned so that the dealers could add phony signatures and pass such works off as valuable paintings.

(E) More seventeenth-century Dutch landscapes were painted than have actually survived, and that is true of those executed by minor artists as well as of those executed by major artists.

PrepTest106 Sec3 Q24

Step 3: The numbers set out in the evidence do seem to support the conclusion, so the author is overlooking the possibility that while there were fewer major artists making these paintings, they still nonetheless created as many paintings as the minor artists. A correct answer to this Strengthen question, then, will eliminate an overlooked possibility, or provide further evidence supporting false attributions.	**Step 4:** (D) is correct. This provides clear motive and opportunity for a scheme that plausibly could avoid detection and result in a large number of excess paintings attributable to major artists.

Wrong answers: (A) 180. This reduces the potential for false attributions. (B) Distortion. The author argues that many landscapes attributed to major artists are actually the work of minor artists, not merely that minor artists assisted by doing prep work. (C) 180. This provides an alternative explanation for why there are currently an equal number of paintings attributed to major and minor artists, despite the greater number and productivity of minor artists of the genre. (E) Distortion. The loss of paintings by both major and minor artists does nothing to make the author's explanation for the apparent discrepancy any more or less likely.

Step 2: 1st Study's Conclusion: Prehistoric birds were cold-blooded. *because* Evidence: Prehistoric birds had growth rings believed to only occur in cold-blooded animals. 2nd Study's Conclusion: Prehistoric birds were warm-blooded. *because* Evidence: Prehistoric birds had dense blood vessels in their bones, which suggests they were active creatures.	**Step 1:** The question stem directs us to find an answer that would support one party in a dispute over another; this indicates a Strengthen/Weaken question (strengthen one argument while weakening the other).

45. A recent study concludes that prehistoric birds, unlike modern birds, were cold-blooded. This challenges a widely held view that modern birds descended from warm-blooded birds. The conclusion is based on the existence of growth rings in prehistoric birds' bodily structures, which are thought to be found only in cold-blooded animals. Another study, however, disputes this view. It concludes that prehistoric birds had dense blood vessels in their bones, which suggests that they were active creatures and therefore had to be warm-blooded.

Which one of the following, if true, would most help to resolve the dispute described above in favor of one party to it?

(A) Some modern warm-blooded species other than birds have been shown to have descended from cold-blooded species.

(B) Having growth rings is not the only physical trait of cold-blooded species.

(C) Modern birds did not evolve from prehistoric species of birds.

(D) Dense blood vessels are not found in all warm-blooded species.

(E) In some cold-blooded species the gene that is responsible for growth rings is also responsible for dense blood vessels.

PrepTest106 Sec3 Q13

Step 3: The two studies use different pieces of evidence to reach opposite conclusions. The correct answer will suggest that one of the pieces of evidence is consistent with either cold-bloodedness or warm-bloodedness, or will raise a reason why in prehistoric birds one of those features would not be indicative of that study's conclusion.	**Step 4:** (E) is correct. This shows that the traits described in each of the studies' evidence are consistent with a single conclusion: cold-bloodedness.

Wrong answers: (A) Outside the Scope. The dispute referenced in the question stem is between the opposing conclusions of warm-blooded versus cold-blooded. The reference in the second sentence to the descent of modern birds is mere contextual information. (B) Distortion. A relevant question would be whether growth rings really are *only* found in cold-blooded species, as thought, not whether cold-blooded species lack any other physical trait besides growth rings, as this answer suggests. (C) Outside the Scope. As with (A), the evolution of modern birds is not relevant to the specific dispute referenced in the question stem regarding whether prehistoric birds were warm or cold-blooded. (D) Distortion. This certainly does not support the conclusion of warm-blooded, but neither does it provide any support for the conclusion of cold-blooded; provides no reason to believe that the presence of dense blood vessels is consistent with cold-bloodedness.

Assumption Family Principle Questions

Prepare

LEARNING OBJECTIVES

In this section, you'll learn to:

- Recognize Principle question stems.
- Distinguish Identify the Principle questions from other Principle question types.
- Use your knowledge of Assumption-based questions to attack Principle Assumption and Principle Strengthen questions.

Now that you've worked with several question types in the Assumption Family, let's turn our attention to Principle questions—a question type that often mimics Assumption Family questions. There has been an average of about five Principle questions per exam in recent years. Principle questions come in three main varieties: Identify the Principle, Apply the Principle, and Parallel Principle. In this section, you will learn to distinguish these three types, as well as how to attack argument-based Identify the Principle questions. You'll learn about Parallel Principle questions later in this chapter, and the remaining types of Principle questions will be covered in Chapter 5.

Recognizing Principle Question Stems

The common thread that appears throughout these three main Principle question types is the presence of a "principle." On the LSAT, a "principle" is a law-like general rule that can be applied not only to the particular situation in an argument but also to other, comparable situations. The question stem for a Principle question will often simply include the word *principle.* The words *proposition* or *policy,* as well as variations on the phrases "most closely conforms to" and "best illustrates," are all strong indicators of a Principle question. In general, any question that asks you to identify or apply a general rule is a Principle question.

Take a look at a few typical Principle question stems:

LSAT Question Stem	Analysis
Which one of the following principles, if established, most helps to justify the conclusion in the passage? *PrepTest105 Sec1 Q14*	"The following principles" indicates this is a Principle question stem.
Which one of the following principles underlies the arbitrator's argument? *PrepTest107 Sec1 Q19*	"The following principles" is a clear indication that this is a Principle question.
The information above conforms most closely to which one of the following principles? *PrepTest105 Sec4 Q12*	"Conforms most closely to" and "following principles" both indicate that this is a Principle question.

Distinguishing Types of Principle Questions

Identify the Principle questions, a subset of which we will be examining in this chapter, present a specific argument or set of events in the stimulus, then ask you to identify an applicable, more generalized principle in the answer choices. Because Identify the Principle questions move from specific in the stimulus to general in the conclusion, using a ⊠ can be a great shorthand note to yourself while tackling Step 1 in these questions.

Apply the Principle questions do just the opposite: They will present a general principle in the stimulus (often expressed as a Formal Logic statement), then ask you to identify a more specific, nonconflicting situation in the correct answer choice. Similarly to Identify the Principle questions, using a ⊠ is a great way to shorthand that you are moving from a general statement in your stimulus to a specific situation in your answer choices.

Parallel Principle questions combine the actions used in Identify and Apply the Principle questions. First, identify the underlying principle in the specific situation in the stimulus. Then, apply that general principle to a new specific situation located in one of the answer choices. Your shorthand for this question type looks like this ◊ and represents moving from a specific stimulus to general and back to specific in the answer choices.

Practice Take a look at the following question stems. Can you identify your specific task in each one?

LSAT Question Stem	My Analysis
46. Which one of the following principles, if established, most helps to justify the conclusion in the passage? *PrepTest105 Sec1 Q14*	
47. Which one of the following principles underlies the arbitrator's argument? *PrepTest107 Sec1 Q19*	
48. The information above conforms most closely to which one of the following principles? *PrepTest105 Sec4 Q12*	
49. This argument most closely conforms to which one of the following principles? *PrepTest101 Sec2 Q22*	
50. Which one of the following judgments most closely conforms to the principle described above? *PrepTest101 Sec3 Q24*	

Expert Analysis for the Practice exercise may be found on the following page. ▶ ▶ ▶

Expert Analysis

Now take a look at how an LSAT Expert would break apart these question stems.

LSAT Question Stem	Analysis
46. Which one of the following principles, if established, most helps to justify the conclusion in the passage? *PrepTest105 Sec1 Q14*	"[W]hich of the following principles" indicates that the "following" answer choices are principles "justify[ing]" the "conclusion" in the stimulus. This is an Identify the Principle question. ^
47. Which one of the following principles underlies the arbitrator's argument? *PrepTest107 Sec1 Q19*	This is an Identify the Principle question. But since the principle in the answer "underlies" the argument in the stimulus, it will be a broad statement of the argument's assumption. ^
48. The information above conforms most closely to which one of the following principles? *PrepTest105 Sec4 Q12*	"[W]hich one of the following principles" indicates that the "following" answer choices are principles that conform to the "information" in the stimulus. This is an Identify the Principle question. ^
49. This argument most closely conforms to which one of the following principles? *PrepTest101 Sec2 Q22*	This is an Identify the Principle question. ^ But note that the stimulus here contains an "argument," which you should break down to evidence and conclusion.
50. Which one of the following judgments most closely conforms to the principle described above? *PrepTest101 Sec3 Q24*	"[T]he principle described above" indicates that there is a general statement in the stimulus to which one of the "following" more specific judgments will conform. This question moves from general to specific, so it is an Apply the Principle question. v

Principle–Assumption and Principle–Strengthen Questions

Prepare As we mentioned earlier, Identify the Principle questions often mimic familiar Assumption Family question types. Specifically, you are likely to see Identify the Principle questions that mimic Assumption and Strengthen questions. For example, consider the following question stem:

> Which one of the following is a principle underlying the advice given to police officers?
>
> *PrepTest107 Sec4 Q17*

This question stems states that there is a principle "underlying" the advice in the stimulus. As a foundation underlies a house (it is unseen, but it holds the house together), so does an assumption underlie an argument (it is unstated, but holds the argument together). Thus, the correct answer will be a necessary assumption, and the stimulus should be attacked as you would attack a Necessary Assumption question stimulus: Find the conclusion and evidence and identify the disconnect. The only difference in approach will come in Step 3, when the scope of your prediction will be broadened. We'll discuss that difference in a moment. First, though, take a look at another example of a Principle question stem that mimics a different question type:

> Which one of the following principles, if valid, most strongly supports the reasoning above?
>
> *PrepTest101 Sec2 Q25*

The phrase "if valid, most strongly supports" sounds very much like phrasing from a Strengthen question stem. In this question, you can expect to see an argument with both a conclusion and evidence. Approach this question in the same way you would approach a Strengthen question, but expect the correct answer choice to be broader in scope and perhaps stronger in wording.

In fact, anticipating the broad wording of the correct answer is the only difference between tackling Assumption and Principle–Assumption questions, and between tackling Strengthen and Principle–Strengthen questions. Because Principle–Assumption questions and Principle–Strengthen questions move from specific situations in the stimulus to broadly worded answer choices (the choices describe principles, after all), once you have broken down the argument into evidence and conclusion and identified the assumption, take a moment to strip that assumption of words specific to the particular situation described in the stimulus. For example, if the stimulus in a Principle–Strengthen question discusses "bank managers," expect the correct answer to be written in terms applicable to any manager, or even any person. Or if the stimulus discusses "fertilization methods of tulips," anticipate a correct answer that discusses the fertilization of all bulbous plants, or even all plants.

Here's how an LSAT expert might analyze a Principle question that mimics a Strengthen question task.

Step 2: Conclusion: The publisher's false claim was not unethical. *because* Evidence: Everyone should know that the publisher's claim was, by definition, impossible.	**Step 1:** The phrase "principle[]...supports the reasoning" indicates a Principle–Strengthen question.

The publisher of a best-selling self-help book had, in some promotional material, claimed that it showed readers how to become exceptionally successful. Of course, everyone knows that no book can deliver to the many what, by definition, must remain limited to the few: exceptional success. Thus, although it is clear that the publisher knowingly made a false claim, doing so should not be considered unethical in this case.

Which one of the following principles, if valid, most strongly supports the reasoning above?

(A) Knowingly making a false claim is unethical only if it is reasonable for people to accept the claim as true.

(B) Knowingly making a false claim is unethical if those making it derive a gain at the expense of those acting as if the claim were true.

(C) Knowingly making a false claim is unethical in only those cases in which those who accept the claim as true suffer a hardship greater than the gain they were anticipating.

(D) Knowingly making a false claim is unethical only if there is a possibility that someone will act as if the claim might be true.

(E) Knowingly making a false claim is unethical in at least those cases in which for someone else to discover that the claim is false, that person must have acted as if the claim were true.

PrepTest101 Sec2 Q2

Step 3: The prediction for a Principle–Strengthen question can simply rephrase the argument with the formulation: "If [this type of evidence], then [this conclusion]." In this case: If a false claim is something everyone knows to be impossible, then making such a claim is not unethical. Said more simply, making a false claim is unethical only when some people might think it could be true.	**Step 4:** (A) is correct. This choice matches the contrapositive of the prediction: If claim unethical, then possibly true.

Wrong answers: (B) The argument does not identify or assume what conditions do make a claim unethical. (C) Outside the Scope. The argument does not refer to or depend on any such balancing of hardships. (D) Distortion. A similar structure as the correct answer but goes astray in focusing on whether it is possible someone might act as if the claim were true, rather than it being actually possible for the claim to be true. (E) Outside the Scope. The argument concerns the possibility of the claim actually being true, not the possibility of discovering it to be false.

Practice Now that we have covered the basics of Principle–Assumption and Principle–Strengthen questions, try your hand at a few examples. Remember to approach them exactly the same way you would approach ordinary Assumption and Strengthen questions in Steps 1 and 2, while broadening your scope in Step 3. The expert analyses follow.

Step 2:	**Step 1:**

51. If an artist receives a public subsidy to support work on a specific project—e.g., making a film—and if this project then proves successful enough to allow the artist to repay the subsidy, is the artist morally obliged to do so? The answer is clearly yes, since the money returned to the agency distributing the subsidies will be welcome as a source of support for other artists deserving of public subsidies.

Which one of the following principles, if established, most helps to justify the conclusion in the passage?

(A) An artist has a moral duty to urge deserving fellow artists to try to obtain public subsidies, especially if those artists' projects promise to be financially successful.

(B) A financially successful artist should acknowledge that financial success is not solely a function of artistic merit.

(C) A subsidy should be understood as creating a debt that, though routinely forgiven, is rightly forgiven only if either the debtor is unable to
repay it or the creditor is not interested in repayment.

(D) The provider of a subsidy should judge as most deserving of subsidies those whose projects are most likely to turn into financial successes.

(E) An artist requesting a subsidy for a potentially profitable project should be required to make a reasonable effort to obtain a bank loan first.

PrepTest105 Sec1 Q1

Step 3:	**Step 4:**

CHAPTER 4

Step 2:	Step 1:

52. Editorial: Our society has a vested interest in maintaining a political system in which candidates are free to adhere to their principles. Yet campaigning for elected office is extremely costly, and because only the wealthiest individuals are able to finance their own political campaigns, most candidates must seek funding from private sources. In so doing, the candidates are almost invariably obliged to compromise their principles. Thus, government itself should assume the cost of candidates' campaigns.

Which one of the following principles, if valid, most helps to justify the conclusion as it is drawn in the argument?

(A) Candidates should not run for elected office if doing so would compel the candidates to compromise their principles.

(B) Candidates wealthy enough to finance their own political campaigns should not be permitted to raise additional funds from private sources.

(C) Voters should not support a candidate if that candidate is known to have accepted funding from private sources.

(D) The government should finance a given activity if doing so will further a vested interest of society.

(E) Private funding for political campaigns should be encouraged only if it redresses an imbalance among candidates' financial means.

PrepTest105 Sec1 Q24

Step 3:	Step 4:

Step 2:	**Step 1:**

53. Arbitrator: The shipping manager admits that he decided to close the old facility on October 14 and to schedule the new facility's opening for October 17, the following Monday. But he also claims that he is not responsible for the business that was lost due to the new facility's failing to open as scheduled. He blames the contractor for not finishing on time, but he too, is to blame, for he was aware of the contractor's typical delays and should have planned for this contingency.

Which one of the following principles underlies the arbitrator's argument?

(A) A manager should take foreseeable problems into account when making decisions.

(B) A manager should be able to depend on contractors to do their jobs promptly.

(C) A manager should see to it that contractors do their jobs promptly.

(D) A manager should be held responsible for mistakes made by those whom the manager directly supervises.

(E) A manager, and only a manager, should be held responsible for a project's failure.

PrepTest107 Sec1 Q19

Step 3:	**Step 4:**

Expert Analysis

Now look at the approach an LSAT expert took.

Step 2: Conclusion: An artist is morally obliged to repay a public subsidy if the artist's project is successful. *because* Evidence: The public agency would welcome the money for use in supporting other artists deserving of public subsidies.	**Step 1:** The question stem directs you to identify a principle to help "justify the conclusion," which indicates a Principle–Strengthen question.

51. If an artist receives a public subsidy to support work on a specific project—e.g., making a film—and if this project then proves successful enough to allow the artist to repay the subsidy, is the artist morally obliged to do so? The answer is clearly yes, since the money returned to the agency distributing the subsidies will be welcome as a source of support for other artists deserving of public subsidies.

Which one of the following principles, if established, most helps to justify the conclusion in the passage?

(A) An artist has a moral duty to urge deserving fellow artists to try to obtain public subsidies, especially if those artists' projects promise to be financially successful.

(B) A financially successful artist should acknowledge that financial success is not solely a function of artistic merit.

(C) A subsidy should be understood as creating a debt that, though routinely forgiven, is rightly forgiven only if either the debtor is unable to repay it or the creditor is not interested in repayment.

(D) The provider of a subsidy should judge as most deserving of subsidies those whose projects are most likely to turn into financial successes.

(E) An artist requesting a subsidy for a potentially profitable project should be required to make a reasonable effort to obtain a bank loan first.

PrepTest105 Sec1 Q14

Step 3: The argument assumes that these circumstances result in a moral obligation to repay: If 1) able to repay and 2) repayment would be welcome, then morally obligated to repay. And, in the contrapositive: If no moral obligation to repay, then 1) not able to repay or 2) repayment not welcome. The correct answer choice will broadly take one of these two forms.	**Step 4:** (C) is correct. This choice matches the contrapositive form of the prediction: For debt to be forgiven (no obligation to repay), then not able to repay or repayment not welcome.

Wrong answers: (A) Distortion. The argument concerns a moral duty to repay, not to urge fellow artists to seek subsidies. (B) Distortion. The argument concerns a moral duty to repay, not to acknowledge financial success. (D) Outside the Scope. The argument is not concerned with which projects are most deserving of subsidies. (E) Outside the Scope. Any eligibility conditions for obtaining the subsidy in the first place are irrelevant to this argument regarding repayment.

Step 2: Conclusion: The government should finance election campaigns. *because* Evidence: Most candidates have to compromise their principles in seeking financing from wealthy private individuals.	**Step 1:** The phrasing "principles, if valid, most helps to justify" indicates a Principle–Strengthen question.

52. Editorial: Our society has a vested interest in maintaining a political system in which candidates are free to adhere to their principles. Yet campaigning for elected office is extremely costly, and because only the wealthiest individuals are able to finance their own political campaigns, most candidates must seek funding from private sources. In so doing, the candidates are almost invariably obliged to compromise their principles. Thus, government itself should assume the cost of candidates' campaigns.

Which one of the following principles, if valid, most helps to justify the conclusion as it is drawn in the argument?

(A) Candidates should not run for elected office if doing so would compel the candidates to compromise their principles.

(B) Candidates wealthy enough to finance their own political campaigns should not be permitted to raise additional funds from private sources.

(C) Voters should not support a candidate if that candidate is known to have accepted funding from private sources.

(D) The government should finance a given activity if doing so will further a vested interest of society.

(E) Private funding for political campaigns should be encouraged only if it redresses an imbalance among candidates' financial means.

PrepTest105 Sec1 Q24

Step 3: The correct answer should set out a rule that states that the government should finance election campaigns in situations where candidates would have to compromise their principles otherwise. The correct choice could be phrased more broadly than the terms of the argument.	**Step 4:** (D) is correct. This choice is stated far more broadly than the terms of the argument, but financing elections falls under the category of financing a "given activity" and avoiding candidates compromising their principles falls under the category of "further[ing] a vested interest of society."

Wrong answers: (A) Distortion. This choice fails to set out a rule that results in government financing election campaigns. (B) Distortion. This choice fails to set out a rule that results in government financing election campaigns. (C) Distortion. This choice fails to set out a rule that results in government financing election campaigns. (E) Distortion. The author argues that campaigns should be funded by the public. He doesn't offer criteria for when private funding should be used.

Step 2: Conclusion: The manager shares at least some blame for the lost business. *because* Evidence: The manager was aware of the typical delays and failed to plan for them.	**Step 1:** The phrase "principle[] underl[ying] the... argument" indicates a Principle–Assumption question.

53. Arbitrator: The shipping manager admits that he decided to close the old facility on October 14 and to schedule the new facility's opening for October 17, the following Monday. But he also claims that he is not responsible for the business that was lost due to the new facility's failing to open as scheduled. He blames the contractor for not finishing on time, but he too, is to blame, for he was aware of the contractor's typical delays and should have planned for this contingency.

Which one of the following principles underlies the arbitrator's argument?

(A) A manager should take foreseeable problems into account when making decisions.

(B) A manager should be able to depend on contractors to do their jobs promptly.

(C) A manager should see to it that contractors do their jobs promptly.

(D) A manager should be held responsible for mistakes made by those whom the manager directly supervises.

(E) A manager, and only a manager, should be held responsible for a project's failure.

PrepTest107 Sec1 Q19

Step 3: The arbitrator assumes that managers who are aware of and then fail to plan for a problem are then responsible for the consequences of that problem. The correct answer in this Principle–Assumption question may use broader language.	**Step 4:** (A) is correct. The contractor's typical delays fall under the category of "foreseeable problems" and planning for contingencies falls under the category of "making decisions."

Wrong answers: (B) 180. The arbitrator ruled that the manager should not depend on the contractor, but instead plan for likely delays. (C) Distortion. The arbitrator ruled that the manager should plan for a delay, not necessarily prevent any such delay. This choice changes the terms of the argument, not just broadens them. (D) Distortion. First, it is unclear whether the manager "directly supervises" the contractor. Second, the problem is contractor delays, not "mistakes." A "delay" does not fall neatly under the category of a "mistake." (E) Distortion. The arbitrator actually rules that the manager shares at least some of the blame, and not that he is solely to blame.

Parallel Flaw Questions

Prepare

LEARNING OBJECTIVE

In this section, you'll learn to:

- Identify and answer Parallel Flaw questions.

Your initial approach to Parallel Flaw questions should be the same as your approach to Flaw questions. Identify the author's conclusion and evidence, and determine why her assumption is flawed. The correct answer will contain an argument that is flawed in precisely the same way. You are likely to see one of the common reasoning errors in Parallel Flaw questions—Causation versus Correlation; Necessity versus Sufficiency; Unrepresentative Sample; and so on. Just as you learned to do in Parallel Reasoning questions (Chapter 3), you can also approach Parallel Flaw questions by identifying the type of conclusion used in the stimulus argument. The correct answer's conclusion type will match.

Be aware that many Parallel Flaw questions will contain Formal Logic. When you see Formal Logic in a Parallel Flaw stimulus, jot down the terms in some sort of shorthand on your scratch paper—you'll see in our explanations that we use letters to represent the various terms in Formal Logic statements. Doing this will help you identify more easily how the argument is flawed and find an answer choice that commits the same reasoning error in the same way. For example, imagine a stimulus that says: "John plays catch whenever he goes to the beach. John said he played catch yesterday, so he must have been at the beach." This argument confuses necessary and sufficient terms. Let (A) replace "John plays catch" and let (B) replace "beach." The argument's structure is now revealed: whenever (B) → (A). Therefore, because (A) → (B). You would then seek an answer choice that messes up Formal Logic terms in the same way.

LSAT STRATEGY

When approaching Parallel Flaw questions:

- Characterize the flaw in the stimulus argument; the correct answer will be flawed in precisely the same way.
- You may compare the conclusion in stimulus argument to those in the answer choice arguments.
- Be on the lookout for flawed Formal Logic.

Here's an example of an LSAT expert's analysis of a Parallel Flaw argument.

Step 2: Conclusion: It is certain that pesticides are contaminating the river. *because* Evidence: Pesticides produced at the plant could cause sterility in otters living in the river, and recently more otters in the river have become sterile.	**Step 1:** The phrase "flaw . . . similar to" indicates a Parallel Flaw question.

A local chemical plant produces pesticides that can cause sterility in small mammals such as otters. Soon after the plant began operating, the incidence of sterility among the otters that swim in a nearby river increased dramatically. Therefore, pesticides are definitely contaminating the river.

Which one of the following arguments contains a flaw in reasoning that is similar to one in the argument above?

(A) The bacteria that cause tetanus live in the digestive tract of horses. Tetanus is a highly infectious disease. Consequently it must be that horses contract tetanus more frequently than do most other animals.

(B) A diet low in calcium can cause a drop in egg production in poultry. When chickens on a local farm were let out in the spring to forage for food, their egg production dropped noticeably. So the food found and eaten by the chickens is undeniably low in calcium.

(C) Animals that are undernourished are very susceptible to infection. Animals in the largest metropolitan zoos are not undernourished, so they surely must not be very susceptible to disease.

(D) Apes are defined by having, among other characteristics, opposable thumbs and no external tail. Recently, fossil remains of a previously unknown animal were found. Because this animal had opposable thumbs, it must have been an ape.

(E) The only animal that could have produced a track similar to this one is a bear. But there are no bears in this area of the country, so this animal track is a fake.

PrepTest104 Sec1 Q11

Step 3: The conclusion is a definite assertion of causation based on evidence of a potential cause. The correct answer will contain a causal argument that contains that same shift from a potential cause to definite cause.	**Step 4:** (B) is correct. This choice contains a shift from a potential cause of the drop in egg production (diet low in calcium) to a claim that the diet must be the cause of the drop in egg production.

Wrong answers: (A) This choice can be eliminated based on the conclusion type: a comparison ("horses . . . more frequently than . . . other animals"). (C) Rather than jumping from a possible cause to a definite cause, this choice commits a Formal Logic flaw; the conclusion is an incomplete contrapositive of the evidence (negates both terms without reversing the sides). (D) This argument assumes that meeting one necessary condition (out of the two mentioned) for being an ape is sufficient to guarantee it is an ape. Not a match. (E) This argument proceeds by eliminating the sole plausible explanation to conclude something is a fake. Not a match.

Practice Now, try a Parallel Flaw question on your own. Work through it using the strategies you've just learned; then check the following page to see how an LSAT expert would approach the same question.

Step 2:	Step 1:

54. Linda says that, as a scientist, she knows that no scientist appreciates poetry. And, since most scientists are logical, at least some of the people who appreciate poetry are illogical.

Which one of the following is most parallel in its reasoning to the flawed reasoning above?

(A) Ralph says that, as an expert in biology, he knows that no marsupial lays eggs. And, since most marsupials are native to Australia, at least some of the animals native to Australia do not lay eggs.

(B) Franz says that, as a father of four children, he knows that no father wants children to eat candy at bedtime. And, since most fathers are adults, at least some of the people who want children to eat candy at bedtime are children.

(C) Yuri says that, as a wine connoisseur, he knows that no wine aged in metal containers is equal in quality to the best wine aged in oak. And, since most California wine is aged in metal containers, California wine is inferior to at least the best French wine aged in oak.

(D) Xi says that, as an experienced photographer, she knows that no color film produces images as sharp as the best black-and-white film. And, since most instant film is color film, at least some instant film produces images less sharp than the best black-and-white film.

(E) Betty says that, as a corporate executive, she knows that no corporate executives like to pay taxes. And, since most corporate executives are honest people, at least some people who like to pay taxes are honest people.

PrepTest107 Sec1 Q23

Step 3:	Step 4:

Expert Analysis

Here's how an LSAT expert applied the Logical Reasoning Method to the question you just tried.

Step 2: Conclusion: Some of the people who appreciate poetry are illogical. *because* Evidence: 1) Most scientists are logical, and 2) no scientists appreciate poetry.	Step 1: The phrase "most parallel... to the flawed reasoning" indicates a Parallel Flaw question.

54. Linda says that, as a scientist, she knows that no scientist appreciates poetry. And, since most scientists are logical, at least some of the people who appreciate poetry are illogical.

Which one of the following is most parallel in its reasoning to the flawed reasoning above?

(A) Ralph says that, as an expert in biology, he knows that no marsupial lays eggs. And, since most marsupials are native to Australia, at least some of the animals native to Australia do not lay eggs.

(B) Franz says that, as a father of four children, he knows that no father wants children to eat candy at bedtime. And, since most fathers are adults, at least some of the people who want children to eat candy at bedtime are children.

(C) Yuri says that, as a wine connoisseur, he knows that no wine aged in metal containers is equal in quality to the best wine aged in oak. And, since most California wine is aged in metal containers, California wine is inferior to at least the best French wine aged in oak.

(D) Xi says that, as an experienced photographer, she knows that no color film produces images as sharp as the best black-and-white film. And, since most instant film is color film, at least some instant film produces images less sharp than the best black-and-white film.

(E) Betty says that, as a corporate executive, she knows that no corporate executives like to pay taxes. And, since most corporate executives are honest people, at least some people who like to pay taxes are honest people.

PrepTest107 Sec1 Q23

CHAPTER 4

Step 3: The evidence supports the deduction that at least *some logical* people do *not appreciate* poetry. The author instead concludes that *some illogical* people *do appreciate* poetry. The conclusion, then, simply negates both terms from the evidence. Look for an answer choice that does the same.	**Step 4:** (B) is correct. This matches the structure of the stimulus. The evidence supports the deduction that at least *some adults* do *not want* children to eat candy at bedtime, but the conclusion states that *some non-adults* do *want* children to eat candy at bedtime.

Wrong answers: (A) 180. This argument is not flawed. The evidence does support a conclusion that at least some of the animals native to Australia do not lay eggs. (C) Distortion. This argument does not contain a blatant flaw, as does the stimulus. It does assume that the "best French wine aged in oak" is equivalent to the "best wine aged in oak." The stimulus does not make a similar assumption. (D) 180. This argument is not flawed. The evidence does support a conclusion that at least some instant film produces images less sharp than the best black-and-white film. (E) Distortion. The evidence in this argument supports the deduction that at least some honest people do not like to pay taxes. The conclusion instead asserts that at least some honest people do like to pay taxes. To match the stimulus, the argument would have to conclude that at least some dishonest people do like to pay taxes.

Parallel Principle Questions

Prepare The final question type we'll discuss in this chapter asks you to identify the principle underlying the argument in the stimulus and then apply the principle to a similar argument in the correct answer. These Parallel Principle questions appear rarely on the LSAT. One has been included on only about half of all recently administered LSATs. Fortunately, Parallel Principle questions are very similar to Parallel Reasoning and Parallel Flaw questions, so if you feel comfortable with those other question types, you should feel comfortable with Parallel Principle questions as well.

In the same way that the stimulus and correct answer in Parallel Flaw questions both contain the same faulty pattern of reasoning, the stimulus and correct answer in Parallel Principle questions both follow the same principle. Parallel Principle questions are similar to Parallel Reasoning and Parallel Flaw questions in that the correct answer will likely discuss a different topic than the stimulus; the only requirement is that the correct answer must be founded on the same principle as the stimulus. To attack Parallel Principle questions efficiently, identify the principle—the broad, general rule—at work in the stimulus and then go through the choices to find the one that applies the identical principle.

Practice Now, try a Parallel Principle question on your own. When you finish, compare your work with the expert's analysis on the next page.

Step 2:	Step 1:

55. Parents should not necessarily raise their children in the ways experts recommend, even if some of those experts are themselves parents. After all, parents are the ones who directly experience which methods are successful in raising their own children.

Which one of the following most closely conforms to the principle that the passage above illustrates?

(A) Although music theory is intrinsically interesting and may be helpful to certain musicians, it does not distinguish good music from bad: that is a matter of taste and not of theory.

(B) One need not pay much attention to the advice of automotive experts when buying a car if those experts are not interested in the mundane factors that concern the average consumer.

(C) In deciding the best way to proceed, a climber familiar with a mountain might do well to ignore the advice of mountain climbing experts unfamiliar with that mountain.

(D) A typical farmer is less likely to know what types of soil are most productive than is someone with an advanced degree in agricultural science.

(E) Unlike society, one's own conscience speaks with a single voice; it is better to follow the advice of one's own conscience than the advice of society.

PrepTest107 Sec4 Q10

Step 3:	Step 4:

Expert Analysis

Here's how an LSAT expert applied the Logical Reasoning Method to the question you just tried.

Step 2: Conclusion: Parents don't need to listen to experts when raising children. Evidence: Parents have the direct experience in seeing what is successful in raising their own children.	**Step 1:** This question stem asks for a situation that "conforms to" the principle "illustrated" above. So the principle is never explicitly stated in the stimulus, but the specific situation in the stimulus and the correct answer choice will each share the same principle—this is a Parallel Principle question.

55. Parents should not necessarily raise their children in the ways experts recommend, even if some of those experts are themselves parents. After all, parents are the ones who directly experience which methods are successful in raising their own children.

Which one of the following most closely conforms to the principle that the passage above illustrates?

(A) Although music theory is intrinsically interesting and may be helpful to certain musicians, it does not distinguish good music from bad: that is a matter of taste and not of theory.

(B) One need not pay much attention to the advice of automotive experts when buying a car if those experts are not interested in the mundane factors that concern the average consumer.

(C) In deciding the best way to proceed, a climber familiar with a mountain might do well to ignore the advice of mountain climbing experts unfamiliar with that mountain.

(D) A typical farmer is less likely to know what types of soil are most productive than is someone with an advanced degree in agricultural science.

(E) Unlike society, one's own conscience speaks with a single voice; it is better to follow the advice of one's own conscience than the advice of society.

PrepTest107 Sec4 Q10

Step 3: Paraphrase the argument in the stimulus in a broad, general form: "If [this evidence], then [this conclusion]": If somebody has direct experience in a matter, then they don't need to listen to experts. The correct answer will contain a specific situation that matches that general rule.	**Step 4:** (C) is correct. The conclusion that one doesn't need to heed experts is backed up by evidence regarding a climber's direct experience.

Wrong answers: (A) There is nothing in this answer choice about direct experience, so it's not a match. (B) While the conclusion here matches the claim that one doesn't need to listen to experts, the evidence provided is not about consumers' direct experiences. (D) 180. This implies that a typical farmer should listen to experts. (E) There is nothing in this choice about having direct experience; additionally, it says not to heed *society*, instead of saying not to heed *experts*.

Identifying Question Stems

Prepare You've seen how the LSAT can test your ability to analyze and evaluate argument-based questions in a number of different ways. On test day, it will be essential for you to be able to differentiate among question types. If you struggle to understand what a question is asking or how to get to the right answer, you'll lose valuable time and energy. Experts know that the path to success in Logical Reasoning is to become familiar with each question type and to know immediately how to attack each question.

Practice For each of the following question stems, identify the question type and mentally characterize the correct answer. Then compare your thinking to the expert analysis that follows.

Question Stem	My Analysis
56. Which of the following, if added to the premises, allows the argument's conclusion to be properly drawn?	
57. Which of the following best characterizes the argument's error of reasoning?	
58. Each of the following, if true, casts doubt on the argument EXCEPT:	
59. In evaluating the argument's conclusion, it would be most valuable to know whether	
60. Which of the following is an assumption required by the argument?	
61. Which of the following, if true, would do most to justify the conclusion drawn above?	
62. Which of the following, if true, most calls into question the argument above?	
63. The reasoning in the argument above is questionable because	

Question Stem	My Analysis
64. Which of the following is an assumption upon which the argument depends?	
65. The argument is vulnerable to criticism on which of the following grounds?	
66. Which of the following lends most support to the argument above?	
67. The conclusion drawn above is unwarranted because	
68. Which of the following principles most helps to justify the reasoning above?	
69. The conclusion of the argument follows logically if which one of the following is presupposed?	
70. Which of the following, if true, most undermines the argument above?	
71. The author makes which one of the following assumptions?	
72. The flawed reasoning in which one of the following is most similar to that in the argument above?	

Expert Analysis

Here's how an LSAT expert would characterize the question stems in that exercise.

Question Stem	Analysis
56. Which of the following, if added to the premises, allows the argument's conclusion to be properly drawn?	Sufficient Assumption question. The correct answer will guarantee the conclusion.
57. Which of the following best characterizes the argument's error of reasoning?	Flaw question. The correct answer will describe the argument's flawed assumption.
58. Each of the following, if true, casts doubt on the argument EXCEPT:	Weaken EXCEPT question. Incorrect choices will each weaken the argument's conclusion. The correct answer will be a strengthener or will have no impact on the conclusion.
59. In evaluating the argument's conclusion, it would be most valuable to know whether	Evaluate question. The correct answer will provide information that, if true, will either strengthen or weaken the conclusion and, if false, will have the opposite effect. Incorrect choices will be irrelevant, having no effect on the conclusion's likelihood.
60. Which of the following is an assumption required by the argument?	Necessary Assumption question. The correct answer will state an assumption that is necessary for the conclusion to stand. Confirm the correct answer using the Denial Test: when a necessary assumption is negated, the conclusion falls apart.
61. Which of the following, if true, would do most to justify the conclusion drawn above?	Strengthen question. The correct answer will strengthen the conclusion by supporting the argument's assumption.
62. Which of the following, if true, most calls into question the argument above?	Weaken question. The correct answer will weaken the conclusion by attacking the argument's assumption.
63. The reasoning in the argument above is questionable because	Flaw question. The correct answer will describe the argument's flawed assumption.

Question Stem	Analysis
64. Which of the following is an assumption upon which the argument depends?	Necessary Assumption question. The correct answer will state an assumption that is necessary for the conclusion to stand. Confirm the correct answer using the Denial Test: when the correct answer is negated, the conclusion falls apart.
65. The argument is vulnerable to criticism on which of the following grounds?	Flaw question. The correct answer will describe the argument's flawed assumption.
66. Which of the following lends most support to the argument above?	Strengthen question. The correct answer will strengthen the conclusion by supporting the argument's assumption.
67. The conclusion drawn above is unwarranted because	Flaw question. The correct answer will describe the argument's flawed assumption.
68. Which of the following principles most helps to justify the reasoning above?	Principle–Strengthen question. The correct answer will strengthen the conclusion in broadly worded terms.
69. The conclusion of the argument follows logically if which one of the following is presupposed?	Sufficient Assumption question. The correct answer will guarantee the conclusion.
70. Which of the following, if true, most undermines the argument above?	Weaken question. The correct answer will weaken the conclusion by attacking the argument's assumption.
71. The author makes which one of the following assumptions?	Necessary Assumption question. The correct answer will state an assumption that is necessary for the conclusion to stand. Confirm the correct answer using the Denial Test: when a necessary assumption is negated, the conclusion falls apart.
72. The flawed reasoning in which one of the following is most similar to that in the argument above?	Parallel Flaw question. The correct answer will contain an argument that is flawed in the same way that the argument in the stimulus is flawed.

Reflect You may find that as you work through more and more argument-based questions, you start to notice the weak points in the arguments that you confront in everyday life—in advertisements, on the news, in written articles, in conversations. That's a good thing! If you are noticing that a television news anchor has just made an assumption, or thinking about how an article in a popular science journal could strengthen its main point, or thinking about how you could knock down a friend's argument against going to see your favorite jazz band with you, or noticing that a subway advertisement leaps to a conclusion without considering alternative possibilities, then you are learning to think like a lawyer. The more you can engage with the arguments you encounter on a daily basis in a skeptical, thoughtful way, the better prepared you will be for the LSAT and for what lies ahead in law school.

Perform

Assumption

Assess your skills on some further examples of Assumption questions. Take no more than 1 minute 30 seconds per question.

1. Naturalist: The recent claims that the Tasmanian tiger is not extinct are false. The Tasmanian tiger's natural habitat was taken over by sheep farming decades ago, resulting in the animal's systematic elimination from the area. Since then naturalists working in the region have discovered no hard evidence of its survival, such as carcasses or tracks. In spite of alleged sightings of the animal, the Tasmanian tiger no longer exists.

Which one of the following is an assumption on which the naturalist's argument depends?

(A) Sheep farming drove the last Tasmanian tigers to starvation by chasing them from their natural habitat.

(B) Some scavengers in Tasmania are capable of destroying tiger carcasses without a trace.

(C) Every naturalist working in the Tasmanian tiger's natural habitat has looked systematically for evidence of the tiger's survival.

(D) The Tasmanian tiger did not move and adapt to a different region in response to the loss of habitat.

(E) Those who have reported sightings of the Tasmanian tiger are not experienced naturalists.

PrepTest123 Sec3 Q9

2. Feathers recently taken from seabirds stuffed and preserved in the 1880s have been found to contain only half as much mercury as feathers recently taken from living birds of the same species. Since mercury that accumulates in a seabird's feathers as the feathers grow is derived from fish eaten by the bird, these results indicate that mercury levels in saltwater fish are higher now than they were 100 years ago.

The argument depends on assuming that

(A) the proportion of a seabird's diet consisting of fish was not as high, on average, in the 1880s as it is today

(B) the amount of mercury in a saltwater fish depends on the amount of pollution in the ocean habitat of the fish

(C) mercury derived from fish is essential for the normal growth of a seabird's feathers

(D) the stuffed seabirds whose feathers were tested for mercury were not fully grown

(E) the process used to preserve birds in the 1880s did not substantially decrease the amount of mercury in the birds' feathers

PrepTest123 Sec3 Q11

3. A new government policy has been developed to avoid many serious cases of influenza. This goal will be accomplished by the annual vaccination of high-risk individuals: everyone 65 and older as well as anyone with a chronic disease that might cause them to experience complications from the influenza virus. Each year's vaccination will protect only against the strain of the influenza virus deemed most likely to be prevalent that year, so every year it will be necessary for all high-risk individuals to receive a vaccine for a different strain of the virus.

Which one of the following is an assumption that would allow the conclusion above to be properly drawn?

(A) The number of individuals in the high-risk group for influenza will not significantly change from year to year.

(B) The likelihood that a serious influenza epidemic will occur varies from year to year.

(C) No vaccine for the influenza virus protects against more than one strain of that virus.

(D) Each year the strain of influenza virus deemed most likely to be prevalent will be one that had not previously been deemed most likely to be prevalent.

(E) Each year's vaccine will have fewer side effects than the vaccine of the previous year since the technology for making vaccines will constantly improve.

PrepTest123 Sec2 Q15

4. An undergraduate degree is necessary for appointment to the executive board. Further, no one with a felony conviction can be appointed to the board. Thus, Murray, an accountant with both a bachelor's and a master's degree, cannot be accepted for the position of Executive Administrator, since he has a felony conviction.

The argument's conclusion follows logically if which one of the following is assumed?

(A) Anyone with a master's degree and without a felony conviction is eligible for appointment to the executive board.

(B) Only candidates eligible for appointment to the executive board can be accepted for the position of Executive Administrator.

(C) An undergraduate degree is not necessary for acceptance for the position of Executive Administrator.

(D) If Murray did not have a felony conviction, he would be accepted for the position of Executive Administrator.

(E) The felony charge on which Murray was convicted is relevant to the duties of the position of Executive Administrator.

PrepTest123 Sec2 Q6

Flaw

Assess your skills on some further examples of Flaw questions. Take no more than 1 minute 30 seconds per question.

5. Advertisement: Fabric-Soft leaves clothes soft and fluffy, and its fresh scent is a delight. We conducted a test using over 100 consumers to prove Fabric-Soft is best. Each consumer was given one towel washed with Fabric-Soft and one towel washed without it. Ninety-nine percent of the consumers preferred the Fabric-Soft towel. So Fabric-Soft is the most effective fabric softener available.

The advertisement's reasoning is most vulnerable to criticism on the grounds that it fails to consider whether

(A) any of the consumers tested are allergic to fabric softeners

(B) Fabric-Soft is more or less harmful to the environment than other fabric softeners

(C) Fabric-Soft is much cheaper or more expensive than other fabric softeners

(D) the consumers tested find the benefits of using fabric softeners worth the expense

(E) the consumers tested had the opportunity to evaluate fabric softeners other than Fabric-Soft

PrepTest123 Sec3 Q8

6. Editorialist: In all cultures, it is almost universally accepted that one has a moral duty to prevent members of one's family from being harmed. Thus, few would deny that if a person is known by the person's parents to be falsely accused of a crime, it would be morally right for the parents to hide the accused from the police. Hence, it is also likely to be widely accepted that it is sometimes morally right to obstruct the police in their work.

The reasoning in the editorialist's argument is most vulnerable to criticism on the grounds that this argument

(A) utilizes a single type of example for the purpose of justifying a broad generalization

(B) fails to consider the possibility that other moral principles would be widely recognized as overriding any obligation to protect a family member from harm

(C) presumes, without providing justification, that allowing the police to arrest an innocent person assists rather than obstructs justice

(D) takes for granted that there is no moral obligation to obey the law

(E) takes for granted that the parents mentioned in the example are not mistaken about their child's innocence

PrepTest123 Sec3 Q18

7. Some anthropologists argue that the human species could not have survived prehistoric times if the species had not evolved the ability to cope with diverse natural environments. However, there is considerable evidence that *Australopithecus afarensis*, a prehistoric species related to early humans, also thrived in a diverse array of environments, but became extinct. Hence, the anthropologists' claim is false.

The reasoning in the argument is most vulnerable to criticism on the grounds that the argument

(A) confuses a condition's being required for a given result to occur in one case with the condition's being sufficient for such a result to occur in a similar case

(B) takes for granted that if one species had a characteristic that happened to enable it to survive certain conditions, at least one related extinct species must have had the same characteristic

(C) generalizes, from the fact that one species with a certain characteristic survived certain conditions, that all related species with the same characteristic must have survived exactly the same conditions

(D) fails to consider the possibility that *Australopithecus afarensis* had one or more characteristics that lessened its chances of surviving prehistoric times

(E) fails to consider the possibility that, even if a condition caused a result to occur in one case, it was not necessary to cause the result to occur in a similar case

PrepTest123 Sec3 Q25

Strengthen/Weaken

Assess your skills on some further examples of Strengthen/Weaken questions. Take no more than 1 minute 30 seconds per question.

8. Although video game sales have increased steadily over the past 3 years, we can expect a reversal of this trend in the very near future. Historically, over three quarters of video games sold have been purchased by people from 13 to 16 years of age, and the number of people in this age group is expected to decline steadily over the next 10 years.

Which one of the following, if true, would most seriously weaken the argument?

(A) Most people 17 years old or older have never purchased a video game.

(B) Video game rentals have declined over the past 3 years.

(C) New technology will undoubtedly make entirely new entertainment options available over the next 10 years.

(D) The number of different types of video games available is unlikely to decrease in the near future.

(E) Most of the people who have purchased video games over the past 3 years are over the age of 16.

PrepTest123 Sec2 Q9

9. A cup of raw milk, after being heated in a microwave oven to 50 degrees Celsius, contains half its initial concentration of a particular enzyme, lysozyme. If, however, the milk reaches that temperature through exposure to a conventional heat source of 50 degrees Celsius, it will contain nearly all of its initial concentration of the enzyme. Therefore, what destroys the enzyme is not heat but microwaves, which generate heat.

Which one of the following, if true, most seriously weakens the argument?

(A) Heating raw milk in a microwave oven to a temperature of 100 degrees Celsius destroys nearly all of the lysozyme initially present in that milk.

(B) Enzymes in raw milk that are destroyed through excessive heating can be replaced by adding enzymes that have been extracted from other sources.

(C) A liquid exposed to a conventional heat source of exactly 50 degrees Celsius will reach that temperature more slowly than it would if it were exposed to a conventional heat source hotter than 50 degrees Celsius.

(D) Milk that has been heated in a microwave oven does not taste noticeably different from milk that has been briefly heated by exposure to a conventional heat source.

(E) Heating any liquid by microwave creates small zones within it that are much hotter than the overall temperature that the liquid will ultimately reach.

PrepTest123 Sec2 Q14

10. A consumer magazine surveyed people who had sought a psychologist's help with a personal problem. Of those responding who had received treatment for 6 months or less, 20 percent claimed that treatment "made things a lot better." Of those responding who had received longer treatment, 36 percent claimed that treatment "made things a lot better." Therefore, psychological treatment lasting more than 6 months is more effective than shorter-term treatment.

Which one of the following, if true, most seriously weakens the argument?

(A) Of the respondents who had received treatment for longer than 6 months, 10 percent said that treatment made things worse.

(B) Patients who had received treatment for longer than 6 months were more likely to respond to the survey than were those who had received treatment for a shorter time.

(C) Patients who feel they are doing well in treatment tend to remain in treatment, while those who are doing poorly tend to quit earlier.

(D) Patients who were dissatisfied with their treatment were more likely to feel a need to express their feelings about it and thus to return the survey.

(E) Many psychologists encourage their patients to receive treatment for longer than 6 months.

PrepTest123 Sec3 Q15

11. Editor: Many candidates say that if elected they will reduce governmental intrusion into voters' lives. But voters actually elect politicians who instead promise that the government will provide assistance to solve their most pressing problems. Governmental assistance, however, costs money, and money can come only from taxes, which can be considered a form of governmental intrusion. Thus, governmental intrusion into the lives of voters will rarely be substantially reduced over time in a democracy.

Which one of the following, if true, would most strengthen the editor's argument?

(A) Politicians who win their elections usually keep their campaign promises.

(B) Politicians never promise what they really intend to do once in office.

(C) The most common problems people have are financial problems.

(D) Governmental intrusion into the lives of voters is no more burdensome in nondemocratic countries than it is in democracies.

(E) Politicians who promise to do what they actually believe ought to be done are rarely elected.

PrepTest123 Sec3 Q19

12. Ethicist: On average, animals raised on grain must be fed sixteen pounds of grain to produce one pound of meat. A pound of meat is more nutritious for humans than a pound of grain, but sixteen pounds of grain could feed many more people than could a pound of meat. With grain yields leveling off, large areas of farmland going out of production each year, and the population rapidly expanding, we must accept the fact that consumption of meat will soon be morally unacceptable.

Which one of the following, if true, would most weaken the ethicist's argument?

(A) Even though it has been established that a vegetarian diet can be healthy, many people prefer to eat meat and are willing to pay for it.

(B) Often, cattle or sheep can be raised to maturity on grass from pastureland that is unsuitable for any other kind of farming.

(C) If a grain diet is supplemented with protein derived from non-animal sources, it can have nutritional value equivalent to that of a diet containing meat.

(D) Although prime farmland near metropolitan areas is being lost rapidly to suburban development, we could reverse this trend by choosing to live in areas that are already urban.

(E) Nutritionists agree that a diet composed solely of grain products is not adequate for human health.

PrepTest123 Sec3 Q21

Assumption-Family Principle

Assess your skills with some further examples of Assumption-Family Principle questions. Take no more than 1 minute 30 seconds per question.

13. Sociologist: Romantics who claim that people are not born evil but may be made evil by the imperfect institutions that they form cannot be right, for they misunderstand the causal relationship between people and their institutions. After all, institutions are merely collections of people.

Which one of the following principles, if valid, would most help to justify the sociologist's argument?

(A) People acting together in institutions can do more good or evil than can people acting individually.

(B) Institutions formed by people are inevitably imperfect.

(C) People should not be overly optimistic in their view of individual human beings.

(D) A society's institutions are the surest gauge of that society's values.

(E) The whole does not determine the properties of the things that compose it.

PrepTest123 Sec3 Q24

Parallel Flaw

Assess your skills with some further examples of Parallel Flaw questions. Take no more than 1 minute 30 seconds per question.

14. All Labrador retrievers bark a great deal. All Saint Bernards bark infrequently. Each of Rosa's dogs is a cross between a Labrador retriever and a Saint Bernard. Therefore, Rosa's dogs are moderate barkers.

Which one of the following uses flawed reasoning that most closely resembles the flawed reasoning used in the argument above?

(A) All students who study diligently make good grades. But some students who do not study diligently also make good grades. Jane studies somewhat diligently. Therefore, Jane makes somewhat good grades.

(B) All type A chemicals are extremely toxic to human beings. All type B chemicals are nontoxic to human beings. This household cleaner is a mixture of a type A chemical and a type B chemical. Therefore, this household cleaner is moderately toxic.

(C) All students at Hanson School live in Green County. All students at Edwards School live in Winn County. Members of the Perry family attend both Hanson and Edwards. Therefore, some members of the Perry family live in Green County and some live in Winn County.

(D) All transcriptionists know shorthand. All engineers know calculus. Bob has worked both as a transcriptionist and as an engineer. Therefore, Bob knows both shorthand and calculus.

(E) All of Kenisha's dresses are very well made. All of Connie's dresses are very badly made. Half of the dresses in this closet are very well made, and half of them are very badly made. Therefore, half of the dresses in this closet are Kenisha's and half of them are Connie's.

PrepTest123 Sec2 Q7

15. We should accept the proposal to demolish the old train station, because the local historical society, which vehemently opposes this, is dominated by people who have no commitment to long-term economic well-being. Preserving old buildings creates an impediment to new development, which is critical to economic health.

The flawed reasoning exhibited by the argument above is most similar to that exhibited by which one of the following arguments?

(A) Our country should attempt to safeguard works of art that it deems to possess national cultural significance. These works might not be recognized as such by all tax-payers, or even all critics. Nevertheless, our country ought to expend whatever money is needed to procure all such works as they become available.

(B) Documents of importance to local heritage should be properly preserved and archived for the sake of future generations. For, if even one of these documents is damaged or lost, the integrity of the historical record as a whole will be damaged.

(C) You should have your hair cut no more than once a month. After all, beauticians suggest that their customers have their hair cut twice a month, and they do this as a way of generating more business for themselves.

(D) The committee should endorse the plan to postpone construction of the new ex-pressway. Many residents of the neighbor-hoods that would be affected are fervently opposed to that construction, and the committee is obligated to avoid alienating those residents.

(E) One should not borrow even small amounts of money unless it is absolutely necessary. Once one borrows a few dollars, the interest starts to accumulate. The longer one takes to repay, the more one ends up owing, and eventually a small debt has become a large one.

PrepTest123 Sec3 Q20

Mixed Perform: Assumption Family Questions

Assess your skills with some further examples of the most important question types introduced in this chapter—Assumption, Flaw, and Strengthen/Weaken. Take no more than 1 minute 30 seconds per question.

16. Atrens: An early entomologist observed ants carrying particles to neighboring ant colonies and inferred that the ants were bringing food to their neighbors. Further research, however, revealed that the ants were emptying their own colony's dumping site. Thus, the early entomologist was wrong.

Atrens's conclusion follows logically if which one of the following is assumed?

(A) Ant societies do not interact in all the same ways that human societies interact.

(B) There is only weak evidence for the view that ants have the capacity to make use of objects as gifts.

(C) Ant dumping sites do not contain particles that could be used as food.

(D) The ants to whom the particles were brought never carried the particles into their own colonies.

(E) The entomologist cited retracted his conclusion when it was determined that the particles the ants carried came from their dumping site.

PrepTest123 Sec3 Q5

17. Many corporations have begun decorating their halls with motivational posters in hopes of boosting their employees' motivation to work productively. However, almost all employees at these corporations are already motivated to work productively. So these corporations' use of motivational posters is unlikely to achieve its intended purpose.

The reasoning in the argument is most vulnerable to criticism on the grounds that the argument

(A) fails to consider whether corporations that do not currently use motivational posters would increase their employees' motivation to work productively if they began using the posters

(B) takes for granted that, with respect to their employees' motivation to work productively, corporations that decorate their halls with motivational posters are representative of corporations in general

(C) fails to consider that even if motivational posters do not have one particular beneficial effect for corporations, they may have similar effects that are equally beneficial

(D) does not adequately address the possibility that employee productivity is strongly affected by factors other than employees' motivation to work productively

(E) fails to consider that even if employees are already motivated to work productively, motivational posters may increase that motivation

PrepTest123 Sec3 Q4

18. Standard aluminum soft-drink cans do not vary in the amount of aluminum that they contain. Fifty percent of the aluminum contained in a certain group (M) of standard aluminum soft-drink cans was recycled from another group (L) of used, standard aluminum soft-drink cans. Since all the cans in L were recycled into cans in M and since the amount of material other than aluminum in an aluminum can is negligible, it follows that M contains twice as many cans as L.

The conclusion of the argument follows logically if which one of the following is assumed?

(A) The aluminum in the cans of M cannot be recycled further.

(B) Recycled aluminum is of poorer quality than unrecycled aluminum.

(C) All of the aluminum in an aluminum can is recovered when the can is recycled.

(D) None of the soft-drink cans in group L had been made from recycled aluminum.

(E) Aluminum soft-drink cans are more easily recycled than are soft-drink cans made from other materials.

PrepTest123 Sec2 Q13

19. Consumer: The latest *Connorly Report* suggests that Ocksenfrey prepackaged meals are virtually devoid of nutritional value. But the *Connorly Report* is commissioned by Danto Foods, Ocksenfrey's largest corporate rival, and early drafts of the report are submitted for approval to Danto Foods' public relations department. Because of the obvious bias of this report, it is clear that Ocksenfrey's prepackaged meals really are nutritious.

The reasoning in the consumer's argument is most vulnerable to criticism on the grounds that the argument

(A) treats evidence that there is an apparent bias as evidence that the *Connorly Report*'s claims are false

(B) draws a conclusion based solely on an unrepresentative sample of Ocksenfrey's products

(C) fails to take into account the possibility that Ocksenfrey has just as much motivation to create negative publicity for Danto as Danto has to create negative publicity for Ocksenfrey

(D) fails to provide evidence that Danto Foods' prepackaged meals are not more nutritious than Ocksenfrey's are

(E) presumes, without providing justification, that Danto Foods' public relations department would not approve a draft of a report that was hostile to Danto Foods' products

PrepTest123 Sec2 Q4

20. Scientist: Earth's average annual temperature has increased by about 0.5 degrees Celsius over the last century. This warming is primarily the result of the buildup of minor gases in the atmosphere, blocking the outward flow of heat from the planet.

Which one of the following, if true, would count as evidence against the scientist's explanation of Earth's warming?

(A) Only some of the minor gases whose presence in the atmosphere allegedly resulted in the phenomenon described by the scientist were produced by industrial pollution.

(B) Most of the warming occurred before 1940, while most of the buildup of minor gases in the atmosphere occurred after 1940.

(C) Over the last century, Earth received slightly more solar radiation in certain years than it did in others.

(D) Volcanic dust and other particles in the atmosphere reflect much of the Sun's radiation back into space before it can reach Earth's surface.

(E) The accumulation of minor gases in the atmosphere has been greater over the last century than at any other time in Earth's history.

PrepTest123 Sec2 Q5

21. Philosopher: An action is morally right if it would be reasonably expected to increase the aggregate well-being of the people affected by it. An action is morally wrong if and only if it would be reasonably expected to reduce the aggregate well-being of the people affected by it. Thus, actions that would be reasonably expected to leave unchanged the aggregate well-being of the people affected by them are also right.

The philosopher's conclusion follows logically if which one of the following is assumed?

(A) Only wrong actions would be reasonably expected to reduce the aggregate well-being of the people affected by them.

(B) No action is both right and wrong.

(C) Any action that is not morally wrong is morally right.

(D) There are actions that would be reasonably expected to leave unchanged the aggregate well-being of the people affected by them.

(E) Only right actions have good consequences.

PrepTest123 Sec2 Q23

22. Political candidates' speeches are loaded with promises and with expressions of good intention, but one must not forget that the politicians' purpose in giving these speeches is to get themselves elected. Clearly, then, these speeches are selfishly motivated and the promises made in them are unreliable.

Which one of the following most accurately describes a flaw in the argument above?

(A) The argument presumes, without providing justification, that if a person's promise is not selfishly motivated then that promise is reliable.

(B) The argument presumes, without providing justification, that promises made for selfish reasons are never kept.

(C) The argument confuses the effect of an action with its cause.

(D) The argument overlooks the fact that a promise need not be unreliable just because the person who made it had an ulterior motive for doing so.

(E) The argument overlooks the fact that a candidate who makes promises for selfish reasons may nonetheless be worthy of the office for which he or she is running.

PrepTest123 Sec3 Q23

23. Hospital executive: At a recent conference on nonprofit management, several computer experts maintained that the most significant threat faced by large institutions such as universities and hospitals is unauthorized access to confidential data. In light of this testimony, we should make the protection of our clients' confidentiality our highest priority.

The hospital executive's argument is most vulnerable to which one of the following objections?

(A) The argument confuses the causes of a problem with the appropriate solutions to that problem.

(B) The argument relies on the testimony of experts whose expertise is not shown to be sufficiently broad to support their general claim.

(C) The argument assumes that a correlation between two phenomena is evidence that one is the cause of the other.

(D) The argument draws a general conclusion about a group based on data about an unrepresentative sample of that group.

(E) The argument infers that a property belonging to large institutions belongs to all institutions.

PrepTest123 Sec2 Q17

24. Historian: The Land Party achieved its only national victory in Banestria in 1935. It received most of its support that year in rural and semirural areas, where the bulk of Banestria's population lived at the time. The economic woes of the years surrounding that election hit agricultural and small business interests the hardest, and the Land Party specifically targeted those groups in 1935. I conclude that the success of the Land Party that year was due to the combination of the Land Party's specifically addressing the concerns of these groups and the depth of the economic problems people in these groups were facing.

Each of the following, if true, strengthens the historian's argument EXCEPT:

(A) In preceding elections the Land Party made no attempt to address the interests of economically distressed urban groups.

(B) Voters are more likely to vote for a political party that focuses on their problems.

(C) The Land Party had most of its successes when there was economic distress in the agricultural sector.

(D) No other major party in Banestria specifically addressed the issues of people who lived in semirural areas in 1935.

(E) The greater the degree of economic distress someone is in, the more likely that person is to vote.

PrepTest123 Sec2 Q19

25. Therapist: Cognitive psychotherapy focuses on changing a patient's conscious beliefs. Thus, cognitive psychotherapy is likely to be more effective at helping patients overcome psychological problems than are forms of psychotherapy that focus on changing unconscious beliefs and desires, since only conscious beliefs are under the patient's direct conscious control.

Which one of the following, if true, would most strengthen the therapist's argument?

(A) Psychological problems are frequently caused by unconscious beliefs that could be changed with the aid of psychotherapy.

(B) It is difficult for any form of psychotherapy to be effective without focusing on mental states that are under the patient's direct conscious control.

(C) Cognitive psychotherapy is the only form of psychotherapy that focuses primarily on changing the patient's conscious beliefs.

(D) No form of psychotherapy that focuses on changing the patient's unconscious beliefs and desires can be effective unless it also helps change beliefs that are under the patient's direct conscious control.

(E) All of a patient's conscious beliefs are under the patient's conscious control, but other psychological states cannot be controlled effectively without the aid of psychotherapy.

PrepTest123 Sec3 Q13

26. Driver: My friends say I will one day have an accident because I drive my sports car recklessly. But I have done some research, and apparently minivans and larger sedans have very low accident rates compared to sports cars. So trading my sports car in for a minivan would lower my risk of having an accident.

The reasoning in the driver's argument is most vulnerable to criticism on the grounds that this argument

(A) infers a cause from a mere correlation

(B) relies on a sample that is too narrow

(C) misinterprets evidence that a result is likely as evidence that the result is certain

(D) mistakes a condition sufficient for bringing about a result for a condition necessary for doing so

(E) relies on a source that is probably not well-informed

PrepTest123 Sec2 Q21

Assess

Use the following criteria to evaluate your results on the Assumption Family Questions Perform quiz.

If, under timed conditions, you correctly answered:

20–26 of the questions: Outstanding! You have demonstrated a strong skill level in Assumption Family questions. For further practice, use any of the Recommended Additional Practice sets, including the Advanced set. If you have time in your study schedule, move on to Chapter 5 on Non-Argument questions. You should also make timed practice with full Logical Reasoning sections a routine part of your LSAT prep.

13–19 of the questions: Good work! You have a solid foundation in Assumption Family questions. For further practice, begin with the Foundations or Mid-Level Recommended Additional Practice set (and, time permitting, work up through the Advanced set, as well). If you have time in your study schedule, move on to Chapter 5 on Non-Argument questions. You should, at this point, make timed practice with full Logical Reasoning sections a routine part of your LSAT prep.

0–12 of the questions: Keep working. Assumption Family questions are central to your LSAT performance (equivalent, on most tests, to the entire Logic Games section). Continued practice will help you improve your score. Begin by reviewing this chapter. Then, try the questions in the Foundations Recommended Additional Practice set. As you continue to progress, move on to the Mid-Level Recommended Additional Practice set. After that, if you have time in your study schedule, move on to Chapter 5 on Non-Argument questions and make timed practice with full Logical Reasoning sections a part of your prep routine.

Recommended Additional Practice: Assumption Family Questions

The following questions provide good practice on recent Assumption Family questions. They are grouped by difficulty as determined from empirical student practice results. Foundations practice has 1- and 2-star questions; Mid-Level practice has 1-, 2-, and 3-star questions; Advanced practice has 2-, 3-, and 4-star questions. All the questions are from PrepTests that are available for digital practice on LawHub with an LSAC LawHub Advantage subscription. Complete explanations and analysis for these questions are available on Kaplan's LSAT Link and LSAT Link+. See **www.kaptest.com/LSAT** to learn more about LSAT Link and LSAT Link+.

Foundations

PrepTest144, Section 3, Questions 1, 9, & 21
PrepTest140, Section 2, Questions 1, 4, 9, & 11
PrepTest139, Section 1, Questions 1, 3, 4, 5, 6, 8, 13, 14, & 24; Section 4, Questions 8, 13, 15, & 22
PrepTest138, Section 2, Questions 2 & 13; Section 3, Questions 1, 9, 16, & 23
PrepTest137, Section 2, Questions 1, 3, 6, 9, & 15; Section 4, Questions 7, 8, 13, & 21
PrepTest136, Section 2, Questions 2, 4, 5, 6, 8, & 13; Section 4, Questions 1, 3, 4, 6, 7, 11, & 16
PrepTest135, Section 1, Questions 1, 3, 6, 8, 13, 14, & 17; Section 4, Questions 2, 3, & 7
PrepTest134, Section 1, Questions 4, 5, 7, & 19; Section 3, Questions 2, 4, & 6
PrepTest133, Section 1, Questions 1, 2, 3, 5, 10, 11, 15, 22, 23, & 25; Section 3, Questions 2, 9, & 14
PrepTest132, Section 2, Questions 2, 3, 5, 7, 9, 12, 23, & 26; Section 4, Questions 3, 5, 15, & 20

Mid-Level

PrepTest144, Section 3, Questions 2, 3, 7, 10, 15, & 25
PrepTest140, Section 2, Questions 3, 6, 10, 15, & 22
PrepTest139, Section 1, Question 7; Section 4, Questions 3, 7, 14, & 18

PrepTest138, Section 2, Questions 4, 5, 7, & 16; Section 3, Questions 3, 5, & 7
PrepTest137, Section 2, Questions 8, 18, & 21; Section 4, Questions 2, 4, 6, 9, 10, 11, & 24
PrepTest136, Section 2, Questions 1, 3, 7, & 10; Section 4, Question 2
PrepTest135, Section 1, Questions 5, 11, 18, 19, 21, & 24; Section 4, Questions 5, 8, 11, 19, 20, 24, & 26
PrepTest134, Section 1, Questions 8, 11, 12, 15, 16, & 17; Section 3, Questions 9, 11, 12, 19, & 24
PrepTest133, Section 1, Questions 16, 18, 19, & 24; Section 3, Questions 6, 15, 17, 21, & 25
PrepTest132, Section 2, Questions 4, 11, 13, 15, 16, & 22; Section 4, Questions 9, 10, 14, 16, 19, & 23

Advanced

PrepTest144, Section 3, Questions 11, 13, 16, 20, & 23
PrepTest140, Section 2, Questions 12, 19, 20, 23, & 25
PrepTest139, Section 1, Questions 17, 19, 20, 22, & 25; Section 4, Questions 11, 16, 17, 19, 21, & 23
PrepTest138, Section 2, Questions 12, 14, 15, 20, 23, 24, & 25; Section 3, Questions 12, 15, 17, 18, 21, & 24
PrepTest137, Section 2, Questions 13, 14, 17, 23, & 25; Section 4, Questions 14, 16, 18, & 25
PrepTest136, Section 2, Questions 11, 12, 15, 17, 19, 21, & 24; Section 4, Questions 8, 12, 17, 20, 22, 24, & 25
PrepTest135, Section 1, Questions 15, 16, & 20; Section 4, Questions 13, 15, 22, & 23
PrepTest134, Section 1, Questions 9, 10, 13, 22, 23, & 24; Section 3, Questions 14, 15, 17, 21, 23, & 26
PrepTest133, Section 1, Question 7; Section 3, Questions 11, 16, 18, 22, 23, & 24
PrepTest132, Section 2, Questions 8, 17, & 25; Section 4, Questions 13, 18, & 22

Answers and Explanations

Assumption

1. (D) Assumption (Necessary) ★★★★

Step 1: Identify the Question Type

Because the correct answer is the "assumption on which the . . . argument depends," this is a Necessary Assumption question.

Step 2: Untangle the Stimulus

Break the argument into evidence and conclusion. The conclusion actually comes at two places: the beginning and end of the stimulus. Whichever place you identify it, the naturalist's main point is that the Tasmanian tiger is extinct. There are two pieces of evidence. First, the tiger was eliminated from its native habitat decades ago, and second, naturalists have found no physical traces of the tiger in this area since its elimination.

Step 3: Make a Prediction

This argument relies on a classic pattern of reasoning. The conclusion is possible, and there's no evidence to contradict it. In other words, absence of evidence is taken to be evidence of absence. Moreover, notice how the argument shifts in scope. The conclusion is broad: The tiger "no longer exists." But the evidence says only that it hasn't been found where it traditionally existed. The author assumes that if you don't find the tiger here, it doesn't exist anywhere. That, in turn, overlooks the possibility that the tigers have survived in a region other than their natural range.

Step 4: Evaluate the Answer Choices

(D) rules out the possibility that the tigers are still alive in some new habitat. It can be confirmed as the correct answer by applying the Denial Test. The denied version would state that the Tasmanian tiger *did* move to a different region. If that were true, then it would make perfect sense why naturalists searching in the tiger's old region found no evidence of it. More importantly, if the Tasmanian tiger moved somewhere else, that would directly contradict the conclusion that the tiger is altogether extinct. Because the denied version directly contradicts the conclusion, that proves that **(D)** is a necessary assumption for the argument.

(A) goes Outside the Scope by introducing starvation. It is not necessary for the argument that any one particular cause, in this case starvation, is what caused the tigers to become extinct. It could also be that the tigers were shot, captured, etc.

(B) is a 180. It weakens the argument by providing an explanation for why naturalists have not found tiger carcasses. Thus, it makes it more likely to be true that the Tasmanian tiger still survives.

(C) is Extreme. The argument relies on the fact that no evidence has been found. The argument doesn't depend on whether all or most or some of the naturalists looked systematically. Even if they have not *all* looked systematically, the tiger could still be extinct. **(C)** does not survive the Denial Test.

(E) While this information supports the naturalist's dismissal of the alleged sightings, it is not necessary to her argument. Using the Denial Test, even if the alleged sightings were from experienced naturalists, they could be wrong and the author could still be correct in concluding that the tiger is extinct based on her reasons.

2. (E) Assumption (Necessary) ★★★★

Step 1: Identify the Question Type

Because the correct answer is the assumption that the argument "depends on," this is a Necessary Assumption question.

Step 2: Untangle the Stimulus

Start by identifying evidence and conclusion. The conclusion ends the stimulus: there is more mercury in saltwater fish than there was 100 years ago. The evidence comes in two pieces. Following the Keyword *since*, we learn that mercury in seabirds' feathers comes from the fish that they eat. From the beginning of the stimulus, we learn feathers from living birds were compared to feathers taken from stuffed birds that lived in the 1880s and the feathers from living birds had twice as much mercury.

Step 3: Make a Prediction

In any argument that depends upon a comparison, examine the items being compared to ensure they are the same things. In this case, if there is no difference between the feathers of living birds and those of stuffed birds, the comparison may be useful. However, if there is something about the preservation process that would affect mercury levels in the stuffed birds, this comparison would be questionable. To draw her conclusion, the author is assuming that the mercury level in the stuffed birds' feathers was not affected by the preservation process.

Step 4: Evaluate the Answer Choices

(E) matches the prediction by ruling out the possibility that the preservation process could have changed the amount of mercury in the stuffed seabird feathers.

(A) is a 180 because it weakens the argument. If seabirds in the 1880s ate fewer fish, then we should expect the level of mercury in their feathers to be lower than the seabird feathers of today, regardless of how much mercury is in the fish. Thus, **(A)** makes it less likely that today's fish have twice as much mercury.

(B) goes Out of Scope by providing an explanation for why the mercury level in fish might change. The argument is about whether or not fish have twice as much mercury now as they did in the 1880s, not about what causes them to have more mercury now. The idea of *pollution* is not in the stimulus.

(C) goes Out of Scope by suggesting a benefit seabirds get from mercury. Whether or not mercury helps seabirds is irrelevant to determining how much mercury is in fish.

(D) is another 180. It weakens the argument because it provides a reason that the feathers from stuffed birds were different from the feathers from live birds. In contrast to **(D)**, the correct answer needs to show that the feathers from the stuffed birds were similar to the feathers recently taken from live birds.

3. (D) Assumption (Sufficient) ★★★★

Step 1: Identify the Question Type

An assumption that would allow the conclusion to be properly drawn is a Sufficient Assumption.

Step 2: Untangle the Stimulus

The author concludes that it will be necessary to vaccinate high-risk individuals every year for a different strain of the flu virus because the vaccination will only protect against the strain anticipated to be most prevalent that year.

Step 3: Make a Prediction

The author jumps from the evidence—that a vaccine for any particular year only protects against the most prevalent strain predicted for that year—to a conclusion that every single year a new vaccination for a different strain will be required. The author ignores the possibility that the same strain might dominate in multiple years and that a previous vaccination will continue to work when that strain shows up again. In order for the author's conclusion to make logical sense, that possibility can't happen. So the correct answer will indicate that repetition of a prevalent strain will not occur.

If you did not recognize that, then for each answer ask if this would guarantee that every year high-risk individuals will need a new vaccine for a new strain. A Sufficient Assumption answer, when added to the evidence, should guarantee that the conclusion is true.

Step 4: Evaluate the Answer Choices

(D) is correct. If every year there will be a new dominant strain of influenza, then the conclusion that every year a different vaccine will be required must be true.

(A) does not guarantee that a vaccine for a different strain of the virus will be needed every year. The *number* of high-risk individuals is irrelevant because the conclusion says all of them (regardless of count) need an annual vaccine.

(B) is Out of Scope. The issue is whether the prevalent strain of the virus will vary year to year, not whether the seriousness of the epidemic will vary from year to year. Additionally, the stimulus doesn't mention anything about *epidemics* at all; it just says the government is trying to limit serious *cases*.

(C) is a Faulty Use of Detail. It restates the evidence, which already indicates that each year's vaccine will protect *only* against the one strain most likely to be prevalent. So, adding this choice to the evidence wouldn't affect anything at all.

(E) is Out of Scope. The number of the vaccinations' side effects does not have any effect on whether a different vaccination will be needed every year.

4. (B) Assumption (Sufficient) ★★★★

Step 1: Identify the Question Type

The "conclusion follows logically if . . . assumed" wording indicates a Sufficient Assumption question, which requires you to select the answer that, in combination with the evidence, would prove the conclusion true. Sufficient Assumption stimuli often contain Formal Logic statements that should be diagrammed.

Step 2: Untangle the Stimulus

Evidence:

If appointment to executive board	→	***undergrad degree***
If felony conviction	→	***~appointment to executive board***

Murray has an undergraduate degree but also a felony conviction.

Conclusion:

Murray cannot be accepted to position of Executive Administrator.

Step 3: Make a Prediction

First, combine the Formal Logic statements of the evidence. The contrapositive of the second statement says:

If appointment to executive board → ***~felony connection.***

Therefore, the combination of both statements says that any person appointed to the executive board must have an undergraduate degree and can't have a felony conviction. The contrapositive would be:

If ~ undergraduate degree to OR felony conviction → ***~appointed executive board***

You know that Murray has a felony conviction. Based on the Formal Logic in the evidence, that means he can't be appointed to the *executive board*. However, the conclusion says he can't become the *Executive Administrator*. The "executive board" and the "Executive Administrator" are not necessarily the same thing. The author assumes either that the requirements are the same for the Executive Administrator position or that the two are somehow connected in another manner.

Step 4: Evaluate the Answer Choices

(B) is correct because it indicates that eligibility requirements are the same for both the board and the Executive Administrator position.

(A) is incorrect because it does not connect the executive board to the Executive Administrator position. Additionally, the argument discusses a *necessary* condition for acceptance to the board while this choice provides a *sufficient* condition.

(C) also is incorrect because it does not connect the executive board to the Executive Administrator position. Additionally, while the argument assumes necessary conditions for the position of Executive Administrator (undergraduate degree and no felony conviction), this choice indicates the absence of a necessary condition.

(D) may be true but, again, it does not connect the executive board to the Executive Administrator position. Also, again, while the argument assumes *necessary* conditions for the position of Executive Administrator, this choice indicates a *sufficient* condition (no felony conviction) for acceptance as the Executive Administrator.

(E) is Out of Scope. Regardless of its relevance to the duties of the position, a felony conviction disqualified Murray. The question is why it disqualified him. This choice, like the other incorrect answers, does not connect the requirements of the board to the requirements of the position.

Flaw

5. (E) Flaw ★☆☆☆

Step 1: Identify the Question Type

Because the correct answer will describe what the argument in the stimulus "fails to consider," this is a Flaw question. Keep an eye out for the advertisement's overlooked alternative.

Step 2: Untangle the Stimulus

Break down the argument into evidence and conclusion. The conclusion is at the end of the stimulus, marked by the Conclusion Keyword *so*. The advertisement's main point is that Fabric-Soft is the most effective fabric softener. The evidence summarizes a test that was performed using Fabric-Soft. Basically, consumers said they preferred towels washed with Fabric-Soft over towels washed without any fabric softener.

Step 3: Make a Prediction

The question stem has already warned you what the flaw in the argument is—an overlooked possibility. The stimulus introduces a survey, which are always questionable on the LSAT. Look for where the survey goes wrong. The conclusion compares Fabric-Soft to all other fabric softeners. But, the survey compares Fabric-Soft to *no* fabric softener, let alone *all* the other fabric softeners. Thus, the advertisement overlooks the fact that no information is actually provided about how Fabric-Soft compares to other fabric softeners.

Step 4: Evaluate the Answer Choices

(E) matches the prediction. To determine whether Fabric-Soft really is the best fabric softener, it would have to be compared against other fabric softeners.

(A) is Out of Scope because it introduces the idea of allergies.

(B) goes Out of Scope by introducing the idea of harm to the environment.

(C) veers Out of Scope with the introduction of cost.

(D) is Out of Scope because it asks about a cost/benefit analysis. The scope of the argument is simply whether or not Fabric-Soft is the most effective, regardless of whether or not consumers want to use fabric softeners in general.

6. (B) Flaw ★★★★

Step 1: Identify the Question Type

Because the correct answer describes how the argument in the stimulus is "vulnerable to criticism," this is a Flaw question.

Step 2: Untangle the Stimulus

Analyze the argument's evidence and conclusion. The conclusion ends the stimulus, indicated by the Keyword *hence*. The author concludes that sometimes getting in the way of police work is morally right. The evidence comes in two pieces. First, it is generally believed that one has the duty to prevent a family member from being harmed. Second, if parents know their child has been falsely accused of a crime, then it would be morally right for them to hide their child from the police.

Step 3: Make a Prediction

The argument shifts scope from evidence about preventing a family member from being harmed to a conclusion about obstructing police work. The author assumes that just because it is morally right to protect family members from harm, and because the police might occasionally pose harm to a family member, it can be morally right to obstruct the police. This assumption overlooks the possibility that there are other moral obligations related to the police. For example, there might be a moral obligation to follow the law or to contest false accusations within the legal system.

Step 4: Evaluate the Answer Choices

(B) matches the prediction. There could be other moral principles related to the police that would outweigh the obligation to protect family members.

(A) is a Distortion. The conclusion is not truly a broad generalization. The editorialist states only that *sometimes* (under the circumstances described in the evidence) it is okay to get in the way of police. The scope of the conclusion is no broader than that of the evidence.

(C) goes Out of Scope by introducing the idea of justice. This stimulus is merely about police work. The argument only assumes that the police arresting an innocent man would result in that person being harmed; not that it would assist justice.

(D) is Extreme. The author never suggests there is *no* moral obligation to obey the law. The argument is merely that there might be times when another moral obligation (to protect family members from harm) outweighs any potential obligation to obey the law.

(E) questions the evidence given, rather than the argument's assumption. In any LSAT question, you must take the evidence for granted. Here, the stimulus clearly states that the parents know their child has been falsely accused. The flaw is that even if the parents know their child has been falsely accused, it is still possible that they have a moral obligation to cooperate with the police.

7. (A) Flaw ★★★★

Step 1: Identify the Question Type

Because the correct answer describes the grounds on which the argument in the stimulus is "most vulnerable to criticism," this is a Flaw question.

Step 2: Untangle the Stimulus

The conclusion is the last sentence, marked by the Keyword *hence*. The anthropologists are wrong. In other words, the human species did not need the ability to cope with many different natural environments to survive prehistoric times. The evidence is that a species related to early humans also had the ability to cope with many different natural environments, but did not survive prehistoric times. The Formal Logic would look like this:

Some anthropologists' view:

If species ~cope with diverse environments → ~survive

If survive → species can cope with diverse environments

The author treats the anthropologists' evidence as this:

If species can cope with diverse environments → survive

So, when the *Australopithecus afarensis* had the ability to cope and did not survive, the author concluded the anthropologists were wrong.

Step 3: Make a Prediction

The conclusion is that the ability to cope with different environments was not necessary for humans to survive. The evidence is that another species with that ability did not survive. However, this evidence has little to do with whether or not coping with different environments is *necessary* for survival. In contrast, the evidence merely shows that coping with different environments is not *sufficient* for survival. If coping with different environments were sufficient for survival then the other species would have survived. Thus, the author assumes that just because coping with different environments is not sufficient for survival, that it is also not necessary. The classic flaw made by this author is confusing necessity and sufficiency.

Step 4: Evaluate the Answer Choices

(A) matches the prediction.

(B) is a Distortion. The author doesn't "take for granted" that an extinct species must share a characteristic with a surviving species. In fact, the author explicitly presents evidence that the other species and humans shared the ability to cope with different environments.

(C) mischaracterizes the argument and is Extreme. First, the author only discusses humans and *Australopithecus afarensis*, not *all* related species. Second, the author never says the two species survived "*exactly* the same" conditions, just that they both had the same characteristic: the ability to thrive in diverse environments.

(D) is probably an accurate claim about the author, but it is not the argument's flaw. The conclusion concerns what is true about humans, not what is true about the other species. For an overlooked possibility to be the correct answer to a Flaw question, it must weaken the argument if true. Whether or not the extinct species at issue had characteristics that lessened its chances of survival would not weaken the argument about the human species.

(E) is a tempting wrong answer, because it includes words such as *condition*, *result*, and *necessary*. However, **(E)** distorts the argument. Our author treated the other anthropologists' claim of necessity (humans had to adapt to diverse environments) as though it was a claim of sufficiency (adapting to diverse environments ensures survival). This choice suggests that the author failed to consider that a condition sufficient in one case could be necessary in another. That simply misstates what the author did in the argument.

Strengthen/Weaken

8. (E) Weaken ★☆☆☆

Step 1: Identify the Question Type

The question stem explicitly directs you to weaken the argument. Identify the assumption and attack it.

Step 2: Untangle the Stimulus

Highlighted by the Contrast Keyword *although*, the author's conclusion is the prediction that "we can expect a reversal of this trend in the very near future." Never leave a vague term (i.e., "this trend") in your paraphrase of the conclusion. Therefore, the author predicts that video game sales will decline in the near future, despite a recent three-year surge. The author's evidence is that the number of 13- to 16-year-olds, historically the prime purchasers of video games, is expected to decline steadily over the next 10 years.

Step 3: Make a Prediction

This argument presents a twist on a classic LSAT argument pattern. A prediction conclusion typically predicts that the future will be like the past, with the built-in assumption that past trends will continue. In this argument, however, the author's conclusion predicts a *divergence* from past trends because the author foresees a changing demographic, a reduction in the number of young teens. Thus, to weaken this argument, you want a choice that indicates the recent three-year trend of increased video game sales will continue, despite the decline in 13- to 16-year-olds.

Step 4: Evaluate the Answer Choices

(E) correctly provides a reason to believe the recent three-year trend of increased video game sales will continue despite the projected decline in 13- to 16-year-olds. While *historically* those young teens bought most of the video games, this choice indicates that the *recent* three-year surge in sales was driven by those older than 16. Therefore, this generation of video game fans is continuing to purchase video games into adulthood.

(A) is a 180, strengthening the argument that video game sales will decline along with the decline in the 13- to 16-year-old age cohort.

(B) is largely irrelevant. It could arguably strengthen or weaken the argument depending on its actual implications. Perhaps a decline in rentals indicates a decline in video game popularity overall, or maybe it indicates that people are choosing to buy instead of rent. Because this answer requires you to make further inferences, and could either weaken or strengthen potentially, it cannot be correct.

(C) is another 180, adding another reason why video game purchases will likely decline.

(D) has no significant effect on the likelihood that video game sales will decline over the next 10 years. All this choice indicates is that the number of video game *types* (not the number of games themselves) will likely *not* decline. While this answer indicates one past condition will continue into the future, there is an extremely tenuous connection, if any, between this fact and the author's conclusion.

9. (E) Weaken ★★★☆

Step 1: Identify the Question Type

The question stem directly asks you to weaken the argument.

Step 2: Untangle the Stimulus

The author concludes that when milk is heated in a microwave oven, the microwaves themselves, not the heat, destroy the lysozyme enzymes in the milk. The evidence is that heating milk in a microwave kills half the enzymes in the milk, but heating milk in a conventional way to the same temperature kills very few of the enzymes.

Step 3: Make a Prediction

This is a causal argument. The author chooses between two potential causes of the destruction of the milk enzymes: heat or microwaves. Because the author concludes the microwaves are at fault, the correct weaken answer choice will provide a reason to believe heat is actually the culprit. The choice will have to explain why heat was a factor when the microwave (but not the conventional heat source) heated the milk. Without specialized technical knowledge, which you do not need, it is impossible to predict more specifically what the correct answer will state.

Step 4: Evaluate the Answer Choices

(E) provides the requisite explanation for how the same overall temperature can kill a larger proportion of enzymes in a microwave than when a conventional heat source is used. Enzymes are caught in hotter zones in the microwaved milk and so experience higher than 50-degree temperatures. In comparison, those isolated higher temperatures don't occur in conventionally heated milk. Thus, it could be the heat itself and not the microwaves directly that kill the enzymes.

(A) shows that increasing the temperature in a microwave is more detrimental to the lysozyme enzyme, but this choice fails in two ways. There is a good deal of similarity between this question and a Paradox question. To correctly weaken this argument, an answer choice must both assert that the heat is the killer and then answer the subsequent paradox of why 50 degrees produces different results in the two heat sources. First, this choice doesn't indicate that something specific about the heat kills the enzymes. Second, this choice does not explain why milk reacts differently when heated by a microwave versus by a conventional heat source.

(B) is irrelevant. Whether enzymes can be replaced has no bearing on what is killing them.

(C) is Out of Scope because it only discusses conventional heating. It does not provide the necessary comparison or distinction between liquid heated to the same overall temperature by a conventional heat source versus by a microwave oven. This choice would be correct if it indicated that a liquid exposed to a *conventional* heat source of 50 degrees will reach that temperature more slowly than a liquid exposed to a *microwave* heat source of 50 degrees. That would bring in the issue of speed between the two heat sources, which could be a reason—other than microwaves themselves—for the difference in enzyme destruction.

(D) is Out of Scope. Taste has nothing to do with discerning what is killing the enzymes.

10. (C) Weaken ★★★★

Step 1: Identify the Question Type

Because the correct answer is the one that "most seriously weakens the argument," this is a Weaken question.

Step 2: Untangle the Stimulus

Break down the argument into evidence and conclusion. The conclusion is the last sentence, marked by the Keyword *therefore*. The author believes that psychological treatments lasting longer than six months work better than those that last less than six months. The evidence is based on a survey in which a slightly larger percentage of people who had received treatment for more than six months claimed that their treatment helped a lot.

Step 3: Make a Prediction

There are two problems with this argument. First, the conclusion is based on a survey, which means you should automatically ask yourself if the survey was representative. The survey shows more people who had longer treatments said they really work. Maybe there is something about that group of people that distorts the results. Additionally, the author assumes that because people *report* that their longer treatment is better, the longer treatment actually is more effective. The weakener will likely suggest an alternative reason why people with longer treatments report better results.

Step 4: Evaluate the Answer Choices

(C) matches the prediction because it suggests that people who like their treatment stay in it longer. Therefore, it is not necessarily the length of treatment that causes better results. Rather, it is the feeling of better results that leads people to stay in treatment longer. This choice actually indicates reverse causality.

(A) is Out of Scope. It introduces the percentage of people in lengthier treatments who said their treatment made things worse. For this statistic to be relevant, we would also need to know the percentage of people in shorter treatments who said their treatments made things worse.

(B) is an Irrelevant Comparison. The results of the survey are reported as percentages, rather than as raw numbers, so it doesn't matter that more people from the group with longer treatments responded.

(D) fails to distinguish between survey respondents in longer versus shorter treatments. If dissatisfied patients from both groups were more likely to respond to the survey, it would help to explain why the percentages of very satisfied patients are relatively low. Nevertheless, it wouldn't explain why more people from the group with longer treatment thought treatment "made things a lot better."

(E) goes Out of Scope by focusing on what psychologists recommend, rather than on what is actually effective.

11. (A) Strengthen ★★★☆

Step 1: Identify the Question Type

Because the correct answer strengthens the argument in the stimulus, this is a Strengthen question.

Step 2: Untangle the Stimulus

Break down the argument into the evidence and conclusion. The conclusion follows *thus*, in the last sentence: it is very difficult to reduce governmental intrusion into the lives of voters in a democracy. The evidence is a three-part chain. Voters elect politicians who promise government assistance. Government assistance requires taxes. Taxes are a governmental intrusion.

Step 3: Make a Prediction

Find the assumption. The conclusion is about the inevitability of governmental intrusion, but the evidence is about what politicians promise before they get elected. Thus, the assumption is that once they are elected, politicians keep their promises to solve problems with governmental assistance. If there is governmental assistance, then there are taxes and governmental intrusion. The correct answer will reinforce this assumption.

Step 4: Evaluate the Answer Choices

(A) matches the prediction. If the elected politicians keep their promises of solving problems with government assistance, then it would lead to taxes and governmental intrusion.

(B) is a 180, because it weakens the argument. If politicians do not do what they promise, then there is no reason to believe that the government will provide assistance and that therefore, governmental intrusion is inevitable.

(C) goes Out of Scope by focusing on what *types* of problems are most common, rather than on whether or not governmental assistance will be used to fix them, resulting in inevitable intrusion.

(D) is an Irrelevant Comparison. The stimulus is only about whether or not governmental intrusion is inevitable in democracies. Other types of governments are immaterial.

(E) is Out of Scope. It focuses on what politicians *believe* and whether it lines up with what they promise, rather than what they actually do once in office. This choice suggests that those politicians who get elected usually don't believe in what they promise, but that doesn't indicate whether or not they keep those promises once in office.

12. (B) Weaken ★★★☆

Step 1: Identify the Question Type

Because the correct answer weakens the argument in the stimulus, this is a Weaken question.

Step 2: Untangle the Stimulus

Analyze the argument's evidence and conclusion. The conclusion ends the stimulus, after the phrase "we must accept the fact that." Basically, the ethicist believes eating meat will soon be considered immoral. The evidence is based on equivalence between meat and grain. When animals are raised on grain, it takes 16 pounds of grain to make one pound of meat. More people could be fed with 16 pounds of grain than with one pound of meat. Further, the population is growing and the supply of grain is limited.

Step 3: Make a Prediction

The conclusion is about *all* meat, but the evidence is only about meat from animals raised on grain. Thus, the author overlooks the possibility that not all meat comes from animals raised on grain. If some meat comes from animals not raised on grain, then eating that meat would not reduce the amount of grain used to feed people. The correct answer will point out that some meat is not raised on grain that could otherwise be used to feed humans.

Step 4: Evaluate the Answer Choices

(B) matches the prediction by pointing out that sheep and cattle can be fed grass instead of grain.

(A) goes Out of Scope by introducing people's preferences. The argument is about whether or not eating meat will be immoral, not about whether or not people will still like it.

(C) focuses on a minor piece of evidence that says a pound of meat is more nutritious than a pound of grain. This answer choice indicates that it's possible to have a nutritious diet without meat, but doesn't address the ethicist's conclusion that a meat diet will soon be immoral.

(D) is initially tempting because it introduces a way people could avoid contributing to the decrease of farmland, which was part of the chain of evidence for why eating meat would become immoral. However, halting suburban development would only affect farmland near metropolitan areas; it could be true that the total amount of farmland would still decrease for other reasons, and the ethicist's conclusion could still follow. Also, **(D)** doesn't provide a reason why using grain to raise meat is acceptable given that the grain could be used to feed humans directly. Even if farmland is maintained, there are still the issues of grain yields leveling off and an expanding population, so **(D)** does not weaken the author's moral argument against eating meat.

(E) goes Out of Scope like **(C)** does by focusing on health, rather than on morality. This choice suggests you shouldn't eat grain alone, but that doesn't mean meat is necessary. There are other types of food beyond grain and meat. Both the nutritionists and the ethicist could be correct.

Assumption-Family Principle

13. (E) Principle (Identify/Strengthen) ★★★★

Step 1: Identify the Question Type

Because the correct answer is the principle that would "help to justify" the argument in the stimulus, this is an Identify the Principle question that resembles a Strengthen question. The correct answer will restate the argument in more general terms, which if true, would make the argument more likely.

Step 2: Untangle the Stimulus

Follow the strategy for approaching a Strengthen question. Analyze the argument's evidence and conclusion. The conclusion is the first sentence. The sociologist believes that romantics are wrong to think people are made evil by institutions. In other words, institutions do not make people evil. The sociologist's reason for believing this comes after the evidence Keywords *after all*: Institutions are just groups of people.

Step 3: Make a Prediction

Boiled down, the argument says collections of people can't make people evil. The assumption is simply that that connection between the evidence and conclusion is accurate. In other words, the author assumes that a collective group (institutions) cannot determine the characteristics of the individuals of which it is made (people). That is, institutions must be shaped by the people in them, and not vice versa. The correct answer will reinforce this assumption in general terms.

Step 4: Evaluate the Answer Choices

(E) matches the prediction. The *whole* would be institutions and the "things that compose it" would be the individual people.

(A) is an Irrelevant Comparison. The stimulus doesn't indicate that institutions are more effective than individuals. Additionally, the argument focuses on whether or not institutions *make* people evil (an attribute), not on how people can *do* the most good or evil (an action).

(B) is Outside the Scope. Even if all institutions are imperfect, **(B)** still doesn't address whether those imperfect institutions can or cannot make people evil.

(C) fails to address whether there is a connection between institutions and people's character. Additionally, the way people should view others is Out of Scope.

(D) veers Out of Scope by introducing the idea of gauging society's values. Additionally, like **(B)** and **(C)**, **(D)** fails to include anything about whether institutions can make people evil.

Parallel Flaw

14. (B) Parallel Flaw ★★★★

Step 1: Identify the Question Type

A question stem that asks you to find the flawed reasoning that resembles the flawed reasoning in the stimulus is a Parallel Flaw question.

Step 2: Untangle the Stimulus

The author concludes that Rosa's dogs are moderate barkers. The evidence is that each dog is a cross of a Lab and a Saint Bernard. Also, the Formal Logic statements at the beginning of the stimulus indicate that all Labs bark a lot and all Saint Bernards bark a little.

Step 3: Make a Prediction

The author assumes without evidence that the mixed dogs will blend the characteristics of each breed. He's overlooking the possibility that one of the traits may be dominant or that some of the mixed dogs might have the barking tendencies of Labs and others those of Saint Bernards. Your task is to find an answer choice that commits that same flaw (i.e., a conclusion that a middle ground between two potential extremes will be the result). **(C)**, **(D)**, and **(E)** all can be eliminated just based on the conclusions, because only **(A)** and **(B)** have conclusions that result in a middle ground.

Step 4: Evaluate the Answer Choices

(B) is correct because just like with Rosa's dogs, the author here assumes that if the cleaner is a mix of the two types of chemicals, then the properties of those chemicals mix. Once again, the author is overlooking the possibility that one of the chemicals might be much stronger than the other: The mixed cleaner could still be very toxic or completely nontoxic (if type B neutralizes the effects of type A, for example).

(A) contains a scope shift that is not present in the stimulus's argument. The evidence tells us about the grades of diligent students and non-diligent students, but Jane is not a part of either of these groups. Unlike the arguments in the stimulus and choice **(B)**, there's no claim that Jane mixes the attributes of diligent and non-diligent students. More importantly, the stimulus says all members of one group were one way and all members of the other group were their opposites. In this argument, the evidence didn't mention all non-diligent students and their bad grades, only some of them and their good grades.

(C) can be eliminated because there is no flaw in its logic.

(D) also can be eliminated because it is essentially not flawed, except to the extent that it ignores the possibility that Bob has forgotten one or both of his skills since he held those jobs. Nevertheless, that flaw is unrelated to the flaw identified in the stimulus assuming a middle ground between two extremes.

(E) describes a necessity-versus-sufficiency flaw, which isn't at play here. Just because all of Kenisha's dresses are well made doesn't mean that all well-made dresses are Kenisha's. The same is true of Connie's poorly made dresses. There may be dresses in the closet belonging to someone else, for example.

15. (C) Parallel Flaw ★★★★

Step 1: Identify the Question Type

Because the correct answer is the argument that demonstrates the same flawed reasoning as the argument in the stimulus, this is a Parallel Flaw question.

Step 2: Untangle the Stimulus

Attack the stimulus as you would a Flaw question. Break down the argument into evidence and conclusion. The conclusion opens the stimulus. The author believes that we should demolish the old train station. The author's evidence is that the historical society does not want to demolish the old train station and the members of the historical society are generally opposed to long-term economic health. Abstractly, the author concludes that we should take an action because the people who oppose it have what he considers a bad characteristic.

Step 3: Make a Prediction

The flaw is a variation on the *ad hominem* attack flaw; that is, the author justifies his recommendation by attacking those who oppose it. Specifically, the author questions the motives of the opposition. The correct answer will model this flawed method of reasoning. Even if you did not see the flaw in this argument, you can still get the point by comparing the answer choice arguments piece by piece against the stimulus. The conclusion recommends a course of action that goes against an opposition group that the author distrusts for a particular reason. This alone will likely be enough to distinguish the right answer. The author fails to consider any reasons for *not* demolishing the train station and relies solely on his belief that preserving old buildings will impede economic health.

Step 4: Evaluate the Correct Answer

(C) matches the prediction. The only reason the author of **(C)** suggests that you have your hair cut no more than once a month is because of the self-interested motives of beauticians, who suggest you have your hair cut more than once a month.

(A) is incorrect because it doesn't refer to an opposition group. This argument mentions groups that might not *recognize* art as significant, but concludes that we shouldn't let that deter us in our preservation efforts. This argument might not have very strong evidence, but it doesn't commit any *reasoning* errors.

(B) fails like **(A)** by failing to mention an opposition group. The author of **(B)** does not oppose anyone else, and although the argument may not be terribly convincing, it commits no *reasoning* error.

(D) fails to match the stimulus because the author's recommendation is based on complying with the point of view of the residents. In other words, both of the points of view in **(D)** want the same thing.

(E) goes awry for two reasons. First, it has the same problem as **(A)** and **(B)**—there is only one point of view in the stimulus. Second, the conclusion here is qualified by a condition, signaled by the word *unless*. The stimulus's conclusion didn't mention any exceptions to the recommendation (not even absolute necessity), so the conclusion types do not match.

Mixed Perform: Assumption Family Questions

16. (C) Assumption (Sufficient) ★★★★

Step 1: Identify the Question Type

The correct answer is the assumption that makes the conclusion follow logically. In other words, if the assumption is true, then the conclusion is true. Thus, this is a Sufficient Assumption question.

Step 2: Untangle the Stimulus

Atrens puts the conclusion at the very end of the stimulus, after the conclusion Keyword *thus*. It says the entomologist was wrong, but you can't let your summary of the conclusion be that vague. Added to the first sentence, the conclusion essentially says ants were not bringing food to their neighbors. The evidence is that research showed the ants were emptying their dumping site.

Step 3: Make a Prediction

Find the mismatched concepts. The conclusion says that whatever the ants were doing, it was not food delivery. The evidence says the ants were emptying their dumping site. The assumption must create a connection between these two ideas. The author assumes that the two actions are mutually exclusive or, in other words, that stuff from one ant's dumping site cannot be food for another ant.

Step 4: Evaluate the Answer Choices

(C) matches the prediction.

(A) veers Out of Scope by contrasting ants to humans.

(B) is also Out of Scope, introducing a new term: gifts. Another assumption would be required to connect bringing food to bringing gifts. Additionally, the new study merely casts doubt on the idea that the ants were bringing food in that situation, but it has nothing to do with their *capacity* to give gifts.

(D) goes Out of Scope by focusing on what the receiving ants did with the particles, rather than on what the particles were. The receiving ants' actions don't indicate whether or not the particles were food.

(E) is Out of Scope, focusing on what the entomologist did after learning about the additional research. Even if the entomologist retracted his claims, it doesn't necessarily follow that Atrens's conclusion is correct.

17. (E) Flaw ★☆☆☆

Step 1: Identify the Question Type

This is a Flaw question because the correct answer describes how the argument in the stimulus is "vulnerable to criticism." Identify what's wrong about the gap between the evidence and conclusion, and keep common flaws in mind.

Step 2: Untangle the Stimulus

Break down the argument into evidence and conclusion. The conclusion comes at the end of the stimulus, marked by the conclusion Keyword *so*. Basically, the conclusion is that corporations that hang motivational posters are not likely to boost the motivation of their workers. The evidence is that almost all workers at those companies are already motivated.

Step 3: Make a Prediction

Start by finding the author's assumption. Here, the conclusion is that the posters will not *boost* workers' motivation. The evidence is that workers are already motivated. The author must be assuming that there aren't degrees of motivation. This overlooks the possibility that workers who are already motivated could become even more motivated. Additionally, the conclusion is about all workers, while the evidence is about "almost all." It's possible that the posters could work on that small group of workers who are not yet motivated. The correct answer will point out one of these overlooked alternatives.

Step 4: Evaluate the Answer Choices

(E) matches the prediction. It could be true that motivational posters lead already motivated workers to become even more motivated.

(A) is Out of Scope because it introduces corporations that do not use motivational posters. The argument focuses only on those corporations that *do* use motivational posters. Ignoring those others is not a flaw.

(B) describes a representativeness flaw, which is not at play here. Both the author's evidence and conclusion are limited to the same corporations.

(C) is not a flaw. While the author does ignore other possible benefits, that oversight doesn't affect the conclusion, which is solely about the posters' influence on motivation.

(D) is Out of Scope. The argument is focused only on whether posters will increase motivation to work productively, not whether they'll affect productivity itself. Whether or not productivity may be affected by other factors is irrelevant.

18. (C) Assumption (Sufficient) ★★☆☆

Step 1: Identify the Question Type

The "conclusion . . . follows logically if . . . assumed" formulation indicates a Sufficient Assumption question.

Step 2: Untangle the Stimulus

The stimulus presents two groups of aluminum cans: group M and group L. The conclusion states that group M contains twice as many cans as group L. The evidence for this is rather convoluted, so break it down piece by piece.

First, standard aluminum cans contain the same amount of aluminum. Both groups M and L contain standard aluminum cans (therefore, the amount of aluminum in each can in each group is the same). Second, half of the aluminum used to make the cans in group M came from the recycled cans of group L. Third, *all* the cans in group L were recycled and turned into cans in group M. Finally, materials other than aluminum in cans are insignificant.

Step 3: Make a Prediction

If half of the aluminum in group M came from the entirety of group L, then half came from elsewhere. In other words, group M must contain twice as much aluminum as group L did. The author thinks this means group M contains twice as many cans at group L did. Indeed, the logic seems sound. So, there must be something very basic to this calculation that is being assumed because the numbers seem to add up correctly. The author must be making a subtle scope shift between double the *aluminum* and double the *cans*. Look for an answer choice that, if added, proves that these two are actually equivalent. The correct answer may do this by eliminating an overlooked reason why they would not be comparable.

Step 4: Evaluate the Answer Choices

(C) is correct. Sure, the numbers add up correctly, but only if it is as straightforward as it seems. The ignored possibility is that some aluminum is lost during the recycling process. In that case, the number of cans in group M would not be exactly twice as many as in group L. However, once this choice confirms that that possibility is not occurring, it proves group M has twice as many cans. The hint at this assumption in the stimulus was the evidence that a negligible amount of other materials is added. That could have led you to ponder whether any aluminum was lost.

(A) is Out of Scope. Whether the group M cans could be recycled further does not at all affect the comparison between the number of cans in each group.

(B) also is Out of Scope. The aluminum's *quality* is irrelevant to the numbers comparison. The evidence says cans do not vary in the amount of aluminum they contain, regardless of what grade it is.

(D) is Out of Scope in the same way that **(A)** is. The stimulus is restricted to group L's transformation into group M. The future of group M—in answer choice **(A)**—and the past of group L—in this answer choice—are both irrelevant.

(E) is an Irrelevant Comparison to cans of other materials. The ease of recycling does not affect whether the math adds up nicely.

19. (A) Flaw ★☆☆☆

Step 1: Identify the Question Type

The phrase "vulnerable to criticism" is one of the most common phrases indicating a Flaw question. Be on the lookout for a disconnect between the evidence and conclusion, and keep classic LSAT flaws in mind.

Step 2: Untangle the Stimulus

The consumer concludes that Ocksenfrey's meals are nutritious. A report indicates that the meals are *not* nutritious, but the consumer asserts that the source of the report makes it biased.

Step 3: Make a Prediction

Two classic LSAT flaws intersect in this argument.

First, there is no actual evidence supporting the claim that Ocksenfrey meals are nutritious. All the consumer has done is cast doubt on a negative report. Assuming the consumer is correct, the report's dismissal leaves us with a complete lack of evidence. The absence, or disproving, of evidence does not support or prove the opposite, yet on the LSAT, authors often assume it does.

Additionally, even though in real life it may be relevant to point out a bias, the LSAT considers it a flaw to make an *ad hominem* attack against the source of an argument rather than address the substance of that argument. The consumer does that here, jumping from an assertion of bias in those producing the report to a complete refutation of its claims.

Step 4: Evaluate the Answer Choices

(A) is correct. It is in line with the prediction and is an accurate description of the argument. Many correct answers to Flaw questions are simply accurate descriptions of the argument. A good test for Flaw answer choices is to ask: "Does the author do this?"

(B) describes a representativeness flaw and does not pass the basic test just described: "Does the author do this?" There is no indication that a nonrepresentative sample of the meals was used in the report. Both the evidence and the conclusion stick to the same scope: prepackaged meals. Even though you could speculate that bias led to the improper selection of unhealthy examples of meals, this will not be the correct answer unless there is some concrete indication of that in the stimulus.

(C) may be true, but isn't correct. To be correct, an "ignored possibility" answer to a Flaw question must, if true, weaken the argument. The author may indeed have failed to consider this possibility, but even if it were true it would not impact the consumer's claim that the meals are nutritious.

(D) is similarly not a flaw. Even if such evidence were submitted, the level of nutrition as compared to Danto's meals does not impact an absolute claim that Ocksenfrey's meals are, or are not, qualitatively nutritious. The conclusion does not make a comparative claim, so comparisons are irrelevant.

(E) is Out of Scope. This answer choice discusses reports that are hostile to *Danto's* meals, while the stimulus deals with a report that is hostile to *Ocksenfrey's* meals. The consumer doesn't mention or assume anything about how Danto's public relations department would react to a report on that company's own products.

20. (B) Weaken ★★★★

Step 1: Identify the Question Type

A question stem that asks you to identify evidence against an argument is a Weaken question. This stem asks you to weaken the scientist's explanation. The classic way to weaken an argument with an explanatory conclusion is to provide an alternative explanation.

Step 2: Untangle the Stimulus

As is often the case for a Strengthen or Weaken question, the question stem directs you to the conclusion, i.e., the "explanation of Earth's warming." The first sentence simply states that the Earth has warmed by 0.5 degrees Celsius. The second sentence contains the scientist's explanation: The warming is caused by the accumulation of gases in the atmosphere, which blocks the planet from releasing heat.

Step 3: Make a Prediction

This is a classic LSAT argument pattern in which an author points out an interesting phenomenon and then provides a causal explanation for that phenomenon. The built-in assumption is that no other explanation exists. The typical way to weaken such an argument is to look for any of the classic alternatives to causation: The causation is reversed, a third factor causes both, or the correlation is merely coincidence. You don't need to predict the specific cause; just keep in mind that you need an answer that indicates one of those three situations is at play.

Step 4: Evaluate the Answer Choices

(B) is correct. A great way to weaken a claim of causality is to show the result preceded the purported cause. If the bulk of the warming occurred *before* the greatest buildup of the gases, then it is less likely that the buildup caused the warming.

(A) is Out of Scope. The argument is concerned only with the cause of the global warming, not the cause of the gas buildup. Additionally, it never mentions industrial pollution, so the amount of gases that arose from pollution (whether it's "some" or "most" or "all") is irrelevant.

(C) is appealing as it might initially seem to provide an alternative explanation for the warming: increased solar radiation. However, all this choice really indicates is that solar radiation was not constant year over year. To provide an alternative explanation for the *average* increase in Earth's temperature over the past century, there would need to be a trend of an *average* increase in solar radiation over the past century, not just yearly fluctuations.

(D) is irrelevant because it includes no reference to time or change. There is no indication that the amount of volcanic dust increased or decreased over the past century, so this choice can't explain the changing temperature.

(E) is a 180 because it strengthens the argument. If the buildup of minor gases was uncharacteristically greater in the past century, then it is more likely that the built-up gases may be responsible for the trapping of heat and, therefore, also responsible for higher temperatures.

21. (C) Assumption (Sufficient) ★★★★

Step 1: Identify the Question Type

The "conclusion follows logically if . . . assumed" phrasing indicates a Sufficient Assumption question. Choose the answer that, if combined with the evidence, proves the conclusion to be true. Sufficient Assumption questions often contain Formal Logic that needs to be mapped out, especially when the question falls in the danger zone, as this one does.

Step 2: Untangle the Stimulus

The philosopher concludes that actions that can reasonably be expected to not affect the general well-being of those affected by them are right. The philosopher supports this conclusion by several Formal Logic statements.

Evidence:

If increase aggregate well-being	→	***morally right***
If reduce aggregate well-being	→	***morally wrong***
If morally wrong	→	***reduce aggregate well-being***

(Note: The first sentence just has a single word indicating Formal Logic, *if*, but the second sentence has the "if but only if" form, which means you must diagram it twice. First translate the statement using the *if* and ignoring the "only if," then translate it using the "only if" and ignoring the *if*.)

Step 3: Make a Prediction

Look at the second sentence of the stimulus. It includes the rare but informative "if and only if." In addition to saying that actions that reduce aggregate well-being are morally wrong, the statement indicates that *only* actions that reduce aggregate well-being can be called morally wrong. In other words, any other actions must be something other than morally wrong. The conclusion, for example, mentions actions that don't change the aggregate well-being. Based on the Formal Logic, those actions must therefore be something other than morally wrong. But does that necessarily mean that they are, as the conclusion asserts, morally right? Or is there another possibility? Arguably, actions could be morally neutral. If that's possible, then the philosopher's conclusion doesn't logically have to follow. For the philosopher's logic to be correct, then morality must be binary (right or wrong), and there cannot be a "neutral" possibility. The correct answer will state that assumption.

Step 4: Evaluate the Answer Choices

(C) matches the prediction that if something is not morally wrong, then it has to be morally right. This eliminates the possibility of moral neutrality, which guarantees the philosopher's conclusion that an unchanged aggregate well-being (which cannot be morally bad) must be morally right.

(A) is a Faulty Use of Detail. Assuming that "morally wrong" and "wrong" actions are synonymous, this answer merely restates existing evidence. Restated evidence cannot provide the missing link between the evidence and conclusion.

(B) says actions can't be wrong *and* right, but it doesn't say actions have to be wrong *or* right. It does not eliminate the possibility of moral neutrality and thus does not guarantee the conclusion.

(D) is incorrect because philosophizing about actions that would leave the aggregate well-being unchanged does not require that such actions exist. And, even if that were the case, that would be a necessary assumption of the argument, rather than a sufficient assumption that would prove the conclusion true. The mere existence of such actions would not guarantee that they are morally right.

(E) is Out of Scope. It mentions "good consequences," a term that doesn't appear in the stimulus. Even if you assume that "good consequences" is synonymous with "increase the aggregate well-being," then this choice merely restates the first Formal Logic statement. Furthermore, this choice doesn't remove the possibility of moral neutrality.

22. (D) Flaw ★★★★

Step 1: Identify the Question Type

Because the correct answer "accurately describes a flaw in the argument," this is a Flaw question.

Step 2: Untangle the Stimulus

Break down the argument into the evidence and conclusion. Following the conclusion Keyword *clearly*, at the end of the stimulus, the conclusion is that political candidates' speeches are selfish and the promises contained therein are unreliable. The evidence is that political candidates give speeches to get elected.

Step 3: Make a Prediction

The author suggests that just because politicians have selfish motives for making promises that those promises may be unreliable. This overlooks the possibility that politicians might reliably keep their promises after they are elected. After all, there could be some additional reason that motivates politicians to keep their campaign promises.

Step 4: Evaluate the Answer Choices

(D) matches the prediction. Just because politicians make promises to get elected does not necessarily mean they will not keep those promises.

(A) distorts the logic of the argument. The argument says if promises are selfishly motivated, then they are unreliable. This answer choice negates that logic without reversing it. Even if you didn't see the Formal Logic, the conclusion is only about unreliable promises. The author doesn't conclude anything about reliable promises and what would make them so.

(B) is Extreme. The author says such promises are *unreliable*, not that they are *never* kept.

(C) is Out of Scope. The argument in the stimulus is not a causal argument. Even if the author's argument was phrased as "selfish motivations cause promises to be unreliable," this answer still would not be correct. The author never confuses that causal relationship with the reverse: Unreliable promises cause motivations to be selfish.

(E) goes Outside the Scope by introducing the idea of "worthy for office." The stimulus focuses on whether the promises politicians make in speeches are unreliable, not on how well suited for office the politicians are.

23. (B) Flaw ★★★★

Step 1: Identify the Question Type

This question stem contains a slight modification of the very common Flaw question phrase "vulnerable to criticism."

Step 2: Untangle the Stimulus

The hospital executive concludes with the recommendation to make protection of client confidentiality the hospital's highest priority. The evidence is the assertion by several computer experts that unauthorized access to computer data is the most significant threat faced by large institutions, including universities and hospitals.

Step 3: Make a Prediction

It might strike you as odd that a hospital is prioritizing computer security over, say, saving lives, merely on the advice of computer experts. The computer experts' analysis of the threat of unauthorized access might be real, but their overall understanding of other threats facing hospital management is likely little to none. Otherwise, the basic test for Flaw question answers is to ask if the author actually does what the answer describes.

Step 4: Evaluate the Answer Choices

(B) is correct because it accurately describes the argument and its inadequacy. The argument relies on the guidance of experts whose expertise is in computers, not in overall hospital management. To accurately pinpoint the most significant threat faced by a hospital, an expert should have some experience in medicine and hospital administration.

(A) does not relate to the argument, which is focused on identifying the highest priority. The *cause* of unauthorized access to confidential data is not discussed, nor is a possible *solution*. Therefore, the executive can't possibly mix up those two.

(C) describes a classic causal flaw, which is not at play here. There is simply no evidence of two things being correlated nor a conclusion that one thing causes another within the argument.

(D) refers to a representativeness flaw, which is unrelated to this argument. According to this choice, the argument draws a *general* conclusion about a group; however, the hospital executive's conclusion is specific to his one hospital.

(E) also fails to describe the argument. The stimulus discusses large institutions only, not institutions in general. The computer experts' advice was for large institutions, such as hospitals, so the hospital executive was right to consider his hospital a proper target of the advice, but he was flawed in assessing the validity of the advice.

24. (A) Strengthen (EXCEPT) ★★★★

Step 1: Identify the Question Type

The question stem directly indicates that this is a Strengthen EXCEPT question, for which you need to identify the one answer choice that does *not* strengthen the argument. The correct answer could weaken or have no effect on the argument.

Step 2: Untangle the Stimulus

The historian explicitly indicates in the last sentence that her conclusion is that the Land Party's success in 1935 was due to addressing the concerns of farmers and small business owners, and the depth of the economic problems those groups faced.

Notice this paraphrase defines the vague terms in the conclusion, such as "that year" and "these groups." The historian's evidence is relatively extensive. First, 1935 was the only year the Land Party was successful. Second, the majority of support came from rural and semirural areas, where the majority of Banestria's population lived. Third, the economic woes of farmers and small businesses were particularly acute that year. Finally, the Land Party specifically targeted farmers and small businesses.

Step 3: Make a Prediction

This is a classic LSAT argument pattern. The author observes an interesting phenomenon, i.e., the Land Party's only victory was in 1935, and then concludes with an explanation for that event. In other words, the author makes a causal argument. The built-in assumption is that there is no other explanation. The classic weakener will suggest an alternative explanation, while strengtheners will bolster the proffered explanation or *eliminate* alternative explanations. Remember the correct EXCEPT answer could also be irrelevant.

Step 4: Evaluate the Answer Choices

(A) is correct. What the Land Party did in preceding elections is largely irrelevant to determining whether the specific factors the author identified in the 1935 election were responsible for that year's victory. The correct answer to an EXCEPT question is often the odd one out. Notice that this choice is the only one focused on urban groups, which were not part of the author's explanation for the Land Party's victory in 1935.

(B) strengthens the author's assumption that focusing on the economic problems of farmers and small business owners caused those groups to vote for the Land Party in 1935.

(C) also strengthens the author's explanation that the Land Party's success in the national election in 1935 was due to economic conditions. This choice indicates that the Land Party's successes at other levels (not national) also occurred during periods of economic distress. This choice reinforces the correlation.

(D) strengthens the assumption that addressing the economic concerns of the rural areas garnered their votes for the Land Party, because no other party bothered.

(E) strengthens the idea that economic distress produced the rare Land Party victory in 1935 by increasing the likelihood that the constituents the party targeted would actually vote.

25. (B) Strengthen ★★★★

Step 1: Identify the Question Type

Because the correct answer "would most strengthen" the argument in the stimulus, this is a Strengthen question.

Step 2: Untangle the Stimulus

The conclusion is at the beginning of the second sentence, marked by the Keyword *thus*. Basically, the therapist's main point is that cognitive psychotherapy, which changes conscious beliefs, is more effective than other forms of therapy, which change unconscious beliefs. After *since*, the evidence is that only conscious beliefs are under a patient's direct conscious control.

Step 3: Make a Prediction

The conclusion is all about the effectiveness of a type of therapy. The evidence, however, deals with the patient's ability to control his beliefs. The author is assuming that the effectiveness of a therapy is related to the patient's ability to control his beliefs. To strengthen the argument, a fact is needed to confirm this connection or to rule out the ability to improve by changing unconscious beliefs.

Step 4: Evaluate the Answer Choices

(B) matches the prediction.

(A) is a 180. If changing unconscious beliefs can *frequently* solve some psychological problems, the assumption that effectiveness depends on conscious control of beliefs is undermined.

(C) is Out of Scope because the argument is about whether or not cognitive therapy is more effective than therapies that do not focus on changing conscious beliefs. Whether or not there are other forms of therapy that also focus on changing conscious beliefs is irrelevant.

(D) is Extreme. The therapist's argument is comparative, i.e., cognitive therapy is more likely to be effective than therapies focused on the unconscious. **(D)** says that no therapy focused on the unconscious will be effective unless it also changes conscious beliefs under the patient's control. The author could acknowledge that at times some therapies focused exclusively on the unconscious may have success, while maintaining his argument that cognitive therapy is *likely* to be more effective.

(E) goes Out of Scope by failing to distinguish between psychotherapies that focus on changing conscious beliefs and psychotherapies that focus on changing unconscious beliefs. Nothing in **(E)** suggests which of those types of therapy would be most useful for controlling those psychological states that "cannot be controlled effectively without the aid of psychotherapy."

26. (A) Flaw ★★★★

Step 1: Identify the Question Type

"Vulnerable to criticism" indicates a Flaw question. Notice how the conclusion goes beyond or deviates from the evidence. Keep in mind the common LSAT flaws.

Step 2: Untangle the Stimulus

The author concludes that trading in his sports car will lower his risk of having an accident. The evidence is that minivans and sedans have low accident rates compared to sports cars.

Step 3: Make a Prediction

This is a variation on a causal argument. The issue is whether the type of car causes accidents or whether the type of driver who chooses that type of car causes accidents.

Step 4: Evaluate the Answer Choices

(A) is correct. Only **(A)** and **(D)** relate to causation. This choice accurately describes the argument. There is evidence of a correlation between the type of car and the number of accidents in which it is involved. The author jumps from that correlation to a conclusion that the car type is responsible for the likelihood of accidents. However, it could just as easily be that the type of driver who selects that type of car is responsible for the accident rate.

(B) describes a representativeness flaw. However, there is no indication of the size or range of the sample, so this flaw is not at play here. This could be correct only if the stimulus actually indicates an inadequate sample size; *no* mention of sample size is not sufficient.

(C) indicates that the driver's conclusion is extreme, but that is not an accurate description of the argument. The driver is consistent, using evidence regarding the likelihood of an accident to reach a conclusion that also involves the likelihood of an accident. The driver does not conclude that he is certain to have *no* accidents in a minivan or sedan.

(D) also does not match the argument. The driver does not conclude that trading in the sports car for a minivan or sedan is the *only* way to reduce the risk of an accident, which is what this choice suggests. To assert something is a necessary condition is to assert that it is the only way to accomplish a goal. Additionally, from the evidence, it's not even clear if switching to a minivan or sedan would be *sufficient* to accomplish the driver's goal.

(E) is incorrect because there is no indication of this in the stimulus. The driver never mentions his research sources. Unlike in a Weaken question, in which the correct answer choice adds evidence that hurts an argument, the correct answer in a Flaw question must reference a problem *already* existing within the stimulus.

CHAPTER 5

Non-Argument Questions

Not all questions in the Logical Reasoning sections involve analyzing or evaluating arguments. A significant number of questions test your ability to make deductions; we will call these Inference questions, an inference—in LSAT terms—being a valid deduction from a set of statements or assertions. Inference questions give you a set of facts or assertions and ask for what must be true based on the facts or what follows logically from them. Other questions give you a general principle and ask for a specific case that correctly applies the principle, or they supply a case and ask you to infer the principle upon which it was decided. A small number of questions give you two paradoxical or seemingly inconsistent statements and ask for a fact that would help explain or reconcile the apparent inconsistency.

Let's break it down by the numbers. Inference questions account for just over 13 percent of the Logical Reasoning sections, around six or seven questions per test. Add to that one or two Principle questions calling for inferences and typically three or four Paradox questions per test, and the material in this chapter constitutes a healthy chunk of the Logical Reasoning sections.

These questions are not based on arguments; there's no need for you to determine conclusion and evidence here or to try to figure out what an author is assuming. Rather, these questions all reward you for seeing the implications of facts and assertions. In non-argument questions, you're interested in what *follows from* the statements in the stimulus, not in what you could add to the stimulus to make it stronger, weaker, or more complete.

Making Deductions and Inference Questions

Here's an example of a typical LSAT Inference question. Feel free to try it now or just read through it to get a sense of what these questions require. You'll see this question explained in detail a little later in the chapter. In this section, you will learn how to handle questions such as this one; you'll learn what the testmaker is asking for and how to untangle the stimulus effectively.

The axis of Earth's daily rotation is tilted with respect to the plane of its orbit at an angle of roughly 23 degrees. That angle can be kept fairly stable only by the gravitational influence of Earth's large, nearby Moon. Without such a stable and moderate axis tilt, a planet's climate is too extreme and unstable to support life. Mars, for example, has only very small moons, tilts at wildly fluctuating angles, and cannot support life.

If the statements above are true, which one of the following must also be true on the basis of them?

(A) If Mars had a sufficiently large nearby moon, Mars would be able to support life.

(B) If Earth's Moon were to leave Earth's orbit, Earth's climate would be unable to support life.

(C) Any planet with a stable, moderate axis tilt can support life.

(D) Gravitational influences other than moons have little or no effect on the magnitude of the tilt angle of either Earth's or Mars's axis.

(E) No planet that has more than one moon can support life.

PrepTest106 Sec1 Q14

By asking for an answer that must be true based on the statements in the stimulus, the LSAT is asking you to make a valid deduction from those statements. Now, you make deductions every day. You might wake up to find the ground wet and water dripping from the trees and deduce that it rained during the night. You might find a piece of pie you left in the refrigerator gone, and given that the only person in the house was your roommate, deduce that she ate your pie. But many of the deductions we make in real life are based on partial information and hunches. In most cases, they're very likely, but they may or may not be true.

A deduction, as defined on the LSAT, applies logic more rigorously than most real-life deductions. To illustrate the difference between the kind of deduction rewarded by an LSAT question and the kind we make in everyday life, suppose a house guest told you, "I don't eat ice cream." Given this fact about your guest, you might speculate, "she must be on a diet," or "I wonder if she's lactose intolerant." Either is possible. However, neither of your reasonable speculations would be a valid deduction on the LSAT because neither *must be true* and neither follows unequivocally from the statement itself. On the LSAT, a valid inference, were it negated, would contradict the given information. So, if the LSAT asked you for an inference based on your guest's statement, the correct answer would be something like "if the only dessert I serve after dinner tonight is ice cream, she won't eat any dessert." This fact is conditional, a little convoluted, and may even seem obvious, but it must be true given that your guest does not eat ice cream.

While all of the questions covered in this chapter deal with what follows from the statements in the stimulus, let's begin with Inference questions. They're the most numerous of the questions covered here, and more importantly, they're the ones that most directly reward you for assessing statements and making valid deductions based on them.

Prepare

LEARNING OBJECTIVES

In this section, you'll learn to:

- Make valid inferences from a single statement of fact.
- Combine two or more statements to make valid inferences.
- Recognize and use Keywords to make valid inferences.
- Recognize and use Formal Logic to make valid inferences.
- Recognize and use uncertain statements to make valid inferences.
- Identify and answer Inference questions.

What Inference Question Stems Ask For

An *inference* on the LSAT is a deduction made from facts given in the question. For LSAT purposes, treat *inference* and *deduction* as synonyms. With a few exceptions, the stimulus of an Inference question serves the same role that rules play in a logic puzzle. In many cases, the correct answer to an Inference question is a fact that *must be true* given the statements that the testmaker provides.

The question stem in the previous sample question was very direct: If the stimulus is true, the right answer must be true also. Here are a few other representative Inference question stems along with the LSAT expert's analysis.

LSAT Question	Analysis
Which one of the following is most strongly supported by the information above? *PrepTest104 Sec1 Q12*	The "information above" (statements in the stimulus) supports the correct answer (the valid inference). Remember that Strengthen questions could also use the word *support* in the question stem. Strengthen questions ask you to support the conclusion or argument above, while Inference questions ask you to support one of the following answers.
Which one of the following can be properly inferred from the passage? *PrepTest106 Sec3 Q1*	The correct answer is a valid deduction ("properly inferred") from the statements in the stimulus.
Which one of the following is a conclusion that can be properly drawn from the information above? *PrepTest104 Sec4 Q17*	This stimulus will be composed of assertions that act as evidence without a conclusion. The correct answer, then, will be a valid conclusion (deduction) drawn from those statements.

All of these stems ask for essentially the same thing: the answer choice that *must be true* if the facts in the stimulus are true. (Note that from time to time, the test will ask for the choice that *must be false* or *could be true* based on the statements. We'll cover those relatively rare question stems before the end of the section.) A precise understanding of what the testmaker is asking for leads to a handful of important observations about Inference questions that make learning how to make deductions more meaningful.

LSAT STRATEGY

Some facts to remember about LSAT inferences:

- An inference follows only from the facts given. No outside knowledge is required.
- An inference need not be mind-blowing. Sometimes it will be simple, even obvious.
- An inference may come from a single fact, or it may require combining multiple facts. It may not be necessary to take into account all the facts given in the stimulus.

Every Inference question stem contains a strong reminder of these strategy points: The correct answer must be based entirely and exclusively on the statements in the stimulus. Thus, it makes a lot of sense to untangle the stimulus by looking for the strongest statements (those that lead to the strongest deductions) and by looking for statements that can be combined (those that share the same terms, for example).

Cataloging and Paraphrasing Statements in the Stimulus

Without an argument to analyze—that is, without an explicit conclusion and evidence to identify—untrained test takers may find themselves at a loss when approaching Inference stimuli. Added to this confusion is the fact that Inference stimuli often use wordy, complicated, or confusing language. The LSAT expert, however, untangles the Inference stimulus efficiently by asking, "What do I *know* to be true?" Asking this question focuses the expert's attention on two criteria: (1) She notes statements that are the most concrete, and (2) she spots statements that can be combined. As always, the LSAT expert actively paraphrases convoluted statements to be sure she understands precisely what the statement does *and does not* assert.

Note the Most Concrete Statements

Think back for a moment to the example we used earlier, your guest's statement: "I don't eat ice cream." You were able to draw a valid inference from that statement because it was so strong. Had she said, "I don't know—maybe I'll have some ice cream," you could not draw a conclusion about what she might have for dessert. When untangling an Inference stimulus, the LSAT expert is always on the lookout for the most concrete statements.

LSAT Question	Analysis
Sharks have a higher ratio of cartilage mass to body mass than any other organism. They also have a greater resistance to cancer than any other organism. Shark cartilage contains a substance that inhibits tumor growth by stopping the development of a new blood network. In the past 20 years, none of the responses among terminal cancer patients to various therapeutic measures has been more positive than the response among those who consumed shark cartilage. *PrepTest106 Sec1 Q11*	The strongest statements here are the superlatives regarding sharks in the first two sentences. Since the rest of the passage is focused on cancer as well, the second sentence stands out: "[sharks] have a greater resistance to cancer than *any* other organism."

Identifying the strongest statements can have immediate benefits. On the next page, take a look at the full question from which that stimulus came, and notice how an LSAT expert approached it. Make sure to first note that the question asks for what must be *false*, rather than what must be true.

Step 2: The strongest statement is in the second sentence: "[sharks] have a great resistance to cancer than any other organism." The final sentence is also a forceful statement regarding the unmatched cancer resistance of sharks, in this case as a therapeutic measure.	**Step 1:** The phrasing "could be true EXCEPT" indicates an Inference question that asks for what *must be false*.

Sharks have a higher ratio of cartilage mass to body mass than any other organism. They also have a greater resistance to cancer than any other organism. Shark cartilage contains a substance that inhibits tumor growth by stopping the development of a new blood network. In the past 20 years, none of the responses among terminal cancer patients to various therapeutic measures has been more positive than the response among those who consumed shark cartilage.

If the claims made above are true, then each of the following could be true EXCEPT:

(A) No organism resists cancer better than sharks do, but some resist cancer as well as sharks.

(B) The organism most susceptible to cancer has a higher percentage of cartilage than some organisms that are less susceptible to cancer.

(C) The substance in shark cartilage that inhibits tumor growth is found in most organisms.

(D) In the past 20 years many terminal cancer patients have improved dramatically following many sorts of therapy.

(E) Some organisms have immune systems more efficient than a shark's immune system.

PrepTest106 Sec1 Q11

Step 3: The wrong answers here all could be true, while the correct answer will contradict something in stimulus. Look first for an answer that contradicts the most concrete statement that sharks are the animals most resistant to cancer. Eliminate Outside the Scope answer choices, since they could be true.	**Step 4:** (A) is correct. The first clause of this answer is consistent with the concrete statement regarding shark supremacy in resisting cancer, but the second clause contradicts that supremacy by indicating that some species are just as good at resisting cancer as sharks.

Wrong answers: (B) Outside the Scope. There is no information about the most susceptible species. Also, it cannot be deduced from the information that the ratio of cartilage to body mass is the reason for the shark's resistance to cancer. (C) It is possible that most organisms also contain the tumor-inhibiting substance, even if they do not match sharks in levels of effectiveness. (D) Such patients using other therapies could have improved dramatically, even if not as dramatically as those on shark therapy. (E) Outside the Scope. The stimulus focuses only on cancer resistance, not entire immune systems.

In this case, the correct answer is supported because it contradicts a single, strong statement in the stimulus. From time to time, the testmaker will reward you for making simple, straightforward inferences. Note, too, that the stimulus provides some basis for speculation that answer choices (B), (C), (D), and (E) also would be false statements. But for a *must be false* question such as this one, ask yourself: "even if this answer choice seems to go *somewhat* against the grain of the information, could it still *possibly* be true?" If it *could be true* then you have to get rid of it.

Practice First, use the question stem to characterize the one correct and four incorrect answers. Then, catalog the statements in this Inference stimulus. Identify the strongest, most concrete assertion(s) you find. As a hint, the most concrete statement in this stimulus is also highlighted by a Contrast Keyword phrase, which we will focus on shortly.

Step 2:	**Step 1:**

1. Letter to the Editor: Your article on effective cockroach control states that vexone is effective against only one of the more than 4,000 cockroach species that infest North America: the German cockroach. In actuality, vexone has been utilized effectively for almost a decade against all of the species that infest North America. In testing our product, Roach Ender, which contains vexone, we have conducted many well-documented studies that prove this fact.

Each of the following statements conflicts with the letter writer's view EXCEPT:

PrepTest106 Sec3 Q12

Expert Analysis for the Practice exercise may be found on the following page. ▶ ▶ ▶

Expert Analysis

Here's how an LSAT expert might analyze the question stem and stimulus you just saw. You can also see her analysis of the answer choices accompanying this question.

Step 2: The first sentence has a concrete statement, but recognize it as the view of another voice; it is not the author's. The contrast phrase "[i]n actuality" leads into the author's statements and her most concrete statement: Vexone has been effective against *all* North American cockroach species. The third sentence is merely an assertion that studies exist that document vexone's effectiveness.	**Step 1:** The phrase "conflicts with . . . EXCEPT" indicates an Inference question asking for what does *not* contradict information in the stimulus.

1. Letter to the Editor: Your article on effective cockroach control states that vexone is effective against only one of the more than 4,000 cockroach species that infest North America: the German cockroach. In actuality, vexone has been utilized effectively for almost a decade against all of the species that infest North America. In testing our product, Roach Ender, which contains vexone, we have conducted many well-documented studies that prove this fact.

Each of the following statements conflicts with the letter writer's view EXCEPT:

(A) Vexone is effective against only two species of cockroach that infest North America.

(B) Not all of the major species of cockroach that infest North America can be controlled by Roach Ender.

(C) Every species of cockroach that infests North America can be controlled by vexone.

(D) The cockroach infestations that have been combated with vexone have not included all of the cockroach species that infest North America.

(E) Roach Ender was tested against exactly 4,000 cockroach species that infest North America.

PrepTest106 Sec3 Q12

Step 3: The most concrete statement in the stimulus holds that vexone is effective against *all* species of cockroach. The correct answer could simply agree with that statement, and it is likely that at least some of the wrong answers will contradict that concrete statement.	**Step 4:** (C) is correct. This answer comports with the concrete statement that vexone is effective against *all* such species.

Wrong answers: (A) This answer contradicts the concrete statement that vexone is effective against *all* such species. (B) This answer also contradicts the concrete statement that vexone is effective against *all* such species. (D) This answer also contradicts the concrete statement that vexone is effective against *all* such species. (E) This answer contradicts the letter, which states that studies have demonstrated vexone to be effective against all of the *more than* 4,000 cockroach species found in North America.

CHAPTER 5

Combine Statements to Make Valid Inferences

In most cases, you won't be able to get the correct answer to an Inference question by rephrasing a single statement; when this happens, you'll need to combine two or more statements in order to predict the correct answer. Even so, it is still crucial to pay attention to the strength or concreteness of the statements in the stimulus. Imagine you learn two facts: (1) All practicing attorneys are eligible for the state bar's insurance plan, and (2) Joe graduated from a law school in the state. From those statements, the best you can say is that Joe may be eligible for the bar's insurance plan. After all, he may or may not be a practicing attorney. But, make the second statement more concrete as it applies to the first statement—Joe is a practicing attorney in the state—and you can easily conclude that Joe is eligible for the plan.

Take a look at an LSAT expert's analysis of an example stimulus from a real LSAT Inference question.

LSAT Question	Analysis
These days, drug companies and health professionals alike are focusing their attention on cholesterol in the blood. The more cholesterol we have in our blood, the higher the risk that we shall die of a heart attack. The issue is pertinent since heart disease kills more North Americans every year than any other single cause. At least three factors—smoking, drinking, and exercise—can each influence levels of cholesterol in the blood. *PrepTest107 Sec1 Q6*	The stimulus provides two causal relationships: 1) Increased cholesterol results in increased risk of death from heart attack, and 2) smoking, drinking, and exercise can each affect cholesterol levels. Combining these statements yields: smoking, drinking, and exercise can each influence the risk of death from heart attack.

The final sentence in the stimulus can be combined with the second because the two sentences both discuss how *levels of cholesterol* factor into two separate causal relationships. You can combine those statements to yield a chain of causation.

Take a look at the full question from which we drew that stimulus. You'll see that the correct answer directly rewards making the logical combination of statements the expert noted.

Step 2: The stimulus provides two causal relationships: 1) Increased cholesterol results in increased risk of death from heart attack, and 2) smoking, drinking, and exercise can each affect cholesterol levels.	**Step 1:** Rather than asking for what the author *did conclude*, this question asks for what "*can be properly concluded*," indicating an Inference question.

These days, drug companies and health professionals alike are focusing their attention on cholesterol in the blood. The more cholesterol we have in our blood, the higher the risk that we shall die of a heart attack. The issue is pertinent since heart disease kills more North Americans every year than any other single cause. At least three factors—smoking, drinking, and exercise—can each influence levels of cholesterol in the blood.

Which one of the following can be properly concluded from the passage?

(A) If a person has low blood cholesterol, then that person's risk of fatal heart disease is low.

(B) Smoking in moderation can entail as great a risk of fatal heart disease as does heavy smoking.

(C) A high-cholesterol diet is the principal cause of death in North America.

(D) The only way that smoking increases one's risk of fatal heart disease is by influencing the levels of cholesterol in the blood.

(E) The risk of fatal heart disease can be altered by certain changes in lifestyle.

PrepTest107 Sec1 Q6

Step 3: Combining the two causal relationships yields a chain of causation: Smoking, drinking, and exercise can each influence cholesterol levels, which, in turn, affect the risk of death from heart attack. The typical Inference answer will focus on the endpoints (three factors influence risk of fatal heart attack), rather than the connecting term (levels of cholesterol).	**Step 4:** (E) is correct. This answer matches the prediction by linking "changes in lifestyle" (which would encompass changes in smoking, drinking, and exercise habits) to the risk of fatal heart disease.

Wrong answers: (A) Distortion. The LSAT demands distinguishing an absolute value ("low" risk) from a relative value ("lower" risk). The stimulus only deals with relative or comparable risk levels. This answer could also be viewed as an incomplete contrapositive of the first causal relationship in the stimulus (negates both terms without reversing the sides). (B) Irrelevant Comparison. While smoking is cited as a factor affecting cholesterol levels in the blood, nothing in the passage distinguishes the effects of moderate versus heavy smoking. (C) Extreme. It cannot be deduced that high-cholesterol is the "*principal* cause of death in North America." Indeed, the stimulus says nothing about a high-cholesterol *diet*, just levels in the blood, wherever they come from. (D) Extreme. The stimulus does not preclude the possibility that smoking may increase the risk of fatal heart disease in other ways.

Practice Try another example. First, use the question stem to characterize the one correct and four incorrect answers. Then, catalog the statements in the stimulus and note which two statements can be combined.

Step 2:	**Step 1:**

2. Poppy petals function to attract pollinating insects. The pollination of a poppy flower triggers the release into that flower of a substance that causes its petals to wilt within one or two days. If the flower is not pollinated, the substance will not be released and the petals will remain fresh for a week or longer, as long as the plant can nourish them. Cutting an unpollinated poppy flower from the plant triggers the release into the flower of the same substance whose release is triggered by pollination.

The statements above, if true, most strongly support which one of the following?

PrepTest106 Sec1 Q16

Expert Analysis

Here's how an LSAT expert might analyze the question stem and stimulus you just saw. You can also see his analysis of the answer choices accompanying this question.

Step 2: Catalog the statements: (1) Poppy petals attract pollinating insects, (2) pollination triggers a substance causing petals to wilt within two days, (3) if not pollinated then petals can remain fresh for a week or more, and (4) cutting an unpollinated flower releases the same substance as pollination.	**Step 1:** A question stem that asks you to use the "statements above" to "support" an answer indicates an Inference question.

2. Poppy petals function to attract pollinating insects. The pollination of a poppy flower triggers the release into that flower of a substance that causes its petals to wilt within one or two days. If the flower is not pollinated, the substance will not be released and the petals will remain fresh for a week or longer, as long as the plant can nourish them. Cutting an unpollinated poppy flower from the plant triggers the release into the flower of the same substance whose release is triggered by pollination.

The statements above, if true, most strongly support which one of the following?

(A) Pollinating insects are not attracted to wilted poppy flowers.

(B) Even if cut poppies are given all necessary nutrients, their petals will tend to wilt within a few days.

(C) Flowers of all plants release the substance that causes wilting when they are cut, although the amount released may vary.

(D) The pollen on pollinated poppy flowers prevents their petals from absorbing the nutrients carried to them by their stems.

(E) Poppy plants are unable to draw nutrients from soil or water after the substance that causes wilting has been released.

PrepTest106 Sec1 Q16

Step 3: Since cutting an unpollinated flower releases the same substance as pollination does, one can deduced that cutting an unpollinated flower will also cause the petals to wilt.	**Step 4:** (B) is correct. This follows from the prediction (in other words, the deduction made in Step 3).

Wrong answers: (A) Distortion. The information indicates that pollination causes wilting, but does not say anything about the effect of wilting on the attractiveness of flowers to pollinating insects. (C) Outside the Scope. There is no information about plants other than poppies. (D) Distortion. It is the substance released following pollination, and not the pollen itself, that is responsible for the wilting. There is no other information regarding the effect of pollen. (E) Distortion. The stimulus does not indicate how the substance causes the poppy flowers to wilt. The reference to nutrients did not apply to the effects on pollinated plants.

In the examples we just looked at, two or more statements shared common terms and thus combined to produce valid inferences that must be true based on the statements in the stimulus. Always look to combine statements when possible in Inference questions.

Using Keywords to Make Valid Inferences

Interestingly, the skills required to dominate Logical Reasoning Inference questions are often the same skills needed to do well in Reading Comprehension. In Reading Comprehension, as you will learn in future chapters, we rely heavily on Keywords to ascertain the structure of a passage and to recognize what will be important in answering questions. You will see a preview of that in this segment as we apply those Reading Comprehension style skills to Logical Reasoning Inference questions. As you saw when we discussed concrete statements, the answer to an Inference question can derive from a single statement. Now we will see how the testmaker often highlights that vital statement using an Emphasis Keyword, such as *importantly* or *unfortunately*. Even more important are Contrast Keywords—words like *but, yet,* or *despite* or phrases such as *on the other hand*. These Keywords tell you that the author considers two terms or concepts to be at odds, and they allow you to see how to potentially connect such statements. Take a look at an LSAT expert's analysis of the following LSAT Inference stimulus.

LSAT Question	Analysis
Ideally, scientific laws should display the virtues of precision and generality, as do the laws of physics. However, because of the nature of their subject matter, laws of social science often have to use terms that are imprecise: for example, one knows only vaguely what is meant by "republicanism" or "class." As for generality, laws that apply only in certain social systems are typically the only ones possible for the social sciences. *PrepTest105 Sec4 Q15*	"Ideally" and "should" emphasize the first sentence as the author's assertion of the scientific ideals of precision and generality. "However" highlights the contrast in the following two sentences, which respectively indicate the limits on precision and generality.

The Keywords very explicitly set out the structure of the passage. First, the author forcefully asserts the scientific ideals of precision and generality. Next, "however" highlights the contrasting limitations on achieving precision and generality that follow. These statements do not combine neatly to form a clear deduction, so the answer may derive from a single statement. Which statement is both emphasized and the most concrete?

Here's how the LSAT expert might analyze the entire question.

Step 2: "Ideally" and "should" emphasize the first sentence as the author's assertion of the scientific ideals of precision and generality. "However" highlights the contrast in the following two sentences, which respectively indicate the limits on precision and generality.	**Step 1:** A question stem that directs using "information above" to "support" an answer indicates an Inference question.

Ideally, scientific laws should display the virtues of precision and generality, as do the laws of physics. However, because of the nature of their subject matter, laws of social science often have to use terms that are imprecise: for example, one knows only vaguely what is meant by "republicanism" or "class." As for generality, laws that apply only in certain social systems are typically the only ones possible for the social sciences.

Which one of the following statements is most strongly supported by the information above?

(A) All else being equal, a precise, general scientific law is to be preferred over one that is not general.

(B) The social sciences would benefit if they redirected their focus to the subject matter of the physical sciences.

(C) Terms such as "class" should be more precisely formulated by social scientists.

(D) Social scientists should make an effort to construct more laws that apply to all societies.

(E) The laws of social science are invariably not truly scientific.

PrepTest105 Sec4 Q15

Step 3: The statements do not neatly combine to yield a deduction. The first sentence is both emphasized ("ideally") and the most concrete. Scan for a match to the first sentence; if necessary, assess each answer by attempting to find direct support in the stimulus.	**Step 4:** (A) is correct. This is a restatement of the first sentence and, thus, directly supported by the passage.

Wrong answers: (B) Distortion. This suggests that the social sciences essentially should cease to exist, which is not indicated in the stimulus. (C) Distortion. While the author acknowledges the imprecision of social science terms, he makes no recommendation for increasing the precision of their definitions. According to the passage, social science will just be stuck with some vague terms. (D) Distortion. The author does not make any suggestions about the types of laws social scientists should or should not formulate. (E) Extreme. The information supports a deduction that laws of social science do not meet the scientific *ideal*, but this choice goes too far in stating they are "invariably not *truly* scientific."

The correct answer is clearly supported by the author's most concrete statement, while three of the wrong answers (B, C, and D) are distortions or contradictions of the less concrete statements in the stimulus. Answer choice (E) attempts to combine the statements in a way suggested by the contrast word "however," but it states the deduction too forcefully.

Practice First, use the question stem to characterize the one correct and four incorrect answers. Then, catalog the statements in the stimulus, using Keywords to combine statements where possible.

Step 2:	**Step 1:**

3. Physical education should teach people to pursue healthy, active lifestyles as they grow older. But the focus on competitive sports in most schools causes most of the less competitive students to turn away from sports. Having learned to think of themselves as unathletic, they do not exercise enough to stay healthy.

Which one of the following is most strongly supported by the statements above, if they are true?

PrepTest107 Sec4 Q3

Expert Analysis

Here's how an LSAT expert might analyze the question stem and stimulus you just saw. You can also see her analysis of the answer choices accompanying this question.

Step 2: "But" contrasts the laudable goal of physical education with the unfortunate result of physical education's focus on competitive sports. The third sentence provides the reason: In a competitive environment, less competitive students see themselves as unathletic and in turn stop exercising.	**Step 1:** A question that asks you to use the "statements above" to "support" an answer indicates an Inference question.

3. Physical education should teach people to pursue healthy, active lifestyles as they grow older. But the focus on competitive sports in most schools causes most of the less competitive students to turn away from sports. Having learned to think of themselves as unathletic, they do not exercise enough to stay healthy.

Which one of the following is most strongly supported by the statements above, if they are true?

(A) Physical education should include noncompetitive activities.

(B) Competition causes most students to turn away from sports.

(C) People who are talented at competitive physical endeavors exercise regularly.

(D) The mental aspects of exercise are as important as the physical ones.

(E) Children should be taught the dangers of a sedentary lifestyle.

PrepTest107 Sec4 Q3

Step 3: The Contrast Keyword—"[b]ut"—points out a dilemma: Physical education should promote healthy, active lifestyles, but its focus on competitive sports has the opposite effect on less competitive students. The correct answer will follow from this dilemma. It could either summarize the problem or offer a solution.	**Step 4:** (A) is correct. Because a focus on competitive sports prevents P.E. from doing what it should for some students, it follows that P.E. should include noncompetitive activities as well.

Wrong answers: (B) Extreme. The stimulus only states that competition causes "most *of the less competitive* students to turn away from sports." There is no information about the population of students as a whole. (C) Distortion. The stimulus states that the unathletic "do not exercise enough to stay healthy," but it is silent as to the exercise habits of the talented competitors. (D) Irrelevant Comparison. The stimulus does not make this comparison. (E) Outside the Scope. The passage does not imply that teaching students about the *dangers* of too little exercise is effective or recommended.

Using Formal Logic to Make Valid Inferences

Think back to the work you did on Formal Logic in Chapter 1 and it will be clear why the testmaker often uses Formal Logic in Inference stimuli. While challenging to read and interpret, conditional Formal Logic statements are easy to combine in ways that reveal their implications. From "If A, then B" and "If B, then C," you can deduce "If A, then C" with absolute confidence. Sometimes, Logical Reasoning inferences are just that straightforward, although you can expect to encounter some pretty convoluted language in these stimuli. Your familiarity with Formal Logic will be an enormous benefit on many Inference questions. Once you recognize that a stimulus contains Formal Logic, its statements are easy to catalog and assess. You can, of course, even jot them down in Formal Logic shorthand on your scratch paper.

With that in mind, take a look at how an LSAT expert would analyze the stimulus from the first Inference question you saw in this chapter.

LSAT Question	Analysis
The axis of Earth's daily rotation is tilted with respect to the plane of its orbit at an angle of roughly 23 degrees. That angle can be kept fairly stable only by the gravitational influence of Earth's large, nearby Moon. Without such a stable and moderate axis tilt, a planet's climate is too extreme and unstable to support life. Mars, for example, has only very small moons, tilts at wildly fluctuating angles, and cannot support life. *PrepTest106 Sec1 Q14*	Two Formal Logic Statements: (1) stable angle → moon has gravitational influence (2) no stable angle → climate not support life

At this point, the LSAT expert seeks to combine the two Formal Logic statements, but recognizes that they do not link up neatly as written. However, taking the contrapositive of the second statement would allow them to link up through the *stable angle* term, yielding:

Climate support life → stable angle → moon has gravitational influence

This means that for the Earth's climate to support life, the moon must be exerting a gravitational influence; equally true, we know that without the moon's gravitational influence, the Earth's climate would not support life. Rather than testing each answer choice, the LSAT expert seeks out the answer choice containing that formal logic deduction.

Step 2: Two Formal Logic Statements: (1) Earth's stable angle → moon has gravitational influence (2) no stable angle → climate not support life	**Step 1:** The phrases "If the statements above are true" and "must also be true" indicate an Inference question.

The axis of Earth's daily rotation is tilted with respect to the plane of its orbit at an angle of roughly 23 degrees. That angle can be kept fairly stable only by the gravitational influence of Earth's large, nearby Moon. Without such a stable and moderate axis tilt, a planet's climate is too extreme and unstable to support life. Mars, for example, has only very small moons, tilts at wildly fluctuating angles, and cannot support life.

If the statements above are true, which one of the following must also be true on the basis of them?

(A) If Mars had a sufficiently large nearby moon, Mars would be able to support life.

(B) If Earth's Moon were to leave Earth's orbit, Earth's climate would be unable to support life.

(C) Any planet with a stable, moderate axis tilt can support life.

(D) Gravitational influences other than moons have little or no effect on the magnitude of the tilt angle of either Earth's or Mars's axis.

(E) No planet that has more than one moon can support life.

PrepTest106 Sec1 Q14

Step 3: Contraposing the second statement and then combining the statements yields the deduction: If Earth's climate supports life → moon has gravitational influence Or Without moon's influence → Earth's climate cannot support life	**Step 4:** (B) is Correct. This matches the deduction from combining the formal logic statements: No moon → Earth not support life.

Wrong answers: (A) It cannot be known what would result if Mars *did* have a large moon. This answer treats the necessary condition of having a large moon as a sufficient condition, but there may be other prerequisites for supporting life. (C) As with answer choice (A), this answer confuses the necessity of a stable angle with being sufficient to support life. (D) Beyond knowing that a moon's influence is necessary for a stable tilt, there is no information as to what degree other gravitational influences play a role. (E) While a moon is necessary, the stimulus does not specify that there must be *exactly one* moon in order to support life. Two moons, or more, might be better than one, or at least as good, for stability.

In that example, two Formal Logic statements linked neatly together in A → B → C form; at least once the contrapositive of the second statement was taken. Sometimes there are additional variables, or there might be a factual statement to combine with the Formal Logic.

Practice First, use the question stem to characterize the one correct and four incorrect answers. Then, catalog the statements in the stimulus. Translate any Formal Logic statements you find and determine whether and how they can be combined. Also, note if there is a factual statement that *triggers* a Formal Logic rule.

Step 2:	**Step 1:**

4. Editorialist: Drivers with a large number of demerit points who additionally have been convicted of a serious driving-related offense should either be sentenced to jail or be forced to receive driver re-education, since to do otherwise would be to allow a crime to go unpunished. Only if such drivers are likely to be made more responsible drivers should driver re-education be recommended for them. Unfortunately, it is always almost impossible to make drivers with a large number of demerit points more responsible drivers.

If the editorialist's statements are true, they provide the most support for which one of the following?

PrepTest107 Sec4 Q12

Step 2:	**Step 1:**

5. A poem is any work of art that exploits some of the musical characteristics of language, such as meter, rhythm, euphony, and rhyme. A novel, though it may be a work of art in language, does not usually exploit the musical characteristics of language. A symphony, though it may be a work of art that exploits the musical characteristics of sounds, rarely involves language. A limerick, though it may exploit some musical characteristics of language, is not, strictly speaking, art.

The statements above, if true, most strongly support which one of the following?

PrepTest104 Sec1 Q20

Expert Analysis

Here's how an LSAT expert might analyze the question stem and stimulus you just saw. You can also see his analysis of the answer choices accompanying this question.

Step 2: Two Formal Logic Statements about drivers with many demerits: another conviction → i) jail or ii) driver re-education re-education → likelihood of increased responsibility Factual Statement: Increased responsibility is nearly impossible for such drivers.	**Step 1:** A question that asks you to use the "statements above" to "support" an answer indicates an Inference question.

4. Editorialist: Drivers with a large number of demerit points who additionally have been convicted of a serious driving-related offense should either be sentenced to jail or be forced to receive driver re-education, since to do otherwise would be to allow a crime to go unpunished. Only if such drivers are likely to be made more responsible drivers should driver re-education be recommended for them. Unfortunately, it is always almost impossible to make drivers with a large number of demerit points more responsible drivers.

If the editorialist's statements are true, they provide the most support for which one of the following?

(A) Drivers with a large number of demerit points who have been convicted of a serious driving-related offense should be sent to jail.

(B) Driver re-education offers the best chance of making drivers with a large number of demerit points responsible drivers.

(C) Driver re-education is not harsh enough punishment for anyone convicted of a serious driving-related offense who has also accumulated a large number of demerit points.

(D) Driver re-education should not be recommended for those who have committed no serious driving-related offenses.

(E) Drivers with a large number of demerit points but no conviction for a serious driving-related offense should receive driver re-education rather than jail.

PrepTest107 Sec4 Q12

Step 3: The fact that it is nearly impossible to increase the level of responsibility of repeat offenders dictates that only one of the two possible results can occur: jail.	**Step 4:** (A) is correct: Two options were identified: re-education or jail. However, re-education depends on the possibility of increasing a driver's responsibility. Since that is nearly impossible, the only option left is jail.

Wrong answers: (B) While technically it is possible that driver education is the *best chance*, there is no support for this assertion; only that increasing the responsibility level of such drivers is nearly impossible. (C) Distortion. The concern is the effectiveness of re-education in increasing driver responsibility levels, not whether it is *harsh* enough. (D) Outside the Scope. The stimulus does not discuss drivers who have no serious driving-related offenses. (E) Outside the Scope. As with choice (D), the stimulus does not discuss drivers who have no serious driving-related offenses.

Expert Analysis

Here's how an LSAT expert might analyze the question stem and stimulus you just saw. You can also see her analysis of the answer choices accompanying this question.

Step 2: Formal Logic statement: Exploit musical aspect of language → Poem Characteristics of three items: Novel: possible work of art in language; does not usually exploit musical aspects Symphony: possible work of art that exploits musical aspects of sound, but rarely of language Limerick: not art	**Step 1:** A question that asks you to use the "statements above" to "support" an answer indicates an Inference question.

5. A poem is any work of art that exploits some of the musical characteristics of language, such as meter, rhythm, euphony, and rhyme. A novel, though it may be a work of art in language, does not usually exploit the musical characteristics of language. A symphony, though it may be a work of art that exploits the musical characteristics of sounds, rarely involves language. A limerick, though it may exploit some musical characteristics of language, is not, strictly speaking, art.

The statements above, if true, most strongly support which one of the following?

(A) If a creation is neither a poem, nor a novel, nor a symphony, then it is not a work of art.

(B) An example of so-called blank verse, which does not rhyme, is not really a poem.

(C) If a novel exploits meter and rhyme while standing as a work of art, then it is both a novel and a poem.

(D) Limericks constitute a nonartistic type of poetry.

(E) If a symphony does not exploit the musical characteristics of sound, then it is not a work of art.

PrepTest104 Sec1 Q20

Step 3: The most concrete information from among the three examples is that a limerick is not art; thus, limericks do not meet the sufficient conditions set out in the stimulus. As to novels and symphonies, while they do not typically meet the sufficient conditions set out to establish what is a poem, there does exist the possibility that each of them could meet those conditions. Anticipate an answer that allows you to know that either a novel or a symphony meets the sufficient conditions for being designated a poem.	**Step 4:** (C) is correct. If a novel, in addition to being based in language, is a work of art that exploits meter and rhyme, then it meets the sufficient conditions set out in the stimulus and, thus, must be a poem.

Wrong answers: (A) Distortion. The stimulus does not dictate that nothing beyond a poem, novel, or symphony could be a work of art. (B) The stimulus does not discuss *blank verse* and rhyming is not a singular necessary condition to qualify as poem. Thus, this answer is not supported. (D) The stimulus defines poems as works of art, without any discussion of *nonartistic* types of poetry. (E) The stimulus does not indicate that exploiting musical characteristics of sound is a necessary condition for a symphony to be a work of art, as this choice suggests.

Using Uncertain Statements to Make Valid Inferences

The process of making inferences from Formal Logic statements rewards your skills of deduction. You use conditional assertions to assess the truth of other statements or combined if/then statements to reveal unstated certainties. For you, as a well-trained test taker, words like *any*, *all*, and *none* signal clear Formal Logic relationships of necessity and sufficiency. In many Inference questions, however, you will also have to deal with statements that are less absolute, statements that use words like *most, many, several,* and *some.*

The good news is that the LSAT follows reliable conventions that can help to create inferences out of statements containing these indeterminate terms. The word *most*, for example, means any amount greater than 50 percent. The word *some*, on the other hand, signifies one or more (i.e., *some* = not none). Note that both of these words—*most* and *some*—have the possibility of also meaning *all*. Although this runs counter to our normal usage and our instincts, it is important to understand how the LSAT uses these words, especially because they can be used to create inferences in some predictable ways. Other indeterminate words—*several*, *many*, and *few*—should be treated in the same way. Don't try to give them any special meaning; they're inclusive of every possibility between *two* and *all*.

LSAT STRATEGY

Levels of Certainty

Here are the types of statements you'll encounter in Inference stimuli, arranged from most concrete to least:

- **Unqualified Assertions** (e.g., *Bob is an attorney* or *Monday will be a rainy day*)
- **Conditional Statements/Formal Logic** (e.g., *If the company hopes to meet its budget, then it must cut travel costs* or *McLaren will lose the election unless the county sees record voter turnout*)
- **Statements with "most"**—this means *more than half* but could include *all* (e.g., *Most of Company Y's employees are college graduates* or *A majority of the respondents preferred the new logo*)
- **Statements with "some" or "few"**—this means anywhere from one to all, just not zero (e.g., *Some architects are painters*)

It's rare for a stimulus to be comprised exclusively of uncertain statements. You might, on occasion, see something along the lines of "Most pizza restaurants in town are family-run businesses, and most pizza restaurants in town employ more than 10 people." Do you see what that allows you to infer? Right, at least one family-run business in town employs more than 10 people. Most of the time, however, the testmaker will include stronger statements—assertions of fact or conditional Formal Logic statements—along with statements containing less certain terms like *many* or *most*.

Here's an LSAT expert's analysis of a stimulus containing statements with varying degrees of certainty.

LSAT Question	Analysis
Critic: Most chorale preludes were written for the organ, and most great chorale preludes written for the organ were written by J. S. Bach. One of Bach's chorale preludes dramatizes one hymn's perspective on the year's end. This prelude is agonizing and fixed on the passing of the old year, with its dashed hopes and lost opportunities. It does not necessarily reveal Bach's own attitude toward the change of the year, but does reflect the tone of the hymn's text. People often think that artists create in order to express their own feelings. Some artists do. Master artists never do, and Bach was a master artist. *PrepTest107 Sec4 Q22*	Cataloging the statements: Two uncertain statements: i) *most* preludes written for organ ii) *most* great preludes for organ by Bach An example regarding one Bach prelude A statement about what other people *often* think Two concrete statements: i) master artists never create to express their own feelings ii) Bach was a master artist

This stimulus contains examples of all the levels of certainty—some ("often"), most, Formal Logic (If an artist is a master artist, then he never creates in order to express his own feelings), as well as an unqualified assertion ("Bach was a master artist"). Which statements do you think are most likely to yield a deduction about what *must be true* (or false)? Take a look at the LSAT expert's analysis on the following page.

Here's the LSAT expert's analysis of the full question associated with that stimulus.

Step 2: Cataloging the statements: Two uncertain statements: i) most preludes written for organ ii) most great preludes for organ by Bach An example regarding one Bach prelude A statement about what other people often think Two concrete statements: i) master artists never create to express their own feelings ii) Bach was a master artist	**Step 1:** The phrase "CANNOT be true" indicates an Inference question asking for what *must be false*.

Critic: Most chorale preludes were written for the organ, and most great chorale preludes written for the organ were written by J. S. Bach. One of Bach's chorale preludes dramatizes one hymn's perspective on the year's end. This prelude is agonizing and fixed on the passing of the old year, with its dashed hopes and lost opportunities. It does not necessarily reveal Bach's own attitude toward the change of the year, but does reflect the tone of the hymn's text. People often think that artists create in order to express their own feelings. Some artists do. Master artists never do, and Bach was a master artist.

If the critic's statements are true, then on the basis of them which one of the following CANNOT be true?

(A) Bach believed that the close of the year was not a time for optimism and joyous celebration.

(B) In composing music about a particular subject, Bach did not write the music in order to express his own attitude toward the subject.

(C) In compositions other than chorale preludes, Bach wrote music in order to express his feelings toward various subjects.

(D) Most of Bach's chorale preludes were written for instruments other than the organ.

(E) Most of the great chorale preludes were written for instruments other than the organ.

PrepTest107 Sec4 Q22

Step 3: The last two statements yield a deduction: Bach never created art to express his own feelings. Check for an answer that contradicts that deduction before considering the less certain information that makes up the bulk of the stimulus.	**Step 4:** (C) is correct. This answer contradicts the deduction that can be derived from the concrete statements at the end of the stimulus: Bach never wrote music to express his feelings.

Wrong answers: (A) The stimulus indicates that we do not know "Bach's own attitude toward the change of the year." This could be true. (B) 180. Based on the deduction at the end of the stimulus, this choice qualifies as a *must be true*. (D) While it is true that Bach wrote most of the *great* choral preludes for the organ, it is still possible that Bach wrote an even larger number of preludes for other instruments. (E) While it is true that most chorale preludes were written for the organ, it is still possible that most *great* choral preludes were written for other instruments.

Answer choice (C) is correct because it directly contradicts the deduction that can be made from the last sentence and its two concrete statements. The other answers either are in agreement with the stimulus or are statements that could be true. Answering this question efficiently and confidently is a result of prioritizing the more certain statements, especially any that can be combined to yield a deduction. On the next page, take a look at an example in which you are required to use less definite information to answer an Inference question.

Practice First, use the question stem to characterize the one correct and four incorrect answers. Then, catalog the statements in the stimulus. Look for statements of greater and lesser certainty. Catalog the statements from most certain to least and determine what can be logically inferred.

Step 2:	**Step 1:**

6. Dr. Z: Many of the characterizations of my work offered by Dr. Q are imprecise, and such characterizations do not provide an adequate basis for sound criticism of my work.

Which one of the following can be properly inferred from Dr. Z's statement?

PrepTest101 Sec3 Q15

The word "many" on the LSAT is an uncertain term which, along with words such as *some* and *few*, should be interpreted as *at least one*. All of these words tell us very little about numbers and quantities, and should be distinguished from the more concrete term "most," which means more than half. The second clause—"such characterizations"—is unqualified and should be interpreted as *all such characterizations*.

Expert Analysis

Here's how an LSAT expert might analyze the question stem and stimulus you just saw. You can also see her analysis of the answer choices accompanying this question.

Step 2: Cataloging the statements:	Step 1: The phrase "properly inferred" indicates an Inference question. The correct answer must be true based on the statements in the stimulus.
One Formal Logic statement: Imprecise characterization → not adequate basis for sound criticism One uncertain statement: *Many* of Dr. Q's characterizations are imprecise.	

6. Dr. Z: Many of the characterizations of my work offered by Dr. Q are imprecise, and such characterizations do not provide an adequate basis for sound criticism of my work.

Which one of the following can be properly inferred from Dr. Z's statement?

(A) Some of Dr. Q's characterizations of Dr. Z's work provide an adequate basis for sound criticism of Dr. Z's work.

(B) All of Dr. Q's characterizations of Dr. Z's work that are not imprecise provide an adequate basis for sound criticism of Dr. Z's work.

(C) All of the characterizations of Dr. Z's work by Dr. Q that do not provide an adequate basis for sound criticism of Dr. Z's work are imprecise.

(D) If the characterization of someone's work is precise, then it provides a sound basis for criticizing that work.

(E) At least one of Dr. Q's characterizations of Dr. Z's work fails to provide an adequate basis for sound criticism of that work.

PrepTest101 Sec3 Q15

Step 3: Since many of Dr. Q's characterizations are imprecise, the formal logic rule dictates that those characterizations are not an adequate basis for sound criticism.	**Step 4:** (E) is correct. This choice matches the prediction.

Wrong answers: (A) At least some of Dr. Q's characterizations are *not* an adequate basis, and it is possible that all of them are inadequate. (B) Distortion. It can be deduced that precision is necessary for providing an adequate basis, not that it is sufficient, as this choice indicates. (C) The formal logic in this choice reverses the direction of the arrow of the statement in the stimulus. (D) Distortion. It can be deduced that precision is necessary for providing an adequate basis, not that it is sufficient, as this choice indicates.

Reflect In day-to-day life, we make inferences all the time, but we are seldom as rigorous as the LSAT requires us to be. Over the coming days, pay attention to the unstated implications of statements you hear and read, anything from television news analysis to your friends' conversations. Try to assess what can be inferred or deduced from them. Are the inferences logical and supported by the statements themselves, or are you bringing in outside information? Are the deductions within the scope of the statements, or are they actually too extreme to be supported?

Inference Questions

You are just about ready to tackle some full Inference questions in practice, but first, do a quick review of what the question stems ask for. Throughout the previous examples, you saw the LSAT expert characterize the one right and four wrong answer choices before diving into his evaluation. While most LSAT Inference questions ask for a deduction that must be true, some questions create a twist by asking instead for a fact that could be true or must be false. Take a moment to drill on this important step with a handful of different Inference question stems.

Practice Consider the following question stems and characterize the one correct and four incorrect answer choices for each. When you're done, turn the page and check your analysis against that of the LSAT expert.

LSAT Question	My Analysis
7. If the statements above are true, which one of the following must also be true? *PrepTest107 Sec1 Q18*	
8. Each of the following is supported by the information above EXCEPT: *PrepTest106 Sec3 Q4*	
9. Which one of the following is most strongly supported by the nutritionist's statements? *PrepTest107 Sec1 Q8*	
10. Which one of the following is strictly implied by the above? *PrepTest105 Sec4 Q17*	

Expert Analysis

Here's how an LSAT expert would characterize the answer choices for each of those question stems.

LSAT Question	Analysis
7. If the statements above are true, which one of the following must also be true? *PrepTest107 Sec1 Q18*	Correct answer choice: Must be true based on the stimulus. Wrong answer choices: Could be false based on the stimulus.
8. Each of the following is supported by the information above EXCEPT: *PrepTest106 Sec3 Q4*	Correct answer choice: Unsupported by the stimulus. Wrong answer choices: Supported by information in the stimulus.
9. Which one of the following is most strongly supported by the nutritionist's statements? *PrepTest107 Sec1 Q8*	Correct answer choice: Strongly supported by the statements in the stimulus. Wrong answer choices: Unsupported by the stimulus.
10. Which one of the following is strictly implied by the above? *PrepTest105 Sec4 Q17*	Correct answer choice: Must be true based on the stimulus. Wrong answer choices: Could be false based on the stimulus.

In every section of the test, the LSAT expert makes a habit of characterizing right and wrong answers before untangling the stimulus. This is especially important to avoid confusion in EXCEPT questions. If you find it helpful, you could even jot down a shorthand note, such as "MBT" for *must be true*, on your scratch paper as a reminder. Don't be overly concerned with the EXCEPT variations, though; over the past five years, they've represented just over 3 percent of the Inference questions in released exams.

Frequently (especially in high-difficulty questions), it is not immediately obvious that an answer choice must be true. In that case, testing whether each answer could be false helps to eliminate wrong choices. An answer choice that must be false can often be found by eliminating any answer choice that is possible in light of the facts.

Practice Now it's time to practice your skills on some more Inference questions. For each question, work on recognizing and (when possible) combining concrete statements. Note how Keywords indicate an author's perspective on facts in the stimulus. If there is Formal Logic, combine statements and form contrapositives. When there are uncertain statements, slow down and understand what could be true, but does not have to be true. Use the corresponding blanks to record your thinking for each step and then, after each question, compare your work to the thinking of an LSAT expert on the following pages.

Step 2:	**Step 1:**

11. Nutritionist: Many people claim that simple carbohydrates are a reasonable caloric replacement for the fatty foods forbidden to those on law-fat diets. This is now in doubt. New studies show that, for many people, a high intake of simple carbohydrates stimulates an overproduction of insulin, a hormone that is involved in processing sugars and starches to create energy when the body requires energy, or, when energy is not required, to store the resulting by-products as fat.

Which one of the following is most strongly supported by the nutritionist's statements?

(A) People on low-fat diets should avoid consumption of simple carbohydrates if they wish to maintain the energy that their bodies require.

(B) People who produce enough insulin to process their intake of simple carbohydrates should not feel compelled to adopt low-fat diets.

(C) People who consume simple carbohydrates should limit their intake of foods high in fat.

(D) People who wish to avoid gaining body fat should limit their intake of foods high in simple carbohydrates.

(E) People who do not produce an excessive amount of insulin when they consume foods high in simple carbohydrates will not lose weight if they restrict only their intake of these foods.

PrepTest107 Sec1 Q8

Step 3:	**Step 4:**

Step 2:	**Step 1:**

12. Everyone who is excessively generous is not levelheaded, and no one who is levelheaded is bold.

Which one of the following is strictly implied by the above?

(A) Everyone who is excessively generous is not bold.

(B) Everyone who is not bold is excessively generous.

(C) No one who is not bold lacks excessive generosity.

(D) If someone is levelheaded, then that person is neither bold nor excessively generous.

(E) If someone is not levelheaded, then that person is either bold or excessively generous.

PrepTest105 Sec4 Q17

Step 3:	**Step 4:**

Step 2:	**Step 1:**

13. Some planning committee members—those representing the construction industry—have significant financial interests in the committee's decisions. No one who is on the planning committee lives in the suburbs, although many of them work there.

If the statements above are true, which one of the following must also be true?

(A) No persons with significant financial interests in the planning committee's decisions are not in the construction industry.

(B) No person who has significant financial interest in the planning committee's decisions lives in the suburbs.

(C) Some persons with significant financial interests in the planning committee's decisions work in the suburbs.

(D) Some planning committee members who represent the construction industry do not work in the suburbs.

(E) Some persons with significant financial interests in the planning committee's decisions do not live in the suburbs.

PrepTest107 Sec1 Q18

Step 3:	**Step 4:**

Step 2:	**Step 1:**

14. Editorial: The government claims that the country's nuclear power plants are entirely safe and hence that the public's fear of nuclear accidents at these plants is groundless. The government also contends that its recent action to limit the nuclear industry's financial liability in the case of nuclear accidents at power plants is justified by the need to protect the nuclear industry from the threat of bankruptcy. But even the government says that unlimited liability poses such a threat only if injury claims can be sustained against the industry; and the government admits that for such claims to be sustained, injury must result from a nuclear accident. The public's fear, therefore, is well founded.

If all of the statements offered in support of the editorial's conclusion correctly describe the government's position, which one of the following must also be true on the basis of those statements?

Ⓐ The government's claim about the safety of the country's nuclear power plants is false.

Ⓑ The government's position on nuclear power plants is inconsistent.

Ⓒ The government misrepresented its reasons for acting to limit the nuclear industry's liability.

Ⓓ Unlimited financial liability in the case of nuclear accidents poses no threat to the financial security of the country's nuclear industry.

Ⓔ The only serious threat posed by a nuclear accident would be to the financial security of the nuclear industry.

PrepTest107 Sec1 Q21

Step 3:	**Step 4:**

Step 2:	**Step 1:**

15. Raising the humidity of a room protects furniture, draperies, and computers from damage caused by excessively dry air. Further, it can make people feel warmer, helps the body's defenses against viruses, and alleviates some skin rashes.

Each of the following is supported by the information above EXCEPT:

(A) Humidity can be bad for computers.

(B) A room can be too dry for the optimal maintenance of its furnishings.

(C) Dry air can feel cooler than humid air of the same temperature.

(D) Increased humidity can be beneficial to the skin.

(E) The human immune system can benefit from humidity.

PrepTest106 Sec3 Q4

Step 3:	**Step 4:**

Expert Analysis

Here's how an LSAT expert looked at the questions you just tried.

Step 2	Step 1
Step 2: Other people claim carbs are a reasonable replacement for fatty foods, but the nutritionist casts doubt on that claim. The evidence indicates two causal relationships: i) high intake of simple carbohydrates results in excess insulin ii) insulin is involved in production of energy or storage of excess as fat	**Step 1:** A question stem directing the use of statements above to support an answer indicates an Inference question.

11. Nutritionist: Many people claim that simple carbohydrates are a reasonable caloric replacement for the fatty foods forbidden to those on law-fat diets. This is now in doubt. New studies show that, for many people, a high intake of simple carbohydrates stimulates an overproduction of insulin, a hormone that is involved in processing sugars and starches to create energy when the body requires energy, or, when energy is not required, to store the resulting by-products as fat.

Which one of the following is most strongly supported by the nutritionist's statements?

(A) People on low-fat diets should avoid consumption of simple carbohydrates if they wish to maintain the energy that their bodies require.

(B) People who produce enough insulin to process their intake of simple carbohydrates should not feel compelled to adopt low-fat diets.

(C) People who consume simple carbohydrates should limit their intake of foods high in fat.

(D) People who wish to avoid gaining body fat should limit their intake of foods high in simple carbohydrates.

(E) People who do not produce an excessive amount of insulin when they consume foods high in simple carbohydrates will not lose weight if they restrict only their intake of these foods.

PrepTest107 Sec1 Q8

Step 3	Step 4
Step 3: Though the stimulus is in the form of an argument, focus on the factual evidence in this Inference question. Combined, the statements produce a chain of causation: High intake of simple carbohydrates can lead to the storage of excess body fat.	**Step 4:** (D) is correct. The information establishes a causal chain from the intake of simple carbohydrates to the storage of excess body fat.

Wrong answers: (A) 180. The stimulus indicates that a diet of simple carbohydrates can provide the energy the body requires. (B) Distortion. The reasons some people need to be on low-fat diets are not indicated and are not related to the concerns regarding simple carbohydrates and insulin. (C) Outside the Scope. The only question in the stimulus is whether those who already limit their intake of fat should replace it with simple carbohydrates. (E) The stimulus provides no information to support speculation regarding what happens to people who do not produce excess insulin.

Step 2: Two Formal Logic statements: i) excessively generous → not levelheaded ii) levelheaded → not bold	**Step 1:** The phrase "implied by" indicates an Inference question.

12. Everyone who is excessively generous is not levelheaded, and no one who is levelheaded is bold.

Which one of the following is strictly implied by the above?

(A) Everyone who is excessively generous is not bold.

(B) Everyone who is not bold is excessively generous.

(C) No one who is not bold lacks excessive generosity.

(D) If someone is levelheaded, then that person is neither bold nor excessively generous.

(E) If someone is not levelheaded, then that person is either bold or excessively generous.

PrepTest105 Sec4 Q17

Step 3: The two Formal Logic statements do not link in a chain. However, take the contrapositive of the first statement and combine it with the second sentence to deduce the following: Anyone who is levelheaded is both not bold and not excessively generous.	**Step 4:** (D) is correct. Taking the contrapositive of the first statement shows that levelheadedness triggers not excessively generous and in the second statement levelheadedness triggers not bold, so both must be true.

Wrong answers: (A) This answer incorrectly links the two statements in a chain as though "not levelheaded" equaled "levelheaded." (B) This answer commits the same error as choice (A); it also erroneously changes the direction of the connection. (C) This answer is identical in meaning to choice (B). (E) None of the statements or their contrapositives has the term "not levelheaded" as a trigger, so this does not have to be true.

Step 2: Catalog the statements:	Step 1: The phrase "must also be true" indicates an Inference question.
Formal Logic statement: Planning committee → Not live in suburbs Uncertain Statements: *Some* on planning committee have financial interest in committee decisions. *Some* on planning committee work in the suburbs.	

13. Some planning committee members—those representing the construction industry—have significant financial interests in the committee's decisions. No one who is on the planning committee lives in the suburbs, although many of them work there.

If the statements above are true, which one of the following must also be true?

(A) No persons with significant financial interests in the planning committee's decisions are not in the construction industry.

(B) No person who has significant financial interest in the planning committee's decisions lives in the suburbs.

(C) Some persons with significant financial interests in the planning committee's decisions work in the suburbs.

(D) Some planning committee members who represent the construction industry do not work in the suburbs.

(E) Some persons with significant financial interests in the planning committee's decisions do not live in the suburbs.

PrepTest107 Sec1 Q18

Step 3: The two uncertain statements cannot be combined together to make a deduction. However, either uncertain statement could be combined with the Formal Logic statement to yield two deductions: i) *some* who work in the suburbs do not live in the suburbs, and, ii) *some* with financial interest in committee decisions do not live in the suburbs.	**Step 4:** (E) is correct. If some people on the planning committee have significant financial interests in their decisions and all people on the planning committee do not live in the suburbs, then it must be true that some people with significant financial interests in committee decisions do not live in the suburbs.

Wrong answers: (A) Extreme. It's not supported that *every* person with a significant financial interest in committee decisions is in the construction industry. The information does not preclude others outside the construction industry from having such interests in committee decisions. (B) Extreme. It's not supported that *every* person with significant financial interest in committee decisions does not live in the suburbs. (C) This answer improperly purports to combine the two uncertain statements. (D) This cannot be deduced for certain because it is possible that all planning committee members work in the suburbs.

Step 2: The Keyword "also" helps focus on the two separate claims about nuclear power: i) It is entirely safe; and ii) limiting the nuclear industry's financial liability is justified. The Keyword "but" highlights the paradoxical nature of needing to grant liability limitations to something that is completely safe.	Step 1: The phrase "must also be true" indicates an Inference question. The question stem further directs you to only accept the editorial's evidence as true, not its conclusion. Catalog the editorial's evidence, and use it to decide which answer also must be true.

14. Editorial: The government claims that the country's nuclear power plants are entirely safe and hence that the public's fear of nuclear accidents at these plants is groundless. The government also contends that its recent action to limit the nuclear industry's financial liability in the case of nuclear accidents at power plants is justified by the need to protect the nuclear industry from the threat of bankruptcy. But even the government says that unlimited liability poses such a threat only if injury claims can be sustained against the industry; and the government admits that for such claims to be sustained, injury must result from a nuclear accident. The public's fear, therefore, is well founded.

If all of the statements offered in support of the editorial's conclusion correctly describe the government's position, which one of the following must also be true on the basis of those statements?

(A) The government's claim about the safety of the country's nuclear power plants is false.

(B) The government's position on nuclear power plants is inconsistent.

(C) The government misrepresented its reasons for acting to limit the nuclear industry's liability.

(D) Unlimited financial liability in the case of nuclear accidents poses no threat to the financial security of the country's nuclear industry.

(E) The only serious threat posed by a nuclear accident would be to the financial security of the nuclear industry.

PrepTest107 Sec1 Q21

Step 3: An important LSAT concept, such as a paradox, in an Inference stimulus will likely be the focus of the correct answer. Here the government is making contradictory claims regarding nuclear power.	Step 4: (B) is correct. This merely restates the idea that the government's claims are contradictory.

Wrong answers: (A) One of the claims must be false, but it is not known which one based on the evidence. Even though the author concludes that the claim about safety must be false, the question stem dictates that the answer should not be based on that conclusion but rather on the "statements offered in support the . . . conclusion." (C) As with choice (A), you cannot know which of the two claims by the government is false. (D) 180. The information suggests that unlimited liability at least could pose a threat to the financial security of the nuclear industry. (E) 180. The information suggests that at least one of the government's claims, potentially the claim regarding the safety of nuclear power, is false.

Step 2: Cataloging the statements reveals that the stimulus is a list of benefits derived from raising the humidity.	Step 1: A question directing the use of "information above" to "support" an answer indicates an Inference question; in this case, select the choice that is *not* supported by the stimulus.

15. Raising the humidity of a room protects furniture, draperies, and computers from damage caused by excessively dry air. Further, it can make people feel warmer, helps the body's defenses against viruses, and alleviates some skin rashes.

Each of the following is supported by the information above EXCEPT:

(A) Humidity can be bad for computers.

(B) A room can be too dry for the optimal maintenance of its furnishings.

(C) Dry air can feel cooler than humid air of the same temperature.

(D) Increased humidity can be beneficial to the skin.

(E) The human immune system can benefit from humidity.

PrepTest106 Sec3 Q4

Step 3: Since the stimulus consists entirely of a list of *benefits* of raising the humidity, what would *not* be supported by the information is something negative about a rise in humidity.	Step 4: (A) is correct. The stimulus in no way suggests that humidity can be bad.

Wrong answers: (B) The indication that raising the humidity can help protect furnishings supports this. (C) The indication that raising humidity can make people feel warmer supports this. (D) The stimulus indicates increased humidity can alleviate skin rashes. (E) The stimulus indicates increased humidity can help defend against viruses.

Reflect For some students, Inference questions can be among some of the most challenging types of questions on the LSAT. Some students find it difficult to avoid bringing in outside information and knowledge. Others are tempted by answer choices that make overly strong deductions. Practice your Inference question skills whenever you read magazine articles or newspaper editorials. Catalog facts and paraphrase the author's statements. Ask yourself whether the author has drawn valid deductions from the facts she cites. Or maybe she exaggerated certain statements. Or maybe she even relied on assumptions and outside knowledge to make inferences that were not directly supported. No matter how strong your analytical skills are now, you'll likely become a much more rigorous and critical reader in law school. Consider your practice with Inference questions as a head start in your legal education (and as an added bonus, you'll also be improving your LSAT score).

Principle Questions Asking for Inferences

In Chapter 4, you learned about Principle questions that reward the same skills tested in Assumption and Strengthen questions—the ability to identify the assumption that underlies the argument. Other Principle questions, however, mimic Inference questions. The stimulus in these Principle questions may state a principle and ask you to identify a specific case that appropriately applies the principle, or the stimulus may present a specific case and ask you to infer the principle from which that case follows. Either way, you'll be rewarded for approaching these questions with the same skills you learned and practiced for standard Inference questions.

Most recent tests have featured one Apply the Principle–Inference question and one or two Identify the Principle–Inference questions.

Here's a typical question asking you to infer the principle illustrated by the specific case described in the stimulus.

Nearly everyone has complained of a mistaken utility bill that cannot easily be corrected or of computer files that cannot readily be retrieved. Yet few people today would tolerate waiting in long lines while clerks search for information that can now be found in seconds, and almost no one who has used a word processor would return to a typewriter.

The information above conforms most closely to which one of the following principles?

(A) The fact that people complain about some consequences of technology cannot be taken as a reliable indication that they would choose to live without it.

(B) If people do not complain about some technology, then it is probably not a significant factor in their daily lives.

(C) The degree to which technologies elicit complaints from people is always an accurate measure of the extent to which people have become dependent on them.

(D) The complaints people make about technological innovations are more reliable evidence of the importance of those innovations than the choices people actually make.

(E) The less willing people are to do without technology the more likely they are to complain about the effects of the technology.

PrepTest105 Sec4 Q12

Note that the question stem asks for an answer containing a principle that *conforms to* the scenario or individual case described in the stimulus. That tells you that the correct answer will represent a broad rule that can be applied to the specific situation in the stimulus. Apply the Principle questions swap the places of the narrow case and the broad rule. These questions state a broad rule in the stimulus and ask you to identify the answer choice containing a narrow case that correctly applies the principle. In both formats, you can think of your job as identifying the one answer choice that provides a perfect one-to-one matchup with the stimulus.

Prepare

LEARNING OBJECTIVES

In this section, you'll learn to:

- Infer a principle (general rule) from a specific case that illustrates it.
- Identify a specific case that appropriately applies a principle (general rule).
- Identify and answer Identify the Principle–Inference questions.
- Identify and answer Apply the Principle questions.

Infer a Principle (General Rule) from a Specific Case that Illustrates It

The stimuli for Principle questions that ask you to identify the principle illustrated by a specific case tend to fall into two broad categories: (1) cases that describe a set of actions and outcomes, and (2) cases that make recommendations. Take a look at an example of each.

Cases that Describe Actions and Outcomes

Let's use the introductory question to illustrate how to attack Infer a Principle questions for stimuli that describe a specific situation, action, or outcome. You want to try to generalize the case into a rule covering other, similar cases. In discussing the relative merits of computers, in very broad terms, what is the author pointing out? Can you paraphrase the outcome generally without using the specific subject matters (utility bills, computer files, waiting in line, typewriters) mentioned in the stimulus?

Take a look at an LSAT expert's thinking as it relates to this stimulus.

Step 2: The contrast word "yet" highlights a paradox: While people are often frustrated with certain inconveniences of modern technologies, they don't want to return to older modes of technology. Generalization: People may complain about the *new way* despite not wanting to return to the *old way*.	**Step 1:** The Keywords "conforms closely to . . . principles" indicate that this is a Principle question.
Nearly everyone has complained of a mistaken utility bill that cannot easily be corrected or of computer files that cannot readily be retrieved. Yet few people today would tolerate waiting in long lines while clerks search for information that can now be found in seconds, and almost no one who has used a word processor would return to a typewriter.	The information above conforms most closely to which one of the following principles? *PrepTest105 Sec4 Q12*

The LSAT expert first recognizes all the helpful hints that can be gleaned from Principle question stems. The question stem tells her that the answer choices contain the principle or broad generalization, while the stimulus merely contains "information," which will often be referred to as a "situation." Because the question stem here did not ask us to analyze the "reasoning" or "argument," there is no need to untangle the stimulus into evidence and conclusion. Instead, our prediction here will consist of putting the specific situation into very broad terms. The correct answer might be in somewhat more specific language and possibly use some terminology from the stimulus, but it could well be as generalized as the LSAT expert's prediction.

(A) The fact that people complain about some consequences of technology cannot be taken as a reliable indication that they would choose to live without it.

(B) If people do not complain about some technology, then it is probably not a significant factor in their daily lives.

(C) The degree to which technologies elicit complaints from people is always an accurate measure of the extent to which people have become dependent on them.

(D) The complaints people make about technological innovations are more reliable evidence of the importance of those innovations than the choices people actually make.

(E) The less willing people are to do without technology the more likely they are to complain about the effects of the technology.

PrepTest105 Sec4 Q12

Answer choice (A) neatly matches the prediction. Principle questions can be very intuitive. Don't overthink them and don't be intimidated by all the variations in the question stems (principle in stimulus, principle in answers, argument based, or non-argument based). In each case, you are just matching a situation to a generalization, and the question stems almost always will provide you clear guidance on what you will find in the stimulus and the answer choices.

Cases that Make Recommendations

Sometimes, a Principle question may ask you to infer a general rule from a specific case in which the author advances a recommendation, prediction, or value judgment—in other words, when the author makes an argument. Your task then becomes to paraphrase that argument in general terms. Rather than complicating, this simplifies your task because there is a routine way to paraphrase any argument: If [this type of Evidence], then [this Conclusion].

Take a look at the following example.

Step 2: Conclusion: Universities should use only open-source software. *because* Evidence: i) Open-source software better embodies values of scholarship; ii) scholarship is central to mission of universities. Paraphrase of Principle: If some tool or resource better embodies values central to mission of a university (or some organization) then it should be used.	**Step 1:** The Keywords "reasoning most closely conforms to . . . principles" tells us this is a Principle question. Because it mentions the commentator's "reasoning," we know that the stimulus will be in *conclusion, because evidence* form.
Commentator: In academic scholarship, sources are always cited, and methodology and theoretical assumptions are set out, so as to allow critical study, replication, and expansion of scholarship. In open-source software, the code in which the program is written can be viewed and modified by individual users for their purposes without getting permission from the producer or paying a fee. In contrast, the code of proprietary software is kept secret, and modifications can be made only by the producer, for a fee. This shows that open-source software better matches the values embodied in academic scholarship, and since scholarship is central to the mission of universities, universities should use only open-source software.	The commentator's reasoning most closely conforms to which one of the following principles? *PrepTest123 Sec3 Q14*

What a relief that you only need to paraphrase the *reasoning* in this stimulus! The LSAT expert used the evidence Keywords and phrases ("this shows that" and "since") and the conclusion-indicating opinion word "should" to home in on the last sentence. Do you see the match for the prediction?

(A) Whatever software tools are most advanced and can achieve the goals of academic scholarship are the ones that should alone be used in universities.

(B) Universities should use the type of software technology that is least expensive, as long as that type of software technology is adequate for the purposes of academic scholarship.

(C) Universities should choose the type of software technology that best matches the values embodied in the activities that are central to the mission of universities.

(D) The form of software technology that best matches the values embodied in the activities that are central to the mission of universities is the form of software technology that is most efficient for universities to use.

(E) A university should not pursue any activity that would block the achievement of the goals of academic scholarship at that university.

PrepTest123 Sec3 Q14

Answer choice (C) is right on point! The argument is all about choosing what best matches the values central to the mission of the university. The author's reason is not what is *most advanced* (choice (A)), or what is *least expensive* (choice (B)). And answer choice (D) misses the argument's recommendation to actually *use* the technology, rather than simply judging something as the *most efficient* to use. Finally, answer choice (E) states what universities should not do, which is outside the scope of the argument in the stimulus, which was all about what universities *should* do.

Now let's look at Apply the Principle questions, in which the stimuli contain broad rules and the answer choices present specific situations.

Identify a Specific Case that Applies a Principle (General Rule)

Apply the Principle questions, more than most LSAT questions, mirror the kind of deductions a student makes on a law school exam. For example, as a first-year law student, you will learn the elements of the tort of battery: the intentional offensive touching of a person without consent. The exam question will present you with some facts. Your task will be to match the facts to the elements of battery to determine if the defendant described in the exam's fact pattern is liable for the offense. Was the victim touched? Was the touch intentional? Was the intentional touch offensive? Did the victim give consent to be touched? If you determine that the given facts correctly match each of the elements of the rule, you can conclude that the defendant is liable. But, if even one of those elements is missing, the defendant will prevail.

In the same way, Apply the Principle questions will present you with one or more rules, very often in the form of conditional Formal Logic statements. Your task is to examine five cases (the five answer choices) and select the one that perfectly matches or applies the rule(s) articulated in the stimulus.

Take a look at how an LSAT expert analyzes an Apply the Principle question. Focus on how he identifies the principles or general rules found in the stimulus.

Step 2:	Step 1:
Step 2: The stimulus contains a single statement in conditional Formal Logic: If harmful substance and available to the public → should tax at levels to discourage use If don't tax at levels to discourage use → either not harmful or not available to public	**Step 1:** The Keywords "application of the . . . principle" indicate that this is an Apply the Principle question.

Politician: Governments should tax any harmful substance that is available to the general public at a level that the tax would discourage continued use of the substance.

Which one of the following is an application of the politician's principle of taxation?

(A) The tax on products containing sugar is raised in an effort to raise revenue to be applied to the health costs resulting from the long-term use of these products.

(B) The tax on certain pain relievers that, even though harmful, are available over the counter is raised, since studies have shown that the demand for these products will not be affected.

(C) The tax on a pesticide that contains an organic compound harmful to human beings is raised to give people an incentive to purchase pesticides not containing the compound.

(D) The tax on domestically produced alcoholic beverages is not raised, since recent studies show that the tax would have a negative impact on the tourist industry.

(E) The tax on products that emit fluorocarbons, substances that have proven to be harmful to the earth's ozone layer, is lowered to stimulate the development of new, less environmentally harmful ways of using these substances.

PrepTest104 Sec4 Q1

Step 3: In Apply the Principle questions, it is common for the principle to be a Formal Logic rule. The correct answer will match the statement in the stimulus: *If a substance is harmful and available to the public, it should be taxed at a level that discourages its use.*	**Step 4:** (C) is correct. The product mentioned here is harmful and, apparently, available to the public. The politician's principle holds that such a product should be taxed to discourage its use.

Wrong answers: (A) Distortion. Here, the tax is used to *raise revenue*, not to *discourage the use* of the harmful substance. (B) Distortion. This choice fails to apply the politician's principle because the tax will *not* discourage use. (D) Distortion. This answer choice doesn't state that alcohol is harmful or that it is available to the general public. If it were both, the politician would hold that it should be taxed at a rate that discourages use. The politician makes no exception for *other* negative impacts. (E) Distortion. Nothing in the politician's principle tells us when taxes on a product should be lowered.

Identify the Principle–Inference and Apply the Principle Questions

When an LSAT expert confronts a question stem identifying a Principle question calling for an inference, the first thing she's likely to note is whether the broad, general rule is in the stimulus or in the correct answer. Take a look at the thinking that helps a well-trained test taker distinguish between "Identify the Principle–Inference" questions and their "Apply the Principle" cousins.

Which one of the following is an application of the politician's principle of taxation? *PrepTest104 Sec4 Q1*	The correct answer will be a specific case that applies the principle (broad rule) of taxation stated in the stimulus. This is an Apply the Principle question. v
The commentator's reasoning most closely conforms to which one of the following principles? *PrepTest123 Sec3 Q14*	The correct answer will rephrase the specific argument ("reasoning") above into a more broad and generalized principle. This is an Identify the Principle question. ^

Practice Practice identifying your task in the following question stems. For each, make sure you can accurately say whether the stimulus contains the broad principle and the answer choices contain specific cases, or vice versa.

LSAT Question	My Analysis
16. The reasoning above conforms most closely to which one of the following principles? *PrepTest105 Sec4 Q24*	
17. Which one of the following judgments most closely conforms to the principle cited above? *PrepTest104 Sec4 Q3*	
18. Which one of the following is an application of the economic principle above? *PrepTest106 Sec1 Q10*	
19. Which one of the following most closely conforms to the principle the ethicist endorses? *PrepTest106 Sec3 Q23*	

Expert Analysis for the Practice exercise may be found on the following page. ▶ ▶ ▶

Expert Analysis

Here's how the LSAT expert would examine each of those question stems and what she would anticipate about the rest of the question.

LSAT Question	Analysis
16. The reasoning above conforms most closely to which one of the following principles? *PrepTest105 Sec4 Q24*	The correct answer is a broad principle that summarizes the argument ("reasoning") above. This is an Identify the Principle question.
17. Which one of the following judgments most closely conforms to the principle cited above? *PrepTest104 Sec4 Q3*	The correct answer will be a decision ("judgment") about a specific case that matches the broad principles set forth in the stimulus. This is an Apply the Principle question.
18. Which one of the following is an application of the economic principle above? *PrepTest106 Sec1 Q10*	The correct answer will be a specific application of the broad economic principle described in the stimulus. This is an Apply the Principle question.
19. Which one of the following most closely conforms to the principle the ethicist endorses? *PrepTest106 Sec3 Q23*	The correct answer will conform to the broad ethical principle described in the stimulus. This is an Apply the Principle question.

Practice Apply the Kaplan Method to the following questions. After each, compare your work to the thinking of an LSAT expert on the following pages.

Step 2:	**Step 1:**

20. It is a principle of economics that a nation can experience economic growth only when consumer confidence is balanced with a small amount of consumer skepticism.

Which one of the following is an application of the economic principle above?

(A) Any nation in which consumer confidence is balanced with a small amount of consumer skepticism will experience economic growth.

(B) Any nation in which the prevailing attitude of consumers is not skepticism will experience economic growth.

(C) Any nation in which the prevailing attitude of consumers is either exclusively confidence or exclusively skepticism will experience economic growth.

(D) Any nation in which the prevailing attitude of consumers is exclusively confidence will not experience economic growth.

(E) Any nation in which consumer skepticism is balanced with a small amount of consumer confidence will experience economic growth.

PrepTest106 Sec1 Q10

Step 3:	**Step 4:**

Step 2:	**Step 1:**

21. A just government never restricts the right of its citizens to act upon their desires except when their acting upon their desires is a direct threat to the health or property of other of its citizens.

Which one of the following judgments most closely conforms to the principle cited above?

(A) A just government would not ban the sale of sports cars, but it could prohibit unrestricted racing of them on public highways.

(B) An unjust government would abolish many public services if these services did not require compulsory labor.

(C) A just government would provide emergency funds to survivors of unavoidable accidents but not to survivors of avoidable ones.

(D) A just government would not censor writings of Shakespeare, but it could censor magazines and movies that criticize the government.

(E) An unjust government would incarcerate one of its citizens even though it had been several years since that citizen harmed someone.

PrepTest104 Sec4 Q3

Step 3:	**Step 4:**

Step 2:	**Step 1:**

22. If an external force intervenes to give members of a community political self-determination, then that political community will almost surely fail to be truly free, since it is during the people's struggle to become free by their own efforts that the political virtues necessary for maintaining freedom have the best chance of arising.

The reasoning above conforms most closely to which one of the following principles?

(A) Political freedom is a virtue that a community can attain through an external force.

(B) Self-determination is not the first political virtue that the members of a community achieve in their struggle to become free.

(C) A community cannot remain free without first having developed certain political virtues.

(D) Political self-determination is required if a community is to remain truly free.

(E) Real freedom should not be imposed on a community by external forces.

PrepTest105 Sec4 Q24

Step 3:	**Step 4:**

Step 2:	**Step 1:**

23. Ethicist: It is widely believed that it is always wrong to tell lies, but this is a rule almost no one fully complies with. In fact, lying is often the morally appropriate thing to do. It is morally correct to lie when telling the truth carries the reasonable expectation of producing considerable physical or psychological harm to others.

Which one of the following most closely conforms to the principle the ethicist endorses?

(A) When Juan asked Judy if the movie they were going to was *North by Northwest*, Judy said yes, though she knew that *Persona* was playing instead. This was the only way Juan would see the film and avoid losing an opportunity for an aesthetically pleasing experience.

(B) A daughter asked her father which candidate he supported, McBride or Chang. Though in fact he preferred Chang, the father responded by saying he preferred McBride, in order to avoid discussion.

(C) A husband told his wife he felt ready to go on a canoe trip, though he had recently had severe chest pains; his wife had determined a year ago that they would go on this trip, so to ask to cancel now would be inconvenient.

(D) A young boy asked his mother if she loved his older sister more than she loved him. The mother said she loved them both to the same degree, even though it was not true.

(E) A friend invited Jamal to a party, but Jamal was afraid that he might see his ex-wife and her new husband there. To spare himself emotional pain, as well as the embarrassment of telling his friend why he did not want to go, Jamal falsely claimed he had to work.

PrepTest106 Sec3 Q23

Step 3:	**Step 4:**

Expert Analysis

Here's how an LSAT expert tackled the questions you just saw. Review her analysis step-by-step, following the Logical Reasoning Method. The more consistently you approach both your practice and review, the faster and more confident you'll be on test day.

Step 2: The stimulus contains a single statement in conditional Formal Logic: If economic growth → confidence and skepticism in balance If confidence and skepticism NOT in balance → NO economic growth	**Step 1:** A principle question with the broad rule in the stimulus and an application of the rule in the choices. Apply the Principle.

20. It is a principle of economics that a nation can experience economic growth only when consumer confidence is balanced with a small amount of consumer skepticism.

Which one of the following is an application of the economic principle above?

(A) Any nation in which consumer confidence is balanced with a small amount of consumer skepticism will experience economic growth.

(B) Any nation in which the prevailing attitude of consumers is not skepticism will experience economic growth.

(C) Any nation in which the prevailing attitude of consumers is either exclusively confidence or exclusively skepticism will experience economic growth.

(D) Any nation in which the prevailing attitude of consumers is exclusively confidence will not experience economic growth.

(E) Any nation in which consumer skepticism is balanced with a small amount of consumer confidence will experience economic growth.

PrepTest106 Sec1 Q10

Step 3: The principle in the stimulus was in Formal Logic form, so the correct answer should match the conditional rule or its contrapositive.	**Step 4:** (D) is correct. All confidence (not balanced) → No growth. This matches the contrapositive.

Wrong answers: (A) Balance → Growth. This choice changes the direction of arrow. (B) Not mostly skeptical → Growth. This choice also changes the direction of the arrow. (C) All confidence or all skepticism (not balanced) → Growth. Distorts the contrapositive. A lack of balance should result in *no* growth. (E) As with choice (A), this choice reverses the direction of the arrow, and, further, distorts the desired balance of confidence with a small amount of skepticism.

Step 2: A rule: a just government never restricts the right of its citizens to act on desires. And an exception: when acting upon desires threatens other citizens' health or property.	**Step 1:** "[M]ost closely conforms to the principle cited above" indicates that in this Principle question, there will be a principle (broad rule) above, and the correct answer will follow that rule. This is an Apply the Principle question.

21. A just government never restricts the right of its citizens to act upon their desires except when their acting upon their desires is a direct threat to the health or property of other of its citizens.

Which one of the following judgments most closely conforms to the principle cited above?

(A) A just government would not ban the sale of sports cars, but it could prohibit unrestricted racing of them on public highways.

(B) An unjust government would abolish many public services if these services did not require compulsory labor.

(C) A just government would provide emergency funds to survivors of unavoidable accidents but not to survivors of avoidable ones.

(D) A just government would not censor writings of Shakespeare, but it could censor magazines and movies that criticize the government.

(E) An unjust government would incarcerate one of its citizens even though it had been several years since that citizen harmed someone.

PrepTest104 Sec4 Q3

Step 3: The exception to the rule doesn't tell us that the government will definitely restrict rights when citizens threaten others' health or property. It's simply a possibility. The firm and hard rule here is that if a citizen does not threaten others' health or property, then a just government will not restrict that person's rights.	**Step 4:** (A) is correct. This follows the rule (and its potential exception) to the letter.

Wrong answers: (B) Outside the Scope. The stimulus doesn't define the behavior of unjust governments. (C) Outside the Scope. The stimulus discusses citizens' desires, not what should be done in the event of an accident. (D) Movies that criticize the government hardly fall under the category of "direct threat to the health or property of other . . . citizens." (E) Outside the Scope. The stimulus doesn't define the behavior of unjust governments.

Step 2: Conclusion: If external forces intervene, then a political community is not truly free. *because* Evidence: One's own struggle to be free develops virtues necessary for maintaining freedom.	**Step 1:** A Principle question in which the stimulus contains *reasoning* and the answers contain *broad principles* is an Identify the Principle question. The correct answer should match the form: If [this Evidence], then [this Conclusion].

22. If an external force intervenes to give members of a community political self-determination, then that political community will almost surely fail to be truly free, since it is during the people's struggle to become free by their own efforts that the political virtues necessary for maintaining freedom have the best chance of arising.

The reasoning above conforms most closely to which one of the following principles?

(A) Political freedom is a virtue that a community can attain through an external force.

(B) Self-determination is not the first political virtue that the members of a community achieve in their struggle to become free.

(C) A community cannot remain free without first having developed certain political virtues.

(D) Political self-determination is required if a community is to remain truly free.

(E) Real freedom should not be imposed on a community by external forces.

PrepTest105 Sec4 Q22

Step 3: The correct answer should indicate: If NOT develop certain political virtues → NOT truly free or the contrapositive: If truly free → developed certain political virtues	**Step 4:** (C) is correct. Translating "without" to "if not," this sentence conforms to "if don't develop certain political virtues → won't be truly free."

Wrong answers: (A) This is a 180. The author believes the intervention of external forces interferes with developing the virtues necessary for freedom. (B) The argument is not concerned with the sequence of achieving different virtues. (D) This is a Distortion. The author indicates that political self-determination, if given by an external force, is not sufficient to be free and that other virtues are necessary. (E) The argument is not concerned with freedom being *imposed*, but with whether an external force *giving* freedom is effective in the long run.

Step 2: Broad rule: If telling the truth would cause considerable physical or psychological harm to others, then it's morally correct to lie.	Step 1: "[M]ost closely conforms to the principle" indicates that this is an Apply the Principle question. There will be a principle (broad rule) above, and the correct answer will follow that rule.

23. Ethicist: It is widely believed that it is always wrong to tell lies, but this is a rule almost no one fully complies with. In fact, lying is often the morally appropriate thing to do. It is morally correct to lie when telling the truth carries the reasonable expectation of producing considerable physical or psychological harm to others.

Which one of the following most closely conforms to the principle the ethicist endorses?

(A) When Juan asked Judy if the movie they were going to was *North by Northwest*, Judy said yes, though she knew that *Persona* was playing instead. This was the only way Juan would see the film and avoid losing an opportunity for an aesthetically pleasing experience.

(B) A daughter asked her father which candidate he supported, McBride or Chang. Though in fact he preferred Chang, the father responded by saying he preferred McBride, in order to avoid discussion.

(C) A husband told his wife he felt ready to go on a canoe trip, though he had recently had severe chest pains; his wife had determined a year ago that they would go on this trip, so to ask to cancel now would be inconvenient.

(D) A young boy asked his mother if she loved his older sister more than she loved him. The mother said she loved them both to the same degree, even though it was not true.

(E) A friend invited Jamal to a party, but Jamal was afraid that he might see his ex-wife and her new husband there. To spare himself emotional pain, as well as the embarrassment of telling his friend why he did not want to go, Jamal falsely claimed he had to work.

PrepTest106 Sec3 Q23

Step 3: Find an answer choice in which someone lies in order to avoid causing physical or psychological harm to others.	Step 4: (D) is correct. The mother lies to prevent psychological harm to her son.

Wrong answers: (A) Judy does not lie to prevent physical or psychological harm to Juan. (B) The father does not lie to prevent physical or psychological harm to his daughter. (C) The husband does not lie to prevent physical or psychological harm to his wife. (E) Jamal lies to prevent physical or psychological harm to *himself*, but not to others.

Reflect Congratulations on acquiring another valuable LSAT (and law school) skill. In the coming days, pay attention to conversations you have in which people apply or infer principles from specific events and situations. Even simple statements can provide practice for these Principle/Inference question types. For example, if you hear a father tell a child, "You should clean up your room because I told you to," he's implying the principle that children should obey their parents. On the other hand, if you hear a mom say, "You need to clean up your room because everyone in this family has responsibilities," she's implying a different principle. What is it?

We generalize rules from specific cases all the time, and we often expect people to act in a certain way or have a particular response because of general rules we follow. As you encounter situations of this type, take the time to make the implied rules explicit to yourself and to note the principles upon which people are acting even when they haven't articulated those principles.

Resolving Discrepancies and Paradox Questions

One more non-argument-based Logical Reasoning question type, the Paradox question, features a stimulus that contains two seemingly contradictory statements. That's the essence of a paradox, a situation that seems impossible, inconsistent, or contradictory but actually isn't. The correct answer to an LSAT Paradox question will always be a fact that, if true, will help explain how the apparent discrepancy can be resolved, that is, how the two problematic facts can be shown to be consistent. Over the past five years, most LSATs have included three or four Paradox questions.

Take a look at a typical LSAT Paradox question. Go ahead and try it now. You'll see this question explained in full a little later in the chapter.

Because of the recent recession in Country A, most magazines published there have experienced decreases in advertising revenue, so much so that the survival of the most widely read magazines is in grave doubt. At the same time, however, more people in Country A are reading more magazines than ever before, and the number of financially successful magazines in Country A is greater than ever.

Which one the following, if true, most helps to resolve the apparent discrepancy in the information above?

(A) Most magazines reduce the amount they charge for advertisements during a recession.

(B) The audience for a successful television show far exceeds the readership of even the most widely read magazine.

(C) Advertising is the main source of revenue only for the most widely read magazines; other magazines rely on circulation for their revenue.

(D) Because of the recession, people in Country A have cut back on magazine subscriptions and are reading borrowed magazines.

(E) More of the new general interest magazines that were launched this year in Country A have survived than survived in previous years.

PrepTest104 Sec1 Q7

Notice that the question stem asks you to resolve the apparent discrepancy in the stimulus. Two terms should really stand out: "resolve" and "apparent discrepancy." Virtually every Paradox question will ask you to explain, resolve, or reconcile two statements. The fact that these statements merely *appear* contradictory or inconsistent tells you that they can actually be compatible.

Prepare

LEARNING OBJECTIVES

In this section, you'll learn to:

- Identify and paraphrase an apparent contradiction.
- Infer what must be true to resolve an apparent contradiction.
- Identify and answer Paradox questions.
- Identify and answer Paradox EXCEPT questions.

Identify and Paraphrase an Apparent Contradiction and Infer What Must Be True to Resolve It

Before you can spot the answer choice that will explain or resolve the paradox in the stimulus, you must be sure you've correctly understood the seeming discrepancy. To make sure you are clear on the scope and terms of the situation, always paraphrase the paradox in your own words. Once you've got a clear picture of the situation, you can predict the kind of fact that will help explain that the facts or statements are actually compatible.

Take a look at how an LSAT expert identifies and paraphrases the paradoxes found in a couple of Paradox question stimuli. You'll see that there is almost always a Contrast Keyword signaling the facts or assertions apparently in conflict. Let's start with the stimulus from the example at the beginning of this section.

LSAT Question	Analysis
Because of the recent recession in Country A, most magazines published there have experienced decreases in advertising revenue, so much so that the survival of the most widely read magazines is in grave doubt. At the same time, however, more people in Country A are reading more magazines than ever before, and the number of financially successful magazines in Country A is greater than ever. *PrepTest104 Sec1 Q7*	Fact 1: Most magazines, including those that are most widely read, are suffering critical losses in ad revenue. *Yet* Fact 2: The number of financially successful magazines is greater than ever. Paradox: How can it be that most magazines are losing ad revenue but the number of successful magazines is growing?

Can you anticipate the kind of fact that might help resolve the apparent discrepancy here? Note that the LSAT expert was precise when forming her paraphrase of the paradox. It would distort the stimulus to say that the magazines are losing "money" or becoming "less profitable." Instead, she notes that most magazines are losing ad revenue. But is that the only way magazines can generate income? What if we learned that more magazines were being sold at newsstands? Or what if we discovered that magazine subscriptions were on the rise? And do magazines have to increase revenue to be successful? What if they've lost ad revenue but have found a way to cut production costs so significantly that their profits have actually increased? The LSAT expert recognizes

CHAPTER 5

that there are many different ways the paradox could be resolved, but she doesn't spend a great amount of time thinking through them. Instead, her prediction is much simpler: The correct answer will be anything that explains the central paradox outlined in the stimulus.

Here's another example. Read the stimulus and review the expert's analysis of it.

LSAT Question	Analysis
When a community opens a large shopping mall, it often expects a boost to the local economy, and in fact a large amount of economic activity goes on in these malls. Yet the increase in the local economy is typically much smaller than the total amount of economic activity that goes on in the mall. *PrepTest106 Sec1 Q17*	Fact 1: Communities expect a boost in the local economy after opening a shopping mall. *Yet* Fact 2: The increase in the local economy is smaller than the amount of economic activity occurring in the mall. Paradox: Why does the local economy not receive an economic boost equal to or larger than the amount of economic activity in the new mall?

If you find yourself scratching your head after reading a Paradox stimulus, good for you. That means you've really spotted the apparent contradiction. But remember that there is *always* a way to reconcile or resolve the discrepancy in these LSAT questions. What fact might explain why the local economy doesn't receive a boost, if the mall is a hub of economic activity? Again, you'll find the answer by sticking close to the terms of the stimulus. The two facts aren't really talking about the same thing. In Fact 1, we learn that local economies expect to see a *boost*, or increase in their economy. In Fact 2, the scope of the stimulus shifts to the *total amount of economic activity* at the shopping malls. But do we know if the economic activity, as large as it might be, is providing a boost to the local economy? What if the stores in the mall are all running a deficit? What if the mall only has economic activity because of investment from the local economy? Stay focused on the big difference between the two facts when you evaluate the answer choices to this paradox later in the chapter.

Now try doing the same kind of analysis on your own.

Prepare Untangle the following stimuli. Identify the two facts that the author believes are in conflict. Paraphrase the paradox or apparent discrepancy the facts raise. Then anticipate the kind of fact(s) that would explain, resolve, or reconcile the seeming contradiction.

LSAT Question	My Analysis
24. The symptoms of hepatitis A appear no earlier than 60 days after a person has been infected. In a test of a hepatitis A vaccine, 50 people received the vaccine and 50 people received a harmless placebo. Although some people from each group eventually exhibited symptoms of hepatitis A, the vaccine as used in the test is completely effective in preventing infection with the hepatitis A virus. *PrepTest107 Sec1 Q10*	
25. The indigenous people of Tasmania are clearly related to the indigenous people of Australia, but were separated from them when the land bridge between Australia and Tasmania disappeared approximately 10,000 years ago. Two thousand years after the disappearance of the land bridge, however, there were major differences between the culture and technology of the indigenous Tasmanians and those of the indigenous Australians. The indigenous Tasmanians, unlike their Australian relatives, had no domesticated dogs, fishing nets, polished stone tools, or hunting implements like the boomerang and the spear-thrower. *PrepTest107 Sec1 Q25*	
26. Generally speaking, if the same crop is sown in a field for several successive years, growth in the later years is poorer than growth in the earlier years, since nitrogen in the soil becomes depleted. Even though alfalfa is a nitrogen-fixing plant and thus increases the amount of nitrogen in the soil, surprisingly, it too, if planted in the same field year after year, grows less well in the later years than it does in the earlier years. *PrepTest106 Sec1 Q8*	

Did you take advantage of the Contrast Keywords in each example? If so, you likely spotted the apparent contradiction. Having done that, were you able to see how the paradox might be resolved? Compare your analysis to that of the LSAT expert on the next page.

Expert Analysis

Here's how an LSAT expert untangled the stimuli you just saw. Take note of the expert's paraphrasing of the paradox in each example and how she anticipates the apparent discrepancies may be resolved.

LSAT Question	Analysis
24. The symptoms of hepatitis A appear no earlier than 60 days after a person has been infected. In a test of a hepatitis A vaccine, 50 people received the vaccine and 50 people received a harmless placebo. Although some people from each group eventually exhibited symptoms of hepatitis A, the vaccine as used in the test is completely effective in preventing infection with the hepatitis A virus. *PrepTest107 Sec1 Q10*	Fact 1: A vaccine is completely effective in preventing hepatitis A infection. *Yet* Fact 2: Some people who received the vaccine eventually exhibited symptoms of hepatitis A. Paradox: If the vaccine is completely effective in preventing hepatitis A infection, how could people who received the vaccine later show symptoms of hepatitis A?
25. The indigenous people of Tasmania are clearly related to the indigenous people of Australia, but were separated from them when the land bridge between Australia and Tasmania disappeared approximately 10,000 years ago. Two thousand years after the disappearance of the land bridge, however, there were major differences between the culture and technology of the indigenous Tasmanians and those of the indigenous Australians. The indigenous Tasmanians, unlike their Australian relatives, had no domesticated dogs, fishing nets, polished stone tools, or hunting implements like the boomerang and the spear-thrower. *PrepTest107 Sec1 Q25*	Fact 1: Indigenous peoples of Tasmania and Australia are clearly related and are only separated by the disappearance of a land bridge. *Yet* Fact 2: Two thousand years after the disappearance of the land bridge, Australians had a number of impressive cultural and technological inventions that the Tasmanians did not. Paradox: Why would there be such great differences between two groups of people, despite their being related and only separated two thousand years ago?
26. Generally speaking, if the same crop is sown in a field for several successive years, growth in the later years is poorer than growth in the earlier years, since nitrogen in the soil becomes depleted. Even though alfalfa is a nitrogen-fixing plant and thus increases the amount of nitrogen in the soil, surprisingly, it too, if planted in the same field year after year, grows less well in the later years than it does in the earlier years. *PrepTest106 Sec1 Q8*	Fact 1: Alfalfa doesn't deplete the soil of nitrogen. *Yet* Fact 2: Alfalfa shows the same reduction in crop yield after years in the same field as do crops that deplete nitrogen. Paradox: Why does alfalfa production decline over the years (just like other plants), even though it has solved the problem from the loss of nitrogen?

You will see the complete questions accompanying the stimuli for these questions a little later in this section.

As you reflect on the stimuli you just untangled, take a moment to consider a key distinction. In an Inference question, the stimulus provides facts that are mutually consistent and can be combined to create a new deduction. By contrast, a Paradox question provides facts that appear to be incompatible but actually are not. Allow your paraphrase of the apparent discrepancy or paradox to guide your prediction of the correct answer. Ask what is in need of explanation. Indeed, you should be able to say, "The fact that *x* and *y* are both true is confusing." Then, when you select the correct answer, you can say, "Okay. This clears it up."

Paradox Questions and Paradox EXCEPT Questions

Paradox question stems overwhelmingly use one of three verbs: *resolve*, *reconcile*, or *explain*. Sometimes, there will be an extra word in the question stem indicating that it is a discrepancy, anomaly, or paradox. Other times, the content of the paradox will even be mentioned in the question stem. Rarely, the test will ask a Paradox EXCEPT question, asking for the only answer that doesn't help to reconcile the seeming contradiction. Take a look at how an LSAT expert analyzes Paradox question stems.

LSAT Question	Analysis
Which one of the following, if true, most helps to explain the discrepancy described above? *PrepTest106 Sec1 Q17*	The correct answer will be a fact that reconciles the apparent discrepancy—a Paradox question.
Each of the following, if true, contributes to reconciling the apparent discrepancy indicated above EXCEPT: *PrepTest101 Sec3 Q14*	The four wrong answers will provide facts that help explain the apparent discrepancy. The correct answer will not explain it (either by deepening the paradox or by being Outside the Scope)—a Paradox EXCEPT question.

Practice Practice Step 1 of the Logical Reasoning Method on a handful of Paradox question stems. Take note of the verbs signaling a Paradox question. Is there any additional guidance in the stem helping you see what to look for as you untangle the stimulus? How would you characterize the correct and incorrect answer choices?

LSAT Question	My Analysis
27. Which one of the following, if true, most helps resolve the apparent discrepancy in the information above? *PrepTest107 Sec1 Q10*	
28. Which one of the following, if true, most helps to explain the similarity described above between alfalfa and non-nitrogen-fixing plants? *PrepTest106 Sec1 Q8*	
29. Each of the following, if true, would contribute to an explanation of differences described above EXCEPT: *PrepTest107 Sec1 Q25*	

Expert Analysis

Here's how the LSAT expert viewed each of those question stems.

LSAT Question	Analysis
27. Which one of the following, if true, most helps resolve the apparent discrepancy in the information above? *PrepTest107 Sec1 Q10*	The correct answer will be a fact that reconciles the apparent discrepancy in the stimulus above—a Paradox question.
28. Which one of the following, if true, most helps to explain the similarity described above between alfalfa and non-nitrogen-fixing plants? *PrepTest106 Sec1 Q8*	The correct answer will be a fact that explains why alfalfa acts in a way similar to non-nitrogen-fixing plants—a Paradox question.
29. Each of the following, if true, would contribute to an explanation of differences described above EXCEPT: *PrepTest107 Sec1 Q25*	The four incorrect answers will explain the differences described in the stimulus. The correct answer will deepen the mystery or discuss something beyond the scope of the stimulus—a Paradox EXCEPT question.

Notice that the LSAT expert used the question stem not only to identify the question type but also to anticipate how she would need to approach the stimulus. Paradox EXCEPT questions ask for an answer choice that does *not* resolve the contradiction. Wrong answer choices provide four possible explanations, and the correct answer will likely be Outside the Scope of the facts or will only talk about one of the facts.

LSAT STRATEGY

Remember this about Paradox questions:

- The statements in a Paradox question stimulus appear to be contradictory only because a fact is missing that explains how everything can be true.
- The correct answer to a Paradox question must account for both of the apparently contradictory facts and not merely state that the situation described is common or that one of the facts in the paradox is easy to understand.

Paradox questions run the gamut of difficulty levels. Don't become complacent if you find that some of the Paradox questions you practice seem obvious or easy. That's true of all question types. The best test takers are rigorous and vigilant against sloppy reading or taking something for granted. Taking time to understand the nature of the paradoxical facts in the stimulus is essential to recognizing what is needed to explain them.

Before you practice full Paradox questions, take a look at the LSAT expert's analysis of the questions associated with the stimuli you've seen in this section. Pay close attention to how the expert predicts the kind of fact she will find in the correct answer and to why she eliminated each of the wrong answers in these questions.

Step 2: Fact 1: A vaccine is completely effective in preventing hepatitis A infection. *Yet* Fact 2: Some people who received the vaccine eventually exhibited symptoms of hepatitis A.	**Step 1:** The Keywords "most helps to resolve the apparent discrepancy" indicate that this is a Paradox question.

The symptoms of hepatitis A appear no earlier than 60 days after a person has been infected. In a test of a hepatitis A vaccine, 50 people received the vaccine and 50 people received a harmless placebo. Although some people from each group eventually exhibited symptoms of hepatitis A, the vaccine as used in the test is completely effective in preventing infection with the hepatitis A virus.

Which one of the following, if true, most helps resolve the apparent discrepancy in the information above?

(A) The placebo did not produce any side effects that resembled any of the symptoms of hepatitis A.

(B) More members of the group that had received the placebo recognized their symptoms as symptoms of hepatitis A than did members of the group that had received the vaccine.

(C) The people who received the placebo were in better overall physical condition than were the people who received the vaccine.

(D) The vaccinated people who exhibited symptoms of hepatitis A were infected with the hepatitis A virus before being vaccinated.

(E) Of the people who developed symptoms of hepatitis A, those who received the vaccine recovered more quickly, on average, than those who did not.

PrepTest107 Sec1 Q10

Step 3: The correct choice will answer this question: If the vaccine is completely effective in preventing hepatitis A infection, how could people who received the vaccine later show symptoms of hepatitis A?	**Step 4:** (D) is correct. This solves the mystery. The vaccine prevents hepatitis A, but nowhere in the stimulus does it say it cures it.

Wrong answers: (A) What the placebo did or didn't do won't explain why people getting the vaccine showed symptoms. (B) What happened to the placebo group won't solve the mystery. (C) What happened to the placebo group won't solve the mystery. (E) Recovering more or less quickly doesn't explain why some who received the vaccine still showed symptoms.

Step 2: Fact 1: Alfalfa doesn't deplete the soil of nitrogen. *Yet* Fact 2: Alfalfa shows the same reduction in crop yield after years in the same field as do crops that deplete nitrogen.	**Step 1:** The Keywords "most helps to explain" indicates that this is a Paradox question.

Generally speaking, if the same crop is sown in a field for several successive years, growth in the later years is poorer than growth in the earlier years, since nitrogen in the soil becomes depleted. Even though alfalfa is a nitrogen-fixing plant and thus increases the amount of nitrogen in the soil, surprisingly, it too, if planted in the same field year after year, grows less well in the later years than it does in the earlier years.

Which one of the following, if true, most helps to explain the similarity described above between alfalfa and non-nitrogen-fixing plants?

(A) Some kinds of plants grow more rapidly and are more productive when they are grown among other kinds of plants rather than being grown only among plants of their own kind.

(B) Alfalfa increases the amount of nitrogen in the soil by taking nitrogen from the air and releasing it in a form that is usable by most kinds of plants.

(C) Certain types of plants, including alfalfa, produce substances that accumulate in the soil and that are toxic to the plants that produce those substances.

(D) Alfalfa increases nitrogen in the soil in which it grows only if a certain type of soil bacteria is present in the soil.

(E) Alfalfa is very sensitive to juglone, a compound that is exuded from the leaves of black walnut trees.

PrepTest106 Sec1 Q8

Step 3: The correct choice will answer this question: Why does alfalfa production decline over the years (just like other plants), even though it has solved the problem from the loss of nitrogen?	**Step 4:** (C) is correct. An "accumulation of toxins" explains why alfalfa yields decrease over time if planted in the same field despite alfalfa's ability to increase nitrogen in the soil.

Wrong answers: (A) This information might not even pertain to alfalfa, and so can't explain the mystery. (B) This explains how alfalfa increases nitrogen levels in the soil, but not why yields decrease. (D) Without knowing whether the bacteria is beneficial or harmful, it's impossible to determine if this explains alfalfa's decreased yields. (E) This fact does nothing to explain why alfalfa (despite its being a nitrogen-fixing plant) grows less well when planted in the same field year after year.

Step 2: Fact 1: Indigenous peoples of Tasmania and Australia are clearly related and are only separated by the disappearance of a land bridge. *Yet* Fact 2: Two thousand years after the disappearance of the land bridge, Australians had a number of impressive cultural and technological inventions that the Tasmanians did not.	**Step 1:** The Keywords "contribute to an explanation" indicate that this is a Paradox question. "EXCEPT" alerts us to the fact that the four wrong answers will help resolve the apparent discrepancy, while the correct answer will either have no impact or deepen the mystery.

The indigenous people of Tasmania are clearly related to the indigenous people of Australia, but were separated from them when the land bridge between Australia and Tasmania disappeared approximately 10,000 years ago. Two thousand years after the disappearance of the land bridge, however, there were major differences between the culture and technology of the indigenous Tasmanians and those of the indigenous Australians. The indigenous Tasmanians, unlike their Australian relatives, had no domesticated dogs, fishing nets, polished stone tools, or hunting implements like the boomerang and the spear-thrower.

Each of the following, if true, would contribute to an explanation of differences described above EXCEPT:

(A) After the disappearance of the land bridge the indigenous Tasmanians simply abandoned certain practices and technologies that they had originally shared with their Australian relatives.

(B) Devices such as the spear-thrower and the boomerang were developed by the indigenous Tasmanians more than 10,000 years ago.

(C) Technological innovations such as fishing nets, polished stone tools, and so on, were imported to Australia by Polynesian explorers more recently than 10,000 years ago.

(D) Indigenous people of Australia developed hunting implements like the boomerang and the spear-thrower after the disappearance of the land bridge.

(E) Although the technological and cultural innovations were developed in Australia more than 10,000 years ago, they were developed by groups in northern Australia with whom the indigenous Tasmanians had no contact prior to the disappearance of the land bridge.

PrepTest107 Sec1 Q25

Step 3: The four wrong choices will answer this question: Why would there be such great differences between two groups of people, despite their being related and only separated two thousand years ago? The correct answer will either deepen the mystery or have no impact.	**Step 4:** (B) is correct. This does nothing to explain why later, after the groups were separated, only one group would continue to use these tools.

Wrong answers: (A) This would explain the difference. (C) This would explain the difference. (D) This would explain the difference. (E) This would explain the difference.

Now, try some full Paradox questions. As you untangle each stimulus, paraphrase the apparent discrepancy in your own words. While you may not be able to predict the exact fact that the correct answer will contain, make sure you're preparing yourself to evaluate the choices by predicting the kind of fact that the right answer needs to have.

Practice For each of the following, apply the Logical Reasoning Method to a Paradox question. Use the corresponding blanks to record your thinking for each step. After each, compare your work to the thinking of an LSAT expert on the following pages.

Step 2:	Step 1:

30. Because of the recent recession in Country A, most magazines published there have experienced decreases in advertising revenue, so much so that the survival of the most widely read magazines is in grave doubt. At the same time, however, more people in Country A are reading more magazines than ever before, and the number of financially successful magazines in Country A is greater than ever.

Which one the following, if true, most helps to resolve the apparent discrepancy in the information above?

(A) Most magazines reduce the amount they charge for advertisements during a recession.

(B) The audience for a successful television show far exceeds the readership of even the most widely read magazine.

(C) Advertising is the main source of revenue only for the most widely read magazines; other magazines rely on circulation for their revenue.

(D) Because of the recession, people in Country A have cut back on magazine subscriptions and are reading borrowed magazines.

(E) More of the new general interest magazines that were launched this year in Country A have survived than survived in previous years.

PrepTest104 Sec1 Q7

Step 3:	Step 4:

Step 2:	**Step 1:**

31. When a community opens a large shopping mall, it often expects a boost to the local economy, and in fact a large amount of economic activity goes on in these malls. Yet the increase in the local economy is typically much smaller than the total amount of economic activity that goes on in the mall.

Which one of the following, if true, most helps to explain the discrepancy described above?

(A) When large shopping malls are new they attract a lot of shoppers but once the novelty has worn off they usually attract fewer shoppers than does the traditional downtown shopping district.

(B) Most of the money spent in a large shopping mall is spent by tourists who are drawn specifically by the mall and who would not have visited the community had that mall not been built.

(C) Most of the jobs created by large shopping malls are filled by people who recently moved to the community and who would not have moved had there been no job offer in the community.

(D) Most of the money spent in a large shopping mall is money that would have been spent elsewhere in the same community had that mall not been built.

(E) Most of the jobs created by the construction of a large shopping mall are temporary, and most of the permanent jobs created are low paying.

PrepTest106 Sec1 Q17

Step 3:	**Step 4:**

Step 2:	Step 1:

32. Birds startled by potential predators generally try to take cover in nearby vegetation. Yet many birds that feed at bird feeders placed in suburban gardens are killed when, thus startled, they fly away from the vegetation in the gardens and into the windowpanes of nearby houses.

Which one of the following, if true, most helps to explain the anomalous behavior of the birds that fly into windowpanes?

(A) Predator attacks are as likely to occur at bird feeders surrounded by dense vegetation as they are at feeders surrounded by little or no vegetation.

(B) The bird feeders in some suburban gardens are placed at a considerable distance from the houses.

(C) Large birds are as likely as small birds to fly into windowpanes.

(D) Most of the birds startled while feeding at bird feeders placed in suburban gardens are startled by loud noises rather than by predators.

(E) The windowpanes of many houses clearly reflect surrounding vegetation.

PrepTest106 Sec3 Q3

Step 3:	Step 4:

Step 2:	Step 1:

33. People always seem to associate high prices of products with high quality. But price is not necessarily an indicator of quality. The best teas are often no more expensive than the lower-quality teas.

Which one of the following, if true, does most to explain the apparent counterexample described above?

(A) Packing and advertising triple the price of all teas.

(B) Most people buy low-quality tea, thus keeping its price up.

(C) All types of tea are subject to high import tariffs.

(D) Low-quality teas are generally easier to obtain than high-quality teas.

(E) The price of tea generally does not vary from region to region.

PrepTest104 Sec4 Q8

Step 3:	Step 4:

Step 2:	Step 1:

34. In an effort to boost sales during the summer months, which are typically the best for soft-drink sales, Foamy Soda lowered its prices. In spite of this, however, the sales of Foamy Soda dropped during the summer months.

Each of the following, if true, contributes to reconciling the apparent discrepancy indicated above EXCEPT:

(A) The soft-drink industry as a whole experienced depressed sales during the summer months.

(B) Foamy Soda's competitors lowered their prices even more drastically during the summer months.

(C) Because of an increase in the price of sweeteners, the production costs of Foamy Soda rose during the summer months.

(D) A strike at Foamy Soda's main plant forced production cutbacks that resulted in many stores not receiving their normal shipments during the summer months.

(E) The weather during the summer months was unseasonably cool, decreasing the demand for soft drinks.

PrepTest101 Sec3 Q14

Step 3:	Step 4:

Expert Analysis

Check your work by studying the LSAT expert's analysis of the questions you just practiced. Review the analysis by following the steps of the Logical Reasoning Method and pay attention to why the expert eliminated each wrong answer (even if you got the question correct).

Step 2: Fact 1: Most magazines, including those most widely read, are suffering critical losses in ad revenue. *Yet* Fact 2: The number of financially successful magazines is greater than ever.	**Step 1:** The phrase "resolve the apparent discrepancy" indicates a Paradox question.

30. Because of the recent recession in Country A, most magazines published there have experienced decreases in advertising revenue, so much so that the survival of the most widely read magazines is in grave doubt. At the same time, however, more people in Country A are reading more magazines than ever before, and the number of financially successful magazines in Country A is greater than ever.

Which one the following, if true, most helps to resolve the apparent discrepancy in the information above?

(A) Most magazines reduce the amount they charge for advertisements during a recession.

(B) The audience for a successful television show far exceeds the readership of even the most widely read magazine.

(C) Advertising is the main source of revenue only for the most widely read magazines; other magazines rely on circulation for their revenue.

(D) Because of the recession, people in Country A have cut back on magazine subscriptions and are reading borrowed magazines.

(E) More of the new general interest magazines that were launched this year in Country A have survived than survived in previous years.

PrepTest104 Sec1 Q7

Step 3: The correct choice will answer this question: How can it be that most magazines are losing ad revenue but the number of successful magazines is growing?	**Step 4:** (C) is correct. This choice describes an alternative factor that explains the financial success of certain magazines, despite the loss of ad revenue.

Wrong answers: (A) This helps explain the decrease in ad revenue but does nothing to explain the mystery of the financial success of certain magazines. (B) Irrelevant Comparison. This helps explain the bad financial straits of some magazines, but does nothing to explain the mystery of the financial success of certain magazines. (D) 180. This makes it even more unfathomable that some magazines are enjoying financial success in the face of declining ad revenues. (E) This fact does nothing to explain *why* more magazines are financially successful despite the loss in advertising revenue.

Step 2: Fact 1: Communities expect a boost in the local economy after opening a shopping mall. *Yet* Fact 2: The increase in the local economy is smaller than the amount of economic activity occurring in the mall.	**Step 1:** The phrase "explain the discrepancy" indicates a Paradox question.

31. When a community opens a large shopping mall, it often expects a boost to the local economy, and in fact a large amount of economic activity goes on in these malls. Yet the increase in the local economy is typically much smaller than the total amount of economic activity that goes on in the mall.

Which one of the following, if true, most helps to explain the discrepancy described above?

(A) When large shopping malls are new they attract a lot of shoppers but once the novelty has worn off they usually attract fewer shoppers than does the traditional downtown shopping district.

(B) Most of the money spent in a large shopping mall is spent by tourists who are drawn specifically by the mall and who would not have visited the community had that mall not been built.

(C) Most of the jobs created by large shopping malls are filled by people who recently moved to the community and who would not have moved had there been no job offer in the community.

(D) Most of the money spent in a large shopping mall is money that would have been spent elsewhere in the same community had that mall not been built.

(E) Most of the jobs created by the construction of a large shopping mall are temporary, and most of the permanent jobs created are low paying.

PrepTest106 Sec1 Q17

Step 3: The correct choice will answer this question: Why does the local economy not receive an economic boost equal to or larger than the amount of economic activity in the new mall?	**Step 4:** (D) is correct. This is the flip side of choices (B) and (C). Rather than adding economic activity to the local economy, the new mall is simply displacing previously existing economic activity.

Wrong answers: (A) This explains why the economic benefits of a new mall would not be long lasting, but does not explain the discrepancy between the amount of financial activity in the mall and the lesser level of benefits to the local economy. (B) 180. This suggests that the economic activity at the new mall should be purely additive to the local economy. (C) Another 180. As with choice (B), this suggests that the economic activity at the new mall should be purely additive to the local economy. (E) As with choice (A), this explains why the economic benefits of a new mall would not be long lasting, but does not explain the discrepancy between the amount of financial activity in the mall and the lesser level of benefits to the local economy.

Step 2: Fact 1: When startled, birds want to fly to vegetation. *Yet* Fact 2: When startled, birds in suburbs often instead fly into windowpanes.	**Step 1:** The phrase "helps to explain" indicates a Paradox question.

32. Birds startled by potential predators generally try to take cover in nearby vegetation. Yet many birds that feed at bird feeders placed in suburban gardens are killed when, thus startled, they fly away from the vegetation in the gardens and into the windowpanes of nearby houses.

Which one of the following, if true, most helps to explain the anomalous behavior of the birds that fly into windowpanes?

(A) Predator attacks are as likely to occur at bird feeders surrounded by dense vegetation as they are at feeders surrounded by little or no vegetation.

(B) The bird feeders in some suburban gardens are placed at a considerable distance from the houses.

(C) Large birds are as likely as small birds to fly into windowpanes.

(D) Most of the birds startled while feeding at bird feeders placed in suburban gardens are startled by loud noises rather than by predators.

(E) The windowpanes of many houses clearly reflect surrounding vegetation.

PrepTest106 Sec3 Q3

Step 3: The correct choice will answer this question: Why do birds, when startled, fly into windowpanes despite wanting to fly to vegetation?	**Step 4:** (E) is correct. This choice provides *a reason why* birds seeking vegetation would strike a windowpane.

Wrong answers: (A) This does nothing to explain *why* the birds fly into windowpanes. (B) 180. This just makes it more mysterious *why* birds would fly such a distance to strike a windowpane. (C) Irrelevant Comparison. Such a distinction doesn't explain *why* any birds would fly into windowpanes. (D) This choice also does not explain *why* birds would fly into windowpanes regardless of what startles them.

Step 2: Fact 1: Higher quality usually means higher price. *Yet* Fact 2: Higher quality teas are often no more expensive than lower quality teas.	**Step 1:** The phrase "explain the apparent counterexample" indicates a Paradox question.

33. People always seem to associate high prices of products with high quality. But price is not necessarily an indicator of quality. The best teas are often no more expensive than the lower-quality teas.

Which one of the following, if true, does most to explain the apparent counterexample described above?

(A) Packing and advertising triple the price of all teas.

(B) Most people buy low-quality tea, thus keeping its price up.

(C) All types of tea are subject to high import tariffs.

(D) Low-quality teas are generally easier to obtain than high-quality teas.

(E) The price of tea generally does not vary from region to region.

PrepTest104 Sec4 Q8

Step 3: The correct choice will answer this question: Why do low-quality teas costs as much as high-quality teas?	**Step 4:** (B) is correct. This provides a distinction between the different quality teas that explains why the low-quality varieties cost as much as the high-quality varieties.

Wrong answers: (A) Something that applies to all teas cannot explain what is raising the price of low-quality teas relative to high-quality. (C) As with (A), this cannot explain the discrepancy because it applies to all teas. (D) 180. This deepens the mystery because this is a further reason why low-quality teas should be cheaper. (E) Irrelevant Comparison. The cost of teas generally across different regions does not address the discrepancy between the price of low- and high-quality teas.

Step 2: Fact 1: Foamy Soda lowered its prices during the prime soda season, summer. *Yet* Fact 2: Sales of Foamy Soda dropped.	**Step 1:** The phrase "reconcil[e] the apparent discrepancy" indicates a Paradox question. In this case, a Paradox EXCEPT.

34. In an effort to boost sales during the summer months, which are typically the best for soft-drink sales, Foamy Soda lowered its prices. In spite of this, however, the sales of Foamy Soda dropped during the summer months.

Each of the following, if true, contributes to reconciling the apparent discrepancy indicated above EXCEPT:

(A) The soft-drink industry as a whole experienced depressed sales during the summer months.

(B) Foamy Soda's competitors lowered their prices even more drastically during the summer months.

(C) Because of an increase in the price of sweeteners, the production costs of Foamy Soda rose during the summer months.

(D) A strike at Foamy Soda's main plant forced production cutbacks that resulted in many stores not receiving their normal shipments during the summer months.

(E) The weather during the summer months was unseasonably cool, decreasing the demand for soft drinks.

PrepTest101 Sec3 Q14

Step 3: The four wrong choices will each provide an answer to this question: Why would Foamy Soda's sales drop despite the fact that it is summer and the fact that Foamy has lowered its prices? The correct answer will deepen the mystery, or have no impact.	**Step 4:** (C) is correct. This could hurt Foamy Soda's profit margins, but does nothing to explain why its *sales* would decline.

Wrong answers: (A) This is a reason for lower soda sales. (B) Steeper price cuts by competitors could explain Foamy Soda's sales losses. (D) Foamy Soda can't sell what doesn't get to the stores. (E) This is a reason for lower soda sales across the board.

Reflect Keep an eye out for apparent discrepancies, seeming contradictions, and paradoxes in your day-to-day life. The next time a friend sees something that puzzles him and asks you, "How can that be?" take the opportunity to practice your Paradox question skills. Find facts that show how the situation can be resolved, reconciled, or explained. You may be surprised to discover how often we fail to explain paradoxes but instead respond by saying things like, "Oh, that happens all the time; don't be surprised," or how often we explain only one side of the discrepancy (just as wrong answers do on the LSAT) and fail to clear up the paradox at all.

Summary

Congratulations. Over the last three chapters, you've learned how to answer all of the Logical Reasoning question types on the LSAT. Continue to improve your performance on non-argument-based questions with the items in the Perform quiz following this section. When you're ready to move on, you'll find an LSAT Channel Spotlight that covers Logical Reasoning section management; it will give you the best strategies for being efficient and effective with your time, not getting bogged down, and using the 35 minutes in each Logical Reasoning section to get the most points possible.

Perform

Inference

Assess your skills on some further examples of Inference questions. Take no more than 1 minute 30 seconds per question.

1. Flavonoids are a common component of almost all plants, but a specific variety of flavonoid in apples has been found to be an antioxidant. Antioxidants are known to be a factor in the prevention of heart disease.

Which one of the following can be properly inferred from the passage?

(A) A diet composed largely of fruits and vegetables will help to prevent heart disease.

(B) Flavonoids are essential to preventing heart disease.

(C) Eating at least one apple each day will prevent heart disease.

(D) At least one type of flavonoid helps to prevent heart disease.

(E) A diet deficient in antioxidants is a common cause of heart disease.

PrepTest106 Sec3 Q1

2. In response to requests made by the dairy industry, the government is considering whether to approve the synthetic hormone BST for use in dairy cows. BST increases milk production but also leads to recurring udder inflammation, decreased fertility, and symptoms of stress in cows who receive the hormone. All of these problems can be kept under control with constant veterinary care, but such levels of veterinary help would cost big farms far less per cow than they would small farms.

If the statements above are true, which one of the following claims is most strongly supported by them?

(A) The government is unlikely to approve the synthetic hormone BST for use in cows.

(B) The proportion of cows that suffer from udder inflammation, decreased fertility, and symptoms of stress is currently greater on big dairy farms than on small ones.

(C) At the present time milk from cows raised on small farms is safer to drink than milk from cows raised on big farms.

(D) The milk from cows who receive BST will not be safe for people to drink.

(E) Owners of big farms stand to gain more from government approval of BST than do owners of small farms.

PrepTest101 Sec3 Q7

3. A century in certain ways is like a life, and as the end of a century approaches, people behave toward that century much as someone who is nearing the end of life does toward that life. So just as people in their last years spend much time looking back on the events of their life, people at a century's end ______.

Which one of the following most logically completes the argument?

(A) reminisce about their own lives

(B) fear that their own lives are about to end

(C) focus on what the next century will bring

(D) become very interested in the history of the century just ending

(E) reflect on how certain unfortunate events of the century could have been avoided

PrepTest123 Sec2 Q3

4. Advertisers have learned that people are more easily encouraged to develop positive attitudes about things toward which they originally have neutral or even negative attitudes if those things are linked, with pictorial help rather than exclusively through prose, to things about which they already have positive attitudes. Therefore, advertisers are likely to ______.

Which one of the following most logically completes the argument?

(A) use little if any written prose in their advertisements

(B) try to encourage people to develop positive attitudes about products that can be better represented pictorially than in prose

(C) place their advertisements on television rather than in magazines

(D) highlight the desirable features of the advertised product by contrasting them pictorially with undesirable features of a competing product

(E) create advertisements containing pictures of things most members of the target audience like

PrepTest123 Sec3 Q10

5. Proponents of the electric car maintain that when the technical problems associated with its battery design are solved, such cars will be widely used and, because they are emission-free, will result in an abatement of the environmental degradation caused by auto emissions. But unless we dam more rivers, the electricity to charge these batteries will come from nuclear or coal-fired power plants. Each of these three power sources produces considerable environmental damage. Thus, the electric car ______.

Which one of the following most logically completes the argument?

(A) will have worse environmental consequences than its proponents may believe

(B) will probably remain less popular than other types of cars

(C) requires that purely technical problems be solved before it can succeed

(D) will increase the total level of emissions rather than reduce it

(E) will not produce a net reduction in environmental degradation

PrepTest123 Sec2 Q8

6. If the economy is weak, then prices remain constant although unemployment rises. But unemployment rises only if investment decreases. Fortunately, investment is not decreasing.

If the statements above are true, then which one of the following must be false?

(A) Either the economy is weak or investment is decreasing.

(B) If unemployment rises, the prices remain constant.

(C) The economy is weak only if investment decreases.

(D) Either the economy is weak or prices are remaining constant.

(E) Either unemployment is rising or the economy is not weak.

PrepTest106 Sec1 Q20

7. If the price it pays for coffee beans continues to increase, the Coffee Shoppe will have to increase its prices. In that case, either the Coffee Shoppe will begin selling noncoffee products or its coffee sales will decrease. But selling noncoffee products will decrease the Coffee Shoppe's overall profitability. Moreover, the Coffee Shoppe can avoid a decrease in overall profitability only if its coffee sales do not decrease.

Which one of the following statements follows logically from the statements above?

(A) If the Coffee Shoppe's overall profitability decreases, the price it pays for coffee beans will have continued to increase.

(B) If the Coffee Shoppe's overall profitability decreases, either it will have begun selling noncoffee products or its coffee sales will have decreased.

(C) The Coffee Shoppe's overall profitability will decrease if the price it pays for coffee beans continues to increase.

(D) The price it pays for coffee beans cannot decrease without the Coffee Shoppe's overall profitability also decreasing.

(E) Either the price it pays for coffee beans will continue to increase or the Coffee Shoppe's coffee sales will increase.

PrepTest123 Sec3 Q22

8. Philosopher: Nations are not literally persons; they have no thoughts or feelings, and, literally speaking, they perform no actions. Thus they have no moral rights or responsibilities. But no nation can survive unless many of its citizens attribute such rights and responsibilities to it, for nothing else could prompt people to make the sacrifices national citizenship demands. Obviously, then, a nation ______.

Which one of the following most logically completes the philosopher's argument?

(A) cannot continue to exist unless something other than the false belief that the nation has moral rights motivates its citizens to make sacrifices

(B) cannot survive unless many of its citizens have some beliefs that are literally false

(C) can never be a target of moral praise or blame

(D) is not worth the sacrifices that its citizens make on its behalf

(E) should always be thought of in metaphorical rather than literal terms

PrepTest123 Sec3 Q16

9. Editorialist: News media rarely cover local politics thoroughly, and local political business is usually conducted secretively. These factors each tend to isolate local politicians from their electorates. This has the effect of reducing the chance that any particular act of resident participation will elicit a positive official response, which in turn discourages resident participation in local politics.

Which one of the following is most strongly supported by the editorialist's statements?

(A) Particular acts of resident participation would be likely to elicit a positive response from local politicians if those politicians were less isolated from their electorate.

(B) Local political business should be conducted less secretively because this would avoid discouraging resident participation in local politics.

(C) The most important factor influencing a resident's decision as to whether to participate in local politics is the chance that the participation will elicit a positive official response.

(D) More-frequent thorough coverage of local politics would reduce at least one source of discouragement from resident participation in local politics.

(E) If resident participation in local politics were not discouraged, this would cause local politicians to be less isolated from their electorate.

PrepTest123 Sec2 Q22

10. Modern science is built on the process of posing hypotheses and testing them against observations—in essence, attempting to show that the hypotheses are incorrect. Nothing brings more recognition than overthrowing conventional wisdom. It is accordingly unsurprising that some scientists are skeptical of the widely accepted predictions of global warming. What is instead remarkable is that with hundreds of researchers striving to make breakthroughs in climatology, very few find evidence that global warming is unlikely.

The information above provides the most support for which one of the following statements?

(A) Most scientists who are reluctant to accept the global warming hypothesis are not acting in accordance with the accepted standards of scientific debate.

(B) Most researchers in climatology have substantial motive to find evidence that would discredit the global warming hypothesis.

(C) There is evidence that conclusively shows that the global warming hypothesis is true.

(D) Scientists who are skeptical about global warming have not offered any alternative hypotheses to explain climatological data.

(E) Research in global warming is primarily driven by a desire for recognition in the scientific community.

PrepTest123 Sec2 Q18

Principle (Inference)

Assess your skills on some further examples of Principle questions that reward you for making valid inferences. Take no more than 1 minute 30 seconds per question.

11. Jablonski, who owns a car dealership, has donated cars to driver education programs at area schools for over five years. She found the statistics on car accidents to be disturbing, and she wanted to do something to encourage better driving in young drivers. Some members of the community have shown their support for this action by purchasing cars from Jablonski's dealership.

Which one of the following propositions is best illustrated by the passage?

(A) The only way to reduce traffic accidents is through driver education programs.

(B) Altruistic actions sometimes have positive consequences for those who perform them.

(C) Young drivers are the group most likely to benefit from driver education programs.

(D) It is usually in one's best interest to perform actions that benefit others.

(E) An action must have broad community support if it is to be successful.

PrepTest123 Sec3 Q6

12. Situation: Someone living in a cold climate buys a winter coat that is stylish but not warm in order to appear sophisticated.

    Analysis: People are sometimes willing to sacrifice sensual comfort or pleasure for the sake of appearances.

The analysis provided for the situation above is most appropriate for which one of the following situations?

(A) A person buys an automobile to commute to work even though public transportation is quick and reliable.

(B) A parent buys a car seat for a young child because it is more colorful and more comfortable for the child than the other car seats on the market, though no safer.

(C) A couple buys a particular wine even though their favorite wine is less expensive and better tasting because they think it will impress their dinner guests.

(D) A person sets her thermostat at a low temperature during the winter because she is concerned about the environmental damage caused by using fossil fuels to heat her home.

(E) An acrobat convinces the circus that employs him to purchase an expensive outfit for him so that he can wear it during his act to impress the audience.

PrepTest123 Sec3 Q1

CHAPTER 5

13. Ethicist: The most advanced kind of moral motivation is based solely on abstract principles. This form of motivation is in contrast with calculated self-interest or the desire to adhere to societal norms and conventions.

The actions of which one of the following individuals exhibit the most advanced kind of moral motivation, as described by the ethicist?

(A) Bobby contributed money to a local charity during a charity drive at work because he worried that not doing so would make him look stingy.

(B) Wes contributed money to a local charity during a charity drive at work because he believed that doing so would improve his employer's opinion of him.

(C) Donna's employers engaged in an illegal but profitable practice that caused serious damage to the environment. Donna did not report this practice to the authorities, out of fear that her employers would retaliate against her.

(D) Jadine's employers engaged in an illegal but profitable practice that caused serious damage to the environment. Jadine reported this practice to the authorities out of a belief that protecting the environment is always more important than monetary profit.

(E) Leigh's employers engaged in an illegal but profitable practice that caused serious damage to the environment. Leigh reported this practice to the authorities only because several colleagues had been pressuring her to do so.

PrepTest123 Sec2 Q7

14. Car companies solicit consumer information on such human factors as whether a seat is comfortable or whether a set of controls is easy to use. However, designer interaction with consumers is superior to survey data; the data may tell the designer why a feature on last year's model was given a low rating, but data will not explain how that feature needs to be changed in order to receive a higher rating.

The reasoning above conforms most closely to which one of the following propositions?

(A) Getting consumer input for design modifications can contribute to successful product design.

(B) Car companies traditionally conduct extensive postmarket surveys.

(C) Designers aim to create features that will appeal to specific market niches.

(D) A car will have unappealing features if consumers are not consulted during its design stage.

(E) Consumer input affects external rather than internal design components of cars.

PrepTest123 Sec2 Q24

Paradox

Assess your skills on some further examples of Paradox questions. Take no more than 1 minute 30 seconds per question.

15. Cats spend much of their time sleeping; they seem to awaken only to stretch and yawn. Yet they have a strong, agile musculature that most animals would have to exercise strenuously to acquire.

Which one of the following, if true, most helps to resolve the apparent paradox described above?

(A) Cats have a greater physiological need for sleep than other animals.

(B) Many other animals also spend much of their time sleeping yet have a strong, agile musculature.

(C) Cats are able to sleep in apparently uncomfortable positions.

(D) Cats derive ample exercise from frequent stretching.

(E) Cats require strength and agility in order to be effective predators.

PrepTest107 Sec1 Q4

16. After replacing his old gas water heater with a new, pilotless, gas water heater that is rated as highly efficient, Jimmy's gas bills increased.

Each of the following, if true, contributes to an explanation of the increase mentioned above EXCEPT:

(A) The new water heater uses a smaller percentage of the gas used by Jimmy's household than did the old one.

(B) Shortly after the new water heater was installed, Jimmy's uncle came to live with him, doubling the size of the household.

(C) After having done his laundry at a laundromat, Jimmy bought and started using a gas dryer when he replaced his water heater.

(D) Jimmy's utility company raised the rates for gas consumption following installation of the new water heater.

(E) Unusually cold weather following installation of the new water heater resulted in heavy gas usage.

PrepTest123 Sec3 Q2

17. During the nineteenth century, the French academy of art was a major financial sponsor of painting and sculpture in France; sponsorship by private individuals had decreased dramatically by this time. Because the academy discouraged innovation in the arts, there was little innovation in nineteenth century French sculpture. Yet nineteenth century French painting showed a remarkable degree of innovation.

Which one of the following, if true, most helps to explain the difference between the amount of innovation in French painting and the amount of innovation in French sculpture during the nineteenth century?

(A) In France in the nineteenth century, the French academy gave more of its financial support to painting than it did to sculpture.

(B) The French academy in the nineteenth century financially supported a greater number of sculptors than painters, but individual painters received more support, on average, than individual sculptors.

(C) Because stone was so much more expensive than paint and canvas, far more unsponsored paintings were produced than were unsponsored sculptures in France during the nineteenth century.

(D) Very few of the artists in France in the nineteenth century who produced sculptures also produced paintings.

(E) Although the academy was the primary sponsor of sculpture and painting, the total amount of financial support that French sculptors and painters received from sponsors declined during the nineteenth century.

PrepTest123 Sec2 Q25

Assess

Use the following criteria to evaluate your results on the Non-Argument Questions Perform quiz.

If, under timed conditions, you correctly answered:

14–17 of the questions: Outstanding! You have demonstrated a strong skill level in Non-Argument questions. For further practice, use any of the Recommended Additional Practice sets, including the Advanced set. In addition, make timed practice with full Logical Reasoning sections a routine part of your study schedule.

9–13 of the questions: Good work! You have a solid foundation in Non-Argument questions. For further practice, begin with the Foundations or Mid-Level Recommended Additional Practice set (and, time permitting, work up through the Advanced set, as well). In addition, make timed practice with full Logical Reasoning sections a routine part of your study schedule.

0–8 of the questions: Keep working. While Non-Argument questions are not as common as those in the Assumption Family, making improvements here can have a big impact on your overall LSAT score. To master Non-Argument questions, you will need continued practice. Begin by reviewing this chapter. Then, try the questions in the Foundations Recommended Additional Practice set. As you continue to progress, move on to the Mid-Level Recommended Additional Practice set. Finally, make time in your study schedule to do timed practice on full Logical Reasoning sections.

Recommended Additional Practice: Non-Argument Questions

All of the following questions will provide good practice on recent Non-Argument questions. They are grouped by difficulty as determined from empirical student practice results. Foundations practice has 1- and 2-star questions; Mid-Level practice has 1-, 2-, and 3-star questions; Advanced practice has 2-, 3-, and 4-star questions. All the questions are from PrepTests that are available for digital practice on LawHub with an LSAC LawHub Advantage subscription. Complete explanations and analysis for these questions are available on Kaplan's LSAT Link and LSAT Link+. See **www.kaptest.com/LSAT** to learn more about LSAT Link and LSAT Link+.

Foundations

PrepTest 144, Section 3, Questions 5, 6, 8, 12, & 14
PrepTest 139, Section 1, Question 10; Section 4, Question 2
PrepTest 138, Section 2, Question 1; Section 3, Question 6
PrepTest 137, Section 2, Questions 2, 5, 7, 11, & 24
PrepTest 136, Section 2, Question 14
PrepTest 135, Section 1, Questions 4, 7, & 12; Section 4, Questions 1, 9, 10, & 18
PrepTest 134, Section 1, Question 18; Section 3, Questions 1, 3, 8, & 13
PrepTest 133, Section 1, Questions 4, 9, & 12; Section 3, Questions 3, 5, 7, & 12
PrepTest 132, Section 2, Question 1; Section 4, Questions 2, 7, & 11

Mid-Level

PrepTest 144, Section 3, Question 22
PrepTest 140, Section 2, Questions 2, 7, 13, & 18
PrepTest 139, Section 1, Question 16; Section 4, Questions 5 & 6
PrepTest 138, Section 2, Questions 3, 6, 8, & 18; Section 3, Questions 2 & 13
PrepTest 137, Section 2, Question 4; Section 4, Questions 3, 5, & 17

PrepTest 136, Section 2, Questions 9 & 23; Section 4, Questions 10 & 14
PrepTest 135, Section 1, Question 25; Section 4, Question 6
PrepTest 134, Section 1, Questions 2, 6, & 20
PrepTest 133, Section 1, Question 6; Section 3, Question 13
PrepTest 132, Section 2, Questions 6 & 21; Section 4, Questions 6 & 26

Advanced

PrepTest 144, Section 3, Question 24
PrepTest 140, Section 2, Questions 14 & 21
PrepTest 139, Questions 12, 15, 18, & 21; Section 4, Questions 9 & 20
PrepTest 138, Section 2, Question 10; Section 3, Questions 4, 10, 14, & 19
PrepTest 137, Section 4, Questions 15, 20, & 23
PrepTest 136, Section 2, Question 22; Section 4, Questions 15, 18, & 21
PrepTest 134, Section 3, Questions 18, 20, & 22
PrepTest 133, Section 1, Question 20; Section 3, Questions 8 & 26
PrepTest 132, Section 2, Questions 18, 19, 20, & 24; Section 4, Questions 8, 17, & 24

Answers and Explanations

Inference

1. (D) Inference ★★★★

Step 1: Identify the Question Type

This question asks what can be "properly inferred," indicating an Inference question. The correct answer must be true based on the information given in the stimulus.

Step 2: Untangle the Stimulus

This brief paragraph contains three facts: First, that almost all plants contain flavonoids; second, that there is a specific flavonoid in apples that's an antioxidant; and third, that antioxidants can help prevent heart disease.

Step 3: Make a Prediction

With Inference stimuli, be on the lookout for words or terms that connect statements. Here, you learn that the flavonoid in apples is an antioxidant and that antioxidants can be a factor that helps prevent heart disease. Anticipate that the correct answer will link apples or flavonoids with the prevention of heart disease. Be prepared, however, to eliminate answers with extreme language. From this stimulus, you can infer that the flavonoid in apples *may help* prevent heart problems, not that they'll cure them or that someone eating apples will never have a heart attack.

Step 4: Evaluate the Answer Choices

(D) fits all of the information in the passage. If apples contain a flavonoid that is an antioxidant, and antioxidants help prevent heart disease, then there is at least one type of flavonoid that helps prevent heart disease.

(A) is too broad. The stimulus contains nothing about diets rich in fruits and vegetables in general. You learn about only one flavonoid in apples. Be careful of statements like this one that sound reasonable based on the "real world," but aren't supported by the stimulus.

(B) is Extreme. Only one type of flavonoid is mentioned in the stimulus as an antioxidant—flavonoids, in general, are not cited as beneficial. Also, **(B)**'s phrase "are essential to" is much stronger than the cautious language of the stimulus.

(C) is Extreme. An apple a day may keep the doctor away, but **(C)**'s prescription is more extreme than the stimulus warrants. "Known to be a factor in prevention" does not translate into "will prevent." Moreover, there's nothing here to support the specific "at least one apple per day" recommendation. Although apples contain the beneficial flavonoid, it is unknown what quantity of apples would need to be consumed to get the antioxidant benefit.

(E) is Outside the Scope. The stimulus deals with the *prevention* of heart disease, not at all with its *cause*.

2. (E) Inference ★★★★

Step 1: Identify the Question Type

When a question stem asks for an answer choice that *supports* the argument, you have a Strengthen question. Here, however, you are asked to find the answer choice that is "*supported by*" the stimulus, so this is an Inference question.

Step 2: Untangle the Stimulus

The dairy industry wants the government to approve the use of BST to increase milk production, but BST causes several side effects. "[C]onstant veterinary care" can control all of these side effects. However, such care would cost small farms more per cow than it would cost big farms.

Step 3: Make a Prediction

With Inference questions, it is not always possible to predict the correct answer exactly, but often you can string some thoughts together and anticipate where the testmaker is going. Because the big farms will have to spend less money per cow than small farms on veterinary care, they won't incur as much relative expense as the small farms will if the government approves BST. The big farms should make out better because they're going to get increased milk production with BST's use and pay less per cow to ward off the side effects.

Step 4: Evaluate the Answer Choices

(E) is correct and must be true based on the last sentence in the stimulus.

(A) is incorrect because nothing in the stimulus mentions the actual likelihood that the government will approve BST. The stimulus simply states that the government "is considering whether to approve" BST.

(B) is an Irrelevant Comparison. This laundry list of ailments represents the side effects of the proposed hormone BST, but you do not know whether any cows—on farms of whatever size—are *currently* suffering from them. Even if they are, there is no evidence that a greater percentage of ailing cows live on big farms rather than on little farms.

(C) is an Irrelevant Comparison. The safety of milk at the present time is not discussed; the stimulus simply mentions the negative health effects of BST on cows and how those effects might be controlled.

(D) is Outside the Scope. The stimulus never mentions anything about whether milk from cows treated with BST will be safe to drink.

3. (D) Inference ★☆☆☆

Step 1: Identify the Question Type

Treat a question that asks you to fill in the blank for a conclusion of an argument as an Inference question. The correct answer should act as a logical conclusion, falling neatly within the scope of what has already been stated without extrapolation.

Step 2: Untangle the Stimulus

The argument begins by analogizing a century to a life, equating how people act as the end of a century approaches with how they act near the end of their life. Then the author states that people at the end of their life start looking back at the events of their life.

Step 3: Make a Prediction

You need to complete the analogy that the author has set up, resisting any urge to extrapolate or get creative. The author equates people's actions at the end of a century with those at the end of their lives; thus, if they look back on their life events, they should also look back on the events of an ending century.

Step 4: Evaluate the Answer Choices

(D) matches the prediction that people will contemplate events of the past century.

(A) repeats what people do at the end of their lives and does not complete the analogy to the end of a century.

(B) might have made sense in 1999 when Y2K was a rampant worry, but it does not logically complete the analogy. *Fear* is Out of Scope.

(C) is a 180. Completing the analogy requires looking back on the century just as one looks back on one's own life. This answer would only work if the stimulus said people at the end of their lives focus on what will happen after they die.

(E) is a Distortion. While the answer choice correctly incorporates reminiscing on past events, the stimulus doesn't mention anything about focusing on unfortunate events or second-guessing any events.

4. (E) Inference ★★☆☆

Step 1: Identify the Question Type

Because the correct answer "logically completes the argument," it is the statement that must be true based on information in the stimulus. Thus, this is an Inference question.

Step 2: Untangle the Stimulus

Paraphrase the information in the stimulus. Advertisers know that people are more likely to develop positive feelings about things if those things are linked to something else people already like. This is true even if people start out with neutral or even negative feelings. Pictures forge this link better than words do.

Step 3: Make a Prediction

Given that pictures effectively create positive links, it would make sense that advertisers would create advertisements that use pictures of things toward which people already have positive feelings.

Step 4: Evaluate the Answer Choices

(E) matches the prediction.

(A) is a Distortion. Just because pictures work *better* than prose for linking products to things people already like does not mean advertisers would use *little* or *no* prose. After all, advertisers might use pictures to make the link and prose for some other purpose.

(B) is another Distortion. The stimulus is about linking products to positive images, not whether the products themselves are easily represented pictorially.

(C) is an Irrelevant Comparison. The stimulus doesn't discuss where ads are placed, just that they should include images. Both television and magazines would therefore be appropriate media, though you have no way to know which is used more.

(D) goes Out of Scope by introducing the idea of contrasting advertisers' products with things that people do not like. The stimulus focuses exclusively on linking advertisers' products to things people like.

5. (A) Inference ★★★☆

Step 1: Identify the Question Type

Treat a question that asks you to fill in the blank at the end of an argument with a conclusion as an Inference question. The correct answer, when tagged onto the argument, should fall neatly within the scope of what has already been stated.

Step 2: Untangle the Stimulus

Proponents of the electric car believe that because the cars are emission-free, their wide use will result in less environmental degradation from auto emissions. In contrast (indicated by the Keyword "but"), the author points out that the electricity to charge electric car batteries will come from hydroelectric dams, nuclear energy, or coal power plants, all of which produce considerable environmental damage. Then, the author makes a conclusion regarding the electric car that you must complete.

Step 3: Make a Prediction

Do not get too creative when adding a conclusion at the end of an argument. Typically, the answer should be consistent with what has already been stated or flow from a logical deduction. In this case, complete the contrast that the author is setting up. Proponents of the electric car believe that they will reduce environmental damage from car emissions, but the author points out an indirect way electric cars will continue causing environmental damage. When assessing answers, remember to treat this like an Inference question and be very wary of answers that are Out of Scope or Extreme.

Step 4: Evaluate the Answer Choices

(A) is correct. It completes the disagreement the author has with the proponents of electric cars. This type of modest, safe answer is exactly what you want in an Inference question. The author must believe this is true because the proponents don't consider a negative result that he sees.

(B) is an Irrelevant Comparison. It speculates about the future popularity of electric cars versus other cars, which you cannot determine. This argument is merely about the environmental effects of electric cars.

(C) is a Faulty Use of Detail. This refers to the first sentence, which details the proponents' view, not the author's. Additionally, success and its requirements are Out of Scope.

(D) is Extreme. While the author does not believe that electric cars are *emission-free*, due to their indirect effect on emissions, the author does not go so far as to claim that electric cars *will* increase the *total* emissions currently being released.

(E), while slightly more modest than **(D)**, is also Extreme. It must be true that the author believes the electric car will not produce as great a reduction in environmental degradation as the proponents of electric cars believe. Nevertheless, the author's statements leave open the possibility that the electric car could, on balance, be at least a little better for the environment than gasoline-powered cars.

6. (A) Inference ★★★★

Step 1: Identify the Question Type

This is an unusual twist on an Inference question. As with any Inference question, the correct answer choice will be logically based on what the stimulus provides, which here consists merely of statements rather than a complete argument. However, the correct answer here "must be false" (i.e., impossible). That means the wrong answers will all be possible, if not definitely true.

Step 2: Untangle the Stimulus

The first two claims are pure Formal Logic and should be interpreted properly. According to the first, if the economy is weak, two effects would follow: Prices would be constant and unemployment would rise. By the contrapositive, if the prices *don't* stay constant *or* unemployment does *not* rise, then the economy is *not* weak:

If economy weak → prices constant AND unemployment rises

If ~prices constant OR ~unemployment rises →
~economy weak

In the second claim, "only if" signals a necessary condition. That means for unemployment to rise, investment *must* decrease. By contrapositive, if investment does *not* decrease, then unemployment will *not* rise:

If unemployment rises → investment decreases
If ~investment decrease → ~unemployment rise

The final claim is a given: Investment is *not* decreasing.

Step 3: Make a Prediction

That final claim sets off a string of deductions using the earlier Formal Logic. Fact 1: Investment is not decreasing. The second claim's contrapositive leads to Fact 2: Unemployment is not rising. The first claim's contrapositive leads to Fact 3: The economy is not weak. The only factor not accounted for is prices, which may or may not be constant. That cannot be determined. Remember that the correct answer *must* be false. Most likely, it will directly conflict with the three given, or deduced, facts.

Step 4: Evaluate the Answer Choices

(A) is impossible, making it the correct answer. It's a given that investment is *not* decreasing, and that leads to the deduction that the economy is *not* weak. Neither option in this answer is true, which means it must be false.

(B) is possible because unemployment has no stated effect on prices.

(C) is a 180. By the first two claims, a weak economy requires a rise in unemployment, which in turn, requires a decrease in investment. This answer must be *true*, which makes it a wrong answer for this question.

(D) is possible. While it's true that the economy is *not* weak, which denies the first option of this answer, it's still possible the prices are constant. That leaves the possibility of truth, meaning **(D)** cannot be guaranteed false.

(E) is another 180. Because unemployment is *not* rising, the contrapositive of the first sentence allows for the deduction that the economy is indeed not weak. That means the second option is definitely true, making the entire statement valid.

7. (C) Inference ★★★★

Step 1: Identify the Question Type

Because the correct answer is the statement that "follows logically" from the statements in the stimulus, this is an Inference question. The correct answer must be true based on the information in the stimulus.

Step 2: Untangle the Stimulus

Notice that the first sentence begins with *[i]f*, as do the first two answer choices. Expect this stimulus to be built of Formal Logic statements. Translate them as you read the stimulus.

If coffee beans cost increases	→	***increase prices***
If increase prices	→	***add noncoffee products OR coffee sales decrease***
If add noncoffee products	→	***overall profits decrease***
If ~overall profits decrease	→	***~coffee sales decrease***

Step 3: Make a Prediction

Start by looking for connections between the Formal Logic statements. Notice that the first two statements can be combined into one chain:

If coffee beans cost increases → increase prices → add noncoffee products OR coffee sales decrease

Based on the third sentence and the contrapositive of the fourth sentence, both adding noncoffee products and decreasing coffee sales would result in decreased overall profits. Therefore, if the cost of coffee beans increases, then no matter what the Coffee Shoppe does, the shop's profitability will decline.

Step 4: Evaluate the Answer Choices

(C) matches the prediction.

(A) reverses the Formal Logic of the deduction without negating. In the stimulus, a decrease in overall profitability is a *necessary* result, not a sufficient condition.

(B) reverses the Formal Logic of the last two sentences without negating. In the stimulus, losing profitability is a necessary result in both the third and fourth sentences, never a sufficient condition.

(D) is a 180. The stimulus says that if the price of coffee beans *increases*, then profitability decreases. This says that if the price of coffee beans *decreases*, then profitability decreases. The stimulus doesn't provide any information about what would happen if the cost of coffee beans goes down. Presumably though, even without consulting the Formal Logic, it would be unlikely that a decrease in overhead costs would cause a decrease in overall profitability.

(E) goes Out of Scope by introducing the idea of the Coffee Shoppe *increasing* its coffee sales. That idea simply is not in the stimulus. The stimulus only discusses a decrease in coffee sales. Even a negation of *decrease* would only be "not decrease." There's no way to know about an increase.

8. (B) Inference ★★★★

Step 1: Identify the Question Type

Because the correct answer is the one that "logically completes the . . . argument," this is an Inference question. The correct answer must be true based on the information in the stimulus.

Step 2: Untangle the Stimulus

Paraphrase the information in the stimulus. First, the philosopher suggests that because nations do not think, feel, or act, they are not persons. Because they are not persons, they have no moral rights or responsibilities. However, the philosopher says a nation needs many citizens to think the nation *does* have moral rights and responsibilities, because only that would lead people to make sacrifices for their nation.

Step 3: Make a Prediction

Connect the ideas in the stimulus together. Nations do not literally have moral rights and responsibilities. But, if nations are going to survive, then citizens need to think that they do. Thus, it appears that a nation needs its citizens to believe something that is not literally true.

Step 4: Evaluate the Answer Choices

(B) matches the prediction. Translated into Formal Logic, it reads:

If a nation survives → many citizens have literally false beliefs

(A) is Out of Scope. It suggests that something else would need to motivate citizens to make sacrifices. But based on the stimulus, it could be true that the false belief that a nation has moral rights is adequate to motivate citizens.

(C) mentions moral praise and blame, both of which are Out of Scope. Neither appears in the stimulus.

(D) goes Out of Scope by introducing the value judgment that nations are not worth the sacrifices citizens make for them. While the philosopher argues that the sacrifices citizens make for nations might be based on a false belief, it still could be true that nations are worth those sacrifices.

(E) is Extreme. While the stimulus does suggest that in the case of moral rights and responsibilities, it makes sense for citizens to think of the nation metaphorically, the stimulus only covers this one scenario. It could be true that in plenty of other cases, it makes better sense to think of the nation in literal terms.

9. (D) Inference ★★★★

Step 1: Identify the Question Type

A question stem that asks you to use the statements above to support one of the answers (direction of support flowing downward) is an Inference question. Look for Formal Logic deductions or try to combine pieces of information.

Step 2: Untangle the Stimulus

While not in Formal Logic form, the statements create a chain of causality. The media doesn't thoroughly cover local politics, and political business is conducted secretively. That leads to isolating local politicians from the electorate. That leads to a reduced chance that public participation will get a positive response from officials. Finally, that discourages resident participation in local politics.

Step 3: Make a Prediction

Typically, when presented with a chain of events, line them up sequentially (as these conveniently already are) and focus on the endpoints. So, the editorialist believes that the lack of media coverage and secret nature of local politics eventually results in discouraging resident participation in local politics. The correct answer will likely relate to that connection. Otherwise, check each answer choice against the stimulus to see if it *must* be true.

Step 4: Evaluate the Answer Choices

(D) is correct. Because infrequent media coverage of local politics triggers a chain of results that tends to discourage resident involvement in local politics, increasing such coverage would reduce "at least" that one cause.

(A) is subtly Extreme. The stimulus only indicates that some level of isolation has the effect of reducing the chance of a positive official response. From that, it cannot be deduced that less isolation would be *likely* to produce a positive response. If this choice said "more likely" (comparative) it would be correct. But *likely* (absolute) goes too far.

(B) is incorrect. The opinionated recommendation language (*should*) is a red flag. The editorialist merely presents a causal chain; she doesn't present her own opinion about preserving or changing that chain. Additionally, the phrase "this *would avoid* discouraging resident participation" is Extreme. Compare that language to the correct answer **(D)**: "reduce at least one source of discouragement."

(C) is Extreme. The phrase "most important factor" is a large red flag here. Beware of Inference question answer choices that mention the "most important" or "primary" factor. You can know that the possibility of positive official response is *a* factor in resident participation, but not that it is the *most important* factor.

(E) is incorrect. It superficially appears to be the contrapositive of the causal chain, but because the statements in the stimulus are not stated absolutely, it is inappropriate to indicate that the absence of a result *causes* the absence of a trigger. For example, a brick thrown through a window always causes the glass to break. However, while the contrapositive says the absence of broken glass is sufficient to know that a brick has not been thrown through the window, you cannot assert that the absence of broken glass *caused* the brick to not be thrown.

10. (B) Inference ★★★

Step 1: Identify the Question Type

A question that directs you to use information from the stimulus to *support* an answer choice (the direction of support flowing down) is an Inference question.

Step 2: Untangle the Stimulus

The first couple of sentences focus on the importance in science of testing hypotheses and gaining recognition from overthrowing conventional wisdom. Subsequently, the author indicates that though predictions of global warming are widely accepted, some scientists remain skeptical. Finally, though hundreds of researchers are striving to make breakthroughs in that area, very few have found evidence against the likelihood of global warming.

Step 3: Make a Prediction

The correct answer to an Inference question is not always readily predictable. In the absence of Formal Logic or a clear deduction resulting from combining two pieces of information, inventory the facts and note any emphasized information. In this stimulus, the second and fourth sentences are the most emphasized and absolute: "*Nothing brings more recognition* than overthrowing conventional wisdom" and it's *remarkable* that hundreds of scientists are focusing on climatology yet few find evidence against global warming. Combined, those statements suggest that a scientist could make her mark by being the one to disprove global warming. In the absence of that choice, approach each answer by asking, "Does the stimulus support this statement?"

Step 4: Evaluate the Answer Choices

(B) is correct. The author indicates that global warming is "widely accepted" with only a few finding evidence against it, and that "[n]othing brings more recognition than overthrowing conventional wisdom." Thus, recognition would act as a motive for scientists to discredit the conventional wisdom that global warming is likely. The use of the qualifier *most* is acceptable here, because, based on the stimulus, all scientists in climatology have this motive to some degree.

(A) is a 180. The author states that science is built on attempting to show that hypotheses are incorrect, and then says it is "accordingly unsurprising" that some scientists are skeptical of global warming predictions.

(C) is Extreme. The author says global warming predictions are widely accepted, but also acknowledges that a few have found counter evidence. This answer goes too far in asserting that global warming has been *conclusively* proven true.

(D) is Out of Scope. The stimulus does not indicate whether or not skeptics have offered any alternative hypotheses.

(E) is Extreme. The word *primarily* is a red flag in Inference answers. While the author believes that recognition is a motivator of scientists—and indeed recognition is the only motivation the author mentions—the author never compares the importance of this motivator to other motivations. You cannot assume that because an LSAT author mentions only one factor, it is the primary or most important factor.

Principle (Inference)

11. (B) Principle (Identify/Inference) ★☆☆☆

Step 1: Identify the Question Type

Because the correct answer is the *proposition* "best illustrated by the passage," this is a Principle question. You have to determine the principle illustrated by the stimulus and then find it in the answer choices, which means this is an Identify the Principle question.

Step 2: Untangle the Stimulus

The question stem describes the stimulus as a *passage*, so don't necessarily expect to find an argument in the stimulus. Read it like you would an Inference question, paraphrasing the information as you go. First, Jablonski has a longstanding practice of donating cars to the local schools' drivers ed programs. Second, Jablonski donated the cars in order to encourage better driving in hopes of decreasing car accidents. Third, some people have bought cars from Jablonksi because they support her donations of cars to the schools.

Step 3: Make a Prediction

The correct answer will summarize the information from the stimulus in more general terms. So, someone (Jablonski) who did a good deed (donating cars to the schools) with a good intention (stopping car accidents) also profited from the good deed (because locals bought cars from Jablonski).

Step 4: Evaluate the Answer Choices

(B) matches the prediction. Because *altruistic* means "helping others," Jablonski's action certainly qualifies. Not only did her good deed help local students, she also profited from it when locals bought cars from her.

(A) is not supported by the stimulus. There may be many ways to reduce accidents. Jablonski just happens to support driver education.

(C) makes a claim that is not supported by the stimulus. It may be that older drivers, too, could benefit from driver education.

(D) is Extreme because it says altruistic actions are *usually* in one's best interest. The stimulus describes one situation where altruistic actions benefited the person performing them; you cannot infer from a single situation that altruistic actions usually work out in one's best interest.

(E) goes Out of Scope by introducing the idea of what makes an action successful. The stimulus does not include information about whether or not Jablonski's action actually accomplished its intention of preventing car accidents. Additionally, while the stimulus says *some* members of the community showed their support for her actions, that doesn't necessarily mean there was *broad* support.

12. (C) Principle (Apply/Inference) ★☆☆☆

Step 1: Identify the Question Type

Despite a lack of usual terms, this is a Principle question. However, it's interesting in that the stimulus provides both a specific situation and an "analysis." So, you'll need to treat the analysis as a broad principle and find a specific situation in the answers that conforms to that rule, which is what makes it an Apply the Principle question. However, it could also be construed as an Identify and Apply the Principle question. The situation paragraph in the stimulus can be used to identify the principle, which is confirmed in the analysis paragraph. Then another situation that matches that same principle can be found in the answer choices. Under either categorization, the correct answer will contain a specific situation that would also be covered by the principle.

Step 2: Untangle the Stimulus

The principle presented in the analysis is that people sometimes choose appearances over comfort or pleasure. The situation of someone living in a cold climate that buys a coat that is stylish but not warm is an example of that principle.

Step 3: Make a Prediction

The correct answer will present someone else who chooses appearances over comfort or pleasure.

Step 4: Evaluate the Answer Choices

(C) matches the prediction. The couple chooses a wine to appear more impressive, rather than selecting their favorite wine, which is more pleasurable (better tasting) and more comfortable (cheaper).

(A) is Out of Scope. The person in this answer choice does not choose based on appearances. In fact, **(A)** does not indicate why the person chooses the automobile over public transportation. Nor does it indicate that public transportation would be more comfortable or pleasurable than driving to work.

(B) is Out of Scope because the parent chooses based on color and comfort, not safety. The stimulus does not include the idea of safety. Additionally, comfort is sought, not sacrificed as it is in the stimulus.

(D) is Out of Scope because the person chooses based on environmental concerns, not appearances, over comfort (warmth). The stimulus does not include the idea of environmental concerns.

(E) is Out of Scope because even though the acrobat acquires something for its appearance (the impressive outfit), there is no information suggesting that any comfort or pleasure was sacrificed.

13. (D) Principle (Apply/Inference) ★☆☆☆

Step 1: Identify the Question Type

The stimulus asks for an individual whose actions exemplify the ethicist's criteria for "the most advanced kind of moral motivation." Taking the ethicist's criteria as a rule or principle, apply it to the actions described in each answer choice. Only the correct answer will feature a person acting in accordance with the ethicist's description of the "most advanced" morality.

Step 2: Untangle the Stimulus

The stimulus defines the "most advanced kind of moral motivation" straightaway: It is "based solely on abstract principles." The second sentence defines what is not "most advanced": "calculated self-interest" and conformity to social norms.

Step 3: Make a Prediction

The correct answer will describe someone behaving in a way that is motivated solely by abstract principles and that is not motivated by self-interest, a desire to conform, or both.

Step 4: Evaluate the Answer Choices

(D) is an example of a person who behaves according to a belief that protecting the environment is more important than money. The individual here is motivated by an abstract ideal and shuns self-interest, so this answer meets the ethicist's definition of advanced moral motivation.

(A) has a person who acts because he fears he will look stingy. This self-interested adherence to social norms is the opposite of what the ethicist would consider to be advanced moral motivation.

(B) is incorrect because it has a person who acts to improve his employer's opinion of him. This is an example of acting from self-interest, the opposite of the ethicist's advanced moral motivation.

(C) is also incorrect because Donna is acting in self-interest. She fears retaliation from her employers, so according to the ethicist's criteria, she is not acting in accordance with advanced moral motivation.

(E) is incorrect because Leigh is acting to conform to her colleague's expectations while avoiding the abstract ideal. Desiring to adhere to social norms and conventions goes against the ethicist's definition of advanced moral motivation.

14. (A) Principle (Identify/Inference) ★★★★

Step 1: Identify the Question Type

The word *proposition*, like policy, rule, or generalization, indicates a Principle question. Because the question stem indicates the general principle is located in the answer choices, the stimulus will contain a specific situation. Your job is to broaden that specific situation into a rule. Oftentimes, the correct answer will merely summarize the reasoning in general terms.

Step 2: Untangle the Stimulus

The author's conclusion, indicated by the Contrast Keyword *[h]owever*, is that "designer interaction with consumers is superior to survey data." Contrast Keywords also often highlight the most important piece of evidence; in this case, *but* emphasizes that survey data can't explain to designers how to change a feature to improve customer satisfaction.

Step 3: Make a Prediction

The author says survey data can't help designers understand how to improve features and then argues that interaction with consumers is *superior*. The author's reasoning indicates that interaction with consumers *can* help designers understand how to improve features. The correct answer should focus on consumer interaction helping designers improve a product.

Step 4: Evaluate the Answer Choices

(A) matches the prediction. It incorporates the argument's conclusion regarding "interaction with consumers" and the evidence regarding changes to a product to "receive a higher rating."

(B) avoids the main point of the argument: that consumer interaction is beneficial.

(C) is Out of Scope. There is no reference to "specific market niches."

(D) is Extreme. The author prefers one type of consumer feedback over another, but he does not indicate that failure to consult consumers will guarantee that a product has unappealing features.

(E) is an Irrelevant Comparison. The argument does not distinguish between external and internal design components.

Paradox

15. (D) Paradox ★★★★

Step 1: Identify the Question Type

The question stem calls for the answer choice that will resolve or explain an apparent paradox. Remember that Paradox questions rarely have a conclusion or evidence. Rather, they consist of a set of seemingly contradictory facts. Find the answer choice that makes those facts make sense together.

Step 2: Untangle the Stimulus

The stimulus says that cats mostly just stretch and yawn. The Keyword *[y]et* signals the unexpected, paradoxical fact. Cats, the stimulus continues, have a strong musculature that most animals would need lots of exercise to acquire.

Step 3: Make a Prediction

You don't need to have a specifically worded prediction, just articulate what the correct answer must do. Here, it will explain how cats do nothing but sleep, stretch, and yawn all the time yet have a strong, agile musculature.

Step 4: Evaluate the Answer Choices

(D) is correct. It shows how both parts of this stimulus could be true. If cats get ample exercise from frequent stretching, that helps to explain how they get the exercise necessary to maintain their agile musculature.

(A) is incorrect because it tells you only why cats sleep; it doesn't tell you how such a somnolent lifestyle manages to provide them with an agile musculature.

(B) is a 180. It deepens the mystery because it indicates that other animals are similar to cats in this respect. It doesn't help explain the main puzzle: *how* cats get adequate exercise from sleeping. **(B)** just asserts that cats aren't unique.

(C) cites yet another fact about cats, but it doesn't explain how it would contribute to their strong, agile musculature. Be careful not to add several additional assumptions to an answer choice to try to make it more relevant than it is.

(E) is Out of Scope. It says *why* cats need a strong, agile, musculature, but it doesn't say *how* they get it.

16. (A) Paradox (EXCEPT) ★☆☆☆

Step 1: Identify the Question Type

Because the correct answer will not explain the increase mentioned in the stimulus, this is a Paradox EXCEPT question. The correct answer will deepen the paradox or go outside the scope of the stimulus. The four incorrect answers will resolve the paradox.

Step 2: Untangle the Stimulus

Start by identifying the paradox. After Jimmy bought an efficient gas heater, his gas bill went up.

Step 3: Make a Prediction

Because they are more concrete than the correct answer, predict the four incorrect answers in Logical Reasoning EXCEPT questions. Here, each incorrect answer will resolve the paradox by explaining why Jimmy's gas bill increased. Here, likely something about the gas heater, the gas, or Jimmy's lifestyle would explain the increase. When you find an answer that explains why Jimmy's gas bill went up, eliminate it. If you find an answer that does not explain why Jimmy's gas bill went up, choose it.

Step 4: Evaluate the Answer Choices

(A) deepens the paradox. This choice confirms that the gas heater uses a smaller percentage of gas, and so an increased bill makes even less sense. Thus, this is the correct choice because it does not explain the paradox.

(B) resolves the paradox by providing a reason why Jimmy's gas use would go up: More people may be using hot water, so more gas is likely consumed.

(C) resolves the paradox. Jimmy's laundry would increase the amount of water that needs to be heated every month, not to mention the additional gas cost from the dryer.

(D) resolves the paradox. If gas itself costs more, then Jimmy's gas bill would reasonably increase, possibly even if the water heater uses less gas than before.

(E) resolves the paradox. It confirms that gas usage was particularly heavy in general after installation, whether from the gas water heater or perhaps his home's gas furnace.

17. (C) Paradox ★★☆☆

Step 1: Identify the Question Type

A question stem that asks you to *explain* a difference is a Paradox question. This question stem points out the two seemingly contradictory facts to be reconciled.

Step 2: Untangle the Stimulus

In the nineteenth century, much of the funding for the arts came from the French Academy of Art, which discouraged innovation. Accordingly, French sculpture of that time showed little innovation. However, French painting showed lots of innovation.

Step 3: Make a Prediction

The stimulus provides a reason for the limited innovation in French sculpture. You need an answer choice that explains the large amount of innovation in French painting that arose despite the discouragement of the French academy, which funded both sculpture and painting. Your prediction doesn't need to identify a specific explanation; a general prediction is usually best and sufficient for a Paradox question.

Step 4: Evaluate the Answer Choices

(C) provides a factor that accounts for innovation in French painting despite the disapproval of the French academy of art. Painters, unlike sculptors, did not need funding to afford the inexpensive tools of their trade and were thus free to be creative.

(A) is a 180. The academy discouraged innovation, so those who were most beholden to the academy would have been most likely to see their creativity stifled.

(B) is a 180 similar to **(A)**. If individual painters received more support from the academy than sculptors did, then it would seem painters would be more likely to have their creativity stifled.

(D) is Out of Scope. The lack of overlap doesn't explain why the innovation levels between the groups varied.

(E) does not provide a distinction between painters and sculptors. The fact that overall funding decreased for both types of artists doesn't explain why painters were more innovative.

CHANNEL SPOTLIGHT

Logical Reasoning—Managing the Section

By The LSAT Channel Faculty

Watch the video lesson for this Spotlight in your online Study Plan.

Throughout the LSAT, there is an inherent tension between speed and accuracy. The Logical Reasoning sections are no exception, of course. With 25 questions to read, analyze, and evaluate in just 35 minutes, you have, on average, only about 1 minute 20 seconds per question. Given those tight constraints, every test taker feels some degree of time pressure. Great test takers, however, maximize their scores in Logical Reasoning not only by mastering the question types and their associated skills, but also by managing the section to prioritize easier and more familiar questions. Top scorers train themselves to avoid "ego battles" with individual questions and to make the best decisions about where to spend their valuable time in the section.

In the video lesson that accompanies this Spotlight, you'll learn how LSAT experts use the format of the Logical Reasoning section to their advantage. Some of the concepts you'll see here—such as triage and strategic skipping and guessing—are similar to those LSAT experts use in the Reading Comprehension section. Because of the structural differences between the Reading Comprehension and Logical Reasoning sections, however, it is important for you to learn how to deploy these strategies effectively in Logical Reasoning. To do that, you need a little background on how the testmaker arranges the questions within the Logical Reasoning section.

The Danger Zone

Kaplan collects and analyzes performance data on every LSAT released by LSAC. When several tests' worth of performance results for Logical Reasoning are aggregated, an important pattern emerges in the Logical Reasoning section.

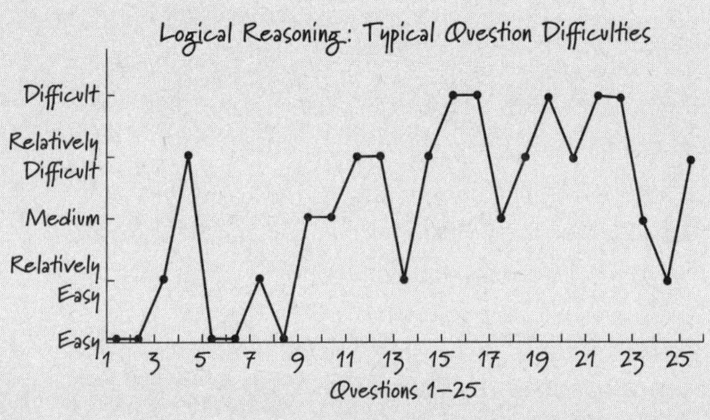

On every LSAT, some of the test's easiest—and hardest—questions are found in the Logical Reasoning section. While it is generally fair to say that the questions increase in difficulty as you progress through a section, the data reveal a more nuanced arrangement.

In many sections, a single difficult question is placed among the first eight or so questions. Likewise, one or two easier questions routinely appear among the section's final four or five questions. The most important revelation, however, is that, in most Logical Reasoning sections, there is a concentration of high-difficulty questions that runs roughly from Question 15 to Question 21. At Kaplan, we refer to that band of the section as the Danger Zone. It is here that test takers are most likely to get questions incorrect, and it is here that they are most likely to lose control of time management.

In the Spotlight video, the LSAT expert will provide additional insight into the Danger Zone, and the patterns of questions typically found there. For now, keep the definition of the Danger Zone in mind as you learn the fundamentals of Logical Reasoning section management.

Triage in Logical Reasoning

Triage is a process used to determine priorities for action. In the Reading Comprehension section, you'll learn to triage (at least initially) among whole passages. In other words, you are choosing to prioritize or deprioritize blocks of 5–7 questions at a time. That approach won't work in Logical Reasoning where every question is independent and comes with its own stimulus. Trying to prioritize among 25 questions (or even among five to ten of them) before starting to answer any of them would be a waste of time. In the Logical Reasoning section, your best approach is to work question by question, but with the skill and familiarity to quickly and confidently identify the ones you may want to skip initially, flag, and come back to.

To triage effectively in Logical Reasoning, you will need to know your personal strengths and weaknesses. At least some of your prioritization will be based on preference. If you are comfortable and accurate with Formal Logic, you can confidently attack questions with conditional statements as soon as you see them. If that is an area of trepidation for you, you'll flag a question containing Formal Logic and come back to it as time permits. The same considerations apply to any question type. Capitalize on your strengths by getting to the questions you're likely to get right, whatever they may be.

Beyond playing to your individual strengths as a test taker, it's valuable to remember the Danger Zone pattern discussed above. You can confidently assume that *most* of the early questions will be straightforward, but you should also expect to find a relatively hard question in the mix. When you encounter that first difficult and time-consuming question, don't let it stop your momentum. If you spend two or three minutes on a single question at this point, you are already throwing off your timing for the whole section. Likewise, make sure you give yourself a chance to answer the questions at the end of the section; at least one or two of them is likely to be easier than what has come before. Most importantly, remember where the Danger Zone is found, typically Questions 15–21. Some test takers find it advantageous to work through the first fourteen questions in an LR section, and then skip to the end and work backward to Question 15. If that approach seems like it might be helpful to you, try it out the next time you practice a full, timed Logical Reasoning section.

Strategic Skipping and Guessing in Logical Reasoning

In Logical Reasoning, where you must evaluate each question individually, triage and strategic skipping go hand in hand. Just keep this principle in mind: Strategic skipping and guessing means skipping and guessing when it is in your interest do so. To put it another way, don't get into an "ego battle" with any Logical Reasoning question. Every question on the LSAT is worth the same value. There is no bonus for answering hard questions. One of the quickest ways to lose control of time management in Logical Reasoning is to overinvest in a single question, and one of the main reasons test takers do that is because they feel they must solve that question. The result is that these test takers wind up skipping and guessing out of frustration, or after investing two minutes or more in a difficult question.

It is far better to make the decision to skip a question quickly and confidently. Remember, you are only skipping the question temporarily. When you do this, use the flag tool to mark the question so that you can come back to it after you've racked up all the easier and faster points available to you. When you get low on time, you can always click to bubble in a guess for any question you've skipped, and you can do so proudly, with the knowledge that you've guessed only on a question that would have been difficult to get anyway. Don't forget to select an answer for every question (even if it is just a guess) as there is no wrong-answer penalty on the LSAT.

Practicing Logical Reasoning Section Management and Assessing Your Skills

To get the feel for the section-management strategies you'll learn in this Spotlight video lesson, you'll need to put them into practice on real Logical Reasoning sections. The LSAT expert will give you good techniques and exercises that will help you evaluate your timed performance and find the areas in which you can improve. If you are using LSAC PrepTests as part of your preparation, set aside at least two or three tests to use for "timing" practice. You need not do the entire test in one sitting, but you will need to clear 35 minutes from your schedule for uninterrupted timed section practice. Follow the best practices from this Spotlight and the accompanying video lesson, and evaluate your section management along with your performance on individual questions. Logical Reasoning requires a combination of mastery and timing skills. Review your section performance thoroughly, studying the questions you got right as well as those you got wrong. Using Kaplan's complete explanations will help you identify your individual strengths and your areas of opportunity. Remember that complete explanations for every LSAT PrepTest in LSAC's LawHub library are available via Kaplan's LSAT Link too. See **www.kaptest.com/lsat/courses/lsat-self-study** for more information.

PART THREE

Reading Comprehension

CHAPTER 6

The Kaplan Reading Comprehension Method

Every administration of the LSAT features one scored Reading Comprehension section. There are always four passages, each around 450–500 words long and with typically a set of 6–8 questions, for a total of 26–28 questions in the section. For many first-time LSAT test takers, Reading Comprehension is the section that feels most familiar, so it should be no surprise if it is your strongest section initially. Reading Comprehension is the section most similar to other tests you've probably taken, such as the SAT or ACT. Given that the Reading Comprehension section tasks you with reading academic material and answering questions about it, the section may even remind you a bit of standard college class tests.

This superficial similarity to other kinds of testing, however, masks some unique features of LSAT Reading Comprehension. Moreover, LSAT test takers' initial comfort with Reading Comprehension often leads them to ignore this section to the detriment of their overall LSAT score. From over 40 years of experience working with LSAT test takers, we at Kaplan know that Reading Comprehension is the section in which many test takers have the hardest time improving their performance. After all, having been good readers throughout their academic careers, LSAT test takers are reluctant to change the way in which they read to suit the types of questions the LSAT testmaker asks.

We also know, however, that LSAT Reading Comprehension tests reading and reasoning skills that can be learned and mastered. Mastering them requires that you understand what is being tested and adopt a strategic reading approach to distinguish the text relevant to LSAT questions from the details and general background information the test questions largely ignore. And once you understand what the test is asking for, learning to read and answer Reading Comprehension questions quickly and accurately will take practice—a lot of practice.

A Strategic Approach to LSAT Reading Comprehension

Notice that we referred to the kind of reading that the expert test taker does as *strategic*. This is an important concept for all that follows. Rather than *deep* or *critical* reading, the kind you might do for a difficult seminar course in college, your job on the LSAT is to get the big picture of a passage—the author's Purpose and Main Idea—and to zero in on how the author makes key points and illustrates ideas or concepts. You're not preparing to have an in-depth conversation about the passage; you're preparing to answer LSAT questions. Take a look at one, and we'll discuss what it reveals about this important LSAT section.

According to the passage, the statements of Picasso and Braque indicate that

(A) they had a long-standing interest in politics

(B) they worked actively to bring about social change

(C) their formal innovations were actually the result of chance

(D) their work was a deliberate attempt to transcend visual reality

(E) the formal aspects of their work were of little interest to them

PrepTest107 Sec2 Q3

In a moment, you'll see the passage from which this question came. For now, start your analysis by looking at the question stem. First off, it begins with "[a]ccording to the passage." You will always be able to answer LSAT Reading Comprehension questions from the text you're given; outside knowledge of the subject matter is neither expected nor rewarded. How many future law students are likely to have any expertise in the subject of early modernist painters, anyway? Even more important, the question references statements made in the passage and asks what they "indicate." *How* the author uses a detail or *why* she has included it is far more relevant to LSAT questions than what might be true about the detail.

Now, let's put that question into its context on the test. On the next page, you'll see the passage followed by three of the questions from its question set. Try it out on your own. Read the passage and, on a separate piece of scratch paper, take down whatever notes seem relevant and helpful. Try to answer the questions that accompany it. Don't take too much time, though—no more than 5–6 minutes. We'll spend the rest of this chapter using this passage and its questions to illustrate how an LSAT expert reads and analyzes a Reading Comprehension passage and subsequently answers its questions efficiently and effectively. Along the way, you'll learn the Kaplan Reading Comprehension Method, the approach you'll use to tackle many more passages in the two chapters that follow this one.

For some years before the outbreak of World War I, a number of painters in different European countries developed works of art that some have described as prophetic: paintings that by challenging viewers' habitual ways of perceiving the world of the present are thus said to anticipate a future world that would be very different. The artistic styles that they brought into being varied widely, but all these styles had in common a very important break with traditions of representational art that stretched back to the Renaissance.

So fundamental is this break with tradition that it is not surprising to discover that these artists—among them Picasso and Braque in France, Kandinsky in Germany, and Malevich in Russia—are often credited with having anticipated not just subsequent developments in the arts, but also the political and social disruptions and upheavals of the modern world that came into being during and after the war. One art critic even goes so far as to claim that it is the very prophetic power of these artworks, and not their break with traditional artistic techniques, that constitutes their chief interest and value.

No one will deny that an artist may, just as much as a writer or a politician, speculate about the future and then try to express a vision of that future through making use of a particular style or choice of imagery; speculation about the possibility of war in Europe was certainly widespread during the early years of the twentieth century. But the forward-looking quality attributed to these artists should instead be credited to their exceptional aesthetic innovations rather than to any power to make clever guesses about political or social trends. For example, the clear impression we get of Picasso and Braque, the joint founders of cubism, from their contemporaries as well as from later statements made by the artists themselves, is that they were primarily concerned with problems of representation and form and with efforts to create a far more "real" reality than the one that was accessible only to the eye. The reformation of society was of no interest to them as artists.

It is also important to remember that not all decisive changes in art are quickly followed by dramatic events in the world outside art. The case of Delacroix, the nineteenth-century French painter, is revealing. His stylistic innovations startled his contemporaries—and still retain that power over modern viewers—but most art historians have decided that Delacroix adjusted himself to new social conditions that were already coming into being as a result of political upheavals that had occurred in 1830, as opposed to other artists who supposedly told of changes still to come.

1. According to the passage, the statements of Picasso and Braque indicate that

   (A) they had a long-standing interest in politics
   (B) they worked actively to bring about social change
   (C) their formal innovations were actually the result of chance
   (D) their work was a deliberate attempt to transcend visual reality
   (E) the formal aspects of their work were of little interest to them

2. The art critic mentioned in the second paragraph would be most likely to agree with which one of the following statements?

   (A) The supposed innovations of Picasso, Braque, Kandinsky, and Malevich were based on stylistic discoveries that had been made in the Renaissance but went unexplored for centuries.

   (B) The work of Picasso, Braque, Kandinsky, and Malevich possessed prophetic power because these artists employed the traditional techniques of representational art with unusual skill.

   (C) The importance of the work of Picasso, Braque, Kandinsky, and Malevich is due largely to the fact that the work was stylistically ahead of its time.

   (D) The prophecies embodied in the work of Picasso, Braque, Kandinsky, and Malevich were shrewd predictions based on insights into the European political situation.

   (E) The artistic styles brought into being by Picasso, Braque, Kandinsky, and Malevich, while stylistically innovative, were of little significance to the history of post–World War I art.

3. Which one of the following characteristics of the painters discussed in the second paragraph does the author of the passage appear to value most highly?

   (A) their insights into pre–World War I politics

   (B) the visionary nature of their social views

   (C) their mastery of the techniques of representational art

   (D) their ability to adjust to changing social conditions

   (E) their stylistic and aesthetic accomplishments

PrepTest107 Sec2 Qs 2, 3, and 7

Using a Roadmap to Answer Reading Comprehension Questions

Reflect a moment on your performance. How long did you spend reading the passage? Did you distinguish certain parts of the passage as more important or more likely to be asked about in the questions? When you turned to the questions, were you surprised by what they asked? Did you have a good idea where in the passage the relevant text could be found?

By the time you've learned and mastered the Reading Comprehension Method, you'll find that you can create a helpful Roadmap as you read the passage. To Roadmap passages effectively, LSAT experts note Keywords within the passage and jot down brief notes on their scratch paper to help them focus on the relevant parts of the passage and quickly research the answers to questions. In fact, if you learn to read as strategically as the best experts, you'll find that you can anticipate many, if not most, of the questions even before you read them.

To learn how to read Reading Comprehension passages strategically and to make good, useful Roadmaps of the passage, it's important to see how LSAT experts use Roadmaps to answer questions. Take a look at how an LSAT expert approached the questions from the passage you just tried. Don't worry if you're not sure why the expert noted certain words in the passage at this point. You'll learn to read and analyze as she did when we introduce the Reading Comprehension Method in full, and you'll practice it extensively in the next two chapters.

First up is the question you saw at the beginning of this chapter.

. . . But the forward-looking quality attributed to these artists should instead be credited to their exceptional aesthetic innovations rather than to any power to make clever guesses about political or social trends. For example, the clear impression we get of Picasso and Braque, the joint founders of cubism, from their contemporaries as well as from later statements made by the artists themselves, is that they were primarily concerned with problems of representation and form and with efforts to create a far more "real" reality than the one that was accessible only to the eye. The reformation of society was of no interest to them as artists.

#3:

Artist CAN picture a future vision.

But preWWI's were artistic innovators, not political guessers.

P + B cared about form, not social-political prediction.

1. According to the passage, the statements of Picasso and Braque indicate that

   (A) they had a long-standing interest in politics

   (B) they worked actively to bring about social change

   (C) their formal innovations were actually the result of chance

   (D) their work was a deliberate attempt to transcend visual reality

   (E) the formal aspects of their work were of little interest to them

PrepTest107 Sec2 Q3

Question Analysis: (Research) The statements of Picasso and Braque are found in the third paragraph. The author emphasizes their interest in the form and technique of art, and their attempt to "create a far more 'real' reality."

(Predict) The author says they weren't much interested in predicting or fomenting societal change.

(Answer) (D) is correct. This is supported by the text following the emphatic "primarily concerned with" language.

Wrong answers: (A) 180. This runs counter to the author's point in the passage. (B) 180. This is contradicted by the paragraph's final sentence. (C) Outside the Scope. If anything, the passage implies that they thought about art and worked actively to change it. (E) 180. According to the passage, these artists were "primarily concerned with . . . representation and form."

Notice how the LSAT expert uses his "map" of the passage to research the text and predict the correct answer. The detail cited in the question stem ("the statements of Picasso and Braque") is evidence for the author's main point. So, the correct answer will have to illustrate that point (and wrong answers—such as (A) and (B) in this case—may contradict that main point). Moreover, the expert has taken note of the author's emphasis (by highlighting the Keyword "primarily") on the painters' interest in artistic form and their attempts to transcend reality. LSAT experts become so strategic at reading LSAT passages that they will often spot language in the passage that will be asked about in the question set, even before they have read the question stems.

The second question you answered asked about a different part of the passage and, more importantly, about the opinion of someone other than the author of the passage.

So fundamental is this break with tradition that it is not surprising to discover that these artists—among them Picasso and Braque in France, Kandinsky in Germany, and Malevich in Russia—are often credited with having anticipated not just subsequent developments in the arts, but also the political and social disruptions and upheavals of the modern world that came into being during and after the war. One art critic even goes so far as to claim that it is the very prophetic power of these artworks, and not their break with traditional artistic techniques, that constitutes their chief interest and value.

#2:
Some critics went further:
argued that artists predicted a chaotic future
prophecy more impt than art.

2. The art critic mentioned in the second paragraph would be most likely to agree with which one of the following statements?

(A) The supposed innovations of Picasso, Braque, Kandinsky, and Malevich were based on stylistic discoveries that had been made in the Renaissance but went unexplored for centuries.

(B) The work of Picasso, Braque, Kandinsky, and Malevich possessed prophetic power because these artists employed the traditional techniques of representational art with unusual skill.

(C) The importance of the work of Picasso, Braque, Kandinsky, and Malevich is due largely to the fact that the work was stylistically ahead of its time.

(D) The prophecies embodied in the work of Picasso, Braque, Kandinsky, and Malevich were shrewd predictions based on insights into the European political situation.

(E) The artistic styles brought into being by Picasso, Braque, Kandinsky, and Malevich, while stylistically innovative, were of little significance to the history of post–World War I art.

PrepTest107 Sec2 Q2

Question Analysis: (Research) In Paragraph 2, the author characterizes the views of critics (with whom he disagrees) who think that the pre-WWI painters were most interesting because of their works' "prophetic power" in areas such as politics and society.

(Predict) The correct answer will match this point of view.

(Answer) (D) is correct. This matches the view of the critics (and opposes that of the author).

Wrong answers: (A) Outside the Scope. It is the author, not the critics, who is interested in the painters' stylistic breakthroughs. What's more, the author says that these painters broke with the styles that had begun during the Renaissance. (B) Outside the Scope. We don't know if the critics attributed the painters' prophetic power to particular techniques. Even if they did, it would not be the representational techniques that the pre-WWI painters rejected. (C) 180. This view is closer to that of the author, who finds the painters' break with traditional techniques to constitute their "chief interest and value." The critics were more interested in the paintings' "prophetic power." (E) 180. The statement in this answer contradicts both the critics *and* the author, both of whom find the painters' work significant.

It is very common to find multiple opinions and points of view expressed in LSAT Reading Comprehension passages. The author may agree or disagree in whole or in part with the other positions he cites or describes. LSAT experts always keep track of who thinks what. The preceding question was about a view the author seeks to discredit, but sure enough, one of the wrong answers—(C)—accurately reflected the author's argument. Pay attention to multiple voices in the text of the passage, and make sure you know whose viewpoint is being called for in the question stem.

The third question also rewarded your ability to keep track of the points of view and to accurately summarize them. But this time, the question asks about the author's position.

So fundamental is this break with tradition that it is not surprising to discover that these artists—among them Picasso and Braque in France, Kandinsky in Germany, and Malevich in Russia—are often credited with having anticipated not just subsequent developments in the arts, but also the political and social disruptions and upheavals of the modern world that came into being during and after the war. One art critic even goes so far as to claim that it is the very prophetic power of these artworks, and not their break with traditional artistic techniques, that constitutes their chief interest and value.

. . . But the forward-looking quality attributed to these artists should instead be credited to their exceptional aesthetic innovations rather than to any power to make clever guesses about political or social trends.

#2:
Some critics went further:
argued that artists predicted a chaotic future
prophecy more impt than art.
#3:
Artist CAN picture a future vision.
But preWWI's were artistic innovators, not political guessers.
P + B cared about form, not social-political prediction.

3. Which one of the following characteristics of the painters discussed in the second paragraph does the author of the passage appear to value most highly?

(A) their insights into pre–World War I politics
(B) the visionary nature of their social views
(C) their mastery of the techniques of representational art
(D) their ability to adjust to changing social conditions
(E) their stylistic and aesthetic accomplishments

PrepTest107 Sec2 Q7

Question Analysis: (Research) While the painters are first discussed in Paragraph 2, the author continues to explain his appreciation of them in Paragraph 3.

(Predict) The author thinks the stylistic and technical break with tradition is what is most valuable about their work. He puts little stock in the view that they were "prophets" of politics or society.

(Answer) (E) is correct. This agrees with the author's position as it is presented in Paragraphs 2 and 3.

Wrong answers: (A) 180. This contradicts the author's position. This is what the critics find so intriguing. (B) 180. This contradicts the author's position. This is more of what the critics find so intriguing. (C) Distortion. The author values the painters' break with representational art. We don't know if he thinks they mastered it first. (D) Faulty Use of Detail. The author seems to appreciate Delacroix's response to societal change, but Delacroix is discussed in Paragraph 4, and this question asks about the pre-WWI artists discussed in Paragraph 2.

It is not uncommon for your research on one Reading Comprehension question to help you predict the correct answer to another. Here, your work on Questions 2 and 3 are just two sides of the same coin. LSAT experts know that the testmaker often presents questions that reward your ability to characterize multiple points of view. The notes that the expert jotted down in the margins of the passage helped him research and predict both of those questions efficiently and effectively.

The LSAT expert *never* considered the possibility that two or more answers were technically correct and then tried to choose the one that was more correct. He stuck to the principle of "one right; four demonstrably wrong" in all cases. It may be hard to accept that the correct and incorrect answers are just as clear-cut in Reading Comprehension as they are in Logical Reasoning, but they are.

Now that you've seen how the LSAT expert uses the Roadmap to research the passage and predict the correct answer, let's examine the entire process from start to finish.

The Kaplan Reading Comprehension Method

To handle four passages in 35 minutes and to get as many right answers as possible from this section, you need to have an approach that you can use consistently. There are five steps to the Kaplan Reading Comprehension Method. The first is all about reading and Roadmapping the passage. The next four steps provide the fastest and surest way to answer each question correctly.

THE KAPLAN READING COMPREHENSION METHOD

STEP 1 **Read the Passage Strategically**—note Keywords and jot down paragraph notes to summarize the portions of the passage relevant to LSAT questions; summarize the author's Topic/Scope/Purpose/Main Idea.

STEP 2 **Read the Question Stem**—identify the question type, characterize the correct and incorrect answers, and look for clues to guide your research.

STEP 3 **Research the Relevant Text**—based on the clues in the question stem, consult your Roadmap; for open-ended questions, refer to your Topic/Scope/Purpose/Main Idea summaries.

STEP 4 **Predict the Correct Answer**—based on your research (or, for open-ended questions, your Topic/Scope/Purpose/Main Idea summaries), predict the meaning of the correct answer.

STEP 5 **Evaluate the Answer Choices**—select the choice that matches your prediction of the correct answer, or eliminate the four wrong answer choices.

As you practice, make it your goal to complete Step 1 in about 3–4 minutes, leaving 4–5 minutes for the question set. If you've completed the chapters on Logical Reasoning, Steps 2–5 of the Reading Comprehension Method should look pretty familiar. They're identical to the steps for handling a Logical Reasoning question, with the exception of Step 3. In Reading Comprehension, you will already have read and Roadmapped the passage before you analyze the question stem. Discipline yourself to *research* targeted parts of the passage (that is, to consult the Roadmap you've already made) based on the clues in the stem. Test takers who *reread* the passage (or big chunks of it) for each question run out of time; it's clear that these test takers do not trust their original reading of the passage and aren't reading strategically from the start.

Step 1—Read the Passage Strategically

Reading strategically means reading not to memorize factual details but to get LSAT questions correct. As you've already seen, the LSAT is far more interested in *how* the author uses a detail than in *what* the facts about the detail are. Similarly, the LSAT is interested in your ability to discern *why* the author is writing the passage (or some portion of it)—his Purpose in writing, if you will. The first step of the Reading Comprehension Method targets the parts of the passage the test is likely to ask about and, when mastered, allows you to read the passage one time and be ready to research and answer every question.

There are two aspects to Strategic Reading, one physical and one mental.

The Physical Roadmap—Keywords and Paragraph Notes

As an LSAT expert reads a Reading Comprehension passage, she reads actively, ready to highlight or underline Keywords, words that indicate the structure of the passage. As you learn to identify Keywords, your reading will become much more strategic because Keywords prompt you to read actively, interrogating why the author is emphasizing a certain point or contrasting one idea with another. There are six categories of Keywords you should look for. You'll see them highlighted in every sample Roadmap you review in this book and elsewhere in your Kaplan materials.

LSAT STRATEGY

Strategic Reading Keywords

- **Emphasis/Opinion**—words that signal that the author finds a detail noteworthy, words that signal the author has a positive or negative opinion, or any other subjective or evaluative language on the author's part (e.g., *especially, crucial, unfortunately, disappointing, I suggest, it seems likely*)
- **Contrast**—words indicating that the author thinks two details or ideas are incompatible or illustrate conflicting points (e.g., *but, yet, despite, on the other hand*)
- **Logic**—words that indicate an argument, either the author's or someone else's (e.g., *thus, therefore, because*)
- **Illustration**—words indicating an example offered to clarify or support another point (e.g., *for example, this shows, to illustrate*)
- **Sequence/Chronology**—words showing an order to certain steps in a process or to developments over time (e.g., *traditionally, in the past, recently, today, first, second, finally, earlier, since*)
- **Continuation**—words indicating that a subsequent example or detail supports the same point or illustrates the same idea (e.g., *moreover, in addition, and, also, further*)

As you review sample Roadmaps, you'll see that the LSAT experts seldom note the sorts of factual information you would likely pinpoint in a conventional textbook for a subject-matter course in school. Instead, their focus on Keywords helps them discern the structure of the passage and thus the author's point of view and purpose in writing.

The other thing the LSAT expert does is to use her pen to jot down brief, abbreviated paragraph notes wherever she encounters an important point in the text. As you review the LSAT experts' Roadmaps, don't make too much of the specific wording. They may be as simple as "Ex" for an example or as thorough as a short description. Everyone will have slightly different notes on their scratch paper. The important thing is that your notes are simple, accurate, and legible, and that they target the author's key points and are not just a list of facts that repeats the passage.

Some test takers wonder why they should take notes at all. The answer is simple: Your job in strategic reading is to highlight the parts of the passage that will help you answer LSAT questions. If you leave a passage entirely blank, you haven't distinguished the parts you're likely to need when researching the questions. Likewise, if you have highlighted or underlined almost everything in the passage, you haven't distinguished what's relevant in that case either. The LSAT expert leaves the passage marked up and jots down notes on the scratch paper in a way that is extremely helpful when it comes to answering the questions.

The Mental Roadmap—Summarizing Topic/Scope/Purpose/Main Idea

While the LSAT expert's stylus and pen are occupied noting Keywords and jotting down notes, her mind is also keeping track of the author's "big picture" in the passage. The most helpful way to grasp the big picture is to build a summary as you read. Pay attention to the four concepts outlined below. You'll usually encounter them in the text in the order they're presented in the strategy box.

LSAT STRATEGY

Reading Comprehension—the "big picture"

- **Topic**—the overall subject of the passage
- **Scope**—the particular aspect of the Topic on which the author focuses
- **Purpose**—the author's reason for writing the passage (express this as a verb—e.g., *to refute, to outline, to evaluate, to critique*)
- **Main Idea**—the author's conclusion or overall takeaway; if you combine the author's Purpose and Scope, you'll usually have a good sense of the Main Idea.

On test day, there is no need for you to write down these summaries. Just make sure you can clearly articulate the author's Purpose and Main Idea within the scope of the passage so that you can predict the correct answers to Global questions and Inference questions that ask you for the author's overall point of view or opinion. During practice sessions, it is a good idea to jot down your summaries of the author's Purpose and Main Idea so that you can compare them to the summaries outlined in the explanations. You'll quickly start to see when and why your summaries were too broad or too narrow or missed the scope of the passage.

Take a look now at an LSAT expert's strategic reading and Roadmap for the passage on the pre-WWI European painters. We'll take Step 1 paragraph by paragraph. In the left-hand column, you'll see the physical Roadmap of Keywords and Paragraph Notes. In the right-hand "Analysis" column, you get some idea of what the LSAT expert was thinking as he read the passage.

LSAT Passage	Analysis
For some years before the outbreak of World War I, a number of painters in different European countries developed works of art that some have described as prophetic: paintings that by challenging viewers' habitual ways of perceiving the world of the present are thus said to anticipate a future world that would be very different. The artistic styles that they brought into being varied widely, but all these styles had in common a very important break with traditions of representational art that stretched back to the Renaissance. #1: PreWWI painters challenged views of world. Huge departure from old trad.	**Step 1:** The passage's **Topic** is a group of pre–World War I European painters. "Some" art historians or critics (but not necessarily the author) consider their paintings "prophetic." The author, however, emphasizes ("very important") their break with traditional, representational art. That break, and the author's assessment of it, is likely to be the passage's **Scope**.

Take note of how the LSAT expert zeroes in on Keywords in order to ask what the author is trying to present and why. You'll usually, as the LSAT expert did here, find the Topic and Scope in the first paragraph. Don't force these summaries, however. If the Scope doesn't emerge until the second paragraph, that's okay.

By the end of the first paragraph, the LSAT expert is fairly confident that the "very important" break with tradition constitutes the passage's Scope. This is confirmed at the beginning of the second paragraph, where the author calls the break "[s]o fundamental."

LSAT Passage	Analysis
So fundamental is this break with tradition that it is not surprising to discover that these artists—among them Picasso and Braque in France, Kandinsky in Germany, and Malevich in Russia—are often credited with having anticipated not just subsequent developments in the arts, but also the political and social disruptions and upheavals of the modern world that came into being during and after the war. One art critic even goes so far as to claim that it is the very prophetic power of these artworks, and not their break with traditional artistic techniques, that constitutes their chief interest and value. #2: Some critics went further: argued that artists predicted a chaotic future prophecy more impt than art.	**Step 1 (cont.):** The author underscores the Scope of the passage: The pre-WWI painters' break with tradition was "so fundamental" that it led some critics (again, not the author) to think that the painters were actually predicting political and societal changes. The author, however, thinks that the painters' "chief interest and value" was in their artistic and technical breakthroughs.

LSAT experts always read actively. They anticipate where the author will go in the subsequent paragraph. They note which points need further clarification or support. By the end of the second paragraph, the expert knows the author's position and how it differs from that of the critics, so he may be a little surprised by the first sentence of the third paragraph.

LSAT Passage	Analysis
No one will deny that an artist may, just as much as a writer or a politician, speculate about the future and then try to express a vision of that future through making use of a particular style or choice of imagery; speculation about the possibility of war in Europe was certainly widespread during the early years of the twentieth century. But the forward-looking quality attributed to these artists should instead be credited to their exceptional aesthetic innovations rather than to any power to make clever guesses about political or social trends. For example, the clear impression we get of Picasso and Braque, the joint founders of cubism, from their contemporaries as well as from later statements made by the artists themselves, is that they were primarily concerned with problems of representation and form and with efforts to create a far more "real" reality than the one that was accessible only to the eye. The reformation of society was of no interest to them as artists. #3: Artist CAN picture a future vision. But preWWI's were artistic innovators, not political guessers. P + B cared about form, not social-political prediction.	**Step 1 (cont.):** Paragraph 3 begins with a concession by the author: Of course the painters, just like everyone else, were interested in political and social developments. Then, the author resumes his argument. The author's **Purpose** and **Main Idea** are signaled by the Keyword "[b]ut": The painters were predictive ("forward-looking") in terms of artistic style and technique, not in the realms of politics and society. The author supports this conclusion with examples: the statements of Picasso, Braque, and their peers. These statements reveal an emphasis ("they were *primarily* concerned with") on the technical problems of art (how does one create "a far more 'real' reality"?), not on societal reformation.

The author begins the third paragraph with a small concession (of course, everyone was thinking about war), but then he resumes his argument in earnest. For the LSAT expert, the structure of the third paragraph is pure gold: The Keyword "[b]ut" is a good indication that the author's Main Point will follow, and the Keyword phrase "[f]or example" signals his primary evidence. You even saw, in the expert's handling of Question 3, how the Emphasis Keyword "primarily" helped the expert predict the correct answer and zero in on the correct choice.

In a passage like this one, where the Main Point is made and supported before the final paragraph, it may be harder to predict what the end of the passage will cover. It might provide additional support for the author's position or discuss the implications of his findings. Here, the LSAT expert notes "also important to remember" in the fourth paragraph's first line.

LSAT Passage	Analysis
It is also important to remember that not all decisive changes in art are quickly followed by dramatic events in the world outside art. The case of Delacroix, the nineteenth-century French painter, is revealing. His stylistic innovations startled his contemporaries—and still retain that power over modern viewers—but most art historians have decided that Delacroix adjusted himself to new social conditions that were already coming into being as a result of political upheavals that had occurred in 1830, as opposed to other artists who supposedly told of changes still to come. *PrepTest107 Sec2 Qs 1-7* #4: Sometimes political change precedes artistic change ex. Delacroix	**Step 1 (cont.):** The passage's final paragraph offers further evidence ("also important") in the form of a parallel example. The author considers Delacroix's work "revealing" in that it shows that changes in art aren't always followed by changes in society. Delacroix was artistically novel, but his work was a reflection of social changes already occurring, not an attempt to predict or trigger future changes.

As you learn to emulate the LSAT expert's approach in Step 1, you'll find yourself summarizing the Purpose and Main Idea without even having to stop and remind yourself to do so.

You'll see more examples of LSAT experts' strategic reading and Roadmapping in the next chapter. But keep Step 1 in perspective. You don't get LSAT points directly from the Roadmap, and there's no such thing as an objectively right or wrong Roadmap. The Roadmap is a tool to help you answer questions correctly, quickly, and confidently. If, upon completing Step 1, you find yourself ready for the question set and able to move through it efficiently, you're Roadmapping well.

Steps 2–5—Answering Reading Comprehension Questions

Several standard question types accompany Reading Comprehension passages—Global, Inference, Detail, Logic Reasoning, and Logic Function. You'll learn the characteristics of each of these in the next chapter, along with strategies specific to each.

Earlier in this chapter, you saw how the LSAT expert consulted his Roadmap to answer three of the questions associated with the passage on pre-WWI European painters. Now, take a look at how the expert answered the remaining questions associated with this passage. This time, though, we'll be explicit about the expert's thinking during Steps 2 through 5 of the Reading Comprehension Method. Whenever you need to refer to the passage, turn to the preceding pages and refresh your memory of the expert's Roadmap.

The first question associated with this passage is much broader than any you've seen up to this point. It's a Global question that illustrates how the LSAT expert's summaries of the passage's Big Picture turn directly into points.

Step 3: (Research) While Roadmapping, we summarized the author's Main Point.	**Step 2:** (Question Type) This is a Global question calling for the author's "main idea."

Which one of the following most accurately states the main idea of the passage?

(A) Although they flourished independently, the pre–World War I European painters who developed new ways of looking at the world shared a common desire to break with the traditions of representational art.

(B) The work of the pre–World War I European painters who developed new ways of looking at the world cannot be said to have intentionally predicted social changes but only to have anticipated new directions in artistic perception and expression.

(C) The work of the pre–World War I European painters who developed new ways of looking at the world was important for its ability to predict social changes and its anticipation of new directions in artistic expression.

(D) Art critics who believe that the work of some pre–World War I European painters foretold imminent social changes are mistaken because art is incapable of expressing a vision of the future.

(E) Art critics who believe that the work of some pre–World War I European painters foretold imminent social changes are mistaken because the social upheavals that followed World War I were impossible to predict.

PrepTest107 Sec2 Q1

Step 4: (Predict) The Main Point summary will serve as a prediction of the correct answer: The painters, through their break with representational art, were predictive ("forward-looking") in terms of artistic style and technique, not in the realms of politics and society.	**Step 5:** (Answer) (B) is correct. This reflects the author's position accurately vis-à-vis the artists and the other critics. It matches the prediction perfectly.

Wrong answers: (A) This choice is too narrow to reflect the Main Point. It doesn't address the critics' view ("prophetic power") or the author's position that the break with tradition led to the future of art. (C) Distortion. This choice blends the views of the critics ("predict social changes") and the author ("anticipation of new directions in [art]"). (D) Outside the Scope. The passage never gets into whether art can express the future. The author calls the pre-WWI painters' predictions "clever guesses about political and social trends," but that doesn't mean he thinks all art is *incapable* of such a vision. (E) Distortion. The author thinks the critics are wrong because they find the pre-WWI painters' work more interesting for its "predictive power" than for its artistic innovation. He never says that World War I could not have been predicted.

Note that the LSAT expert could comfortably have stopped and moved on once he had read answer choice (B). Having summarized the passage's Big Picture in Step 1, he was prepared for a Global question and could be confident that this answer was correct.

Not surprisingly, since the fourth and final paragraph of the passage offered only a further example to support the author's main point, there was just one question here that addressed that paragraph. Take a look at how the LSAT expert attacked it.

Step 3: (Research) Delacroix is discussed in the fourth paragraph and serves as a distinct but parallel example of an artist dealing with social change.	**Step 2:** (Question Type) This is a Logic Function question asking why ("in order to") the author mentions an example.

The author presents the example of Delacroix in order to illustrate which one of the following claims?

(A) Social or political changes usually lead to important artistic innovations.

(B) Artistic innovations do not necessarily anticipate social or political upheavals.

(C) Some European painters have used art to predict social or political changes.

(D) Important stylistic innovations are best achieved by abandoning past traditions.

(E) Innovative artists can adapt themselves to social or political changes.

PrepTest107 Sec2 Q4

Step 4: (Predict) The author says that it is "important to remember that not all . . . changes in art are . . . followed by dramatic events in the world outside art." He then cites Delacroix as an artist who adjusted his style to changes already happening in the outside world.	**Step 5:** (Answer) (B) is correct. Sometimes artistic innovations *follow* social changes. The case of Delacroix is an example.

Wrong answers: (A) Extreme. The author does not claim that societal changes lead to artistic innovation more often than not ("usually"). (C) Outside the Scope. Some artists may have done this, but the author doesn't use Delacroix as an example of such artists. (D) Outside the Scope. The author never attempts to argue about the *best* way to achieve artistic innovation. (E) Distortion. The case of Delacroix may show that this statement is true, but that is not *why* the author discusses Delacroix. He's interested in showing that artistic innovation isn't always about trying to predict the future.

Here, again, the physical Roadmap (the Keywords noted by the LSAT expert and the paragraph notes he jotted down) allowed the expert to research the passage quickly and to predict the correct answer before evaluating the choices. The expert knew that the testmaker would likely ask one question about this peripheral example.

The next question is another Global question, but this time, instead of asking about the author's Purpose or Main Idea, it rewards the test taker who can sum up the passage's structure. As you review the expert's analysis, go back and compare the answers to the Keywords and margin notes on the original Roadmap.

Step 3: (Research) The Roadmap serves as an outline of the passage.	**Step 2:** (Question Type) This is a Global question looking for an accurate outline of the passage.

Which one of the following most accurately describes the contents of the passage?

(A) The author describes an artistic phenomenon; introduces one interpretation of this phenomenon; proposes an alternative interpretation and then supports this alternative by criticizing the original interpretation.

(B) The author describes an artistic phenomenon; identifies the causes of that phenomenon; illustrates some of the consequences of the phenomenon and then speculates about the significance of these consequences.

(C) The author describes an artistic phenomenon; articulates the traditional interpretation of this phenomenon; identifies two common criticisms of this view and then dismisses each of these criticisms by appeal to an example.

(D) The author describes an artistic phenomenon; presents two competing interpretations of the phenomenon; dismisses both interpretations by appeal to an example and then introduces an alternative interpretation.

(E) The author describes an artistic phenomenon; identifies the causes of the phenomenon; presents an argument for the importance of the phenomenon and then advocates an attempt to recreate the phenomenon.

PrepTest107 Sec2 Q5

Step 4: (Predict) Here, the author introduces the pre-WWI European painters, presents the reason some critics find them important, contradicts those critics with his own idea of why the painters are important, and then supports his position with examples.	**Step 5:** (Answer) (A) is correct. This outline follows the passage accurately step-by-step, paragraph-by-paragraph.

Wrong answers: (B) Distortion. The author does not discuss the "consequences" of the break with tradition, nor does he speculate about their "significance." (C) Distortion. The author does not provide two criticisms of the critics' position (or "traditional interpretation," as it is called here), and he certainly does not dismiss such criticism. His main point is about why the critics are wrong. (D) Distortion. This overcomplicates things. The author gives one opposing view and counters it with his own. There's no third "alternative" in the passage. (E) Distortion. This answer is wrong in everything except its first statement, most noticeably when it says that the author "advocates an attempt to recreate" the pre-WWI painters' work.

Note how each answer choice begins identically. An LSAT expert knows that this pattern makes a focus on the end of each answer choice the more strategic approach.

There is one more short question associated with this passage. Like many LSAT Reading Comprehension questions, it begins with "[a]ccording to the author." But pay attention to what it is actually asking.

Step 3: (Research) The details about the pre-WWI painters are found primarily in paragraphs 2 and 3.	**Step 2:** (Question Type) This is a Detail question, but one in which the four wrong answers are details that the author associated with the pre-WWI painters; the correct answer, on the other hand, is *not* something that the author claims these artists included in their work.

According to the author, the work of the pre-World War I painters described in the passage contains an example of each of the following EXCEPT:

(A) an interest in issues of representation and form

(B) a stylistic break with traditional art

(C) the introduction of new artistic techniques

(D) the ability to anticipate later artists

(E) the power to predict social changes

PrepTest107 Sec2 Q6

Step 4: (Predict) It is impossible to predict what the author does not cite as an example of something the pre-WWI painters did. However, if an answer choice is something that the critics would say, it will be correct.	**Step 5:** (Answer) (E) is correct. This is in the passage, but it is a claim made by the critics, not by the author.

Wrong answers: (A) The author does mention this in Paragraph 3. (B) The author does mention this at the end of Paragraph 1 and the beginning of Paragraph 2. (C) The author does mention this near the end of Paragraph 2. (D) The author does mention this in Paragraph 2 as well.

The majority of Reading Comprehension questions start with something like "[a]ccording to the passage" or "[b]ased on the passage," and support for the correct answer is present in the text. Take your cue from the LSAT expert: Note the clues in the stem, research the passage, and predict the correct answer. Never answer based on what you think you remember from the passage or what "sounds right" to you. Learn to make a helpful Roadmap and then use it to identify precisely what the correct answer must say.

Reading Comprehension Wrong Answer Types

As you were reviewing the LSAT expert's work on the pre-WWI European painters passage, you may have noticed certain wrong answer types popping up over and over again. This is not by chance. Just as you saw in Logical Reasoning, the testmaker uses certain patterns of distracters test after test, question after question. Take a few minutes to learn about the wrong answer types most common in Reading Comprehension before you move on to the next chapter.

Not every wrong answer you see will fit neatly into one of the types you see described here. After all, sometimes when a question asks for what the passage suggests, the wrong answer will just be something the author does *not* suggest, without clearly being a 180 or Extreme. Other wrong answers might fit more than one category. Still, it's worth your time to learn the wrong answer types in the list that follows. You'll see them referred to many times in the questions illustrated in the coming chapters.

LSAT STRATEGY

Reading Comprehension—Wrong Answer Types

- **Outside the Scope**—a choice containing a statement that is too broad, too narrow, or beyond the purview of the passage
- **Extreme**—a choice containing language too emphatic (*all, never, every, none*) to be supported by the passage
- **Distortion**—a choice that mentions details or ideas from the passage but mangles or misstates the relationship between them given or implied by the author
- **180**—a choice that directly contradicts what the correct answer must say
- **Faulty Use of Detail**—a choice that accurately states something from the stimulus but in a manner that incorrectly answers the question
- **Half-Right/Half-Wrong**—a choice in which one clause follows from the passage but another clause contradicts or distorts the passage

Along the way, you'll see a handful of wrong answers that appear to defy categorization. When that happens, we'll still explain clearly how the LSAT expert can recognize them as demonstrably incorrect. Whenever a wrong answer does fit clearly into one of the types outlined above, however, we'll note that too.

Now that you see the value of approaching each Reading Comprehension passage and question set with a deliberate and repeatable method, we'll practice applying it to more passages and question sets in the next chapter. We'll build on what you've learned here by diving deeper into each step of the Reading Comprehension Method. Additionally, you'll see examples of passages that fit a handful of rhetorical or structural patterns the testmaker uses over and over. As you become more familiar with these passage structures, your strategic reading will become even more targeted. In some passages, for example, you will focus on the author's disagreement with a critic. In others, you'll see that the author has no personal opinion to express but rather is simply interested in explaining other experts' ideas on a subject. In any case, remember that the LSAT questions will focus on the author's Purpose and Main Idea and will reward you for paying attention to *why* the author has included a detail or *how* he's using it within the text. We'll outline the common Reading Comprehension question types in Chapter 7 as well.

CHANNEL SPOTLIGHT

Same Road, Different Maps

By The LSAT Channel Faculty

Watch the video lesson for this Spotlight in your online Study Plan.

When you are first learning to read LSAT Reading Comprehension passages strategically, it can be difficult to assess how effective your Roadmaps are in helping you answer the questions quickly and accurately. You will see sample Roadmaps that look a little different from what you came up with, and you'll wonder whether you're getting at the right stuff within the passage. That's natural. Every test taker's Roadmap for a Reading Comprehension passage will look a little different, but all effective Roadmaps share a focus on passage structure and the author's Scope and Purpose. When you see sample Roadmaps in this book and in Kaplan explanations, they are just that: *samples* of an LSAT expert's work.

To illustrate the range of styles that effective Roadmaps might cover, the following pages present four expert Roadmaps of an official LSAT passage. Each one was created by an experienced LSAT instructor who scored in the 95th percentile or better on the test. The point isn't that one of them is better than any other, but that, despite their stylistic differences, they were all effective for the test takers who made them.

In the video lesson that accompanies this Spotlight, an LSAT Channel expert will help you review these Roadmaps with an eye to the characteristics they share. It will help you focus on what experts are after, and it will dispel your concern that there is a right or wrong way to highlight or underline Keywords or abbreviate your paragraph notes (provided that they are accurate, of course).

Remember, no one other than you ever sees the Roadmap (or any other notes in your test booklet, for that matter). Don't aspire to some undefinable goal of perfection or worry that your work looks a little different from someone else's. Your goal is to have your notes or sketches be useful, accurate, succinct, and strategic throughout the test.

Sample Roadmap A

A proficiency in understanding, applying, and even formulating statutes—the actual texts of laws enacted by legislative bodies—is a vital aspect of the practice of law, but statutory law is often given too little attention by law schools. Much of legal education, with its focus on judicial decisions and analysis of cases, can give a law student the impression that the practice of law consists mainly in analyzing past cases to determine their relevance to a client's situation and arriving at a speculative interpretation of the law relevant to the client's legal problem.

Lawyers discover fairly soon, however, that much of their practice does not depend on the kind of painstaking analysis of cases that is performed in law school. For example, a lawyer representing the owner of a business can often find an explicit answer as to what the client should do about a certain tax-related issue by consulting the relevant statutes. In such a case the facts are clear and the statutes' relation to them transparent, so that the client's question can be answered by direct reference to the wording of the statutes. But statutes' meanings and their applicability to relevant situations are not always so obvious, and that is one reason that the ability to interpret them accurately is an essential skill for law students to learn.

Another skill that teaching statutory law would improve is synthesis. Law professors work hard at developing their students' ability to analyze individual cases, but in so doing they favor the ability to apply the law in particular cases over the ability to understand the interrelations among laws. In contrast, the study of all the statutes of a legal system in a certain small area of the law would enable the student to see how these laws form a coherent whole. Students would then be able to apply this ability to synthesize in other areas of statutory law that they encounter in their study or practice. This is especially important because most students intend to specialize in a chosen area, or areas, of the law.

One possible argument against including training in statutory law as a standard part of law school curricula is that many statutes vary from region to region within a nation, so that the mastery of a set of statutes would usually not be generally applicable. There is some truth to this objection; law schools that currently provide some training in statutes generally intend it as a preparation for practice in their particular region, but for schools that are nationally oriented, this could seem to be an inappropriate investment of time and resources. But while the knowledge of a particular region's statutory law is not generally transferable to other regions, the skills acquired in mastering a particular set of statutes are, making the study of statutory law an important undertaking even for law schools with a national orientation.

PrepTest131 Sec4 Qs9–15

#1:
Law Sch needs to do more teaching of how to "read" laws, not just apply precedents
students get wrong impression

#2:
Ex. of how a lawyer needs to understand law's wording

#3:
"Put it all together"
another reason for policy

#4:
Counter-Arg: Laws vary all over US; could hurt nat'l schools
Counter-Counter-Arg.: NO – learning to "read" laws is helpful everywhere

Sample Roadmap B

A proficiency in understanding, applying, and even formulating statutes—the actual texts of laws enacted by legislative bodies—is a vital aspect of the practice of law, but statutory law is often given too little attention by law schools. Much of legal education, with its focus on judicial decisions and analysis of cases, can give a law student the impression that the practice of law consists mainly in analyzing past cases to determine their relevance to a client's situation and arriving at a speculative interpretation of the law relevant to the client's legal problem.

Lawyers discover fairly soon, however, that much of their practice does not depend on the kind of painstaking analysis of cases that is performed in law school. For example, a lawyer representing the owner of a business can often find an explicit answer as to what the client should do about a certain tax-related issue by consulting the relevant statutes. In such a case the facts are clear and the statutes' relation to them transparent, so that the client's question can be answered by direct reference to the wording of the statutes. But statutes' meanings and their applicability to relevant situations are not always so obvious, and that is one reason that the ability to interpret them accurately is an essential skill for law students to learn.

Another skill that teaching statutory law would improve is synthesis. Law professors work hard at developing their students' ability to analyze individual cases, but in so doing they favor the ability to apply the law in particular cases over the ability to understand the interrelations among laws. In contrast, the study of all the statutes of a legal system in a certain small area of the law would enable the student to see how these laws form a coherent whole. Students would then be able to apply this ability to synthesize in other areas of statutory law that they encounter in their study or practice. This is especially important because most students intend to specialize in a chosen area, or areas, of the law.

One possible argument against including training in statutory law as a standard part of law school curricula is that many statutes vary from region to region within a nation, so that the mastery of a set of statutes would usually not be generally applicable. There is some truth to this objection; law schools that currently provide some training in statutes generally intend it as a preparation for practice in their particular region, but for schools that are nationally oriented, this could seem to be an inappropriate investment of time and resources. But while the knowledge of a particular region's statutory law is not generally transferable to other regions, the skills acquired in mastering a particular set of statutes are, making the study of statutory law an important undertaking even for law schools with a national orientation.

PrepTest131 Sec4 Qs9–15

#1:
Stat. law gets insufficient
attention in law school
Instead case analysis

#2:
Actual practice: just look up
statutes
Must know how to interpret

#3:
Teaching stat. law
good for synthesis

#4:
Critics arg.—not national
Auth response: skills transferable,
even if statutes aren't

Sample Roadmap C

A proficiency in understanding, applying, and even formulating statutes—the actual texts of laws enacted by legislative bodies—is a vital aspect of the practice of law, but statutory law is often given too little attention by law schools. Much of legal education, with its focus on judicial decisions and analysis of cases, can give a law student the impression that the practice of law consists mainly in analyzing past cases to determine their relevance to a client's situation and arriving at a speculative interpretation of the law relevant to the client's legal problem.

Lawyers discover fairly soon, however, that much of their practice does not depend on the kind of painstaking analysis of cases that is performed in law school. For example, a lawyer representing the owner of a business can often find an explicit answer as to what the client should do about a certain tax-related issue by consulting the relevant statutes. In such a case the facts are clear and the statutes' relation to them transparent, so that the client's question can be answered by direct reference to the wording of the statutes. But statutes' meanings and their applicability to relevant situations are not always so obvious, and that is one reason that the ability to interpret them accurately is an essential skill for law students to learn.

Another skill that teaching statutory law would improve is synthesis. Law professors work hard at developing their students' ability to analyze individual cases, but in so doing they favor the ability to apply the law in particular cases over the ability to understand the interrelations among laws. In contrast, the study of all the statutes of a legal system in a certain small area of the law would enable the student to see how these laws form a coherent whole. Students would then be able to apply this ability to synthesize in other areas of statutory law that they encounter in their study or practice. This is especially important because most students intend to specialize in a chosen area, or areas, of the law.

One possible argument against including training in statutory law as a standard part of law school curricula is that many statutes vary from region to region within a nation, so that the mastery of a set of statutes would usually not be generally applicable. There is some truth to this objection; law schools that currently provide some training in statutes generally intend it as a preparation for practice in their particular region, but for schools that are nationally oriented, this could seem to be an inappropriate investment of time and resources. But while the knowledge of a particular region's statutory law is not generally transferable to other regions, the skills acquired in mastering a particular set of statutes are, making the study of statutory law an important undertaking even for law schools with a national orientation.

PrepTest131 Sec4 Qs9–15

#1:
L-schools teach cases, but need to teach statutes too!

#2:
Legal practice not just about cases

#3:
Stat interp. would also help with synth.

#4:
Despite regional variance, stat. interp. skills are import.

Sample Roadmap D

A proficiency in understanding, applying, and even formulating statutes—the actual texts of laws enacted by legislative bodies—is a vital aspect of the practice of law, but statutory law is often given too little attention by law schools. Much of legal education, with its focus on judicial decisions and analysis of cases, can give a law student the impression that the practice of law consists mainly in analyzing past cases to determine their relevance to a client's situation and arriving at a speculative interpretation of the law relevant to the client's legal problem.

Lawyers discover fairly soon, however, that much of their practice does not depend on the kind of painstaking analysis of cases that is performed in law school. For example, a lawyer representing the owner of a business can often find an explicit answer as to what the client should do about a certain tax-related issue by consulting the relevant statutes. In such a case the facts are clear and the statutes' relation to them transparent, so that the client's question can be answered by direct reference to the wording of the statutes. But statutes' meanings and their applicability to relevant situations are not always so obvious, and that is one reason that the ability to interpret them accurately is an essential skill for law students to learn.

Another skill that teaching statutory law would improve is synthesis. Law professors work hard at developing their students' ability to analyze individual cases, but in so doing they favor the ability to apply the law in particular cases over the ability to understand the interrelations among laws. In contrast, the study of all the statutes of a legal system in a certain small area of the law would enable the student to see how these laws form a coherent whole. Students would then be able to apply this ability to synthesize in other areas of statutory law that they encounter in their study or practice. This is especially important because most students intend to specialize in a chosen area, or areas, of the law.

One possible argument against including training in statutory law as a standard part of law school curricula is that many statutes vary from region to region within a nation, so that the mastery of a set of statutes would usually not be generally applicable. There is some truth to this objection; law schools that currently provide some training in statutes generally intend it as a preparation for practice in their particular region, but for schools that are nationally oriented, this could seem to be an inappropriate investment of time and resources. But while the knowledge of a particular region's statutory law is not generally transferable to other regions, the skills acquired in mastering a particular set of statutes are, making the study of statutory law an important undertaking even for law schools with a national orientation.

PrepTest131 Sec4 Qs9–15

¶1:
Statutes:
- vital
- neglected by law schools
- gives false impression

¶2:
law ≠ case
analysis

¶3:
synthesis impt. skill

¶4:
possible arg. against author's point:
- some truth
- but wrong

CHAPTER 7

Reading Comprehension: Passage Types and Question Types

In this chapter, you'll learn the specific skills involved in applying the Reading Comprehension Method to passages and their question sets. Along the way, you'll discover that the LSAT uses certain patterns over and over, both in the way passages are structured and in the types of questions the test asks.

If you have already worked in or completed the chapters on Logical Reasoning, this chapter will feel different. That's because it's difficult to practice Reading Comprehension skills outside the context of full passages. We won't be able to atomize the skills as neatly in this chapter as we have in others. That makes it very important for you to study the Learning Objectives at the beginning of each section and keep them in mind as you're reviewing the expert analysis of the LSAT material. Don't hesitate to mark the pages where Learning Objectives are introduced and refer to them often to keep the goals of the lessons at the front of your mind.

Because LSAT Reading Comprehension passages are often densely written and because the questions shift their focus from the passage as a whole to details scattered throughout the text, it's easy to miss the forest for the trees in this section. To remain strategic and effective in Reading Comprehension, you must proactively engage the material. Don't sit back and read passively, waiting for the author's point to come to you. LSAT experts constantly question and challenge the author as they read. They anticipate where the passage will go and even the questions that the testmaker will ask. That's not easy, but it will make a huge difference in law school, where you will do a similar kind of targeted, interrogative, and skeptical reading. Start training yourself as a strategic reader now and you'll be well ahead of the game on test day and in your first year as a law student.

Job one in gaining this expertise is to internalize the Reading Comprehension Method. Use it unfailingly until it becomes second nature.

THE KAPLAN READING COMPREHENSION METHOD

STEP 1 **Read the Passage Strategically**—note Keywords and jot down paragraph notes to summarize the portions of the passage relevant to LSAT questions; summarize the author's Topic/Scope/Purpose/ Main Idea.

STEP 2 **Read the Question Stem**—identify the question type, characterize the correct and incorrect answers, and look for clues to guide your research.

STEP 3 **Research the Relevant Text**—based on the clues in the question stem, consult your Roadmap; for open-ended questions, refer to your Topic/Scope/Purpose/Main Idea summaries.

STEP 4 **Predict the Correct Answer**—based on your research (or, for open-ended questions, your Topic/ Scope/Purpose/Main Idea summaries), predict the meaning of the correct answer.

STEP 5 **Evaluate the Answer Choices**—select the choice that matches your prediction of the correct answer, or eliminate the four wrong answer choices.

The first big section of this chapter will concentrate on Step 1: the active reading and note taking you'll need to do in order to answer all of the passage's questions efficiently. As you learn and practice Step 1, we'll also introduce common passage structures you'll see in LSAT passages.

The second section of the chapter will cover Steps 2–5. You'll learn and practice the most effective ways to answer Reading Comprehension questions. As you do so, you'll learn the characteristics of the question types the testmaker uses in this section.

At the end of the chapter, you'll have a chance to practice a complete passage-and-question set and compare your work to that of an LSAT expert step-by-step. Chapter 8 contains four more full passages, so you'll have ample opportunity to put all that you learn here to work.

Strategic Reading and Reading Comprehension Passage Types

Prepare With four passages in the 35-minute Reading Comprehension section, you have about 8½ minutes per passage. Of that, you'll spend between three and four minutes on Step 1 of the Reading Comprehension Method, reading the passage strategically and creating a Roadmap. In Chapter 6, you saw an example of how this targeted reading and note taking sets you up to answer the questions quickly and confidently. Let's quickly outline and explain the skills associated with Step 1.

Strategic Reading and Roadmapping Skills

If you ask most untrained test takers how they start out in Reading Comprehension, they would probably say something like, "I read the passage, I guess." That's accurate, as far as it goes. If you ask LSAT experts, however, their answer would be more nuanced: "I prepare myself to answer all of the passage's questions." Step 1 is not just reading; it's reading strategically, and that's a complex task. You'll be taking note of Keywords that reveal the author's opinion and the passage structure, you'll make paragraph notes to correspond with the most important points in the passage, and you'll summarize the author's Purpose and Main Idea. Here's the good news: Each of those tasks has a handful of manageable, learnable skills associated with it.

LEARNING OBJECTIVES

In this portion of the chapter, you'll learn to use:

Keywords

- Identify Keywords from six categories (Emphasis/Opinion, Contrast, Logic, Illustration, Sequence/Chronology, Continuation).
- Use Keywords to accurately paraphrase the text (author's purpose, passage structure, etc.).
- Use Keywords to accurately predict where the passage will go (scope and purpose of remaining paragraphs, for example).
- Use Keywords to predict points in the passage to which LSAT questions will refer.

Margin Notes

- Identify text that warrants a paragraph note.
- Capture key content in a brief, accurate note on your scratch paper.

"Big Picture" Summary—Topic/Scope/Purpose/Main Idea

- Read a passage to identify the author's Topic and Scope.
- Read a passage to identify the author's Purpose.
- Read a passage to identify the author's Main Idea.

Why Use Keywords?

The short, but very compelling, answer is that Keywords indicate points of view and important spots in the passage's structure, and knowing where those are is often the key to distinguishing between right and wrong answers on the test. Here's why. Take two simple statements:

> Jessica earned an outstanding LSAT score. Jessica is going to attend Gilligan University Law School next fall.

If that was all you knew, you could not answer this typical LSAT question: "With which one of the following statements about Gilligan University Law School would the author most likely agree?" You know two facts about Jessica, but nothing about the author's point of view toward her future alma mater. Add a Contrast Keyword, however, and the answer to the LSAT question is clear:

> Jessica earned an outstanding LSAT score; *despite this fact*, she will attend Gilligan University Law School next fall.

Now, you know that the correct answer to the LSAT question would be something along the lines of "It's unexpected that Gilligan would be the choice of someone with an outstanding LSAT score." On the other hand, what if the two facts were connected by a Logic Keyword?

> *Because* Jessica earned an outstanding LSAT score, she will attend Gilligan University Law School next fall.

This signals a profound difference in the author's point of view. The correct answer now would be something like, "Gilligan University Law School generally requires a high LSAT score for admission." Consider the implications of these examples: In both cases, the facts were absolutely identical, yet the correct answers to the LSAT question were polar opposites. Keywords signal an author's purpose or position, they highlight what she wants to emphasize, and they reveal how she is making her argument. These are the aspects of the text that LSAT questions focus upon.

LSAT Reading Comprehension questions never ask for factual details that a test taker might just happen to know from the outside world. Take the following assertion, for example:

> During the Civil War, President Lincoln deliberately sought out the advice of cabinet members whose opinions were at odds with his own.

The LSAT will not ask, "Which of the following is true of Lincoln's cabinet?" and expect you to report on the multiplicity of opinions. After all, you may be able to answer a question like that without reading the passage at all. Indeed, it would not even matter if you were a history major who could write an essay on the subject and challenge the statement about Lincoln with facts of your own. LSAT Reading Comprehension is not a test of expertise; like the rest of the LSAT, it's a test of skill.

Now, put the statement about Lincoln into the context of an LSAT passage:

> Effective leaders allow for open dialogue. For example, during the Civil War, President Lincoln deliberately sought out the advice of cabinet members whose opinions were at odds with his own.

From this, the LSAT might draw a question such as "The author most likely refers to Lincoln and his cabinet in order to . . ." The correct answer, you'll notice, must start with a verb. Because the sentence on Lincoln is prefaced with the Illustration Keywords "[f]or example," the correct answer here would say something like "to illustrate one characteristic of effective leaders." Regardless of how much (or how little) you know about leadership or the Lincoln administration, strategic reading will get you the LSAT point.

As you learned in Chapter 6, there are six types of Keywords you'll want to identify and use as you are reading LSAT passages. In the chart that follows, the categories are listed roughly in order of importance.

LSAT STRATEGY

Strategic Reading Keywords

- **Emphasis/Opinion**—words that signal that the author finds a detail noteworthy, words that signal the author has a positive or negative opinion, or any other subjective or evaluative language on the author's part (e.g., *especially, crucial, unfortunately, disappointing, I suggest, it seems likely*)
- **Contrast**—words indicating that the author thinks two details or ideas are incompatible or illustrate conflicting points (e.g., *but, yet, despite, on the other hand*)
- **Logic**—words that indicate an argument, either the author's or someone else's (e.g., *thus, therefore, because*)
- **Illustration**—words indicating an example offered to clarify or support another point (e.g., *for example, this shows, to illustrate*)
- **Sequence/Chronology**—words showing an order to certain steps in a process or to developments over time (e.g., *traditionally, in the past, recently, today, first, second, finally, earlier, since*)
- **Continuation**—words indicating that a subsequent example or detail supports the same point or illustrates the same idea (e.g., *moreover, in addition, and, also, further*)

As you start to recognize Keywords as a part of your strategic reading approach, concentrate first on Emphasis/Opinion and Contrast signals. You'll see that they are most often associated with LSAT questions because they most directly reveal the author's point of view and purpose in including a detail in the passage. Once you're comfortable recognizing those categories, move on to Logic (these should be familiar to you from working with Logical Reasoning questions) and Illustration. Finally, add the Sequence/Chronology and Continuation signals to your repertoire. You'll find that you understand LSAT passages more quickly and are able to stay focused on the most important aspects of the passages as you read.

As you review the LSAT experts' analyses of the passages that follow, pay attention to where the experts noted Keywords and used them to understand the passages.

Why Take Paragraph Notes?

LSAT passages are around 450–500 words long, and while they stay focused on a single Topic and Scope, they abound in details and often reflect two or more points of view. Labeling the key points of a passage by paragraph on your scratch paper makes it much easier for you to target your research for individual questions. Unlike in some precollege tests, the order of LSAT Reading Comprehension questions doesn't necessarily correspond to the order of the passage. Question 2 might take you to the third paragraph, question 3 might point back to the first paragraph, and question 4 might ask for an answer about the passage as a whole. Paragraph notes help you navigate the passage quickly to find the text relevant to a specific question.

No two test takers' scratch paper notes will look identical. Even two high-scoring LSAT experts who routinely ace the Reading Comprehension section will not jot down exactly the same words or phrases. So, don't construct the unrealistic idea of a "perfect Roadmap" in your mind. The experts' notes will have some things in common, however.

Take another look at the work of one expert on the opening paragraph of the passage about pre-World War I European painters.

For some years before the outbreak of World War I, a number of painters in different European countries developed works of art that some have described as prophetic: paintings that by challenging viewers' habitual ways of perceiving the world of the present are thus said to anticipate a future world that would be very different. The artistic styles that they brought into being varied widely, but all these styles had in common a very important break with traditions of representational art that stretched back to the Renaissance.

PrepTest107 Sec2 Qs 1-7

¶1:
PreWWI painters challenged views of world.
Huge departure from old trad.

Notice that the expert has accounted for both points of view here: those of the critics—just referred to as "some" at this point in the passage—and of the author. LSAT experts are always cognizant of multiple points of view within a passage, and they know that the testmaker will reward them for keeping track of who thinks what.

At times, you may have as little as one note per paragraph. Something like "Prof. Brown's hypothesis" or "steps in the process" may suffice if the scope of a paragraph is limited and its organization clear. When the author uses a single paragraph to portray two or more ideas, examples, or theories, however, multiple notes may be in order. Take a look at how an LSAT expert Roadmapped a paragraph in which the author evaluates a scientific hypothesis:

The first alternative seems unlikely. One possible model for such an inertial system might involve an internal magnetic compass to measure the directional leg of each journey. Birds transported to the release site wearing magnets or otherwise subjected to an artificial magnetic field, however, are only occasionally affected. Alternately, if pigeons measure their displacement by consciously keeping track of the direction and degree of acceleration and deceleration of the various turns, and timing the individual legs of the journey, simply transporting them in the dark, with constant rotations, or under complete anesthesia ought to impair or eliminate their ability to orient. These treatments, however, have no effect. Unfortunately, no one has yet performed the crucial experiment of transporting pigeons in total darkness, anesthetized, rotating, and with the magnetic field reversed all at the same time.

PrepTest104 Sec3 Qs 15-21

#2:
Alt. #1 not likely
both models tested w/ neg results
ultimate test not done yet.

That's a dense paragraph outlining the reasons the author is skeptical of a proposed scientific explanation. It presents two possible models, along with details about experiments performed to test them. And, for most LSAT test takers, none of this subject matter is at all familiar. Still, the LSAT expert has left herself a very navigable map. She has clearly noted the author's opinions, and in conjunction with the Keywords marked in the passage, she has jotted down notes sufficient to locate the two models and their experiments should a question ask about them. You'll see this passage later in the chapter. As you examine more expert Roadmaps, take the time to study their paragraph notes and reflect on why successful test takers note certain details.

Why Summarize the Author's Topic, Scope, Purpose, and Main Idea?

The answer here isn't much different than it has been for the other features of the Roadmap. We summarize the big picture of the passage because the LSAT asks questions that reward you for having these summaries in mind. Global questions ask for the Purpose or Main Idea directly:

> Which one of the following most accurately states the main point of the passage?
>
> The primary purpose of the passage is to

In fact, as you'll see when we discuss the Reading Comprehension question types below, we recommend that you answer a passage's Global questions first among any of the questions accompanying a passage. That way, the big picture of the passage is still fresh in your mind.

Global questions aren't the only ones that are made easier by having overall summaries in your mind. Open-ended Inference questions asking for a statement with which the author would agree and those asking about the author's attitude also benefit from having the passage succinctly summarized:

> It can be inferred that the author would be most likely to agree that
>
> The passages most strongly suggest that the author of Passage B would agree with which of the following statements in Passage A?

Both of those are questions in which knowing the authors' overall Scope, Purpose, and Main Idea will help you to identify the correct answer, eliminate wrong answers, or both.

Whenever you see an LSAT expert's physical Roadmap (highlighted or underlined Keywords and paragraph notes), you'll also have a chance to consider his "mental Roadmap" (the big picture summary) as you review his analysis of the passage. Don't gloss over the way in which the LSAT expert paraphrases and condenses the author's points and perspective. Strong paraphrasing is perhaps the most important indication of active, strategic reading.

LSAT STRATEGY

Reading Comprehension—the "big picture"

- **Topic**—the overall subject of the passage
- **Scope**—the particular aspect of the Topic that the author is focusing on
- **Purpose**—the author's reason for writing the passage (express this as a verb—e.g., *to refute, to outline, to evaluate, to critique*)
- **Main Idea**—the author's conclusion or overall takeaway; if you combine the author's Purpose and Scope, you'll usually have a good sense of the Main Idea.

Summary: Step 1—Read the Passage Strategically

Now, think back to the LSAT expert's answer to the question about how she starts out in Reading Comprehension: "I prepare myself to answer all of the passage's questions." Step 1 is a complex process, but each of its elements has a clear objective: Note and paraphrase the parts of the passage that will help get correct answers. The Roadmap an expert produces (on the testing screen, on her scratch paper, and in her mind) is a tool for answering the questions. Keep that as your primary objective and you'll improve your strategic reading skills and your Reading Comprehension score.

LSAT Reading Comprehension Passage Types

Before turning to examples and practice with passages, take a few minutes to learn about the common passage structures you'll see in LSAT Reading Comprehension. There are two ways to categorize LSAT Reading Comprehension passages: by subject matter and by passage structure.

Subject Matter

Every LSAT Reading Comprehension section contains four passages, and it's true that nearly every section has one passage each in the areas of natural science, social science, humanities, and law. Most future law students come from undergraduate backgrounds in the social sciences or the humanities, so there may be an instinctive preference for passages on topics from these areas and a concomitant distrust of one's ability in natural science passages dealing with physics, chemistry, or biology. Empirical data show, however, that there is little, if any, correlation between subject matter areas and difficulty levels. If you encounter a passage and have a subjective preference for the topic, that's fine, but don't make subject matter more important than it is. Learn to read all Reading Comprehension passages strategically, and you'll be at a decided advantage over much of your competition on the exam.

Passage Structures

For you as a test taker, organizing Reading Comprehension passages by their structures may be a much more meaningful taxonomy. The passage structure offers you a clue to the author's purpose in writing the passage, and that in turn gives you a start in creating a helpful Roadmap. There are four structures you should recognize, listed here from most to least common.

READING COMPREHENSION PASSAGE TYPES

- **Theory/Perspective**—The passage focuses on a thinker's theory or perspective on some part of the Topic; typically (though not always), the author disagrees, and critiques the opponent's perspective or defends his own.
- **Event/Phenomenon**—The passage focuses on an event, a breakthrough development, or a problem that has arisen; when a solution to the problem is proposed, the author most often agrees with the solution (and that represents the passage's Main Idea).
- **Debate**—The passage outlines two opposing positions (neither of which is the author's) on some aspect of the Topic; the author may side with one of the positions, may remain neutral, or may critique both. (This structure has been rare on recent LSATs.)
- **Biography**—The passage discusses something about a notable person; the aspect of the person's life emphasized by the author reflects the Scope of the passage.

In this chapter, you'll see examples of each of the first three structures. The passages you will work on in Chapter 8 and throughout the Practice Library offer additional examples. Many years ago, Debate passages were much more common than they have been on tests since around 2008. This may be because it was in 2007 that the testmaker introduced the paired Comparative Reading passages that now accompany one of the four question sets on LSAT exams. At any rate, if you use older materials and tests during your LSAT preparation, be aware that you may overestimate the likelihood of encountering this passage structure.

Step 1 in Action: Strategic Reading Examples and Practice

In this section, you'll see three Reading Comprehension passages. In each one, you'll have a chance to practice Step 1 of the Reading Comprehension Method; that is, you'll read the passage strategically and create a Roadmap. On the test, you'll take 3–4 minutes for this step, but don't worry if you take a little longer at this point. It's more important to practice the strategic reading skills and to get comfortable with this new and different way of approaching a piece of text. Along the way, we'll give you clues about how to approach passages with different structures. Additionally, you'll see a note about Comparative Reading when you have the opportunity to try out a set of paired passages (something you'll do just once in a full Reading Comprehension section).

Theory/Perspective Passages

Passages with this structure account for over half of all passages on recent LSATs, and that means they account for over half of the points you can get from the Reading Comprehension section. As previously noted, Theory/Perspective passages outline an opinion of someone other than the author on some aspect of the passage's Topic. Once you identify the presence of another opinion, pay attention to the author's response. Does he agree or disagree? Why? What arguments and evidence does the author or his opponent offer? Use paragraph notes to keep track of the differing opinions in the passage. Summarize the author's Purpose (most likely, to critique his opponent's position or defend his own) and Main Idea ("the opposing view is faulty because . . ." or "my view prevails because . . .").

Perhaps, as you were reading that, it occurred to you that the passage from Chapter 6 on the pre-World War I European painters is a Theory/Perspective passage. There, the author told you about the opinion of critics who believe that the painters were interesting because they seemed to predict the political and social future of Europe. The author of the passage disagreed with that perspective. He argued that the painters were noteworthy for their interest in aesthetic and technical innovations, and that they should not be considered "prophets" of politics and society.

Keep that passage in mind as you practice with a new Theory/Perspective passage on the following pages.

Practice Read and Roadmap the following passage. As you read, highlight or underline Keywords within the passage and record paragraph notes highlighting the key opinions or main points of each paragraph. When you're finished, compare your work to the LSAT expert's Roadmap and analysis on the following pages.

Personal names are generally regarded by European thinkers in two major ways, both of which deny that names have any significant semantic content. In philosophy and linguistics, John Stuart Mill's formulation that "proper names are meaningless marks set upon . . . persons to distinguish them from one another" retains currency; in anthropology, Claude Lévi-Strauss's characterization of names as being primarily instruments of social classification has been very influential. Consequently, interpretation of personal names in societies where names have other functions and meanings has been neglected. Among the Hopi of the southwestern United States, names often refer to historical or ritual events in order both to place individuals within society and to confer an identity upon them. Furthermore, the images used to evoke these events suggest that Hopi names can be seen as a type of poetic composition.

Throughout life, Hopis receive several names in a sequence of ritual initiations. Birth, entry into one of the ritual societies during childhood, and puberty are among the name-giving occasions. Names are conferred by an adult member of a clan other than the child's clan, and names refer to that name giver's clan, sometimes combining characteristics of the clan's totem animal with the child's characteristics. Thus, a name might translate to something as simple as "little rabbit," which reflects both the child's size and the representative animal.

More often, though, the name giver has in mind a specific event that is not apparent in a name's literal translation. One Lizard clan member from the village of Oraibi is named Lomayayva, "beautifully ascended." This translation, however, tells nothing about either the event referred to—who or what ascended—or the name giver's clan. The name giver in this case is from Badger clan. Badger clan is responsible for an annual ceremony featuring a procession in which masked representations of spirits climb the mesa on which Oraibi sits. Combining the name giver's clan association with the receiver's home village, "beautifully ascended" refers to the splendid colors and movements of the procession up the mesa. The condensed image this name evokes—a typical feature of Hopi personal names—displays the same quality of Western Apache place names that led one commentator to call them "tiny imagist poems."

Hopi personal names do several things simultaneously. They indicate social relationships—but only indirectly—and they individuate persons. Equally important, though, is their poetic quality; in a sense they can be understood as oral texts that produce aesthetic delight. This view of Hopi names is thus opposed not only to Mill's claim that personal names are without inherent meaning but also to Lévi-Strauss's purely functional characterization. Interpreters must understand Hopi clan structures and linguistic practices in order to discern the beauty and significance of Hopi names.

PrepTest104 Sec3 Qs 8-14

Expert Analysis for the Practice exercise may be found on the following page. ▶ ▶ ▶

Expert Analysis

Now, compare your Roadmap to that of an LSAT expert. Look for places in which you missed an important Keyword or mischaracterized a point in the passage. Think of the Analysis column as the expert's internal monologue, paraphrasing the passage while reading. Use it to assess whether your big picture summary is accurate and useful.

LSAT Passage	Analysis
Personal names are generally regarded by European thinkers in two major ways, both of which deny that names have any significant semantic content. In philosophy and linguistics, John Stuart Mill's formulation that "proper names are meaningless marks set upon . . . persons to distinguish them from one another" retains currency; in anthropology, Claude Lévi-Strauss's characterization of names as being primarily instruments of social classification has been very influential. Consequently, interpretation of personal names in societies where names have other functions and meanings has been neglected. Among the Hopi of the southwestern United States, names often refer to historical or ritual events in order both to place individuals within society and to confer an identity upon them. Furthermore, the images used to evoke these events suggest that Hopi names can be seen as a type of poetic composition.	**Step 1:** The first paragraph lays out the entire big picture for this passage. The **Topic** is the scholarship of personal names. The **Scope** will focus on Hopi names. The author's **Purpose/Main Idea** is to show that Hopi names illustrate the shortcomings of the two major European theories about personal names. The paragraph starts with the two theories. Mill (philosophy/linguistics) says names are arbitrary; we just use them to keep people separate. Lévi-Strauss (anthropology) says names are used for social classification. The author says Hopi names are different in two ways: 1) They go beyond mere individual identity by being associated with rituals or events, and 2) they use images and so, are poetic. We can anticipate seeing those differences explained in the next two paragraphs.
#1: Names: Euro views = meaningless differentiators or social classif tool. Euro ignores addl uses: names giving I.D. names as poetry.	

LSAT Passage	Analysis
Throughout life, Hopis receive several names in a sequence of ritual initiations. Birth, entry into one of the ritual societies during childhood, and puberty are among the name-giving occasions. Names are conferred by an adult member of a clan other than the child's clan, and names refer to that name giver's clan, sometimes combining characteristics of the clan's totem animal with the child's characteristics. Thus, a name might translate to something as simple as "little rabbit," which reflects both the child's size and the representative animal. #2: How Hopi get names thru rites. Names I.D. clan and kid's traits.	As expected, this paragraph outlines how the Hopi confer names through rituals. Their names refer to a person's clan and to his or her individual characteristics or events from his or her life. Thus, Hopi names contain "meaning" beyond merely identifying a person.
More often, though, the name giver has in mind a specific event that is not apparent in a name's literal translation. One Lizard clan member from the village of Oraibi is named Lomayayva, "beautifully ascended." This translation, however, tells nothing about either the event referred to—who or what ascended—or the name giver's clan. The name giver in this case is from Badger clan. Badger clan is responsible for an annual ceremony featuring a procession in which masked representations of spirits climb the mesa on which Oraibi sits. Combining the name giver's clan association with the receiver's home village, "beautifully ascended" refers to the splendid colors and movements of the procession up the mesa. The condensed image this name evokes—a typical feature of Hopi personal names—displays the same quality of Western Apache place names that led one commentator to call them "tiny imagist poems." #3: Long ex. of poetry found in specific naming	This paragraph goes into more detail about what the author considers Hopi names' second distinguishing characteristic: They are poetic. The Hopi often give names that are not literal. The author cites a detailed example to illustrate this and concludes that (like Apache place names) Hopi names may be considered "tiny imagist poems."

LSAT Passage	Analysis
Hopi personal names do several things simultaneously. They indicate social relationships—but only indirectly—and they individuate persons. Equally important, though, is their poetic quality; in a sense they can be understood as oral texts that produce aesthetic delight. This view of Hopi names is thus opposed not only to Mill's claim that personal names are without inherent meaning but also to Lévi-Strauss's purely functional characterization. Interpreters must understand Hopi clan structures and linguistic practices in order to discern the beauty and significance of Hopi names. *PrepTest104 Sec3 Qs 8-14* #4: Sums up how Hopi names' meaning and poetry depart from Mill's ("arbitrary") and L-S's ("social class only") views	Here, the author reiterates his thesis (or Main Idea) and his evidence for it. Because they 1) indirectly indicate social relationships and 2) have poetic qualities, Hopi names do not fit into Mill's "names are just arbitrary" theory or Lévi-Strauss's functional "social classification" theory.

The next time you see a Theory/Perspective structure, the subject matter may be drawn from natural science or law, rather than social science (as it was here) or humanities (as it was with the pre-World War I painters). You could also find that the author's response to the theory or perspective surfaces later in the passage. That said, you'll encounter similar patterns that will help you stay focused on the two points of view and highlight the pieces of the passage that will be tested in the question set.

You'll see the questions associated with this passage a little later in the chapter. For now, continue to practice Roadmapping, this time on a passage with a different structure.

Event/Phenomenon Passages

On recent tests, the Event/Phenomenon structure has appeared in a little over 25 percent of the passages. While not as common as the Theory/Perspective structure, this is still significant. Here, the author will inform you about a recent event, a change that has occurred over time, or a problem or dilemma. Always ask whether the author presents an interpretation of the event or change or a solution to the problem (identified as her own solution or someone else's proposal). These passages are often neutral and detail heavy—note names, dates, or places as you see them, but don't lose sight of the big picture by getting too caught up in the small stuff.

Before practicing the next passage (or more properly, passages), it's important that we take a moment to discuss Comparative Reading because that's the format you're about to see.

LSAT STRATEGY

A Note on Comparative Reading

One time per section, the LSAT presents a Comparative Reading selection. Instead of seeing a single 450- to 500-word passage, you'll see two shorter passages labeled Passage A and Passage B. The two passages always share a common Topic and sometimes a common Scope. The passages almost always differ, however, in terms of Purpose and Main Idea. That doesn't mean that the two authors must oppose each other. Indeed, it's often not clear that either passage was written in response to (or even with knowledge of) the other. It may be that Passage A presents an argument against a theory while Passage B presents a model for testing the validity of such theories. It could be that Passage A identifies a problem confronting biologists and Passage B offers a solution to the problem. Of course, a good, old-fashioned debate could take place as well, with Passage A arguing that a proposed law will be good for the country and Passage B contending that it will be bad.

Regardless of how the passages are related, your approach to Comparative Reading should differ little from your approach to Reading Comprehension passages in general. You'll still begin by reading strategically and Roadmapping the passages. The primary difference in preparing yourself to answer the questions comes right after you finish your Roadmaps but before you tackle the question set. Because almost all of the questions associated with these paired passages ask you to compare the passages in some way, you need to take a moment to briefly catalog the similarities and differences between Passage A and Passage B. Here are a handful of questions to ask and answer before diving into the questions:

- Are the passages different in Scope, Purpose, or Main Idea? The answer will generally be yes; make sure to characterize the differences.
- Do the passages share common details, examples, or evidence? The answer is often yes, but beware, the two authors may reach very different conclusions or make different recommendations based on the same underlying facts.
- If either author makes a contention or recommendation, how would the other author respond to it? The test is fond of Inference questions that ask whether one author would agree or disagree with something the other said.
- Do the two passages share a common principle? If yes, paraphrase the principle. If no, characterize how the authors approach the Topic differently.

Comparing and contrasting the two passages should only take a few seconds, but it will leave you much better prepared to research and answer the questions that follow.

Practice With that in mind, read and Roadmap the following Comparative Reading passages. Highlight or underline Keywords within the passage, and record your paragraph notes on a separate piece of scratch paper. After you finish reading and Roadmapping the passages individually, take a minute or two to compare and contrast the two passages. Then check your work against the LSAT expert's analysis that follows.

Passage A is from a source published in 2004, and Passage B is from a source published in 2007.

Passage A

Millions of people worldwide play multiplayer online games. They each pick, say, a medieval character to play, such as a warrior. Then they might band together in quests to slay magical beasts; their avatars appear as tiny characters striding across a Tolkienesque land.

The economist Edward Castronova noticed something curious about the game he played: it had its own economy, a bustling trade in virtual goods. Players generate goods as they play, often by killing creatures for their treasure and trading it. The longer they play, the wealthier they get.

Things got even more interesting when Castronova learned about the "player auctions." Players would sometimes tire of the game and decide to sell off their virtual possessions at online auction sites.

As Castronova stared at the auction listings, he recognized with a shock what he was looking at. It was a form of currency trading! Each item had a value in the virtual currency traded in the game; when it was sold on the auction site, someone was paying cold hard cash for it. That meant that the virtual currency was worth something in real currency. Moreover, since players were killing monsters or skinning animals to sell their pelts, they were, in effect, creating wealth.

Passage B

Most multiplayer online games prohibit real-world trade in virtual items, but some actually encourage it, for example, by granting participants intellectual property rights in their creations.

Although it seems intuitively the case that someone who accepts real money for the transfer of a virtual item should be taxed, what about the player who only accumulates items or virtual currency within a virtual world? Is "loot" acquired in a game taxable, as a prize or award is? And is the profit in a purely in-game trade or sale for virtual currency taxable? These are important questions, given the tax revenues at stake, and there is pressure on governments to answer them, given that the economies of some virtual worlds are comparable to those of small countries.

Most people's intuition probably would be that accumulation of assets within a game should not be taxed even though income tax applies even to noncash accessions to wealth. This article will argue that income tax law and policy support that result. Loot acquisitions in game worlds should not be treated as taxable prizes and awards, but rather should be treated like other property that requires effort to obtain, such as fish pulled from the ocean, which is taxed only upon sale. Moreover, in-game trades of virtual items should not be treated as taxable barter.

By contrast, tax doctrine and policy counsel taxation of the sale of virtual items for real currency, and, in games that are intentionally commodified, even of in-world sales for virtual currency, regardless of whether the participant cashes out. This approach would leave entertainment value untaxed without creating a tax shelter for virtual commerce.

PrepTest140 Sec3 Qs 7-13

Expert Analysis

Now, compare your Roadmap to that of an LSAT expert. Look for places in which you missed an important Keyword or mischaracterized a point in the passage. Compare your big picture summary to those of the LSAT expert and review her notes on how these paired passages are similar and how they are different.

LSAT Passage	Analysis
Passage A is from a source published in 2004, and Passage B is from a source published in 2007.	
Passage A Millions of people worldwide play multiplayer online games. They each pick, say, a medieval character to play, such as a warrior. Then they might band together in quests to slay magical beasts; their avatars appear as tiny characters striding across a Tolkienesque land. ¶1: Multiplayer online gaming popular	**Step 1:** The short first paragraph appears to be background information: multiplayer role-playing games are popular.
The economist Edward Castronova noticed something curious about the game he played: it had its own economy, a bustling trade in virtual goods. Players generate goods as they play, often by killing creatures for their treasure and trading it. The longer they play, the wealthier they get. ¶2: EC notes: economy within game	Here, the **Topic** starts to take shape: An economist noticed that players in these games collect virtual goods.
Things got even more interesting when Castronova learned about the "player auctions." Players would sometimes tire of the game and decide to sell off their virtual possessions at online auction sites. ¶3: Also odd: auction stuff when bored!	This paragraph narrows the **Scope** of the passage: Virtual goods are auctioned/sold online.

LSAT Passage	Analysis
As Castronova stared at the auction listings, he recognized with a shock what he was looking at. It was a form of currency trading! Each item had a value in the virtual currency traded in the game; when it was sold on the auction site, someone was paying cold hard cash for it. That meant that the virtual currency was worth something in real currency. Moreover, since players were killing monsters or skinning animals to sell their pelts, they were, in effect, creating wealth. #4: EC: Wow: this is $ trade, virtual wealth converted to real	And, here in the final paragraph, we get the **Purpose** and **Main Idea**–to reveal an economist's startling discovery: Virtual items have value in "real-world" currency; thus, the "work" players are doing in the game creates wealth.
Passage B Most multiplayer online games prohibit real-world trade in virtual items, but some actually encourage it, for example, by granting participants intellectual property rights in their creations. #5: A few games push real trade	From the outset, this passage addresses the same **Topic** and **Scope** as Passage A: the trade/sale of virtual items from online games. It adds a fact not contained in Passage A: some games forbid, while others encourage, these sales.
Although it seems intuitively the case that someone who accepts real money for the transfer of a virtual item should be taxed, what about the player who only accumulates items or virtual currency within a virtual world? Is "loot" acquired in a game taxable, as a prize or award is? And is the profit in a purely in-game trade or sale for virtual currency taxable? These are important questions, given the tax revenues at stake, and there is pressure on governments to answer them, given that the economies of some virtual worlds are comparable to those of small countries. #6: Shld virtual goods be taxed? How about profits? Govts. pressed to decide	The author of Passage B has a distinct **Purpose**: to raise "important questions" about the taxability of commerce in virtual items. Note the three distinct questions here.

LSAT Passage	Analysis
Most people's intuition probably would be that accumulation of assets within a game should not be taxed even though income tax applies even to noncash accessions to wealth. This article will argue that income tax law and policy support that result. Loot acquisitions in game worlds should not be treated as taxable prizes and awards, but rather should be treated like other property that requires effort to obtain, such as fish pulled from the ocean, which is taxed only upon sale. Moreover, in-game trades of virtual items should not be treated as taxable barter. #7: A: Don't tax items that stay in virtual world.	The author starts to formulate his **Main Idea** (almost in the style of a thesis statement): In-game trade of virtual items should not be taxable. The author draws an analogy: Acquiring virtual items in a game is like catching fish; we don't tax fish until they are sold.
By contrast, tax doctrine and policy counsel taxation of the sale of virtual items for real currency, and, in games that are intentionally commodified, even of in-world sales for virtual currency, regardless of whether the participant cashes out. This approach would leave entertainment value untaxed without creating a tax shelter for virtual commerce. #8: A: Tax when virtual goods sold for real $. *PrepTest140 Sec4 Qs7-13*	In the final paragraph, however, the author of Passage B expands on his **Main Idea**: When virtual items are sold for "real-world" currency, or when they are commodified within a game, they should be taxable. The author's main support for his argument is that having this system allows the games to remain fun but not become virtual "tax shelters."

Compare/Contrast the Passages

The relationship between the two passages is pretty simple: Passage A announces the discovery of a new economic phenomenon, while Passage B explores practical legal questions raised by that phenomenon.

Passage A is neutral; its author describes the economist's "shock" at discovering virtual goods with real-world value, but neither the author nor the economist offers any judgment on the discovery. Passage B's author, on the other hand, makes an argument. The argument's conclusion is a recommendation about when trade in virtual items should and should not be taxed.

Passage A contains facts (e.g., how virtual items are auctioned and traded) not found in Passage B. Passage B reveals differences among games (some encourage trading while others forbid it) not discussed in Passage A. The economist in Passage A takes note of in-game activities ("skinning animals to sell their pelts" (paragraph 4)), while the author of Passage B compares such activities to "real-world" work ("[pulling] fish . . . from the ocean" (paragraph 3)).

Taken together, these passages illustrate Event/Phenomenon passages very well. Even in a regular, single passage, this would be a common Event/Phenomenon structure: A discovery is noted, a problem arises from it, and the author proposes a solution.

You'll see the questions for these paired passages a little later in the chapter. Look forward to applying your analysis of the similarities and differences between the two short passages on several questions. Now, return to a standard-length LSAT passage to look at the third and last of the passage structures with which you'll practice.

Debate Passages

This passage structure is less common than the previous two, constituting somewhere around 10 percent of recent passages. You're unlikely to see more than one of these in a Reading Comprehension section, and on some tests, they may be absent altogether. Make sure to distinguish Debate passages from Theory/Perspective passages that may focus on the point of view of a particular individual. In Debate passages, there will be two (or more) views distinct from that of the author. The author may remain neutral, simply explaining the debate, or he may choose one side or the other. Most often, however, he will declare one side more promising or more likely, but conclude that the debate is not yet settled.

Practice With that in mind, read and Roadmap the following passage. Mark Keywords within the passage, and record your paragraph notes on a separate piece of scratch paper. When you're finished, compare your work to that of the LSAT expert on the following pages.

Homing pigeons can be taken from their lofts and transported hundreds of kilometers in covered cages to unfamiliar sites and yet, when released, be able to choose fairly accurate homeward bearings within a minute and fly home. Aside from reading the minds of the experimenters (a possibility that has not escaped investigation), there are two basic explanations for the remarkable ability of pigeons to "home": the birds might keep track of their outward displacement (the system of many short-range species such as honeybees); or they might have some sense, known as a "map sense," that would permit them to construct an internal image of their environment and then "place" themselves with respect to home on some internalized coordinate system.

The first alternative seems unlikely. One possible model for such an inertial system might involve an internal magnetic compass to measure the directional leg of each journey. Birds transported to the release site wearing magnets or otherwise subjected to an artificial magnetic field, however, are only occasionally affected. Alternately, if pigeons measure their displacement by consciously keeping track of the direction and degree of acceleration and deceleration of the various turns, and timing the individual legs of the journey, simply transporting them in the dark, with constant rotations, or under complete anesthesia ought to impair or eliminate their ability to orient. These treatments, however, have no effect. Unfortunately, no one has yet performed the crucial experiment of transporting pigeons in total darkness, anesthetized, rotating, and with the magnetic field reversed all at the same time.

The other alternative, that pigeons have a "map sense," seems more promising, yet the nature of this sense remains mysterious. Papi has posited that the map sense is olfactory: that birds come to associate odors borne on the wind with the direction in which the wind is blowing, and so slowly build up an olfactory map of their surroundings. When transported to the release site, then, they only have to sniff the air en route and/or at the site to know the direction of home. Papi conducted a series of experiments showing that pigeons whose nostrils have been plugged are poorly oriented at release and home slowly.

One problem with the hypothesis is that Schmidt-Koenig and Phillips failed to detect any ability in pigeons to distinguish natural air (presumably laden with olfactory map information) from pure, filtered air. Papi's experimental results, moreover, admit of simpler, nonolfactory explanations. It seems likely that the behavior of nostril-plugged birds results from the distracting and traumatic nature of the experiment. When nasal tubes are used to bypass the olfactory chamber but allow for comfortable breathing, no disorientation is evident. Likewise, when the olfactory epithelium is sprayed with anesthetic to block smell-detection but not breathing, orientation is normal.

PrepTest104 Sec3 Qs15-21

Expert Analysis for the Practice exercise may be found on the following page. ▶ ▶ ▶

Expert Analysis

Now, compare your Roadmap to that of an LSAT expert. Look for places in which you missed an important Keyword or mischaracterized a point in the passage. Use the Analysis column reflecting the expert's internal monologue to assess whether your big picture summary is accurate and useful.

LSAT Passage	Analysis
Homing pigeons can be taken from their lofts and transported hundreds of kilometers in covered cages to unfamiliar sites and yet, when released, be able to choose fairly accurate homeward bearings within a minute and fly home. Aside from reading the minds of the experimenters (a possibility that has not escaped investigation), there are two basic explanations for the remarkable ability of pigeons to "home": the birds might keep track of their outward displacement (the system of many short-range species such as honeybees); or they might have some sense, known as a "map sense," that would permit them to construct an internal image of their environment and then "place" themselves with respect to home on some internalized coordinate system. ¶1: How pigeons find home? 2 poss. ways: O.D. (bee-like navig.) or M.S. (inner map coords).	**Step 1:** The **Topic**—homing pigeons—and the **Scope**—the question of how they home—are clear from the first paragraph. After dismissing a rather harebrained sugges-tion (maybe they read human minds!), the author presents two reasonable hypotheses: 1) outward displacement (which other species, such as honey-bees, use), and 2) "map sense." We can anticipate that the next two paragraphs will evaluate these hypotheses in more detail.

LSAT Passage	Analysis
The first alternative seems unlikely. One possible model for such an inertial system might involve an internal magnetic compass to measure the directional leg of each journey. Birds transported to the release site wearing magnets or otherwise subjected to an artificial magnetic field, however, are only occasionally affected. Alternately, if pigeons measure their displacement by consciously keeping track of the direction and degree of acceleration and deceleration of the various turns, and timing the individual legs of the journey, simply transporting them in the dark, with constant rotations, or under complete anesthesia ought to impair or eliminate their ability to orient. These treatments, however, have no effect. Unfortunately, no one has yet performed the crucial experiment of transporting pigeons in total darkness, anesthetized, rotating, and with the magnetic field reversed all at the same time.	The author finds outward displacement "unlikely" but admits that it has not been 100 percent ruled out. She cites two possible models for outward displacement: Homing pigeons may have "an internal magnetic compass," or they may keep track of turns and acceleration. When tested, neither model was supported by the findings. "Unfortunately," says the author, no one has done the complete rule-out experiment of impairing, simultaneously, all of the pigeons' potential modes of tracking outward displacement. That's why the author won't say the hypothesis is completely disproven. Because the author thinks outward displacement is "unlikely," she will give her evaluation of the "map sense" in the next paragraph.
#2: O.D. not likely both models tested w/ neg results ultimate test not done yet.	

LSAT Passage	Analysis
The other alternative, that pigeons have a "map sense," seems more promising, yet the nature of this sense remains mysterious. Papi has posited that the map sense is olfactory: that birds come to associate odors borne on the wind with the direction in which the wind is blowing, and so slowly build up an olfactory map of their surroundings. When transported to the release site, then, they only have to sniff the air en route and/or at the site to know the direction of home. Papi conducted a series of experiments showing that pigeons whose nostrils have been plugged are poorly oriented at release and home slowly. #3: M.S. more likely but still ?? Papi's idea: smell directs birds Experiments support idea	As expected, here's the author's evaluation of pigeons' "map sense." This hypothesis she finds "promising." Nonetheless, "map sense" "remains mysterious." So, our author doesn't think the map sense has been completely explained. The rest of the paragraph details how a scientist named Papi tested an olfactory model for the map sense with some success.
One problem with the hypothesis is that Schmidt-Koenig and Phillips failed to detect any ability in pigeons to distinguish natural air (presumably laden with olfactory map information) from pure, filtered air. Papi's experimental results, moreover, admit of simpler, nonolfactory explanations. It seems likely that the behavior of nostril-plugged birds results from the distracting and traumatic nature of the experiment. When nasal tubes are used to bypass the olfactory chamber but allow for comfortable breathing, no disorientation is evident. Likewise, when the olfactory epithelium is sprayed with anesthetic to block smell-detection but not breathing, orientation is normal. *PrepTest104 Sec3 Qs 15-21* #4: problems with Papi idea S-K&P: no ev of birds analyzing air P's results undercut by other tests & expls.	This paragraph outlines three criticisms of Papi's experiments (signaled by the Keywords "[o]ne problem," "moreover," and "[l]ikewise"). The criticisms come from a pair of scientists: Schmidt-Koenig and Phillips. They tested pigeons using filtered air (no smells, in other words) and found no difference in their ability to home. They also suggested that Papi's experiments had traumatized the birds, and so they performed two tests that blocked the pigeons' olfactory senses without injuring them. The results, again, undermined Papi's model. There is no explicit thesis statement or conclusion sentence in this passage. The author's **Purpose**, as shown by Paragraphs 2–4 is to *evaluate* the two main hypotheses. Her **Main Point** is that pigeons probably home using a map sense (outward displacement is unlikely), but that we don't yet know what kind of map they use.

Instead of viewing this as a natural science passage (and thus focusing on how much he doesn't know about the complex models and experiments), the LSAT expert identifies this as a classic Debate passage. Doing so demystifies the subject matter and makes it easier to understand the author's Purpose and the overall organization of the passage.

Keep the expert's summaries and paragraph notes in mind when you turn to the questions associated with this passage in the next section of this chapter.

Reflect

In all three of the examples you just looked at, the LSAT expert:

- Used Keywords to discern the structure of the passage and note the author's purpose for offering certain details and examples.
- Took down brief, accurate paragraph notes highlighting the points in the passage most likely to surface in the questions.
- Summarized the author's Topic, Scope, Purpose, and Main Idea while reading the passage.

Keep those examples in mind as you practice additional Reading Comprehension passages. For all of the passages included in this book, you'll find sample Roadmaps and complete discussions of the passages in addition to explanations of individual questions. In practice, don't hesitate to spend 3–4 minutes reading and Roadmapping a passage and then compare your work in Step 1 to that of the LSAT expert reflected in the explanations. After you review the strategic reading step, you'll feel much more confident going into the question set.

It is possible to practice the kind of strategic reading you'll do on the LSAT with almost anything you read, at least anything academic or nonfiction. Next time you're perusing a newspaper editorial, a well-written commentary piece, or an article in a science magazine, roadmap it. Try to imagine, or even write, the kinds of questions the LSAT would ask about the piece you've just finished. Look for places in which the author has used Contrast, Illustration, or Opinion Keywords in ways that would allow for the testmaker to ask an Inference or Logic Function question. Learning to read in a new way will not happen overnight, but if you start to read this way consistently, by test day, you'll be far ahead of the average test taker.

CHANNEL SPOTLIGHT

Keywords are Road Signs

By The LSAT Channel Faculty

Watch the video lesson for this Spotlight in your online Study Plan.

Kaplan's strategic reading approach for Reading Comprehension puts a lot of emphasis on the strategy of noting Keywords. What makes these words "key" is that they focus your attention on the author's Purpose and on the structure of the passage. Emphasis/Opinion Keywords—such as *unfortunately, surprisingly*, and *crucial*—express the author's attitude toward a subject or tell you what the author encourages the reader to focus on. Contrast Keywords—such as *but, yet*, and *despite*—highlight concepts or ideas that the author considers incompatible or signal a disagreement between two opinions. Logic Keywords—for example *thus, therefore*, and *because*—and Illustration Keywords—such as *for example*—outline arguments and indicate where and how the author attempts to support her positions.

Spotting those Keywords, and learning to quickly identify what they signal, is valuable to you as an LSAT test taker because the test neither requires nor rewards outside knowledge. LSAT Reading Comprehension questions ask very little about the *what* of a passage—that is, about the facts, dates, or names in the passage—but instead ask you to recognize *why* the author wrote it and *how* she makes and supports her points. Learning to use Keywords as "road signs" that guide your reading will make you more strategic, and thus, more efficient.

When you first start practicing for the LSAT, passages with content that is familiar to you will seem easier and more comfortable to work with. But, on Test Day, you have no control over the topics that will be covered in the Reading Comprehension section. In the video that accompanies this Spotlight, an LSAT Channel expert will help you understand how using Keywords allows you to read strategically even when the subject matter of a passage is complex and unfamiliar. Start by reading the excerpt from a passage about punk rock (of all things) that follows. Then, watch the video lesson to see how reading that passage strategically can make an official LSAT passage on an obscure science topic much easier to comprehend.

Using Keywords

The idea that the British punk rock bands of the 1970s were wholly original—some would say "unprecedented"—has long dominated the annals of rock musicology. This view has been reinforced by an accident of history: many American fans first heard punk rock performed by these British groups. Bands such as the Sex Pistols, the Clash, and Damned burst on to the music scene in the late 1970s and early 1980s and became immediately influential; only over the next decade did many American fans become familiar with the music of American bands such as the New York Dolls, the Ramones, or Suicide, who had recorded and performed years before the British groups formed. Because of the enormous power of the first British punk rock that reached the United States, some American fans overlooked the very tangible influence that these earlier American bands had on their British counterparts. Rock fans and writers failed to consider both the musical similarities (including the raw, stripped down sound and simple, three-chord song structures) and the very different social and political environments (for example, the massive and often violent labor strikes in mid-1970s Britain) that reveal these bands' mutual influence.

More recent books and documentaries, such as Legs McNeil and Gillian McCain's *Please Kill Me* and *End of the Century—The Story of the Ramones* call into question the standard view that punk rock originated in England. These works' investigation of the underground music scene in Manhattan in the mid-1970s, especially at the now legendary CBGBs, lead to a number of questions. For example . . .

Darwin's conception of early prehistoric humans as confident, clever hunter-gatherers has long dominated anthropology. His theory has been reinforced by an accident of history: the human fossil record has been found largely in reverse order. Remains of humans' most recent forebears, who lived 35,000 to 100,000 years ago, were discovered in 1856; over the next century, discoveries yielded fossils of hominids from progressively earlier eras. Because the first-discovered fossil hominids, the Neanderthals, genuinely resembled modern humans, anthropologists from Darwin on have confused the life-styles of today's nonindustrial peoples with those of our distant hominid forebears. These anthropologists have failed to consider both the sophistication of modern hunter-gatherer societies (including their use of fire, clothing, shelter, weapons, tools, language, and complex strategies) and the ways in which their environments differ from prehistoric ones (for example, in containing fewer large animal predators).

Recent intellectual developments, such as the new field of taphonomy, have called into question the traditional hypothesis that early hominids outsmarted the predators with whom they competed for meat and that they mastered their world through hunting. Taphonomy investigates the transformation of skeletal remains into fossil—it asks, for example, whether bone piles have been deposited by predators, hunters, or floodwaters, and whether hyenas' teeth scar animal bones differently than do human tools.

Taphonomy has been utilized by some researchers in studying a group of animal fossils, hominid fossils, and stone tools that were almost two million years old. By comparing the microscopic features of linear grooves on the fossilized animal bones with similar grooves on modern bones, the researchers found that cut marks made by stone tools differed from the marks of other taphonomic agents, such as carnivores' teeth or sedimentary abrasion. They also found that the markings of stone tools on many of the fossilized animal bones did not occur systematically at the joints and that the toothmarks of animal carnivores often underlay rather than overlay the cut marks.

The researchers hypothesized from this evidence that early hominids were scavengers of meat left from carnivore kills, rather than hunters of live prey. From patterns of wear on fossilized hominid teeth, the researchers further deduced that early hominids, like other scavengers, ate fruit primarily and meat only occasionally. Early hominids could have been well adapted for scavenging: agility in climbing trees helped them escape predators and gain superior vantage points, and an upright mode of walking enabled them to scan the ground for carcasses and to carry useful scavenging tools. According to these researchers, Darwin's vision of early prehistoric hunters may be familiar and appealing, but the fossil record suggests a revised picture of less-confident early hominids who often perched in trees and who foraged and scavenged alone or in small groups.

PrepTest108 Sec4 Qs 21–27

Reading Comprehension Question Strategies

The universal characteristic of LSAT Reading Comprehension questions is this: *they reward you for having read and understood the passage.* That may sound almost tautological—Reading Comprehension questions are obviously about whether I comprehended the reading?! Well, yes. But that obvious truth masks a subtler, more important one: Reading Comprehension questions do *not* reward what you (or anyone else) knew *before* reading the passage. The questions are always worded such that they must be answered from the text. We'll keep coming back to that truth, and we'll build the strategies for answering the questions based on the text throughout this section.

Reading Comprehension Question Types

Prepare The LSAT testmaker uses five main types of questions in the Reading Comprehension section. You'll learn to recognize them shortly. Moreover, depending on the wording of the question stem, many of those question types may contain clues that will allow you to target your research to specific portions of the text.

LEARNING OBJECTIVES

In this portion of the chapter, you'll learn to:

- Recognize Global questions.
- Recognize Inference questions.
- Recognize Detail questions.
- Recognize Logic Function questions.
- Recognize Logic Reasoning questions.
- Determine whether the question stem contains research clues.

Let's define and see examples of each Reading Comprehension question type. As we go through the question types, pay attention to the analysis that the LSAT expert does for Step 2—reading the question stem and looking for clues—of the Reading Comprehension Method.

Global Questions

Global questions ask about the passage as a whole. They are designed to test your comprehension of the author's Main Idea or Purpose. These questions lack research clues, naturally, as they take the entire passage into account. To predict the correct answer, use your summary of the Purpose or Main Idea. Nearly all passages contain one Global question, and it is usually (but not always) the first question in the set. Occasionally, you'll encounter a passage with two Global questions. In such cases, one is likely to be the first question in the set and the other at (or near) the end of the question set. Very rarely, you'll find a passage with no Global question accompanying it.

LSAT Question Stem	Analysis
Which one of the following most accurately expresses the main point of the passage?	**Step 2:** "[M]ain point"—a Global question. Use the Main Idea summary to predict the correct answer and evaluate the choices.
The primary purpose of the passage is to	**Step 2:** "[P]rimary purpose"—a Global question. Use the Purpose summary to predict the correct answer and evaluate the choices.

The language of Global question stems is fairly standardized. You may find small variations, but expect to see "main point" or "primary purpose" most often.

One rare variation on the Global question asks you to describe the organization of the passage. You actually saw an example of this type among the questions accompanying the pre-World War I European painters passage in Chapter 6.

LSAT Question Stem	Analysis
Which one of the following most accurately describes the organization of the passage?	**Step 2:** "[D]escribes the organization of the passage"—a Global question variant. Consult the Roadmap to outline the overall structure and use that to evaluate the choices.

This is the one type of Global question that benefits from research. Whereas the standard "main point" and "primary purpose" Global questions can be answered with your big picture summary, "organization" Global questions need you to match the correct answer to the flow of the passage. It's helpful with "organization" Global questions to consult the Roadmap before you evaluate the choices.

Inference Questions

Inference questions account for a little less than half of the points in Reading Comprehension. In a typical 27-question section, there will be anywhere from 10 to 12 Inference questions, although one recent test had 14. Inference questions are characterized by language in the stem telling you that the correct answer *is based on* or *follows from* the passage without necessarily being stated in the passage.

LSAT Question Stem	Analysis
Based on the passage, the author would be most likely to agree with which one of the following statements about unified field theory?	**Step 2:** "Based on the passage" and "most likely to agree"—an Inference question. "[U]nified field theory" is the research clue.
The passage suggests which one of the following about the behavior of migratory water fowl?	**Step 2:** "The passage suggests"—an Inference question. "[M]igratory water fowl" is the research clue.
Given the information in the passage, to which one of the following would radiocarbon dating techniques likely be most applicable?	**Step 2:** "Given the information in the passage" and "likely be . . . applicable"*—an Inference question. The correct answer follows from the passage. "[R]adiocarbon dating techniques" is the research clue.

*When a question stem asks you to apply something from the passage, treat it as an Inference question. The correct answer still follows from the information in the passage; it's just applied to a new or hypothetical context in the correct answer.

In each of these cases, the expert notes research clues in the question stem. She will be able to quickly check her Roadmap at those points and use the text to predict the correct answer. Other Inference questions are open-ended and call for a different approach to evaluating the choices.

LSAT Question Stem	Analysis
It can be inferred that the author would be most likely to agree that	**Step 2:** "[I]nferred"—an Inference question. No research clues. Evaluate the choices using the Scope, Purpose, and Main Idea summaries *or* use the answer choices as research clues and check them against the text.
Which one of the following statements is most strongly supported by the passage?	**Step 2:** "[S]upported by the passage"—an Inference question. No research clues. Evaluate the choices using the Scope, Purpose, and Main Idea summaries *or* use the answer choices as research clues and check them against the text.

In these questions, no targeted research clue is present. When you see an Inference question of this type, quickly check the answer choices. If they all relate to the same portion of the passage, you can simply use them as research clues and test each one against the text. If the answer choices seem vague, broad, or scattered, start by checking them against your Scope, Purpose, and Main Idea summaries. Eliminate all those with which the author would not agree. That will either leave you with the one correct choice or will narrow down the number of choices you need to research.

One other variant on the Inference question is fairly common: the Author's Attitude question. A strong strategic reader, who has identified Emphasis/Opinion Keywords in the passage, can research these questions quickly.

LSAT Question Stem	Analysis
The author's attitude toward the use of DNA evidence in appeals by convicted felons is most accurately described as	**Step 2:** "[A]uthor's attitude"—an Inference question about the author's attitude. "[T]he use of DNA evidence in appeals by convicted felons" is the research clue. Look for Opinion Keywords that indicate the author's view.
The author's stance regarding monetarist economic theories can most accurately be described as one of	**Step 2:** "[A]uthor's stance"—an Inference question about the author's attitude. "[M]onetarist economic theories" is the research clue. Look for Opinion Keywords that indicate the author's view.

You may see other slight variations in the wording of Inference question stems, but don't let that throw you. The feature they all have in common is that the correct answer follows from the passage without being directly stated in it.

Detail Questions

Detail questions are less common than Inference questions. You'll typically see 4–5 per test, though not every passage will necessarily be accompanied by a Detail question. The identifying characteristic of the Detail question stem is that, in some way, it tells you that the correct answer will closely paraphrase something stated explicitly in the passage: "according to the passage" and "the passage states" are common phrasings of these questions.

LSAT Question Stem	Analysis
According to the passage, some critics have criticized Gilliam's films on the grounds that	**Step 2:** "According to the passage"—a Detail question. "[C]ritics have criticized Gilliam's films on the grounds that" is the research clue.
The passage states that a role of a municipality's comptroller in budget decisions by the city council is to	**Step 2:** "The passage states"—a Detail question. "[A] municipality's comptroller in budget decisions by the city council" is the research clue.
The author identifies which one of the following as a commonly held but false preconception?	**Step 2:** "[I]dentifies which one"—a Detail question. "[C]ommonly held but false preconception" is the research clue.

Almost all Detail questions contain research clues; after all, you're looking for a detail. Do not, however, think that questions highlighting a word or phrase in the passage are Detail questions. When the question stem shares the same words highlighted in the passage, it is usually asking for an Inference that can be drawn from what is said there, or it is a Logic Function question asking you *why* the author has included that particular detail or *how* she has used it.

Be ready to encounter 1–2 Detail EXCEPT questions. Not every test includes one of these, but if you should see one, treat it as the LSAT expert does in these examples.

LSAT Question Stem	Analysis
The passage does NOT provide evidence that Mead utilizes which one of the following techniques in one or more of her ethnographies?	**Step 2:** "NOT provide evidence"—a Detail EXCEPT question. Use the answer choices as research clues and eliminate the four stated in the passage.
The author attributes each of the following to the Federalists EXCEPT:	**Step 2:** "The author attributes each . . . EXCEPT"— a Detail EXCEPT question. Use the answer choices as research clues and eliminate the four stated in the passage.

Because all four wrong answers are included in the text, you can use the answer choices as research clues. Eliminate any answers that are stated. If, as you're checking the choices, you find a choice with which the author would clearly disagree or that falls completely outside the scope of the passage, you can choose it with confidence as the correct answer.

Logic Function Questions

Logic Function questions are less common than Detail questions. You'll usually see around three of these in a Reading Comprehension section. These questions will always include a research clue, and it's easy to see why. The question stem points you to a portion of the passage—a detail, a reference, or a paragraph—and asks you *why* the author included it or *how* it functions within the passage.

LSAT Question Stem	Analysis
The author of the passage mentions declining inner-city populations most likely in order to	**Step 2:** "[I]n order to"—a Logic Function question. The correct answer states *why* the author mentions declining inner-city populations. The research clue is the highlighted text.*
The author's discussion of Rimbaud's travels in the Mediterranean in the third paragraph functions primarily to	**Step 2:** "[F]unctions primarily to"—a Logic Function question. The correct answer states why the author discusses Rimbaud's Mediterranean travels. "[T]he third paragraph" is the research clue.
Which one of the following best states the function of the third paragraph of the passage?	**Step 2:** "[S]tates the function"—a Logic Function question. "[T]hird paragraph" is the research clue. This is almost like a mini-Global question asking for the purpose of Paragraph 3 instead of the "primary purpose" of the entire passage.

*Note: When the question stem has a highlighted reference to the passage, the same word(s) or phrase will be highlighted in the passage while you are working on that question. The highlight will disappear when you move to another question or passage. Highlighted-text questions replace the old paper-and-pencil questions that referred to specific line numbers. Keep that in mind when you're practicing on older released tests.

Be careful on Logic Function questions to avoid answer choices that accurately reflect what the passage said about the detail or reference but do not explain *why* the author included it.

Logic Reasoning Questions

These questions are slightly more common than Logic Function questions. You'll likely see 3–4 per section. It's very unlikely that every passage will have a Logic Reasoning question in its question set. The distinguishing characteristic of Logic Reasoning questions in Reading Comprehension is that they mirror the task of a question type typically found in the Logical Reasoning section. Take a look at the LSAT expert's analyses of a couple of questions to see this illustrated.

LSAT Question Stem	Analysis
Which one of the following would, if true, most strengthen the claim made by the author in the final sentence of the passage?	**Step 2:** "[I]f true, most strengthen"—a Logic Reasoning question mirroring a Strengthen question from the LR sections. Research the passage around the referenced sentence.
Which one of the following pairs of proposals is most closely analogous to the pair of studies discussed in the passage?	**Step 2:** "[M]ost closely analogous"—a Logic Reasoning question mirroring a Parallel Reasoning question from the LR sections. "[T]he pair of studies" is the research clue.

The most common Logical Reasoning question types mirrored by Reading Comprehension Logic Reasoning questions are Strengthen/Weaken, Parallel Reasoning, Method of Argument, and Principle (with the first two types in the list being far more common than the others). When you encounter one of these questions in the Reading Comprehension section, use the same approach you would in the Logical Reasoning sections, treating the referenced portion of the passage as the question's stimulus.

A note about research clues. In her analyses of the question stems, the LSAT expert identified research clues wherever they were present. Knowing where to look in the passage for the text relevant to the correct answer will make you faster and more accurate throughout the question set. As you prepare to do more practice with Reading Comprehension question stems, learn to spot these five types of research clues.

LSAT STRATEGY

Reading Comprehension Research Clues

- **Highlighted Text**—research around the highlighted detail; look for Keywords indicating why the text in question has been included or how it's used.
- **Paragraph References**—consult your Roadmap to see the paragraph's scope and function.
- **Quoted Text** (often accompanied by a line reference)—check the context of the quoted term or phrase; ask what the author meant by it in the passage.
- **Proper Nouns**—check the context of the person, place, or thing; ask whether the author had a positive, negative, or neutral evaluation of it; ask why it was included in the passage.
- **Content Clues**—terms, concepts, or ideas highlighted in the passage, but not included as direct quotes in the question stem; these will almost always refer you to something the author emphasized or stated an opinion on.

You'll see these research clues in action when we turn to Steps 3 and 4 of the Reading Comprehension Method. For now, get a little practice with Step 2 using the questions that accompany the Hopi Personal Names passage.

Practice For each of the following, identify the question type and state whether the question stem includes a research clue. You can check your work against the expert analysis on the following pages.

LSAT Question	My Analysis
1. Which one of the following statements most accurately summarizes the passage's main point?	**Step 2:**
2. The author most likely refers to Western Apache place names in order to	**Step 2:**
3. Which one of the following statements describes an example of the function accorded to personal names under Lévi-Strauss's view?	**Step 2:**
4. The primary function of the second paragraph is to	**Step 2:**
5. Based on the passage, with which one of the following statements about Mill's view would the author of the passage be most likely to agree?	**Step 2:**
6. It can be inferred from the passage that each of the following features of Hopi personal names contributes to their poetic quality EXCEPT:	**Step 2:**
7. The author's primary purpose in writing the passage is to *PrepTest104 Sec3 Qs8-14*	**Step 2:**

Expert Analysis

Here's how an LSAT expert would analyze each of those question stems.

LSAT Question	Analysis
1. Which one of the following statements most accurately summarizes the passage's main point?	**Step 2:** "[M]ain point"—A Global question asking for the author's Main Idea. Consult the big picture summary.
2. The author most likely refers to Western Apache place names in order to	**Step 2:** "[I]n order to"—This is a Logic Function question asking how or why the author cited a particular detail. The highlighted text provides the research clue.
3. Which one of the following statements describes an example of the function accorded to personal names under Lévi-Strauss's view?	**Step 2:** An Inference question asking us to apply what the passage says about Lévi-Strauss's theory of names. "Lévi-Strauss's view" is the research clue.
4. The primary function of the second paragraph is to	**Step 2:** "[P]rimary function . . . is to"—A Logic Function question asking for the purpose of a full paragraph. The paragraph reference is the research clue.
5. Based on the passage, with which one of the following statements about Mill's view would the author of the passage be most likely to agree?	**Step 2:** "Based on the passage . . . with which . . . would the author . . . agree?"—An Inference question rewarding an understanding of the author's opinion about Mill's theory. "Mill's view" is the research clue.
6. It can be inferred from the passage that each of the following features of Hopi personal names contributes to their poetic quality EXCEPT:	**Step 2:** "[C]an be inferred . . . EXCEPT"—This is an Inference EXCEPT question. The four wrong answers will follow from the passage. The correct answer will not. The Hopi names' "poetic quality" is the research clue.
7. The author's primary purpose in writing the passage is to *PrepTest104 Sec3 Qs8-14*	**Step 2:** "[P]rimary purpose"—A Global question calling for the author's purpose in writing the passage. Consult the big picture summary.

How did you do? You'll have more opportunities to perform Step 2, interpreting the question stems and looking for research clues, as you work through the questions from the passages on Online Gaming and Homing Pigeons later in the chapter. For now, though, let's take the questions from the Hopi Personal Names passage and work through the next two steps of the Reading Comprehension Method: Step 3—Research the Relevant Text; and Step 4—Predict the Correct Answer.

Researching Reading Comprehension Questions and Predicting the Correct Answer

Prepare In Reading Comprehension, poorly trained test takers often lose a lot of points (and, just as importantly, a lot of time) because they essentially answer questions by rereading the passage. They aren't sure quite where to find the correct answer and wind up looking all over the passage in response to each answer choice. You *should* answer the questions based on the passage, of course, but there is a big difference between researching the relevant text and simply rereading the passage.

LEARNING OBJECTIVES

In this part of the chapter, you'll learn to:

- Identify and employ five kinds of research clues (highlighted text, paragraph reference, quoted text, proper names, and content clues) in question stems to research the relevant text in a passage.
- Research the relevant text and accurately predict the correct answer to Inference questions featuring referent reading clues.
- Use Topic, Scope, Purpose, and Main Idea summaries to predict the correct answer to Global questions.
- Use Topic, Scope, Purpose, and Main Idea summaries to predict broadly the correct answer to Inference questions lacking referent reading clues.

Step 3 is where you earn the payoff for the time you spend reading the passage strategically and creating a helpful Roadmap. Take a look at how an LSAT expert handles Steps 3 and 4 in the Hopi Personal Names passage. For reference, we've reprinted the expert's Roadmap and Step 1 analysis. Consult it along with the expert to see how he's working through the Research and Prediction steps.

LSAT Passage

Personal names are generally regarded by European thinkers in two major ways, both of which deny that names have any significant semantic content. In philosophy and linguistics, John Stuart Mill's formulation that "proper names are meaningless marks set upon . . . persons to distinguish them from one another" retains currency; in anthropology, Claude Lévi-Strauss's characterization of names as being primarily instruments of social classification has been very influential. Consequently, interpretation of personal names in societies where names have other functions and meanings has been neglected. Among the Hopi of the southwestern United States, names often refer to historical or ritual events in order both to place individuals within society and to confer an identity upon them. Furthermore, the images used to evoke these events suggest that Hopi names can be seen as a type of poetic composition.

¶1:
Names: Euro views =
meaningless differentiators
or social classif tool.
Euro ignores add'l uses:
names giving I.D.
names as poetry.

Analysis

Step 1: The first paragraph lays out the entire big picture for this passage. The **Topic** is the scholarship of personal names. The **Scope** will focus on Hopi names. The author's **Purpose/Main Idea** is to show that Hopi names illustrate the shortcomings of the two major European theories about personal names.

The paragraph starts with the two theories. Mill (philosophy/linguistics) says names are arbitrary; we just use them to keep people separate. Lévi-Strauss (anthropology) says names are used for social classification.

The author says Hopi names are different in two ways: 1) They go beyond mere individual identity by being associated with rituals or events, and 2) they use images and so, are poetic. We can anticipate seeing those differences explained in the next two paragraphs.

LSAT Passage	Analysis
Throughout life, Hopis receive several names in a sequence of ritual initiations. Birth, entry into one of the ritual societies during childhood, and puberty are among the name-giving occasions. Names are conferred by an adult member of a clan other than the child's clan, and names refer to that name giver's clan, sometimes combining characteristics of the clan's totem animal with the child's characteristics. Thus, a name might translate to something as simple as "little rabbit," which reflects both the child's size and the representative animal. #2: How Hopi get names thru rites. Names I.D. clan and kid's traits.	As expected, this paragraph outlines how the Hopi confer names through rituals. Their names refer to a person's clan and to his or her individual characteristics or events from his or her life. Thus, Hopi names contain "meaning" beyond merely identifying a person.
More often, though, the name giver has in mind a specific event that is not apparent in a name's literal translation. One Lizard clan member from the village of Oraibi is named Lomayayva, "beautifully ascended." This translation, however, tells nothing about either the event referred to—who or what ascended—or the name giver's clan. The name giver in this case is from Badger clan. Badger clan is responsible for an annual ceremony featuring a procession in which masked representations of spirits climb the mesa on which Oraibi sits. Combining the name giver's clan association with the receiver's home village, "beautifully ascended" refers to the splendid colors and movements of the procession up the mesa. The condensed image this name evokes—a typical feature of Hopi personal names—displays the same quality of Western Apache place names that led one commentator to call them "tiny imagist poems." #3: Long ex. of poetry found in specific naming	This paragraph goes into more detail about what the author considers Hopi names' second distinguishing characteristic: They are poetic. The Hopi often give names that are not literal. The author cites a detailed example to illustrate this and concludes that (like Apache place names) Hopi names may be considered "tiny imagist poems."

LSAT Passage	Analysis
Hopi personal names do several things simultaneously. They indicate social relationships—but only indirectly—and they individuate persons. Equally important, though, is their poetic quality; in a sense they can be understood as oral texts that produce aesthetic delight. This view of Hopi names is thus opposed not only to Mill's claim that personal names are without inherent meaning but also to Lévi-Strauss's purely functional characterization. Interpreters must understand Hopi clan structures and linguistic practices in order to discern the beauty and significance of Hopi names. *PrepTest104 Sec3 Qs8-14*	Here, the author reiterates his thesis (or Main Idea) and his evidence for it. Because they 1) indirectly indicate social relationships and 2) have poetic qualities, Hopi names do not fit into Mill's "names are just arbitrary" theory or into Lévi-Strauss's functional "social classification" theory.
#4: Sums up how Hopi names' meaning and poetry depart from Mill ("arbitrary") and L-S ("social class only") views.	

Note: The highlighting near the end of the third paragraph corresponds to Question 2.

LSAT Question	Analysis
Which one of the following statements most accurately summarizes the passage's main point?	**Step 2:** A Global question asking for the author's Main Idea. **Step 3:** Consult the big picture summary. **Step 4:** The author's Main Idea is that Hopi names, because of their ritual and poetic qualities, illustrate the shortcomings of the two major European theories about personal names.
The author most likely refers to Western Apache place names in order to	**Step 2:** This is a Logic Function question asking how or why the author cited a particular detail. **Step 3:** When the author refers to Apache place names at the end of Paragraph 3, he tells us that another scholar described Apache place names as "tiny imagist poems." The author thinks that description is also applicable to Hopi personal names. **Step 4:** The function of the detail is to *apply* a scholar's description of Apache place names to Hopi personal names.
Which one of the following statements describes an example of the function accorded to personal names under Lévi-Strauss's view?	**Step 2:** An Inference question asking us to apply what the passage says about Lévi-Strauss's theory of names. **Step 3:** Lévi-Strauss's theory is described in the first paragraph: Names are "instruments of social classification." **Step 4:** The correct answer will provide an example of a name revealing something about a person's place in society.
The primary function of the second paragraph is to	**Step 2:** A Logic Function question asking for the purpose of a full paragraph. **Step 3:** The second paragraph outlined ways in which Hopi names refer to events in a person's life, and so, go beyond simply identifying the person. **Step 4:** The correct answer will say something along the lines of: "provide evidence/examples of Hopi names having meaning beyond that of a simple identity 'tag.'"

LSAT Question	Analysis
Based on the passage, with which one of the following statements about Mill's view would the author of the passage be most likely to agree?	**Step 2:** An Inference question rewarding an understanding of the author's opinion about Mill's theory. **Step 3:** The author describes Mill's theory in Paragraphs 1 and 4: Names are arbitrary, meaningless beyond the fact that they identify individuals. **Step 4:** The author finds Mill's individual identity theory unacceptable because it is too narrow to cover the types of meaning and poetic value found in Hopi names.
It can be inferred from the passage that each of the following features of Hopi personal names contributes to their poetic quality EXCEPT	**Step 2:** This is an Inference EXCEPT question. The four wrong answers will follow from the passage. The correct answer will not. **Step 3:** The author discussed Hopi names' poetic qualities near the end of Paragraph 1, throughout Paragraph 3, and at the beginning of Paragraph 4. **Step 4:** We cannot predict an answer NOT found in the passage. We will test each answer choice and eliminate those that follow from the passage's comments on poetic quality.
The author's primary purpose in writing the passage is to *PrepTest104 Sec3 Qs8–14*	**Step 2:** A Global question calling for the author's purpose in writing the passage. **Step 3:** Consult the big picture summary. **Step 4:** The author's purpose is to illustrate how Hopi names reveal the shortcomings of the two major European theories of personal names.

You'll see the answer choices for these questions shortly, when we discuss Step 5 of the Reading Comprehension Method. It is actually very good for you to practice predicting the correct answers without seeing the answer choices. As you work through additional passages in Chapter 8, you may find it very helpful to cover up the answer choices until you've predicted the correct answer, especially if you find it difficult to fully invest in Step 4 of the Method.

Step-by-step, you're building the Reading Comprehension skills. By the end of the chapter, you'll be able to tackle full passages, from reading and Roadmapping all the way through answering the questions.

Practice Before moving on to the answer choices, try Steps 2–4 on the passages discussing Online Gaming. For your convenience, we'll reprint the paired Comparative Reading passages and the expert's Roadmap and analysis. Review those briefly before you dive into the question stems. When you've completed Steps 2–4, check your work against that of the LSAT expert on the following pages.

LSAT Passage	Analysis
Passage A is from a source published in 2004, and Passage B is from a source published in 2007.	
Passage A Millions of people worldwide play multiplayer online games. They each pick, say, a medieval character to play, such as a warrior. Then they might band together in quests to slay magical beasts; their avatars appear as tiny characters striding across a Tolkienesque land. #1: Multiplayer online gaming popular	**Step 1:** The short first paragraph appears to be background information: Multiplayer role-playing games are popular.
The economist Edward Castronova noticed something curious about the game he played: it had its own economy, a bustling trade in virtual goods. Players generate goods as they play, often by killing creatures for their treasure and trading it. The longer they play, the wealthier they get. #2: EC notes: economy within game	Here, the **Topic** starts to take shape: An economist noticed that players in these games collect virtual goods.
Things got even more interesting when Castronova learned about the "player auctions." Players would sometimes tire of the game and decide to sell off their virtual possessions at online auction sites. #3: Also odd: auction stuff when bored!	This paragraph narrows the **Scope** of the passage: Virtual goods are auctioned/sold online.

LSAT Passage	Analysis
As Castronova stared at the auction listings, he recognized with a shock what he was looking at. It was a form of currency trading! Each item had a value in the virtual currency traded in the game; when it was sold on the auction site, someone was paying cold hard cash for it. That meant that the virtual currency was worth something in real currency. Moreover, since players were killing monsters or skinning animals to sell their pelts, they were, in effect, creating wealth. #4: EC: Wow: this is $ trade, virtual wealth converted to real	And here in the final paragraph, we get the **Purpose** and **Main Idea**–to reveal an economist's startling discovery: Virtual items have value in "real-world" currency; thus, the "work" players are doing in the game creates wealth.
Passage B Most multiplayer online games prohibit real-world trade in virtual items, but some actually encourage it, for example, by granting participants intellectual property rights in their creations. #5: A few games push real trade	From the outset, this passage addresses the same **Topic** and **Scope** as Passage A: the trade/sale of virtual items from online games. It adds a fact not contained in Passage A: Some games forbid, while others encourage, these sales.
Although it seems intuitively the case that someone who accepts real money for the transfer of a virtual item should be taxed, what about the player who only accumulates items or virtual currency within a virtual world? Is "loot" acquired in a game taxable, as a prize or award is? And is the profit in a purely in-game trade or sale for virtual currency taxable? These are important questions, given the tax revenues at stake, and there is pressure on governments to answer them, given that the economies of some virtual worlds are comparable to those of small countries. #6: Shld virtual goods be taxed? How about profits? Govts. pressed to decide	The author of Passage B has a distinct **Purpose**: to raise "important questions" about the taxability of commerce in virtual items. Note the three distinct questions here.

LSAT Passage	Analysis
Most people's intuition probably would be that accumulation of assets within a game should not be taxed even though income tax applies even to noncash accessions to wealth. This article will argue that income tax law and policy support that result. Loot acquisitions in game worlds should not be treated as taxable prizes and awards, but rather should be treated like other property that requires effort to obtain, such as fish pulled from the ocean, which is taxed only upon sale. Moreover, in-game trades of virtual items should not be treated as taxable barter. #7: A: Don't tax items that stay in virtual world.	The author starts to formulate his **Main Idea** (almost in the style of a thesis statement): In-game trade of virtual items should not be taxable. The author draws an analogy: Acquiring virtual items in a game is like catching fish; we don't tax fish until they are sold.
By contrast, tax doctrine and policy counsel taxation of the sale of virtual items for real currency, and, in games that are intentionally commodified, even of in-world sales for virtual currency, regardless of whether the participant cashes out. This approach would leave entertainment value untaxed without creating a tax shelter for virtual commerce. *PrepTest140 Sec4 Qs7–13* #8: A: Tax when virtual goods sold for real $.	In the final paragraph, however, the author of Passage B expands on his **Main Idea**: When virtual items are sold for "real-world" currency, or when they are commodified within a game, they should be taxable. The author's main support for his argument is that having this system allows the games to remain fun but not become virtual "tax shelters."

Compare/Contrast the Passages

The relationship between the two passages is pretty simple: Passage A announces the discovery of a new economic phenomenon, while Passage B explores practical legal questions raised by that phenomenon.

Passage A is neutral; its author describes the economist's "shock" at discovering virtual goods with real-world value, but neither the author nor the economist offers any judgment on the discovery. Passage B's author, on the other hand, makes an argument. The argument's conclusion is a recommendation about when trade in virtual items should and should not be taxed.

Passage A contains facts (e.g., how virtual items are auctioned and traded) not found in Passage B. Passage B reveals differences among games (some encourage trading, while others forbid it) not discussed in Passage A. The economist in Passage A takes note of in-game activities ("skinning animals to sell their pelts" (paragraph 4)), while the author of Passage B compares such activities to "real-world" work ("[pulling] fish . . . from the ocean" (paragraph 3)).

Note: The highlighted phrases "skinning animals" (Passage A, paragraph 4) and "fish pulled from the ocean" (Passage B, paragraph 3) correspond to Question 9. The highlighted phrase "games that are intentionally commodified" (Passage B, paragraph 4) corresponds to Question 14.

LSAT Question	My Analysis
8. Which one of the following pairs of titles would be most appropriate for passage A and passage B, respectively?	**Step 2:** **Step 3:** **Step 4:**
9. Which one of the following most accurately expresses how the use of the phrase "skinning animals" in passage A relates to the use of the phrase "fish pulled from the ocean" in passage B?	**Step 2:** **Step 3:** **Step 4:**
10. With regard to their respective attitudes toward commerce in virtual items, passage A differs from passage B in that passage A is more	**Step 2:** **Step 3:** **Step 4:**

LSAT Question	My Analysis
11. Based on what can be inferred from their titles, the relationship between which one of the following pairs of documents is most analogous to the relationship between passage A and passage B?	**Step 2:** **Step 3:** **Step 4:**
12. The passages were most likely taken from which one of the following pairs of sources?	**Step 2:** **Step 3:** **Step 4:**
13. Which one of the following most accurately describes the relationship between the two passages?	**Step 2:** **Step 3:** **Step 4:**
14. Based on passage B, which one of the following is a characteristic of some "games that are intentionally commodified"? *PrepTest140 Sec4 Qs7–13*	**Step 2:** **Step 3:** **Step 4:**

Expert Analysis for the Practice exercise may be found on the following page. ▶ ▶ ▶

Expert Analysis

Here's how the LSAT expert analyzed each of those question stems. Compare your work to his. Did your identification of the question types match? Did you know where in the passage to find the relevant text for those questions containing research clues?

LSAT Question	Analysis
8. Which one of the following pairs of titles would be most appropriate for passage A and passage B, respectively?	**Step 2:** The passages' "titles" would reflect their Main Ideas, so this is a Global question. **Step 3:** Consult the big picture summary to predict the correct answer. **Step 4:** Passage A is about an economist making the shocking discovery of a new form of wealth. Passage B presents a model for how to tax trade in virtual items.
9. Which one of the following most accurately expresses how the use of the phrase "skinning animals" in passage A relates to the use of the phrase "fish pulled from the ocean" in passage B?	**Step 2:** This question asks you to determine how a phrase was used and to apply it to another phrase. Thus, it is an Inference question. **Step 3:** Passage A cited "skinning animals" as a type of in-game "work," while Passage B used catching fish as a real-world analogy to in-game work. **Step 4:** The correct answer will describe the relationship noted in the Step 3 research.
10. With regard to their respective attitudes toward commerce in virtual items, passage A differs from passage B in that passage A is more	**Step 2:** An Inference question about both authors' attitudes. **Step 3:** Passage A describes the economist's "shock" (paragraph 4). Passage B addresses the subject by raising "important questions" (paragraph 2). **Step 4:** The correct answer will say something along the lines of "startled and excited."
11. Based on what can be inferred from their titles, the relationship between which one of the following pairs of documents is most analogous to the relationship between passage A and passage B?	**Step 2:** The correct answer will apply the relationship between the two passages to that between two distinct documents. This is a Logic Reasoning question that rewards Parallel Reasoning skills. **Step 3:** Consult the big picture summary of both passages, and compare them. **Step 4:** The correct answer will describe a document that announces a new discovery, and then one that asks practical, legal questions raised by the discovery.

CHAPTER 7

LSAT Question	Analysis
12. The passages were most likely taken from which one of the following pairs of sources?	**Step 2:** This is an Inference question. It asks you to use the passages' content and style to infer the type of literature from which each was culled. **Step 3:** Passage A is informal and narrative; it feels like it comes from a popular newspaper or magazine. Passage B's author states that this text is from the beginning of an "article" that is going to go into more detail about law and policy, as would be the case in a law journal. **Step 4:** The correct answer will likely say: Passage A—a popular magazine; Passage B—an academic law journal.
13. Which one of the following most accurately describes the relationship between the two passages?	**Step 2:** A Global question rewarding accurate summaries of the two passages and a valid comparison of them. **Step 3:** Consult the big picture summary (the mental Roadmap, if you will). **Step 4:** The correct answer will be something along these lines: Passage A announces a shocking discovery; Passage B identifies important questions raised by the discovery and recommends an answer.
14. Based on passage B, which one of the following is a characteristic of some "games that are intentionally commodified"? *PrepTest140 Sec4 Qs7–13*	**Step 2:** The correct answer will be found in the passage ("Based on the passage, which one . . . is a characteristic . . ."), making this a Detail question. **Step 3:** The author of Passage B describes "intentionally commodified" games in the final paragraph. These games grant intellectual property rights to players who create virtual goods in the game. The author also argues that virtual goods in these games should be taxed when sold for real-world currency or in-game virtual currency. **Step 4:** The correct answer will restate or closely paraphrase something the author of Passage B said about intentionally commodified games.

With all of this work done, evaluating the answer choices will be much easier and much faster. That's what you'll do in the next part of this chapter.

Evaluating Reading Comprehension Answer Choices

Prepare This is what the entire Reading Comprehension Method is set up to do: answer the questions correctly. Pay close attention to how the LSAT expert uses his prediction to make bold, accurate assessments of whether each choice is correct or incorrect.

LEARNING OBJECTIVES

In this portion of the chapter, you'll learn to:

- Use a prediction of the correct answer to evaluate the answer choices.
- Use the Topic, Scope, Purpose, and Main Idea summaries to evaluate the answer choices.
- Evaluate answer choices by efficiently checking them against the passage text.

It is not uncommon for test takers to get bogged down in the Reading Comprehension section, especially as they evaluate the answer choices. Do you find yourself reading through answer choices multiple times, unsure which of two or three tempting choices is correct? The way to overcome that hesitation, and thus to increase your speed and accuracy, is to practice the Reading Comprehension Method. The more comfortable you get researching the passage and making accurate, pointed predictions, the quicker you'll find, and the more confidently you'll select, the correct answer. As you review the LSAT expert's evaluations below, keep all of the work you've done through Steps 1–4 in mind.

Let's start by taking one more look at the Hopi Personal Names passage. We'll reprint the passage, Roadmap, and Step 1 analysis for reference. Along with each question, we'll repeat the expert's Step 2–4 analyses as well. This time, though, we'll add the answer choices and show you how the expert zeroes in on the correct choice.

LSAT Passage	Analysis
Personal names are generally regarded by European thinkers in two major ways, both of which deny that names have any significant semantic content. In philosophy and linguistics, John Stuart Mill's formulation that "proper names are meaningless marks set upon . . . persons to distinguish them from one another" retains currency; in anthropology, Claude Lévi-Strauss's characterization of names as being primarily instruments of social classification has been very influential. Consequently, interpretation of personal names in societies where names have other functions and meanings has been neglected. Among the Hopi of the southwestern United States, names often refer to historical or ritual events in order both to place individuals within society and to confer an identity upon them. Furthermore, the images used to evoke these events suggest that Hopi names can be seen as a type of poetic composition. #1: Names: Euro views = meaningless differentiators or social classif tool Euro ignores addl uses: names giving I.D. names as poetry	**Step 1:** The first paragraph lays out the entire big picture for this passage. The **Topic** is the scholarship of personal names. The **Scope** will focus on Hopi names. The author's **Purpose/Main Idea** is to show that Hopi names illustrate the shortcomings of the two major European theories about personal names. The paragraph starts with the two theories. Mill (philosophy/linguistics) says names are arbitrary; we just use them to keep people separate. Lévi-Strauss (anthropology) says names are used for social classification. The author says Hopi names are different in two ways: 1) They go beyond mere individual identity by being associated with rituals or events, and 2) they use images and so, are poetic. We can anticipate seeing those differences explained in the next two paragraphs.

LSAT Passage	Analysis
Throughout life, Hopis receive several names in a sequence of ritual initiations. Birth, entry into one of the ritual societies during childhood, and puberty are among the name-giving occasions. Names are conferred by an adult member of a clan other than the child's clan, and names refer to that name giver's clan, sometimes combining characteristics of the clan's totem animal with the child's characteristics. Thus, a name might translate to something as simple as "little rabbit," which reflects both the child's size and the representative animal. #2: How Hopi get names thru rites Names I.D. clan and kid's traits	As expected, this paragraph outlines how the Hopi confer names through rituals. Their names refer to a person's clan, and to his or her individual characteristics or events from his or her life. Thus, Hopi names contain "meaning" beyond merely identifying a person.
More often, though, the name giver has in mind a specific event that is not apparent in a name's literal translation. One Lizard clan member from the village of Oraibi is named Lomayayva, "beautifully ascended." This translation, however, tells nothing about either the event referred to—who or what ascended—or the name giver's clan. The name giver in this case is from Badger clan. Badger clan is responsible for an annual ceremony featuring a procession in which masked representations of spirits climb the mesa on which Oraibi sits. Combining the name giver's clan association with the receiver's home village, "beautifully ascended" refers to the splendid colors and movements of the procession up the mesa. The condensed image this name evokes—a typical feature of Hopi personal names—displays the same quality of Western Apache place names that led one commentator to call them "tiny imagist poems." #3: Long ex. of poetry found in specific naming	This paragraph goes into more detail about what the author considers Hopi names' second distinguishing characteristic: They are poetic. The Hopi often give names that are not literal. The author cites a detailed example to illustrate this, and concludes that (like Apache place names) Hopi names may be considered "tiny imagist poems."

CHAPTER 7

LSAT Passage	Analysis
Hopi personal names do several things simultaneously. They indicate social relationships—but only indirectly—and they individuate persons. Equally important, though, is their poetic quality; in a sense they can be understood as oral texts that produce aesthetic delight. This view of Hopi names is thus opposed not only to Mill's claim that personal names are without inherent meaning but also to Lévi-Strauss's purely functional characterization. Interpreters must understand Hopi clan structures and linguistic practices in order to discern the beauty and significance of Hopi names.	Here, the author reiterates his thesis (or Main Idea) and his evidence for it. Because they 1) indirectly indicate social relationships and 2) have poetic qualities, Hopi names do not fit into Mill's "names are just arbitrary" theory or into Lévi-Strauss's functional "social classification" theory.

PrepTest104 Sec3 Qs8–14

#4:
Sums up how Hopi names' meaning and poetry depart from Mill ("arbitrary") and L-S ("social class only") views

Step 3: Consult the big picture summary.	Step 2: A Global question asking for the author's Main Idea.

Which one of the following statements most accurately summarizes the passage's main point?

(A) Unlike European names, which are used exclusively for identification or exclusively for social classification, Hopi names perform both these functions simultaneously.

(B) Unlike European names, Hopi names tend to neglect the functions of identification and social classification in favor of a concentration on compression and poetic effects.

(C) Lacking knowledge of the intricacies of Hopi linguistic and tribal structures, European thinkers have so far been unable to discern the deeper significance of Hopi names.

(D) Although some Hopi names may seem difficult to interpret, they all conform to a formula whereby a reference to the name giver's clan is combined with a reference to the person named.

(E) While performing the functions ascribed to names by European thinkers, Hopi names also possess a significant aesthetic quality that these thinkers have not adequately recognized.

PrepTest104 Sec3 Q8

Step 4: The author's Main Idea is that Hopi names, because of their ritual and poetic qualities, illustrate the shortcomings of the two major European theories about personal names.	Step 5: (E) is correct. This choice briefly summarizes the author's argument that Hopi names' ritual and poetic qualities reveal the shortcomings of the major European theories about names.

Wrong answers: (A) Distortion. The passage is not about what European names do, but what scholars say all names do. Additionally, this choice doesn't touch on the ritual or poetic features that the author thinks make Hopi names illustrative. (B) Distortion. The author does not say that Hopi names don't identify individuals. Indeed, he says the opposite. Moreover, this answer choice says nothing about the European theories about names. (C) Distortion. This choice mirrors the author's recommendation at the very end of the passage, but it doesn't capture the passage's Main Idea, that Hopi names illustrate the shortcomings of the major European theories. (D) This choice is far too narrow in Scope. It focuses on only one of the two distinguishing features of Hopi names, and it says nothing about the European theories.

Step 3: When the author refers to Apache place names at the end of Paragraph 3, he tells us that another scholar described Apache place names as "tiny imagist poems." The author thinks that description is also applicable to Hopi personal names.	**Step 2:** This is a Logic Function question asking how or why the author cited a particular detail.

The author most likely refers to Western Apache place names in order to

(A) offer an example of how names can contain references not evident in their literal translations

(B) apply a commentator's characterization of Western Apache place names to Hopi personal names

(C) contrast Western Apache naming practices with Hopi naming practices

(D) demonstrate that other names besides Hopi names may have some semantic content

(E) explain how a specific Hopi name refers subtly to a particular Western Apache site

PrepTest104 Sec3 Q9

Step 4: The function of the detail is to *apply* a scholar's description of Apache place names to Hopi personal names.	**Step 5:** (B) is correct. This choice matches the prediction perfectly.

Wrong answers: (A) Faulty Use of Detail. The author's example is found earlier in Paragraph 3. The detail in question here is another scholar's description of an analogous naming practice. (C) 180. The author thinks the naming practices are similar, not opposed. (D) Distortion. The author's purpose is not to provide further evidence, but simply to apply what he considers an apt description to his evidence. (E) Outside the Scope. The author neither states nor implies that Hopi personal names refer to places named by the Apache.

Step 3: Lévi-Strauss's theory is described in the first paragraph: Names are "instruments of social classification."	**Step 2:** An Inference question asking us to apply what the passage says about Lévi-Strauss's theory of names.

Which one of the following statements describes an example of the function accorded to personal names under Lévi-Strauss's view?

(A) Some parents select their children's names from impersonal sources such as books.

(B) Some parents wait to give a child a name in order to choose one that reflects the child's looks or personality.

(C) Some parents name their children in honor of friends or famous people.

(D) Some family members have no parts of their names in common.

(E) Some family names originated as identifications of their bearers' occupations.

PrepTest104 Sec3 Q10

Step 4: The correct answer will provide an example of a name revealing something about a person's place in society.	**Step 5:** (E) is correct. Identifying a person by his or her occupation fits Lévi-Strauss's social classification theory perfectly.

Wrong answers: (A) Outside the Scope. Lévi-Strauss says nothing about giving people names from books. (B) Outside the Scope. Lévi-Strauss is not said to consider looks or personalities in the meaning of names. (C) Distortion. This type of naming may well happen, but it doesn't fit into Lévi-Strauss's social classification theory. (D) Outside the Scope. This phenomenon is not mentioned in the passage at all.

Step 3: The second paragraph outlines ways in which Hopi names refer to events in a person's life, and so, go beyond simply identifying the person.	**Step 2:** A Logic Function question asking for the purpose of a full paragraph.

The primary function of the second paragraph is to

(A) present reasons why Hopi personal names can be treated as poetic compositions

(B) support the claim that Hopi personal names make reference to events in the recipient's life

(C) argue that the fact that Hopis receive many names throughout life refutes European theories about naming

(D) illustrate ways in which Hopi personal names may have semantic content

(E) demonstrate that the literal translation of Hopi personal names often obscures their true meaning

PrepTest104 Sec3 Q11

Step 4: The correct answer will say something along the lines of: "Provide evidence/examples of Hopi names having meaning beyond that of a simple identity 'tag.'"	**Step 5:** (D) is correct. "[S]emantic content" is a fancy way of saying "meaning."

Wrong answers: (A) Faulty Use of Detail. This choice describes the purpose of Paragraph 3. (B) This choice is too narrow. It doesn't get at the purpose of Paragraph 2, which is to show how Hopi names confer additional meaning. (C) Distortion. The author does not argue that multiple naming events are what distinguish Hopi names; it is, rather, the meaning conferred through the names given. (E) Distortion. Someone unaware of Hopi culture and language might well be confused by a literal translation, but the author did not write Paragraph 2 *in order to* demonstrate this rather obvious fact.

Step 3: The author describes Mill's theory in Paragraphs 1 and 4: Names are arbitrary, meaningless beyond the fact that they identify individuals.	**Step 2:** An Inference question rewarding an understanding of the author's opinion about Mill's theory.

Based on the passage, with which one of the following statements about Mill's view would the author of the passage be most likely to agree?

(A) Its characterization of the function of names is too narrow to be universally applicable.

(B) It would be correct if it recognized the use of names as instruments of social classification.

(C) Its influence single-handedly led scholars to neglect how names are used outside Europe.

(D) It is more accurate than Lévi-Strauss's characterization of the purpose of names.

(E) It is less relevant than Lévi-Strauss's characterization in understanding Hopi naming practices.

PrepTest104 Sec3 Q12

Step 4: The author finds Mill's individual-identity theory unacceptable because it is too narrow to cover the types of meaning and poetic value found in Hopi names.	**Step 5:** (A) is correct. This matches the Step 4 prediction and perfectly captures the author's primary purpose in writing the passage.

Wrong answers: (B) This choice is too narrow. Adding Lévi-Strauss's theory would not be enough to account for the additional meaning and poetic qualities found in Hopi names. (C) Extreme. Mill's theory hasn't *single-handedly* influenced scholars; at a minimum, Lévi-Strauss's has also played a role. (D) Distortion. The author considers both theories inadequate. He doesn't compare their relative accuracy. (E) Distortion. The author considers both theories inadequate. He doesn't compare their relative relevance to Hopi names.

Step 3: The author discussed Hopi names' poetic qualities near the end of paragraph 1, throughout paragraph 3, and at the beginning of paragraph 4.	**Step 2:** This is an Inference EXCEPT question. The four wrong answers will follow from the passage. The correct answer will not.

It can be inferred from the passage that each of the following features of Hopi personal names contributes to their poetic quality EXCEPT:

(A) their ability to be understood as oral texts

(B) their use of condensed imagery to evoke events

(C) their capacity to produce aesthetic delight

(D) their ability to confer identity upon individuals

(E) their ability to subtly convey meaning

PrepTest104 Sec3 Q13

Step 4: We cannot predict an answer NOT found in the passage. We will test each answer choice and eliminate those that follow from the passage's comments on poetic quality.	**Step 5:** (D) is correct. The author associates the identity-conferring qualities of Hopi names with the naming rituals described in paragraph 2, not with their poetic qualities.

Wrong answers: (A) This is supported in paragraph 4. (B) This is supported in paragraph 3. (C) This is supported in paragraph 4. (E) This is supported by the first sentence of paragraph 3, in which the author says that Hopi names refer to events "not apparent in a name's literal meaning."

Step 3: Consult the big picture summary.	**Step 2:** A Global question calling for the author's purpose in writing the passage.

The author's primary purpose in writing the passage is to

(A) present an anthropological study of Hopi names

(B) propose a new theory about the origin of names

(C) describe several competing theories of names

(D) criticize two influential views of names

(E) explain the cultural origins of names

PrepTest104 Sec3 Q14

Step 4: The author's purpose is to illustrate how Hopi names reveal the shortcomings of the two major European theories of personal names.	**Step 5:** (D) is correct. All of the details offered in the passage are given to show that the two major European theories cannot account for certain features of Hopi names.

Wrong answers: (A) Distortion. The passage contains a lot of anthropological data, but its purpose is to critique the predominant theories, not merely to present an ethnographic study. (B) Distortion. The author doesn't get this far in the passage. He shows how the major theories are inadequate, but he doesn't propose a new one. (C) Distortion. The author describes two theories, not several, and his purpose is to demonstrate the inadequacy of the two he presents. (E) Outside the Scope. This goal is never addressed in the passage.

Notice that the expert never compares the answers to one another. She never thinks, "Which is more correct, choice (A) or choice (C)?" Knowing what the correct answer must contain, and having predicted its meaning accurately, she can assess the choices with confidence. Naturally, she may confirm a choice by referring to the text. Likewise, she may do a quick research check to be certain that a wrong answer distorts or contradicts the passage. Never, though, will she engage in multiple rereads as she makes her way through a set of questions.

Practice Now, try Step 5 on your own. Use the work you've already done with the Comparative Reading passages on Online Gaming. Take a few moments to refresh your memory of the passages, the Roadmap, and the expert's strategic reading analysis. Then, turn to the questions one at a time. You've already completed Steps 2–4 here, so review the research you did and predictions you made. Use them to evaluate the answer choices. Avoid comparing answers to one another and keep in mind that the one correct answer will be justified by the passage, while all four wrong answers will not. When you're finished, check your answers and compare your analysis to that of an LSAT expert on the following pages.

LSAT Passage	Analysis
Passage A is from a source published in 2004, and Passage B is from a source published in 2007.	
Passage A Millions of people worldwide play multiplayer online games. They each pick, say, a medieval character to play, such as a warrior. Then they might band together in quests to slay magical beasts; their avatars appear as tiny characters striding across a Tolkienesque land. ¶1: Multiplayer online gaming popular	**Step 1:** The short first paragraph appears to be background information: Multiplayer role-playing games are popular.
The economist Edward Castronova noticed something curious about the game he played: it had its own economy, a bustling trade in virtual goods. Players generate goods as they play, often by killing creatures for their treasure and trading it. The longer they play, the wealthier they get. ¶2: EC notes: economy within game	Here, the **Topic** starts to take shape: An economist noticed that players in these games collect virtual goods.
Things got even more interesting when Castronova learned about the "player auctions." Players would sometimes tire of the game and decide to sell off their virtual possessions at online auction sites. ¶3: Also odd: auction stuff when bored!	This paragraph narrows the **Scope** of the passage: Virtual goods are auctioned/sold online.

LSAT Passage	Analysis
As Castronova stared at the auction listings, he recognized with a shock what he was looking at. It was a form of currency trading! Each item had a value in the virtual currency traded in the game; when it was sold on the auction site, someone was paying cold hard cash for it. That meant that the virtual currency was worth something in real currency. Moreover, since players were killing monsters or skinning animals to sell their pelts, they were, in effect, creating wealth. #4: EC: Wow: this is $ trade, virtual wealth converted to real	And, here in the final paragraph, we get the **Purpose** and **Main Idea**–to reveal an economist's startling discovery: Virtual items have value in "real-world" currency; thus, the "work" players are doing in the game creates wealth.
Passage B Most multiplayer online games prohibit real-world trade in virtual items, but some actually encourage it, for example, by granting participants intellectual property rights in their creations. #1: A few games push real trade	From the outset, this passage addresses the same **Topic** and **Scope** as Passage A: the trade/sale of virtual items from online games. It adds a fact not contained in Passage A: Some games forbid, while others encourage, these sales.
Although it seems intuitively the case that someone who accepts real money for the transfer of a virtual item should be taxed, what about the player who only accumulates items or virtual currency within a virtual world? Is "loot" acquired in a game taxable, as a prize or award is? And is the profit in a purely in-game trade or sale for virtual currency taxable? These are important questions, given the tax revenues at stake, and there is pressure on governments to answer them, given that the economies of some virtual worlds are comparable to those of small countries. #2: Shld virtual goods be taxed? How about profits? Govts. pressed to decide	The author of Passage B has a distinct **Purpose**: to raise "important questions" about the taxability of commerce in virtual items. Note the three distinct questions here.

LSAT Passage	Analysis
Most people's intuition probably would be that accumulation of assets within a game should not be taxed even though income tax applies even to noncash accessions to wealth. This article will argue that income tax law and policy support that result. Loot acquisitions in game worlds should not be treated as taxable prizes and awards, but rather should be treated like other property that requires effort to obtain, such as fish pulled from the ocean, which is taxed only upon sale. Moreover, in-game trades of virtual items should not be treated as taxable barter. #3: A: Don't tax items that stay in virtual world.	The author starts to formulate his **Main Idea** (almost in the style of a thesis statement): In-game trade of virtual items should not be taxable. The author draws an analogy: Acquiring virtual items in a game is like catching fish; we don't tax fish until they are sold.
By contrast, tax doctrine and policy counsel taxation of the sale of virtual items for real currency, and, in games that are intentionally commodified, even of in-world sales for virtual currency, regardless of whether the participant cashes out. This approach would leave entertainment value untaxed without creating a tax shelter for virtual commerce. *PrepTest140 Sec4 Qs7–13* #4: A: Tax when virtual goods sold for real $.	In the final paragraph, however, the author of Passage B expands on his **Main Idea**: When virtual items are sold for "real world" currency, or when they are commodified within a game, they should be taxable. The author's main support for his argument is that having this system allows the games to remain fun but not become virtual "tax shelters."

Compare/Contrast the Passages

The relationship between the two passages is pretty simple: Passage A announces the discovery of a new economic phenomenon, while Passage B explores practical legal questions raised by that phenomenon.

Passage A is neutral; its author describes the economist's "shock" at discovering virtual goods with real-world value, but neither the author nor the economist offers any judgment on the discovery. Passage B's author, on the other hand, makes an argument. The argument's conclusion is a recommendation about when trade in virtual items should and should not be taxed.

Passage A contains facts (e.g., how virtual items are auctioned and traded) not found in Passage B. Passage B reveals differences among games (some encourage trading, while others forbid it) not discussed in Passage A. The economist in Passage A takes note of in-game activities ("skinning animals to sell their pelts" (paragraph 4)), while the author of Passage B compares such activities to "real-world" work ("[pulling] fish . . . from the ocean" (paragraph 3)).

CHAPTER 7

Note: The highlighted phrases "skinning animals" (Passage A, paragraph 4) and "fish pulled from the ocean" (Passage B, paragraph 3) correspond to Question 16. The highlighted phrase "games that are intentionally commodified" (Passage B, paragraph 4) corresponds to Question 21.

Step 3: Consult the big picture summary to predict the correct answer.	**Step 2:** The passages' "titles" would reflect their Main Ideas, so this is a Global question.

15. Which one of the following pairs of titles would be most appropriate for passage A and passage B, respectively?

(A) "The Economic Theories of Edward Castronova"
"Intellectual Property Rights in Virtual Worlds"

(B) "An Economist Discovers New Economic Territory"
"Taxing Virtual Property"

(C) "The Surprising Growth of Multiplayer Online Games"
"Virtual Reality and the Law"

(D) "How to Make Money Playing Games"
"Closing Virtual Tax Shelters"

(E) "A New Economic Paradigm"
"An Untapped Source of Revenue"

PrepTest140 Sec4 Q7

Step 4: Passage A is about an economist making the shocking discovery of a new form of wealth. Passage B presents a model for how to tax trade in virtual items.	**Step 5:**

Step 3: Passage A cited "skinning animals" as a type of in-game "work," while Passage B used catching fish as a real-world analogy to in-game work.	**Step 2:** This question asks you to determine how a phrase was used and to apply it to another phrase. Thus, it is an Inference question.

16. Which one of the following most accurately expresses how the use of the phrase "skinning animals" in passage A relates to the use of the phrase "fish pulled from the ocean" in passage B?

(A) The former refers to an activity that generates wealth, whereas the latter refers to an activity that does not generate wealth.

(B) The former refers to an activity in an online game, whereas the latter refers to an analogous activity in the real world.

(C) The former, unlike the latter, refers to the production of a commodity that the author of passage B thinks should be taxed.

(D) The latter, unlike the former, refers to the production of a commodity that the author of passage B thinks should be taxed.

(E) Both are used as examples of activities by which game players generate wealth.

PrepTest140 Sec4 Q8

Step 4: The correct answer will describe the relationship noted in the Step 3 research.	**Step 5:**

Step 3: Passage A describes the economist's "shock" (paragraph 4). Passage B addresses the subject by raising "important questions" (paragraph 2).	**Step 2:** An Inference question about both authors' attitudes.

17. With regard to their respective attitudes toward commerce in virtual items, passage A differs from passage B in that passage A is more

Ⓐ critical and apprehensive
Ⓑ academic and dismissive
Ⓒ intrigued and excited
Ⓓ undecided but curious
Ⓔ enthusiastic but skeptical

PrepTest140 Sec4 Q9

Step 4: The correct answer will say something along the lines of "startled and excited."	**Step 5:**

Step 3: Consult the big picture summary of both passages, and compare them.	**Step 2:** The correct answer will apply the relationship between the two passages to that between two distinct documents. This is a Logic Reasoning question that rewards Parallel Reasoning skills.

18. Based on what can be inferred from their titles, the relationship between which one of the following pairs of documents is most analogous to the relationship between passage A and passage B?

    (A) "Advances in Artificial Intelligence"
    "Human Psychology Applied to Robots"

    (B) "Internet Retailers Post Good Year"
    "Lawmakers Move to Tax Internet Commerce"

    (C) "New Planet Discovered in Solar System"
    "Planet or Asteroid: Scientists Debate"

    (D) "Biologists Create New Species in Lab"
    "Artificially Created Life: How Patent Law Applies"

    (E) "A Renegade Economist's Views on Taxation"
    "Candidate Runs on Unorthodox Tax Plan"

PrepTest140 Sec4 Q10

Step 4: The correct answer will describe a document that announces a new discovery, and then one that asks practical, legal questions raised by the discovery.	**Step 5:**

Step 3: Passage A is informal and narrative; it feels like it comes from a popular newspaper or magazine. Passage B's author states that this text is from the beginning of an "article" that is going to go into more detail about law and policy, as would be the case in a law journal.	Step 2: This is an Inference question. It asks you to use the passages' content and style to infer the type of literature from which each was culled.

19. The passages were most likely taken from which one of the following pairs of sources?

(A) passage A: a magazine article addressed to a general audience
passage B: a law journal article

(B) passage A: a technical journal for economists
passage B: a magazine article addressed to a general audience

(C) passage A: a science-fiction novel
passage B: a technical journal for economists

(D) passage A: a law journal article
passage B: a speech delivered before a legislative body

(E) passage A: a speech delivered before a legislative body
passage B: a science-fiction novel

PrepTest140 Sec4 Q11

Step 4: The correct answer will likely say: "Passage A—a popular magazine; Passage B—an academic law journal."	Step 5:

Step 3: Consult the big picture summary (the mental Roadmap, if you will).	**Step 2:** A Global question rewarding accurate summaries of the two passages and a valid comparison of them.

20. Which one of the following most accurately describes the relationship between the two passages?

    (A) Passage A summarizes a scholar's unanticipated discovery, while passage B proposes solutions to a problem raised by the phenomenon discovered.

    (B) Passage A explains an economic theory, while passage B identifies a practical problem resulting from that theory.

    (C) Passage A reports on a subculture, while passage B discusses the difficulty of policing that subculture.

    (D) Passage A challenges the common interpretation of a phenomenon, while passage B reaffirms that interpretation.

    (E) Passage A states a set of facts, while passage B draws theoretical consequences from those facts.

PrepTest140 Sec4 Q12

Step 4: The correct answer will be something along these lines: "Passage A announces a shocking discovery; Passage B identifies important questions raised by the discovery and recommends an answer."	**Step 5:**

Step 3: The author of Passage B describes "intentionally commodified" games in the final paragraph. These games grant intellectual property rights to players who create virtual goods in the game. The author also argues that virtual goods in these games should be taxed when sold for real-world currency or in-game virtual currency.	**Step 2:** The correct answer will be found in the passage ("Based on the passage, which one . . . is a characteristic . . ."), making this a Detail question.

21. Based on passage B, which one of the following is a characteristic of some "games that are intentionally commodified"?

    (A) The game allows selling real items for virtual currency.

    (B) The game allows players to trade avatars with other players.

    (C) Players of the game grow wealthier the longer they play.

    (D) Players of the game own intellectual property rights in their creations.

    (E) Players of the game can exchange one virtual currency for another virtual currency.

PrepTest140 Sec4 Q13

Step 4: The correct answer will restate or closely paraphrase something the author of Passage B said about intentionally commodified games.	**Step 5:**

Expert Analysis

Here's how an LSAT expert answered the questions from the Online Gaming passage. Compare your analysis of the correct and incorrect answers to his.

Step 3: Consult the big picture summary to predict the correct answer.	**Step 2:** The passages' "titles" would reflect their Main Ideas, so this is a Global question.

15. Which one of the following pairs of titles would be most appropriate for passage A and passage B, respectively?

(A) "The Economic Theories of Edward Castronova"
"Intellectual Property Rights in Virtual Worlds"

(B) "An Economist Discovers New Economic Territory"
"Taxing Virtual Property"

(C) "The Surprising Growth of Multiplayer Online Games"
"Virtual Reality and the Law"

(D) "How to Make Money Playing Games"
"Closing Virtual Tax Shelters"

(E) "A New Economic Paradigm"
"An Untapped Source of Revenue"

PrepTest140 Sec4 Q7

Step 4: Passage A is about an economist making the shocking discovery of a new form of wealth. Passage B presents a model for how to tax trade in virtual items.	**Step 5:** (B) is correct. This answer matches the predictions and accurately summarizes the two articles.

Wrong answers: (A) The description of Passage A is Extreme: We learn only about Castronova's discovery, not his theories. This choice also distorts Passage B, which is about taxation, not IP law. (C) Distortion. Passage A is about the economist's surprise over the trade of virtual items, not the popularity of the games from which they come. Passage B is about tax law, specifically. (D) Distortion. Passage A doesn't provide any tips for exploiting trade in virtual items. Passage B wants to *prevent*, not close, one potential tax shelter. (E) Extreme/Distortion. The term "[p]aradigm" is too broad to fit Passage A. Passage B is about taxing an already "tapped" source of revenue.

Step 3: Passage A cited "skinning animals" as a type of in-game "work," while Passage B used catching fish as a real-world analogy to in-game work.	**Step 2:** This question asks you to determine how a phrase was used, and to apply it to another phrase. Thus, it is an Inference question.

16. Which one of the following most accurately expresses how the use of the phrase "skinning animals" in passage A relates to the use of the phrase "fish pulled from the ocean" in passage B?

(A) The former refers to an activity that generates wealth, whereas the latter refers to an activity that does not generate wealth.

(B) The former refers to an activity in an online game, whereas the latter refers to an analogous activity in the real world.

(C) The former, unlike the latter, refers to the production of a commodity that the author of passage B thinks should be taxed.

(D) The latter, unlike the former, refers to the production of a commodity that the author of passage B thinks should be taxed.

(E) Both are used as examples of activities by which game players generate wealth.

PrepTest140 Sec4 Q8

Step 4: The correct answer will describe the relationship noted in the Step 3 research.	**Step 5:** (B) is correct. This choice correctly describes the in-game activity from Passage A and the real-world analogy applied in Passage B.

Wrong answers: (A) Half-Right/Half-Wrong. In both passages, the referenced activities are said to generate wealth. (C) Distortion. The author of Passage B thinks real-world fish should only be taxed *when sold*, and thus, would say the same thing about the in-game pelts. (D) Distortion. The author of Passage B thinks real-world fish should only be taxed *when sold*, and thus, would say the same thing about the in-game pelts. (E) Half-Right/Half-Wrong. In Passage B, catching fish is offered as a real-world analogy to in-game activities.

Step 3: Passage A describes the economist's "shock" (paragraph 4). Passage B addresses the subject by raising "important questions" (paragraph 2).	**Step 2:** An Inference question about both authors' attitudes.

17. With regard to their respective attitudes toward commerce in virtual items, passage A differs from passage B in that passage A is more

(A) critical and apprehensive

(B) academic and dismissive

(C) intrigued and excited

(D) undecided but curious

(E) enthusiastic but skeptical

PrepTest140 Sec4 Q9

Step 4: The correct answer will say something along the lines of "startled and excited."	**Step 5:** (C) is correct. This captures the economist's wonder and curiosity at his discovery.

Wrong answers: (A) 180. The economist in Passage A seems neither critical nor apprehensive about the trade in virtual items. (B) 180. The economist may have academic interest in the phenomenon, but the passage describes his excitement and contains no dismissive tone. (D) Distortion. The economist notices something "curious," in the sense of unusual or intriguing, but his response is not undecided; it is enthusiastic. (E) Half-Right/Half-Wrong. The economist does appear enthusiastic, but not skeptical. Indeed, the passage describes wonder at his discovery.

Step 3: Consult the big picture summary of both passages, and compare them.	**Step 2:** The correct answer will apply the relationship between the two passages to that between two distinct documents. This is a Logic Reasoning question that rewards Parallel Reasoning skills.

18. Based on what can be inferred from their titles, the relationship between which one of the following pairs of documents is most analogous to the relationship between passage A and passage B?

(A) "Advances in Artificial Intelligence"
"Human Psychology Applied to Robots"

(B) "Internet Retailers Post Good Year"
"Lawmakers Move to Tax Internet Commerce"

(C) "New Planet Discovered in Solar System"
"Planet or Asteroid: Scientists Debate"

(D) "Biologists Create New Species in Lab"
"Artificially Created Life: How Patent Law Applies"

(E) "A Renegade Economist's Views on Taxation"
"Candidate Runs on Unorthodox Tax Plan"

PrepTest140 Sec4 Q10

Step 4: The correct answer will describe a document that announces a new discovery and then one that asks practical, legal questions raised by the discovery.	**Step 5:** (D) is correct. The first document announces a new phenomenon. The second raises legal questions that apply to the phenomenon.

Wrong answers: (A) This choice mischaracterizes both passages. Passage A isn't about advances in understanding a phenomenon; it is about discovering one. And Passage B is about *legal* questions a new phenomenon raises. (B) This choice mischaracterizes both passages. Passage A isn't an announcement of economic boon, and Passage B isn't about a legislative response. (C) Half-Right/Half-Wrong. The first document here might be parallel to Passage A, but Passage B doesn't describe a debate about the new phenomenon. (E) Distortion. Passage A neither states nor implies that the economist is a renegade. And Passage B doesn't apply the discovery to a political campaign.

Step 3: Passage A is informal and narrative; it feels like it comes from a popular newspaper or magazine. Passage B's author states that this text is from the beginning of an "article" that is going to go into more detail about law and policy, as would be the case in a law journal.	**Step 2:** This is an Inference question. It asks you to use the passages' content and style to infer the type of literature from which each was culled.

19. The passages were most likely taken from which one of the following pairs of sources?

(A) passage A: a magazine article addressed to a general audience
passage B: a law journal article

(B) passage A: a technical journal for economists
passage B: a magazine article addressed to a general audience

(C) passage A: a science-fiction novel
passage B: a technical journal for economists

(D) passage A: a law journal article
passage B: a speech delivered before a legislative body

(E) passage A: a speech delivered before a legislative body
passage B: a science-fiction novel

PrepTest140 Sec4 Q11

Step 4: The correct answer will likely say: "Passage A—a popular magazine; Passage B—an academic law journal."	**Step 5:** (A) is correct. This matches the prediction perfectly.

Wrong answers: (B) 180. Passage A is noteworthy for its lack of technical jargon. Passage B promises to go much deeper than would a general-audience magazine. (C) 180/Distortion. Passage A is decidedly nonfiction. Passage B is addressed more to lawyers than to economists. (D) Outside the Scope/Distortion. Passage A doesn't touch on any legal topics. Passage B is explicitly an article, not a speech. (E) Outside the Scope. Nothing in Passage A implies that legislative recommendations are to follow. Passage B is clearly nonfiction.

Step 3: Consult the big picture summary (the mental Roadmap, if you will).	**Step 2:** A Global question rewarding accurate summaries of the two passages and a valid comparison of them.

20. Which one of the following most accurately describes the relationship between the two passages?

    (A) Passage A summarizes a scholar's unanticipated discovery, while passage B proposes solutions to a problem raised by the phenomenon discovered.

    (B) Passage A explains an economic theory, while passage B identifies a practical problem resulting from that theory.

    (C) Passage A reports on a subculture, while passage B discusses the difficulty of policing that subculture.

    (D) Passage A challenges the common interpretation of a phenomenon, while passage B reaffirms that interpretation.

    (E) Passage A states a set of facts, while passage B draws theoretical consequences from those facts.

PrepTest140 Sec4 Q12

Step 4: The correct answer will be something along these lines: "Passage A announces a shocking discovery; Passage B identifies important questions raised by the discovery and recommends an answer."	**Step 5:** (A) is correct. This matches the Step 4 prediction.

Wrong answers: (B) Outside the Scope. We learn nothing of the economist's theories, and the questions in Passage B are the result of a discovery, not of a theory. (C) Distortion. Online gaming communities might be considered a subculture, but Passage A isn't a report on them. Passage B proposes a model for taxation, not difficulties in enforcement. (D) Outside the Scope. Passage A does not challenge anyone's interpretation, nor does Passage B reaffirm Passage A in any way. (E) Distortion. Passage A does communicate facts, although "states" seems too dry a description of its tone. Passage B does not outline consequences; it raises questions and provides an answer.

Step 3: The author of Passage B describes "intentionally commodified" games in the final paragraph. These games grant intellectual property rights to players who create virtual goods in the game. The author also argues that virtual goods in these games should be taxed when sold for real-world currency or in-game virtual currency.	**Step 2:** The correct answer will be found in the passage ("Based on the passage, which one . . . is a characteristic . . ."), making this a Detail question.

21. Based on passage B, which one of the following is a characteristic of some "games that are intentionally commodified"?

(A) The game allows selling real items for virtual currency.

(B) The game allows players to trade avatars with other players.

(C) Players of the game grow wealthier the longer they play.

(D) Players of the game own intellectual property rights in their creations.

(E) Players of the game can exchange one virtual currency for another virtual currency.

PrepTest140 Sec4 Q13

Step 4: The correct answer will restate or closely paraphrase something the author of Passage B said about intentionally commodified games.	**Step 5:** (D) is correct. This is stated explicitly in the first paragraph of Passage B.

Wrong answers: (A) Distortion. The issue is the sale of virtual items for real currency. This choice gets that backwards. (B) Outside the Scope. There is nothing about avatars in either passage. (C) Faulty Use of Detail. This is a fact mentioned in Passage A (paragraph 2). (E) Distortion. The passages address the sale of virtual items for either virtual or real currency. Virtual-to-virtual *currency exchanges* are not mentioned.

It's good to build up your practice step-by-step as you're learning the Method. If you continue to practice these steps diligently, by test day, following the steps will be second nature.

Practice Now you're ready to try Steps 2–5 on a question set. Here, you see the Debate passage on Homing Pigeons, complete with the Roadmap and strategic reading analysis. This time, all of the questions associated with that passage are included. Take a few minutes to refresh your memory of the passage and then work through the entire question set. Don't time yourself. Record your analysis for each Step of the Reading Comprehension Method involved in handling the question set. When you're done, compare your work to the expert analysis that follows.

LSAT Passage	Analysis
Homing pigeons can be taken from their lofts and transported hundreds of kilometers in covered cages to unfamiliar sites and yet, when released, be able to choose fairly accurate homeward bearings within a minute and fly home. Aside from reading the minds of the experimenters (a possibility that has not escaped investigation), there are two basic explanations for the remarkable ability of pigeons to "home": the birds might keep track of their outward displacement (the system of many short-range species such as honeybees); or they might have some sense, known as a "map sense," that would permit them to construct an internal image of their environment and then "place" themselves with respect to home on some internalized coordinate system. #1: How pigeons find home? 2 poss. ways: O.D. (bee-like navig.) or M.S. (inner map coords.)	Step 1: The **Topic**—homing pigeons—and the **Scope**—the question of how they home—are clear from the first paragraph. After dismissing a rather harebrained suggestion (maybe they read human minds!), the author presents two reasonable hypotheses: 1) outward displacement (which other species, such as honeybees, use), and 2) "map sense." We can anticipate that the next two paragraphs will evaluate these hypotheses in more detail.

LSAT Passage	Analysis
The first alternative seems unlikely. One possible model for such an inertial system might involve an internal magnetic compass to measure the directional leg of each journey. Birds transported to the release site wearing magnets or otherwise subjected to an artificial magnetic field, however, are only occasionally affected. Alternately, if pigeons measure their displacement by consciously keeping track of the direction and degree of acceleration and deceleration of the various turns, and timing the individual legs of the journey, simply transporting them in the dark, with constant rotations, or under complete anesthesia ought to impair or eliminate their ability to orient. These treatments, however, have no effect. Unfortunately, no one has yet performed the crucial experiment of transporting pigeons in total darkness, anesthetized, rotating, and with the magnetic field reversed all at the same time. #2: O.D. not likely both models tested w/ neg results ultimate test not done yet.	The author finds outward displacement "unlikely" but admits that it has not been 100 percent ruled out. She cites two possible models for outward displacement: Homing pigeons may have "an internal magnetic compass," or they may keep track of turns and acceleration. When tested, neither model was supported by the findings. "Unfortunately," says the author, no one has done the complete rule-out experiment of impairing, simultaneously, all of the pigeons' potential modes of tracking outward displacement. That's why the author won't say the hypothesis is completely disproven. Because the author thinks outward displacement "unlikely," she will give her evaluation of the "map sense" in the next paragraph.
The other alternative, that pigeons have a "map sense," seems more promising, yet the nature of this sense remains mysterious. Papi has posited that the map sense is olfactory: that birds come to associate odors borne on the wind with the direction in which the wind is blowing, and so slowly build up an olfactory map of their surroundings. When transported to the release site, then, they only have to sniff the air en route and/or at the site to know the direction of home. Papi conducted a series of experiments showing that pigeons whose nostrils have been plugged are poorly oriented at release and home slowly. #3: M.S. more likely but still ?? Papi's idea: smell directs birds Experiments support idea	As expected, here's the author's evaluation of pigeons' "map sense." This hypothesis she finds "promising." Nonetheless, "map sense" "remains mysterious." So, our author doesn't think the map sense has been completely explained. The rest of the paragraph details how a scientist named Papi tested an olfactory model for the map sense with some success.

LSAT Passage	Analysis
One problem with the hypothesis is that Schmidt-Koenig and Phillips failed to detect any ability in pigeons to distinguish natural air (presumably laden with olfactory map information) from pure, filtered air. Papi's experimental results, moreover, admit of simpler, nonolfactory explanations. It seems likely that the behavior of nostril-plugged birds results from the distracting and traumatic nature of the experiment. When nasal tubes are used to bypass the olfactory chamber but allow for comfortable breathing, no disorientation is evident. Likewise, when the olfactory epithelium is sprayed with anesthetic to block smell-detection but not breathing, orientation is normal.	This paragraph outlines three criticisms of Papi's experiments (signaled by the keywords "[o]ne problem," "moreover," and "[l]ikewise"). The criticisms come from a pair of scientists: Schmidt-Koenig and Phillips. They tested pigeons using filtered air (no smells, in other words) and found no difference in their ability to home. They also suggested that Papi's experiments had traumatized the birds, and so they performed two tests that blocked the pigeons' olfactory senses without injuring them. The results, again, undermined Papi's model.
PrepTest104 Sec3 Qs 15–21	There is no explicit thesis statement or conclusion sentence in this passage. The author's **Purpose**, as shown by Paragraphs 2–4 is to *evaluate* the two main hypotheses. Her **Main Point** is that pigeons probably home using a map sense (outward displacement is unlikely), but that we don't yet know what kind of map they use.
¶4: Problems with Papi idea S-K&P: no ev of birds analyzing air P's results undercut by other tests & expls.	

Note: The highlighted word "possibility" in paragraph 1 corresponds to Question 24. The highlighted phrase "the system of many short-range species such as honeybees" in paragraph 1 corresponds to Question 26. The highlighted term "first alternative" in paragraph 2 corresponds to Question 25.

Step 3:	Step 2:

22. Which one of the following best states the main idea of the passage?

    (A) The ability of pigeons to locate and return to their homes from distant points is unlike that of any other species.

    (B) It is likely that some map sense accounts for the homing ability of pigeons, but the nature of that sense has not been satisfactorily identified.

    (C) The majority of experiments on the homing ability of pigeons have been marked by design flaws.

    (D) The mechanisms underlying the homing ability of pigeons can best be identified through a combination of laboratory research and field experimentation.

    (E) The homing ability of pigeons is most likely based on a system similar to that used by many short-range species.

PrepTest104 Sec3 Q15

Step 4:	Step 5:

Step 3:	Step 2:

23. According to the passage, which one of the following is ordinarily true regarding how homing pigeons "home"?

    (A) Each time they are released at a specific site they fly home by the same route.

    (B) When they are released they take only a short time to orient themselves before selecting their route home.

    (C) Each time they are released at a specific site they take a shorter amount of time to orient themselves before flying home.

    (D) They travel fairly long distances in seemingly random patterns before finally deciding on a route home.

    (E) Upon release they travel briefly in the direction opposite to the one they eventually choose.

PrepTest104 Sec3 Q16

Step 4:	Step 5:

Step 3:	Step 2:

24. Which one of the following experiments would best test the "possibility" referred to in the first paragraph?

   (A) an experiment in which the handlers who transported, released, and otherwise came into contact with homing pigeons released at an unfamiliar site were unaware of the location of the pigeons' home

   (B) an experiment in which the handlers who transported, released, and otherwise came into contact with homing pigeons released at an unfamiliar site were asked not to display any affection toward the pigeons

   (C) an experiment in which the handlers who transported, released, and otherwise came into contact with homing pigeons released at an unfamiliar site were asked not to speak to each other throughout the release process

   (D) an experiment in which all the homing pigeons released at an unfamiliar site had been raised and fed by individual researchers rather than by teams of handlers

   (E) an experiment in which all the homing pigeons released at an unfamiliar site were exposed to a wide variety of unfamiliar sights and sounds

PrepTest104 Sec3 Q17

Step 4:	Step 5:

Step 3:	Step 2:

25. Information in the passage supports which one of the following statements regarding the "first alternative" for explaining the ability of pigeons to "home"?

(A) It has been conclusively ruled out by the results of numerous experiments.

(B) It seems unlikely because there are no theoretical models that could explain how pigeons track displacement.

(C) It has not, to date, been supported by experimental data, but neither has it been definitively ruled out.

(D) It seems unlikely in theory, but recent experimental results show that it may in fact be correct.

(E) It is not a useful theory because of the difficulty in designing experiments by which it might be tested.

PrepTest104 Sec3 Q18

Step 4:	Step 5:

Step 3:	Step 2:

26. The author refers to "the system of many short-range species such as honeybees" most probably in order to

(A) emphasize the universality of the ability to home

(B) suggest that a particular explanation of pigeons' homing ability is worthy of consideration

(C) discredit one of the less convincing theories regarding the homing ability of pigeons

(D) criticize the techniques utilized by scientists investigating the nature of pigeons' homing ability

(E) illustrate why a proposed explanation of pigeons' homing ability is correct

PrepTest104 Sec3 Q19

Step 4:	Step 5:

Step 3:	Step 2:

27. Which one of the following, if true, would most weaken Papi's theory regarding homing pigeons' homing ability?

(A) Even pigeons that have been raised in several different lofts in a variety of territories can find their way to their current home when released in unfamiliar territory.

(B) Pigeons whose sense of smell has been partially blocked find their way home more slowly than do pigeons whose sense of smell has not been affected.

(C) Even pigeons that have been raised in the same loft frequently take different routes home when released in unfamiliar territory.

(D) Even pigeons that have been transported well beyond the range of the odors detectable in their home territories can find their way home.

(E) Pigeons' sense of smell is no more acute than that of other birds who do not have the ability to "home."

PrepTest104 Sec3 Q20

Step 4:	Step 5:

Step 3:	Step 2:

28. Given the information in the passage, it is most likely that Papi and the author of the passage would both agree with which one of the following statements regarding the homing ability of pigeons?

   (A) The map sense of pigeons is most probably related to their olfactory sense.

   (B) The mechanism regulating the homing ability of pigeons is most probably similar to that utilized by honeybees.

   (C) The homing ability of pigeons is most probably based on a map sense.

   (D) The experiments conducted by Papi himself have provided the most valuable evidence yet collected regarding the homing ability of pigeons.

   (E) The experiments conducted by Schmidt-Koenig and Phillips have not substantially lessened the probability that Papi's own theory is correct.

PrepTest104 Sec3 Q21

Step 4:	Step 5:

Expert Analysis for the Practice exercise may be found on the following page. ▶ ▶ ▶

Expert Analysis

Here's how the LSAT expert performed Steps 2–5 on the passage about Homing Pigeons. Compare your work to that of the expert. Don't check merely to see whether you got the correct answers. Ask questions that help you dig into your mastery of these important steps in the Reading Comprehension Method. Did you recognize each question type? Where there were research clues, did you use them to research the passage? Did you predict the correct answer whenever possible?

Step 3: Consult the big picture summary.	**Step 2:** A Global question calling for the author's main idea.

22. Which one of the following best states the main idea of the passage?

    (A) The ability of pigeons to locate and return to their homes from distant points is unlike that of any other species.

    (B) It is likely that some map sense accounts for the homing ability of pigeons, but the nature of that sense has not been satisfactorily identified.

    (C) The majority of experiments on the homing ability of pigeons have been marked by design flaws.

    (D) The mechanisms underlying the homing ability of pigeons can best be identified through a combination of laboratory research and field experimentation.

    (E) The homing ability of pigeons is most likely based on a system similar to that used by many short-range species.

PrepTest104 Sec3 Q15

Step 4: The author's Main Point is that pigeons probably home using a map sense (outward displacement is unlikely), but that we don't yet know what kind of map they use.	**Step 5:** (B) is correct. This matches the big picture summary of the passage, and thus, our Step 4 prediction.

Wrong answers: (A) Outside the Scope. Not only is this far too narrow to represent the passage's Main Idea, but it is also something the author never said. (C) Extreme/180. First, we have no idea whether the experiments described in the passage represent a *majority* of the experiments on homing by pigeons. Second, the experiments described in paragraph 2 were, apparently, well designed; their results make outward displacement less likely to explain pigeons' homing abilities. (D) Outside the Scope. The author does not opine on the *best* way to identify pigeons' homing mechanisms. More importantly, this is not the point of the passage. (E) 180. The system used by short-range species such as honeybees (paragraph 1) is outward displacement, the explanation the author finds *un*likely (paragraph 2).

Step 3: The author states facts known about pigeons' homing ability only at the beginning of paragraph 1. After that, she discusses only possible explanations for *how* they home.	**Step 2:** "According to the passage . . ." signals a Detail question. The correct answer will come directly from the text.

23. According to the passage, which one of the following is ordinarily true regarding how homing pigeons "home"?

(A) Each time they are released at a specific site they fly home by the same route.

(B) When they are released they take only a short time to orient themselves before selecting their route home.

(C) Each time they are released at a specific site they take a shorter amount of time to orient themselves before flying home.

(D) They travel fairly long distances in seemingly random patterns before finally deciding on a route home.

(E) Upon release they travel briefly in the direction opposite to the one they eventually choose.

PrepTest104 Sec3 Q16

Step 4: The correct answer will say something akin to the first sentence of the passage: "Pigeons can home from many kilometers away; when released, they take under a minute to orient themselves, and then fly home."	**Step 5:** (B) is correct. This matches the passage's first sentence perfectly.

Wrong answers: (A) Outside the Scope. The author never tells us if pigeons use the same route home. (C) Outside the Scope. The author does not discuss this issue one way or the other. (D) 180. This statement contradicts the opening lines of the passage, which say that the pigeons orient within one minute. (E) Outside the Scope. The author makes no mention of pigeons flying in the direction opposite to their home.

Step 3: The hypothesis referenced in this question stem is that pigeons read the minds of their handlers.	**Step 2:** This question asks you to identify an experiment that would test the hypothesis from line 6. This makes it an Inference question.

24. Which one of the following experiments would best test the "possibility" referred to in the first paragraph?

(A) an experiment in which the handlers who transported, released, and otherwise came into contact with homing pigeons released at an unfamiliar site were unaware of the location of the pigeons' home

(B) an experiment in which the handlers who transported, released, and otherwise came into contact with homing pigeons released at an unfamiliar site were asked not to display any affection toward the pigeons

(C) an experiment in which the handlers who transported, released, and otherwise came into contact with homing pigeons released at an unfamiliar site were asked not to speak to each other throughout the release process

(D) an experiment in which all the homing pigeons released at an unfamiliar site had been raised and fed by individual researchers rather than by teams of handlers

(E) an experiment in which all the homing pigeons released at an unfamiliar site were exposed to a wide variety of unfamiliar sights and sounds

PrepTest104 Sec3 Q17

Step 4: The correct answer will describe an experiment that could disprove the mind-reading hypothesis.	**Step 5:** (A) is correct. If the pigeons' handlers do not know where the pigeons' home is, and if the pigeons are still able to home, we could disprove the mind-reading hypothesis.

Wrong answers: (B) Distortion. This would help disprove the hypothesis that pigeons are able to home because humans are affectionate toward them. (C) Distortion. This would help disprove the hypothesis that pigeons are able to home because they can understand human language or verbal cues. (D) Distortion. This would help disprove the hypothesis that pigeons are able to home because of their relationship with a specific individual. (E) Distortion. This would help disprove the hypothesis that pigeons are able to home because they recognize familiar sights and sounds.

Step 3: The "first alternative" is outward displacement, discussed throughout paragraph 2.	**Step 2:** This is an Inference question. The correct answer follows from information in the passage.

25. Information in the passage supports which one of the following statements regarding the "first alternative" for explaining the ability of pigeons to "home"?

(A) It has been conclusively ruled out by the results of numerous experiments.

(B) It seems unlikely because there are no theoretical models that could explain how pigeons track displacement.

(C) It has not, to date, been supported by experimental data, but neither has it been definitively ruled out.

(D) It seems unlikely in theory, but recent experimental results show that it may in fact be correct.

(E) It is not a useful theory because of the difficulty in designing experiments by which it might be tested.

PrepTest104 Sec3 Q18

Step 4: The author thinks outward displacement is unlikely to be the mechanism by which pigeons home, but she admits that it has not been 100 percent ruled out.	**Step 5:** (C) is correct. This follows from the author's opinion that outward displacement is "unlikely" but has not been ruled out by the "crucial experiment."

Wrong answers: (A) 180. No one has yet performed the "crucial experiment" that would definitely disprove outward displacement. (B) 180. The author presents two theoretical models in paragraph 2: an internal magnetic compass and the measurement of acceleration and turns. (D) 180. The experimental results in paragraph 2 all weaken the likelihood that pigeons use outward displacement. (E) 180. Given the results discussed in paragraph 2, it appears that experimenters have had no trouble testing outward displacement.

Step 3: The reference from the question stem is associated with outward displacement. When the author first cites outward displacement as one of the two "basic explanations," she notes that outward displacement is the system used by honeybees and other short-range homing species.	**Step 2:** This is a Logic Function question asking *how* or *why* the author cited a particular detail.

26. The author refers to "the system of many short-range species such as honeybees" most probably in order to

(A) emphasize the universality of the ability to home

(B) suggest that a particular explanation of pigeons' homing ability is worthy of consideration

(C) discredit one of the less convincing theories regarding the homing ability of pigeons

(D) criticize the techniques utilized by scientists investigating the nature of pigeons' homing ability

(E) illustrate why a proposed explanation of pigeons' homing ability is correct

PrepTest104 Sec3 Q19

Step 4: By bringing up the fact that other species are able to home through outward displacement, the author suggests a reason why scientists may want to investigate whether this could also explain homing pigeons' homing abilities.	**Step 5:** (B) is correct. This is precisely how the reference to honeybees and other short-range species is used in the first paragraph.

Wrong answers: (A) Extreme. The author never claims that all animals can home and certainly doesn't cite honeybees, a single species, to try to emphasize that point. (C) 180. While the author considers outward displacement "unlikely," her evaluation of the hypothesis doesn't come up until paragraph 2. At the point in the passage where she mentions honeybees, she is trying to show that outward displacement is one of two "basic explanations" that deserve testing. (D) Faulty Use of Detail. The author's critiques of scientists' experiments are found at the end of paragraph 2 and in paragraph 4. (E) 180. Outward displacement is the explanation the author considers "unlikely" to be valid.

Step 3: Papi's model is found in paragraph 3. He thinks that pigeons home through an olfactory map sense. They smell their way home, if you will.	**Step 2:** This is a Logic Reasoning question, worded like a Weaken question would be in the Logical Reasoning sections.

27. Which one of the following, if true, would most weaken Papi's theory regarding homing pigeons' homing ability?

(A) Even pigeons that have been raised in several different lofts in a variety of territories can find their way to their current home when released in unfamiliar territory.

(B) Pigeons whose sense of smell has been partially blocked find their way home more slowly than do pigeons whose sense of smell has not been affected.

(C) Even pigeons that have been raised in the same loft frequently take different routes home when released in unfamiliar territory.

(D) Even pigeons that have been transported well beyond the range of the odors detectable in their home territories can find their way home.

(E) Pigeons' sense of smell is no more acute than that of other birds who do not have the ability to "home."

PrepTest104 Sec3 Q20

Step 4: The correct answer will provide a set of facts that makes it unlikely that pigeons use a "smell map" to find their way home.	**Step 5:** (D) is correct. If pigeons are taken to places with wholly unfamiliar smells and yet are still able to home, Papi's model is less likely to explain their "map sense."

Wrong answers: (A) Outside the Scope. This doesn't address smell as a factor in the pigeons' homing ability. (B) 180. This supports Papi's model. (C) Outside the Scope. This doesn't address smell as a factor in the pigeons' homing ability. (E) Irrelevant Comparison. Papi's hypothesis does not require that pigeons have a better developed sense of smell than other birds have. A bird of prey, for example, might have an extremely acute sense of smell, but would use it to hunt rather than to home.

Step 2: This is an Inference question; the correct answer follows from the passage. Note that this question is similar to a Point at Issue question from Logical Reasoning, but it asks for a point of *agreement* between two people rather than a point of disagreement.

Step 3: Papi's position is found in paragraph 3. The author's point of view is best expressed through our big picture summary.

28. Given the information in the passage, it is most likely that Papi and the author of the passage would both agree with which one of the following statements regarding the homing ability of pigeons?

(A) The map sense of pigeons is most probably related to their olfactory sense.

(B) The mechanism regulating the homing ability of pigeons is most probably similar to that utilized by honeybees.

(C) The homing ability of pigeons is most probably based on a map sense.

(D) The experiments conducted by Papi himself have provided the most valuable evidence yet collected regarding the homing ability of pigeons.

(E) The experiments conducted by Schmidt-Koenig and Phillips have not substantially lessened the probability that Papi's own theory is correct.

PrepTest104 Sec3 Q21

Step 4: The author and Papi would agree that pigeons probably home through the use of a "map sense." Only Papi, however, would claim that the map was olfactory in nature.

Step 5: (C) is correct. Both the author and Papi consider map sense the most promising explanation for pigeons' homing ability.

Wrong answers: (A) Half-Right/Half-Wrong. Papi would agree with this statement; the author would not. (B) 180. The system used by honeybees is outward displacement, an explanation that both the author and Papi would find unlikely. (D) Distortion. Presumably Papi would think his own experiments pretty valuable, but the author is unconvinced. (E) Distortion. We have no idea whether Papi thinks Schmidt-Koenig and Phillips's experiments have damaged his model. Presumably, the author thinks so, since she cites their work to demonstrate why the precise nature of the map sense "remains mysterious."

Reflect Take a moment to reflect on how you built your skills to the point where you could more efficiently tackle that last question set. You're certainly not yet as fast and confident as you will be after more practice, but already, by concentrating on the steps of the Reading Comprehension Method, you're almost certainly taking a straighter, more effective line to the correct answer.

CHAPTER 8

Reading Comprehension Perform Quiz

Now that you've mastered the steps in the Reading Comprehension Method, it's time to assess yourself on what you've learned, by practicing with passages and question sets you haven't seen. In the pages that follow, you'll find four new passages. Among these passages, you'll find both standard and Comparative Reading passages, you'll see further examples of the common structural patterns found on the LSAT, and you'll get more exposure to all of the Reading Comprehension question types. This set of passages is representative of the various passage patterns and subject matter that has appeared on official LSATs over the past five years.

Notes on the Reading Comprehension Perform Quiz

The passages in this chapter are arranged by difficulty (from easiest to hardest). To assess passage difficulty, we calculated the average difficulty of all questions from each passage's question set. That said, don't place undue emphasis on the difficulty assessment of entire passages. Even the easiest passages may have one or more very difficult questions, and the hardest may have a couple of "gimmes." As you review, check the difficulty level of each question and read the explanations to see what may have made it easier or harder for the majority of test takers. Because the passages are organized by difficulty, if you take them in order, you will encounter different patterns and subject matter at random, just as you will on the exam. That is a good reminder that subject matter alone does not determine the difficulty of Reading Comprehension questions and that different subject areas are easier or harder for different individuals.

As you tackle the Reading Comprehension passages and questions in this chapter, keep the following pointers in mind.

Use the Reading Comprehension Method consistently. Chapter 7 was organized around the Reading Comprehension Method introduced in Chapter 6. That's because having a consistent, strategic approach is essential in this section of the test. Be conscious of each step as you work. If you practice without instilling the Method and its associated strategies, you're likely to repeat your old patterns, and that means continuing to be frustrated by the same Reading Comprehension pitfalls over and over again.

THE KAPLAN READING COMPREHENSION METHOD

STEP 1 **Read the Passage Strategically**—note Keywords and jot down paragraph notes to summarize the portions of the passage relevant to LSAT questions; summarize the author's Topic/Scope/Purpose/Main Idea.

STEP 2 **Read the Question Stem**—identify the question type, characterize the correct and incorrect answers, and look for clues to guide your research.

STEP 3 **Research the Relevant Text**—based on the clues in the question stem, consult your Roadmap; for open-ended questions, refer to your Topic/Scope/Purpose/Main Idea summaries.

STEP 4 **Predict the Correct Answer**—based on your research (or, for open-ended questions, your Topic/Scope/Purpose/Main Idea summaries), predict the meaning of the correct answer.

STEP 5 **Evaluate the Answer Choices**—select the choice that matches your prediction of the correct answer, or eliminate the four wrong answer choices.

As you try these passages, pay special attention to your work in Step 1 of the Method. To better simulate digital testing, underline or highlight text on the page, but take your paragraph notes on a separate piece of scratch paper. Many test takers underestimate the importance of strategic reading. If you find that you are encountering questions that surprise you or for which you have little idea of where in the passage the relevant information would be, it's likely that you needed a stronger Roadmap or better big-picture summaries back in Step 1.

Review your work thoroughly. Complete explanations for the passages and questions in this chapter follow right after the Perform quiz. Take the time to study them even if you get all of a passage's questions correct. Review how expert test takers Roadmapped the passage, the Keywords they highlighted, the paragraph notes they jotted down, and how they summarized the author's overall Purpose and Main Idea. You may well discover that with more effective strategic reading, your work on the questions could have been both faster and more accurate. Of course, when you miss a question, determine whether the problem came from a misunderstanding or oversight in the question, or whether you misread or overlooked a key piece of the passage.

Another way in which you can effectively use the explanations is to first complete Step 1—create a Roadmap and summarize the author's Purpose and Main Idea. Then, review just that much of the explanations for the passage before you even try the questions. This will let you focus on how you're doing in Step 1, laying the crucial groundwork for effective management of the question set. After you're sure that you understand the passage in a way that will help you get LSAT points, try the questions and review them as well. This approach is helpful when you find a particular passage frustrating and you feel that you're making little progress working through the questions.

Finally, each question's difficulty is ranked in the explanations—from ★★★★ for the toughest questions to ★ for the easiest. Consulting these rankings will tell you a lot about the passages and questions you're practicing. You might, for example, discover a very hard question in an otherwise easy passage. In that case, you'll focus your review on what made that question confusing for test takers while reassuring yourself that your overall approach was on target. Conversely, you may find a passage in which, say, four out of six questions rate ★★★ or ★★★★. In that case, you'll know the passage was tough for everyone, which means you should spend extra time reviewing the Roadmap and big-picture summaries to discover how the testmaker made a passage so challenging.

Timing. On Test Day, you'll have about 8½ minutes per passage. Naturally, that kind of time pressure can make even routine reading feel stressful. As you're assessing your skills on individual passages, keep those timing restrictions in mind. At this point, keep your work on each passage to no more than 10 minutes. Speed will come with familiarity, practice, and (believe it or not) patience. When you take full tests or try 35-minute Reading Comprehension sections, time yourself strictly. But don't be in such a rush to get faster that you fail to gain the efficiencies that come from practicing the methodical application of good Reading Comprehension strategy. The LSAT Channel Spotlight following Chapter 8 will address timing in depth and will introduce you to strategies to effectively manage the 35-minute Reading Comprehension section that you'll complete on Test Day. In the following Perform quiz, time yourself on the passages one by one to perfect your approach.

Perform

For decades, there has been a deep rift between poetry and fiction in the United States, especially in academic settings; graduate writing programs in universities, for example, train students as poets or as writers of fiction, but almost never as both. Both poets and writers of fiction have tended to support this separation, in large part because the current conventional wisdom holds that poetry should be elliptical and lyrical, reflecting inner states and processes of thought or feeling, whereas character and narrative events are the stock-in-trade of fiction.

Certainly it is true that poetry and fiction are distinct genres, but why have specialized education and literary territoriality resulted from this distinction? The answer lies perhaps in a widespread attitude in U.S. culture, which often casts a suspicious eye on the generalist. Those with knowledge and expertise in multiple areas risk charges of dilettantism, as if ability in one field is diluted or compromised by accomplishment in another.

Fortunately, there are signs that the bias against writers who cross generic boundaries is diminishing; several recent writers are known and respected for their work in both genres. One important example of this trend is Rita Dove, an African American writer highly acclaimed for both her poetry and her fiction. A few years ago, speaking at a conference entitled "Poets Who Write Fiction," Dove expressed gentle incredulity about the habit of segregating the genres. She had grown up reading and loving both fiction and poetry, she said, unaware of any purported danger lurking in attempts to mix the two. She also studied for some time in Germany, where, she observes, "Poets write plays, novelists compose libretti, playwrights write novels—they would not understand our restrictiveness."

It makes little sense, Dove believes, to persist in the restrictive approach to poetry and fiction prevalent in the U.S., because each genre shares in the nature of the other. Indeed, her poetry offers example after example of what can only be properly regarded as lyric narrative. Her use of language in these poems is undeniably lyrical—that is, it evokes emotion and inner states without requiring the reader to organize ideas or events in a particular linear structure. Yet this lyric expression simultaneously presents the elements of a plot in such a way that the reader is led repeatedly to take account of clusters of narrative details within the lyric flow. Thus while the language is lyrical, it often comes to constitute, cumulatively, a work of narrative fiction. Similarly, many passages in her fiction, though undeniably prose, achieve the status of lyric narrative through the use of poetic rhythms and elliptical expression. In short, Dove bridges the gap between poetry and fiction not only by writing in both genres, but also by fusing the two genres within individual works.

1. Which one of the following most accurately expresses the main point of the passage?

   (A) Rita Dove's work has been widely acclaimed primarily because of the lyrical elements she has introduced into her fiction.

   (B) Rita Dove's lyric narratives present clusters of narrative detail in order to create a cumulative narrative without requiring the reader to interpret it in a linear manner.

   (C) Working against a bias that has long been dominant in the U.S., recent writers like Rita Dove have shown that the lyrical use of language can effectively enhance narrative fiction.

   (D) Unlike many of her U.S. contemporaries, Rita Dove writes without relying on the traditional techniques associated with poetry and fiction.

   (E) Rita Dove's successful blending of poetry and fiction exemplifies the recent trend away from the rigid separation of the two genres that has long been prevalent in the U.S.

2. Which one of the following is most analogous to the literary achievements that the author attributes to Dove?

(A) A chef combines nontraditional cooking methods and traditional ingredients from disparate world cuisines to devise new recipes.

(B) A professor of film studies becomes a film director and succeeds, partly due to a wealth of theoretical knowledge of filmmaking.

(C) An actor who is also a theatrical director teams up with a public health agency to use street theater to inform the public about health matters.

(D) A choreographer defies convention and choreographs dances that combine elements of both ballet and jazz dance.

(E) A rock musician records several songs from previous decades but introduces extended guitar solos into each one.

3. According to the passage, in the U.S. there is a widely held view that

(A) poetry should not involve characters or narratives

(B) unlike the writing of poetry, the writing of fiction is rarely an academically serious endeavor

(C) graduate writing programs focus on poetry to the exclusion of fiction

(D) fiction is most aesthetically effective when it incorporates lyrical elements

(E) European literary cultures are suspicious of generalists

4. The author's attitude toward the deep rift between poetry and fiction in the U.S. can be most accurately described as one of

(A) perplexity as to what could have led to the development of such a rift

(B) astonishment that academics have overlooked the existence of the rift

(C) ambivalence toward the effect the rift has had on U.S. literature

(D) pessimism regarding the possibility that the rift can be overcome

(E) disapproval of attitudes and presuppositions underlying the rift

5. In the passage the author conjectures that a cause of the deep rift between fiction and poetry in the United States may be that

(A) poets and fiction writers each tend to see their craft as superior to the others' craft

(B) the methods used in training graduate students in poetry are different from those used in training graduate students in other literary fields

(C) publishers often pressure writers to concentrate on what they do best

(D) a suspicion of generalism deters writers from dividing their energies between the two genres

(E) fiction is more widely read and respected than poetry

6. In the context of the passage, the author's primary purpose in mentioning Dove's experience in Germany at the end of the third paragraph is to

(A) suggest that the habit of treating poetry and fiction as nonoverlapping domains is characteristic of English-speaking societies but not others

(B) point to an experience that reinforced Dove's conviction that poetry and fiction should not be rigidly separated

(C) indicate that Dove's strengths as a writer derive in large part from the international character of her academic background

(D) present an illuminating biographical detail about Dove in an effort to enhance the human interest appeal of the passage

(E) indicate what Dove believes to be the origin of her opposition to the separation of fiction and poetry in the U.S.

7. It can be inferred from the passage that the author would be most likely to believe which one of the following?

(A) Each of Dove's works can be classified as either primarily poetry or primarily fiction, even though it may contain elements of both.

(B) The aesthetic value of lyric narrative resides in its representation of a sequence of events, rather than in its ability to evoke inner states.

(C) The way in which Dove blends genres in her writing is without precedent in U.S. writing.

(D) Narrative that uses lyrical language is generally aesthetically superior to pure lyric poetry.

(E) Writers who successfully cross the generic boundary between poetry and fiction often try their hand at genres such as drama as well.

8. If this passage had been excerpted from a longer text, which one of the following predictions about the near future of U.S. literature would be most likely to appear in that text?

(A) The number of writers who write both poetry and fiction will probably continue to grow.

(B) Because of the increased interest in mixed genres, the small market for pure lyric poetry will likely shrink even further.

(C) Narrative poetry will probably come to be regarded as a sub-genre of fiction.

(D) There will probably be a rise in specialization among writers in university writing programs.

(E) Writers who continue to work exclusively in poetry or fiction will likely lose their audiences.

PrepTest123 Sec4 Qs1–8

The two passages discuss recent scientific research on music. They are adapted from two different papers presented at a scholarly conference.

Passage A

Did music and human language originate separately or together? Both systems use intonation and rhythm to communicate emotions. Both can be produced vocally or with tools, and people can produce both music and language silently to themselves.

Brain imaging studies suggest that music and language are part of one large, vastly complicated, neurological system for processing sound. In fact, fewer differences than similarities exist between the neurological processing of the two. One could think of the two activities as different radio programs that can be broadcast over the same hardware. One noteworthy difference, though, is that, generally speaking, people are better at language than music. In music, anyone can listen easily enough, but most people do not perform well, and in many cultures composition is left to specialists. In language, by contrast, nearly everyone actively performs and composes.

Given their shared neurological basis, it appears that music and language evolved together as brain size increased over the course of hominid evolution. But the primacy of language over music that we can observe today suggests that language, not music, was the primary function natural selection operated on. Music, it would seem, had little adaptive value of its own, and most likely developed on the coattails of language.

Passage B

Darwin claimed that since "neither the enjoyment nor the capacity of producing musical notes are faculties of the least [practical] use to man . . . they must be ranked amongst the most mysterious with which he is endowed." I suggest that the enjoyment of and the capacity to produce musical notes are faculties of indispensable use to mothers and their infants and that it is in the emotional bonds created by the interaction of mother and child that we can discover the evolutionary origins of human music.

Even excluding lullabies, which parents sing to infants, human mothers and infants under six months of age engage in ritualized, sequential behaviors, involving vocal, facial, and bodily interactions. Using face-to-face mother-infant interactions filmed at 24 frames per second, researchers have shown that mothers and infants jointly construct mutually improvised interactions in which each partner tracks the actions of the other. Such episodes last from one-half second to three seconds and are composed of musical elements—variations in pitch, rhythm, timbre, volume, and tempo.

What evolutionary advantage would such behavior have? In the course of hominid evolution, brain size increased rapidly. Contemporaneously, the increase in bipedality caused the birth canal to narrow. This resulted in hominid infants being born ever-more prematurely, leaving them much more helpless at birth. This helplessness necessitated longer, better maternal care. Under such conditions, the emotional bonds created in the premusical mother-infant interactions we observe in *Homo sapiens* today—behavior whose neurological basis essentially constitutes the capacity to make and enjoy music—would have conferred considerable evolutionary advantage.

9. Both passages were written primarily in order to answer which one of the following questions?

   (A) What evolutionary advantage did larger brain size confer on early hominids?

   (B) Why do human mothers and infants engage in bonding behavior that is composed of musical elements?

   (C) What are the evolutionary origins of the human ability to make music?

   (D) Do the human abilities to make music and to use language depend on the same neurological systems?

   (E) Why are most people more adept at using language than they are at making music?

10. Each of the two passages mentions the relation of music to

(A) bonding between humans
(B) human emotion
(C) neurological research
(D) the increasing helplessness of hominid infants
(E) the use of tools to produce sounds

11. It can be inferred that the authors of the two passages would be most likely to disagree over whether

(A) the increase in hominid brain size necessitated earlier births
(B) fewer differences than similarities exist between the neurological processing of music and human language
(C) brain size increased rapidly over the course of human evolution
(D) the capacity to produce music has great adaptive value to humans
(E) mother-infant bonding involves temporally patterned vocal interactions

12. The authors would be most likely to agree on the answer to which one of the following questions regarding musical capacity in humans?

(A) Does it manifest itself in some form in early infancy?
(B) Does it affect the strength of mother-infant bonds?
(C) Is it at least partly a result of evolutionary increases in brain size?
(D) Did its evolution spur the development of new neurological systems?
(E) Why does it vary so greatly among different individuals?

13. Which one of the following principles underlies the arguments in both passages?

(A) Investigations of the evolutionary origins of human behaviors must take into account the behavior of nonhuman animals.
(B) All human capacities can be explained in terms of the evolutionary advantages they offer.
(C) The fact that a single neurological system underlies two different capacities is evidence that those capacities evolved concurrently.
(D) The discovery of the neurological basis of a human behavior constitutes the discovery of the essence of that behavior.
(E) The behavior of modern-day humans can provide legitimate evidence concerning the evolutionary origins of human abilities.

14. Which one of the following most accurately characterizes a relationship between the two passages?

(A) Passage A and passage B use different evidence to draw divergent conclusions.
(B) Passage A poses the question that passage B attempts to answer.
(C) Passage A proposes a hypothesis that passage B attempts to substantiate with new evidence.
(D) Passage A expresses a stronger commitment to its hypothesis than does passage B.
(E) Passage A and passage B use different evidence to support the same conclusion.

PrepTest123 Sec4 Qs9–14

The World Wide Web, a network of electronically produced and interconnected (or "linked") sites, called pages, that are accessible via personal computer, raises legal issues about the rights of owners of intellectual property, notably those who create documents for inclusion on Web pages. Some of these owners of intellectual property claim that unless copyright law is strengthened, intellectual property on the Web will not be protected from copyright infringement. Web users, however, claim that if their ability to access information on Web pages is reduced, the Web cannot live up to its potential as an open, interactive medium of communication.

The debate arises from the Web's ability to link one document to another. Links between sites are analogous to the inclusion in a printed text of references to other works, but with one difference: the cited document is instantly retrievable by a user who activates the link. This immediate accessibility creates a problem, since current copyright laws give owners of intellectual property the right to sue a distributor of unauthorized copies of their material even if that distributor did not personally make the copies. If person A, the author of a document, puts the document on a Web page, and person B, the creator of another Web page, creates a link to A's document, is B committing copyright infringement?

To answer this question, it must first be determined who controls distribution of a document on the Web. When A places a document on a Web page, this is comparable to recording an outgoing message on one's telephone answering machine for others to hear. When B creates a link to A's document, this is akin to B's giving out A's telephone number, thereby allowing third parties to hear the outgoing message for themselves. Anyone who calls can listen to the message; that is its purpose. While B's link may indeed facilitate access to A's document, the crucial point is that A, simply by placing that document on the Web, is thereby offering it for distribution. Therefore, even if B leads others to the document, it is A who actually controls access to it. Hence creating a link to a document is not the same as making or distributing a copy of that document. Moreover, techniques are already available by which A can restrict access to a document. For example, A may require a password to gain entry to A's Web page, just as a telephone owner can request an unlisted number and disclose it only to selected parties. Such a solution would compromise the openness of the Web somewhat, but not as much as the threat of copyright infringement litigation. Changing copyright law to benefit owners of intellectual property is thus ill-advised because it would impede the development of the Web as a public forum dedicated to the free exchange of ideas.

15. Which one of the following most accurately expresses the main point of the passage?

(A) Since distribution of a document placed on a Web page is controlled by the author of that page rather than by the person who creates a link to the page, creating such a link should not be considered copyright infringement.

(B) Changes in copyright law in response to the development of Web pages and links are ill-advised unless such changes amplify rather than restrict the free exchange of ideas necessary in a democracy.

(C) People who are concerned about the access others may have to the Web documents they create can easily prevent such access without inhibiting the rights of others to exchange ideas freely.

(D) Problems concerning intellectual property rights created by new forms of electronic media are not insuperably difficult to resolve if one applies basic commonsense principles to these problems.

(E) Maintaining a free exchange of ideas on the Web offers benefits that far outweigh those that might be gained by a small number of individuals if a radical alteration of copyright laws aimed at restricting the Web's growth were allowed.

16. Which one of the following is closest in meaning to the term "strengthened" as that term is used in the passage?

    (A) made more restrictive
    (B) made uniform worldwide
    (C) made to impose harsher penalties
    (D) dutifully enforced
    (E) more fully recognized as legitimate

17. With which one of the following claims about documents placed on Web pages would the author be most likely to agree?

    (A) Such documents cannot receive adequate protection unless current copyright laws are strengthened.
    (B) Such documents cannot be protected from unauthorized distribution without significantly diminishing the potential of the Web to be a widely used form of communication.
    (C) The nearly instantaneous access afforded by the Web makes it impossible in practice to limit access to such documents.
    (D) Such documents can be protected from copyright infringement with the least damage to the public interest only by altering existing legal codes.
    (E) Such documents cannot fully contribute to the Web's free exchange of ideas unless their authors allow them to be freely accessed by those who wish to do so.

18. Based on the passage, the relationship between strengthening current copyright laws and relying on passwords to restrict access to a Web document is most analogous to the relationship between

    (A) allowing everyone use of a public facility and restricting its use to members of the community
    (B) outlawing the use of a drug and outlawing its sale
    (C) prohibiting a sport and relying on participants to employ proper safety gear
    (D) passing a new law and enforcing that law
    (E) allowing unrestricted entry to a building and restricting entry to those who have been issued a badge

19. The passage most strongly implies which one of the following?

    (A) There are no creators of links to Web pages who are also owners of intellectual property on Web pages.
    (B) The person who controls access to a Web page document should be considered the distributor of that document.
    (C) Rights of privacy should not be extended to owners of intellectual property placed on the Web.
    (D) Those who create links to Web pages have primary control over who reads the documents on those pages.
    (E) A document on a Web page must be converted to a physical document via printing before copyright infringement takes place.

20. According to the passage, which one of the following features of outgoing messages left on telephone answering machines is most relevant to the debate concerning copyright infringement?

    (A) Such messages are carried by an electronic medium of communication.

    (B) Such messages are not legally protected against unauthorized distribution.

    (C) Transmission of such messages is virtually instantaneous.

    (D) People do not usually care whether or not others might record such messages.

    (E) Such messages have purposely been made available to anyone who calls that telephone number.

21. The author's discussion of telephone answering machines serves primarily to

    (A) compare and contrast the legal problems created by two different sorts of electronic media

    (B) provide an analogy to illustrate the positions taken by each of the two sides in the copyright debate

    (C) show that the legal problems produced by new communication technology are not themselves new

    (D) illustrate the basic principle the author believes should help determine the outcome of the copyright debate

    (E) show that telephone use also raises concerns about copyright infringement

22. According to the passage, present copyright laws

    (A) allow completely unrestricted use of any document placed by its author on a Web page

    (B) allow those who establish links to a document on a Web page to control its distribution to others

    (C) prohibit anyone but the author of a document from making a profit from the document's distribution

    (D) allow the author of a document to sue anyone who distributes the document without permission

    (E) should be altered to allow more complete freedom in the exchange of ideas

PrepTest123 Sec4 Qs15–22

In tracing the changing face of the Irish landscape, scholars have traditionally relied primarily on evidence from historical documents. However, such documentary sources provide a fragmentary record at best. Reliable accounts are very scarce for many parts of Ireland prior to the seventeenth century, and many of the relevant documents from the sixteenth and seventeenth centuries focus selectively on matters relating to military or commercial interests.

Studies of fossilized pollen grains preserved in peats and lake muds provide an additional means of investigating vegetative landscape change. Details of changes in vegetation resulting from both human activities and natural events are reflected in the kinds and quantities of minute pollen grains that become trapped in sediments. Analysis of samples can identify which kinds of plants produced the preserved pollen grains and when they were deposited, and in many cases the findings can serve to supplement or correct the documentary record.

For example, analyses of samples from Long Lough in County Down have revealed significant patterns of cereal-grain pollen beginning by about 400 A.D. The substantial clay content of the soil in this part of Down makes cultivation by primitive tools difficult. Historians thought that such soils were not tilled to any significant extent until the introduction of the moldboard plough to Ireland in the seventh century A.D. Because cereal cultivation would have required tilling of the soil, the pollen evidence indicates that these soils must indeed have been successfully tilled before the introduction of the new plough.

Another example concerns flax cultivation in County Down, one of the great linen-producing areas of Ireland during the eighteenth century. Some aspects of linen production in Down are well documented, but the documentary record tells little about the cultivation of flax, the plant from which linen is made, in that area. The record of eighteenth-century linen production in Down, together with the knowledge that flax cultivation had been established in Ireland centuries before that time, led some historians to surmise that this plant was being cultivated in Down before the eighteenth century. But pollen analyses indicate that this is not the case; flax pollen was found only in deposits laid down since the eighteenth century.

It must be stressed, though, that there are limits to the ability of the pollen record to reflect the vegetative history of the landscape. For example, pollen analyses cannot identify the species, but only the genus or family, of some plants. Among these is madder, a cultivated dye plant of historical importance in Ireland. Madder belongs to a plant family that also comprises various native weeds, including goosegrass. If madder pollen were present in a deposit it would be indistinguishable from that of uncultivated native species.

23. Which one of the following most accurately expresses the main point of the passage?

(A) Analysis of fossilized pollen is a useful means of supplementing and in some cases correcting other sources of information regarding changes in the Irish landscape.

(B) Analyses of historical documents, together with pollen evidence, have led to the revision of some previously accepted hypotheses regarding changes in the Irish landscape.

(C) Analysis of fossilized pollen has proven to be a valuable tool in the identification of ancient plant species.

(D) Analysis of fossilized pollen has provided new evidence that the cultivation of such crops as cereal grains, flax, and madder had a significant impact on the landscape of Ireland.

(E) While pollen evidence can sometimes supplement other sources of historical information, its applicability is severely limited, since it cannot be used to identify plant species.

24. The passage indicates that pollen analyses have provided evidence against which one of the following views?

    (A) The moldboard plough was introduced into Ireland in the seventh century.

    (B) In certain parts of County Down, cereal grains were not cultivated to any significant extent before the seventh century.

    (C) In certain parts of Ireland, cereal grains have been cultivated continuously since the introduction of the moldboard plough.

    (D) Cereal grain cultivation requires successful tilling of the soil.

    (E) Cereal grain cultivation began in County Down around 400 A.D.

25. The phrase "documentary record" as it is used in the first and third paragraphs of the passage primarily refers to

    (A) documented results of analyses of fossilized pollen

    (B) the kinds and quantities of fossilized pollen grains preserved in peats and lake muds

    (C) written and pictorial descriptions by current historians of the events and landscapes of past centuries

    (D) government and commercial records, maps, and similar documents produced in the past that recorded conditions and events of that time

    (E) articles, books, and other documents by current historians listing and analyzing all the available evidence regarding a particular historical period

26. The passage indicates that prior to the use of pollen analysis in the study of the history of the Irish landscape, at least some historians believed which one of the following?

    (A) The Irish landscape had experienced significant flooding during the seventeenth century.

    (B) Cereal grain was not cultivated anywhere in Ireland until at least the seventh century.

    (C) The history of the Irish landscape during the sixteenth and seventeenth centuries was well documented.

    (D) Madder was not used as a dye plant in Ireland until after the eighteenth century.

    (E) The beginning of flax cultivation in County Down may well have occurred before the eighteenth century.

27. Which one of the following most accurately describes the relationship between the second paragraph and the final paragraph?

    (A) The second paragraph proposes a hypothesis for which the final paragraph offers a supporting example.

    (B) The final paragraph describes a problem that must be solved before the method advocated in the second paragraph can be considered viable.

    (C) The final paragraph qualifies the claim made in the second paragraph.

    (D) The second paragraph describes a view against which the author intends to argue, and the final paragraph states the author's argument against that view.

    (E) The final paragraph offers procedures to supplement the method described in the second paragraph.

PrepTest123 Sec4 Qs23–27

Assess

Use the following criteria to evaluate your results on the Reading Comprehension Perform quiz.

If, under timed conditions, you correctly answered:

21–27 of the questions: Outstanding! You have demonstrated a strong skill level in Reading Comprehension. For further practice, use any of the Recommended Additional Practice sets, including the Advanced set. In addition, find room in your study schedule to do timed practice on full Reading Comprehension sections.

14–20 of the questions: Good work! You have a solid foundation in Reading Comprehension. For further practice, begin with the Foundations or Mid-Level Recommended Additional Practice set (and, time permitting, work up through the Advanced set, as well). After that, begin making timed practice on full Reading Comprehension sections a routine part of your LSAT preparation.

0–13 of the questions: Keep working. Reading Comprehension is central to your LSAT score. Continued practice offers you the best chance to make steady improvement in this section. Begin by reviewing the Reading Comprehension chapters with a focus on the steps of the Reading Comprehension Method. Pinpoint the areas in which you can make the greatest improvements. Then try the passages in the Foundations Recommended Additional Practice set. As you continue to progress, move on to the Mid-Level Recommended Additional Practice set. After that, if you have time in your study schedule, try to make timed practice on full Reading Comprehension sections a routine part of your LSAT preparation.

Recommended Additional Practice: Reading Comprehension

All of the following passages will provide good practice on recent Reading Comprehension passages. They are grouped by difficulty as determined from empirical student practice results. All the passages are from PrepTests that are available for digital practice on LawHub with an LSAC LawHub Advantage subscription. Complete explanations and analysis for these passages and questions are available on Kaplan's LSAT Link and LSAT Link+. See **www.kaptest.com/LSAT** to learn more about LSAT Link and LSAT Link+.

Foundations

PrepTest 141, Section 3, Passage 1: The Discovery of Prions
PrepTest 141, Section 3, Passage 2: Katherine Dunham's Contribution to Modern Dance
PrepTest 139, Section 3, Passage 1: Keeping Small Farms Profitable
PrepTest 137, Section 1, Passage 1: The Biography of Lorenzo Tucker
PrepTest 137, Section 1, Passage 3: The Effects of Species Invasion
PrepTest 135, Section 3, Passage 1: Latina Autobiography in the 1980s
PrepTest 135, Section 3, Passage 2: The Archivist's Dilemma
PrepTest 134, Section 4, Passage 1: Utility and Criminal Deterrence
PrepTest 134, Section 4, Passage 2: Mexican-American Proverbs
PrepTest 133, Section 4, Passage 2: Kate Chopin
PrepTest 133, Section 4, Passage 4: Objectivist Historians
PrepTest 132, Section 1, Passage 1: Earthquake-Dating by Lichenometry

Mid-Level

PrepTest 139, Section 3, Passage 2: Forward into Photography's Past
PrepTest 139, Section 3, Passage 3: Patents—The Tech Company's Best Defense
PrepTest 138, Section 1, Passage 1: The Corrido

PrepTest 138, Section 1, Passage 2: How Plants Evolved Secondary Substances
PrepTest 136, Section 1, Passage 2: Reliability of Fingerprint Identification
PrepTest 135, Section 3, Passage 4: Restoring Europe's Farmland
PrepTest 134, Section 4, Passage 3: Evolutionary Psychology and Altruism
PrepTest 134, Section 4, Passage 4: Dostoyevsky and the Radicals
PrepTest 133, Section 4, Passage 1: "Tradition" and Sea Otter Pelts
PrepTest 133, Section 4, Passage 3: Ocean Floor Discoveries
PrepTest 132, Section 1, Passage 2: Custom-Made Medical Illustrations as Evidence
PrepTest 132, Section 1, Passage 4: The Fiction of Sarah Orne Jewett

Advanced

PrepTest 141, Section 3, Passage 3: Happiness and Wealth
PrepTest 141, Section 3, Passage 4: Factors in Risk-Reduction Policy-Making
PrepTest 139, Section 3, Passage 4: *Calvaria major* and the Dodo Bird
PrepTest 138, Section 1, Passage 3: Modeling Smith's Pin Factory
PrepTest 138, Section 1, Passage 4: Selective Enforcement of Laws
PrepTest 137, Section 1, Passage 2: The Autobiography of Nisa
PrepTest 137, Section 1, Passage 4: The Paradox of Omnipotence
PrepTest 136, Section 1, Passage 1: Digital Publishing
PrepTest 136, Section 1, Passage 3: Ellington's Jazz and Morrison's *Jazz*
PrepTest 136, Section 1, Passage 4: Discovery of Nuclear Fission
PrepTest 135, Section 3, Passage 3: Blackmail in Two Legal Contexts
PrepTest 132, Section 1, Passage 3: Dental Caries and Archaeology

CHAPTER 8

Answers and Explanations

Passage 1—Poetry and Fiction

Step 1: Read the Passage Strategically

Sample Roadmap

For decades, there has been a deep rift between poetry and fiction in the United States, especially in academic settings; graduate writing programs in universities, for example, train students as poets or as writers of fiction, but almost never as both. Both poets and writers of fiction have tended to support this separation, in large part because the current conventional wisdom holds that poetry should be elliptical and lyrical, reflecting inner states and processes of thought or feeling, whereas character and narrative events are the stock-in-trade of fiction.

Certainly it is true that poetry and fiction are distinct genres, but why have specialized education and literary territoriality resulted from this distinction? The answer lies perhaps in a widespread attitude in U.S. culture, which often casts a suspicious eye on the generalist. Those with knowledge and expertise in multiple areas risk charges of dilettantism, as if ability in one field is diluted or compromised by accomplishment in another.

Fortunately, there are signs that the bias against writers who cross generic boundaries is diminishing; several recent writers are known and respected for their work in both genres. One important example of this trend is Rita Dove, an African American writer highly acclaimed for both her poetry and her fiction. A few years ago, speaking at a conference entitled "Poets Who Write Fiction," Dove expressed gentle incredulity about the habit of segregating the genres. She had grown up reading and loving both fiction and poetry, she said, unaware of any purported danger lurking in attempts to mix the two. She also studied for some time in Germany, where, she observes, "Poets write plays, novelists compose libretti, playwrights write novels—they would not understand our restrictiveness."

It makes little sense, Dove believes, to persist in the restrictive approach to poetry and fiction prevalent in the U.S., because each genre shares in the nature of the other. Indeed, her poetry offers example after example of what can only be properly regarded as lyric narrative. Her use of language in these poems is undeniably lyrical—that is, it evokes emotion and inner states without requiring the reader to organize ideas or events in a particular linear structure. Yet this lyric expression simultaneously presents the elements of a plot in such a way that the reader is led repeatedly to take account of clusters of narrative details within the lyric flow. Thus while the language is lyrical, it often comes to constitute, cumulatively, a work of narrative fiction. Similarly, many passages in her fiction, though undeniably prose, achieve the status of lyric narrative through the use of poetic rhythms and elliptical expression. In short, Dove bridges the gap between poetry and fiction not only by writing in both genres, but also by fusing the two genres within individual works.

¶1:

Poetry v. fiction clash in US. Poets don't wr. fic & v.v.—diff. qualities.

¶2:

Why the clash? Culture disdains generalists.

¶3:

Au: Good that clash is ending. Ex.: R. Dove does both, approves of mixing genres.

¶4:

RD believes they share a lot, & her work demos that. Her fiction lyrical, her poems tell stories.

Discussion

Paragraph 1 jumps right into the **Topic**: the division between poetry and fiction in the United States. The Scope and Purpose won't become clear until later in the passage, but the first paragraph does narrow the Topic a bit by focusing on how writers have perpetuated the division between fiction and poetry.

Paragraph 2 suggests a possible reason for the division: U.S. culture doesn't think much of generalists. You also get a taste of the author's perspective in the last sentence, ". . . as if ability in one field is diluted or compromised by accomplishment in another." This suggests that the author thinks ability is not diminished by involvement in multiple fields, and starts to suggest the Scope of the passage.

Paragraph 3 starts with another strong indication of the author's view, the Keyword *[f]ortunately*. The author thinks it's a good thing that the boundaries are starting to break down. The rest of the paragraph (and, indeed, the rest of the passage) is devoted to the example of Rita Dove, an author whose work blends elements traditionally associated with poetry and those traditionally associated with fiction. Here, the Scope and Purpose should become clearer. The **Scope**, or specific aspect of the Topic explored by the author, is the move toward the breakdown of the barrier between poetry and fiction, as represented by Rita Dove. The author's **Purpose** is simply to illustrate the trend toward breaking down the poetry/fiction divide. The **Main Idea** is that Rita Dove is an example of a trend in which the rigid boundaries between poetry and fiction in America are starting to erode.

The author's attitude suggests that she advocates for further breakdown of the barrier, but the rest of the passage doesn't quite go that far. Rather than advocating anything, paragraph 4 simply explains how Dove not only writes in both genres, but also melds elements of poetry and fiction in some of her work.

1. (E) Global ★☆☆☆

Step 2: Identify the Question Type

This is a Global question because it asks you to identify the passage's "main point."

Step 3: Research the Relevant Text

The entire text is relevant when answering a Global question. Use your understanding of the passage's big picture from Step 1 to predict your answer.

Step 4: Make a Prediction

Use the author's statements of opinion to confirm the Main Idea, which is that Rita Dove's work is evidence that the rift between fiction and poetry is diminishing.

Step 5: Evaluate the Answer Choices

(E) is a match for this prediction. It even uses the word *exemplifies*, which perfectly captures the author's use of Rita Dove as an example.

(A) is a Distortion. The author makes no claim that the blending of elements is the reason Dove's work has been well received.

(B) is too narrow. The particular elements of Dove's writing described in the middle of paragraph 4 are just details. A list of subsidiary details will never be correct when a question asks you for the main point of the entire passage.

(C) is also a Distortion. The bias in the United States is against writers who cross genres, not against writers who use lyrical language in fiction.

(D) is too narrow. There's no mention of the poetry/fiction rift that forms the foundation for the passage. Furthermore, Rita Dove's techniques aren't necessarily nontraditional; she just uses them across genres.

2. (D) Logic Reasoning (Parallel Reasoning) ★☆☆☆

Step 2: Identify the Question Type

The phrase "most analogous to" also appears in Parallel Reasoning questions in the Logical Reasoning section, so this is the same type of question.

Step 3: Research the Relevant Text

Rita Dove is mentioned in both paragraphs 3 and 4, but paragraph 4 is probably more relevant because paragraph 3 mainly discusses Dove's background and her views on segregating poetry and fiction.

Step 4: Make a Prediction

In paragraph 4, the author tells us that Dove uses techniques typically associated with poetry in her narrative fiction, and vice versa. Our correct answer, then, will be about an artist or practitioner who crosses genres or disciplines in the creation of individual works.

Step 5: Evaluate the Answer Choices

(D), in which a choreographer combines elements of two different types of dance, is parallel to Dove's attempts to write works that combine elements of poetry and fiction. **(D)** is therefore correct.

(A)'s combination element might be tempting, but this ultimately distorts the author's point—Dove's writing doesn't combine "traditional and nontraditional" methods.

(B)'s "theoretical knowledge" is Outside the Scope of the passage. The rift the author discusses isn't between academics and practitioners, but between practitioners of two different literary genres.

(C) has no true blending of genres; instead, one medium is consciously used to promote another.

(E) doesn't discuss two genres; guitar solos aren't exactly a departure from rock. **(E)** also introduces the element of work that's not original, something that doesn't come into play at all in the passage.

3. (A) Detail ★☆☆☆

Step 2: Identify the Question Type

This is a Detail question because it begins with the phrase "[a]ccording to the passage." The focus is simply on what the author states directly.

Step 3: Research the Relevant Text

The author talked about widely held views regarding poetry and fiction in the United States in both of the first two paragraphs.

Step 4: Make a Prediction

The author directly mentions two prevailing views: In the first paragraph, that poetry should be lyrical and elliptical while fiction should be rooted in character and narrative; and in the second paragraph, that American culture is suspicious of generalists.

Step 5: Evaluate the Answer Choices

(A) is a match for the first paragraph.

(B) is a Distortion. The author discusses the differences between the genres, but never makes a value judgment. Also, no evidence is given that university writing programs favor one genre over another.

(C) is another Distortion; the first paragraph says that fiction programs and poetry programs tend to be operated independently, but says nothing about the balance between the two.

(D)'s use of the phrase "most aesthetically effective" is too strong; the author does speak favorably of the outcome when fiction (at least, Dove's fiction) incorporates lyrical elements, but makes no comparison to fiction that doesn't employ lyrical language.

(E) is Outside the Scope. The views of Europeans are never mentioned; it's U.S. culture that the author says is suspicious of generalists.

4. (E) Inference ★☆☆☆

Step 2: Identify the Question Type

Any question that asks about the author's attitude toward a particular part of the passage is an Inference question.

Step 3: Research the Relevant Text

The "deep rift" between poetry and fiction in the United States is discussed mainly in the first two paragraphs and briefly at the beginning of paragraph 3.

Step 4: Make a Prediction

Fortunately, the beginning of the third paragraph tells you that the author's not a fan of the rift between poetry and fiction, and that she's glad to see it diminishing. Also, the end of paragraph 2 suggests skepticism from the author toward the idea that crossing genres dilutes a writer's competence in either genre.

Step 5: Evaluate the Answer Choices

(E) correctly characterizes the author's negative position toward the "attitudes and presuppositions underlying the rift."

(A) is unsupported. The author isn't perplexed about what caused the rift; she tells us explicitly in paragraph 2.

(B) is Extreme and Outside the Scope of the passage. *Astonishment* is too strong a word, and there's no reason to believe that the author thinks academics are unaware of the rift.

(C) suggests that the author is conflicted about her position on the rift, but there's no sign of ambivalence; the author makes her position on the division crystal clear.

(D) is unsupported. The final sentence of the passage announces that one writer, at least, bridges the gap. If the author were truly pessimistic, then the hopeful example of Rita Dove would be left out of the passage entirely.

5. (D) Detail ★☆☆☆

Step 2: Identify the Question Type

This is a Detail question because it asks about what the author conjectures, and not about what the author implies or suggests.

Step 3: Research the Relevant Text

Your Roadmap quickly tells you that the cause of the deep rift between poetry and fiction is discussed in paragraph 2.

Step 4: Make a Prediction

The third sentence in paragraph 2 says that the poetry-fiction rift is likely due to a widespread attitude in American culture that is skeptical of the generalist; in the case of literature, that would be a writer who works in and blends elements of multiple genres.

Step 5: Evaluate the Answer Choices

(D) matches this prediction perfectly.

(A) is Outside the Scope. The author never discusses how poets and fiction writers see each other's work.

(B) is a Distortion. The author does tell us that the programs for poetry and fiction are usually segregated, but she doesn't discuss teaching methods, nor does she imply that the methods are the cause of the rift. Furthermore, she does not discuss "other literary fields" beyond poetry and fiction.

(C) is also Outside the Scope. The author doesn't blame publishers and doesn't mention the pressure they may or may not exert on writers.

(E) might be a view held by someone, somewhere, but the author doesn't advance that view.

6. (B) Logic Function ★☆☆☆

Step 2: Identify the Question Type

The phrase "primary purpose" might have led you to label this a Global question, but this is a Logic Function question because it asks about the author's purpose for including a particular detail, not for writing the passage as a whole.

Step 3: Research the Relevant Text

The end of paragraph 3 is of course relevant, but in order to understand the author's purpose in mentioning a particular experience, we have to understand the purpose of the passage as a whole and of the paragraph in which the reference occurs.

Step 4: Make a Prediction

The mention of Rita Dove's experience in Germany comes on the heels of a description of her disbelief at the aversion to blending genres. The Germany reference simply builds on that, providing some background and context for her different perspective on crossing genre lines.

Step 5: Evaluate the Answer Choices

(B) is therefore correct.

(A) is a Distortion. The author does locate the rift between poetry and fiction in specific American attitudes, but the author never broadens those attitudes to all English-speaking cultures.

(C) is a Distortion. Any praise the author reserves for Dove and her work is given in the context of her blending of poetry and fiction, not of her studies abroad.

(D) might be correct if the author were writing a profile of Rita Dove. However, Dove is being used as an example in the passage, so the author gains nothing by drumming up "human interest" in Dove or her life.

(E) ignores the fourth sentence of paragraph 3, which mentions that Dove grew up reading both poetry and fiction and was unaware of any problems with mixing elements of the two. It's hard to make the case, therefore, that her experience in Germany was the origin of her position on the poetry-fiction rift.

7. (A) Inference ★★★☆

Step 2: Identify the Question Type

Two clues indicate that this is an Inference question: the word *inferred* and the phrase "author would be most likely to believe."

Step 3: Research the Relevant Text

The question stem doesn't help much in guiding your research, other than to point you to places where the author gives her point of view (that is, primarily paragraphs 2 through 4).

Step 4: Make a Prediction

When an Inference stem doesn't give you any clues to help you research the passage, don't work from memory or hunch. Use the content clues in the answer choices to guide your research. Don't stop until you find the answer choice that *must* be true based on the author's statements.

Step 5: Evaluate the Answer Choices

(A) is a valid inference. In paragraph 4, the author refers to each of the works she mentions as either poetry or fiction, even while describing how it incorporates elements of the other genre. **(A)** is therefore correct.

(B) is a Distortion. The author talks about these two effects of lyric narrative in paragraph 4, but she's focused on the value of the blend, not on a comparison of one effect to the other.

(C) is Extreme. "Without precedent" is a tip-off; such strong language is rarely warranted in an Inference question. Although the author doesn't specifically reference another writer who blends elements of the two genres, she says that Dove is merely one example of a trend.

(D) is an Irrelevant Comparison; the author doesn't set up any value comparisons among the various types of writing she discusses.

(E) seems reasonable, but doesn't have to be true. The only place the author talked about other forms like drama was in the reference to Dove's experience in Germany and its being mentioned as an example of boundary crossing.

8. (A) Inference ★☆☆☆

Step 2: Identify the Question Type

This is an Inference question because it asks you to determine how the author might continue the passage beyond the last paragraph. Use the author's stated opinion to predict how she might view the future of U.S. literature.

Step 3: Research the Relevant Text

The author's viewpoint toward the future of U.S. literature is clearest at the very beginning of paragraph 3.

Step 4: Make a Prediction

The opening sentence of paragraph 3 says that the divisions between poetry and fiction are eroding. In fact, the author uses the extended example of Rita Dove to prove that point. The correct answer will be consistent with this idea.

Step 5: Evaluate the Answer Choices

(A) is entirely consistent with the beginning of paragraph 3. If the author says that "the bias against writers who cross generic boundaries is diminishing," she must expect that the trend is likely to continue.

(B) is Outside the Scope. The market for poetry has no bearing on the author's predictions concerning whether writers will continue to cross genres.

(C) goes too far; the author doesn't talk about the relationship between narrative poetry and the fiction genre as a whole; you only know that she thinks the boundaries are coming down.

(D) is a 180. It contradicts the passage because this is precisely the trend the author says we're finally breaking free of.

(E) is Extreme and Outside the Scope; the focus throughout the passage is on the writers, not on the audiences.

Passage 2—Evolutionary Value of Music

Step 1: Read the Passage Strategically

Sample Roadmap

Passage A

Did music and human language originate separately or together? Both systems use intonation and rhythm to communicate emotions. Both can be produced vocally or with tools, and people can produce both music and language silently to themselves.

Brain imaging studies suggest that music and language are part of one large, vastly complicated, neurological system for processing sound. In fact, fewer differences than similarities exist between the neurological processing of the two. One could think of the two activities as different radio programs that can be broadcast over the same hardware. One noteworthy difference, though, is that, generally speaking, people are better at language than music. In music, anyone can listen easily enough, but most people do not perform well, and in many cultures composition is left to specialists. In language, by contrast, nearly everyone actively performs and composes.

Given their shared neurological basis, it appears that music and language evolved together as brain size increased over the course of hominid evolution. But the primacy of language over music that we can observe today suggests that language, not music, was the primary function natural selection operated on. Music, it would seem, had little adaptive value of its own, and most likely developed on the coattails of language.

¶1:
Music & lang start together? Similarities.
¶2:
Brain ev: they use same system. > sims than diffs.
Big diff: People gen. better at lang.
¶3:
Au: They prob. developed together. Lang took primacy, music followed.

Passage B

Darwin claimed that since "neither the enjoyment nor the capacity of producing musical notes are faculties of the least [practical] use to man . . . they must be ranked amongst the most mysterious with which he is endowed." I suggest that the enjoyment of and the capacity to produce musical notes are faculties of indispensable use to mothers and their infants and that it is in the emotional bonds created by the interaction of mother and child that we can discover the evolutionary origins of human music.

Even excluding lullabies, which parents sing to infants, human mothers and infants under six months of age engage in ritualized, sequential behaviors, involving vocal, facial, and bodily interactions. Using face-to-face mother-infant interactions filmed at 24 frames per second, researchers have shown that mothers and infants jointly construct mutually improvised interactions in which each partner tracks the actions of the other. Such episodes last from one-half second to three seconds and are composed of musical elements—variations in pitch, rhythm, timbre, volume, and tempo.

What evolutionary advantage would such behavior have? In the course of hominid evolution, brain size increased rapidly. Contemporaneously, the increase in bipedality caused the birth canal to narrow. This resulted in hominid infants being born ever-more prematurely, leaving them much more helpless at birth. This helplessness necessitated longer, better maternal care. Under such conditions, the emotional bonds created in the premusical mother-infant interactions we observe in *Homo sapiens* today—behavior whose neurological basis essentially constitutes the capacity to make and enjoy music—would have conferred considerable evolutionary advantage.

#1:

Darwin: music a mystery. Au: It evolved to foster mom/kid bonds.

#2:

Mom/kid ritual interactions, with mus. elements.

#3:

Advantage? Bigger brain ® earlier birth ® more care needed. Music creates > emotional bonds.

Discussion

In Comparative Reading, your work has an added element: After determining **Purpose** and **Main Idea** for each passage, you need to understand the relationship between the two passages. Most, if not all, of the questions will focus in some way on this relationship.

Passage A begins with a question that reveals the **Scope** of the passage: the question of whether music and language developed together. The paragraph structure is straightforward: The author poses the question in paragraph 1; introduces research indicating the similarities (and one difference) in paragraph 2; and concludes in paragraph 3 that music and language likely evolved together, but that language is the primary driver of natural selection. Passage A's **Purpose**: to set forth evidence that music and language likely developed in tandem. Its **Main Idea**: Given the common neurological basis for music and language, it seems likely that they developed together as brain size increased, but music developed "on the coattails of language."

Passage B starts out with a quote from Darwin, but you get a strong statement of the author's belief before the end of paragraph 1: Music has evolutionary benefits in the bonding of mothers and infants. Paragraph 2 is devoted to research on mother-infant interactions and paragraph 3 to the possible evolutionary benefits. Passage B's **Purpose**: to argue that the ability to produce music has evolutionary benefits related to emotional bonding between mother and child. Its **Main Idea**: Music is likely a bonding mechanism that has conferred evolutionary advantage.

Remember that your work isn't done—you must define the relationship between the passages before moving on. The author of passage A believes that music developed in tandem with language, but regards music as almost an unnecessary side effect of language with no evolutionary benefit. The author of passage B believes that music represents a useful ability that confers an evolutionary benefit by solidifying the mother/infant relationship. The authors thus disagree regarding the evolutionary significance and advantages of musical ability in humans.

Both passages have the same **Topic** (music), and both are concerned with the development of musical ability in humans, but the data presented differs greatly: Passage A focuses on neurological data, while passage B concerns itself primarily with observed human behavior.

9. (C) Global ★☆☆☆

Step 2: Identify the Question Type

The word *primarily* indicates that the question is asking about the passages as a whole, which is the scope of a Global question.

Step 3: Research the Relevant Text

Although the question refers to both passages, it's only asking you to use the work you've already done in Step 1, just like every other Global question in the RC section.

Step 4: Make a Prediction

You should have already determined that both passages are concerned with how and why our musical abilities evolved.

Step 5: Evaluate the Answer Choices

(C) matches this prediction.

(A) is too broad. The passages are concerned specifically with the development of music; there are presumably many advantages of larger brain size outside the scope of these passages.

(B) introduces an issue addressed only in passage B. In Comparative Reading questions concerned with both passages, many wrong answers will focus only on one of the two passages.

(D) poses a question that is answered in passage A, but not passage B. Furthermore, passage A only answers this question in the interest of answering the larger question posed in the first paragraph.

(E) can be eliminated because it's discussed only in passage A, but even there, the question isn't answered.

10. (B) Detail ★★★☆

Step 2: Identify the Question Type

This is a Detail question because it asks about what the passages mention explicitly.

Step 3: Research the Relevant Text

Anything mentioned in either passage concerning music is relevant to answering this question. That doesn't narrow your research very much, so save your research for the answer choices.

Step 4: Make a Prediction

Predicting this answer could be incredibly time-consuming because the question stem doesn't give enough content clues to focus your research. When this happens, save your research for the answer choices. Don't select an answer until you can find a reference to it in each passage, as the question stem demands.

Step 5: Evaluate the Answer Choices

(B) is correct, although it's easy to overlook. Passage A doesn't delve deeply into the emotional ramifications of music as passage B does, and it's easy to gloss right over the reference in the second sentence of Passage A.

(A) is wrong because bonding between humans is mentioned only in passage B.

(C) is wrong because only passage A discusses neurological research.

(D) is wrong because only passage B addresses the helplessness of hominid infants.

(E) is mentioned in passage A only.

11. (D) Inference ★★★★

Step 2: Identify the Question Type

Any question asking what the passages would be "most likely" to agree or disagree over is an Inference question. The passages weren't necessarily written in direct response to each other, so you'll have to infer points of agreement and disagreement.

Step 3: Research the Relevant Text

Whenever you're reading Comparative Reading passages, remember to take some time during Step 1 of the Reading Comprehension Method to predict larger points of agreement and disagreement between the passages; they're almost guaranteed to come up in the questions.

Step 4: Make a Prediction

You can't always predict the answer to Inference questions, but based on your global understanding of the passages, this one should be pretty straightforward. The authors disagree about the reason for the development of musical ability: Author A sees it as a tag-along to language which doesn't serve much purpose of its own, while author B thinks it confers an important evolutionary benefit.

Step 5: Evaluate the Answer Choices

(D) paraphrases this well.

(A) raises an issue only discussed in passage B. You have no idea what the author of passage A thinks about this.

(B) only focuses on something from passage A. Passage B doesn't tackle the neurological data, nor does it discuss the relationship between music and language.

(C) is a Distortion. Passage B says directly that brain size increased rapidly (near the beginning of its third paragraph); passage A says only that it increased. That's a difference, but not a disagreement; you don't know what author A thinks about the rate of increase. It's possible this is a point of agreement between the authors.

(E) introduces mother-infant bonding, which isn't mentioned at all in passage A.

12. (C) Inference ★★★★

Step 2: Identify the Question Type

Like the previous question, this one focuses on agreement or disagreement between the two authors, so this is also an Inference question.

Step 3: Research the Relevant Text

The content clue "musical capacity in humans" isn't terribly helpful for research because that's the scope of both passages. However, your global understanding of the passages could come in handy here.

Step 4: Make a Prediction

The area of overlap between the two passages is relatively small, so even if you can't predict the right answer, you know that it needs to deal with subject matter covered by both passages.

Step 5: Evaluate the Answer Choices

(C) is correct. Although the authors interpret the role of brain size differently, each points to a role that hominid brain development had in the evolution of musical ability; both passages do so near the beginnings of their respective third paragraphs.

(A) is an area covered only by passage B. Passage A doesn't take a position on this.

(B) also covers territory only discussed in passage B. Mothers and infants aren't mentioned at all in passage A.

(D) is not touched upon in either passage.

(E) is only touched upon in passage A, and even there, the author doesn't say *why* musical ability varies among individuals.

13. (E) Logic Reasoning (Principle) ★★★★

Step 2: Identify the Question Type

Like its analogous question type in Logical Reasoning, this question asks for a principle underlying both passages.

Step 3: Research the Relevant Text

This question stem provides no content clues to help you research, so any part of the passage could form the basis of the correct answer. The correct answer will likely come from your broader assessment of the passages.

Step 4: Make a Prediction

Because the question stem focuses on a principle underlying both passages, look for points of agreement or common methods of argument. Both passages come to conclusions about the evolutionary significance of music and the likelihood that music conferred evolutionary advantages. You might predict something like "modern traits can be explained on the basis of the evolutionary advantages they might confer."

Step 5: Evaluate the Answer Choices

(E) is the closest to that prediction and has the additional advantage of referring to modern-day humans, another overlap between the passages.

(A) would be correct if the authors cited the behavior of nonhuman animals as part of their data. That's not happening, so you have no evidence that either author believes this.

(B) is Extreme ("all human capacities"). **(B)** need not be true in order for either author to make his/her argument.

(C) is a principle underlying passage A, but not passage B, which does not allude to the concurrent development of language.

(D), like **(C)**, introduces neurological foundations of behavior. Neither passage, however, claims that discovering the neurological basis of a behavior constitutes discovery of the behavior's "essence."

14. (A) Logic Reasoning (Method of Argument) ★★★★

Step 2: Identify the Question Type

Don't be thrown by the wording in the question type. Even if you identified this as a Global question, the task is still the same: determine in general terms what each passage does in relation to the other. The *relationship* question is very common in Comparative Reading, so learning to attack it effectively will earn you points on Test Day.

Step 3: Research the Relevant Text

There's no specific place to research this answer; instead, use the relationship between the passages that you determined during Step 1 to answer this question.

Step 4: Make a Prediction

The data presented by the two authors was very different in nature; their conclusions differed as well. The key difference is their view of the evolutionary significance of musical ability; even though the answer choices are general, knowing that they fundamentally disagree on their main point should help you eliminate choices.

Step 5: Evaluate the Answer Choices

(A) sums up the passages' relationship neatly and is therefore correct.

(B) is a Distortion. Not only does passage A actually answer the question it poses, but passage B also sets out to answer a slightly different question—the question of whether music has evolutionary benefit.

(C) is nearly a 180. Passage B doesn't support passage A—it reaches an entirely different conclusion.

(D) is unsupported. Both authors are clear and consistent in the presentation of their cases; if anything, passage B is more strongly worded because passage A uses tentative language like "it would seem" (paragraph 3).

(E) is a 180 because the passages' conclusions differ.

Passage 3—Copyright Law and the World Wide Web

Step 1: Read the Passage Strategically

Sample Roadmap

The World Wide Web, a network of electronically produced and interconnected (or "linked") sites, called pages, that are accessible via personal computer, raises legal issues about the rights of owners of intellectual property, notably those who create documents for inclusion on Web pages. Some of these owners of intellectual property claim that unless copyright law is strengthened, intellectual property on the Web will not be protected from copyright infringement. Web users, however, claim that if their ability to access information on Web pages is reduced, the Web cannot live up to its potential as an open, interactive medium of communication.

The debate arises from the Web's ability to link one document to another. Links between sites are analogous to the inclusion in a printed text of references to other works, but with one difference: the cited document is instantly retrievable by a user who activates the link. This immediate accessibility creates a problem, since current copyright laws give owners of intellectual property the right to sue a distributor of unauthorized copies of their material even if that distributor did not personally make the copies. If person A, the author of a document, puts the document on a Web page, and person B, the creator of another Web page, creates a link to A's document, is B committing copyright infringement?

To answer this question, it must first be determined who controls distribution of a document on the Web. When A places a document on a Web page, this is comparable to recording an outgoing message on one's telephone answering machine for others to hear. When B creates a link to A's document, this is akin to B's giving out A's telephone number, thereby allowing third parties to hear the outgoing message for themselves. Anyone who calls can listen to the message; that is its purpose. While B's link may indeed facilitate access to A's document, the crucial point is that A, simply by placing that document on the Web, is thereby offering it for distribution. Therefore, even if B leads others to the document, it is A who actually controls access to it. Hence creating a link to a document is not the same as making or distributing a copy of that document. Moreover, techniques are already available by which A can restrict access to a document. For example, A may require a password to gain entry to A's Web page, just as a telephone owner can request an unlisted number and disclose it only to selected parties. Such a solution would compromise the openness of the Web somewhat, but not as much as the threat of copyright infringement litigation. Changing copyright law to benefit owners of intellectual property is thus ill-advised because it would impede the development of the Web as a public forum dedicated to the free exchange of ideas.

#1:

IP issues for doc. creators b/c of www. IP owners: "Tighten © laws." www users: "No! Web must stay free."

#2:

Problem: linking ability betw. docs. Immed. access complicates ©. Infringes?

#3:

Big Q: Who owns www distrib? Analogy to outgoing phone msg. Owners = distributors but linking ≠ distrib. Ex: PW. Au: Owner restrictions better than tougher laws.

Discussion

Beware of familiar topics! Intellectual property on the Web, the **Topic** of this Law passage, is a well-known topic and nearly everyone has an opinion; remember to stay focused on what's presented in the passage, not your own opinions.

Paragraph 1 sets forth the conflict. Some owners of intellectual property rights feel stronger protection is required, but Web users fear this will limit the potential of the Web. The paragraph ends with a strong sense of the **Scope** (the conflict over strengthening copyright law). The author's Purpose doesn't emerge right away, but you can guess that she'll probably take a side.

Paragraph 2 explains the root of the issue: Web page links, and the problems created by the instant accessibility these links afford. The author also poses what she sees as the underlying question in the debate over increased protection—does linking to someone else's Web page constitute copyright infringement?

Paragraph 3 provides an analysis, by analogy, that demonstrates the author's view. According to the author, linking to a Web page is not copyright infringement. This statement reveals the author's **Purpose**: to analyze the need for increased copyright protection and advise against it. The **Main Idea** is therefore that changing copyright law to further protect owners would impede development of the Web and is thus ill-advised.

15. (A) Global ★★★★

Step 2: Identify the Question Type

This is a Global question because it asks you for the "main point" of the passage.

Step 3: Research the Relevant Text

The entire passage is relevant in a Global question. Instead of rereading a specific part, base your prediction on the Main Idea you determined during Step 1.

Step 4: Make a Prediction

From Step 1, you can see that the passage sets up a critical question in the debate over the need for increased copyright protection: are an owner's rights infringed by someone linking to his Web page? The author's answer is that those rights are not infringed, and that thus there is no reason to increase protection.

Step 5: Evaluate the Answer Choices

(A) is a match for this idea.

(B) goes further than the passage does by distorting the passage's final sentence—the author never provides a condition that, if satisfied, would make changes to copyright law anything but ill-advised. Furthermore, the introduction of the term *democracy* is Outside the Scope.

(C) both overemphasizes and misrepresents a detail from late in paragraph 3. The author only mentions the ability to restrict access to Web documents as an alternative to strengthening copyright law. Furthermore, the author says that if an owner did restrict access, the openness of the Web would be compromised.

(D) is too broad. The passage isn't about resolution of problems concerning intellectual property rights in the electronic age generally. Rather, the passage concerns only one such problem. Also, the author never points to basic commonsense principles as a cure-all.

(E) has its focus in the wrong place. The author does argue against changing the law, but not because such changes would benefit only a small number of individuals. You don't know from the passage how many people create Web documents.

16. (A) Inference ★☆☆☆

Step 2: Identify the Question Type

This is an Inference question because it asks for the meaning of a word as it's used in the passage. The author doesn't state the word's meaning directly, so you'll need to infer its meaning from context.

Step 3: Research the Relevant Text

You'll need to read around the highlighted term to predict what the author means by *strengthened.*

Step 4: Make a Prediction

The relevant sentence lays out the position that unless copyright law is *strengthened*, some owners of content will not be protected. The immediate counterpoint is that Web users don't want their access reduced. Therefore, *strengthened* means "made to create additional limitations on access."

Step 5: Evaluate the Answer Choices

(A) is a match.

(B) is Outside the Scope. The passage doesn't discuss the geographic uniformity of copyright laws.

(C) is also Outside the Scope. The passage doesn't discuss penalties for violating copyright laws.

(D) concerns enforcement of laws, which is Outside the Scope.

(E) touches on the legitimacy of current intellectual property law, but the passage focuses on the desire for *additional* restrictions in the law and the arguments against such restrictions.

17. (E) Inference ★★★★

Step 2: Identify the Question Type

Any question that asks what the author would be "most likely to agree with" is an Inference question.

Step 3: Research the Relevant Text

Documents placed on Web pages are discussed briefly in paragraphs 1 and 2, but the author discusses them primarily in paragraph 3.

Step 4: Make a Prediction

The author says a few things in paragraph 3 about documents placed on the Web: They're still controlled by their owners; linking to them isn't copyright infringement; and restrictions on access to those documents "would compromise the openness of the Web," as would copyright infringement litigation. Even if you can't predict the correct answer, you know that it will be a statement that *must* be true based on these claims made by the author.

Step 5: Evaluate the Answer Choices

(E) is correct because it must be true based on the author's statements in the passage's penultimate and final sentences.

(A) is a 180. The passage's final sentence explicitly states that copyright laws should not be strengthened. Furthermore, the author offers passwords as a possible safeguard for authors who want to better protect their documents.

(B) is a subtle Distortion: The passage says that password protection would compromise the openness of the Web *somewhat*, not that it would *significantly* threaten to reduce the number of people using the Web for communication.

(C) is Extreme. The author has provided a suggested means of limiting access (a required password), so she wouldn't agree that limiting access is impossible.

(D) contradicts the author's view. The last sentence of the passage clearly indicates that the author considers changes to copyright law potentially harmful to public interest.

18. (C) Logic Reasoning (Parallel Reasoning) ★★★★

Step 2: Identify the Question Type

This resembles a Parallel Reasoning question from the Logical Reasoning section because it asks you to find the answer choice providing a relationship "most analogous to" one put forth in the passage.

Step 3: Research the Relevant Text

"Relying on passwords to restrict access to a Web document" is a content clue leading you to the second half of paragraph 3.

Step 4: Make a Prediction

The author sees tightening the laws as far more damaging to the potential of the Web than password protection is; password protection restricts access and creates some limitations on free exchange and development, but it's better than changing the law and creating even greater limitations. The correct answer will deal with the relationship between a legal solution and a non-legal, self-help solution to unrestricted access.

Step 5: Evaluate the Answer Choices

(C) is analogous to the passage and therefore correct. Prohibiting a sport is a restrictive legal remedy, and relying on participants to play safely is a self-help remedy that allows greater access while protecting those playing the game.

(A) only addresses the password issue (the self-help remedy), not the relationship to strengthening current copyright laws (the legal remedy). Allowing everyone use of a facility would have the opposite effect of tightening restrictions in copyright law.

(B) might be tempting at first because it describes two different plans of attack on restricting the same activity, but both courses of action offered by **(B)** are laws. In the passage's scenario, it's tougher laws versus protections created by the owners themselves.

(D) involves legislation and enforcement of a law, but offers nothing analogous to the self-devised passwords from the passage.

(E) is like **(A)** in that it only offers an analogue to the Web passwords. Allowing unrestricted access to a building is analogous to repealing copyright laws, not strengthening them.

19. (B) Inference ★★☆☆

Step 2: Identify the Question Type

This is an Inference question because it asks you to determine what the passage *implies*.

Step 3: Research the Relevant Text

This question stem doesn't have any content clues to guide your research. Therefore, be prepared to save your research for Step 5 as you evaluate the answer choices.

Step 4: Make a Prediction

The passage implies plenty of things, so prediction might be tough here. However, keep in mind that a valid inference is a statement that *must* be true based on the passage. Make sure you can find direct textual support for an answer choice before you select it.

Step 5: Evaluate the Answer Choices

(B) is a valid inference and therefore correct. Copyright infringement is unlawful distribution, and the author's analogy in paragraph 3 establishes that linking is not copyright infringement, presumably because control over a document's distribution remains in the hands of its owner.

(A) is unsupported. "Creators of links to Web pages" and "owners of intellectual property" are discussed as two different groups in paragraph 3, but the passage gives no reason why there couldn't be people who are members of both groups.

(C) is Outside the Scope of the passage. Privacy rights aren't mentioned at all; this passage is about copyright infringement.

(D) is a 180. It contradicts the author's view, illustrated by the analogy in paragraph 3. The author believes that control rests in the hands of the documents' creators, not those who link to the pages containing those documents.

(E) is Outside the Scope; no evidence is given that the format of the document in question affects the issue of who controls the rights to distribute it.

20. (E) Detail ★☆☆☆

Step 2: Identify the Question Type

The phrase "according to the passage" indicates a Detail question.

Step 3: Research the Relevant Text

This question stem offers a clear content clue ("features of outgoing messages left on telephone answering machines") leading you to the second sentence in paragraph 3.

Step 4: Make a Prediction

The question asks for the feature of outgoing phone messages that makes them relevant to the copyright debate. The phrase "this is akin to" points to that feature. The person who possesses the telephone number leaves the outgoing message available to anyone who calls the number, just as the owner of a document leaves that document available to anyone who visits the Web page.

Step 5: Evaluate the Answer Choices

(E) matches this prediction.

(A) is merely coincidental. That both telephones and Web pages are electronic means of communication doesn't figure into the author's argument.

(B) is unsupported. Not only does the author not address legal protections for phone messages, but she also states that no unauthorized distribution takes place.

(C)'s reference to instantaneous distribution is in the discussion of Web pages in paragraph 2. It's not related to the phone message analogy.

(D) is Outside the Scope. Recording isn't at issue; the issue that makes outgoing phone messages relevant to Web copyright issues is access and distribution.

21. (D) Logic Function ★★☆☆

Step 2: Identify the Question Type

The phrase "serves primarily to" indicates a Logic Function question. The correct answer won't detail what the author says about telephone answering machines, but why the author included them in the passage in the first place.

Step 3: Research the Relevant Text

The author discusses telephone answering machines near the beginning of paragraph 3.

Step 4: Make a Prediction

The second sentence of paragraph 3 contains the phrase "this is comparable to" before launching into the answering machine discussion. This means that answering machines are being used as an analogy. The author offers the telephone analogy to illustrate the point that no unauthorized distribution occurs when one provides a link to an existing Web page.

Step 5: Evaluate the Answer Choices

(D) is a match, even though it is phrased in more general terms.

(A) is a Distortion. Remember the context; the whole passage is about whether increased copyright protections are required for Web pages. Telephones are relevant only as an analogy.

(B) is wrong because the answering machine analogy is offered in support of the author's position, not the other side.

(C) misstates the author's purpose. He does not use the telephone analogy to demonstrate that similar copyright issues predate the Internet.

(E) also misstates the author's purpose. He doesn't use the analogy to prove a point about copyright as it relates to telephone usage, but rather to illustrate his point about copyright on websites.

22. (D) Detail ★★★★

Step 2: Identify the Question Type

The words "according to the passage" indicate that this is a Detail question.

Step 3: Research the Relevant Text

"Present copyright laws" is a content clue that means the same as "current copyright laws," which are mentioned in the passage's second paragraph.

Step 4: Make a Prediction

The passage gives you only one piece of direct information: Copyright holders can sue for unauthorized distribution.

Step 5: Evaluate the Answer Choices

(D) correctly paraphrases this idea.

(A) is a Distortion. There are some new issues with content on the Web, but according to the passage, current law clearly prohibits unauthorized distribution.

(B) contradicts the author's view that the owner or publisher of a document controls access to it.

(C) is Outside the Scope. It is a trap for those prone to bringing in outside knowledge; the profit issue is batted around a lot in the debate over copyright issues, but it's not mentioned in this passage.

(E) is a 180. The author advocates leaving copyright law as it is, not loosening (or tightening) its restrictions further.

Passage 4—Pollen Analysis and the Irish Landscape

Step 1: Read the Passage Strategically

Sample Roadmap

In tracing the changing face of the Irish landscape, scholars have traditionally relied primarily on evidence from historical documents. However, such documentary sources provide a fragmentary record at best. Reliable accounts are very scarce for many parts of Ireland prior to the seventeenth century, and many of the relevant documents from the sixteenth and seventeenth centuries focus selectively on matters relating to military or commercial interests.

Studies of fossilized pollen grains preserved in peats and lake muds provide an additional means of investigating vegetative landscape change. Details of changes in vegetation resulting from both human activities and natural events are reflected in the kinds and quantities of minute pollen grains that become trapped in sediments. Analysis of samples can identify which kinds of plants produced the preserved pollen grains and when they were deposited, and in many cases the findings can serve to supplement or correct the documentary record.

For example, analyses of samples from Long Lough in County Down have revealed significant patterns of cereal-grain pollen beginning by about 400 A.D. The substantial clay content of the soil in this part of Down makes cultivation by primitive tools difficult. Historians thought that such soils were not tilled to any significant extent until the introduction of the moldboard plough to Ireland in the seventh century A.D. Because cereal cultivation would have required tilling of the soil, the pollen evidence indicates that these soils must indeed have been successfully tilled before the introduction of the new plough.

Another example concerns flax cultivation in County Down, one of the great linen-producing areas of Ireland during the eighteenth century. Some aspects of linen production in Down are well documented, but the documentary record tells little about the cultivation of flax, the plant from which linen is made, in that area. The record of eighteenth-century linen production in Down, together with the knowledge that flax cultivation had been established in Ireland centuries before that time, led some historians to surmise that this plant was being cultivated in Down before the eighteenth century. But pollen analyses indicate that this is not the case; flax pollen was found only in deposits laid down since the eighteenth century.

It must be stressed, though, that there are limits to the ability of the pollen record to reflect the vegetative history of the landscape. For example, pollen analyses cannot identify the species, but only the genus or family, of some plants. Among these is madder, a cultivated dye plant of historical importance in Ireland. Madder belongs to a plant family that also comprises various native weeds, including goosegrass. If madder pollen were present in a deposit it would be indistinguishable from that of uncultivated native species.

¶1:
Irish landscp traced thru hist docs, but frag. + unreliable.

¶2:
Pollen fossils an addl way to track. What pollen grains can show.

¶3:
Ex. cereal pollen in Co. Down. Hist. says soil not tilled before 600s. Pollen says it was.

¶4:
Ex. flax pollen in Co. Down. Records scarce. Hist. says flax grown pre 1700s. Pollen says not.

¶5:
Limits on what pollen can reveal, ex. madder, which pollen can't tell from other species.

Discussion

Paragraph 1 of this Natural Science passage introduces limitations on the traditional study of Ireland's landscape: accounts of the landscape are scarce, and where they do exist, they are incomplete. That provides our **Topic** (the historical Irish landscape), but Scope and Purpose are still wide open.

Paragraph 2 introduces a supplemental source of information that will eventually become the **Scope** of the passage: studies of fossilized pollen grains, and what they can tell us about changes in the landscape. The paragraph outlines the information pollen grains can provide about the vegetative history of a region, and then relates that information to the historical record. The author seems to value the pollen evidence for its ability to "supplement or correct" the historical record.

Paragraphs 3 and 4 provide examples of how pollen grain information has changed beliefs about some aspects of historical land development. Don't worry too much about the details of these paragraphs—you can come back to them if a question asks you to.

Finally, paragraph 5 notes that pollen analysis isn't without its own limitations and gives an example. It's not until the end that we can be sure of the author's **Purpose**, which is largely informative: to explain the impact of a new information source on our understanding of the evolution of the Irish landscape. The **Main Idea** reflects this: The author believes that studies of fossilized pollen can be useful for supplementing or correcting the historical record when studying changes in Ireland's landscape.

23. (A) Global ★★★☆

Step 2: Identify the Question Type

Any question asking for the "main point" of the passage is a Global question.

Step 3: Research the Relevant Text

The entire passage is relevant in a Global question. Use your knowledge of the passage's big picture (Topic, Scope, Purpose, Main Idea) to predict your answer.

Step 4: Make a Prediction

As you know from Step 1, the Main Idea of the passage is that fossilized pollen records can sometimes help make more accurate determinations than can the historical record when it comes to the development of the Irish landscape.

Step 5: Evaluate the Answer Choices

(A) is a match for this prediction.

(B) is a Distortion. The analysis of historical documents is what led historians to their mistaken hypotheses in the first place.

(C) incorrectly shifts the passage's focus from the historical development of Ireland's landscape to the identification of plant species. Furthermore, paragraph 5 tells you that pollen analysis can't identify the species of some plants.

(D) misuses some of the passage's details. The idea that cultivation of cereal, flax, and madder had a significant impact on the Irish landscape was never in question.

(E)'s phrase "severely limited" is Extreme, and its tone is all wrong. The author presents the pollen analysis as a valuable additional tool, even though it has some limitations.

24. (B) Detail ★★★☆

Step 2: Identify the Question Type

The phrase "the passage indicates" signals a Detail question.

Step 3: Research the Relevant Text

The words "provided evidence against which one of the following views" is a content clue. Research wherever the author has described a claim that was challenged by any of the pollen evidence. Your Roadmap tells you that paragraphs 3 and 4 contain sentences that describe those claims.

Step 4: Make a Prediction

Pollen evidence from paragraph 3 refutes the view that soils weren't successfully tilled and cereals cultivated in County Down before the seventh century (paragraph 3), and the pollen evidence in paragraph 4 refutes the view that flax was cultivated in Down before the eighteenth century (paragraph 4).

Step 5: Evaluate the Answer Choices

(B) is a match for the historians' view from paragraph 3.

(A) is a Distortion. The moldboard plough is referenced in paragraph 3, but isn't part of what the pollen evidence contradicted.

(C) is also a Distortion. The evidence presented relates to the period predating the plough, not after. Also, no one in the passage espouses the view that cereal cultivation continued unabated since the moldboard plough was introduced.

(D) is mentioned in paragraph 3, but it's mentioned not as a view of the historians, but as a pure fact.

(E) is a tempting 180, because this is the information provided *by* the pollen fossils, but that's not what you were asked for. You were asked for the view the pollen fossil evidence argued *against*, not what it argued *for*.

25. (D) Inference ★★★★

Step 2: Identify the Question Type

This is an Inference question because it asks you to infer the meaning of a word or phrase as it's used by the author in context.

Step 3: Research the Relevant Text

Questions with highlighted text often require context. Don't limit yourself to just the highlighted term or phrase, but delve into the rest of the passage as needed. There are two references to the "documentary record" cited in the question stem, but they both refer back to an earlier part of the passage: the "fragmentary record" provided by "documentary sources" introduced in the first paragraph.

Step 4: Make a Prediction

The historical record referred to by the author is the record that the fossilized pollen data is supplementing and, in some cases, correcting; it's the history that was recorded at the time, much of it military and commercial, according to the author in paragraph 1.

Step 5: Evaluate the Answer Choices

(D) is a perfect match.

(A) mentions pollen, which isn't part of the documentary record. The author discusses pollen because the documentary record is incomplete.

(B) also refers to the pollen evidence, but such evidence isn't part of the documentary record. Rather, it supplements and/or corrects the documentary record according to the end of paragraph 2.

(C) fails when it brings up "current historians." The documentary record was created during the relevant time period, not reconstructed later.

(E) again mentions "current historians"; the documentary record consists of documents from the actual time. These documents are studied by current historians, not created by them.

26. (E) Detail ★★★★

Step 2: Identify the Question Type

The question stem begins with the phrase "the passage indicates"; this categorical wording indicates a Detail question.

Step 3: Research the Relevant Text

This question focuses on the beliefs of some historians. Look for where you identified these historians' views in your Roadmap. The third and fourth paragraphs will provide the basis for your prediction.

Step 4: Make a Prediction

Paragraph 3 says that historians believed that soils in County Down weren't tilled until the seventh century A.D., when the moldboard plough was introduced to Ireland. Paragraph 4 says that historians believed that flax was being cultivated in County Down before the eighteenth century.

Step 5: Evaluate the Answer Choices

(E) perfectly paraphrases the historians' belief about flax cultivation.

(A) is Outside the Scope. Flooding isn't mentioned anywhere in the passage. Also, the seventeenth century is mentioned only in connection with recordkeeping, in the first paragraph.

(B) is too broad. The historians believed cereal wasn't cultivated in one part of Ireland before the seventh century because the soil in this location was hard to till.

(C) is directly contradicted by the end of paragraph 1, which says that sixteenth- and seventeenth-century records of the Irish landscape focus "selectively on matters relating to military or commercial interests."

(D) misuses the details concerning madder. Madder is mentioned, but in the context of the limitations of the pollen evidence; there's nothing in the passage concerning views about when it was first used as a dye plant.

27. (C) Logic Reasoning (Method of Argument) ★★★★

Step 2: Identify the Question Type

Like questions that concern the relationship between the passages in Comparative Reading, this question asks about the relationship between two paragraphs. That makes this a Method of Argument question.

Step 3: Research the Relevant Text

Use your Roadmap to determine the purpose of the second paragraph and the final paragraph, and then predict how those relate to each other.

Step 4: Make a Prediction

The final paragraph, which talks about the limitations of pollen fossil data, is intended to qualify the second paragraph, which introduces pollen fossil data as a valuable new addition to the analysis of the development of the Irish landscape.

Step 5: Evaluate the Answer Choices

(C) is a match.

(A) is a Distortion. The final paragraph doesn't support the idea set forth in paragraph 2, but explains its limitations.

(B) might be tempting because it uses the word *problem*, but the problem in the final paragraph isn't going to be solved; it's simply a limitation on the information that's available through this method.

(D) is a 180. The author never argues against the view that the pollen fossil is a valuable addition to the record. In fact, the whole passage is set up to argue for that view.

(E) is Outside the Scope. The final paragraph doesn't offer any procedures, just some limitations.

Reading Comprehension Passage Acknowledgments

Acknowledgment is made to the following sources from which material has been adapted for use in this book:

Valerie A. Hall, "The Development of the Landscape of Ireland over the Last Two Thousand Years: Fresh Evidence from Historical and Pollen Analytical Studies." ©1997 by Chronicon, UCC.

Francis Haskell, "Art & the Apocalypse." ©1993 by NYREV, Inc.

Leandra Lederman, "'Stranger than Fiction': Taxing Virtual Worlds." ©2007 by New York University Law Review.

Timothy Miller, *How to Want What You Have*. ©1995 by Timothy Miller.

Carol Muske, "Breaking Out of the Genre Ghetto." ©1995 by Poetry in Review Foundation.

Clive Thompson, "Game Theories." ©2004 by The Walrus Magazine.

Peter Whiteley, "Hopuutungwni: 'Hopi Names' as Literature." ©1992 by the Smithsonian Institution.

CHANNEL SPOTLIGHT

Reading Comprehension—Managing the Section

By The LSAT Channel Faculty

Watch the video lesson for this Spotlight in your online Study Plan.

When it comes to time management and efficiency on the LSAT, the stakes may be highest in the Reading Comprehension section. The reason is simple: Typically, there are more questions in this section than there are in any other section of the test. Since the LSAT administered in June 2007, there have been 27 questions in the Reading Comprehension section of every officially released LSAT test. Compare that to just 24-26 questions in each Logical Reasoning section. Of course, the Reading Comprehension section is still just 35 minutes long. With more questions to answer in the same amount of time, you may feel even more pressure to speed up and more stress about running out of time. For an LSAT expert, however, the 27 questions in the Reading Comprehension section signal a greater opportunity, and thus, a bigger advantage for a test taker with sharply honed section-management skills.

Of course, the layout of the Reading Comprehension section is quite different than that found in Logical Reasoning sections. This has advantages and disadvantages. In place of the 25 or so discrete questions, you have four passages, on which you should average about 8 ½ minutes per passage. Moreover, as you will see, the location and distribution of the hardest is also quite different between the Reading Comprehension and Logical Reasoning sections. In the video that accompanies this Spotlight, you'll get an in-depth analysis of the section that will help you apply the section-management strategies and tactics LSAT experts use to maximize their scores. Here's some of what you'll see.

Triage in Reading Comprehension

Analysis of students' performance on recently released LSATs shows that the most common order of difficulty for the passages in those tests' Reading Comprehension sections is 1-2-4-3 (arranged from easiest to hardest). That order was slightly more common than 1-2-3-4. If you default to doing the passages in one of those two orders, chances are you're tackling the section strategically. The strongest indicator that a passage will be easier to comprehend is clear organization. This will often be signaled by Keywords. If a passage begins with "Some believe . . . however . . ." and has supporting paragraphs with "for example" or "this is illustrated by," you will be able to put your finger on the author's Main Idea directly. Any time that a passage's first paragraph contains a definitive topic sentence or thesis, and you can see that the body is made up of shorter, focused paragraphs, the passage will likely be easy to Roadmap, whatever its topic.

Personal preference, however, does have a role to play in your Reading Comprehension triage decisions.

After all, Reading Comprehension passages deal with real-world subject matter, and while the test neither requires nor rewards outside knowledge, certain topics and vocabulary may just be more (or less) comfortable for you. It's fine to make that part of your triage calculus, but be decisive and confident in your decision to deprioritize a passage. If you read the first 15–20 lines of a passage on a complicated science or law topic and you feel like your head is swimming, move on to the next passage. After you've completed that one, come back to the passage that was initially intimidating. You'll often find that you are more prepared to read the first passage strategically at that point.

Strategic Skipping and Guessing in Reading Comprehension

This is the aspect of section management in which Reading Comprehension shows the greatest divergence from Logical Reasoning. In Logical Reasoning, the section's hardest questions tend to cluster in the "Danger Zone." In Reading Comprehension, the most difficult questions are more spread around, and passages tend to have a broad mix of easy and hard questions. That means that you need to prepare yourself to skip and guess at different points along the way in the Reading Comprehension section. Open-ended Inference questions with no research clues or a complicated Detail EXCEPT questions are likely to be time-consuming, even in passages that were relatively easy to read and Roadmap. If temporarily skipping one or two of the section's hardest questions preserves the time you need to handle an additional passage (and the six or seven questions associated with it), that will almost certainly be worth your while.

There is another upside to the question distribution in Reading Comprehension. The corollary to finding difficult questions associated with the easier passages is that you're also more likely to find easy questions associated with the complex and dense ones. Practice managing your time with the goal of getting to every passage, thus giving yourself the opportunity to answer all of the section's easier questions. Just as with the other sections of the LSAT, guess on questions when it is in *your interest* to do so.

Practicing Reading Comprehension Section Management and Assessing Your Skills

After you watch this Spotlight's video lesson, you'll want to practice the section-management skills and strategies you've learned. If you are using LSAC PrepTests as part of your preparation, set aside at least two or three tests to use for "timing" practice. You need not do the entire test in one sitting, but you will need to clear 35 minutes from your schedule for uninterrupted timed section practice. As you work on improving your section management, keep the lessons from this Spotlight in mind, and use the techniques and exercises suggested by the LSAT Channel expert. Timing practice is the ideal mode for improving both your overall efficiency and your mastery of the question types within the section. Review your section performance thoroughly, studying the questions you got right as well as those you got wrong. Using Kaplan's complete explanations will help you spot areas in which you need additional mastery practice, questions on which you could have worked more quickly or confidently, and places in which you simply made preventable mistakes. Remember that complete explanations for every LSAT PrepTest in LSAC's LawHub library are available via Kaplan's LSAT Link too. See **www.kaptest.com/lsat/courses/lsat-self-study** for more information.

PART FOUR

LSAT Argumentative Writing

CHANNEL SPOTLIGHT

How Law Schools Use Your LSAT Argumentative Writing Essay

By The LSAT Channel Faculty

Watch the video lesson for this Spotlight in your online Study Plan.

Do Law Schools Actually Read the Argumentative Writing Response?

Yes, of course they do.

Actually, "My goodness, yes, of course," was the response of a law school admissions director from a prestigious East Coast institution. She seemed surprised one would even ask whether LSAC and its members would go to all the trouble and expense of creating, writing, administering, and distributing a writing exercise in which none of them was interested. In fact, in 2024, LSAC revamped the LSAT Writing section, specifically in response to requests from law school admissions officers. The LSAT Argumentative Writing task, launched in 2024, is precisely tailored to what law school admissions officers said they wanted to see to assess applicants' readiness for law school.

But there may still be cynics, so let's start by addressing them first. **Yes, they read it**, and they take it seriously.

Now, not everyone reads it with the same interest, at the same point in the application review process, or with the same purpose in mind. But saying that some law schools give your LSAT Argumentative Writing response a quicker look, while others invest it with greater importance, is very different from the cavalier assumption that LSAT Writing is superfluous and deserves no attention.

What Are Law Schools Looking to Gauge, and Why?

This Spotlight and the accompanying video will tell you exactly what law schools are looking for, why the LSAT Argumentative Writing task serves their purposes, and how to approach the exercise as practically and systematically as the rest of this book has persuaded you to approach the primary, multiple-choice LSAT.

As admissions officers evaluate your LSAT Argumentative Writing response, they are trying to pinpoint one or more of the following, and some are looking for all three. If you hit all the bases, you'll have nothing to fear. They want to assess:

Your relationship with the English language. The easier and more fluent your writing under tightly-timed, reference-book-free circumstances, the more likely it is that the predominant mode of your law school training won't be a strain for you.

Your affinity for argument. Because most applicants haven't engaged in formal debate, law schools like to see that you have a sense of how to create a persuasively phrased conclusion, you know how to support it with appropriate evidence, and you are able to explain the connections between the two.

The degree of help you received on your Personal Statement. Seeing your LSAT Argumentative Writing response side by side with your Personal Statement gives admissions officers a clue as to how much (or how little) of the personal statement is in your own voice.

CHAPTER 9

LSAT Argumentative Writing

How is LSAT Argumentative Writing Administered?

In August of 2024, at the same time that the LSAC began administering the LSAT with two scored Logical Reasoning sections and one scored Reading Comprehension section—and retired the once-feared Logic Games section—it also debuted LSAT Argumentative Writing. Like previous versions of the LSAT Writing section, LSAT Argumentative Writing is completed by students on their own computers, using browser-based proctoring software, and is launched from their LSAC accounts. Upon registration for LSAC's LawHub Advantage, you will receive access to practice prompts for the LSAT Argumentative Writing task as well. Since you will take your actual Argumentative Writing section using the LawHub interface, this is a great way to practice!

Your official LSAT Argumentative Writing section goes live eight days prior to the day of your official exam and can be completed up to one year from your official test date. Don't wait too long, though, because all applicants are required to have an Argumentative Writing essay on file before their LSAT multiple-choice score is sent to either the applicant or the applicant's selected law schools.

You can get all of the details about how the LSAT Argumentative Writing essay is administered at **www.lsac.org/lsat/frequently-asked-questions-about-lsat/frequently-asked-questions-about-lsat-writing**. You will need a computer or laptop running Windows or Mac OS, for which you have administrator rights, with a webcam, a microphone, only one connected monitor, and an internet connection. You will also need a valid international passport or a government-issued photo ID from the United States of America, Canada, or U.S. Territories. The FAQs on the LSAC page cover these technical and ID requirements, accommodated testing questions, and other issues.

The proctoring software monitors your screen as you enter text. It also records the feed from your webcam and microphone to ensure that you are working unassisted as you complete the LSAT Argumentative Writing section.

How is the Exercise Structured?

The structure of LSAT Argumentative Writing is always the same. You will be introduced to a **Debatable Issue** and given background information about that issue. You will then be presented with a **Key Question** about that issue. The Key Question will always be one that can be answered in a variety of ways: that is, there will be a wide range of potential answers to the Key Question.

You will then be presented with four **Perspectives** on the Key Question. Each Perspective will be identified as coming from a person or source who is interested in the Key Question. Each Perspective will make a claim about how the Key Question should be answered, and will often provide supporting information, details, or discussion. The four Perspectives, taken together, reveal that there are differing ideologies, beliefs and values concerning the Key Question.

Your job is to carve out your own position on the Key Question, and to argue in support of that position using information from at least one of the Perspectives. You are expected to discuss the complexities of the Debatable Issue and encouraged to address at least one potential counterargument.

What is My Role or Persona in All of This?

To put it simply: You are you! The Argumentative Writing task encourages students to write as themselves, and to express their own opinions on the Key Question. In fact, the instructions for the LSAT Argumentative Writing specifically instruct you to "incorporate any knowledge or experiences you might have regarding this issue, your own values, and your critical evaluation of the arguments and ideas contained in the other perspectives." You should not feel pressure to write as if you were already an attorney: use your own unique perspective and voice in your response.

LSAT ARGUMENTATIVE WRITING STRATEGY

Because the Key Question is by design a question that can be answered in a wide variety of ways by people with different backgrounds and values, be careful not to present your position as the only valid response. While you should absolutely argue that your position is the correct answer to the Key Question, you should not disparage those who might reach a different conclusion or write as though no other position is possible.

The Test Begins: The Prewriting Analysis Period

First things first: Make sure that you treat the brainstorming and planning portion of your exam as an important part of the process. The LSAC considers this portion of the exam so important that students are given a 15-minute "prewriting analysis period" prior to their 35 minutes of writing time.

When you launch your LSAT Argumentative Writing exam, you will first be given the opportunity to read a set of directions. These never change, so no need to invest time here if you have prepared! Once you click to advance past these directions, your 15-minute "prewriting analysis period" begins. You will have access to the Debatable Issue, Key Question, Perspectives, and additional directions. Again, these directions never change, so there is no need to invest time there—focus entirely on the issue and perspectives.

During your prewriting time, you can digitally highlight and underline in the Debatable Issue, Key Question, and Perspectives. You will also have access to a digital "scratch paper" section, as physical scratch paper is not permitted. All markups you make, and everything entered on your digital scratch paper, will be available during both your prewriting and writing time. A few important notes, however:

- During your writing time, your digital scratch paper will be condensed into a smaller area. Although you will be able to scroll through everything you have entered, only a small portion of your digital scratch paper will be visible at once.
- During your writing time, you will not be able to copy and paste from your digital scratch paper to your main written response.

You must remain on the prewriting analysis screen for at least 5 minutes, and may remain there for up to 15 minutes, after which your writing time will begin automatically. However, you should plan to remain in prewriting mode for the full 15 minutes and use every second of that available planning time. As you will see shortly, there's lots to do!

Approaching the Issue: Reading, Brainstorming, and Planning

Once your prewriting time begins, you will want to divide up your time into roughly three five-minute phases: Reading, Brainstorming, and Planning. During these three phases, you will mark up the Debatable Issue, Key Question, and Perspectives, and make notes on your digital scratch paper.

Prewriting: Reading

First, you will want to read through the Debatable Issue and Key Question. Read to see what sparks your interest. What comes to mind as you read the Debatable Issue? What emotional response do you have to the Key Question? Use the digital highlighting and underlining tools liberally to mark the portions that speak to you as you read. Try it by poring over this Debatable Issue and Key Question available on LawHub:

PURPOSE OF COLLEGE

The principal aim of an undergraduate liberal arts education has traditionally been to cultivate a student's understanding of a broad range of important areas of knowledge, from the fine arts to the sciences, philosophy, language, economics—these things have been seen as crucial to understanding, and participating in, the larger world beyond the classroom. Some, however, believe that this kind of education has failed to provide students with the practical skills necessary to succeed in an increasingly competitive and career-focused society, suggesting we need to reconsider what university programs should look like. Such proposals are often framed as a pragmatic response to trends in the economy and predictions about the skills, knowledge, and training that will best serve students' career readiness. Given this proposed shift in emphasis toward skills-based education, it's worth considering what the overall goal of an undergraduate education should be.

KEY QUESTION: To what extent do colleges and universities serve their students' best interests when they emphasize career preparation?

At this point, you may have an idea of how you will want to respond to the Key Question. If so, it is fine to continue your reading with that position in mind, but don't commit yet. As a good advocate, you want to weigh everything you can—within time limits—before carving out your final position. While it is great to have an idea already of how you will respond, reserve final judgment until you have read and considered at least some of the Perspectives.

Here is what one test taker noted down on their digital scratch paper as they read the Debatable Issue and Key Question:

lib. arts purpose
fail on career skills?
Is career prep students best interest?

Note that they didn't feel the need to write in complete sentences, or even complete words. Remember, the law schools will receive only your response, not your digital scratch paper, as part of your application package. Your digital scratch paper is just for you!

Next, begin reading the Perspectives. Again, read each to see what sparks your interest. What comes to mind as you read each Perspective? Does anything bring you joy or make you angry? As before, use the digital highlighting and underlining tools liberally to mark the portions that speak to you as you read. Try it with these Perspectives:

Perspective 1—an excerpt from a career advice blog

"Recruiting talent for a variety of organizations across industries, I've witnessed how the demands of today's job market make the cultivation of practical skills and specialized training more important than ever. If a student's time at university is an investment that ought to prepare them for the future, then surely career readiness must factor highly into what such institutions aim to provide. Schools that recognize this and adapt will produce graduates who are better equipped to explore a wide array of career paths, and who can adapt to changing job roles within ever-evolving industries. That's the way for today's student to make a meaningful contribution to society—by being well-equipped to grow and change within an economic reality that is itself always growing and changing."

Perspective 2—an excerpt from a university's promotional brochure

"In college, I began making my way through this world and crafting a life for myself that reflects my values. But what are my values, and how did I come to hold these values rather than others? Once I realized I didn't have to unquestioningly accept the norms and values that had been given to me, I was free to decide for myself which values I wanted to hold on to, which to leave behind, and even which new values I felt drawn to. College provided the context in which I could reflect on my values, the reasons and evidence for them, and whether they are the right values for me. Would my classmates and I have been able to test out our ideas and ideals so effectively if my university was only focused on practical career skills? I don't believe so—such work requires a dedicated exploration of ideas and knowledge for their own sake."

Perspective 3—an excerpt from a textbook on the sociology of education

"Across cultures, higher education has served primarily to aid the process of socialization by instilling cultural values, norms, and behaviors, thereby integrating people into the fabric of their respective societies. A university degree provides more than just those so-called 'soft' skills necessary for making white-collar work function smoothly, like interpersonal communication and teamwork. This emblem of accomplishment, the college degree, also provides a social signal that one is befitted to the upper-middle class, if not higher. By serving as class membership badges, undergraduate degrees perpetuate social stratification and hierarchies, with the result that access to opportunity is determined largely not by merit, but more so by one's ability to conform to a particular set of values—in short, to 'fit in.' In this manner, college places subtle constraints on students that go far beyond the more well-known problem of financial barriers to access."

Perspective 4—an excerpt from a journal on higher education

"The traditional structure of higher education needs a transformative overhaul. The modern university has its origins in medieval schools, which stressed rote memorization and obedience to the centralized authority of teachers, reflecting the broader civic and political context of those schools. But in today's world, we don't accept such a rigid, top-down system in our civic and political life. We expect citizens to be agents in the evolution of their communities.

Likewise, there's no reason to accept it in our educational lives. Instead, we ought to honor the agency of students in orchestrating their own educational experience. Some colleges have begun to change in the right direction, emphasizing dialogue over monologue and problem-solving over sheer information retention. This new form of relationship between student and university is critical, where teachers collaborate with students to discover new truths together, where student learning is based on their own guided learning experiences, and where curricula are created around topics that engage students' intrinsic motivation to learn. This moves us closer to creating the flourishing, diverse society we need."

As you read through these Perspectives, did some things catch your attention more than others? Did some things speak to you or irritate you more? Here is what our test taker noted down on their digital scratch paper as they read:

P1 CAREER BLOG:
Internal contradiction
"Specialized training" v "wide array of career paths"
"Adapt to changing roles"

P2 UNIVERSITY BROCHURE:
Explore ideas = deciding own values

P3 SOCIOLOGY OF EDUCATION:
Shouldn't degree tell you has knowledge and skills?

P4 JOURNAL ON HIGHER ED:
X

Notice that our test taker did not pay equal attention to each Perspective. In fact, they made no notes at all on Perspective 4, because nothing in that one jumped out at them, or connected with their own perspective and thinking. That's ok: in fact, that's the idea! You will not have time to mention, let alone analyze, all four Perspectives in your response, and you are only required to mention one. If a Perspective doesn't speak to you, move on.

Some experts have even found that they don't always read all four Perspectives. After all, time is tight and that is a lot of text! If you find after reading two or three Perspectives that you have a good idea of the position you want to take and a few things from Perspectives that will be relevant, it's ok to skim, or even stop reading the Perspectives and move on to the next phase of your prewriting time: Brainstorming.

Prewriting: Brainstorming

During roughly your second 5 minutes of prewriting time, you will move on to brainstorming about what to write. Here is where your own personal experiences, knowledge, and values should really come into play. Whatever you know, or have experienced and learned, about people and the world is fodder for your essay, because all of that is what fundamentally guides your judgment.

First, take a moment to think about your own life experiences, knowledge, and values. Have you, your family, or friends had any experiences which bear on the Debatable Issue and Key Question? Does the Debatable Issue directly or indirectly relate to your identity, or any communities of which you are a member? Would certain responses to the Key Question implicate your values, life, goals, and ideals?

Here is what our test taker wrote on their digital scratch paper as they brainstormed on these questions:

- Cousin—needed special engineer skills
- Music major—many not musicians
- My values: people should get value for big $$ tuition
- have to get people to hire you, degree has to do that (P3 rebuttal)

Next, it's time to brainstorm on how you will answer the Key Question. If you already have your answer in mind, you're all set. If not, take time now to think of one or two possible positions you can take.

Keep in mind that it doesn't matter what position you take, as the Key Question is designed to have a variety of answers. What matters to the law school admissions officers reading your response is whether you bring sound analysis and independent thought to your response. So, when deciding which of your brainstormed positions to write about, think not only about what you agree with, but also about what you can support.

ARGUMENTATIVE WRITING STRATEGY

If you are considering multiple potential responses to the Key Question, which response should you choose? That's easy: the one you think you'd have an easier time writing. The goal of the essay isn't to solve the puzzle of how much of college education should be focused on career readiness. It's to get you a step closer to law school. You'll have a more impressive piece of writing if you choose a response for which you can make the strongest possible argument for your case.

Look at it this way: you're going to be an attorney one day. Attorneys, by definition, have to be able to argue every side of a question. You could do a fine job defending multiple different responses to the Key Question, so don't sweat it. Pick the one you want to write—the one that'll be more fun, the one that'll show you off better.

Speaking of support, the last step of brainstorming is thinking about how you can support your position. If you have not already done so along the way, think about and note down examples and arguments, both from the Perspectives and from your own life, that you can offer in support of your position. And don't forget to think critically, as well: brainstorm at least one possible counterargument to your proposed position, and how you could rebut that counterargument.

ARGUMENTATIVE WRITING STRATEGY

Neither LSAC nor the law schools that receive your response will be fact-checking your response, so there's no need to adhere to the strictly factual. Have an anecdote you'd like to share, but you aren't 100% sure you have all the details correct? Share it anyhow! Have a story about someone else's experience that would really support your position, but don't want to mention them in your response? Write that it happened to a sibling, or to you. It is ok to tweak the details in your examples ~~in order~~ to better support your position, present things professionally, or minimize distractions.

Below is what our test taker wrote as they brainstormed the position they will take. Notice that their thoughts are becoming more fleshed-out at this point, with more full phrases and complete ideas. They're starting to think ahead to how they will phrase things when their writing time begins. Once you are done brainstorming, you will have a deeper understanding of how you will address the Key Question. You will also have come up with some ideas, and perhaps even some phrases, likely to end up in your response. Here's what they wrote:

Students need to be prepared to enter their careers, but also able to pivot.

Sounds like the basis for a vigorous argument, but we are also told to address a potential counterargument. What might that be, and how might they demolish it?

Counter: The world needs skilled workers ("practical skills & specialized training")

Rebuttal: Even advocates for this (P1) admit that the skills workers really need are the ability to adapt

Wow, they've planned a great rebuttal of that counterargument! So, they are all set, right? They should exit the prewriting screen and begin writing, right?

Well, not quite.

Once you exit the prewriting screen, you are committed. Have the entire essay's flow in mind before you start to write. Once brainstorming is complete, it's time to move on not to writing, but to the final phase of prewriting: planning.

Prewriting: Planning

The final phase of your prewriting time—about the last five minutes—should be spent planning and outlining what you will write. Your planning should involve thinking through—and jotting down on your scratch paper—the points you think you'll want to make.

ARGUMENTATIVE WRITING STRATEGY

More Argumentative Writing responses fail for lack of planning than for any other reason.

The primary thing you will want to accomplish during the planning phase of prewriting is to create an outline of the points you will make, and how you will support them. Your outline should be in the order in which you want the points to appear in your essay. Before deciding that your outline is complete, you should make sure that it includes each of the following:

1. Your answer to the Key Question
2. A place to discuss at least one Perspective
3. Examples or stories to support each point
4. A place to discuss a counterargument and rebuttal

Here is what our test taker entered as an outline on their digital scratch paper:

Intro

P1
Colleges need to give students what they paid for
- High tuition costs
- Specialized careers
- Cousin chemical engineering story

P2
Need to be prepared to adapt
- Cousin got more than that
- Music college story

P3
College degree has to convince people to hire you (Perspect. 3)
- Do better at merit-based admissions
- Then, let college degrees mean you have broad skills

P4
Counter: need career skills (Perspect. 1)
Rebuttal: Perspect. 1 admits need to adapt

Conclusion

Once your outline is ready, you still need to acknowledge the reality that you may not have time to write everything you have planned. You should take a moment to number your body paragraphs in order of importance, which will likely be different from the order in which you want them to appear in your essay. During your writing time, after drafting your introduction and conclusion, you will draft your body paragraphs in that order. That way, if you begin to run out of time, you can be sure that your best ideas have made it into your response.

Make the point that you believe is strongest—the one you can best support—your number one. Make the counterargument and rebuttal your number two. If neither of these discusses a Perspective, add a point including such a discussion as your number three. Otherwise, number any remaining paragraphs in order of strength and importance. Here's how our test taker turned their outline into a writing plan:

> Intro
>
> P1–1
> Colleges need to give students what they paid for
> - High tuition costs
> - Specialized careers
> - Cousin chemical engineering story
>
> P2–3
> Need to be prepared to adapt
> - Cousin got more than that
> - Music college story
>
> P3–4
> College degree has to convince people to hire you—Perspect. 3
> - Do better at merit-based admissions
> - Then, let college degrees mean you have broad skills
>
> P4–2
> Counter: need career skills (Perspect. 1)
> Rebuttal: Perspect. 1 admits need to adapt
>
> Conclusion

At this point, your prewriting time may be done! If you still have time remaining, you can begin planning out a topic sentence. You can even type out your topic sentence, to be re-typed into your writing area once writing time begins. However, since most students won't have time to do this during their prewriting time, we'll discuss your topic sentence during the writing time.

Writing Your Essay

Once your prewriting time has expired (or you click to advance to the writing screen early) your writing time begins. Your digital scratch paper is now located on the left-hand side of the screen, under the Debatable Issue, Key Question, and Perspectives. You can scroll to view any portion of your digital scratch paper, or select "Writing only" mode to hide the prompt and digital scratch paper to create a larger writing screen.

You will type out your response on this writing screen. Here is where it gets real: it is this text which the admissions offices at your law schools will receive in connection with your LSAT score.

How should I actually write my response?

Begin by writing out your Introduction and your Conclusion. These should each be a statement or restatement of your response to the Key Question. A dynamite introduction will fully state the position being taken, and give the reader an idea of what to expect in the coming essay. Here's what our test taker wrote:

> To truly serve their students' best interests, colleges and universities must find a balance between career-specific preparation and a broader development of skills and knowledge. Both components are essential for students to flourish.

Dynamite introduction! They have carved out a position—both kinds of education are necessary—and left the reader with an idea of what is coming: an explanation of why each is important.

Wait a minute, that's "dynamite"? What about recapping the Key Question first? What about an introduction to the Debatable Issue?

Naah, you don't need all that stuff. The Debatable Issue and Key Question are right there for the reader to consult as they see fit. Jump right in and announce your position.

ARGUMENTATIVE WRITING STRATEGY

Don't waste time recapping the Debatable Issue and Key Question, which is there for the reader's reference if they want it. Cut to the chase.

Next, add in supporting body paragraphs, in the number in which you ordered them, as time permits. As you write, link your points and paragraphs with Keywords: "First of all"... "Additionally"... "But"... "However"... "Finally."

ARGUMENTATIVE WRITING STRATEGY

Readers love to see structural Keywords because their use indicates that you are an organized thinker and disciplined writer. Even for someone merely skimming the response, such Keywords jump out and make a most favorable impression.

May I see an example?

I'll give you one better and show you two. For starters, here is the essay our test taker wrote using the outline we saw above. The writer did not, of course, highlight the structural signals as you see below; we did that to make the point that judicious use of Keywords really shapes your essay along classical lines.

As you read, keep an eye on our expert assessment in the right-hand column.

To truly serve their students' best interests, colleges and universities must find a balance between career-specific preparation and a broader development of skills and knowledge. Both components are essential for students to flourish.	*Great introduction, cuts right to the point, both are important*
Students should feel confident that a college education in a particular field will provide the specific skills needed to enter and thrive in that career. Students often spend tens of thousands of dollars on their college education, and should receive value for that investment. My cousin, for instance, wanted to pursue a career in chemical engineering. His college program provided extensive coursework specific to this field, which allowed him to obtain a chemical-engineering position after graduation. The specialized career preparation he received was precisely what was needed to enter his chosen field.	*Strong, specific support*
At the same time, however, students would be ill-served by an exclusive focus on career preparation. Many if not most college-educated individuals no longer spend the entirety of their working life in a single career, or even a single industry. My cousin also received instruction at college in history, two languages, business, and the arts. Should he choose, down the line, to leave chemical engineering, he will have the background that he needs to begin that journey. In fact, many college graduates do not even begin their careers in the field for which they trained and studied in college. I studied music as an undergraduate. **Granted**, many of my classmates have used their music education to go on to careers as performers, composers, conductors, and music educators. **That said**, many more of my classmates graduated and instead accepted jobs in other fields. I count among my music-degree-holding fellow students a business executive, a literature teacher, a pastor, a marketing manager, and the owner of a pottery studio. Had our education focused solely on career-specific preparation, my classmates would not have had the skills necessary to pursue these opportunities and succeed.	*Here comes the other side of that "both"* *Uses lived and community experience—nice!*

CHAPTER 9

Indeed, even a career advice blog which concludes that "the cultivation of practical skills and specialized training [is] more important than ever" implicitly acknowledges that career-focused training is not enough. **While arguing** that career readiness "must factor highly into what such institutions aim to provide," the blog states in the same paragraph that schools should "produce graduates who are better equipped to explore a wide array of career paths, and who can adapt to changing job roles within ever-evolving industries." Producing such graduates does not involve only the specialized training that the blog demands, **but instead** requires that colleges provide students with broad knowledge, as well as soft skills fostered by such a broad education, including a willingness to learn and the confidence to change. Adaptability does not come from a narrow field of view, but from experience adapting to the varying demands of a broad field of study.	*Counterargument and rebuttal—yes!*
It is a broad-based education, across a wide range of topics, which provides students with the "soft skills" and adaptability which career-readiness advocates acknowledge that students need. For this reason, colleges and universities would be remiss if they did not provide students not only preparation for their chosen career, but also with the opportunity to obtain a wide variety of skills and knowledge. Colleges should thus structure their programs to provide each student with a balance between these two laudable goals.	*And bringing it home*

In sum, that's a solid piece of work. Notice that although our test taker planned for four body paragraphs, they did not have time to include all those points. They still, however, wrote a robust and strong response, even without including everything they planned. There is no need to write a novel: a smaller number of points, written well, is better than a larger number of points, but poorly supported.

But wait, this response argues for a balanced approach, rather than choosing a "winner" between a broad education and career preparation. Is that allowed?

Absolutely! The Debatable Issue and Key Question are designed to allow for a broad variety of responses, not an either/or. Advocating for a balanced or mixed answer is allowed. In fact, moderate, qualified, or balanced positions are often easier to effectively support.

But now, to show you a different take on the Debatable Issue and Key Question, here's a second test-taker's response:

There is no doubt that colleges and universities owe it to their students to prepare them for career success beyond graduation. Those students have not just invested their time and money into the school, but also tied their fate to the reputation and future standing of the institution. It is in both the school and the students' interest for graduates to be as prepared as possible to thrive after earning their degree. However, in an age of constant innovation and disruption, we have to consider what makes a student truly "prepared" for that success.	*Great introduction, leaves them wanting more*
Those who advocate for career training in school—for the "cultivation of practical skills and specialized training" above all else—ignore the realities of the modern world. Yes, our society needs skilled workers, but their position is short-sighted at best. What happens to the student whose education is focused on giving them the skills to manage an office or run a research team, who finds a few years into their career that their job can now be done by an AI or an algorithm? Where does that specifically trained worker turn next? If their only hope is to return to school, then the education system has already failed them.	*Acknowledge a counterargument—yes!* *Solid use of supporting detail*
Additionally, who is to say what skills will be most useful for the unknown careers of tomorrow? When I began my undergraduate career, it was most practical to pursue advanced math training as preparation for my desired career. Within years of graduation, it was clear that computer coding skills were suddenly the fundamental requirement for those on the same path. Fortunately for me, I had already changed my mind and pursued other paths—but had I not, I would have found myself obsolete in my own field in less time than it took to earn my degree.	*Brought in personal lived experience—great!*

It is indeed an admirable goal to make students "equipped to explore a wide variety of career paths," but in that very goal is the key to what higher education should be focused on. It is the nature of people to change their mind, to have varied interests, and to explore more than one path in their lifetime. It is the nature of our world to evolve and devalue some skills as others rise to prominence. To best serve their students, colleges and universities need to prepare graduates who are capable of evolution along with the world around them.	*Bringing it back to the Key Questions*
This ability to evolve does not come from any particular set of skills for career specialization. It comes instead from a confidence in oneself, from an understanding of historical context, and from a steadiness in one's core values as circumstances become less steady. Higher education can and does help students develop all of these things through exposure to new ideas, new people, and new experiences. Through the fire of discovery, thought, and continued challenge, students forge a sense of their own self and develop the ability to adapt to new situations without abandoning their values and goals. This not only sets each individual up for long-term success, it is also the greatest benefit higher education can give to society.	*Good transition—nice connection to prior paragraph* *Strong closing statement*

Another solid response.

So, is one of these samples far superior to the other?

By no means. Either one would bring a smile to admissions officers' faces. Each is well planned, well argued, and easy to read. Each, though, has its own unique strengths. The first response makes more liberal use of Keywords, points out a logical inconsistency in one of the Perspectives, and uses a broader range of specific examples. The second response makes the counterargument and rebuttal more explicit, has a beautiful command of language, and makes constant reference back to the Key Question. The second response uses full, robust opening and closing paragraphs as part of its argument, while the first response uses shorter, more streamlined, opening and closing paragraphs. Responses do not need to reach the same conclusion, or have the same strengths, to succeed.

What about proofreading?

We're glad you asked! You'll want to make sure that you reserve at least 5 minutes at the end of your writing time for proofreading. It is ok to have some lingering errors—it's a timed essay, after all—but you will want to do a quick look-see for subject/verb agreement, dangling modifiers, unclear pronoun antecedents, unclear transitions, and "left behind" partial sentences and thoughts. This is a great time to make sure you've used plenty of Keywords and connected each paragraph to the one before.

Some experts prefer to proofread each paragraph as they write it, rather than saving all proofreading for the end. These experts, however, still leave 2–3 minutes at the end for a final skim-through to ensure that the response is well organized.

Bear in mind that the Argumentative Writing screen will close when your 35 minutes expires. Don't attempt elaborate rewrites or expansions in the final minute or two, as you risk running out of time with an unfinished sentence or paragraph.

I'm concerned about my primary, multiple-choice LSAT score, and I don't want to take time away from the test to work on and practice writing because it doesn't affect that score. Why should I take time to practice?

Even Kaplan LSAT faculty members—including several J.D.s and experienced attorneys—had to practice Argumentative Writing before they were able to crank out first-class essays in the time allowed. The LSAT Argumentative Writing section is a specialized task that requires some trial and error to gain expertise. However, if you need more persuasion to take Argumentative Writing seriously, how about these arguments?

- **Students consistently report that planning and writing a practice response helps them with LSAT Logical Reasoning.** That should make sense. In creating an LSAT Argumentative Writing response, you are putting an argument together. In LR, you are taking arguments apart. Work on one task ought to inform your command of the other, and students tell us that it does.

LAW SCHOOL APPLICATION STRATEGY

The smart move is to do everything you can so that no single aspect of your application is anything less than first-rate.

- **Working on the LSAT Argumentative Writing task offers a pleasant break from multiple-choice testing.** You can stop juggling (A) (B) (C) (D) (E) for a while without feeling guilty that you're goofing off.
- **Your stiffest competition for admissions is probably taking the LSAT Argumentative Writing section very seriously.** Those with high GPAs, great recommendations, and anticipated excellent multiple-choice LSAT results know that lots and lots of applicants boast the same numerical and qualitative credentials. As such, they look for any opportunity to stand out from the pack, and the LSAT Argumentative Writing section is one such opportunity.

Using the English language to make a case for a position should be right in your wheelhouse—if you truly have the mind and soul of an attorney. You should relish this chance to be a skillful advocate and make the most of it.

PART FIVE

Countdown to Test Day

CHAPTER 10

Test Day

Here in Part V of this book, you'll learn about how to get ready for your official LSAT administration.

You're getting near the end of this book, so finish up strong!

Planning for Your Test Administration

Is it starting to feel like your whole life is a buildup to the LSAT? You've known about it for years, worried about it for months, and now spent weeks (at least) in solid preparation for it. As the test gets closer, you may find your anxiety building. Don't worry; after the preparation you've done, you're in good shape for the test. The key to calming any pre-test jitters is to be prepared for the road to test day and beyond.

Test Modality

The first question is where you'll be testing. LSAC has been offering the LSAT as a remotely proctored, take-at-home test since 2021. That is the most popular testing modality, and likely the one you'll be using. Here's the page for more information about remote testing: **www.lsac.org/lsat/about/remote-modality**. Starting in 2023, however, LSAC began providing an in-person testing option that allows students to take their test at a Prometric testing center. For more information about this option, visit **www.lsac.org/lsat/ about/test-center-modality**. Whichever modality you choose, your LSAT will be identical to that of all other test takers in your administration; the timing, length, sections, and indeed, questions are the same regardless of where you take your LSAT.

Score Preview

Another decision you need when planning your official LSAT is whether to register for LSAC's Score Preview option. Score Preview allows you to see your LSAT score before deciding whether to cancel your score on a given administration. With Score Preview, you have six days after scores are released to choose to keep your score (in which case it is released to all schools to which you apply) or to cancel (in which case, your record will indicate a canceled test, but no score will be reported). Schools will not know whether you chose to cancel after seeing your score. At the time of this writing, the cost of score preview is $45 if you purchase prior to the test dates of your administration, and $75 if you choose to purchase within the specified period after your test (approximately 10 days, and definitely before scores from your test administration are released). For more information, visit **www.lsac.org/lsat/lsat-scoring/lsat-score-preview**.

A word of caution: While the Score Preview option has many benefits, don't be cavalier about it. A test canceled under Score Preview still counts as an administered LSAT on your record. You are allowed to take the LSAT only five times during the current rolling five-year reporting period and only seven times in your lifetime, so don't just "wing it" because you purchased Score Preview and wind up throwing away one of your allotted administrations.

Schedule your test well in advance. The registration deadlines are posted here **www.lsac.org/LSATdates**. With your test date in place, you can plan your study schedule (remember, there are helpful tips and tools for that in your online companion for this book) and set your sights on success.

The Week Before the Test

Your goal during the week before the LSAT is to set yourself up for success on test day. Up until this point, you have been working to build your LSAT potential, but test day is about achievement.

LSAT STRATEGY

Things to Do Leading Up to Test Day:

- Get your body on schedule for the time of your test, and do LSAT questions at that same time of day.
- Eat, sleep, and exercise.
- Prepare your testing area and test your equipment.
- Make sure roommates or family know your test date and time to ensure a distraction-free environment.
- Check **www.lsac.org** for the most recent test day guidelines.
- Decide whether to take the test or withdraw.

Prepping yourself for success begins with taking care of your basic needs: food, sleep, and exercise. It's easy to get caught up in the stress of balancing your life with LSAT practice, but if taking an extra hour to study every night leaves you sleep deprived and exhausted on test day, it's hurting you more than helping. Figure out what time you need to go to sleep the night before the exam, and make sure you're in bed at that time *every night* the week before the exam, especially if you're a night owl who gets a second wind late in the evening. If possible, start doing some LSAT work—even if it's only a few problems—at the same time that you will be taking your test. Finally, if you are someone who regularly engages in physical activity, this is *not* the week to stop. Physical activity helps lower stress and increases production of dopamine and norepinephrine, two neurotransmitters that improve memory, attention, and mood!

During this week, you should also decide on and set up the room and desk you'll use to take the test, especially if that space is different from the room or desk you normally use to study. Take a practice test (or at least a timed section) with this configuration to ensure that it is as quiet and comfortable as you imagine. If you live with roommates or family members, let them know about your testing schedule to ensure they'll be able to give you the privacy and quiet you'll need during your LSAT. Taking those steps now will pay off by preventing unexpected situations when it matters most.

LSAC REQUIREMENTS

Acceptable Identification: www.lsac.org/lsat/taking-lsat/identification-accepted-lsat-admission

LSAC photo requirements: www.lsac.org/jd/lsat/day-of-test/photo-requirements

Also, at least a week prior to your test, make sure to double-check your registration against the government-issued ID you'll be showing to the proctor on camera. Be sure that the names match and that the ID isn't expired! (As of the time this book went to press, LSAC accepts photo IDs that expired *within 90 days of the test date*, but check the LSAC website for the latest information.) If the names don't match, contact LSAC *immediately* so you can remedy the situation. If that isn't fixed by test day, you may not be allowed to take the exam. You will also need a passport-style photograph to upload to your LSAC account. The deadline to upload the photo is approximately one month before test day. Confirm your photo upload deadline by checking the LSAC website. LSAC is strict about the photo requirements, so Kaplan recommends that you have your photos taken professionally at a place that specializes in passport photos.

PLAN YOUR REMAINING STUDY TIME

- Balance stress management and study.
- Study areas of greatest strength, not only areas of greatest opportunity.
- The majority of your work should be under timed conditions—either full-length LSATs or Timing practice on full sections.
- Be sure you are familiar with the digital test interface (by practicing with tests in LSAC's LawHub).
- Still review the Answers and Explanations for every practice problem (using Kaplan's LSAT Link or Link+).
- Remember that you are going to law school!

The kind of practice that you do the week before the exam is important. Resist the temptation to focus on your weaknesses, and instead focus primarily on shoring up your strengths. The reality is that you are more likely to grab a few points in your strengths at the last minute than you are in the areas you struggle with the most. Of course, work on all sections of the LSAT during this time.

Keep in mind that the LSAT is a test of timing and endurance. In the days leading up to the test, most of your work should be under timed conditions, and you should try to fit in a complete test or two if you have the time in your schedule. Having said that, do not fall into the trap of doing nothing but full-length tests right before the LSAT. Just as world-class athletes don't engage in exhausting practice sessions right before a match or race, you need to balance practice and fatigue. Watch your stress levels, too: Taking too many exams can lead to a stress spiral that is hard to climb out of.

Finally, the week before the exam is the time to decide whether you are ready to take your test. As of this writing, LSAC's policy allows you to withdraw your registration all the way up until 11:59 p.m. Eastern time on the night before your exam without it showing up on your record. There is no right or wrong answer to the question of whether you are ready to take your exam, but if you are having any doubts, ask yourself two questions:

- What is the lowest score I would be okay with an admissions officer seeing?
- Am I scoring at least that high now?

You can choose your goals in life, but you can't always choose your timelines. If the answer to the second question is a resounding no, then it may be in your best interest to change your test date. Though there is a modest benefit to applying early, submitting a score that is well below a school's median is more likely to result in a faster rejection than a surprise admission. Don't expect any miracles on test day. It's possible that your score will suddenly jump up to an all-time high on the day of the exam, but it isn't likely. More to the point, it's risky.

The Day Before the Test

The day before the test is as important as the six days before it. The first instinct of most test takers is to cram as much as possible in hopes of grabbing a few last-second points. But the LSAT isn't a test that can be crammed for. You should think of test day as game day. Make sure you can reach your potential when it counts. Relax the day before the test to hit your peak performance when it matters most.

LSAT STRATEGY

The day before the test:

- Relax! Read a book, watch a movie, take a walk, or go shopping.
- Don't take any full-length tests, and preferably don't study at all.
- Gather the things you'll want during the test—your government-issued ID (required), five sheets of blank scratch paper, a few sharp pencils, tissues, etc.
- Eat a healthy meal for dinner and get plenty of sleep.

The advice in that LSAT Strategy callout is hard to follow, but trust Kaplan's decades of experience with tens of thousands of students. Make the day before the test a wonderful, relaxing day. There's a good chance that during the last few weeks or months, the stress of balancing LSAT prep with the rest of your busy life has meant you've had less time to yourself or with your family and loved ones. Spend a day with your significant other or kids. Go to the spa or spend the day watching a movie marathon. Whatever you do, make sure the day is as restful and relaxing as possible. Put your LSAT materials away and leave them there because, while you aren't going to cram your way to a good score, you may cram your way to a bad one. Think of how you normally feel when you get a score on something that is less than you hoped for. Now imagine how it would feel the day before the exam and what that kind of anxiety could do to you. The benefits to studying the day before are almost nonexistent, but the risks are sky-high.

Don't forget to cap off the day with a healthy dinner and a good night's sleep. It's not going to be easy to fall asleep the night before the test, so make sure you are in bed on time. Resist the urge to stare at a television or computer screen: They tend to make it even harder to sleep. For what it's worth, however, the most important night's sleep isn't the night before the test; it's two nights before the test. For various reasons, the effects of sleep deprivation tend to skip a day, so getting a great night's sleep two nights before the exam will help make sure that you are well rested the day of the test!

The Morning of the Test

Use test day morning to relax, focus, and gather your confidence before the test. Get up early to give yourself some time to wake up, have breakfast, and prepare your testing space. If you have an afternoon testing time, plan your morning accordingly. A relaxed morning is a much better start than a frantic, stressful one. Make sure breakfast has a good balance of protein and carbohydrates. You'll need the energy later!

Dress comfortably in a way you don't mind being seen on camera. The proctors will take your picture and a picture of your photo ID and will be watching you throughout the exam. Remember too that you may not wear a hat or a hood (unless it is subject to a religious exemption) or sunglasses, and you may not have a purse, bag, briefcase, or backpack in the room with you during your LSAT.

LSAT STRATEGY

On the morning of the test:

- Get up early enough that you don't have any rush to get ready before your testing time.
- Eat a healthy breakfast.
- Dress comfortably for your space, and remember that you will be on camera throughout the test.
- Clear any forbidden objects from your testing area.

LSAC strictly forbids several other kinds of items from being on the desk or in the room where you are testing. The proctor will have you point your camera around the room to ensure forbidden items are not present. The full rules for the test are given in LSAC's candidate agreement: **www.lsac.org/about/lsac-policies/lsaccandidate-agreement**. Read it carefully prior to test day.

LSAT FACTS

The following items are prohibited:

- Cell phones
- Electronic devices of any kind, including tablets, digital watches, exercise devices, and timers
- Headphones or earbuds (plain foam ear plugs are permitted with your proctor's approval)
- Backpacks, bags, or purses
- Mechanical pencils
- Papers or books (other than five sheets of plain scratch paper)
- Hats and hoods (other than religious items)

Note: The strategies outlined here and on the following page refer to the remotely proctored ("test-at-home") experience. If you are taking the LSAT in a testing center, please see **www.lsac.org/lsat/about/test-center-modality**.

During Check-in and the Test

Without a doubt, the best part of the "take-at-home" LSAT experience is the fact that there is no need to travel to a testing site, worry about parking, wait to check in, and watch as other nervous test takers (Prometric sites administer a wide variety of tests) go through the same thing. Still, there are several requirements you must meet for your testing space and equipment. You can find the complete LSAC test day checklist for remote test takers here: **www.lsac.org/lsat/taking-lsat/remote-checklist.**

LSAC requires you to open your proctoring application 30 minutes before the start of your test. You can join the session for your test a few minutes early, but if you're more than 10 minutes early, you'll see a wait screen until the proctor joins and activates your session. To start your LSAT, you will log in to your proctoring software (LSAC provides instructions for making an account) and click "Start Session." Follow the setup process—there's a tech check, photo-ID verification, and installation of a test-recovery app—and then you'll meet a proctor who will direct you to LSAC's LawHub (you'll already be familiar with it from ample practice), where you'll launch your LSAT.

You'll need your LSAC username and password to log in, so make sure you remember them. The proctor will have you read the rules out loud and check a box to indicate your agreement. At this point, the proctor will enter a password that activates a start button on your screen.

Click that, and your LSAT test will begin.

LSAT FACTS

Pre-test procedures:

- Log in to your proctoring software (LSAC will provide instructions for making an account) at least 30 minutes prior to your testing time.
- Follow the setup process—you'll need a Prometric username and password, then there's a tech check followed by photo ID verification, and then you can click on the launch test button.
- That will direct you to LSAC's LawHub, where you'll use your LSAC username and password to log in.
- You'll need to read and agree to a certifying statement, and then you can . . .
- Click BEGIN to start your official LSAT.

Once the test begins let all your practice and preparation take over. Identify the questions and use the Kaplan methods, strategies, and tactics you've learned for each section and question type. Use the expert section-management techniques from your LSAT Channel Spotlight sessions, and rock your LSAT test day.

After the first two sections, you'll have a 10-minute break. Follow the proctor's permission before moving around or leaving the room. You cannot use any electronic device during the intermission, and you may not use the computer you are testing on for any other purpose.

The testing process will begin again after a full 10 minutes has elapsed. There's another check-in process with the proctor, and once that's completed, you can resume the test with Section 3. Again, let all your preparation take over. If you've trained and practiced like a Kaplan LSAT expert, there won't be any surprises on the test, and you'll be confident you're ready for these last two sections.

After the fourth section of the test is complete, you'll rip up your scratch paper, and hit a SUBMIT button to make it official. Take a moment to relax and breathe. Congratulations! You have finished the scored sections of the LSAT. The only section that now remains is LSAT Argumentative Writing, which you will take at some point relatively soon after your test. Though the Argumentative Writing task can be a nice addition to your application, it is nowhere near as important as what you'll have just accomplished.

LSAT STRATEGY

During the test:

- Let all your training and preparation take over.
- Identify the questions, and use the Kaplan methods, strategies, and tactics you've learned for each section and question type.
- Use the section management techniques you've learned from Kaplan LSAT experts.
- Answer every question.
- Relax during the break.
- Don't worry about how you're scoring. Don't try to figure out which section is the experimental one. Focus only on what's in front of you.

After the test, your focus will likely shift to the Law School application process: writing a winning Personal Statement, soliciting excellent Letters of Recommendation, pulling together your undergraduate transcripts, a resume, and more. Kaplan can be a valuable partner on this stage of your law school journey as well. To find out more about how working with a Kaplan's admissions consultant can help your application stand out, visit **www.kaptest.com/lsat/practice/law-school-admissions-consulting** or call 1-800-KAPTEST.